Practical CakePHP Projects

Kai Chan and John Omokore
with Richard K. Miller

Apress®

Practical CakePHP Projects

Copyright © 2009 by Kai Chan and John Omokore with Richard K. Miller

ISBN-13 (pbk): 978-1-4302-1578-3

ISBN-13 (electronic): 978-1-4302-1579-0

Printed and bound in the United States of America 9 8 7 6 5 4 3 2 1

Trademarked names may appear in this book. Rather than use a trademark symbol with every occurrence of a trademarked name, we use the names only in an editorial fashion and to the benefit of the trademark owner, with no intention of infringement of the trademark.

Java™ and all Java-based marks are trademarks or registered trademarks of Sun Microsystems, Inc., in the US and other countries. Apress, Inc., is not affiliated with Sun Microsystems, Inc., and this book was written without endorsement from Sun Microsystems, Inc.

Lead Editor: Steve Anglin
Technical Reviewer: David Golding
Editorial Board: Clay Andres, Steve Anglin, Mark Beckner, Ewan Buckingham, Tony Campbell, Gary
    Cornell, Jonathan Gennick, Michelle Lowman, Matthew Moodie, Jeffrey Pepper, Frank Pohlmann,
    Ben Renow-Clarke, Dominic Shakeshaft, Matt Wade, Tom Welsh
Project Manager: Richard Dal Porto
Copy Editor: Marilyn Smith
Associate Production Director: Kari Brooks-Copony
Production Editor: Candace English
Compositor: Patrick Cunningham
Proofreader: Martha Whitt
Indexer: Brenda Miller
Artist: April Milne
Cover Designer: Kurt Krames
Manufacturing Director: Tom Debolski

Distributed to the book trade worldwide by Springer-Verlag New York, Inc., 233 Spring Street, 6th Floor, New York, NY 10013. Phone 1-800-SPRINGER, fax 201-348-4505, e-mail orders-ny@springer-sbm.com, or visit http://www.springeronline.com.

For information on translations, please contact Apress directly at 2855 Telegraph Avenue, Suite 600, Berkeley, CA 94705. Phone 510-549-5930, fax 510-549-5939, e-mail info@apress.com, or visit http://www.apress.com.

Apress and friends of ED books may be purchased in bulk for academic, corporate, or promotional use. eBook versions and licenses are also available for most titles. For more information, reference our Special Bulk Sales–eBook Licensing web page at http://www.apress.com/info/bulksales.

The information in this book is distributed on an "as is" basis, without warranty. Although every precaution has been taken in the preparation of this work, neither the author(s) nor Apress shall have any liability to any person or entity with respect to any loss or damage caused or alleged to be caused directly or indirectly by the information contained in this work.

The source code for this book is available to readers at http://www.apress.com.

For Rita
—Kai Chan

For Comfort
—John Omokore

For Marian
—Richard K. Miller

Contents at a Glance

Contents

About the Authors

 **KAI CHAN** started his computing career in the late 1980s. His current interests include programming methodology, the Semantic Web, data visualization, and enterprise systems. Kai holds a Computer Science bachelor's degree and a master's degree in Computer Graphics. He is a cofounder of the Azzian MVC CMS framework. Together with John Omokore and others, he runs a software and training company in London, specializing in various large-scale projects, from SAP to e-commerce web sites. When he has a spare moment, he likes tennis, squash, and long-distance running.

 **JOHN OMOKORE** is a developer, technical consultant, writer, and trainer. John has programming experience in many technologies, including Linux, PHP, MySQL, and Ajax. He has worked on market research data analysis, database development, and related systems. He received his bachelor's degree in Mathematics and is pursuing a postgraduate degree in software engineering at Oxford University in England. John provides consulting and web development services to corporate organizations around the world. He's a cofounder of AlternativeBrains and the Azzian MVC CMS framework and sits on the board of many companies. John lives outside London with his wife, two children, and some animals. His career interests include open source scripting languages, OOP programming, and the use of SAP in large-scale industries (chiefly oil and gas). When not scripting, he enjoys playing chess and squash, visiting the gym, and a bit of socializing.

 **RICHARD K. MILLER** graduated from Brigham Young University with a degree in Business Management but has been interested in technology since he began computer programming at age 10. His experience includes web programming, Internet marketing, and new media strategies. He is the developer of several MediaWiki extensions and WordPress plugins, including the widely used What Would Seth Godin Do plugin.

About the Technical Reviewer

DAVID GOLDING began developing web sites in 1999 and first started using CakePHP on a bet he couldn't complete a web application in five minutes. He is the author of *Beginning CakePHP: From Novice to Professional* (Apress, 2008) and has taught CakePHP even while it was still in early stages of development. David has a degree in European Studies from Brigham Young University and continues work in religious studies and history as a graduate student at Claremont Graduate University. He lives with his wife, Camille, and his son, Kenny, in Southern California.

Acknowledgments

When we first decided to write this book, we really didn't think it would be that difficult a task. After all, we've been coding and writing documentation for years and years. Now having written the book, we can honestly say it has been one of the hardest projects we've done since we wrote our first-ever Hello World program. As such, with tears streaming from our eyes, we would wholeheartedly like to thank all the people involved. It all sounds like a cliché, but it's all true. Thank you to the team at Apress, the Cake Software Foundation, colleagues, friends, families, and neighbors. In no particular order, we would like to thank them individually. They are Steve Anglin, Richard Dal Porto, Matt Wade, Marilyn Smith, Joohn Choe, David Golding, Nancy Wright, Richard K. Miller, Rita Woo, Terry Wells, Dan Jackson, Candace English, and God.

Kai Chan and John Omokore

Thank you to Kai Chan and John Omokore for allowing me to take part in this book. I've enjoyed working with them and the entire Apress team. Thanks to David Golding for getting me involved. I'm thankful for good parents, family, friends, and colleagues, and to God.

Richard K. Miller

Introduction

First off, thank you for picking up this book. Whether you are standing in a bookshop or reading this at home, we assume you probably have a strong interest in developing web sites. In the past few years, the number of web site frameworks has increased dramatically. This is especially true for PHP-based frameworks. Many people have chosen to adopt CakePHP (Cake, for short) for various reasons, such as these:

- PHP programmers are widely available. Most projects have tight deadlines, and you want team members who can quickly pick up a new piece of technology.

- CakePHP is easy to learn. You want a powerful tool that you can easily master.

- CakePHP has good support. Developers frequently post and reply to messages on the Cake forum. And there are always some good discussions happening on the Cake IRC. (To see for yourself, simply download mIRC from http://www.mirc.com/, connect to the server irc.freenode.net, and join the #cakephp channel.)

When you are developing a site using Cake, you often find yourself trawling through tutorials online to see how things are done. We've done that ourselves many times. However, despite the power of the Internet, we still like to look through books. And we think you will find this book a great help in your Cake development endeavors, in addition to all of the material available online.

Most of the applications in this book have been written as a result of some real-world development we have done in the past. We focus on projects that we think are relevant to the future of web development.

Let's take mashups, for example. We should all take an interest in this ever-expanding area of web development. We can honestly say that any successful online web site in the future will need to easily communicate with other applications. Application designers will need to bear this in mind. Matters such as search engine optimization need to be built into the application itself. Cake allows us to think in terms of the high-level architecture instead of the nuts and bolts of a web application.

Who Should Read This Book

Practical CakePHP is a book mainly for developers. To get the most from it, you should be comfortable with a number of web technologies and programming concepts. These include PHP, SQL, HTML, JavaScript, object-oriented programming, and design patterns, as well as the general principles of web development. If you are at the forefront of web development, then this book is for you!

If our book sounds a little too advanced for you, we recommend that you do some preliminary reading. We suggest the following books:

- *Beginning PHP and MySQL: From Novice to Professional, Third Edition,* by W. Jason Gilmore (Apress, 2008)

- *Beginning CakePHP: From Novice to Professional* by David Golding (Apress, 2008)

How This Book Is Organized

Each chapter in this book has been chosen so it will cover the core features in Cake, plus some of the minor features as well. The following is a rough breakdown of what each chapter includes.

- Chapter 1, "Cake Fundamentals," gives you an introduction to Cake. If you are new to the CakePHP framework, this is the place to start.

- Chapter 2, "Blogging," provides you with a simple blogging application. It's perfect for beginners who want to know what a Cake application looks like. If there are two chapters in the book that need to be read in sequence, they are Chapters 1 and 2.

- Chapter 3, "E-Commerce," gives you greater insight into the way Cake is used in a common application. We walk through implementing an online shop using the Cake framework.

- Chapter 4, "A Message Forum Web Service," covers the development of a web services API. We guide you through creating a clean API, so any third party can access your application using standard protocols.

- Chapter 5, "Google Maps and the Traveling Salesman," shows you how the Google Maps API is used with Cake. One of the main features of this chapter's application relates to the classic traveling salesman problem: a salesman needs to visit a number of cities only once and return to where he started.

- Chapter 6, "Mashing Twitter with the Google Translator," emphasizes the importance of web services in modern web application development. In true Web 2.0 and Cake fashion, this chapter's application mashes the Google Ajax Language API with the Twitter API to provide automatic translation of Twitter messages.

- Chapter 7, "Unit Testing and Web Testing," covers one of the hottest topics among web professionals. Cake 1.2 devotes a large section to testing, and this chapter shows you how to take advantage of Cake's integrated unit testing features.

- Chapter 8, "A Cake Control Panel," covers Cake's access control lists and security features. We develop a web-based front end that allows administrators to manage user security.

- Chapter 9, "Translating Stories," provides you with the knowledge to tackle Cake's internationalization and localization features. We develop an application in which news stories are available in other languages, with an administration area where translators can translate stories from a base language to another language.

- Chapter 10, "Adding Automagic Fields," demonstrates extending Cake's use of auto-magic fields like `created`, `modified`, and `title`. We create three new automagic fields.

- Chapter 11, "Cake Tags," shows you our take on an established technology where XML tags are used as a wrapper to coding logic. Using Cake, we develop our own HTML-based tags to display two Yahoo maps.

- Chapter 12, "Dynamic Data Fields," extends the e-commerce chapter with a special product-filtering technique. We take a dynamic data approach to product searches.

- Chapter 13, "Captcha," shows how ASCII Art can be used as a Captcha test. In this chapter's project, the Captcha test is housed in a Cake component so it can be used by other applications.

How to Contact the Authors

The authors can be contacted as follows:

- Kai Chan can be contacted at `kai.chan@edgeable.com`.

- John Omokore can be contacted at `john@omokore.com`.

- Richard K. Miller can be contacted at `richard@richardkmiller.com`.

CHAPTER 1

Cake Fundamentals

Using a framework of some sort has now become the order of the day for building large-scale web applications. Organizations have found that using an in-house framework for web projects enhances code reuse, scalability, quick project turnarounds, and security.

New and evolving frameworks provide rapid application development tools to promote the adoption of particular programming languages. Many frameworks derived from PHP have been popular with programmers in the open source community. CakePHP—Cake for short—is currently one of the fastest-growing rapid application development frameworks. When you are developing large web applications or creating components that you will reuse in many applications, you'll find Cake to be a great help.

In this chapter, we'll highlight some of the concepts, technologies, and tools that Cake relies on, including the PHP scripting language, the Model-View-Controller design pattern, and object-oriented programming techniques. We will also outline the default folder structures and naming conventions and introduce some Cake best practices. And, of course, we'll demonstrate how to write some Cake code.

This chapter will serve as a quick reference that will provide you with a solid foundation on which to build your knowledge of the framework throughout the rest of the book.

Cake Features

Why should you use Cake when there are so many other frameworks in town? There is a number of good reasons for the popularity of Cake PHP. It has a short learning curve in comparison to other frameworks, because Cake is easy to use and understand. Also, because there are so many PHP programmers, Cake has a large community. New users can find many projects to refer to and use.

Here are some features of Cake that make web application development with it easy and fast:

- It uses the Model-View-Controller (MVC) framework for PHP.

- Its database connectivity support includes MySQL and PostgreSQL, as well as many other database platforms.

- Cake is easy to install on most platforms, including Unix and Windows.

- Its MIT license is more flexible than other licenses.

- It uses easy and flexible templating (which allows PHP syntax, with helpers).

- Cake has view helpers to assist in the insertion of often-repeated snippets of HTML and forms code, Ajax, JavaScript, and so on.

- It has components for handling e-mail, authentication, access control, localization, security, sessions, and request handling.

- Cake provides utility classes to manipulate resources such as sets, files, folders, XML, and many others.

- Your URLs are optimized for search engines.

■**Note** For a complete and up-to-date list of Cake features; see the official web site at `http://cakephp.org`. You can also find many discussions regarding how Cake compares with other frameworks, such as Ruby on Rails, symfony, Zend Framework, and CodeIgniter. For a comparison of Cake with the aforementioned frameworks, check `http://frinity.blogspot.com/2008/06/why-choose-cakephp-over-other.html`.

The Ingredients of Cake

In this section, we'll delve into the core concepts and technologies employed by Cake, starting with the MVC design pattern.

The Model-View-Controller Design Pattern

Cake supports the MVC design pattern, which aims to modularize an application into three parts:

- The *model* represents the data for the application.
- The *view* represents the presentation.
- The *controller* ties the model and view together and deals with user input.

Familiarity with the MVC pattern is a plus, but this book does not assume you have any prior knowledge of MVC. This chapter covers how Cake employs the MVC concept.

Rapid Application Development

Along with MVC, Cake took on the philosophy of rapid application development (RAD), sometimes also known as rapid prototyping. RAD is basically a method of decreasing the time taken to design software systems by using many prebuilt skeleton structures. This provides developers with many advantages, including easier maintenance, code reuse, more efficient teamwork, and quick project turnaround. RAD also provides the ability to make rapid changes based on client feedback, decreasing the dangers of feature creep.

Additionally, you can find a lot of off-the-shelf open source code, which you can easily plug into your Cake applications. A great place to start is `http://bakery.cakephp.org`.

PHP 4+

PHP 4+ refers to PHP version 4 and above. PHP has become one of the most important server-side scripting languages on the Web. It is currently a predominant language for the development of web applications. It provides web developers the functionalities to quickly create dynamic web applications. PHP has come a long way since PHP 3 was first introduced more than a decade ago.

The adoption of the Cake framework assumes knowledge of PHP 4. The official PHP manual, at http://www.php.net, provides a complete reference on PHP.

■Note A common problem faced in life with a new adventure is where to go for the right information in order to avoid the mistakes of predecessors. If you are just starting out with PHP, you can refer to the many online PHP forums and repositories, such as the popular PEAR library and the ever-growing http://www. phpclasses.org web site.

Object-Oriented Programming

Object-oriented programming (OOP) can be described as a method of implementation in which the parts of a program are organized as a collection of objects, each of which represents an instance of a class, and whose classes are all members of a hierarchy of classes united via inheritance relationships. For example, a Dog object says() 'woof woof', while a Cat object says() 'meow meow', and they both inherit says() from the Pets class.

The Cake framework supports the three key principles of object-oriented development: encapsulation, inheritance, and polymorphism.

For the simple magic called *encapsulation*, Cake's implementation of one object is protected, or hidden away, from another object to eliminate interference. However, there must be some interaction with other objects in the application, or the object is useless. As in most OOP applications, an object in the Cake framework provides an *interface* to another object to enable this interaction. Listing 1-1 shows the default database configuration class, called DATABASE_CONFIG, which encapsulates $default and $shop database connection arrays.

Listing 1-1. *The Cake Database Configuration Class*

```
class DATABASE_CONFIG {
    var $default = array(
            'driver' => 'mysql',
            'persistent' => 'true',
            'host' => 'localhost',
            'login' => 'admin',
            'password' => 'superadmin',
            'database' => 'userdb',
            'prefix' => ''
```

```
    var $shop = array(
            'driver' => 'mysql',
            'persistent' => 'true',
            'host' => 'localhost',
            'login' => 'user',
            'password' => 'userme',
            'database' => 'shopdb',
            'prefix' => 'sp'
);
```

By default, Cake internally interfaces with the $default connection database. It uses its array parameters for its default database connection unless you explicitly specify a different database connection by assigning the $useDbConfig = '$shop' property in a model class. This explicit interface will enable some interaction with the tables in the shop database.

Cake's support for *inheritance* cannot be overemphasized. It wraps a lot of database manipulation and other utility functions in its default classes in a manner that enables an object to take on the functions of another object and extend or tailor those functions so you don't repeat the same code. We consider this act of charity as one of the greatest benefits to developers, as it undoubtedly ensures fast application development. Therefore, you need to spend some time sharpening your knives by reading a Cake cheat map or its online API (http://api.cakephp.org) to understand what your objects will inherit.

In a controller genealogy, user-defined controller objects inherit from the AppController object. The AppController inherits from Controller object, which extends the Object class. A controller class can be derived from the AppController class, as shown in Listing 1-2. (Controllers are discussed in more detail in the upcoming sections about Cake models, views, and controllers.)

Listing 1-2. *The Application Controller Class*

```
class ProductsController extends AppController {
    function beforeFilter() {
    }
}
```

This default class contains the beforeFilter() method, which can be overridden in any class that extends the AppController class, such as a user-defined controller class. In Listing 1-2, ProductsController extends the AppController class.

And lastly, Cake implements *polymorphism* and ensures that functions within an object can behave differently depending on the input. It basically creates the ability to respond to the same function call in many different ways.

The Cake framework creates many reusable objects. You can use these objects without knowing their internal workings. This is one of the key benefits of using Cake.

▓**Note** For more information about OOP in relation to PHP, refer to the PHP manual at http://www.php.net/oop5.

Dissecting Cake

Before you start baking a Cake application, you will need to download the Cake framework from cakephp.org and install it on your computer. Remember that Cake is based on the PHP scripting language, so you need to have PHP up and running first. If you will be using information stored in a database, you will need to install the database engine. All our examples assume the MySQL database.

Cake's Directory Structure

When you unpack Cake, you will find the following main folder structures:

- app: Contains files and folders for your application. The app folder is your development folder, where your application-specific folders and files reside.

- cake: Contains core Cake libraries. The cake folder contains the core libraries for CakePHP. You should not touch these libraries unless you really know what you are doing.

- docs: Contains Cake document files such as the read me, copyright, and change log text files. You can store your own documentation in this folder.

- vendors: Contains third-party code. The vendors folder can contain third-party libraries, such as the Swift Mailer package for sending e-mail messages.

Separating the default Cake core library folder from the application folder makes it possible for you to have many different applications sharing a single Cake installation. With this folder structure, you can easily upgrade your existing version of Cake without affecting any applications you have written. Table 1-1 details Cake's default folder structure.

Table 1-1. *The Cake Default Folder Structure*

Directory			Description
app/			The parent folder for your application
	config/		Contains configuration files for global structures such as database connections, security, and access control
	controllers/		Contains your application controllers files (e.g., user_ controller.php)
		components/	Contains your user-defined component files
	/index.php		Allows you to deploy Cake with /app as the DocumentRoot
	locale/		Contains locale files that deal with internationalization
	models/		Contains the model files
	plugins/		Contains the plugin files
	tests/		Contains the test folders and files
	tmp/		Used for caches and logs
	vendors/		Contains third-party libraries

Continued

Table 1-1. *Continued*

Directory			Description
views/			Contains view folders and files for presentation (e.g., the .ctp files)
	elements/		Elements, which are bits of views, go here
	errors/		Custom error pages
	helpers/		Helpers
	layouts/		Application layout files
webroot/			The DocumentRoot for the application
	css/		Contains the application style sheet files
	files/		Contains any files
	img/		Contains graphics
	js/		Contains JavaScript files
cake/			Contains Cake core libraries
vendors/			Contains third-party libraries for all applications

The Cake Naming Conventions

Like similar frameworks, Cake employs naming conventions instead of configuration files for many of its workings, such as for its MVC structure. It is good practice to understand and employ the Cake conventions. You can override some of the rules later, when you become a proficient Cake baker.

Cake has naming conventions for the four core objects: controllers, models, views, and tables. It also provides global constants and functions.

Controller Naming

Controller class names must be plural and must have Controller appended, as in ProductsController. If the object has more than one word, the second word must also begin with an uppercase letter, as in OnlineProductsController. Do not use underscores to separate words.

File names must be plural, with _controller appended and the .php extension, as in products_controller.php. If the object has more than one word, the subsequent words must be delimited with underscores, as in online_products_controller.php.

Model Naming

Model class names are singular, as in Product. If the object has more than one word, the second word must also begin with an uppercase letter (camel case), as in OnlineProduct.

File names are singular, with the .php extension, as in product.php. If the object has more than one word, the subsequent words are delimited with underscores, as in online_product.php.

View Naming

View file names take on the action name in the controller. For example, if the object has a method `ProductsController::upgrade()`, the path is `app/views/products/upgrade.ctp`.

Table Naming

Database table names should be plural, with words delimited with underscores, as in `country_codes`. You can override this naming convention by setting the `$useTable` property to your preferred table name. For example, you could set the following:

```
$useTable = 'mytable';
```

where `'mytable'` is the name of a table in a database.

Global Constants

The global constants are categorized into three major parts:

- *Core defines*: For example, `CAKE _SESSION_STRING` defines the Cake application session value.

- *Web root configurable paths*: For example, `WEBROOT_DIR` defines the web root folder where resources such as image and CSS files are stored.

- *Paths*: For example, `VIEWS` defines the parent folder for the presentation files (views).

For example, you can have the following code snippet to read the `example.ctp` page as an array from the `VIEWS` folder:

```
$page = VIEWS . 'example.ctp';
$file = file($page);
```

Global Functions

The global functions serve as wrappers for some utility functions. For example, the following function code snippet performs a simple search and replace operation to add style to $text.

```
$word = "sweet";  // search string - The needle!
$text = "This Cake is as sweet as honey"; // The haystack
// r(...) is the global function
r('$word', "<div class='red'>$word</div>", 'text');
```

The controller should contain most of the business logic, like this:

```
$shopping_basket_balance = $net_price + $tax;
```

Quite often in real applications, the business logic is split into separate parts. However, in Cake, the business logic is often separated into components or vendors, as discussed later in this chapter.

> ■**Note** It is advisable to familiarize yourself with the global constants and functions to avoid reinventing the wheel. To see a complete list of Cake's various classes and functions, visit `http://api.cakephp.org`.

Models

The model is the first of the MVC concepts. Communicating with data stores such as tables, iCal events, structured files, LDAP records, and so on is an inevitable aspect of any large-scale web application, especially when it involves a large number of users. The actions of manipulating data stored in a data store are best done within a model. The model should be involved with just fetching and saving data from data stores. For example, table queries should be placed in the model.

Model Creation

Models are declared using the keyword `class`, followed by the name you wish to give to the model. Just like any PHP class, a user-defined model may contain some properties and methods specific to the implementation of that model as determined by the business requirement.

A user-defined model class should follow the Cake naming convention and predefined rules; for example, a `Product` model class should extend the `AppModel` class. The `AppModel` class extends the `Model` class, which defines Cake's model functionality. For example, the `Product` model class in Listing 1-3 invariably inherits all of the `Model` class properties and methods.

Listing 1-3. *A Sample Model Class*

```
class Product extends AppModel {
}
```

Though the `Product` class in Listing 1-3 appears empty, it is heavily loaded with some of Cake's properties and methods. We will bring some of these useful properties and methods into the limelight throughout this book.

The `AppModel` class is originally defined in the `cake/` directory. To create your own, place it in `app/app_model.php`. This allows methods to be shared among the models. The `Model` class, which `AppModel` extends, is a standard Cake library defined in `cake/libs/model.php`. Model default methods such as the `find()` method are defined in the `Model` class stored in `cake/libs/model/model.php`. Don't start tweaking Cake's default `Model` class until you become an expert baker.

> ■**Note** Refer to the cheat sheet in at `http://cakephp.org/files/cakesheet.pdf` before writing a query method in your `Model` class definition. Alternatively, check the Cake API at `http://api.cakephp.org`. This effort will save you from rewriting existing functionalities and enhance rapid application development. For example, Cake provides a `find('all')` query to retrieve some or all information from a database table.

Let's use an example to demonstrate the four well-known types of operations that you will normally perform on a database (collectively known as CRUD):

- Create a record and insert it into a database table.
- Retrieve records from one or more database tables.
- Update tables.
- Delete records.

First, we will create a table named `departments` and insert some sample data with the SQL shown in Listing 1-4.

Listing 1-4. *The Table Schema for departments*

```
CREATE TABLE IF NOT EXISTS `departments` (
 `id` int(10) unsigned NOT NULL auto_increment,
`name` varchar(255) default NULL,
`region` varchar(255) default NULL,
  PRIMARY KEY (`id`)
) ;

INSERT INTO `departments` (`id`, `name`,`region`) VALUES
(1, 'Customer Services','UK'),
(2, 'Sales','UK'),
(3, 'Press Office','UK'),
(4, 'Investor Relations','US'),
(5, 'Human Resources',NG),
(6, 'Partnership Opportunities','US'),
(7, 'Marketing','UK'),
(8, 'Online Marketing','US');
```

Listing 1-4 contains some records about the name and region of the departments. This table is simple and self-explanatory.

Now that we have a database, we'll perform the first of the CRUD operations. We'll create some records, by using the default `save()` method provided in a model class. Using this method comes at the price of ensuring that the format of the data to be passed to it as a parameter must adhere to the Cake preformatted array structure. Let's take a look at a sample data structure in Listing 1-5.

Listing 1-5. *Cake's Expected $this->data Format*

```
Array
(
    [0] => Array
        (
            [Department] => Array
                (
                    [id] => 9
                    [name] => Warranties
                    [region] => Russia
                )

        )

    [1] => Array
        (
            [Department] => Array
                (
                    [id] => 10
                    [name] => Website
                    [region] => UK
                )
        )
)
```

In Listing 1-5, we've preformatted two additional records to be added to our departments database table. This structure, stored in a PHP variable such as $data or $this-data, will save its values to matching fields in the departments database table. To commit the data in this structure into this table, the save() method is at your service, but the format of $this->data argument is crucial to the success of the operation.

Now that we've created the expected data structure, let's define the Department model class to use this preformatted data and commit the two additional records into the departments table. The Department model class is shown in Listing 1-6.

Listing 1-6. *The Department Model Class*

```php
<?php
class Department extends AppModel {

    var $name = 'Department';
    var $useTable = 'departments';

    function saveMessage($data) {
        if ($this->save($data)) {
            return true;
        } else {
            return false;
        }
    }
}
?>
```

In Listing 1-6, first we declare the Department class that extends AppModel. Next are the properties, starting with the $name property assigned the value Department. This property is necessary if you are running on anything less than PHP 5. The $useTable property specifies the name of the table required for data access or manipulation in the model. Although it isn't required, if omitted, Cake will use a table with the name of the model. For example, if the model name is department, Cake will use the departments table for the model by default. It is important to explicitly specify which database table you are using, especially if Cake's table naming convention is not followed.

The saveMessage() model function call should be done in a controller class. We'll discuss the controller in more detail later in this chapter. In our imaginary controller class, to invoke the saveMessage() method defined in Listing 1-6, we need the following statement:

```
$this->Department->saveMessage($data);
```

This method accepts as a parameter the preformatted array information called $data, as defined in Listing 1-5. Using an If statement, if the $data passed to Cake's save() model function is committed to the departments database table, a Boolean true value is returned; if not, false is returned. You can also save data into a database table in this manner by using Cake's create() model function.

When submitting an HTML form created using the $form object in a view, Cake automatically structures the form fields data submitted to a controller in a format that is similar to that shown in Listing 1-5.

Next, let's delve into the retrieve part of CRUD operations, or data access. To be meaningful, most data-access operations are filtered using some criteria. We're going to add a getDepartment() method to the Department model class, as shown in Listing 1-7.

Listing 1-7. *Retrieving Records Using $region='US' Criteria with the find() Method*

```
function getDepartment($region=null) {

    return $this->find('all',array('conditions'=>array('region'=>$region)));
}
```

In Listing 1-7, we define a getDepartment() method that accepts $region as its parameter. This method employs the service of the Cake's find() method to retrieve some department information based on $region as its parameter. To search for a department in the United States, we'll create the following in a controller class:

```
$this->Department->getDepartment('US');
```

This statement will retrieve and format all the departments in the US region, as shown in Listing 1-8.

Listing 1-8. *Structure of the Return Department Data Where Region Equals US*

```
Array
(
    [0] => Array
        (
            [Department] => Array
                (
                    [id] => 4
                    [name] => Investor Relations
                    [region] => US
                )

        )

    [1] => Array
        (
            [Department] => Array
                (
                    [id] => 6
                    [name] => Partnership Opportunities
                    [region] => US
                )
        )
    [2] => Array
        (
            [Department] => Array
                (
                    [id] => 8
                    [name] => Online Marketing
                    [region] => US
                )
        )

)
```

▓**Note** The formatted array data in Listing 1-8 might appear completely different when there are associations between the Department model class and other model classes that are connected to database tables. In case of associations, the array will include array data from tables of associated models. You will come across preformatted associated data in Chapter 3.

The find() function is one of the most useful Cake functions for data access. It has the following format:

```
find( conditions[array], fields[array], order[string], recursive[int] )
```

This method also accepts the parameters, in the order listed in Table 1-2.

Table 1-2. *The find() Function Parameters*

Name	Description	Default Value
type	Can be set to all, first, count, neighbors, or list to determine what type of data-access operation to carry out	first
conditions	An array of conditions specified as key and value	null
fields	An array of fields of key and value to retrieve	null
order	To specify whether to order fields in ascending (ASC) or descending (DESC) order	null (no SQL ORDER BY clause will be used if no order field is specified)
page	To determine the page number	null
limit	To limit the page result	null
offset	The SQL offset value	null
recursive	Whether to include the associated model	1

You can use many other Cake predefined model methods, such as the query() method or the read() method, which returns a list of fields from the database and sets the current model data (Model::$data) with the record found. Or you can create your own user-defined methods to manipulate data specific to the table a model object uses.

Listing 1-9 shows an alternative way of retrieving information about the departments. This listing will return exactly the same records from the departments table as the one shown in Listing 1-8 when used in our imaginary controller. The difference is that Listing 1-8 uses the find() method, while Listing 1-9 uses the query() method to access data.

Listing 1-9. *Retrieving Records with the query() Method*

```
function getDepartment($region=null) {

    $sql = "SELECT * FROM `departments` WHERE `region` = $region";
    return $this->query($sql);
}
```

One advantage of using the query() method is that you can put an already defined SQL statement, from a legacy system, into this method without going through the trouble of dividing the query parameters into parts, as you would need to do to use the find() method.

Data Validation

Data validation is an essential part of ensuring integrity and accuracy of data submitted by the user, such as via a web form. Cake has built-in validation mechanisms. You specify the validation rules in a model, and Cake automatically applies the rules when a web form is connected to that model. These rules can also be applied to XML data.

First, let's add a simple validation rule to our Department model using the $validate array, as shown in Listing 1-10. The validation rule array is basically an associative array. The keys are the names of the form fields to validate, and the corresponding values represent the rules attached to the form fields. We'll make use of this rule later, in the "Views" section.

Listing 1-10. *The Validation Rule for the Department Model*

```
var $validate = array( 'region' => array(
                            'alphaNumeric' => array(
                                'rule'=>'alphaNumeric',
                                'required'=>true,
                                'message'=>'Enter a region.'
                            )
                        )
                );
```

A field can have multiple validation rules. The $validate array in Listing 1-10 defines a rule for the region field in our Department model. If a user does not submit a valid region field, the model will return an error to the controller and quit committing the data to the departments database table. The message key deals with the error messages during validation. To display the error message on a form, use the form helper's error function:

```
<?php echo $form->error('region');?>
```

This will display the error message "Enter a region" if a user enters a nonalphanumeric value in the region input field.

Apart from the rules employed in Listing 1-10, Cake provides a number of built-in validation rules to check the validity of form inputs and ensure the integrity of information you want to store. Table 1-3 lists a few of the built-in rules provided by Cake.

Table 1-3. *Some of Cake's Built-in Validation Rules*

Rule	Description	Example
cc	Checks for a valid credit card number	'rule'=>array('cc','fast')
date	Checks for a valid date	'rule'=>'date'
email	Checks for a valid e-mail address	'rule'=>'email'
ip	Checks for a valid IP address	'rule'=>'ip'
phone	Checks for a valid phone number	'rule'=>array('phone', null, 'uk')

For a complete list of the validation constants in your Cake build, see the predefined rules in the cake/libs/validation.php file.

You can extend the list of the rules by adding your own user-defined rules. In Listing 1-11, we define a simple custom rule to check if a value is a string.

Listing 1-11. *A Custom Rule Called String*

```
function string($check) {

    return is_string($check);
}
```

Before you apply a custom rule, such as the string rule shown in Listing 1-11, add it to the cake/libs/validation.php file, and then simply add the rule to your model $validate array:

```
var $validate = array('name'=>'string');
```

This will ensure that the name field is a valid string. In upcoming chapters, you will come across more validation rules.

The model object is robust and provides a lot of functionality for database manipulation. However, part of the data retrieved by a model is required for web surfers' consumption. When a user makes a URL request, some response is expected to be displayed in a view, which we'll look at in the following section.

Views

Now that we have some validation rules, let's build an HTML form to ask users to enter department information. The task of building a web form is done in a view.

Views are presentation pages. The HTML or XML documents on the Web are views to the users. However, views can be anything, especially if Cake is used to output other formats like RSS, PDF, and so on (which is certainly possible with the RequestHandler component and parsing extensions in the router). Views render information to the users. Views are composed of a mixture of HTML and PHP code.

By default, a view should be stored under the controller name folder. For example, the view for the add() method in the DepartmentsController is stored as app/views/departments/add.php.

Data from the controller is passed to the view by using the set() method in a controller.

■**Note** Views should be involved only with displaying output. For example, this is where you will see HTML tags and XML tags. Business logic, such as $shopping_basket_balance = $net_price + $tax;, should not be in the view. However, the following is OK in a view: If ($shopping_basket_balance > 1000) { echo 'You are eligible for a discount'; }.

Let's build the view to add information to our departments database table. We are going to use another utility provided by Cake to build forms: the $form object. Listing 1-12 shows the add view.

Listing 1-12. *The Add View for the departments Table*

```
<h1>Add Department</h1>
<?=$form->create('department',array('action'=>'add'));?>
<p>Name:
<?=$form->input('Department.name',array('size'=>'120'));?>
<?=$form->error('name');?></p>
<p>Region:
<?=$form->input('Department.region',array('size'=>'40'));?>
<?=$form->error('region');?></p>
<?=$form->end('Save')?>
```

The view code created using the $form object is stored in /app/views/department/add.ctp.
Remember that the validation rule for this form is created at Listing 1-10.

To display the add view to a user, we need a controller object with a function called add(),
which tries to do exactly what it says: add the form data to our departments database table.

Listing 1-13 shows the action add() method of the DepartmentsController.

Listing 1-13. *The add() Action in the Departments Controller*

```
<?php
class DepartmentsController extends AppController {

    function add() {

        if (!empty($this->data)) {

            $this->Department->create();
            if ($this->Department->save($this->data)) {
                $this->Session->setFlash(➥
__('The Department data has been saved', true));
                $this->redirect(array('action'=>'add'));
            } else {
                $this->Session->setFlash(➥
__('The Department data could not be saved. Please, try again.', true));
            }
        }
    }
}
?>
```

Now that we've built a web form using the HTML helper and created a controller to
handle the add() action, let's demonstrate how data is passed to a view. We'll start by creating
a show action in our Departments controller class. The action method is shown in Listing 1-14.

Listing 1-14. *The show() action in the Departments Controller*

```
function show($region) {

    $this->set('data', $this->Department->getDepartment($region));
}
```

In Listing 1-14, the show() method accepts the $region data as a parameter, and then retrieves departmental data and uses the set() method to prepare the data for the view in Listing 1-15. A view is always named after an action. For example, the show() action in the DepartmentsController of Listing 1-14 will have a view file stored in app/views/department/show.ctp.

Listing 1-15. *A View for the Action show($region) of DepartmentsController*

```
<h1 class="first">

    Our Department: -

    <?php

        foreach($data as $department) {
            echo $department ['Department'] ['name'];
        }
    ?>

</h1>
<p>Our Departments are led by Dr. Cake .</p>
```

The view in Listing 1-15 will display the name of the department (for example, Sales) in the header section of the web page presented to the user.

■**Tip** If you have a number of data items to display in a view, such as $title = "Practical Cake Projects"; $department = "Sales"; and $region = "UK";, using $this->set(compact('title', 'department', 'region')); will enable you to use only one set() function in your controller class to pass all the information to your view. You can then access the individual variable in your view; for example, <?php pr($title); ?>.

An essential part of any framework is the part that handles requests. In the MVC structure, this is handled by the controller.

Controllers

As you've seen, a controller is a class with methods called *actions*. These actions or methods contain most of the logic that responds to user requests in an application. For example, if a user wants to know the number of departments in a particular region, the user needs to access the show() method of DepartmentsController defined in Listing 1-10, by typing the following URL in a browser address bar:

```
localhost/departments/show/US
```

The default structure for accessing a Cake URL is to first specify the controller and then the action. In the preceding URL, departments is the controller, show is the action, and US is a parameter.

By convention, a Cake request should be structured in the following manner:

```
http://[mydomain.com]/[Application]/[Controller]/[Action]/[Param1]/…[ParamN]
```

■**Note** The index()method is the default access point to a controller when a method is not explicitly specified in a user's request. For example, you can load the index() method with codes that will invoke the welcome page of your application. However, do not forget to create a view, or you will get a warning from Cake stating that you should create a view for the action.

Your application's controller classes are expected to extend the AppController class, which in turn extends a core Controller class, which is a standard Cake library. The AppController class is defined in /app/app_controller.php, and it should contain methods that are shared between two or more controllers.

These controllers can include any number of actions. The AppController serves as a global class that can contain properties and methods common to all the user-defined controllers in an application. For example, you can have a method to detect and extract the IP address of a user, and then use the value of this address to determine the flow of the application. Earlier, in Listing 1-2, we used the default controller method called beforeFilter() in our controller class to reference the method defined in the AppController class stored in app/app_controller.php. Another simple example is to set a default page title for an application, as in this example:

```php
<?php
class AppController extends Controller {
    var $pageTitle = 'Chapter 1 - A Bakery Application';
```

Since our user-defined controller extends the AppController, using the statement $this->PageTitle within our controller gives us access to the string 'Chapter 1 - A Bakery Application' assigned to the pageTitle property in the AppController class.

The $uses property is an important property within the controller. It works similarly to the require_once statement in PHP. Basically, once you have created a model (such as Department) and you want to use the model in a controller, you need to include it in the $uses array. For example, where Department and Trade are existing models, you can have the following statement in your controller:

```
$uses = array('Department', 'Trade');.
```

Cake Components

Components are classes defined to carry out specific application tasks to support the controller. Cake comes with many built-in components, such as Acl (for user and group access control), Auth (for user and group authentication), Email, Session, and RequestHandler. Components can also be user-defined. In fact, in large web applications, you will most likely need to build some of your own components to be used by several controllers. All the components that you develop should be stored in the folder app/controllers/components. Components follow the same Cake conventions as controllers.

From a programmer's point of view, components enable you to extend the functionality of Cake. If you find that your component is quite useful and you possess the free open source spirit, you can and should post it on the Cake web site, where there is a public repository of components.

To demonstrate, we'll dive straight in and create our own simple component—a utility to convert an array to an object. Listing 1-16 shows the code to create this component.

Listing 1-16. *A Component to Convert an Array to an Object*

```php
<?php
class ArrayToObjectComponent extends Object{

    function startup(&$controller) {
        $this->Controller = $controller;
    }

    function convert($array, &$obj) {
        foreach ($array as $key => $value) {
            if (is_array($value)) {
                $obj->$key = new stdClass();
                $this->array_to_obj($value, $obj->$key);
            } else {
                $obj->$key = $value;
            }
        }

        return $obj;
    }
}
?>
```

The ArrayToObjectComponent class in Listing 1-16 contains two basic functions, which are stored in app/controllers/components/array_to_object.php:

- The first function, called startup(), is used to instantiate the controller object. This enables all other functions within the component to access information contained in the parent controller. It's basically a callback method used to bring the controller object into the component.

- The second function, convert(), is our user-defined function. It does the work of accepting an array of data and returning the array as an object. You can use this component whenever you want to convert an array to an object.

Everything inside a component should be generic. Do not put controller-specific code, such as a database table name, into components.

You can use components within controllers or other components. To use a component—whether it is a built-in one or one you have created—you need to first declare the component within the $components array in a user-defined controller, another component, or in the AppController class. For example, to use the component in Listing 1-16, include the following statement:

```
var $components = array('ArrayToObject')
```

In Listing 1-17, we make references to the built-in Session component and our ArrayToObject component in the DepartmentsController class.

Listing 1-17. *Using Components in DepartmentsController*

```php
<?php
class DepartmentsController extends AppController
{
    var $uses = array( 'Department');
    var $components = array( 'Session', 'ArrayToObject');

    function display() {
        $arrData = array();
        $arrData   = $this->find('all');
        pr($this->ArrayToObject->convert(arrData, &$obj));
    }
}
?>
```

In Listing 1-17, we convert the result of the data retrieved from our departments database table from an array to an object. First, we use the $uses array to reference the Department model. We then use the $component array to reference the Session component, which is a built-in Cake component, and the ArrayToObject component, which is our user-defined component. Next, we create a display() function that contains a declaration of an array variable called $arrData. We retrieve the department data using the default find() function, store the result in the array, and then pass the array to the convert() method of the ArrayToObject component. Finally, we use the Cake pr() global function to print the resulting object.

Helpers

Cake helpers are classes that help to decrease development time by providing shortcuts to generate presentational elements. Earlier, we used the Cake form helper, which helps with form element creation and data handling. Helper files should be stored in the app/views/helpers folder. Table 1-4 briefly describes some of Cake's built-in helpers. For full documentation of the Cake helpers, check the Cake API at http://api.cakephp.org.

Table 1-4. *Some of Cake's Built-in Helpers*

Helper	Description
HTML	Helps automate creating HTML elements and also enables dynamic generation of HTML tags by accepting and parsing variables. This helper is called in a view by using the $html object. To include a reference to HTML helper, use the variable $helpers = array('Html');. HTML helper functions output HTML elements such as charset, css, div, docType, image, link, meta, nestedList, para, style, tableHeaders, tableCells, and so on.
Form	Helps in form creation and processing. Use the $form object together with its functions to create form elements. For example, to create a form input element, use the $form->input() function. To start the form tag, use the $form->create() function. Other form input element functions include label, checkbox, dateTime, hidden, radio, textarea, and so on. There are many options that can be used in form element functions, such as maxLength, to set the maximum length of an HTML attribute.
Ajax	Helps to simplify Ajax tasks. It requires the statement $javascript->link(array('prototype')) in the view, which references the Prototype JavaScript framework, in order to work properly in a view. You can get a copy of Prototype from http://www.prototypejs.org/download.
JavaScript	Helps to simplify JavaScript tasks, such as to create a JavaScript Object Notation (JSON) object from an array, using $javascript->object(). To attach an event to an element, use $javascript->event().
Paginator	Helps to format data into multiple pages or to sort data based on some parameters. For example, to create a link to the next set of paginated results, use the $paginator->next() function.
Session	Provides functions to deal with session management. For example, to render messages, use $session->flash(). To read all values stored in a given session, use $session->read().
Text	Provides functions to deal with text or string handling. For example, to remove whitespace from the beginning and/or end of text, use the $text->trim() function.
Time	Helps manage dates and times. For example, to check if a given date/time string is today, use the $time->isToday() function.
XML	Helps with XML manipulation. To create XML elements, use the $xml->elem() function. This helper can also be used to convert a result set into XML.

To reference the common helpers that you need in your application, you can specify the following statement in your AppController class:

```
var $helpers = array('Html','Form','Ajax','JavaScript');
```

This will ensure that the `$javascript->link()` function in a layout works properly.

You may need to create your own helper or tweak an existing helper class to provide additional functionality that is not yet supplied by Cake. As an example, Listing 1-18 creates a simple helper called `/app/views/helpers/break.php`. This helper will print a variable and insert a new break after printing.

Listing 1-18. *A Sample Custom Break Helper*

```
class BreakHelper extends AppHelper {
    function newline($val) {
        return $this->output("$val<br />");
    }
}
```

We can use this helper in our `Departments` controller object to insert a break whenever we use the controller's `print()` function, as shown in Listing 1-19.

Listing 1-19. *Using the Sample Break Helper*

```
<?php
class DepartmentsController extends AppController {
    var $name = 'Departments';
    var $helpers = array('Break');

    function print($val) {
        return $this->Break->newline($val);
    }
}
?>
```

First, in Listing 1-19, we reference the break helper by declaring `var $helpers = array('Break');`. Next, we define a `print()` function that accepts a `$val` parameter. This function contains the statement that invokes the break helper's `newline($val)` method, and consequently returns the result with a newline after it.

Plugins

With Cake, you can create a complete MVC package called a *plugin*, which you can integrate into other Cake applications. A plugin is a mini-application with its own controllers, models, views, and other Cake resources. Cake does not have any built-in plugins. You can use third-party plugins, or better still, build your own.

Here, we will create a basic feedback plugin that will provide mailing facility. It will have
the following directory structure:

```
/app
    /plugins
        /feedback
            /controllers
            /models
            /views
            /feedback_app_controller.php
            /feedback_app_model.php
```

where

- /controllers contains plugin controllers.

- /models contains plugin models.

- /views contains plugin views.

- /feedback_app_controller.php is the plugin's AppController, named after the plugin.

- /feedback_app_model.php is the plugin's AppModel, named after the plugin.

■**Note** You must create both an AppController and an AppModel for a plugin to work properly.
If you forget to define the FeedbackAppController class and the FeedbackAppModel, Cake will throw
a "Missing Controller" error.

The feedback plugin's AppController is stored in app/plugins/feedback_app_controller.
php, and its corresponding AppModel class is stored in app/plugins/feedback_app_model.php,
as shown in Listing 1-20.

Listing 1-20. *Feedback App Classes for the Feedback Plugin*

```php
<?php
class FeedbackAppController extends AppController {
    //..
}
?>

<?php
class FeedbackAppModel extends AppModel {
    / /..
}
?>
```

Now, let's create the FeedbackSendController for our feedback plugin. The code in Listing 1-21 is stored in app/plugins/feedback/controllers/feedback_send_controller.php.

Listing 1-21. *The FeedbackSendController to Invoke the send() Method*

```php
<?php
class FeedbackSendController extends FeedbackAppController {
    var $name = 'Feedback';
    var $uses = array( 'Feedback');

    function send($toEmail) {

        $this->set( "result", false );

        if ( $this->Feedback->sendEmail($toEmail) ) {
            $this->set( "result", true );
        }
    }
}
?>
```

Next, we'll create and store the FeedbackSendModel class in the app/plugins/feedback/ models/feedback_send_model.php file, as shown in Listing 1-22.

Listing 1-22. *The FeedbackSendModel That Uses the PHP mail() Function to Send a Message*

```php
<?php
class FeedbackSendModel extends FeedbackAppModel
{
    function sendEmail($recipient) {
        // Here's where we try to send an email message.
        if( mail($recipient, 'Hi', 'What is baking', 'From: sugar@Cake.com') ) {
            return true;
        }
        return false;
    }
}
?>
```

Next, let's create a simple feedback plugin view stored in the app/plugins/feedback/ views/feedback_send/send.ctp file, as shown in Listing 1-23.

Listing 1-23. *The Feedback Email View*

```
<h1>Feedback Email</h1>
<?php
if ( $result ) {
    echo 'Thank you for your feedback.';
} else {
    echo 'Sorry! Our system is down at the moment. Please try again later.';
}
?>
}
?>
```

Now that we have installed the feedback plugin, we can use it. To access the plugin within a Cake application, you can add name of the plugin, then the action, then the parameter to the URL, as follows:

```
http://localhost/feedback/feedbackSend/feedbackSend/send/[emailparam]
```

You can have a default controller with the name of your plugin. If you do that, you can access it via /[plugin]/action. For example, a plugin named users with a controller named UsersController can be accessed at http://[your domain]/users/add if there is no plugin called AddController in your [plugin]/controllers folder.

Plugins will use the layouts from the app/views/layouts folder by default. You will see how to override layouts in Chapter 3.

You can access a plugin within controllers in your Cake application by using the requestAction() function:

```
$sent = $this->requestAction(array('controller'=>'FeedbackSend','action'=>'send'));
```

Vendors

Many modern frameworks adopt the Don't Repeat Yourself (DRY) principle. Lazy (or maybe efficient) programmers don't like to reinvent the wheel! To allow us to sleep in a little longer, Cake has provided a vendors folder. This is where we store third-party applications that don't have any relationship with Cake, such as the phpBB message board application and the Swift Mailer mailing application. This comes in handy, considering the number of utility scripts and programs available in various PHP repositories such as http://www.phpclasses.org.

Cake's technique of including external scripts is as simple as using the following function:

```
App::import('Vendor','file',array('file'=>'fileName.php'));
```

The third parameter of the function accepts an array of file names. Usually, fileName.php is the startup file of the third-party application.

The App::import() function can be used in controllers, models, and views of Cake applications. However, it is important that the call is made before any class definition. The vendors folder provides a standard way to include third-party applications.

As an example, let's create a `spillout.php` script, as shown in Listing 1-24. This script will serve as our third-party script that we'll use in our `ScreenController` later. This script should be stored in the app/vendors folder.

Listing 1-24. *A Script to Display the Content of a File on the Screen*

```php
<?php
class ReadFile {
    protected $file;

    public function __construct($fileName) {
        $this->file = $fileName;
    }

    private function spill() {
        return readfile($this->file);
    }
}
?>
```

Listing 1-24 will simply read the content of the `welcome.html` file and send it to the screen for a user's consumption. We can import this script into our `ScreenController` as shown in Listing 1-25.

Listing 1-25. *The ScreenController to Use a Script as a Vendor*

```php
<?php
    App::import('Vendor','file',array('file'=> 'spillout.php'));
    class ScreenController extends AppController {

    function index() {
        $output = new ReadFile('welcome.html');
        $output->spill();
    }
}
?>
```

In Listing 1-25, we use the `import()` function to load the content of the `spillout.php` file, and then we create an instance of the `ReadFile` class using the `welcome.html` file as its parameter and store it in $output. Finally, we send the content of the file to the screen using `$output->spill();`.

Summary

In this chapter, we briefly introduced you to the main features of Cake. We explained how it is a RAD platform, with the MVC design pattern forming the base foundation. We covered how the Cake MVC structure works, with business logic stored in controllers and components, data access in models, and presentational markup in the view. Additionally, we showed how Cake reduces development time with helpers, plugins, and vendors.

After reading this chapter, you should have an overview of how Cake structures a web application. You should feel confident that learning Cake is one of the best decisions for anyone interested in PHP programming and with a need to write rapid web applications. But do note, sometimes it may be better to write basic methods like "Hello World" in a simple PHP script, rather than using Cake, so that you don't end up killing an ant with a sledge hammer.

In the following chapters, we'll present full-fledged Cake applications, beginning with a simple blogging application.

CHAPTER 2

■■■

Blogging

The Web has revolutionized the way we communicate with friends and strangers. We now freely exchange media content, such as textual information, graphics, audio, and video. One of the ways to exchange such information is known as *blogging*. Blogging uses HTML forms for tasks such as submitting posts, uploading content, and so on.

In the 1990s, blogging started like a kiddie joke, with individuals posting their personal stuff online. Since then, there has been an explosion of blogging web sites. Nowadays, movie stars, politicians, and corporate organizations such as Microsoft host their own blogging sites to communicate their ideas.

This chapter describes how to build your own blogging application. But why would you bother to develop such an application when you can use one of the many free or low-cost solutions, such as Blogger, Movable Type, Textpattern, WordPress, TypePad, or LiveJournal (to name a few)?

The ready-made blogger solutions have common interface design features. Developing your own blogging application allows you to customize the site, giving it a unique look, excluding unnecessary features, and adding features that are not supplied with the prebuilt sites.

In this chapter, we'll build our own blog application, which will enable us to list, add, edit, delete, publish, and unpublish posts. We will use Cake's form helper to automate some tasks, such as to generate form elements, validate user-submitted data, and repopulate invalid form elements with submitted data. We will insert the post data into an XML file to provide RSS service to those with an RSS reader (or aggregator).

To create this blog application, you need a web server that supports PHP and a database server to store some information. If you are new to the concepts and the workings of Cake, read Chapter 1 before continuing with this chapter.

Creating the Database

Building web sites that allow user interactivity sometimes requires working with persistent data, which can be stored in relational databases or local file systems. This requirement applies to building our blog application, as we need to manage the post records. As mentioned in the previous chapter, we'll use the MySQL database server for the examples in this book. We'll use Cake's objects and their methods that allow us to store and retrieve data from a database. For information about how to configure Cake's database connection parameters and connect to a database, see Chapter 1.

Our Blog database will contain a single table named posts. This table will store records of posts. The records include fields for an ID to provide a unique reference for each post, the title of a post, the post's content, the dates that a post was created and modified, and whether or not a post should be published (displayed to the public). Listing 2-1 shows the SQL to create the posts table.

Listing 2-1. *The SQL Statement to Create the posts Table*

```sql
CREATE TABLE IF NOT EXISTS `posts` (
  `id` int(11) NOT NULL auto_increment,
  `title` varchar(50) default NULL,
  `content` text,
  `created` datetime default NULL,
  `modified` datetime default NULL,
  `published` tinyint(1) NOT NULL default '1',
  PRIMARY KEY  (`id`)
);
```

The SQL schema shown in Listing 2-1 will handle basic post information. If you like, you can add more fields, such as a summary field to store summaries of posts.

Now, let's insert some sample post information into our posts table, using the following SQL statements:

```sql
INSERT INTO `posts`➥
(`id`, `title`, `content`, `created`, `modified`, `published`) VALUES
(1, 'Another day Still Looking', 'My Lion ran off',➥
'2008-06-19 18:26:11', '2008-06-19 18:26:11', 1),

(2, 'A good day', 'The Lion is back in one piece.',➥
'2008-06-19 18:31:50', '2008-06-19 18:31:50', 1),

(3, 'Thank GOD', 'Everything belongs to my father',➥
'2008-06-20 18:42:11', '2008-06-20 18:42:11', 1);
```

If you added other fields, be sure to insert their corresponding values with SQL INSERT statements.

▓**Tip** Cake will automatically populate the created and modified fields in a table with the current date information (in our example, the dates when saving and updating posts). In Cake, these fields are called automagic model fields.

Reviewing the Application Structure

Before we start to build the blog application, let's take a brief look at the folder structure and files that will form part of the application. Table 2-1 assumes that other default Cake folders and files also exist in the same environment.

Table 2-1. *The Blog Application Structure*

Directory		Description
app/		The parent folder for the blog application
	config/	Amended database.php file to include our blog database parameters
	controllers/	posts_controller.php file, which contains all the actions, such as add post
	models/	post.php file to deal with our blog application data
	views/posts	index.ctp, add.ctp, edit.ctp, and delete.ctp files

We'll create these files and explain their contents in upcoming sections. For details on Cake's complete file system structure, refer to Chapter 1.

Creating the Post Model

The Post object manages the post data. By using Cake's naming convention, we'll be able to take advantage of the functionality inherently provided by Cake. We'll use that functionality to interact with the posts database table, and access and manipulate the post records. The Post model class, shown in Listing 2-2, is stored in app/models/post.php.

Listing 2-2. *The Post Object That Handles the Post Data (app/models/post.php)*

```php
<?php
class Post extends AppModel
{
    var $name = 'Post';
    var $validate = array( 'title'=>array(
                            'alphaNumeric'=>array(
                                'rule'=>'alphaNumeric',
                                'required'=>true,
                                'message'=>'Enter a title for this post',
                                )
                        ),
                        'content'=>array(
                            'alphaNumeric'=>array(
                                'rule'=>'alphaNumeric',
                                'required'=>true,
                                'message'=>'Enter some content for your post',
                                )
                        )
                );
}?>
```

The Post model class consists of the $name property, used to handle PHP 4 backward-compatibility, and the $validate array property, which contains the validation rules.

In the $validate array, each element's key corresponds to the name of the input element to be validated (for example, title), and its value defines the rules to apply against the input before the post data is saved to the posts table—when the post form is submitted. Listing 2-2 shows the validation rules. We check that the title and the content fields of the form are not empty when the form is submitted. We also check whether the values submitted are alphanumeric. If not, the corresponding error messages set in the validation array against the 'message' keys will be displayed.

The PostsController object, which we will create next, will use the Post model object to access information from the posts table, ensure the integrity of the submitted post information, and then commit the post into the posts database table.

Creating the Posts Controller

Now that the Post model class is created, we need a PostsController object to manage all the post actions. These actions include listing all the posts and providing the user interfaces for adding and editing post data. The controller calls the Post model object created in Listing 2-2 to handle the post data as required.

The PostsController class will contain the methods listed in Table 2-2.

Table 2-2. *The PostsController Class Actions*

Method	Description
index()	Lists all the posts from the posts table and handles the RSS feed for posts
add()	Invokes the add post page and saves validated posts to the posts table
edit()	Invokes the edit post page
disable()	Disables a published post
enable()	Enables a disabled post so it's published
delete()	Removes a post record from the posts table

Listing the Posts

The PostsController class, shown in Listing 2-3, extends the AppController class. This file is stored in app/controllers/posts_controller.php.

Listing 2-3. *The PostsController to Define Post Actions (app/controllers/posts_controller.php)*

```php
<?php
class PostsController extends AppController
{
    var $name = 'Posts';
    function index() {
        $posts = $this->Post->find('all');

        $this->set(compact('posts'));
    }
```

First, we add the index method, which displays the list of posts. By default, this method is called if no other action is called explicitly during a URL request. Along with showing all the published posts, the index page contains links that will enable users to perform operations such as edit, publish, unpublish, and delete a post record.

In Listing 2-3, the index method contains two simple statements. The first uses the Post model object with its default find method to pull all the posts from the posts database table and then store the results in an array called $posts. The second prepares and sets the $posts records so that the views/posts/index.ctp file, shown in Listing 2-4, can display the list of all the posts from the $posts variable.

Listing 2-4. *The View for the Post List (views/posts/index.ctp)*

```php
<div id="center_content">
    <h2>Post Listings</h2>
    <p>Here is a list of the existing posts.</p>
    <div>
    </div>
    <?php
        if ( isset( $posts ) && is_array( $posts ) ) {
    ?>
        <table>
            <tr>
                <td>
                    <b>ID</b>
                </td>
                <td>
                    <b>title</b>
                </td>
                <td>
                    <b>content</b>
                </td>
                <td>
                    <b>Last Modified</b>
                </td>
                <td>
                    <b>published</b>
                </td>
                <td colspan="2"><b>  Action</b></td>
            </tr>
```

```php
<?php foreach ($posts as $post) : ?>
<tr>
    <td><?php echo $post['Post' ][ 'id' ]; ?></td>
    <td><?php echo $post['Post' ][ 'title' ]; ?></td>
    <td><?php echo $post[ 'Post' ][ 'content' ]; ?></td>
    <td><?php echo $post[ 'Post' ][ 'modified' ]; ?></td>
    <td>
        <?php echo $html->link(ife(
                '$post['Post']['published'] == 1',
                'Published',
                'Unpublished'),
                '/posts/'.ife('$post['Post']['published'] == 1',
                'disable','enable').'/'.$post['Post']['id']
                );
        ?>
    </td>
    <td>
        <?php echo $html->link(
                    'Edit',
                    '/posts/edit/'.$post['Post']['id']);?>
    </td>
    <td>
        <?php echo $html->link(
                    'Delete',
                    '/posts/delete/'.$post['Post']['id']);?>
    </td>
</tr>
<? endforeach;?>
<?php
    if ( sizeof( $posts ) == 0 ) {
?>
    <tr style="background-color: #cccccc;">
        <td colspan="6">
            <span style="font-size: 17px;">
                No post found.
            </span>
        </td>
    </tr>
<?php
    }
?>
</table>

<br/>

<?php
    }
?>
</div>
```

The `index.ctp` file in Listing 2-4 starts with the headings of the web page that displays the posts list. We then insert a section of PHP code immediately after these headings. If the `$posts` variable set by the `PostsController` object contains some post records, we first display the headings for the individual elements in the variable. Next, using a `foreach` loop statement to loop through the `$posts` variable, we display a list item for each post. Finally, if the `$post` variable is empty, we simply display the message `No post found`. Figure 2-1 shows an example of a post listing.

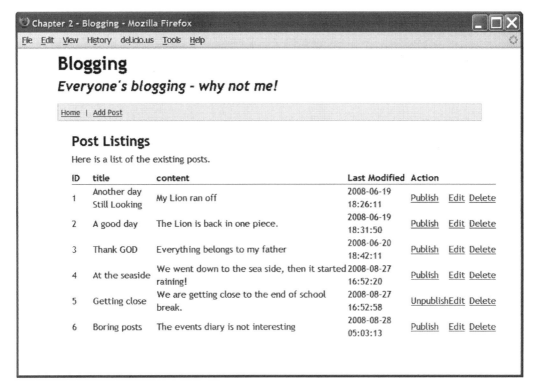

Figure 2-1. *Viewing the post listings page*

This list provides an interface to directly manage individual posts. As shown on the right side of Figure 2-1, the page has links to trigger the publish, edit, and delete actions.

Adding a Post

The next method we need to implement in the `PostsController` class is the `add` method, as shown in Listing 2-5. This method, as the name implies, handles adding post data.

Listing 2-5. *The add Method for Adding Post Data*

```
function add() {

    $actionHeading = 'Add a Post!';
    $actionSlogan = 'Please fill in all fields. Feel free to add your➥
post and express your opinion.';

    $this->set(compact('actionHeading','actionSlogan'));

    if (!empty($this->data)) {
        $this->Post->create();
        if ($this->Post->save($this->data)) {
            $this->Session->setFlash(__('The Post has been saved', true));
            $this->redirect(array('action'=>'index'));
        } else {
            $this->Session->setFlash(➥
__('The Post could not be saved. Please try again.', true));
        }
    }
}
```

In the add method, the first two statements set the heading and slogan for the add view page. This is necessary because we are going to use a single element view to display the forms to add and edit posts. Elements in Cake enable you to reuse views.

Next, we check if the add post form has been submitted. If the form has not been submitted, the add view is displayed. If the submitted data ($this->data) is not empty, using the save method of the Post model object, the application will attempt to create a new post record. The save method automatically uses the validation rules defined in Listing 2-2 to check the integrity of the submitted post. If the post does not pass the validation rules, the error message is set, using the setFlash method of the Session object. Otherwise, the post is saved to the database table, and the success message is set for display in the view.

Next, we'll create the add view and store the codes in views/posts/add.ctp file. The content of the add.ctp file is simply the following code snippet:

```
<?php echo $this->element('add_or_edit');?>
```

The $this->element() method accepts the name of a file stored in the views/elements folder (add_or_edit in this case), without the file extension (without .ctp). It simply transfers the content of add_or_edit.ctp into the add.ctp file. The resulting source code for the add view is shown in Listing 2-6.

Listing 2-6. *The Add View That Provides an Interface to Add a Post (app/views/posts/add.ctp)*

```
<fieldset>
    <legend> <?php __('Add a Post!');?> </legend>
    Please fill in all fields.
    <?php
        echo $form->create('Post');
        echo $form->error( 'Post.title' );
        echo $form->input( 'Post.title',
                        array( 'id' => 'posttitle', 'label' => 'Title:',➥
'size' => '50', 'maxlength' => '255', 'error' => false ) );

        echo $form->error( 'Post.content' );
        echo $form->input( 'Post.content',
                        array( 'id' => 'postcontent', 'type'=>'textarea',➥
'label' => 'Content:', 'rows' => '10', 'error' => false ) );

        echo $form->end( array( 'label' => ' Submit Post ' ) );
    ?>
</fieldset>
```

In Listing 2-6, we start by displaying the heading of the interface for adding a post. We then insert a PHP opening code tag to house the creation of the form using Cake's form helper functionality. First, the `$form->create()` method defines the start tag for our form. Its 'Post' string argument represents the action that will be invoked, such as the URL to which the form data will be submitted. Note that if the method attribute is not specified, the POST method is the default request method.

Next, we start to add the required form input elements using the `$form->error()` method, which deals with the error handling of the form. Its argument, Post.title, is a string that represents the name of the input element, where Post is the model name, followed by a dot (.), and title holds the value of the post's title.

Next is the `$form->input()` method to generate the text input element called title, whose first argument is in the same argument format as the error input element. The second argument of the text input element is an associative array of HTML text input element attributes.

Following that is the code that generates the textarea input element called content using an argument format similar to the title input element discussed previously.

Finally, after we've added the form elements, we can add the form closing tag using the form helper method `$form->end()`. It also accepts an associative array of HTML submit input element attributes.

Figure 2-2 shows an example of an add post form when a user tries to submit a blank form. The error messages are displayed.

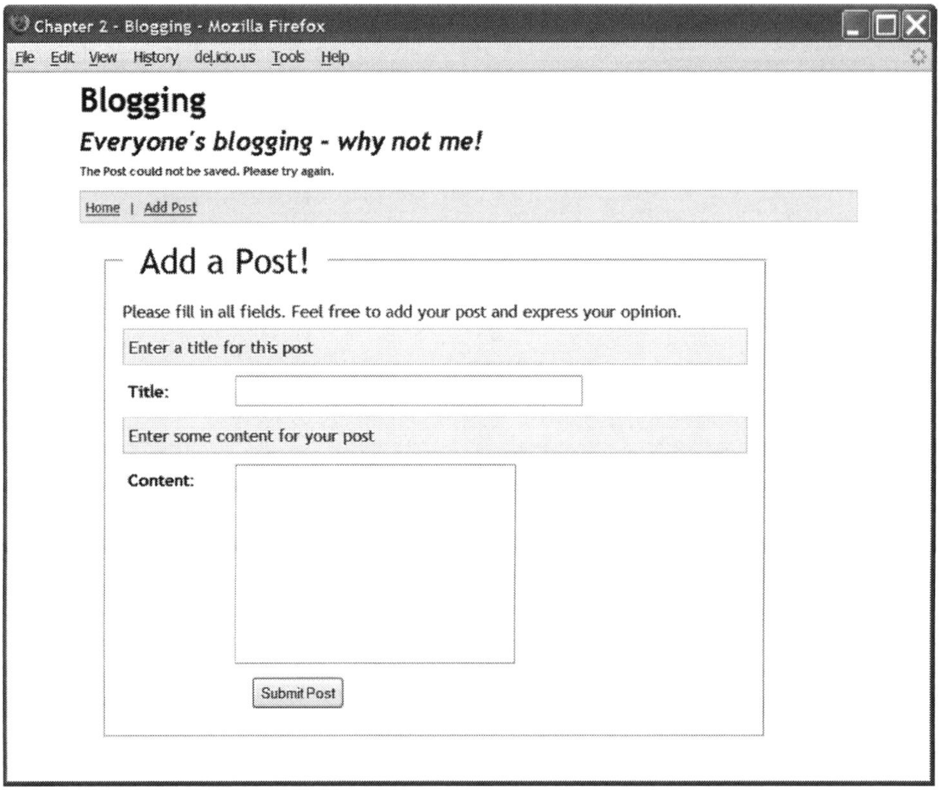

Figure 2-2. *Error messages appear when you try to submit a blank add post form.*

Updating a Post

Sometimes, we are not completely satisfied with our posts and would like to make some amendments. We will create the edit action of the PostsController to handle this task. It uses a supplied post ID (in our case $id) to retrieve the details of a post from the posts database table and repopulates the edit form with the information. This edit method code snippet is shown in Listing 2-7.

Listing 2-7. *The edit Action That Handles a Post Edit Request*

```
function edit($id = null) {

    $actionHeading = 'Edit a Post!';
    $actionSlogan = 'Please fill in all fields. Now you can amend your post.';

    $this->set(compact('actionHeading','actionSlogan'));

    if (!$id && empty($this->data)) {
        $this->Session->setFlash(__('Invalid Post', true));
        $this->redirect(array('action'=>'index'));
    }

    if (!empty($this->data)) {
        if ($this->Post->save($this->data)) {
            $this->Session->setFlash(__('The Post has been saved', true));
            $this->redirect(array('action'=>'index'));
        } else {
            $this->Session->setFlash(__ ➥
('The Post could not be saved. Please try again.', true));
        }
    }

    if (empty($this->data)) {
        $this->data = $this->Post->read(null, $id);
    }
}
```

In Listing 2-7, we first set the heading and slogan for the edit view page. The next step we take is to check whether $id and $this->data (form data) are empty. If so, an error message is stored in our Session object, and the request is redirected to the blog home page. If the submitted form data is not empty, Cake will try to commit the edited post information to the posts database table and then flash appropriate messages upon success or failure. Finally, if only the submitted data is empty, a post's information is pulled with the Post model read method using the supplied $id as the criterion.

Next, we'll create the edit view and store the codes in the views/posts/edit.ctp file. The content of this file is exactly the same as that of the add.ctp file:

```
<?php echo $this->element('add_or_edit');?>
```

Here, we've reused the add_or_edit.ctp element file again to produce the source code for the edit post view, taking advantage of the elements resource of Cake. In principle, the views for adding and editing posts are the same, except for their page headings.

Figure 2-3 shows an example of the edit view for post ID 1.

Figure 2-3. *The view to update post ID 1*

We've built our post forms using one of the key features of Cake: form helpers. These helpers have automated the tasks of generating our form elements, validating the form input, and repopulating the submitted data.

Unpublishing a Post

When you don't want a post record to be displayed on the home page, you can disable the record. Given a post $id, the disable method disables the appropriate post, as shown in Listing 2-8.

Listing 2-8. *The disable Action to Disable a Published Post*

```
function disable($id=null) {
    $post = $this->Post->read(null,$id);
    if (!$id && empty($post)) {
        $this->Session->setFlash(➡
__('You must provide a valid ID number to disable a post.',true));
        $this->redirect(array('action'=>'index'));
    }
    if (!empty($post)) {
        $post['Post']['published'] = 0;
        if ($this->Post->save($post)) {
            $this->Session->setFlash(__('Post ID '.$id.' has been disabled.',true));
```

```
    } else {
        $this->Session->setFlash(__('Post ID '.$id.' was not saved.',true));
    }
    $this->redirect(array('action'=>'index'));
} else {
    $this->Session->setFlash(__('No Post by that ID was found.',true));
    $this->redirect(array('action'=>'index'));
}
}
```

In Listing 2-8, using the request $id, a post record is retrieved from the posts database table and stored in the $post array variable. If the $id value is null or the $post variable is empty, we use the Session object to set the appropriate message and redirect to the blog home page. If there is a valid $id and the $post is not empty, we set the post published element to 0 and update the posts database table. Finally, the Session object sets the appropriate message, and then we redirect to the blog home page.

Publishing a Post

The enable method does the opposite of the disable method. It uses the supplied post ID ($id) to determine which post record to enable, as shown in Listing 2-9.

Listing 2-9. *The enable Action to Enable (Publish) a Disabled Post*

```
function enable($id=null) {
    $post = $this->Post->read(null,$id);
    if (!$id && empty($post)) {
        $this->Session->setFlash(➥
__('You must provide a valid ID number to enable a post.',true));
        $this->redirect(array('action'=>'index'));
    }
    if (!empty($post)) {
        $post['Post']['published'] = 1;
        if ($this->Post->save($post)) {
            $this->Session->setFlash➥
(__('Post ID '.$id.' has been published.',true));
        } else {
            $this->Session->setFlash(__('Post ID '.$id.' was not saved.',true));
        }
        $this->redirect(array('action'=>'index'));
    } else {
        $this->Session->setFlash(__('No Post by that ID was found.',true));
        $this->redirect(array('action'=>'index'));
    }
}
```

In Listing 2-9, the enable method contains the same code sections as that of the disable method in Listing 2-8. The difference is in the enable method, the statement $post['Post']['published'] is set to 1.

Deleting a Post

We can do some housekeeping by removing posts that are no longer needed. We'll use the delete method to remove posts from the posts database table. Listing 2-10 shows the code for the delete method.

Listing 2-10. *The delete Action to Remove Posts*

```
function delete($id = null) {
        if (!$id) {
                $this->Session->setFlash(__('Invalid id for Post', true));
                $this->redirect(array('action'=>'index'));
        }
        if ($this->Post->del($id)) {
                $this->Session->setFlash(__('Post deleted', true));
                $this->redirect(array('action'=>'index'));
        }
    }
}
?>
```

When the delete action is invoked by requesting to delete a post, the dialog box shown in Figure 2-4 appears. Clicking the OK button will permanently remove the selected post record from the database table.

Figure 2-4. *The delete confirmation dialog box*

Creating an RSS Feed

Since we've decided to share our posts with the rest of the world, we can reduce the stress on our blog database by creating an RSS feed—a static XML file that will be updated whenever the posts change.

RSS is an abbreviation for Really Simple Syndication. It is an XML web content syndication format that can be read by using news reader software (or through some online sites and scripts). For the blog application, using an RSS feed means that people can get updated information about your blog without needing to visit your blogging web site. Scripts such as robots can fetch your RSS feed so that your users can be kept informed of changes to your posts.

Essentially, what we'll create is an XML file of the information stored in the posts database table. Remember that our code will be writing to a static file stored somewhere on your web site, so it is important to ensure read-write privileges for the document.

You can generate an RSS feed in several ways, such as with the Document Object Model (DOM), XMLWriter, SimpleXML, and so on. However, Cake provides a helper to handle RSS feeds, so you don't need to worry about how to micromanage them. The RSS helper creates standards-compliant RSS feeds. You invoke its functionality with var $helpers = array('Rss');.

For the RSS feed for our blog application, we first need to include the following in our app/config/routes.php file:

```
Router::parseExtensions( 'rss' );
```

This informs the router to parse out file extensions from the URL. For example, http://localhost/posts.rss would yield a file extension of rss. It is used by RequestHandler components to automatically switch to alternative layouts and templates in order to load the RssHelper with .rss content.

■**Caution** Don't forget to add Router::parseExtensions('rss'); to your app/config/routes.php file and also ensure that you add RequestHandler to your PostsController's $component variable. Things will not go well if the two instructions are not added. However, if you already have Router::parseExtensions, just add the rss string argument. Router::parseExtensions accepts many arguments.

Now we need to perform the following tasks:

- Determine the elements (for example, the data fields) that we want to appear in our RSS feed.

- Create the layout for our RSS/XML view.

- Create the post RSS view.

The first task requires that we tweak the index method in the PostsController class by adding extra lines of code to it. In this case, we will add the channel array data and then fetch the ten most recent post records for public consumption. The content of our new index method is shown in Listing 2-11.

Listing 2-11. *The New index Method of the PostsController Modified for RSS*

```
function index() {
    $posts = $this->Post->find('all');

    $channelData = array(
            'title' => 'Current posts | The blogger',
            'link' => array(
                    'controller' => 'posts', 'action' => 'index', 'ext' => 'rss'),
            'url' => array('controller' => 'posts', 'action' => 'index',➡
'ext' => 'rss'),
            'description' => 'The current posts in our blog',
            'language' => 'en-uk'
                );

    $posts = $this->Post->find('all',
                        array('limit' => 10, 'order' => 'Post.created'));

    $this->set(compact('channelData', 'posts'));
    }
```

In Listing 2-11, the channel and posts information are set for the views and layouts, which we'll create next.

The layout file, app/views/layouts/rss/defaut.ctp, will contain the following code snippet:

```
<?php
    echo $rss->header();

    $channel = $rss->channel(array(), $channelData, $items);

    echo $rss->document(array(), $channel);
?>
```

Since Cake allows views to pass variables to the layout, we've set the $items variable in the layout, instead of following the normal convention of setting variables in a controller.

Next, we will create the RSS view in app/views/posts/rss/index.ctp. This file will contain a function called rss_transform, which accepts the $items (for example, post data) as an argument, and as its name implies, returns a transformed array version of the post data. Listing 2-12 shows the content of the RSS view file.

Listing 2-12. *The Content of the RSS View (app/views/posts/rss/index.ctp)*

```
<?php
    function rss_transform($item) {
        return array('title' => $item['Post']['title'],
            'link' => array('controller' => 'posts', 'action' => 'view',➡
'ext' => 'rss', $item['Post']['id']),
            'guid' => array('controller' => 'posts', 'action' => 'view',➡
```

```
'ext' => 'rss', $item['Post']['id']),
          'description' => strip_tags($item['Post']['content']),
          'pubDate' => $item['Post']['created'],
          );
   }
   $this->set('items', $rss->items($posts, 'rss_transform'));
?>
```

In Listing 2-12, the `$rss->items` helper method converts our post data into an XML format and uses the `set` method to pass the converted XML to the RSS layout. Here, the layout is going to do the work of rendering the output when you make the URL request `posts/index.rss`. Your request should display an XML version of the posts as fetched in the `PostsController` index action. When you choose to view the posts, you can select whether to save a copy of the RSS feed file or display it on the screen. Figure 2-5 shows an example of how this looks in Firefox.

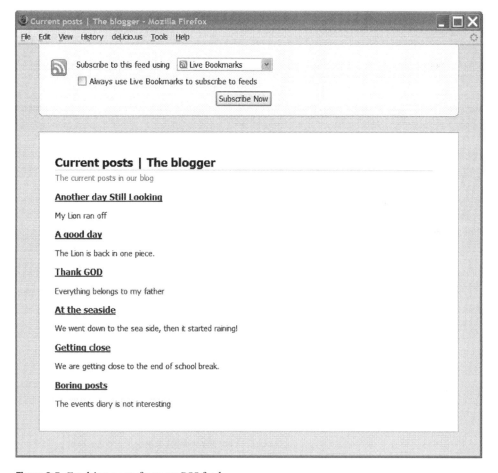

Figure 2-5. *Fetching posts from an RSS feed*

Summary

This chapter described how to build a blogging application using Cake. We first created a posts database table and populated it with some sample posts. We took advantage of Cake's components by creating our posts controller and model classes to perform the necessary tasks: list, add, edit, delete, save, enable, disable, and access data. The corresponding action views were created using the $form object methods. Finally, we created an RSS feed, with the help of the RSS helper, to present some of our posts to the public.

The modularity of the blogging application allows it to be extended by adding more actions to the controller class. For example, you could add an action to upload images.

CHAPTER 3

■■■

E-Commerce

The buzzword e-*commerce*, short for electronic commerce, simply refers to the processing and recording of online transactions. To boast a competitive edge and increase profit, businesses and individuals that peddle services or products must not just have a web presence but also endeavor to sell their merchandise online. There are numerous e-commerce applications based on the PHP scripting language, such as the free, open source osCommerce and Magento. Here, we're going to implement an online shop using the Cake framework.

First, we'll design a skeletal look and feel for our shop, and then we'll create our shop database in MySQL. Next, we'll populate the database with some category and product information. We'll then use Cake features to allow users to select categories and products, add selected products to their shopping cart, click to check out, and, finally, make payments using the popular Google Checkout or PayPal payment system.

This chapter assumes that you're familiar with PHP, MySQL, and Cake. It also assumes that you have set up a development environment that supports these technologies.

The Online Shop Layout

A typical online shop layout is divided into five sections (elements). We'll follow that design and use the Cake view elements listed in Table 3-1. We'll use Cake's features to help us develop these elements of our shop application before stitching them together into the standard layout.

Table 3-1. *View Elements of Online Shop Layout*

Division Name	Description
[Header]	Contains header information, such as the logo and banner
[Left Column]	Displays an expandable category level, sublevel, and product lists
[Center Column]	The main content area of the web site; what it contains depends on the visitor action, so it might show a product description, best-selling products, and so on
[Right Column]	Contains the mini-basket or other elements
[Footer]	Displays summary information about a shop, such as the copyright, contact information, shortcut links, and so on

▓**Tip** To include the left navigation element stored in `app/views/elements/menu.php` in a view, use the code `$this->elements('menu');`.

Two Site Layouts

In this example, we're going to use two different layouts:

- Most of the web pages will show the five sections of the web site as illustrated in Figure 3-1. This first layout is stored in the `app/views/layouts/default.ctp` file as the application default layout.

- The second layout will exclude the right column by collapsing the center and the right columns into one column. This layout stored in `app/views/layouts/checkbase.ctp`. We'll use this layout to display the `checkout` action of the orders controller.

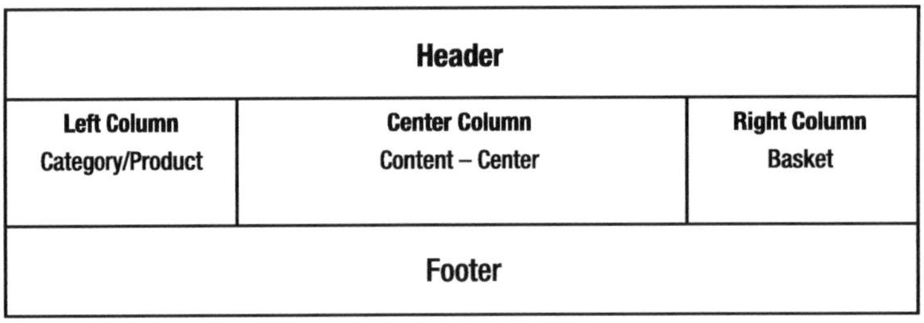

Header		
Left Column **Category/Product**	**Center Column** **Content – Center**	**Right Column** **Basket**
Footer		

Figure 3-1. *The default layout*

▓**Note** One of the aims of this book is to show you how to properly organize elements (code snippets) of an application within the Cake's structure in order to enjoy the benefit of Cake's code reuse and ease of maintenance. However, in this chapter, we will not discuss how our online shop folders and files are organized, as this organization is identical to the structure explained in Chapter 1.

Layout of the Main Content

When a user requests a web page, the `default.ctp` file takes care of the overall look and feel of the web site, which is shown in Figure 3-1. If you want to adapt the main layout of the shop application, just edit the file or create another layout, such as a `checkbase.ctp` file, to suit your needs. However, do not forget to include the `$layout = 'checkbase';` statement in the method of your controller object that requires this new look.

The following code displays only the main content area of the layout:

```
<div id="main_content_container">
    <div id="leftnav"><?php echo $this->element(menu');?></div>
        <div id="main_body_container">
            <?php echo $content_for_layout; ?>
        </div>
    <div id="right_nav_container">
        <?php echo $this->element('basket');?>
    </div>
</div>
```

The `$this->element(menu')` method is used to include the navigation view stored in the app/views/elements/menu.ctp file. This file contains the view logic that generates the category tree menu that is displayed in the left column of the layout. This navigation section of the page is expected to display the product categories at all times. The `$content_for_layout` variable includes the view rendered in response to a user action. The `$this->element('basket')` method displays the mini-basket content in the right column of the layout.

The User Journey

Like any successful dynamic web site, an online shop requires planning and a data store of some sort before jumping into the implementation of the application. These tasks include database design, program flow design, resource planning, and so on. Since we are fortunate to have an existing database schema to use for this example, we will skip the first step of categorizing and normalizing our shop data and move on to explaining the program flow, or user journey.

The online shopping process starts with a customer surfing the Internet and ends with the customer parting with some cash, which ends up in some businessman's online account.

This basic flow for our online shop example looks like this:

1. A user visits our shop.

2. The user browses the categories and products.

3. The user views the product details.

4. The user adds products to the shopping basket.

5. The user clicks to check out and pay.

6. The customer receives an e-mail confirmation notice.

In our example, users do not need to register. They browse categories and products, pay for selected items, and leave the shop.

During the user journey, some vital transaction information is collected and stored in database tables. Needless to say, the tracked data is used for transaction completion and for making other business decisions.

Setting Up the Shop Database

First, we need to connect our application to a MySQL database server. Our configuration, stored in the app/config/database.php file, includes the following array definition:

```
var $default = array('driver' => 'mysql',
        'persistent' => false,
        'host' => 'localhost',
        'login' => 'user',
        'password' => 'password',
        'database' => 'shop',
        'prefix' => '',
);
```

Do not forget to replace the current database access information with your local username and password. If you need more information about how to configure a database connection, see Chapter 1.

We'll create three database tables for our online shop application:

- The categories table stores product categories.

- The products table stores the product descriptions.

- The carts table stores selected product items.

■**Note** We've said that we are not going to collect personal user information in our online shop application. So how do we identify a user? We will create and use a session ID for every unique user request. For information about implementing authentication, see Chapter 8. Also, some common online shop tables, such as the order and order_item tables, are left out of this example. Any table schema not presented in this section is skipped for the sample implementation of this application.

As indicated in Figure 3-1, the left column of our shop layout will present a navigation menu tree that is generated from the product categories data. The categories table and data are created by the SQL statements shown in Listing 3-1.

Listing 3-1. *The categories Table Schema*

```
CREATE TABLE IF NOT EXISTS `categories` (
  `id` int(10) unsigned NOT NULL auto_increment,
  `parent_id` int(11) NOT NULL default '0',
  `name` varchar(50) character NOT NULL,
  `description` varchar(200) character NOT NULL,
  `image` varchar(255) character NOT NULL,
  PRIMARY KEY  (`id`),
  KEY `cat_parent_id` (`parent_id`),
  KEY `cat_name` (`name`)
);
```

```
INSERT INTO `categories` (`id`, `parent_id`, `name`, `description`, `image`) VALUES
(17, 0, 'Jazz', 'Everything from 1890s', ''),
(12, 0, 'Classical', 'From Medieval to Contemporary', ''),
(13, 17, 'Dizzy Gillespie', 'The Trumpeter Master', ''),
(14, 12, 'Mozart', 'The Old Favourite', '');
```

Next, our categories need to relate to some product information, which we'll put in a products table. Listing 3-2 presents the SQL statements to create this table and populate it with some sample data.

Listing 3-2. *The products Table Schema*

```
CREATE TABLE IF NOT EXISTS `products` (
  `id` int(10) unsigned NOT NULL auto_increment,
  `category_id` int(10) unsigned NOT NULL default '0',
  `name` varchar(100) character NOT NULL default '',
  `description` text character NOT NULL,
  `price` decimal(9,2) NOT NULL default '0.00',
  `qty` smallint(5) unsigned NOT NULL default '0',
  `image` varchar(200) character default NULL,
  `thumbnail` varchar(200) character default NULL,
  `created` datetime NOT NULL default '0000-00-00 00:00:00',
  `modified` datetime NOT NULL default '0000-00-00 00:00:00',
  PRIMARY KEY (`id`),
  KEY `cat_id` (`category_id`),
  KEY `name` (`name`)
);

INSERT INTO `products` (`id`, `category_id`, `name`, `description`, ➥
`price`, `qty`, `image`, `thumbnail`, `created`, `modified`) VALUES
(1, 13, 'Dizzy 1990s', 'Best of Dizzy Gillespie in the 1990s', 12.00, ➥
10, NULL, '1.jpg', '0000-00-00 00:00:00', '0000-00-00 00:00:00'),
(2, 14, 'Mozart for Lovers', 'Relax with your loved one with this ➥
double CD.', 15.00, 5, NULL, NULL, '0000-00-00 00:00:00', '0000-00-00 00:00:00'),
(22, 13, 'Dizzy and Stan', 'Live with Dizzy Gillespie and Stan Getz.', ➥
13.00, 10, NULL, '1.jpg', '0000-00-00 00:00:00', '0000-00-00 00:00:00');
```

When a user selects a category, the products linked to this category are displayed. For example, when you select the category called Jazz, you'll see the Dizzy 1990s item and the Dizzy and Stan item listed as products under this category.

Next on the user journey, when a user has selected the type of music she wants to buy and she is happy with the vibes, she adds her selections to a shopping basket. The user-selected items are stored in the carts database table. This table and some sample data are created using the SQL in Listing 3-3.

Listing 3-3. *The carts Table Schema*

```
CREATE TABLE IF NOT EXISTS `carts` (
  `id` int(10) unsigned NOT NULL auto_increment,
  `product_id` int(10) unsigned NOT NULL default '0',
  `qty` mediumint(8) unsigned NOT NULL default '1',
  `ct_session_id` char(32) NOT NULL,
  `created` datetime NOT NULL default '0000-00-00 00:00:00',
  PRIMARY KEY  (`id`),
  KEY `pd_id` (`product_id`),
  KEY `ct_session_id` (`ct_session_id`)
);

INSERT INTO `carts` (`id`, `product_id`, `qty`, `ct_session_id`, `created`) VALUES
(52, 1, 2, '32cabb9d6fb31404a5b736830eac6aa3', '2008-09-24 15:46:53'),
(51, 2, 3, '32cabb9d6fb31404a5b736830eac6aa3', '2008-09-24 15:29:01');
```

■**Tip** Some online shops store configuration information in a table. Alternatively, this information can be stored using Cake's configuration method—for example, `Configure::write('Shop.name', 'Sound Empire');`. To access the shop name, use Cake's configuration `read` method, as in `Configure::read('Shop.name')`. As you can imagine, a shop administrator would find it more difficult to update these configuration parameters than to work with information stored in a database table. Modifying the parameters would require physical file system access and consequently some manipulation fuss.

Interacting with the Online Shop Database

Now that we're connected to the database, created the required tables, and populated them with some sample data, our application needs the information stored in the database in order to provide the initial content of the web pages. For example, the site navigation requires the category data stored in the `categories` table to do its bit. So who handles the tasks of accessing and manipulating information stored in the database? You'll be happy to learn that Cake provides default model functions that serve as shortcuts to database operations. These prebuilt functions allow for easy and fast application development. Now let's start digging out some information.

First, we'll create our custom objects to handle the display of an expandable category level, sublevel, and product lists.

The Category Model

Let's create the Category model class to interact with the categories table data created in Listing 3-1. The beginning of this model is shown in Listing 3-4.

Listing 3-4. *The Beginning of the Category Model (app/models/category.php)*

```
<?php
class Category extends AppModel {
    var $name = 'Category';
    var $hasMany = array('Product');
```

In this model, we have two important properties:

- The $name property will serve as a reference to this model object within the controllers of this application when needed.

- The association property $hasMany simply defines the relationship between the categories table and the products table. In this case, we define that a categories record can relate to many products records. In our application, the category Jazz is associated with the products Dizzy 1990s and Dizzy and Stan (see Listings 3-1 and 3-2). This property is required to ensure an association between the Category and Product model objects.

Now that the Category model class is attached to our categories table data and it has established a relationship with the products table data, we can create some custom methods in the model class to interact with the categories and products tables. These custom methods will internally use Cake's default properties and methods, such as the find method for database create, read, update, and delete (CRUD) operations.

The Category model class will contain three methods to provide information in the final format needed to generate the products category navigation: getCategories, buildCategories, and getChildCategories.

The first method, getCategories, returns the entire category list. This method is shown in Listing 3-5.

Listing 3-5. *The Category Model's getCategories() Method*

```
function getCategories($field='Category.id',$direction='ASC') {
    return $this->find('all',array('order'=>$field.' '.$direction));
}
```

The method in Listing 3-5 is employed whenever we require the list of all the product categories from the categories table, in ascending order of the category IDs. We've provided some parameters, $field and $direction, so that it's possible to use this function in more than one way elsewhere in the application.

Next in this model class is the buildCategories method, which returns the currently selected category and its children categories. This method is shown in Listing 3-6.

Listing 3-6. *The Category Model's buildCategories() Method*

```
function buildCategories($categories, $parentId)
{
    $ChildCategories = array();
    $ids = array();
    foreach ($categories as $category) {
        if ($category['Category']['parent_id'] == $parentId) {
            $ChildCategories[] = $category['Category'];
        }
        $ids[$category['Category']['id']] = $category['Category'];
    }
    $HoldParentId = $parentId;
    while ($HoldParentId != 0) {
        $parent    = array($ids[$HoldParentId]);
        $currentId = $parent[0]['id'];
        $HoldParentId = $ids[$HoldParentId]['parent_id'];
        foreach ($categories as $category) {
            if ($category['Category']['parent_id'] == $HoldParentId && ➥
!in_array($category['Category'], $parent)) {
                $parent[] = $category['Category'];
            }
        }
        array_multisort($parent);
        $n = count($parent);
        $ChildCategories2 = array();
        for ($i = 0; $i < $n; $i++) {
            $ChildCategories2[] = $parent[$i];
            if ($parent[$i]['id'] == $currentId) {
                $ChildCategories2 = array_merge($ChildCategories2,
                                                $ChildCategories);
            }
        }
        $ChildCategories = $ChildCategories2;
    }
    return $ChildCategories;
}
```

This method takes two arguments: an array of the entire category records from the categories table ($categories) and a category's parent ID ($parentId). The getCategories method in Listing 3-5 supplies the $categories array data used as the first argument in the buildCategories method in Listing 3-6.These two Category model methods, together with the $this->passedArgs['c'] obtained from the user request, are used in the CategoriesController class method called menu to generate the application category navigation presented in the left column of the web pages. The CategoriesController is discussed in the next section.

In Listing 3-6, first we declare two array variables: $ChildCategories and $ids. Using a for loop over $categories, if the current category's parent ID equals that passed as an argument ($parentId), we add the current category to the $ChildCategories array variable. We also add the current category to the $ids array, making sure that the $ids array key is the category ID of the current category. This is followed by a while loop to create a parent category and append children categories appropriately. Finally, the function formats and returns the current category list, which includes only the currently selected category and its children. This function is made so it can also handle deep category levels (more than two levels).

Next, we create the getChildCategories method, as shown in Listing 3-7. This method returns a list of the entire category IDs that belong to the children of a specified category.

Listing 3-7. *The Category Model's getChildCategories() Method*

```
function getChildCategories($categories, $id, $recursive = true)
{
    if ($categories == NULL) {
        $categories = $this->getCategories();
    }
    $n     = count($categories);
    $child = array();
    for ($i = 0; $i < $n; $i++) {
        $catId    = $categories[$i]['id'];
        $parentId = $categories[$i]['parent_id'];
        if ($parentId == $id) {
            $child[] = $catId;
            if ($recursive) {
            $child = array_merge($child,
                            $this->getChildCategories($categories, $catId));
            }
        }
    }
    return $child;
}
```

The arguments supplied to the getChildCategories method contain the following information, in the order presented here:

- $categories: All the category lists stored in the categories table.

- $id: A category ID that requires its children category IDs.

- $recursive: Whether it should include all levels deep of children categories in the operation. Its default value is the Boolean true.

Next in this method we use an if statement to check for a valid category list, if the getChildCategories method is not supplied with a valid category argument. This means that if there is no category information from the categories table stored in the $categories array, we use the getCategories method to generate the entire category list and assign the result to the $categories variable.

Next, we count the number of elements in the $categories array and assign the result to the $n variable. We then declare an array variable called $child, which will contain a list of the children category IDs.

We then loop over the $categories array variable with a for loop and assign a category ID and its parent ID to $catId and $parentId, respectively. Next, using an If statement, we check that the current parent ID ($parentId) we've extracted is the one for which we want to obtain children category IDs. If the $parentId is the same as the one passed to the getChildCategories method as an argument ($id), we add the current category ID to the $child array variable. By default, this method will use itself to perform the same tasks based on the current category ID, unless the $recursive argument is set to Boolean false. Lastly, this method will return the $child array variable containing all children category IDs of a specified category parent ID.

The getChildCategories method in Listing 3-7 is used within the ProductsController class method called lists to provide this function with a list of category IDs. This function uses the list of category IDs, formatted as {1,2,3}, to fetch a list of all products that belong to these category IDs, presented in the middle column of the web page. The ProductsController is discussed a little later in this chapter.

The Categories Controller

Now that we've created the Category model, let's delve into the CategoriesController class, as shown in Listing 3-8.

Listing 3-8. *The CategoriesController Class (app/controllers/categories_controller.php)*

```php
<?php
class CategoriesController extends AppController {
    var $name = 'Categories';
    function getAll() {
        return $this->Category->getCategories();
    }
    function menu() {
        $categories = $this->getAll();
        return $this->Category->buildCategories($categories,
                                    $this->passedArgs['c']);
    }
}
?>
```

In the CategoriesController, we make use of the services provided by the methods defined in the Category model, discussed in the previous section. Additionally, one of the properties inherited from the AppController is the $uses array. This array includes an element that provides a reference to the Category model.

Next, we declare the getAll method, which simply provides the list of all the categories information from the categories table. This method returns the result of the $this->Category->getCategories() statement when called by another object.

The last method provided by the CategoriesController is menu. As the name implies, it helps with the creation of the categories navigation (menu) shown in the left column of the web site. The first statement of this method stores the categories information in the $categories array using the getAll method previously defined in this class. This array variable, as well as the current category ID (supplied by $this->passedArgs['c']), is then passed to the buildcategories() method to create an array formatted for the menu view. The array returned by the buildcategories method on the home page of the web site is structured as follows:

```
Array
(
    [0] => Array
        (
            [id] => 12
            [parent_id] => 0
            [name] => Classical
            [description] => From Medieval to Contemporary
            [image] =>
        )

    [1] => Array
        (
            [id] => 17
            [parent_id] => 0
            [name] => Jazz
            [description] => Everything from 1890s
            [image] =>
        )
)
```

This array structure contains two first-level category records; that is, categories with their parent IDs equal to an integer value of 0 (zero).

Next, we call the menu method of the CategoriesController within the app/views/elements/ menu.ctp file to supply this view script with the categories information required to display the category navigation menu. The view takes the category list (stored in $categories) and displays its content in Cascading Style Sheets (CSS) <ul> and <li> tags in the left column of the layout. Since the category navigation is central to this application—that is, it must always be displayed—we've placed the following code snippet in the default.ctp layout file to include this element of the web site at all times:

```
<div id="leftnav"><?php echo $this->element(menu');?></div>
```

The content of the menu.ctp view file is shown in Listing 3-9.

Listing 3-9. *The Category Navigation View for the Left Column (app/views/elements/menu.ctp)*

```
<ul>
<li><?=$html->link('All Category','/');?></li>
<?php
$categories = $this->requestAction("/categories/menu/c:$catId/p:$pdId/ ");
foreach ($categories as $category) {
    extract($category);
    $level = ($parent_id == 0) ? 1 : 2;
    $url   = '/carts/index/cat_id:' . $id;
    if ($level == 2) {
        $name = "~~~" . $name;
    }
    $listId = '';
```

```php
        if ($id == $catId) {
            $listId = ' id="current"';
        }
?>
<li<?php echo $listId; ?>><?=$html->link($name, $url);?></li>
<?php
}
?>
</ul>
```

In Listing 3-9, the first line begins with the <ul> opening tag. Next, using the $html helper object, we created a link to display the message 'All Category'.

The first line of the <?php opening tag uses Cake's requestAction function. It requests the menu method of the CategoriesController object to provide a list of categories information (stored in the $categories array variable) that match the category and the product IDs passed to this method using the c:$catId and p:$pdId parameters, respectively.

Finally, using a foreach loop, the $categories array content is extracted to generate the category navigation that appears in the left column throughout the application. Figure 3-2 shows the application response when the Classical menu item is selected by a user, with the submenu item Mozart displayed.

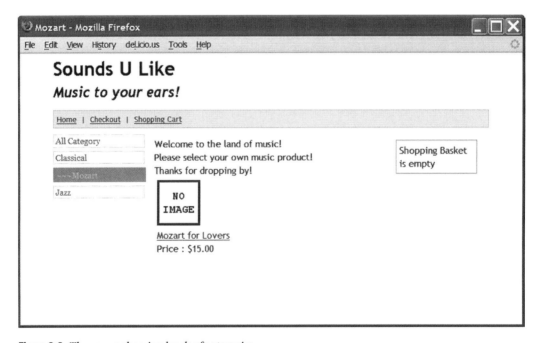

Figure 3-2. *The screen showing levels of categories*

The Product Model

Our next task is to implement the Product model class, which as the name suggests, provides product information from the products table. We will begin with the class properties, as shown in Listing 3-10.

Listing 3-10. *The Beginning of the Product Model (app/models/product.php)*

```php
<?php
class Product extends AppModel
{
    var $name = 'Product';
    var $belongsTo = array('Category');
```

In the $name property, the $belongsTo array variable tells the application that a product record belongs to a category. (The $name property works as described in the earlier discussion of the Category model.)

Next is the lists method, shown in Listing 3-11. This method provides all the product records based on one or more category IDs in the ascending order of product category ID.

Listing 3-11. *The Product Model's lists() Method*

```php
function lists($catIds = NULL) {
    if(is_array($catIds)) {
    $results = $this->find( 'all', array(
        'conditions'=>array('Product.category_id'=>$catIds),
        'order' => 'Product.category_id ASC' ));
    return $results;
    }
}
```

The Products Controller

Now that we've created the Product model class, we need an object to provide some data and services to other objects in our shop application. The ProductsController class, shown in Listing 3-12, defines the lists and view methods to provide these services when called by other objects or scripts within the application.

Listing 3-12. *The ProductsController Class (app/controllers/products_controller.php)*

```php
<?php
class ProductsController extends AppController {
    var $name = 'Products';
    function lists() {
        $categories = $this->Category->find( 'all',
                                    array( 'order' => 'Category.id ASC' ));
        $categories = $this->Category->buildCategories($categories,
                                    $this->passedArgs['c']);
        $children_ids  = $this->Category->getChildCategories($categories,
                                    $this->passedArgs['c'], true);
```

```
            $allCatIds = array_merge(array($this->passedArgs['c']), $children_ids);
            return $this->Product->lists($allCatIds) ;
        }

        function view() {
            $result = $this->Product->find( 'all',
                                        array('conditions'=>array('Product.id'=>
                                              $this->passedArgs['pd_id'] )));
            if (empty ($result) ) {
                $this->redirect(array('controller'=>'/ecommerce', 'action'=>'index'));
            }
            $this->set('product', $result);
        }
    }
?>
```

The lists method in Listing 3-12 returns a list of products based on one or more category IDs. The first statement in this method retrieves all the categories information and stores the result in the $categories array. This array is then used as the first argument of the buildCategories method of the Category model to provide a filtered set of category information, stored in the $categories array variable. The second argument, $this->passedArgs['c'], of this method determines the family of category information that is required.

Next is the getChildCategories method, which accepts the newly created $categories array as the first argument, the current category ID (stored in $this->passedArgs['c']), and a Boolean true. We talked about this method earlier in the discussion of the Category model class (Listing 3-7). Here, this method returns the list of all children category IDs that belong to the category ID supplied as second argument of the method. Next, using the PHP array_merge function, the current category ID and that of the children are merged together and stored in the $allCatIds array variable.

Finally, the $allCatIds variable is passed to the lists method of the Product model, which returns a list of all products that belong to the category IDs available in the $allCatIds variable. The lists method of the ProductsController is called or triggered when a user clicks a category. This method is called in the app/views/elements/products.ctp view file, which is shown in Listing 3-13.

Listing 3-13. *The Product List View for the Center Column (app/views/elements/products.ctp)*

```
<?php
$products = $this->requestAction("/products/lists/c:$catId/");
foreach($products as $product): ?>
<div class="product_container">
<?php
    if ( $product['Product']['thumbnail'] ) {
        $thumbnail = '/img/products/' . $product['Product']['thumbnail'];
    } else {
        $thumbnail = 'no-image-small.png';
    }
```

```
    e( $html->link(
        $html->image($thumbnail, array( 'border' => '0' )),
        array('controller' =>'products',
        'action' => "view/cat_id:$catId/pd_id:".$product['Product']['id']
        ),
        array('escape' => false))); ?>
    <br>
    <? echo $html->link( $product['Product']['name'], ➥
"/products/view/cat_id:$catId/pd_id:".$product['Product']['id'] ); ?>
    <br>Price : $<?=$product['Product']['price'];
?>
</div>
<? endforeach;?>
```

In Listing 3-13, the first line uses Cake's requestAction function to request the lists method of the ProductsController object to provide a list of product information that matches the category ID passed to this method via the c:$catId parameter. The resulting list of products is stored in the $products array variable. Finally, using a foreach loop, the content of the $products array is displayed in the center of the web page. The resulting view is shown in Figure 3-3.

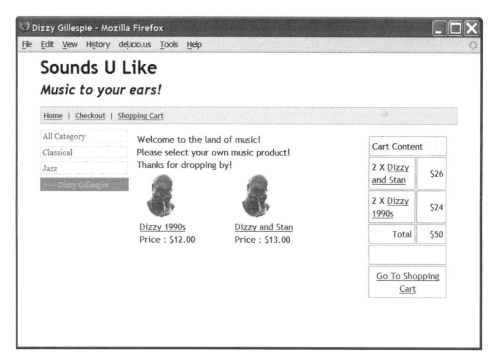

Figure 3-3. *The view rendered when a category ID is selected*

The last method in Listing 3-12, view, uses Cake's set method to automagically pass a full product description to the app/views/products/view.ctp file. Using the default find method against the Product object, our view method retrieves a record of a product from the products table based on a specified product ID (retrieved from $this->passedArgs['pd_id']). This product information is stored in the $result array variable. If $result is empty, then the application redirects the user to the home page; otherwise, the current product information is displayed on the page.

If the product ID is set, then the content of the product details view stored in the app/views/elements/product_details.ctp file will be displayed in the center column. This view file is shown in Listing 3-14.

Listing 3-14. *The Product Details View for the Center Column (app/views/elements/product_details.ctp)*

```php
<?php
    if ( $product[0]['Product']['image'] ) {
        $pd_thumbnail = '/img/products/' . $product[0]['Product']['image'];
    } else {
        $pd_thumbnail = 'no-image-small.png';
    }
    e($html->image($pd_thumbnail,
                    array( 'border' => '0', 'width'=>'150', 'height'=>'150' )));
?>
<br />
<strong><?php echo $product[0]['Product']['name']; ?></strong>
<br />
Price : <?php echo Configure::read('Shop.currency'); ?>
<?php echo $product[0]['Product']['price']; ?><br>
<?php
    if ($product[0]['Product']['qty'] > 0) {
        e($html->link('Add to Shopping Basket',
            '/carts/add/cat_id:'.$catId.'/pd_id:'.$product[0]['Product']['id']));
    } else {
        e('Out Of Stock');
    }
?>
<br />
<?php
    e( nl2br($product[0]['Product']['description']));
?>
```

In Listing 3-14, we use the $product array variable passed in using $this->set('product', $result) from the view method of the ProductsController. It displays the product details in the center of the web page, as shown in the example in Figure 3-4.

The ProductsController and other controllers employ the services of the Product and Category models. Reference to these models is available in the AppController class, as discussed a little later in the chapter.

Figure 3-4. *The index view rendered when a product is selected*

The Cart Model

Next, we'll implement the Cart model class. Along with supplying the content of the shopping cart to the application, the Cart model provides functionalities to manipulate the cart, as well as the checkout section of the application. We will begin with the class properties, shown in Listing 3-15.

Listing 3-15. *The Beginning of the Cart Model (app/models/cart.php)*

```php
<?php
class Cart extends AppModel
{
    var $name = 'Cart';
    var $hasMany = array('Product');
```

The Cart class starts with the class definition, as usual, and then establishes its relationship with the Product model object using var $hasMany = array('Product');. This simply states that a cart can contain one or more products.

We'll create the following methods in the Cart model:

- getCart
- isCartEmpty
- addCart
- updateCart
- cleanUp
- emptyBasket
- doUpdate
- getCartContent

The getCart method supplies all the information stored in the carts table. This method is shown in Listing 3-16.

Listing 3-16. *The Cart Model's getCart() Method*

```
function getCart($pid, $sid) {
    return $this->find( 'all', array(
    'conditions'=>array('Cart.product_id'=>$pid,
                        'Cart.ct_session_id'=>$sid),
                        'order' => 'Cart.id ASC' ));
}
```

The getCart method takes two arguments: $pid (product ID) and $sid (session ID). These are used in Cake's find method to filter the provided carts table records. The product ID is extracted from a user's URL request. The session ID is obtained from Cake's Session object. These variables are extracted in the beforeFilter method of the AppController object, as you will see later in this chapter.

Next is the isCartEmpty method, which checks whether there is at least one record in the carts table. This method is shown in Listing 3-17.

Listing 3-17. *The Cart Model's isCartEmpty() Method*

```
function isCartEmpty($sid = NULL) {
    $result = $this->find('first',
                array('conditions'=>array('Cart.ct_session_id'=>$sid),
                                        'recursive' => 0 ));
    if ( empty( $result ) ) {
        return true;
    }
        return false;
}
```

The isCartEmpty method accepts $sid (session ID) as its argument and uses the find method to check whether the session ID exists in the carts table. If this session ID exists in the carts table, true is returned; otherwise, false is returned, and the message "Shopping Basket is empty" is displayed. The status of the basket section, on the right side of the web site, depends on the value returned by this method.

Next, we need the function to add a product to the carts table, addCart, as shown in Listing 3-18.

Listing 3-18. *The Cart Model's addCart() Method*

```
function addCart($product_id, $sid) {
    $this->data[ 'Cart' ][ 'product_id' ] = $product_id;
    $this->data[ 'Cart' ][ 'qty' ] = 1;
    $this->data[ 'Cart' ][ 'ct_session_id' ] = $sid;

    $this->save();
}
```

The addCart method takes a product ID and the session ID as its arguments. Here, we use Cake's model method save to add the product ID, quantity, and session ID. We do not need to fill in the cart table's created field (see Listing 3-3), as this is one of Cake's magic fields and will be filled in automatically by the model when the save method is called.

Now we need a function to update the quantity of a product in the carts table. This is the updateCart, as shown in Listing 3-19.

Listing 3-19. *The Cart Model's updateCart() Method*

```
function updateCart($product_id, $sid) {
    $sql = "UPDATE carts
    SET qty = qty + 1
    WHERE ct_session_id = '$sid' AND product_id = $product_id";
    $this->query( $sql );
}
```

This is triggered when a user clicks the Add to Shopping Basket link on the product description page. If the displayed product ID and session ID match that of the argument, the record quantity is incremented by one.

Next, we include a function to remove old cart records, cleanUp. Sometimes customers add products to the shopping basket, but don't bother to either complete the transaction or empty the basket. The method shown in Listing 3-20 will handle cleaning up abandoned carts' records.

Listing 3-20. *The Cart Model's cleanUp() Method*

```
function cleanUp() {
    $threeDaysAgo = date('Y-m-d H:i:s',
                        mktime(0,0,0, date('m'),
                                date('d') - 3,
                                date('Y')));

    $delete_condition = "Cart.created < '$threeDaysAgo'";
    $this->deleteAll( $delete_condition, false);
}
```

The cleanUp method deletes records that were added to the basket three days ago from the carts table.

Next is the `emptyBasket` method, shown in Listing 3-21. This method is used as the delete function that is triggered when a user clicks the Delete button on the checkout page.

Listing 3-21. *The Cart Model's emptyBasket() Method*

```
function emptyBasket($cartId = NULL) {
    if ($cartId) {
      $this->delete( $cartId );
    }
}
```

The `emptyBasket` method deletes a record from the carts table based on the cart ID.

We also need to be able to update the quantity of products a customer wants to buy. This functionality is provided by the `doUpdate` method, as shown in Listing 3-22.

Listing 3-22. *The Cart Model's doUpdate() Method*

```
function doUpdate($newQty, $catId) {

    // Update product quantity
    $this->data[ 'Cart' ][ 'qty' ] = $newQty;
    $this->id = $catId;

    $this->save();
}
```

The `doUpdate` method accepts two arguments: $newQty supplies the new quantity of products the customer wants to purchase, and $catId specifies the ID of the carts table record to be updated.

Finally, we add the `getCartContent` method to find out what's in the cart, as shown in Listing 3-23.

Listing 3-23. *The Cart Model's getCartContent() Method*

```
function getCartContent( $sid ) {
    $cartContent = array();
    $sql = "SELECT ct.id, ct.product_id, ct.qty, pd.name, pd.description,
            pd.price, pd.thumbnail, pd.category_id
            FROM carts ct, products pd, categories cat
            WHERE
            ct_session_id = '$sid' AND
            ct.product_id = pd.id AND
            cat.id = pd.category_id";
    $results = $this->query( $sql );
    foreach ($results as $result ) {
        $cartContent[] = $result;
    }
    return $cartContent;
}

}
?>
```

The getCartContent method returns the contents of the carts table where the session ID field value matches the argument $sid. The result, stored in the $cartContent array, contains additional product and category information relating to the retrieved cart's contents. If there is no match, an empty array variable is returned.

Handling User Requests

Now that we have created all the functionality needed to interact with our database, we can begin the process of building our application's controllers to handle user requests. We will need to decipher which action should be invoked and employ Cake's MVC tricks to tie these actions to views that render the appropriate application display. We will start by creating the master controller, called the AppController class. Our online shop controllers will borrow some properties and methods from this master controller to save the time of creating them in each individual controller.

The AppController Class

By default, a Cake controller class extends the AppController class. You've already been introduced to the app/app_controller.php class file in Chapter 1. Our shop AppController class will contain all the common functionality required to centralize request handling and extract session IDs. The global properties and methods defined here are automatically available to the objects of requests or other classes that extend AppController.

Listing 3-24 shows the AppController class properties.

Listing 3-24. *The Beginning of the AppController Class (app/app_controller.php)*

```php
<?php
class AppController extends Controller {
    var $pageTitle = 'Chapter 3 - Ecommerce';
    var $sid;
    var $catId;
    var $pdId;

    var $uses = array('Product', 'Category', 'Cart');
    var $helpers = array( 'Form', 'Html', 'Session', 'Javascript' );
    var $components = array( 'Session', 'RequestHandler', 'Shop' );
```

The $pageTitle property sets an initial page title for this application, which can change according to a user's page request. The $sid property will contain a session ID to identify our application user. As we mentioned earlier, to avoid repetition of code within this book, we've decided not to address authentication in this application. Hence, we've used the $sid variable to represent and track a user from page to page.

The $catId and $pdid properties will be assigned the user-requested category and product values, respectively, when available. If these values are not available, we set the properties to an integer value of 0. Next in Listing 3-24, we include some of Cake's built-in properties, such as the $uses array to require the Product, Category, and Cart model objects. Then we include some helpers and components, which were introduced in Chapter 1.

Next, we override the beforeFilter method, which is triggered first by default, before any other action in our AppController, as shown in Listing 3-25.

Listing 3-25. *The AppController's beforeFilter() Method*

```
function beforeFilter() {

    if ( isset( $this->passedArgs['cat_id'] ) &&
         (int)$this->passedArgs['cat_id'] != 1 ) {
        $this->catId = (int)$this->passedArgs['cat_id'];
    } else {
        $this->catId = 0;
    }

    if ( isset( $this->passedArgs['pd_id'] ) &&
          $this->passedArgs['pd_id'] != '' ) {
        $this->pdId = (int)$this->passedArgs['pd_id'];
    } else {
        $this->pdId = 0;
    }

    $data = $this->Session->read();
    $this->sid = $data['Config']['userAgent'];
    $this->set('catId', $this->catId);
    $this->set('pdId', $this->pdId);
    $this->set('sid', $this->sid);
    $this->setPageTitle();
}
```

In Listing 3-25, the overridden method checks the URL of a user request to extract and then determine the category ID and product ID values. The beforeFilter method ensures that during the course of the application, the $catId and $pdId variables contain some integer values. For example, with this URL:

```
http://localhost/cake/__chapters__/ecommerce/
```

the values of these two properties will default to 0. If the URL is as follows the value of the current category ID will be 12 and the product ID will be 0.

```
http://localhost/cake/__chapters__/ecommerce/ecommerce/index/cat_id:12
```

In this case, the $this->passedArgs['cat_id'] array stores the requested value of cat_id:12 of the URL.

The last statement of the beforeFilter method, $this->setPageTitle(), ensures that as a user moves from page to page, the current page title is reflected.

The setPageTitle method, which sets the current page title, is shown in Listing 3-26.

Listing 3-26. *The AppController's setPageTitle() Method*

```
function setPageTitle() {
    if ( $this->pdId > 0 ) {
        $result = $this->Product->find('all',
                        array('conditions'=>array('Product.id' => $this->pdId )));
        $this->pageTitle = $result[0]['Product']['name'];
    } elseif ( $this->catId > 0 ){
        $result = $this->Category->find('all',
                        array('conditions'=>array('Category.id' => $this->catId )));
        $this->pageTitle = $result[0]['Category']['name'];
    }
}
```

If the current product ID value ($this->pdId) is greater than zero, the value of $this->pdId is used to query the products table in order to extract the corresponding product name. The $pageTitle property is then assigned the appropriate product name. If the current category ID value is greater than zero, then the category ID ($this->catId) is used to pull the corresponding category name from the categories table, and finally, this category name is used as the page title. If the function fails to set a page title, the $pageTitle remains Chapter 3 - Ecommerce, as defined in the property section of the AppController.

Now that we have defined the properties and functionalities that we require in our AppController class, let's tie things together to enable users to navigate our shop.

The Home Page

The starting point is the definition of our preferred home page. The app/config/routes.php file contains information about handling user requests for our application. We use the following line in our routes file:

```
Router::connect('/', array('controller' => 'carts', 'action' => 'index'));
```

This defines a controller (carts) and an action (index) within the CartsController class that serve as our shop's home page. When a user types the URL http://localhost/cake/__chapters__/ecommerce/ in a web browser address bar or clicks the Home link on the web site, the request is handled by the index action of the CartsController object.

We'll create the CartsController in the following section.

The Carts Controller

Listing 3-27 shows the carts controller for our shop application.

Listing 3-27. *The CartsController Class (app/controllers/carts_controller.php)*

```
<?php
class CartsController extends AppController {
    var $name = 'Carts';
    function index() {
    }
}
?>
```

The CartsController class begins by extending the AppController class. It then sets its $name property to Carts to ensure backward compatibility with PHP 4.

By default, the index action is mapped to the app/views/carts/index.ctp view file. Remember that the layout of our shop contains a middle section, or center column. Our index.ctp view handles what is rendered in this area of the web site layout. The content of this view file is shown is shown in Listing 3-28.

Listing 3-28. *The View for the Center Column Content (app/views/carts/index.ctp)*

```php
<?php
    e( 'Welcome to the land of music!
    <br />
    Please select your own music product!
    <br />
    Thanks for dropping by!<br />');
    if ($pdId) {
        e( $this->element('product_details'));
    } else if ($catId) {
        e( $this->element('products'));
    } else {
        e( $this->element('categories'));
    }
?>
```

In Listing 3-28, we first render our welcome message using the e() function, which is a Cake convenience method for PHP's echo statement. You can change this message to suit your needs. Next, we use the current values of the product ID ($pdId) and category ID ($catId), as defined in the beforeFilter method of the AppController class (Listing 3-25), to logically control the view that is finally displayed to web surfers.

When a user visits our shop for the first time, the values of the product ID and category ID will be set to zero, as defined in the beforeFilter method of the AppController, since the user has not yet selected a category or a product from the home page. For this scenario, the view logic will render the content stored at app/views/elements/categories.ctp. We will also have this scenario when a user clicks the Home link of the web site. The content of this view is shown in Listing 3-29.

Listing 3-29. *The Category List View for the Center Column (app/views/elements/categories.ctp)*

```php
<?php
$categories = $this->requestAction("/categories/getAll");
foreach($categories as $category): ?>
<div class="product_container">
<?
    if ( $category['Category']['image'] ) {
        $cat_thumbnail = '/img/products/' . $category['Category']['image'];
    } else {
        $cat_thumbnail = 'no-image-small.png';
    }
```

```
    e( $html->link(
        $html->image($cat_thumbnail, array( 'border' => '0' )),
        array('action' => '/index/cat_id:' . $category['Category']['id']),
        array('escape' => false))); ?>
    <br>
    <? e( $html->link( $category['Category']['name'], ➥
"/carts/index/cat_id:".$category['Category']['id'] )); ?>
</div>
<? endforeach;?>
```

In Listing 3-29, we also use Cake's requestAction method to trigger the getAll method of the CategoriesController. The result of this method is a list of all the category information, which is stored in the $categories array variable. This variable is then looped over to display the list of categories, as shown in Figure 3-5.

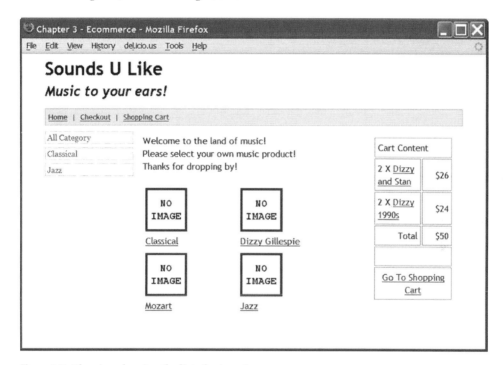

Figure 3-5. *The view showing the list of categories*

Now, we're finished with the left column content—the category navigation—and the center column content. Let's move to the right column, which displays the current shopping basket (cart) content (see Figure 3-5). If there is no information in the carts table, we'll display the message "Shopping Basket is empty" in this area of the page.

The view code to generate the basket content is stored at app/views/elements/basket.ctp. This code is shown in Listing 3-30.

Listing 3-30. *The Basket View for the Right Column (app/views/elements/basket.ctp)*

```php
<table id="minicart">
<?php
$cartContents = $this->requestAction("/carts/getMiniCart/s:$sid");
if ( !empty($cartContents) && is_array($cartContents) ) {
$Total = 0;
?>
<tr>
<td colspan="2">Cart Content</td>
</tr>
<?php
foreach($cartContents as $cartContent) {
    $Total += $cartContent['pd']['price'] * $cartContent['ct']['qty'];
?>
<tr>
<td>
<?=$cartContent['ct']['qty'];?> X
<?=$html->link($cartContent['pd']['name'],
'/products/view/pd_id:'.$cartContent['ct']['product_id'].➥
'cat_id:'.$cartContent['pd']['category_id']);?></td>
<td width="30%" align="right"><?=Configure::read('Shop.currency');?>
<?=$cartContent['pd']['price'] * $cartContent['ct']['qty'];?></td>
</tr>
<?php
    } ?>
<tr>
<td align="right">Total</td>
<td width="30%" align="right">
<?=Configure::read('Shop.currency');?>
<?=$Total;?>
</td>
</tr>
<tr>
<td colspan="2"> </td></tr>
<tr>
<td colspan="2" align="center"><?=$html-> ➥
link(' Go To Shopping Cart','/carts/view');?></td>
</tr>
<?php
} else {
echo '<tr><td width="150">Shopping Basket is empty</td></tr>';
}
?>
</table>
```

Before we delve into the code in Listing 3-30, let's add the product titled Mozart for Lovers to our basket by clicking the Add to Shopping Basket link on the product description page. Adding a product to the basket triggers the CartsController's add method, shown in Listing 3-31.

Listing 3-31. *The CartsController's add() Method*

```
function add() {
    $data = $this->Product->findById( $this->pdId );
    if( empty ( $data ) ) {
        $this->redirect('/');
    } else {
        if ($data['Product']['qty'] <= 0) {
            $this->Session->setFlash('The product you requested is  ➥
no longer in stock');
            $this->redirect('/');
        }
    }
    $sessionData = $this->Cart->getCart($this->pdId, $this->sid);
    if ( empty($sessionData)) {
        $this->Cart->addCart($this->pdId, $this->sid);
    } else {
        $this->Cart->updateCart($this->pdId, $this->sid);
    }
    $this->Cart->cleanUp();
    $this->redirect(array('controller'=>'Products',
                    'action'=>"view/cat_id:$this->catId/pd_id:$this->pdId"));
}
```

In Listing 3-31, the first statement uses Cake's findById model method, which accepts a product ID ($this->pdId) to retrieve a product's information from the products table. This product information is stored in the $data array variable. If $data is empty, the application redirects to the home page.

Next, the script checks if the product quantity is less than or equal to zero. If so, the application uses the Cake Session object's setFlash method to hold the message 'The product you requested is no longer in stock' in the Session object, and then redirects to the home page.

Then the application calls the getCart method of the Carts model object in order to check the existence of this product in the shopping basket. The result of this method is stored in the $sessionData array variable. If the product does not exist in the shopping basket against the current session ID, the addCart() method of the Carts model object is called to insert a new product into the carts table. If the product does exist in the shopping basket, the updateCart method is called to increment the quantity of the product in the carts table by one.

Next, the script seizes the opportunity to do some housecleaning by calling the cleanUp method to remove records that are few days old from the carts table. Finally, the application redirects the user to the current product's description page.

Now that we've added a product to the carts table, let's jump back into the basket view code in Listing 3-30. First, we use the requestAction method to get all the content of the cart from the carts table. This Cake method accepts the string that triggers the CartsController's getMiniCart method, which accepts the session ID (via s:$sid) as an argument and assigns the result to the $cartContents variable. Next, if the $cartContents variable is an array and is not empty, the $Total variable is assigned a value of zero. Finally, using the foreach loop over $cartContents, the current content of the basket now includes the newly added product Mozart for Lovers, costing $15, as shown in Figure 3-6.

Figure 3-6. *The view showing Mozart for Lovers in the shopping basket in the right column*

Checking our user journey, our next action is to proceed to the shopping basket, to check that we are happy with our current product selections. If not, we will amend the selections or completely remove unwanted products from our shopping basket. This interface allows for cart-manipulation processes, such as updating the product quantity, deleting the product, and so on. Let's suppose the user has clicked the Go to Shopping Cart link in Figure 3-6, and modified the cart content by removing the Mozart for Lovers and Dizzy 1990s items from her shopping basket. The new content of the shopping basket is shown in Figure 3-7.

Figure 3-7. *The view showing a sample cart content*

The Order Model

Next, we're going to deal with the orders. We'll start by creating the Order model class, shown in Listing 3-32. Note that this class does not interact with any database table.

Listing 3-32. *The Order Model Class (app/models/order.php)*

```php
<?php
class Order extends AppModel
{
    var $name = 'Order';
    var $useTable = false;
    var $validate = array(
            'name' => array( 'rule' => array( 'between', 2, 255 ),
            'required' => true,
            'message' => 'Please enter a name.' ),
            'address' => array( 'rule' => array( 'between', 4, 255 ),
            'required' => true,
            'message' => 'Please enter an address.' ),
            'comment' => array( 'rule' => array( 'between', 5, 255 ),
            'required' => true,
            'message' => 'Please enter a comment.' ));
}
?>
```

In Listing 3-32, we define the $validate array to ensure input data integrity for the name, address, and comment form elements.

Next, we're going to click the Proceed to Checkout button. Our action will trigger the checkout method of the OrdersController object, which is defined in Listing 3-33.

Listing 3-33. *The OrdersController Class (app/controllers/orders_contoller.php)*

```php
<?php
class OrdersController extends AppController {
    var $name = 'Orders';
    var $uses = array('Order');

    function checkout() {
        $data = $this->passedArgs['cts'];
        $this->set('data', $data);
        $this->layout = 'checkbase';
    }

    function confirm() {
        $this->layout = 'checkbase';
        if (!empty($this->data)) {
            $orders = $this->data;
            $carts = $this->Cart->find('all', array(
            'conditions'=>array('Cart.id'=>$this->data['Order']['cts']),
            'recursive' => 1 ));
            $this->set(compact('carts', 'orders'));
        }
    }
}
?>
```

As usual, the OrdersController class references the Orders model object using the $uses = array("Order"); statement. Next, we define the checkout method, which first extracts the current cart's content IDs from $this->passedArgs['cts'] array, and then stores the result in the $data array. The $data array is passed to the app/views/orders/checkout.ctp view file, shown in Listing 3-34, for display. The last statement of this method changes the default layout to checkbase.

Listing 3-34. *The Checkout View (app/views/orders/checkout.ctp)*

```php
<fieldset>
    <legend>
        <?php echo $this->pageTitle = __('<strong>Checkout</strong>', true); ?>
    </legend>
    <?php
        echo $form->create('Order', array('url'=>'/orders/confirm/') );
        echo $form->error( 'Order.name' );
```

```
        echo $form->input(  'Order.name', array( 'id' => 'ordername',
                            'label' => 'Name:', 'size' => '30',
                            'maxlength' => '255', 'error' => false ) );
        echo $form->error( 'Order.address' );
        echo $form->input(  'Order.address', array( 'id' => 'orderaddress',
                            'type'=>'textarea', 'label' => 'Address:',
                            'rows' => '3', 'error' => false ));
        echo $form->error( 'Order.comment' );
        echo $form->input(  'Order.comment', array( 'id' => 'ordercomment',
                            'type'=>'textarea', 'label' => 'Comment:',
                            'rows' => '5', 'error' => false ) );
        echo $form->error( 'Order.payment' );
        echo $form->input(  'Order.payment', array('type'=>'radio',
                            'options'=>array(1=>'Google', 2=>'Paypal')));
        echo $form->input( 'cts', array('type'=>'hidden', 'value'=>$data) );
        echo $form->end( array( 'label' => ' Confirm Order ' ) );
    ?>
</fieldset>
<br />
<?php echo $this->element('checkout'); ?>
```

In Listing 3-34, the code is divided into two main parts. The first part uses Cake's $form object to render the checkout form. The second part renders the current content of the shopping basket, similar to the basket view code (Listing 3-30). Listing 3-34 produces the checkout form shown in Figure 3-8.

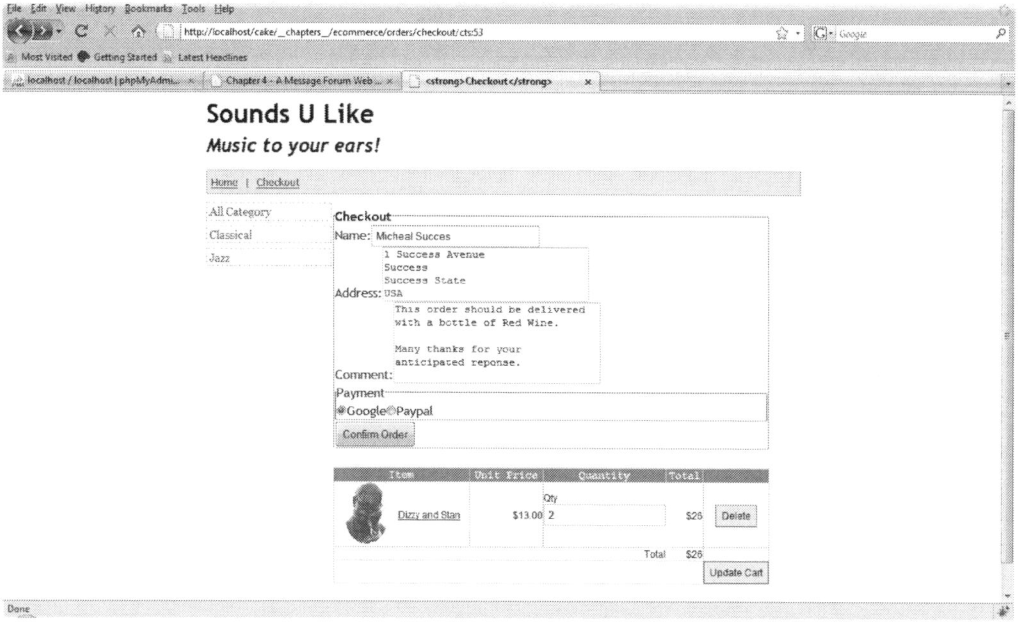

Figure 3-8. *The checkout page*

When the user clicks the Confirm Order button on the checkout page, the confirm method of the OrdersController is triggered. If the submitted form data (stored in $this->data) is not empty, then the form data is stored in the $orders array. Next, we retrieve the current cart content based on the cart ID (extracted from $this->data['Order']['cts']), and the result is stored in the $carts array variable.

▓**Note** It is important to include the statement var $belongsTo = array('Product'); in the Cart model class, because we'll need to submit some vital product information (such as product name, price, and description) to our chosen payment gateway. This statement will ensure that the application includes related product information whenever carts table records are retrieved.

Finally, using Cake's set and compact functions, the two array variables are passed on to the app/views/orders/confirm.ctp file. The structure of the array variables is shown in Listing 3-35.

Listing 3-35. *The Structure of $order and $cart Array Variables*

```
Array
(
    [Order] => Array
        (
            [name] => Micheal Succes
            [address] => 1 Success Avenue
                        Success
                        Success State
                        USA
            [comment] => This order should be delivered with a bottle of Red Wine.
                        Many thanks for your anticipated reponse.
            [payment] => 1
            [cts] => 53
        )
)

Array
(
    [0] => Array
        (
            [Cart] => Array
                (
                    [id] => 53
                    [product_id] => 22
                    [qty] => 2
                    [ct_session_id] => 32cabb9d6fb31404a5b736830eac6aa3
                    [created] => 2008-09-25 23:30:18
                )
```

```
        [Product] => Array
            (
                [id] => 22
                [category_id] => 13
                [name] => Dizzy and Stan
                [description] => Live with Dizzy Gillespie and Stan Getz.
                [price] => 13.00
                [qty] => 10
                [image] => 1.jpg
                [thumbnail] => 1.jpg
                [created] => 0000-00-00 00:00:00
                [modified] => 0000-00-00 00:00:00
            )
        )
)
```

The array structures in Listing 3-35 are passed on to the confirm.ctp view file, as shown in Listing 3-36.

Listing 3-36. *The OrdersController's confirm() Method View*

```php
<?php
    if($order['Order']['payment'] == 1) {
        echo $this->element('google_checkout');
    } else {
        echo $this->element('paypal_checkout');
    }
?>
```

If the order payment method selected equals 1, then the Google Checkout payment form is displayed. If not, the PayPal form is presented.

The Google Checkout Button

Google needs no introduction when it comes to the world of Internet. However, you should be aware that to use Google services, you need to have a Google account, which you probably already do if you use Google Mail, Google Docs, Google Adwords, or any of the numerous other Google offerings.

Shoppers are often frustrated by needing to fill out lengthy online forms before making payments. It is easy to encourage users to check out via the Google Checkout button, which is secure and convenient. When this button is selected, the $carts and $order array variables are passed to the app/views/elements/google_checkout.ctp file, shown in Listing 3-37.

Listing 3-37. *Google Checkout View (app/views/elements/google_checkout.ctp)*

```php
<?php
    echo $form->create('Order',
        array( 'url'=>'https://checkout.google.com/api/checkout/v2/➥
checkoutForm/Merchant/xxxxxxxxxxxxxxx',
                'accept-charset'=>'utf-8' ) );

    $i = 0;

    foreach($carts as $cart) {

        $x = $i+1;

        echo $form->hidden( "item_name_$x",
                        array( 'value'=>$cart['Product']['name']));
        echo $form->hidden( "item_description_$x",
                        array( 'value'=>$cart['Product']['description']));
        echo $form->hidden( "item_quantity_$x",
                        array( 'value'=>$cart['Cart']['qty']));
        echo $form->hidden( "item_price_$x",
                        array( 'value'=>$cart['Product']['price']));
        echo $form->hidden( "item_currency_$x",
                        array( 'value'=>Configure::read('Item.currency')));
        echo $form->hidden( "ship_method_name_$x",
                        array( 'value'=>Configure::read('Order.shipmethod')));
        echo $form->hidden( "ship_method_price_$x",
                        array( 'value'=>Configure::read('Order.shipprice')));
        echo $form->hidden( "tax_rate",
                        array( 'value'=>Configure::read('Order.taxrate')));
        echo $form->hidden( "tax_us_state",
                        array( 'value'=>Configure::read('Order.taxstate')));
    }

    echo $form->hidden('_charset_');

    echo $html->image( 'http://checkout.google.com/buttons/checkout.gif? ➥
merchant_id=xxxxxxxxxxxxxxx&w=180&h=46&style=white&variant=text&loc=en_US',
                        array( 'name'=>'Google Checkout',
                                'alt'=>'Fast checkout through Google',
                                'height'=>'46',
                                'width'=>'180') );

    echo $form->end( array( 'label' => ' Confirm Order ' ) );
?>
```

The view file shown in Listing 3-37 generates a page similar to the one shown in Figure 3-9.

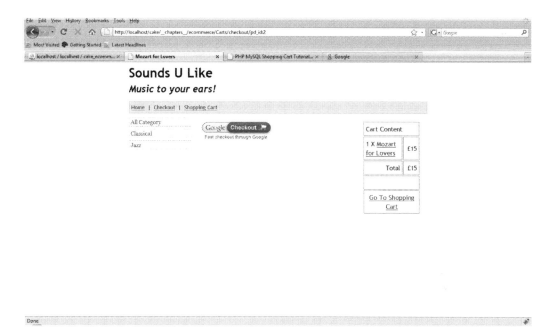

Figure 3-9. *The Google checkout page*

Clicking the Google Checkout button will redirect the user to the Google sandbox environment, as shown in Figure 3-10.

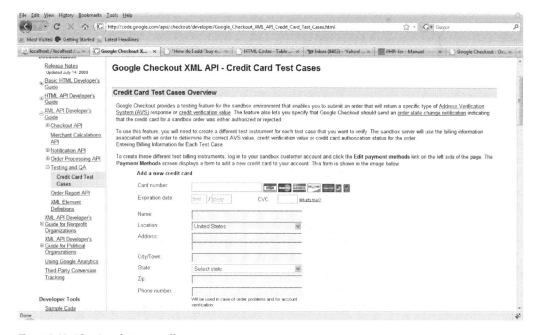

Figure 3-10. *The Google test sandbox*

For more information about processing online sales using Google's payment system, Google Checkout buttons, and the Google sandbox, visit the following sites:

- `https://checkout.google.com/sell/`

- `http://code.google.com/apis/checkout/developer/Google_Checkout_Basic_HTML_Google_Checkout_Buttons.html`

- `http://code.google.com/apis/checkout/developer/Google_Checkout_XML_API_Credit_Card_Test_Cases.html`.

The PayPal Submit Button

PayPal can be regarded as the father of online payment gateways. It's ubiquitous when it comes to online payment choices. Here, we are going to create the payment form, in the app/views/elements/paypal_checkout.ctp file, as shown in Listing 3-38. You can use the Buy-it-Now button form generator on PayPal to create a similar payment form.

Listing 3-38. *The PayPal View (app/views/elements/paypal_checkout.ctp)*

```php
<?php
    echo $form->create('Order',
                        array('url'=>'https://www.paypal.com/cgi-bin/webscr',
                            'id'=>'payPalForm') );
    echo $form->hidden("item_number", array( 'value'=>"The Music Club"));
    echo $form->hidden("cmd", array( 'value'=>"_xclick"));
    echo $form->hidden("no_note", array( 'value'=>"1"));
    echo $form->hidden("business", array( 'value'=>"sales@practicalcakephp.com"));
    echo $form->hidden("currency_code", array( 'value'=>"USD"));
    echo $form->hidden("return", array( 'value'=>"http://practicalcakephp.com"));
    $i = 0;
    foreach($carts AS $cart) {
    $x = $i+1;
    echo $form->hidden("item_number", array( 'value'=>"The Music Club"));
    echo $form->hidden("item_description_$x",
                    array( 'value'=>$cart['Product']['description']));
    echo $form->hidden("item_quantity_$x", array( 'value'=>$cart['Cart']['qty']));
    echo $form->hidden("item_price_$x", array( 'value'=>$cart['Product']['price']));
    }
    echo $form->end( array( 'label' => ' Submit ' ) );
?>
```

The PayPal view is passed the $carts and the $order array variables.

For further information about the numerous services provided by PayPal, visit http://www.paypal.com.

Summary

In this chapter, we went through the process of building an online shop. For this demonstration, we've kept its features to a minimum. However, users can navigate the product category menu, add products to a shopping basket, review the basket contents, and proceed to the checkout form.

We started this chapter by looking at a typical shop layout, the shop user journey, and the creation of the database and tables needed for the shop application. We then proceeded to build all the model classes that interact with the database tables, such as those for categories, products, carts, and so on.

To handle user requests, we built the AppController class with properties and methods that provide functionality common to other controller classes. This helps us to avoid "reinventing the wheel" and to extend other controller classes, such as the category controller of the application. We then built the other controller classes to handle the application requests.

Finally, we created checkout forms to handle payment transactions. We used a Google sandbox as our payment test environment and also created a PayPal form as an alternative payment option.

Building a comprehensive e-commerce web site obviously involves more than what we covered in this chapter. For example, you would want to add an administration area to the web site to facilitate management.

■■■

CHAPTER 4

A Message Forum Web Service

In this chapter, we'll build a Cake-based forum. While there are a lot of popular open source forums such as phpBB, we like the idea of rolling our own. It's a fantastic learning process, and we get to deal with a lot of new subjects that don't come up in our day jobs.

So that our forum will stand out from the crowd, we need a unique selling point. That will be a web service API for our forum. Web services are quite a common feature in many modern web applications, but not that common in many of the forums.

Our Take on Web Services

The term *web services* can have many meanings. For example, simply entering the URL http://www.cakephp.org/ into your browser can be called a web service request, since you're using HTTP GET. The World Wide Web Consortium (W3C) has an official definition for web services (http://www.w3.org/2002/ws/Activity):

> *Web services provide a standard means of interoperating between different software applications, running on a variety of platforms and/or frameworks.*

This meaning is quite general, indicating that web services are a way for computers to talk to each other, which may or may not include the Web.

Before we get to creating our forum, let's clear up what we mean by web services.

Web Service Elements

There are many elements relating to web services. We start with a short explanation of each element to provide a foundation for our particular angle on web services.

- *API*: This acronym stands for application programming interface. In the world of computers, much like the definition of web services, this is quite a general term. For us, it means a set of published functions or methods that can be directly accessed via URLs on the server, such as `http://www.example.com/getWidgets.json` or `http://www.example.com/getWidgets/json`.

- *SOAP*: This stands for Simple Object Access Protocol, and is one of the main protocols of a web service. It piggybacks onto the HTTP protocol, considered too complex and verbose by many developers. Taking the previous example, our SOAP request would look something like this:

```
POST / HTTP/1.1
Host: www.example.com
Content-Type: text/xml; charset="utf-8"
Content-Length: nnnn
SOAPAction: "Some-URI"

<SOAP-ENV:Envelope
  xmlns:SOAP-ENV="http://schemas.xmlsoap.org/soap/envelope/"
  SOAP-ENV:encodingStyle="http://schemas.xmlsoap.org/soap/encoding/">
  <SOAP-ENV:Body>
      <m:getWidgets xmlns:m="Some-URI">
          <type>square</type>
      </m:getWidgets>
  </SOAP-ENV:Body>
</SOAP-ENV:Envelope>
```

- *HTTP*: In a sense, HTTP (Hypertext Transfer Protocol) and SMTP (Simple Mail Transfer Protocol) are the two main protocols people use on the Internet. They surf the Web using the HTTP protocol and read e-mail messages using the SMTP protocol. Many developers have adopted HTTP as their protocol for developing their web services; specifically, just the GET and POST methods within that protocol. This is how we will be developing our API in this chapter's application.

- *XML-RPC*: The Extensible Markup Language Remote Procedure Call was created by David Winer, one of the pioneers in modern web services and blogging. It's similar to SOAP, but simpler. This protocol is not frequently used by developers. The major web applications that support XML-RPC include Flickr and Amazon S3.

- *REST*: This stands for representational state transfer. The term was coined by Roy Fielding, one of the main authors of HTTP. It is not a protocol, but a set of statements about how distributed media should be organized, with the Web being a key example.

Figure 4-1 illustrates how many web developers see web services. On the left side, we have the clients. They can be applications on other servers; desktop applications, which include browsers; and other devices, like mobile cell phones. These clients will most often use HTTP (GET, POST, and so on) to send and request data to and from the server, shown on the right. The way the clients talk to the server is the protocol: XML-RPC, SOAP, RSS, and so on. These protocols are quite specific, since there are standards attached. For example, in RSS, you must end all requests with the .rss extension. The format you will receive will be in a specific format, as defined by the official standards body.

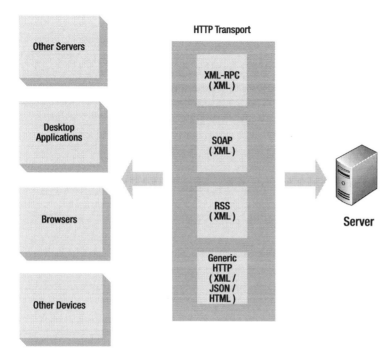

Figure 4-1. *Elements of web services*

However, you can develop your own proprietary protocol using the features of HTTP. Many web service providers have gone this route—Google Maps, Flickr, and Twitter, to name a few.

Mashing different services together is never an easy task. For example, an image will have a different context depending on the application. The use of REST complicates the picture. In Figure 4-1, it sits within generic HTTP, as we regard it as a specific way of using that protocol.

REST and HTTP

Many people have advocated the use of the REST principle with HTTP for web services. In particular, the use of the HTTP methods should conform to the W3C standard. For example, GET methods should not alter any data. Something like http://www.example.com/editUser/?id=1&name=new_name should not be allowed. In REST, this would look like http://www.example.com/User/1. The new name would be supplied as a key/value pair—name=new_name—in the request body, and instead of using GET, we would be using PUT.

In a sense, we see HTTP as being a diluted form of REST. It can get quite confusing, as some meanings can overlap. We see the confusion surrounding REST much as we see the complexity of SOAP. Many developers find REST difficult to use.

To use REST in its full meaning, you must conform to the correct use of the HTTP methods such as GET, POST, PUT, and DELETE. Most browsers support only GET and POST. You can use the other methods via XMLHttpRequest in Ajax scripting, but that just won't be enough to conform to the principles of REST. To end our discussion of REST, the web services that we're going to write in this chapter will not conform to the principles of REST.

▦**Note** The four most important HTTP requests are GET, POST, PUT, and DELETE. GET requests a resource, such as an HTML file. (Requesting the resource must not cause a side effect, such as deleting a record). POST sends data to the resource to be processed. It creates a new resource, updates the resource, or both. We'll consider the PUT operation to be the same as the POST. Elliotte Rusty Harold gives a good explanation at http://www.elharo.com/blog/software-development/web-development/2005/12/08/post-vs-put/. Finally, DELETE just deletes a resource, such as a user account.

We've always liked the principle of KISS, which means we prefer to Keep It Short and Simple. Logical standards like SOAP sometimes are just too logical. As such, like many web APIs, we're just opting for plain old HTTP GET and POST as the two modes that developers can use to access the innards of our forum. Referring to our diagram in Figure 4-1, we're using the generic HTTP method.

Result Return Formats

When we make a web service request, the result can be returned in many formats depending on the client request, including HTML, JSON, XML, and RSS.

You can even specify the result to be returned as a comma-separated list or as a JavaScript-ready document output. For our application, we'll use JSON. Developers can easily use our web services via Ajax or on the server using curl or wget.

Application Requirements

One of the main focal points of our forum application is the API. Therefore, we'll start by thinking about the methods that we will be exposing to the public. The API requests will come from other applications, not individuals using the application via an interface, so we must consider that in our planning.

In our forum application, we want to include some common features that are found in all forums:

- Post messages

- Reply to messages

- View messages

- Search messages

Since our own interface is basically also a client, we need to look at our own front end as if it were a third-party client application that is calling the processing scripts from a distant server. We know there are several ways to make a URL request. The following are the ones we are interested in:

- Requesting a URL via curl or wget; they may also want it returned in a particular format

- Requesting a URL via a browser using HTTP GET or POST

- Requesting a URL via Ajax scripting using HTTP GET or POST; that is, the XMLHttpRequest (XHR) within the browser makes the HTTP call

Some of our actions may support only GET and/or POST. This is similar to many of the other web APIs.

We must have a standard way to respond to requests. For example, in HTTP, the response code 200 is OK, and the response code 404 is resource or page not found. Furthermore, some requests return data, while others carry out particular actions like saving data. We must be able to return data in a consistent manner given different requests.

Threads and Posts

For our forum, we need to decide how discussions should be organized. We simply define a discussion (commonly called a *thread*) as the messages and the subsequent messages (replies) to those messages. Let's look at some of the ways in which messages could be organized.

Organized by Date

Using this method, each message is organized by date order, regardless of to which message it is replying. Users can then see the most up-to-date messages as they come in.

Organizing by date is problematic because we won't know which message a message is replying to. We can overcome this by including the message, but do we include the whole message or just part of it? Perhaps we could allow the users to select the parts they are replying to?

Listing 4-1 shows a code snippet that allows a user to quote part of a message so other users can refer to it.

Listing 4-1. *JavaScript Code to Get Selected Text*

```
 1:    <input type="button" onmousedown="displaySelected();">
 2:
 3:    <script>
 4:
 5:    function displaySelected(){
 6:
 7:        var selectedText = '';
 8:
 9:        if ( window.getSelection ) {
10:            selectedText = window.getSelection();
11:        }
12:        else if (document.selection){
13:            selectedText = document.selection.createRange().text;
14:        }
15:
16:        return selectedText;
17:
18:    }
19:
20:    </script>
```

You might want to use the code in Listing 4-1 if you decide to extend the forum application. It simply retrieves the text a user has selected with the mouse. On line 9, we check whether the user has selected any text on Firefox/Gecko-based browsers. If so, we place the text in to the `selectedText` variable. Line 12 checks for text selection in Internet Explorer/Trident-based browsers.

Organized by First Post

Using the by-first-post organization, we show only new messages, essentially the first messages, as they come in. We won't show the replies. If users want to read the replies, they need to drill down; that is, make another request to a different Cake action.

If a user replies to an old message, it won't be displayed. It will remain relative to that old message. Users will know of that reply only when they drill down to it.

An obvious problem is that active discussions will be followed only by those who participated in it at the early stages, when the discussions were at the top of the page. When new messages arrive, the old messages get pushed down. This is not desirable, since we want many people contributing to a discussion as long as possible. After all, if people are just asking questions on the forum, very few people would bother to read the forum.

Organized by Replies

You can also organize the threads by the number of replies, so the thread that has the greatest number of replies is shown first. If no one has contributed to the thread for a while, it will still stay at the top.

The problem with this organization is that current and active threads are not given priority. So we end up putting too much emphasis on a topic that may no longer be of interest to most people.

Organized by Last Post

Another organization possibility is a slightly different take on the by-first-post organization. Using this method, we order a discussion by its last post, but we show the first post.

This approach has a number of advantages. If a new message comes in, it floats to the top. However, if a reply to an old message is posted, the first post of that discussion floats to the top. In this way, we encourage people to participate in ongoing discussions. If the discussion has been exhausted, it simply floats back down the page.

Organizing the posts by the last post seems to be the most sensible method. In fact, most forums organize discussions this way, and so will our application.

Web Service Requests

Our application will support the following five API requests:

- Fetch one message
- Fetch many messages
- Fetch threads
- Process a message
- Search for messages

These requests will be the ones that we will be publishing in our API documentation. They will all support Ajax from a browser, ordinary HTTP requests from a browser, and curl or wget calls from a server.

Layout

The API is an important component to the application. However, we're not just publishing an API. The application will also be a working forum where users can post messages. In that sense, we're building a client as well as the API services within the same application.

Our application front end will have all the essential features that any forum user will expect. A user can post messages, reply to messages, view topics, and search for messages. The layout of the interface will be similar to that of the other projects in this book. We start with a header, followed by a navigation bar, and then the main content area. When a user goes straight to the site, they will be presented with a view of the current threads, as shown in Figure 4-2.

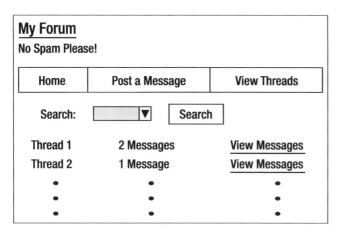

Figure 4-2. *A rough sketch of the forum application layout*

Application Structure

In the previous section, we talked about how we're going to organize our messages according to threads. This relationship is a one-to-many association, where one thread ties together many messages.

The two main database tables in our application are messages and threads. The fields in these tables are shown in Tables 4-1 and 4-2.

Table 4-1. *The Fields in the messages Table*

Field Name	Data Type	Description
id	char(36)	Primary key (note it's a UUID and not an auto-increment field; see the action class MfMessageProcess for an explanation)
name	varchar(255)	Name of the user posting the message
email	varchar(255)	E-mail address of the user
message	mediumtext	The message body itself
reply_to	char(36)	If the message is a reply to another message, this is the reply message ID
Subject	varchar(255)	The subject of the message (replies will have a RE: prefix)
t_created_at	datetime	Automagic field (but we fill this in ourselves; see the action class MfMessageProcess for an explanation)
thread_id	char(36)	The thread this message belongs to

Table 4-2. *The Fields in the threads Table*

Field Name	Data Type	Description
id	char(36)	Primary key (again, UUID and not an auto-increment field)
first_message_id	char(36)	Used so we can easily pick out the first message when it needs to be displayed in the threads listing
last_message_date	datetime	Used so we can order the threads correctly according to the last message date
message_num	int(11)	The number of messages within this thread

■**Note** As we haven't used database transactions in our application, the number in the message_num field of the threads table may not always be completely accurate, but that's not critical at this stage, as it's used only for display purposes.

You'll notice that the threads table includes a few metadata fields to contain data that describes the thread. This helps us to cut down on the number of SQL calls needed to list our threads. Each time a new message is added to a thread, the code updates the last_message_date field with the date of that message. This way, we don't need to look in the messages table for the last message that was posted within a thread.

JSON Web Services

We have specified that we'll be using the JSON format for all our API returns. To get this part of our application working, we need to do some setup.

The Router class must be aware of the JSON extension. We take care of this by adding the following line in the /app/config/routes.php file:

```
Router::parseExtensions( 'json' );
```

Following this, we need to include the RequestHandler component by adding it into our $components variable in our /app/app_controller.php file, so that it's available to all controllers. We also need the Session component. Our $components variable will look like this:

```
var $components = array( 'Session', 'RequestHandler' );
```

Now the RequestHandler will automatically map JSON requests to the correct layout and view. When a JSON request comes in, it will pick the layout file within the folder /app/views/layout/json instead of /app/views/layout. Our JSON layout file is shown in Listing 4-2.

Listing 4-2. *JSON Layout File (/app/views/layout/base.ctp)*

```php
<?php

    // This is used when the call extension is .json
    header( "Pragma: no-cache" );
    header( 'Content-Type: text/x-json' );
    header( "X-JSON: ".$content_for_layout );

    $controller = $this->name;
    $action = $this->action;
    $datetime = date( "Y_M_j__G_i_s_T" );
    $file_name = $controller.'_'.$action.'_'.$datetime;

    header( 'Content-Disposition: attachment; filename="'.$file_name.'.json"' );

    echo $content_for_layout;
?>
```

Any script that requests a JSON return can use the HTTP headers Content-Type and X-JSON to identify whether or not it is a JSON return. However, the $content_for_layout isn't guaranteed to be JSON. We must manually put that into a JSON format.

Once the layout has been picked out, the RequestHandler will look in a json folder within the views folder that corresponds to the controller, similar to how the layout folder structure works. In our application, all the API methods have the same json view. For example, in the view file app/views/mf_fetch_threads/json/index.ctp for the MfFetchThreads controller, we just make use of JavaScript helper to format our result in a JSON format, as shown here:

```php
<?php
    echo $javascript->object( $result );
?>
```

Our Application Controller

Throughout the development of the forum application, we've placed a lot of attention on our web services API. We're going to continue with that line of thought by using a version of the Command design pattern, adapted for the Web, in our controller.

The Command pattern is an object-oriented class design, where we encapsulate each action in a class of its own. Class names are usually nouns, because they represent objects. However, in the Command pattern, the names are verbs, and each class must implement an execution method, traditionally called execute(); in our case, it will be called index(). (See http://en.wikipedia.org/wiki/Command_pattern for more information about the traditional implementation of the Command pattern.)

Why implement the actions as a class? The advantages are not so obvious in a web environment or with small applications. The following are the advantages of this approach:

- Each action class is treated as an API request action. It has a higher status than the verb object.

- The classes are smaller and more manageable.

- Supporting functions for each action are encapsulated within the action's own class. For example, each class has its own validation method.

To use the Command pattern in our controller, we start with a base controller, which acts as the parent class of all the action classes. Code that is common to all the action classes can be placed here. This base class is shown Listing 4-3.

Listing 4-3. *Base Controller (mf_controller.php)*

```
 1:    <?php
 2:
 3:    class MfController extends AppController {
 4:
 5:        var $name = 'Mf';
 6:
 7:        var $uses = array( 'Thread', 'Message', ➥
'MfSearchProcess', 'MfFetchMessage',
 8:                            'MfFetchMessages', 'MfFetchThreads' );
 9:
10:        function _checkAjax() {
11:
12:            if ( $this->RequestHandler->isAjax() ) {
13:
14:                // This must exist: app/views/layouts/json/ajax.ctp
15:                $this->RequestHandler->renderAs( $this, 'json' );
16:            }
17:        }
18:
19:        function index() {
20:
21:        }
22:    }
23:    ?>
```

The _checkAjax method on line 10 is used by the action classes to check whether the API call is an Ajax request. If it is an Ajax request, we render the Ajax layout file in app/views/layouts/json/ajax.ctp.

Following this, each action class extends the MfController class. An example is shown in Listing 4-4. There are quite often other supporting functions that help the main index function.

Listing 4-4. *Example of an Action Class That Extends the Main MfController Class*

```php
1:    <?php
2:
3:    include_once( 'mf_controller.php' );
4:
5:    class MfExampleController extends MfController {
6:
7:        var $name = 'MfExample';
8:
9:        var $result = array(    'result' => '',
10:                                'message' => '',
11:                                'errors' => '',
12:                                'data' => ''
13:                           );
14:
15:        function beforeFilter() {
16:
17:            $this->_checkAjax();
18:        }
19:
20:        function _validation() {
21:
22:            $result = true;
23:
24:            // Do validation
25:
26:            return $result;
27:        }
28:
29:        function index() {
30:
31:            if ( $this->_validation() ) {
32:
33:                // Do business logic
34:            }
35:        }
36:
37:        function beforeRender() {
38:
39:            $this->set( 'result', $this->result );
40:        }
41:    }
42:
43:    ?>
```

When the controller is called, it first checks whether it's an Ajax call in the beforeFilter on line 15. Next, we go in to the main index action on line 29. If the API call validates, we do the business logic. When we're ready to display the results, we package it in the beforeRender action on line 37.

Taking this hypothetical example, when we request a Cake URL, it will look like this:

http://www.example/MfExample/index/param:1/

Now that we've talked about how the controllers are set up, we can show you how we've actually implemented it. Table 4-3 shows all the controller actions we have written.

Table 4-3. *Our Application Controllers*

Controller File	Description
mf_controller.php	Parent controller to all action classes
mf_fetch_post_controller.php	Fetch a message
mf_fetch_posts_controller.php	Fetch several messages
mf_fetch_threads_controller.php	Fetch the threads
mf_post_form_controller.php	Post messages
mf_post_process_controller.php	Process a message
mf_search_process_controller.php	Process a search request

Now, if we were to do this in the traditional Cake way, there would be only two files: message_controller.php, to contain all actions relating to messages, and thread_controller.php, to contain all actions relating to threads. The MessageController would contain actions that fetch one or more posts and handle message posting, and it would contain various supporting functions. In this case, by separating out the actions as classes, we gain better management.

All the action classes have their own corresponding model, as shown in Table 4-4.

Table 4-4. *Action Controllers and the Corresponding Models*

Controller	Model	File
MfController	No associated model	
MfFetchMessageController	MfFetchMessage	app/models/mf_fetch_message.php
MfFetchMessagesController	MfFetchMessages	app/models/mf_fetch_messages.php
MfFetchThreadsController	MfFetchThreads	app/models/mf_fetch_threads.php
MfMessageFormController	MfMessageForm	app/models/mf_message_form.php
MfMessageProcessController	MfMessageProcess	app/models/mf_message_process.php
MfSearchProcessController	MfSearchProcess	app/models/mf_search_process.php

Next, we'll dive right into the heart of each controller and its view, starting with the MfFetchMessageController controller.

Fetch a Message

The MfFetchMessageController is used to find a particular message using its id. The findById method executes a simple SQL SELECT statement to the database and fetches the single message record. The code is shown in Listing 4-5.

Listing 4-5. *Fetch One Message Controller (mf_fetch_message_controller.php)*

```
 1:    <?php
 2:
 3:    include_once( 'mf_controller.php' );
 4:
 5:    class MfFetchMessageController extends MfController {
 6:
 7:        var $name = 'MfFetchMessage';
 8:
 9:        var $result = array(    'result' => '',
10:                                'message' => '',
11:                                'errors' => '',
12:                                'data' => ''
13:                                );
14:
15:        function beforeFilter() {
16:
17:            $this->_checkAjax();
18:        }
19:
20:        function _validation() {
21:
22:            $result = true;
23:
24:            $this->data = array( 'MfFetchMessage' );
25:            $this->data[ 'MfFetchMessage' ][ 'messageId' ] = '';
26:
27:            if ( isset( $this->passedArgs[ 'messageId' ] ) ) {
28:                $this->data[ 'MfFetchMessage' ][ 'messageId' ] = ➥
$this->passedArgs[ 'messageId' ];
29:            }
30:
31:            $this->MfFetchMessage->set( $this->data );
32:
33:            if ( !$this->MfFetchMessage->validates() ) {
34:
35:                $result = false;
36:
37:                $this->result[ 'result' ] = '0';
38:                $this->result[ 'message' ] = ➥
"There are some problems with your request.";
```

```
39:                    $this->result[ 'errors' ] = ➥
$this->MfFetchMessage->validationErrors;
40:               }
41:
42:           return $result;
43:        }
44:
45:        function index() {
46:
47:            if ( $this->_validation() ) {
48:
49:                $message = $this->Message->findById( ➥
$this->data[ 'MfFetchMessage' ][ 'messageId' ] );
50:
51:                if ( $message == '' ) {
52:                    $this->result[ 'result' ] = '0';
53:                    $this->result[ 'message' ] = ➥
'There was a problem fetching the message. Please try again later.';
54:                }
55:                else {
56:
57:                    $this->result[ 'result' ] = '1';
58:                    $this->result[ 'message' ] = ➥
'Message fetched successfully.';
59:                    $this->result[ 'data' ] = $message;
60:                }
61:            }
62:        }
63:
64:        function beforeRender() {
65:
66:            $this->set( 'result', $this->result );
67:        }
68:    }
69:
70:    ?>
```

Each action class returns a set of key/value pairs to the caller. On lines 9 through 12, there are four standard ones that will always be returned:

- result: Whether the request was successful or not: 1 or 0

- message: The human-readable message that goes with the result

- errors: A set of key/value pairs, where the key is the parameter and the value is the error message

- data: If the request is for data, where to look for it

Most of the action classes have three methods: beforeFilter, index, and beforeRender. The beforeFilter method checks whether it's an Ajax call. The parent _checkAjax() method looks like this:

```
function _checkAjax() {

    if ( $this->RequestHandler->isAjax() ) {

        // This must exist: \app\views\layouts\json\ajax.ctp
        $this->RequestHandler->renderAs( $this, 'json' );
    }
}
```

We have manually mapped Ajax calls to JSON returns. If it is an Ajax call, the layout \app\ views\layouts\json\ajax.ctp is used. We would like to return data to callers in a standard way, of course. However, this is not always possible, Ajax and server-side calls can handle formatted data like JSON, but then HTML messes up the format.

The main index() method is where all the action happens. We have created a _validation() method. Any parameter coming into the action class must be validated, and we make use of Cake's validation as much as we can. To do this, we create a model specifically for our action class called MfFetchMessage, as shown in Listing 4-6.

Listing 4-6. *MfFetchMessageController Model (app/models/mf_fetch_message.php)*

```
<?php

class MfFetchMessage extends AppModel
{
    // Mainly for PHP4 users
    var $name = 'MfFetchMessage';

    var $useTable = false;

    var $validate = array( 'messageId' => array(
                                'rule' => array( 'between', 36, 36 ),
                                'required' => true,
                                'message' => 'Please provide a message id ➥
of 36 characters in length.' )
                            );
}

?>
```

Once the validation has passed, we go ahead and carry out the business logic within index. When that's done, the beforeRender() method is called. This method sets the $result variable for the views. Of course, we could have just as easily set the result in index(), but following the idea of the Command pattern, we're keeping code decoupled and standardized.

Our view for the MfFetchMessageController is quite simple. It takes $result['data'] and formats it in HTML, ready to be displayed. It's worth highlighting that the JSON output also makes use of the $result variable, but in that case, it formats the output in JSON notation instead of HTML. Our HTML view is shown in Listing 4-7.

Listing 4-7. *Fetch One Message View (app/views/mf_fetch_message/index.ctp)*

```php
<?php

    if ( isset( $result[ 'data' ][ 'Message' ] ) ) {

        echo '<div class="message">';

            echo '<div class="message_header">';
                echo '<h3>'.$result[ 'data' ][ 'Message' ] ➥
[ "subject" ].'</a></h3>';
                echo ' <h6>By '.$result[ 'data' ][ 'Message' ] ➥
[ "email" ].'</h6>';
            echo '</div>';

            $message_id = $result[ 'data' ][ 'Message' ][ "id" ];
            $thread_id = $result[ 'data' ][ 'Message' ][ "thread_id" ];

            echo '<div class="message" short_message="" ➥
full_message="" fetched="0" id="message_'.$message_id.'">';

                echo $result[ 'data' ][ 'Message' ][ "message" ];

                $reply_link = $html->link( 'Reply', ➥
'/cake/__chapters__/message_forum/MfMessageForm/index/ ➥
reply_to:'.$message_id.'/thread_id:'.$thread_id.'/' );
                echo '<div>'.$reply_link.'</div>';

            echo '</div>';

        echo '</div>';
    }
?>
```

Fetch Several Messages

At present, our MfFetchMessagesController, shown in Listing 4-8, helps us to find queries based on the thread ID.

■**Note** We can quite easily see the fetch several messages action being deprecated, in favor of using the MfMessageProcessController as a generic "find any messages" class. We'll leave that as an exercise for the reader.

Listing 4-8. *Fetch Several Messages Controller (mf_fetch_messages_controller.php)*

```php
1:    <?php
2:
3:    include_once( 'mf_controller.php' );
4:
5:    class MfFetchMessagesController extends MfController {
6:
7:        var $name = 'MfFetchMessages';
8:
9:        // The message results
10:       var $messages = array();
11:
12:       // The message results ordered with indent indicator
13:       var $messagesOrdered = array();
14:
15:       var $result = array(    'result' => '',
16:                               'message' => '',
17:                               'errors' => '',
18:                               'data' => ''
19:                               );
20:
21:       function beforeFilter() {
22:
23:           $this->_checkAjax();
24:       }
25:
26:       function _validation() {
27:
28:           $result = true;
29:
30:           $this->data = array( 'MfFetchMessages' );
31:           $this->data[ 'MfFetchMessages' ][ 'threadId' ] = '';
32:
33:           if ( isset( $this->passedArgs[ 'threadId' ] ) ) {
34:               $this->data[ 'MfFetchMessages' ][ 'threadId' ] = ➥
$this->passedArgs[ 'threadId' ];
35:           }
36:
37:           $this->MfFetchMessages->set( $this->data );
38:
39:           if ( !$this->MfFetchMessages->validates() ) {
40:
41:               $result = false;
42:
43:               $this->result[ 'result' ] = '0';
44:               $this->result[ 'message' ] = ➥
"There are some problems with your request.";
```

```
45:                    $this->result[ 'errors' ] = ➥
$this->MfFetchMessage->validationErrors;
46:                }
47:
48:            return $result;
49:        }
50:
51:        function index() {
52:
53:            if ( $this->_validation() ) {
54:
55:                $conditions = array ();
56:
57:                if ( isset( $this->data[ 'MfFetchMessages' ] ➥
[ 'threadId' ] ) ) {
58:
59:                    $threadId = ➥
$this->data[ 'MfFetchMessages' ][ 'threadId' ];
60:                    $conditions[] = array( ➥
"Message.thread_id =" => $threadId );
61:                }
62:
63:                $messages = $this->Message->find( 'all',
64:                            array( 'conditions' => $conditions,
65:                                    null,
66:                                    'order' => 'Message.t_created_at ASC'
67:                                    ) );
68:
69:                if ( $messages == '' ) {
70:
71:                    $this->result[ 'result' ] = '0';
72:                    $this->result[ 'message' ] = ➥
'There was a problem fetching the threads. Please try again later.';
73:                }
74:                else {
75:
76:                    $this->messages = $messages;
77:
78:                    $this->_sortMessages();
79:
80:                    $this->result[ 'result' ] = '1';
81:                    $this->result[ 'message' ] = ➥
'Messages fetched successfully.';
82:                    $this->result[ 'data' ] = $this->messagesOrdered;
83:                }
84:            }
85:
```

```
86:                $this->set( 'result', $this->result );
87:          }
88:
89:        function beforeRender() {
90:
91:                $this->set( 'result', $this->result );
92:          }
93:
94:        function _sortMessages( $start_id = '', $level = '' ) {
95:
96:                static $stopRun = 1;
97:
98:                // You never know!
99:                if ( $stopRun++ > 1000 ) {
100:                     return;
101:                }
102:
103:                for( $idx=0; $idx<sizeof( $this->messages ); $idx++ ) {
104:
105:                       if ( !isset( $this->messages[$idx][ 'Done' ] ) ) {
106:
107:                              // Found a root message
108:                              if ( $this->messages[$idx][ 'Message' ] ➡
[ 'reply_to' ] == $start_id ) {
109:
110:                                     $this->messages[$idx][ 'Message' ] ➡
[ 'indent' ] = $level;
111:
112:                                     $this->messagesOrdered[] = ➡
$this->messages[$idx];
113:
114:                                     $message_id = ➡
$this->messages[$idx][ 'Message' ][ 'id' ];
115:
116:                                     // That's done; let's remove it
117:                                     $this->messages[$idx][ 'Done' ] = '1';
118:
119:                                     $this->_sortMessages( $message_id, $level.'.' );
120:                              }
121:                       }
122:                }
123:          }
124:    }
125:
126:    ?>
```

As you can see, the structure of this class is similar to that of the MfFetchMessageController. In this case, we have an extra private method _sortMessages() on line 94, which sorts our message recursively according to replies. We have used a simple full stop to signify the depth of the message within the thread. For peace of mind, we've placed a stopper on line 99 just in case the method goes into an infinite recursive loop.

Again, our view for the MfFetchMessages controller simply takes the $result['data'], loops through the data, and formats the output for HTML display. We've used the indent indicator to indent our messages from the left side of the browser. As we are multiplying the number of full stops by pixel value, the greater the depth, the further away it will be displayed from the left margin (see lines 7 and 9 in Listing 4-9). You can just as easily use em, as that probably makes it more accessible. But hey, we just wanted to make it obvious that you can use pixels instead.

Our view is shown in Listing 4-9.

Listing 4-9. *Fetch Multiple Messages View (app/views/mf_fetch_messages/index.ctp)*

```
 1:    <h2>Messages</h2>
 2:
 3:    <?php
 4:
 5:        foreach ( $result[ 'data' ] as $current_message ) {
 6:
 7:            $indent = strlen( $current_message[ 'Message' ][ "indent" ] )*20;
 8:
 9:            echo '<div style="margin-left: '.$indent.'px;">';
10:
11:            echo '<div class="message_header">';
12:            echo '<h3>'.$current_message[ 'Message' ][ "subject" ].'</a></h3>';
13:            echo ' <h6>By ➡
'.$current_message[ 'Message' ][ "email" ].'</h6>';
14:
15:            echo '</div>';
16:
17:            $message_id = $current_message[ 'Message' ][ "id" ];
18:            $thread_id = $current_message[ 'Message' ][ "thread_id" ];
19:
20:            echo '<div class="message_message" ➡
short_message="" full_message="" fetched="0" id="message_'.$message_id.'">';
21:                echo $current_message[ 'Message' ][ "message" ];
22:                echo '<div ➡
<a href="/cake/__chapters__/message_forum/MfMessageForm/index/ ➡
reply_to:'.$message_id.'/thread_id:'.$thread_id.'/">Reply</a></div>';
23:                echo '</div>';
24:
25:            echo '</div>';
26:        }
27:
28:    ?>
```

Fetch the Threads

We have used the pagination feature within Cake to separate the threads into pages.
Listing 4-10 shows the MfFetchThreadsController.

Listing 4-10. *Fetch the Threads Controller (mf_fetch_threads_controller.php)*

```php
 1:    <?php
 2:
 3:    include_once( 'mf_controller.php' );
 4:
 5:    class MfFetchThreadsController extends MfController {
 6:
 7:        var $name = 'MfFetchThreads';
 8:
 9:        var $paginate = array( 'limit' => 20,
10:                               'order' => array( ➥
'Thread.last_message_date' => 'DESC' ) );
11:
12:        var $result = array(    'result' => '',
13:                                'message' => '',
14:                                'errors' => '',
15:                                'data' => ''
16:                                );
17:
18:        function beforeFilter() {
19:
20:            $this->_checkAjax();
21:        }
22:
23:        function _validation() {
24:
25:            $result = true;
26:
27:            return $result;
28:        }
29:
30:        function index() {
31:
32:            if ( $this->_validation() ) {
33:
34:                $threads = $this->paginate( 'Thread' );
35:
36:                if ( $threads == '' ) {
37:                    $this->result[ 'result' ] = '0';
38:                    $this->result[ 'message' ] = ➥
'There was a problem fetching the threads. Please try again later.';
39:                }
```

```
40:                   else {
41:                       $this->result[ 'result' ] = '1';
42:                       $this->result[ 'message' ] = ➥
'Threads fetched successfully.';
43:                       $this->result[ 'data' ] = $threads;
44:                   }
45:              }
46:          }
47:
48:      function beforeRender() {
49:
50:          $this->set( 'result', $this->result );
51:      }
52:    }
53:
54:    ?>
```

Adding pagination is essentially a three-step process. Referring to our controller class, first you set up the options in the controller via the $paginate variable on line 9. In our case, we limit the number of records returned to 20. We also order the threads according to the last_message_date field in descending order. Next, instead of using the Cake findBy[Field Name] method, we use the paginate method. This takes the model name as its main parameter (see line 34).

The third and final step in using pagination is at the bottom of the view, shown in Listing 4-11. Cake provides a paginate helper (see line 43), which is included by default once the paginate method is used. We simply call the prev and next methods, which will generate the necessary HTML links.

Listing 4-11. *Fetch the Threads View (app/views/mf_fetch_threads.php)*

```
1:    <h2>Threads</h2>
2:
3:    <?php
4:        echo $javascript->link( 'mf_fetch_threads/index' );
5:    ?>
6:
7:    <?php
8:
9:        foreach ( $result[ 'data' ] as $current_message ) {
10:
11:            $message_id = $current_message[ 'Message' ][ "id" ];
12:            $thread_id = $current_message[ 'Message' ][ "thread_id" ];
13:            $message_num = $current_message[ 'Thread' ][ "message_num" ];
14:
15:            echo '<div class="thread_header">';
16:            echo '<h3>'.$current_message[ 'Message' ] ➥
[ "subject" ].'</a></h3>';
```

```
17:                 echo ' <h6>Started By ➥
'.$current_message[ 'Message' ][ "name" ].'</h6>';
18:
19:                     // Number of messages
20:                     echo ' | '.$message_num.' messages';
21:
22:                     // Open link
23:                     echo ' | <span id="open_link_'.$message_id.'"> ➥
<a href="javascript: void(0);" ➥
onclick="getMessage(\''.$message_id.'\',\''.$thread_id.'\');">Open</a></span>';
24:
25:                     // View thread
26:                     echo ' | <a ➥
href="/cake/__chapters__/message_forum/MfFetchMessages/index/threadId:'.➥
$thread_id.'/">List Messages</a>';
27:
28:                     // Loading
29:                     echo ' | <div id="loading_'.$message_id.'"></div>';
30:
31:             echo '</div>';
32:
33:             // Display first message
34:             echo '<div class="thread_message" short_message=""
35:             full_message="" fetched="0" id="message_'.$message_id.'"></div>';
36:         }
37:
38:     ?>
39:
40:     <hr class="paginator_line">
41:
42:     <?php
43:         if ( isset( $paginator ) ) {
44:
45:             echo $paginator->prev( '« Previous ', null,
46:                                     null, array( 'class' => 'disabled' ) );
47:             echo ' ';
48:             echo $paginator->next( ' Next »', null,
49:                                     null, array( 'class' => 'disabled' ) );
50:             echo ' ';
51:             echo $paginator->counter();
52:         }
53:     ?>
```

Line 4 in Listing 4-11 creates an HTML script tag, which will call the JavaScript file located at app/webroot/js/mf_fetch_threads/index.js. This file is shown in Listing 4-12.

Listing 4-12. *JavaScript File Used to Support the Fetching of Threads (app/webroot/js/mf_fetch_threads/index.js)*

```
1:    function getMessage(message_id,thread_id) {
2:
3:        var full_message = ➥
$('message_'+message_id).getAttribute( 'full_message' );
4:
5:        if ( full_message != '' ) {
6:            $('message_'+message_id).innerHTML = full_message;
7:            return false;
8:        }
9:
10:       new Ajax.Request( '/cake/__chapters__/message_forum/MfFetchMessage/ ➥
index/messageId:'+message_id+'/.json',
11:           {   asynchronous:true,
12:               evalScripts:true,
13:               onComplete: function(response,json){
14:
15:                   if ( json[ 'result' ] == '1' ) {
16:
17:                       message_links = ➥
json[ 'data' ][ 'Message' ][ 'message' ];
18:                       message_links += '<div>';
19:                       message_links += '<a href="javascript: ➥
void(0);" onclick="closeMessage(\''+message_id+'\');">Close</a> |';
20:                       message_links += ➥
'<a href="/cake/__chapters__/message_forum/MfFetchMessages/index/ ➥
threadId:'+thread_id+'/">List Messages</a> |';
21:                       message_links += ➥
'<a href="/cake/__chapters__/message_forum/MfMessageForm/index/ ➥
reply_to:'+message_id+'/thread_id:'+thread_id+'/">Reply</a>';
22:                       message_links += '</div>';
23:
24:                       $('message_'+message_id).innerHTML = message_links;
25:
26:                       $('message_'+message_id).setAttribute( ➥
'full_message', $('message_'+message_id).innerHTML );
27:                       $('loading_'+message_id).innerHTML = '';
28:                   }
29:               },
30:               onLoading: function() {
31:
32:                   $('message_'+message_id).setAttribute( ➥
'short_message', $('message_'+message_id).innerHTML );
33:                   $('loading_'+message_id).innerHTML = ➥
'<img src="/cake/__chapters__/message_forum/img/ajax-loader.gif" alt="" /> ➥
loading, please wait.';
34:               }
35:           } );
36:   }
```

```
37:
38:    function closeMessage(message_id) {
39:
40:        var short_message = $('message_'+message_id).↦
getAttribute( 'short_message' );
41:        $('message_'+message_id).innerHTML = short_message;
42:    }
```

When a user clicks the Open link (see line 23 in Listing 4-11), the getMessage function on
line 1 in Listing 4-12 is called. This function makes an Ajax call to the MfFetchMessage method
(see line 10). That method will return the message in JSON format. We start the parsing on
line 13. We finish the process by displaying the message together with some links, on line 24.
A sample of the parsed output is shown in Figure 4-3.

Figure 4-3. *Displaying threads*

Post Messages

Our message posting form, shown in Listing 4-13, posts messages using Ajax by default. However, if the user has JavaScript turned off, it will degrade to standard HTML posting. Because it's not part of our API method calls, its structure doesn't mirror the API action classes. However, in the future we may include this as an API method call where users can use our form instead of writing their own. They can conveniently include the form in the sidebar of their web site—in a blog, for example.

Listing 4-13. *Post a Message Controller (mf_message_form_controller.php)*

```php
<?php

include_once( 'mf_controller.php' );

class MfMessageFormController extends MfController {

    var $name = 'MfMessageForm';

    function index() {

        if ( isset( $this->passedArgs['reply_to'] ) ) {

            $this->data['Message']['reply_to'] = $this->passedArgs['reply_to'];

            $replyMessageId = $this->data['Message']['reply_to'];
            $replyMessage = $this->Message->findById( $replyMessageId );

            if ( !empty( $replyMessage ) ) {

                $this->data['Message']['subject'] = ➥
'RE: '.$replyMessage[ 'Message' ][ 'subject' ];
            }
        }

        if ( isset( $this->passedArgs['thread_id'] ) ) {

            $this->data['Message']['thread_id'] = $this->passedArgs['thread_id'];
        }
    }
}

?>
```

The view for the form is pretty sparse, as shown here:

```php
<?php
    echo $this->element( 'message_form' );
?>
```

As you can see, the view for the message form is separated off into an element, as shown in Listing 4-14.

Listing 4-14. *Message Posting Form as an Element (/app/views/elements/message_form.ctp)*

```
 1:    <?php
 2:        if ( $session->check( 'Message.flash'  ) ) {
 3:            echo '<div class="hilight">';
 4:            $session->flash();
 5:            echo '</div>';
 6:        }
 7:    ?>
 8:
 9:    <!-- TinyMCE -->
10:    <?php
11:        echo $javascript ➡
->link( 'jscripts/tinymce/jscripts/tiny_mce/tiny_mce' );
12:    ?>
13:    <script type="text/javascript">
14:        tinyMCE.init({
15:            mode : "textareas",
16:            theme : "advanced",
17:            theme_advanced_buttons1 : ➡
"bold,italic,underline,separator,strikethrough,justifyleft, ➡
justifycenter,justifyright, justifyfull,bullist,numlist, ➡
undo,redo,link,unlink",
18:            theme_advanced_buttons2 : "",
19:            theme_advanced_buttons3 : "",
20:            theme_advanced_toolbar_location : "top",
21:            theme_advanced_toolbar_align : "left",
22:            theme_advanced_statusbar_location : "bottom",
23:            extended_valid_elements : ➡
"a[name|href|target|title|onclick],img[class|src|border=0|alt| ➡
title|hspace|vspace|width|height|align|onmouseover|onmouseout|name], ➡
hr[class|width|size|noshade],font[face|size|color|style], ➡
span[class|align|style]",
24:            content_css : "/cake/__chapters__/message_forum/css/global.css"
25:
26:        });
27:    </script>
28:    <!-- /TinyMCE -->
29:
30:    <?php
31:        echo $javascript->link( 'elements/message_form' );
32:    ?>
33:
34:    <div id="page_message"></div>
35:
```

```
36:    <div id="message_form">
37:
38:    <?php
39:        echo $ajax->form(   null,
40:                            'post',
41:                            array(  'url' => '/MfMessageProcess/index',
42:                                    'complete' => 'updateForm(request,json);',
43:                                    'before' => 'beforeMessage();'
44:                                 )
45:                            );
46:    ?>
47:
48:    <fieldset style="border:1px solid black; background-image:url( ➥
'/cake/__chapters__/message_forum/app/webroot/img/background.gif' );">
49:        <legend> <?php __('Add a Message!');?> </legend>
50:        Please fill in all fields. Remember, spam and be damned!
51:        <?php
52:            echo $form->error( 'Message.name' );
53:            echo $form->input( 'Message.name', array( ➥
'id' => 'messagename', 'label' => 'Name:', 'size' => '50', ➥
'maxlength' => '255', 'error' => false ) );
54:
55:            echo $form->error( 'Message.email' );
56:            echo 'Your email will not be displayed.';
57:            echo $form->input( 'Message.email', array( ➥
'id' => 'messageemail', 'label' => 'Email:', 'size' => '50', ➥
'maxlength' => '255', 'error' => false ) );
58:
59:            echo $form->error( 'Message.subject' );
60:            echo $form->input( 'Message.subject', array( ➥
'id' => 'messagesubject', 'label' => 'Subject:', 'size' => '50', ➥
'maxlength' => '255', 'error' => false ) );
61:
62:            echo $form->error( 'Message.message' );
63:            echo $form->input( 'Message.message', array( ➥
'id' => 'messagemessage', 'type'=>'textarea', 'label' => 'Message:', ➥
'rows' => '20', 'error' => false ) );
64:
65:            echo $form->hidden( 'Message.reply_to' );
66:            echo $form->hidden( 'Message.thread_id' );
67:        ?>
68:    </fieldset>
69:
70:    <?php echo $form->end( array( 'label' => ' Submit Message ' ) );?>
71:
72:    </div>
```

There are a number of interesting things happening in this element. Before we go any further, we have to admit that this simple form turned out to be quite complex because of the use of Ajax and how it can degrade in the absence of JavaScript.

First, we have included the TinyMCE what you see is what you get (WYSIWYG) web editor. It was either that or the FCKeditor, which is just as good.

Note TinyMCE (http:/tinymce.moxiecode.com) and FCKeditor (http:/www.fckeditor.net) are two of the most popular web-based open source text editors. You will generally use them to replace the HTML textarea tag. They provide editing capabilities much like any desktop word processing editor.

Installing TinyMCE is quite easy. First, download the package from the TinyMCE web site (http://tinymce.moxiecode.com). Then unzip the code into the folder /app/webroot/js/jscripts/.

Next, we need to initialize the editor. This is done from lines 10 to 27 in Listing 4-14. Later, when the form is saved, we also need to trigger TinyMCE to save the content. This is done in the JavaScript helper file (see Listing 4-15, line 47).

In Listing 4-14, we include our JavaScript helper file in the line echo $javascript->link('elements/message_form'); on line 31. The helper file, shown in Listing 4-15, is stored in /app/webroot/js/elements/message_form.js. We have created an elements folder within /app/webroot/js. This allows us to easily pick out which JavaScript file goes with which .ctp file, as we have named the JavaScript file to be the same as the .ctp file that included it.

Listing 4-15. *JavaScript Helper Functions for the Message Posting Form (/app/webroot/js/elements/message_form.js)*

```
 1:
 2:     function updateForm(request,json) {
 3:
 4:         var msg_render = '';
 5:         var result = json['result'];
 6:         var message = json['message'];
 7:         var errors = json['errors'];
 8:
 9:         $('page_message').innerHTML = '<div class="hilight">'+message+'</div>';
10:
11:         $$('.submit input')[0].disabled = false;
12:
13:         // Remove all previous error messages
14:         var current_errors = $$('.error-message');
15:
16:         for( var i=0; i<current_errors.length; i++ ) {
17:             var error_tag = current_errors[i];
18:             error_tag.parentNode.removeChild(error_tag);
19:         }
20:
```

```
21:          // If there are error messages, update these
22:          if ( errors != '' ) {
23:
24:              for( var field_id in errors ){
25:
26:                  // The error message in a div
27:                  var div_error = document.createElement( "div" );
28:                  div_error.className = "error-message";
29:                  div_error.innerHTML = errors[field_id];
30:
31:                  form_ele = $('message'+field_id);
32:                  parent_form_ele = form_ele.parentNode;
33:
34:                  parent_form_ele.insertBefore(   div_error,
35:                                            form_ele.previousSibling );
36:              }
37:          }
38:
39:          // If it was successful, then we clear the form
40:          if ( result == 1 ) {
41:              $('message_form').innerHTML = '';
42:          }
43:      }
44:
45:    function beforeMessage() {
46:
47:          tinyMCE.triggerSave();
48:
49:          $('page_message').innerHTML = ➡
'<div class="hilight">Posting, please wait ... ➡
<img src="/cake/__chapters__/message_forum/img/ajax-loader.gif" alt="" /> ➡
</div>';
50:
51:          $$('.submit input')[0].disabled = true;
52:      }
53:
```

In the updateForm method in Listing 4-15, we basically parse the form process return results, which is in the standard format we described earlier, where the results contain the keys, message, errors, and data. We first remove any errors that were previously there. We do this simply by using the removeChild method on line 18.

We then display any errors by looping through the errors key value and displaying it before the field. The Cake Ajax form can easily do this step for us, but it displays the error messages after the field, and we want the user to read the error first and then see the field to which it refers. We use the DOM method insertBefore to insert a DIV tag, which contains the error message before the field. The web page http://developer.mozilla.org/en/docs/ DOM:element.insertBefore has some good information about DOM methods.

If there are no errors, the form has been posted successfully, and we then clear the form to avoid any trigger-happy user. Additionally, we can display some other useful information there at a later date—maybe some advertisement relating to the posted message, for example.

Before posting the Ajax request, we call the beforeMessage() method on line 45. In that function, we need to manually get TinyMCE to save our message. This happens only because we are using Ajax. If you're using ordinary HTML to post, you won't need to carry out this step with TinyMCE.

After that, we simply add some user interface sugar, starting with a spinning Ajax loader image. Then we disable the submit button.

Returning to our message posting form in Listing 4-14, our next step simply uses the Ajax and form helpers to add some form elements (see line 38). An important point to note is the handling of the error messages relating to the fields. This point applies only when the user browser is not running JavaScript; that is, HTML is being used to post messages. We have turned off the automatic display of the error messages relating to Cake's rendering of the input tags. This is because we want the error messages to be displayed before the input fields. To add the error messages before the field, we manually display the error messages, as in this example:

```
echo $form->error( 'Message.name' );
```

A sample form for adding a message is shown in Figure 4-4.

■**Note** The Ajax helper is a wrapper for Prototype's methods. In the Ajax helper, you can use the update option to specify which div container to update the return result. If you don't use the update option, Cake will use Prototype's Request method. If you do specify an update option, it will use the Updater method.

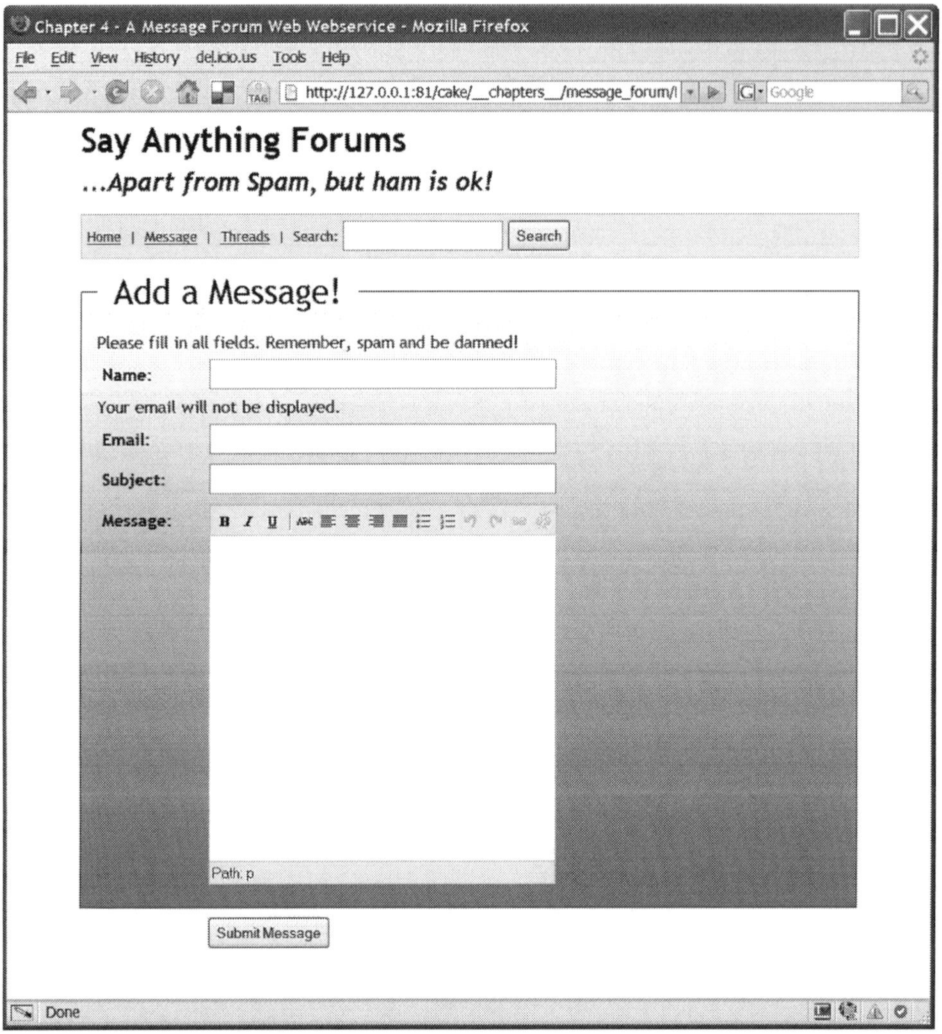

Figure 4-4. *Posting a message*

Process a Message

In the processing or saving of a message, we use a model that directly maps to a table. This is unlike some of the earlier controller actions, where the models were essentially wrapper classes for validation, as MfMessageProcess is an API method that we're exposing. As shown in Listing 4-16, it follows the same class structure as the other API methods.

Listing 4-16. *Save a Message Controller (mf_message_process_controller.php)*

```php
1:    <?php
2:
3:    include_once( 'mf_controller.php' );
4:
5:    class MfMessageProcessController extends MfController {
6:
7:        var $name = 'MfMessageProcess';
8:
9:        var $result = array(    'result' => '',
10:                                'message' => '',
11:                                'errors' => '',
12:                                'data' => ''
13:                                );
14:
15:        function beforeFilter() {
16:
17:            $this->_checkAjax();
18:        }
19:
20:        function _validation() {
21:
22:            $result = true;
23:
24:            if ( !empty( $this->data ) ) {
25:
26:                $this->Message->set( $this->data );
27:
28:                if ( !$this->Message->validates() ) {
29:
30:                    $result = false;
31:
32:                    if ( $this->RequestHandler->requestedWith() == 'form' ) {
33:                        $this->Session->setFlash( __( ➥
'Sorry, there was a problem with your form details, see below.', true ) );
34:                    }
35:
36:                    $this->result[ 'result' ] = '0';
37:                    $this->result[ 'message' ] = ➥
"There are some problems with your request.";
38:                    $this->result[ 'errors' ] = ➥
$this->Message->validationErrors;
39:                }
40:            }
41:
42:            return $result;
43:        }
44:
```

```
45:         function index() {
46:
47:             if ( $this->_validation() ) {
48:
49:                 $message_date = date( 'y-m-d H:i:s', mktime() );
50:                 $message_id = String::uuid();
51:                 $thread_id = String::uuid();
52:                 $origThreadId = $this->data[ 'Message' ][ 'thread_id' ];
53:
54:                 if ( $this->data[ 'Message' ][ 'thread_id' ] ) {
55:                     $thread_id = $this->data[ 'Message' ][ 'thread_id' ];
56:                 }
57:
58:                 $this->Message->create();
59:
60:                 $this->data[ 'Message' ][ 't_created_at' ] = $message_date;
61:                 $this->data[ 'Message' ][ 'thread_id' ] = $thread_id;
62:                 $this->data[ 'Message' ][ 'id' ] = $message_id;
63:
64:                 if ( $this->Message->save( $this->data ) ) {
65:
66:                     if ( $this->RequestHandler->requestedWith() == 'form' ) {
67:                         $this->Session->setFlash( ➡
__( 'Your message has been posted!', true ) );
68:                     }
69:
70:                     $this->result[ 'message' ] = ➡
'Your message has been posted!';
71:                     $this->result[ 'result' ] = '1';
72:                     $this->result[ 'errors' ] = '';
73:
74:                     // Save the thread
75:                     if ( empty( $origThreadId ) ) {
76:
77:                         $threadData = array();
78:                         $threadData[ 'first_message_id' ] = $message_id;
79:                         $threadData[ 'last_message_date' ] = $message_date;
80:                         $threadData[ 'id' ] = $thread_id;
81:                         $threadData[ 'message_num' ] = '1';
82:
83:                         $this->Thread->create();
84:                         $thread_save = $this->Thread->save( $threadData );
85:
86:                         if ( !$thread_save ) {
87:
88:                             $this->Message->delete( $this->data );
89:                         }
90:                     }
```

```
 91:                     else {
 92:                         $this->Thread->threadPlusOne( $origThreadId );
 93:                     }
 94:
 95:                     // Everything seems OK. Let's do a redirect after message.
 96:                     // Is it coming from a standard HTML message form
 97:                     if ( $this->RequestHandler->requestedWith() == 'form' ) {
 98:                         $this->redirect( array( ➥
'controller' => 'MfMessageForm',
 99:                                             'action' => 'index' ) );
100:                         exit();
101:                     }
102:                 }
103:                 else {
104:
105:                     if ( $this->RequestHandler->requestedWith() == 'form' ) {
106:                         $this->Session->setFlash( ➥
__( 'Sorry, there was a problem with your form details, see below.', true ) );
107:                     }
108:
109:                     $this->result[ 'message' ] = ➥
'Sorry, there was a problem with your form details.';
110:                     $this->result[ 'result' ] = '0';
111:                     $this->result[ 'errors' ] = ➥
$this->Message->validationErrors;
112:                 }
113:             }
114:         }
115:
116:         function beforeRender() {
117:
118:             $this->set( 'result', $this->result );
119:         }
120:     }
121:
122:     ?>
```

There isn't much in the process view for HTML requests. It simply displays the message form again, as follows:

```
<?php
    echo $this->renderElement( 'message_form' );
?>
```

In Listing 4-16, we start off with some Cake validation. Once validation is all good (on line 47), we do the business stuff of saving the message. If a user is posting a new message, we also need to create a thread record for it. However, if the message wasn't saved for some reason, we need to remove it from the thread record that we have already saved.

We have used UUIDs to help us with two coding tasks (see lines 50 and 51):

- It allows us to easily delete the thread record if the message record didn't save. This isn't strictly needed, as we can always get the ID quite easily once the thread has been saved.

- Since a thread needs the ID of the last message posted (or the first one if it's a fresh post), and a message needs the ID of the thread, it makes sense for us to generate the IDs within the code, rather than rely on the database to give us IDs. We save on the number of queries we make and have fewer lines of code.

Another feature within the code in Listing 4-16 is the redirect after the post, which is quite a common practice nowadays in order to avoid repeated posts. However, this feature isn't needed in an Ajax call, so we filter this out on lines 32, 66, and 105.

Process a Search Request

Again, the MfSearchProcessController follows the structure of the other API methods, as shown in Listing 4-17.

Listing 4-17. *Search for Messages Controller (mf_search_process_controller.php)*

```php
1:      <?php
2:
3:      include_once( 'mf_controller.php' );
4:
5:      class MfSearchProcessController extends MfController {
6:
7:          var $name = 'MfSearchProcess';
8:
9:          var $paginate = array(  'limit' => 20,
10:                                  'order' => array( ➥
'Message.t_created_at' => 'asc' ) );
11:
12:          var $result = array(    'result' => '',
13:                                  'message' => '',
14:                                  'errors' => '',
15:                                  'data' => '',
16:                                  'search_term' => ''
17:                                  );
18:
19:          var $search_term = '';
20:
21:          function _validation() {
22:
23:              $result = true;
24:
25:              if ( isset( $this->data[ 'MfSearchProcess' ]['search_term'] ) ) {
26:
```

```
27:                      $search_term = ➥
$this->data[ 'MfSearchProcess' ]['search_term'];
28:                  }
29:              elseif ( $this->Session->read( "search_term" ) ) {
30:
31:                  $search_term = $this->Session->read( "search_term" );
32:                  $this->data[ 'MfSearchProcess' ]['search_term'] = ➥
$search_term;
33:                  }
34:              elseif ( isset( $this->passedArgs['search_term'] ) ) {
35:
36:                  $search_term = $this->passedArgs['search_term'];
37:                  $this->data[ 'MfSearchProcess' ]['search_term'] = ➥
$search_term;
38:                  }
39:
40:              $this->MfSearchProcess->set( $this->data );
41:
42:              // Now check search term
43:              if ( !$this->MfSearchProcess->validates() ) {
44:
45:                  $result = false;
46:
47:                  $this->result[ 'result' ] = '0';
48:
49:                  // Since there's only 1 field, for the minute
50:                  // we'll assume it's from the search term
51:                  $validation_error = '';
52:
53:                  if ( isset( $this->MfSearchProcess ➥
->validationErrors[ 'search_term' ] ) ) {
54:                      $validation_error = $this ➥
->MfSearchProcess->validationErrors[ 'search_term' ];
55:                  }
56:
57:                  $message = __( ➥
'Sorry, there was a problem with your search form. '.$validation_error, true );
58:
59:                  $this->result[ 'message' ] = $message;
60:                  $this->result[ 'errors' ] = ➥
$this->MfSearchProcess->validationErrors;
61:              }
62:
63:              $this->result[ 'search_term' ] = ➥
$this->data[ 'MfSearchProcess' ]['search_term'];
64:              $this->search_term = ➥
$this->data[ 'MfSearchProcess' ]['search_term'];
65:
```

```
66:                return $result;
67:            }
68:
69:        function index() {
70:
71:            $messages = array();
72:
73:            if ( $this->_validation() ) {
74:
75:                $conditions = array();
76:
77:                if ( $this->search_term ) {
78:
79:                    $this->Session->write( "search_term", ➥
$this->search_term );
80:
81:                    $search_term = $this->search_term;
82:
83:                    $conditions[] = ➥
array( "MATCH(email,subject,message) AGAINST ('$search_term')" );
84:                }
85:
86:                $messages = $this->paginate( ➥
'Message', array( "or" => $conditions ) );
87:
88:                if ( $messages == '' ) {
89:                    $this->result[ 'result' ] = '0';
90:                    $this->result[ 'message' ] = ➥
'There was a problem with the search. Please try again later.';
91:                }
92:                else {
93:
94:                    $this->result[ 'result' ] = '1';
95:                    $this->result[ 'message' ] = ➥
'Search results fetched successfully.';
96:                    $this->result[ 'data' ] = $messages;
97:                }
98:            }
99:        }
100:
101:        function beforeRender() {
102:
103:            $this->set( 'result', $this->result );
104:        }
105:    }
106:
107:    ?>
```

We first validate to see whether we have a search term on line 73. Once that passes, we use Cake's pagination feature to split the results into pages.

We have used a dummy model MfSearchProcess as a way to validate our search term using Cake's validation function. We need to store the search term in session so it can be used during the pagination when a user selects a different page.

On line 83, we have used MySQL's MATCH AGAINST operator in our queries. This gives a wider range of accurate matches. To use the MySQL MATCH AGAINST operator in your code, you will need to create a full-text index on the database fields using this command:

```
CREATE FULLTEXT INDEX full_text_1 ON messages (email,subject,message);
```

▦Note Avoid using the LIKE operator. The LIKE operator is quite expensive, as it must scan all the fields where the operator is used. Also, it doesn't match variations of the word. For example, if the search term is *running*, it won't search for *run* or *runner*. MySQL has many other search methods besides the standard LIKE. See http://dev.mysql.com/doc/refman/5.0/en/fulltext-search.html for details.

The view for our search function is shown in Listing 4-18.

Listing 4-18. *View Template for the Search Action Class (/app/views/mf_search_process/index.ctp)*

```
<h2>Search Results</h2>

<?php
    if ( $result[ 'result' ] == '0' ) {
        echo '<div class="hilight">';
        echo $result[ 'message' ];
        echo '</div>';
    }
?>

<?php

    if ( $result[ 'data' ] ) {

        foreach ( $result[ 'data' ] as $current_message ) {

            echo '<div class="message_header">';
                echo '<h3>'.$current_message[ 'Message' ] ➥
[ "subject" ].'</a></h3>';
                echo ' <h6>By '.$current_message[ 'Message' ] ➥
[ "email" ].'</h6>';

            echo '</div>';
```

```php
            $message_id = $current_message[ 'Message' ][ "id" ];
            $thread_id = $current_message[ 'Message' ][ "thread_id" ];

            echo '<div class="message_message" short_message="" ➥
full_message="" fetched="0" id="message_'.$message_id.'">';

                echo $text->highlight(   $current_message[ 'Message' ] ➥
[ "message" ],
                                    $result[ 'search_term' ],
                                    '<span class="highlight_search">\1</span>'
                                    );

                echo '<div><span id="open_link_'.$message_id.'"> ➥
<a href="/cake/__chapters__/message_forum/MfFetchMessages/index/ ➥
threadId:'.$thread_id.'/">View in thread</a></div>';
            echo '</div>';
        }
    }
    else {
        echo '<div class="hilight">';
        echo 'No Results';
        echo '</div>';
    }

?>

<hr class="paginator_line">

<?php
    if ( isset( $paginator ) ) {

        $paginator->options(array( ➥
'update' => 'main_content_container', 'indicator' => 'loading'));

        echo $paginator->prev( '« Previous ', null, null, ➥
array( 'class' => 'disabled' ) );
        echo ' ';
        echo $paginator->next( ' Next »', null, null, ➥
array( 'class' => 'disabled' ) );
        echo ' ';
        echo $paginator->counter();
    }
?>
```

The view loops through the message results and formats the output. In the pagination helper methods at the bottom, we have used Ajax for the next and prev links. In Cake, we simply add the following line to Ajaxify the links:

```
$paginator->options(array( 'update' => 'main_content_container',
                           'indicator' => 'loading'));
```

■**Tip** We have used the text helper to highlight our search term. But don't forget there are also some other basic functions in the Cake API that may help you out in other situations. For example, in parts of this application, we have used the __() helper function instead of using echo or even the Cake shorthand echo function function e(). See http://api.cakephp.org/basics_8php.html for details.

Writing the API Documentation

For many developers, writing documentation is never a pleasant experience. But for this chapter, you could say it's the end point. Without the documentation, there's no reason for writing the API. Why bother to structure our actions around the Command pattern? It would have been easier to just write each action within one or two controllers.

The following shows the documentation for the Web Forum API as it would appear on our forum web site.

Welcome to our message forum API. We provide five different methods for you to use. All our method returns use the JSON format. Each request will return four or more keys. The standard four keys returned on every request are as follows:

- result: If 1 is returned, this means the request was processed successfully. If 0 is returned, then see message and errors key.

- message: A human-friendly return message. This will complement the result key.

- errors: This will contain error messages relating to the result. It will be given in key/ value pairs, where the key is the name of the parameter and value contains the error message.

- data: If the request returns data, it will be held in this key.

You must end all URL requests in .json. An example request would look like this:

```
http://www.example.com/MfFetchMessage/ ➥
index/Id:488bb046-2ae8-43c2-af41-0154cbdd56cb/.json
```

And the return response may look like this:

{"result":"1","message":"Message fetched successfully.","errors":"","data": ➥
{"Message":{"id":"488bb046-2ae8-43c2-af41-0154cbdd56cb","name":"John Titor", ➥
"email":"sfsd","message":"<p>Time travel machine. Good working order. Used ➥
only once. 10,000 Ningis ono. if you're interested, please call me at ➥
314 159 2653. <\/p>","reply_to":"","subject":"Hyper Dimensional Resonator ➥
for sale","t_created_at":"2008-07-27 00:16:22", ➥
"thread_id":"488bb046-5004-44e2-9dbd-0154cbdd56cb"}, ➥
"Thread":{"id":"488bb046-5004-44e2-9dbd-0154cbdd56cb", ➥
"first_message_id":"488bb046-2ae8-43c2-af41-0154cbdd56cb", ➥
"last_message_date":"2008-07-27 00:16:22","message_num":"1"}}}

The API documentation follows.

MfFetchMessage

Get one forum message.

Arguments

messageId (Required)—The message ID

HTTP Method

POST

Syntax

http://[domain]/MfFetchMessage/index/messageId:[message_id]/.json

Return

Standard return keys

MfFetchMessages

Note the extra letter s. Get more than one message from the forum. At present, we filter only by the thread ID.

Arguments

threadId (Required)—The thread ID

HTTP Method

POST

Syntax

```
http://[domain]/MfFetchMessages/index/threadId:[thread_id]/.json
```

Return

Standard return keys

MfFetchThreads

Get the forum threads. This returns a set of paginated messages. The messages are sorted according to the date of the last message that was posted within a thread. Each page has 20 messages. At present, this amount is fixed.

Arguments

page (Optional)—The page number starting from 1. Numeric.

HTTP Method

POST

Syntax

```
http://[domain]/MfFetchMessages/index/page:[page_number]/.json
```

Return

Standard return keys

MfMessageProcess

Post a message onto the forum.

Arguments

- name (Optional)—Sender's name. Maximum 255 characters.
- email (Required)—Sender's e-mail address. Maximum 255 characters.
- subject (Required) —Message subject. Maximum 255 characters.
- message (Optional) —Message body. Maximum 16,777,215 characters.

HTTP Method

POST

Syntax

```
http://[domain]/MfMessageProcess/index.json
```

Return

Standard return keys

MfSearchProcess

Search for messages. The results are paginated with 20 messages per page.

Arguments

- searchTerm (Required)—Search term. Maximum 255 characters.
- page (Optional)—Page number. Numeric.

HTTP Method

POST

Syntax

```
http://[domain]/MfSearchProcess/index.json
```

Return

Standard return keys, plus extra search_term key, which contains the search term

Summary

In this application, we've covered several Cake topics, including the use of Ajax, JSON web service returns, Cake pagination, the use of validation in a model with no associated table, and how to include the TinyMCE browser editor. The highlight of the chapter, however, was the building of a web service API.

The application still has a number of features we should add before it can be used in a commercial environment. Here are some suggestions that you can use to further develop the forum application:

- This is an obvious one. Stop spammers! There are many techniques to prevent spam, or at least keep it down to a minimum. In the final chapter in this book, we implement a Captcha authentication test. You can easily integrate this into the forum application. However, this puts the responsibility on every user. If you don't like interrupting the usability of the site, you can employ a filter, like a Bayesian text filter, instead. There are several PHP versions of this filter floating about. For other techniques, see `http://en.wikipedia.org/wiki/Forum_spam`.

- Users should be able to upload images to the forum.

- Users should be able to e-mail updates on a thread. This is particularly important for users who have posted questions.

- Add user accounts. You could then allow only registered users to post messages. However, this might be a barrier to the use of the forum, since it's one more hurdle for users to jump over. Fewer users posting messages means fewer people will find anything interesting on the forum.

- We have to admit that our application has one slightly uncomfortable area. Our client action classes like `mf_post_form_controller.php` and our API action classes like `mf_search_process_controller.php` more or less live within the same domain. They share the same folders and same parent controllers. It's as if they were part of the API, but, of course, they are not. You should separate them out, either into separate controllers or separate folders.

CHAPTER 5

Google Maps and the Traveling Salesman

Some friends of ours are about to go on a big European vacation. They talked about how they've used Google Maps to help them find the location of hotels, restaurants, and local attractions. They wanted to keep friends and families updated of their progress, but didn't want to use e-mail. Furthermore, they weren't sure in which order to visit the places. Being far more enthusiastic than they were, we said we would write an application for them that they can use to enter their destinations, make comments, and plan their journey.

In our application, we're going to be covering many topics. Since we're going to be using Google Maps, client-side JavaScript will be employed. We also want to store the locations and the comments they make. Naturally, we'll be creating some Cake models to represent these data entities. We will also be building a straightforward controller to hold the functions that will manage the locations and comments.

One of the main features of the application relates to a classic computing puzzle called the "traveling salesman problem" (or in our case, the traveling tourist problem). Namely, a salesman needs to visit a number of cities only once, but return back to the same place as where he started. Devise an algorithm to find the shortest route for the whole trip. This part of the application will be done client side using a simple algorithm, but the calculated route will be stored on the database.

Now, to get started, we'll first talk about Google Maps.

Hello Map!

Google Maps is pretty easy to use, so we can dive straight in with the Google Map equivalent of the Hello World program, as shown in Listing 5-1.

Listing 5-1. *A Simple Google Maps Example*

```
1:    <!DOCTYPE html "-//W3C//DTD XHTML 1.0 Strict//EN"➥
"http://www.w3.org/TR/xhtml1/DTD/xhtml1-strict.dtd">
2:    <html xmlns="http://www.w3.org/1999/xhtml">
3:    <head>
4:    <meta http-equiv="content-type" content="text/html; charset=utf-8"/>
5:    <title>Google Maps JavaScript API Example</title>
6:    <script src="http://maps.google.com/maps?file=api&amp;v=2&amp;➥
key=insert_your_key_here" type="text/javascript"></script>
```

```
 7:    <script type="text/javascript">
 8:    function initialize() {
 9:    if ( GBrowserIsCompatible() ) {
10:    var map = new GMap2( document.getElementById( "map_container" ) );
11:    map.setCenter( new GLatLng( 51.49937, -0.14421 ), 13 );
12:    }
13:    }
14:    </script>
15:    </head>
16:    <body onload="initialize()" onunload="GUnload()">
17:    <div id="map_container" style="width: 600px; height: 400px"></div>
18:    </body>
19:    </html>
```

The code in Listing 5-1 displays a 600 × 400 pixel Google Map on the page. The location of the map is set to the coordinates for London, specified by the setCenter() function on line 11. The output from the code in Listing 5-1 is shown in Figure 5-1.

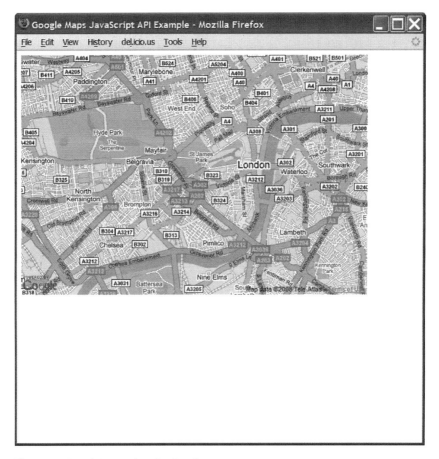

Figure 5-1. *Google Maps showing London*

To get started, we need to include the JavaScript Google Maps API file. This is done using the `<script>` tag on line 6. Within the tag, you must provide your own Google Maps API key. You can get a key (which is free) at `http://maps.google.com`.

Tip If you are developing on a local machine, you can still get a key. For example, you can use `http://127.0.0.1` or `http://localhost`, depending on which local URL you are using.

Once the page has been loaded via the `onload` event on line 16, the `initialize()` function is called.

The `initialize()` method, as defined on line 8, first checks whether we have a compatible browser. If we do, we then go ahead and create an object that will represent a map on the web page. This is done using the `GMap2` class. Additionally, we also need to provide an area where it can display the map; in our case, it's a `<div>` tag with an ID called `map_container` on line 17.

We're not quite finished yet though. In order for a map to be displayed, we need to tell the map object to display a location, and this is done using the `setCenter()` function on line 11, which sets the location and displays the map at the same time. And that's it! Wasn't that easy?

When the browser is closed or when a different page is brought up, the `onunload` event calls `GUnload()`. This Google Map function closes down unwanted connections and is used to avoid memory leaks.

Google Maps Explained

Google Maps is almost exclusively a client-side JavaScript API. Although you can make some server-side calls, that is not encouraged. After all, Google collects better statistics if the calls are made from the browser rather than from the server.

Note To effectively use Google Maps, you need to have some basic knowledge of JavaScript, particularly the object-oriented areas of the language. Two sites to get you started are `http://www.w3schools.com/jS/js_obj_intro.asp` and `http://developer.mozilla.org/en/docs/Introduction_to_Object-Oriented_JavaScript`.

Before we start, let's go over the main features of the API that are relevant to our application.

Geocoding

Geocoding is the process of converting textual locations such as street addresses or place names into geographic coordinates. This is important for a number of reasons. We can locate exact positions on a map, enabling us to place markers accurately. It eliminates confusion where two or more places have the same name.

The Google Maps API includes a class that provides us with a geocoding service. This is the `GClientGeocoder` class.

Google Map Events

Within browsers, JavaScript can be programmed to execute code depending on certain events. In traditional terminology, this is called *event-driven programming*. These events come in many forms: they can be mouse-based, keyboard-based, or even based on other events, such as when a page is completely loaded.

Event-based programming is particularly important in an Ajax environment. Since calls are mostly asynchronous, things don't happen in a nice serial fashion.

■Note Before the use of Ajax, just about every activity on a browser was synchronous. Users had to wait for feedback whenever they generated an event, such as by clicking a link or submitting a form. Essentially, you could make only one call to the server at any one time. With the use of XMLHttpRequest in Ajax, we can now make many calls to the server within a single web page, which makes them all asynchronous. Events can happen independently of each other.

Google Maps defines its own specialized events, which are handled by the API itself. These are separate from the DOM events within a browser, which are more generic. For example, a click event can be attached to any instance of a map, so when a user clicks a map, a call is made to a function, which opens a window with information regarding the location that the user has clicked and additionally stores the coordinates of the location with a call to the server using Ajax. Map events are handled by the GEvent object. We will register events using the addListener() static method.

Map Interface Elements

In the Google Maps API, you can add interface control elements, which allow you to interact with the map. Examples include buttons that you can use to move the map around, instead of using the mouse, and a sliding control bar to zoom in and out of the map. In Google Maps terminology, these are known as *controls*. All the control elements subclass the GControl class. You can define your own control by subclassing this class. For example, you can create a button that makes an Ajax call to your database server, fetching any journey near that location.

Overlays

Objects that move with the map are called *overlays*. These can be pushpins marking the location of a point or graphical lines that show route directions. The API provides several built-in overlay classes, which are listed in Table 5-1.

Markers are interactive in that they can be dragged across the map and placed in a new location. Each marker has an icon attached to it. You can define your own icon or use the default one.

A large number of markers can slow down the display of the map. As a result, the API has a marker manager class called MarkerManager.

Table 5-1. *Map Overlay Objects*

Overlay	Description
GMarker	This class is used to mark a point on the map.
GPolyline	This class is used to lay down lines on the map. There is also a GPolygon class, where the lines form a closed area.
GGroundOverlay	With this class, as well as drawing lines on the map, you can add images on top of them.
GTileLayerOverlay	With this class, the map itself is an overlay. You can modify the map itself with your own version of the map. However, you probably won't be using this very often. The pop-up bubble speech window is a special overlay; only one can exist in any one map instance.

Driving Directions

One useful feature in the Google Maps API is the ability to map out a travel route via several locations. These routes are then marked in blue on the map. This is done via the GDirections class. A very useful feature is the ability of the class to take locations either as textual names or latitude/longitude coordinate points. As an example, Listing 5-2 shows plotting a route from New York to Anchorage. Figure 5-2 shows the route map itself.

Listing 5-2. *Using the Google Maps GDirections Class to Find a Route*

```
 1:     <html>
 2:
 3:     <head>
 4:         <title>Google Maps GDirections Class</title>
 5:
 6:         <script src="http://maps.google.com/maps?file=api&v=2.x&⮡
key= insert_your_key_here " type="text/javascript"></script>
 7:
 8:         <script type="text/javascript">
 9:
10:             function initialize() {
11:                 map = new GMap2(document.getElementById("map_canvas"));
12:                 directions = new GDirections(map);
13:                 directions.load("from: New York, USA to: Anchorage");
14:             }
15:
16:         </script>
17:
18:     </head>
19:
20:     <body onload="initialize()">
21:         <div id="map_canvas" style="width: 400px; height: 480px;"></div>
22:     </body>
23:
24:     </html>
```

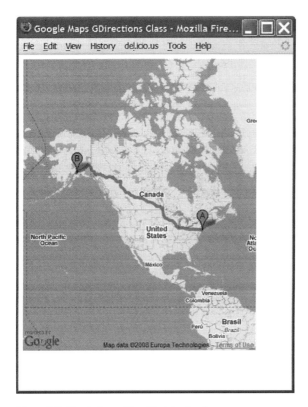

Figure 5-2. *Route from New York to Anchorage*

This GDirections class will be an important component of the project. When a query is sent off to the Google servers, it returns a number of useful items of information. One of which is the distance between the locations. This is very important to us, because it will provide the distance via the roads on the map rather than the straight linear distance between locations. However, if the user were planning to fly, the straight line distance would be more appropriate. In that case, we could easily calculate the distance using the latitude/longitude information.

OK, now that we have explained how Google Maps work, we can start our application by gathering the requirements.

Application Requirements

Our travel application will allow our friends and also the general public to plan their travel journeys and make comments on the places they visit. It will be a web site where they can keep friends and families up-to-date on their travels.

So that our application can be as successful as possible, we will employ a bit of *user-centered design* philosophy, a term originally coined by Donald Norman. We will think of the application in terms of users or personas, rather than application functions. Sometimes these needs also correlate directly with business objectives.

Using our friends as our average persona, we map out their needs and the conclusions that we can draw from them. A user interface can then be created based on these conclusions.

We run through the ways in which our friends will use the site. We start the process by asking them some broad questions. These are mapped out as follows:

- *Scenarios/Needs*: We're going to Europe soon, and we want to keep a blog or journal of some kind to keep family and friends updated.

- *Conclusion*: Users want to be able to enter destinations and make comments about those destinations. We need to save the destinations so they can make comments while they are on their journey. We can continue to draw conclusions from this simple need, but that is probably enough for us.

- *Scenarios/Needs*: We're not sure which places to visit first.

- *Conclusion*: There are numerous conclusions we can draw from this statement. For example, we can map out a user journey based on different personas: art lovers, party people, or a combination of personas. Or we could map a user journey based on age groups, such as for students. But in this case, we will simply employ the traveling salesman algorithm to find the shortest route between each destination.

We will base our interface on what we know from this brief user-centered design exercise.

So far, we have covered the broad issues of the application. Next, we will map out a functional specification that we can use for our Cake application. The functions will include the following:

- There will be a consistent navigation bar at the top, since the focus is on the application.

- Users will be able to plan their journey on the first page of the application by entering their destination.

- There will be a page where they can retrieve a saved journey and make comments.

- There will be a page where families and friends can view their comments.

In addition to these functions, we will add a further twist by allowing users to add tags to their journeys. This will be a comma-separated list of strings or tags, which you can associate with a journey.

From the specification, we have sketched out the simple layout of the application in Figure 5-3.

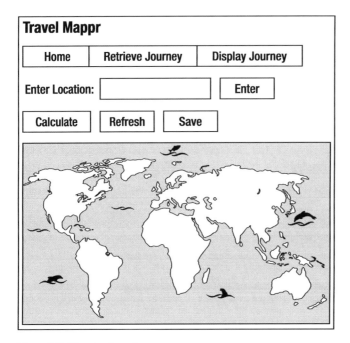

Figure 5-3. *Sketch of our home page*

Application Structure

We will set out to create our journeys controller, which will represent the journeys within the application. It will be responsible for the server-side needs of the application, saving and retrieving user journeys, for example.

Along with the journeys controller, there will be three related models. Remember that the model class names follow the name of the controller. The model class names we will use are Journey, Location, and Tag.

Table 5-2 shows the relationships among the different tables. This will give us an overall picture of how the different data elements are related to each other.

Table 5-2. *Main Database Table Relationships*

Table	Relationship
journeys	Each journey is composed of different locations. Also, each journey can have more than one tag.
locations	One location belongs to only one journey.
tags	One tag belongs to only one journey.

The information in Table 5-2 can also be shown graphically in an entity-relationship diagram, as in Figure 5-4.

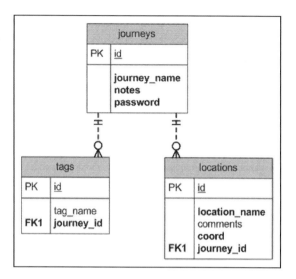

Figure 5-4. *Entity-relationship diagram of application tables*

▓**Tip** Data schemas are quite valuable during development. They help you to visualize the relationships among elements, identify problems, and maybe even improve on the relationships. In our example, we see that a route has one tag line associated with it, but later on, we may also want tags associated with locations. But would this add too much complexity to the application? Always be aware of feature bloat—adding unnecessary features that may be used only by a small percentage of users.

From the data schema, we can create our database tables. Listing 5-3 shows the structure of the journeys table.

Listing 5-3. *The journeys Table Schema*

```
CREATE TABLE `journeys` (
  `id` int(11) NOT NULL auto_increment,
  `journey_name` varchar(255) NOT NULL,
  `notes` text NOT NULL,
  `password` varchar(255) NOT NULL,
  PRIMARY KEY  (`id`)
);
```

The journey_name field stores the journey name that the user enters. The notes field is for comments about the journey itself. Editing a journey can be done only when a correct password is used, so we have created a password field.

Listing 5-4 shows the structure of the locations table.

Listing 5-4. *The locations Table Schema*

```
CREATE TABLE `locations` (
  `id` int(11) NOT NULL auto_increment,
  `location_name` varchar(255) NOT NULL,
  `comments` varchar(255) default NULL,
  `coord` varchar(255) NOT NULL,
  `journey_id` int(11) NOT NULL,
  PRIMARY KEY (`id`)
);
```

The name of the location that the user enters is held in location_name. The comments field stores the comments for a particular location. The coord field is longitude and latitude information taken from geocoding the location name. Finally, journey_id is the foreign key to the journeys table.

Listing 5-5 shows the tags table structure.

Listing 5-5. *The tags Table Schema*

```
CREATE TABLE `tags` (
  `id` int(10) unsigned NOT NULL auto_increment,
  `tag_name` varchar(100) default NULL,
  `journey_id` varchar(255) NOT NULL,
  PRIMARY KEY (`id`)
);
```

The tags table is pretty simple. The tag_name field holds a particular tag name for a journey. The journey_id field is the foreign key to the journeys table.

Cake Models

From the schema in Listings 5-3, 5-4, and 5-5, we created the Cake models, as shown in Listings 5-6, 5-7, and 5-8.

Listing 5-6. *The Journey Model (/app/models/journey.php)*

```
class Journey extends AppModel {

    var $name = 'Journey';

    // The journey data validation
    var $validate = array( 'journey_name' => array(
                        'rule' => array( 'between', 1, 255 ),
                        'required' => true,
                        'message' => 'Your journey name
                                    must be between 1 and 255
                                    characters long.' ) );
```

```
    // Each journey has many locations and also many tags.
    var $hasMany = array(   'Location' => array( 'className' => 'Location' ),
                            'Tag' => array( 'className' => 'Tag' )
                        );
}
```

Listing 5-7. *The Location Model (/app/models/location.php)*

```
class Location extends AppModel {

    var $name = 'Location';

    var $belongsTo = array('Journey');
}
```

Listing 5-8. *The Tag Model (/app/models/tag.php)*

```
class Tag extends AppModel
{
    var $name = 'Tag';

    var $belongsTo = array('Journey');
}
```

All three models are quite straightforward, except Journey, which contains a hasMany association that reflects the schema. A simple validation code has also been added, requiring each journey entry into the database to have a journey_name within it.

The Interface

Like most modern web applications, a large part of our application is written in JavaScript that sits within the browser. Most of the action will initially occur in the browser itself. The server-side code comes into play when the user decides to save or retrieve the journey information.

The Global Layout

We start off by creating the global layout file in /app/views/layouts/default.ctp, as shown in Listing 5-9.

Listing 5-9. *The Global Layout File (/app/views/layouts/default.ctp)*

```
 1:    <!DOCTYPE html PUBLIC "-//W3C//DTD XHTML 1.0 Strict//EN"
 2:    "http://www.w3.org/TR/xhtml1/DTD/xhtml1-strict.dtd">
 3:
 4:    <html xmlns="http://www.w3.org/1999/xhtml">
 5:    <head>
 6:
 7:        <meta http-equiv="content-type" content="text/html; charset=utf-8"/>
 8:
 9:        <!-- page title -->
10:        <title><?php echo $title_for_layout; ?></title>
11:
12:        <!-- page css -->
13:        <?php echo $html->css( 'site' ); ?>
14:
15:        <script src="http://maps.google.com/maps?file=api&amp;v=2&amp;➥
key= insert_your_key_here" type="text/javascript"></script>
16:
17:        <?php
18:            echo $javascript->link( 'scriptaculous-js-1.8.1/lib/prototype' );
19:            echo $javascript->link( '➥
scriptaculous-js-1.8.1/src/scriptaculous.js?load=effects' );
20:
21:            // include site.js
22:            echo $javascript->link( 'site' );
23:        ?>
24:
25:    </head>
26:
27:    <body onload="initialize()" onunload="GUnload()">
28:
29:        <div id="center_content">
30:
31:            <div class="header_wrapper">
32:                <h1>Travel Mappr</h1>
33:                <h4><i>Because life is a journey :)</i></h4>
34:            </div>
35:
36:            <div class="nav_1">
37:                <?php echo $html->link( 'Home', '/base' ); ?>
38:                 | 
39:
40:                <?php echo $html->link( 'Retrieve Journey',
41:                                        '/journeys/retrieve_form' ); ?>
42:                 | 
43:
```

```
44:                <?php echo $html->link( 'Display Journey',
45:                                    '/journeys/display_journey' ); ?>
46:          </div>
47:
48:          <div id="main_content_container">
49:                <?php echo $content_for_layout; ?>
50:          </div>
51:
52:       </div>
53:
54:    </body>
55:    </html>
```

▨**Note** You can create many layouts in the layouts folder and change between them in the same view. Just set the layout variable in the controller action. For example, if you created a new layout file /layouts/ vanilla.ctp, you can change the layout from within your action with this statement: $this->layout = 'vanilla';.

Let's go through the important lines in Listing 5-9. We start by setting the title in line 10. Next, we include our CSS file for our application in line 13.

On line 15, we bring in the Google Maps API. Remember to use your own key that correlates to your domain name.

Following this, we use Cake's JavaScript inclusion method on lines 18 and 19 to include the Prototype and script.aculo.us JavaScript libraries. We also include our site-wide JavaScript file site.js, located in /app/webroot/js/.

Within the main body tag, the page starts off with a simple header followed by a navigation bar using Cake's HTML helper to create the HTML links, as follows:

- Home: This simply takes a user back to the home page.

- Retrieve Journey: Allows a user to retrieve a saved trip from the database.

- Display Journey: A user can display any journey.

To finish, we echo the $content_for_layout variable on line 49. This takes the rendered controller action view content and inserts it into that position.

Home Page

Now that the global layout has been set up, we can create our home page view. We'll use Cake's designated default home page home.ctp, in the folder /app/views/pages/., shown in Listing 5-10.

In our application, users must be able to plot out a journey quite easily. On the home page, we will create a form where users can create their journeys the moment they enter the site.

Listing 5-10. *The Default View (/app/views/pages/home.ctp)*

```
 1:    <p id="journey_helper_message">
 2:        You currently have no journey planned,
 3:        enter a starting location to begin.
 4:    </p>
 5:
 6:    <div>
 7:
 8:        <p>
 9:            Location Name:
10:
11:            <?php echo $form->text( 'LocationName' ); ?>
12:            <?php echo $form->button( 'Enter a Location',
13:                                    array('id'=>'location_name_button'));
14:            ?>
15:        </p>
16:
17:    </div>
18:
19:    <div id="map_functions_wrapper">
20:
21:        <!-- find the best route -->
22:        <?php
23:            echo $form->button( 'Calculate Journey',
24:                                array(  'id'=>'find_route_button' ) );
25:        ?>
26:
27:        <!-- start a new route -->
28:        <?php
29:            echo $form->button( 'Start Again',
30:                                array(  'id'=>'start_again_button' ) );
31:        ?>
32:
33:        <!-- save the route -->
34:        <?php
35:            echo $form->create( null, array(    'id' => 'add_form',
36:                                                'url' => '/journeys/add_form',
37:                                                'class' => 'function_form'
38:                                                ) );
39:
40:            // used to store the location in json format
41:            echo $form->hidden( 'locations' );
42:
43:            echo $form->submit( 'Save Journey', array( 'div' => false ) );
44:
45:            echo $form->end();
```

```
46:         ?>
47:
48:     </div>
49:
50:     <!-- This is where our Google Map will be displayed -->
51:     <div id="map_canvas"></div>
```

In Listing 5-10, we haven't included any form-posting elements apart from the Save Journey button on line 43. All of the other buttons relate entirely to client-side code and will be used in conjunction with the Google Maps functionality. The first button, Enter a Location, on line 12, will save and display the location in Google Maps locally. The Calculate Journey button, on line 23, will use the Google Maps API and JavaScript to calculate the shortest journey. The Start Again button, on line 29, will clear the slate for a new journey to be entered.

When this home page code is processed with the default layout, we get the output shown in Figure 5-5 (with Paris set as the starting location in this example). The code and functionality behind all these buttons will be explained in the next section.

Figure 5-5. *The application home page*

Travel Mappr Manager

Now we're going to talk about the Travel Mappr manager class in /app/webroot/js/site.js. The class will be called TravelMapprManager, and it will handle all the client-side functionality relating to the application. site.js is called from within the default layout default.ctp, as shown on line 21 in Listing 5-9. We use Prototype's API to help us with the creation of the class itself.

▓Note   You may have noticed that Listing 5-10 doesn't contain any onclick events. If you are used to writing onclick or onchange events within HTML code, consider using Prototype's Event.observe method instead. It allows you to separate any JavaScript code from the content.

Listing 5-11 shows the main skeleton structure of our TravelMapprManager class in the site.js file. We have purposely left out many other functions, as commented on line 75. These will be described individually.

Listing 5-11. *The Main JavaScript File Used in Our Application (/app/webroot/js/site.js)*

```
 1:    var TravelMapprManager = Class.create( {
 2:
 3:        // id of container
 4:        map_container : '',
 5:
 6:        /* the current map */
 7:        map : null,
 8:
 9:        /* geocoding location */
10:        geocoder : null,
11:
12:        /* user entered locations */
13:        user_journey : new Array(),
14:
15:        initialize : function( map_container ) {
16:
17:            this.map_container = map_container;
18:
19:            // start the map
20:            Event.observe( window, 'load', this.displayMap.bind(this) );
21:
22:            // observe the map buttons
23:            Event.observe( document, 'dom:loaded',➥
this.initObservers.bind(this) );
24:
25:        },
26:
27:    displayMap : function() {
28:
```

```
29:                 if ( GBrowserIsCompatible() ) {
30:
31:                     if ( $( this.map_container ) ) {
32:
33:                         // create a map instance
34:                         this.map = new GMap2( $( this.map_container ) );
35:
36:                         // add map controls
37:                         this.map.addControl(new GLargeMapControl());
38:                         this.map.addControl(new GMapTypeControl());
39:
40:                         // center the map at a certain location
41:                         this.map.setCenter( new GLatLng( 48.85656, 2.35097 ), 8 );
42:
43:                         // set up a geocoding instance
44:                         this.geocoder = new GClientGeocoder();
45:
46:                         // unload map
47:                         Event.observe( window, 'unload', GUnload );
48:                     }
49:                 }
50:             },
51:
52:     initObservers : function() {
53:
54:             if ( $('location_name_button') ) {
55:                 $('location_name_button').observe(
56:                     'click', this.findLocation.bindAsEventListener(this) );
57:             }
58:
59:             if ( $('find_route_button') ) {
60:                 $('find_route_button').observe(
61:                     'click', this.findBestJourney.bindAsEventListener(this) );
62:             }
63:
64:             if ( $('start_again_button') ) {
65:                 $('start_again_button').observe(
66:                     'click', this.startAgain.bindAsEventListener(this) );
67:             }
68:
69:             if ( $('add_form') ) {
70:                 $('add_form').observe( 'submit',
71:                     this.saveJourney.bindAsEventListener(this) );
72:             }
73:         },
74:
75:     // other functions.
76:     )
```

At the beginning of Listing 5-11 are some variables to hold various journey-related values. When Class.create is called, the initialize method on line 15 is called. This loads and displays the map and also starts observing the map buttons we have created.

Once the DOM has been fully loaded using the dom:loaded event on line 23, the buttons get the click event attached to them.

The findLocation() function will locate the place in Google Maps and display it in the map canvas and also save the details locally in a JavaScript variable.

The findBestJourney()function will carry out the algorithm for finding the shortest journey using the shortest neighbor algorithm.

The startAgain()function will clear reset variables and allow a user to enter a new journey.

Finally, once a journey has been plotted, the saveJourney() function will observe the submit event in the save journey form and post the journey details to the server for saving.

In the following sections, we'll describe each of the missing functions in Listing 5-11, starting with the function that helps us to find a Google map location.

Finding Locations

When a user enters a location name and clicks the Enter a Location button, the findLocation() function, shown in Listing 5-12, is fired.

Listing 5-12. *JavaScript to Find a Google Map Location*

```
 1:    findLocation : function() {
 2:
 3:            loc_name = $( 'LocationName' ).value;
 4:
 5:            if ( loc_name == '' ) {
 6:                alert( "Please enter a location name." );
 7:                return;
 8:            }
 9:
10:            // we only allow a maximum number of locations
11:            if ( this.user_journey.length >= 20 ) {
12:                alert( "    Sorry! We have reached the maximum
13:                        number of locations." );
14:                return;
15:            }
16:
17:            // do geocoding; find the longitude and latitude of the location
18:            if ( this.geocoder ) {
19:
20:                var current_o = this;
21:
22:                this.geocoder.getLatLng(
23:                    loc_name,
24:                    function( point ) {
25:
```

```
26:                          if ( !point ) {
27:                              alert( loc_name + " not found" );
28:                          } else {
29:
30:                              // store the location
31:                              current_o.storeLocation( loc_name, point );
32:
33:                              // center the location on the map and
34:                              // add pushpin marker
35:                              current_o.map.setCenter( point, 13 );
36:                              var marker = new GMarker( point );
37:                              current_o.map.addOverlay( marker );
38:                          }
39:                      }
40:                  );
41:              }
42:          },
43:
44:      storeLocation : function( loc_name, point ) {
45:
46:              var new_loc = new Array();
47:
48:              new_loc['coord'] = point.lat()+','+point.lng();
49:              new_loc['loc_name'] = loc_name;
50:
51:              this.user_journey.push( new_loc );
52:
53:              // update the journey message
54:              this.updateJourneyMessage()
55:          },
```

This function starts with a couple of error-handling lines. Then we make the geocoding API call geocoder.getLatLng on line 22. If the Google API call finds the location, we store it using our storeLocation() function on line 44. We simply hold the location name and coordinate in an array and push it into a global array. Finally, we set the map to show the location and add a pushpin marker, starting from line 35.

Figure 5-6 shows an example of what a user should see after entering a location.

In the next section, we'll look at the algorithm for our traveling salesman/tourist problem. It's the shortest distance between locations. Even so, it's pretty long, so you may want to jump to the next section and come back to the algorithm later.

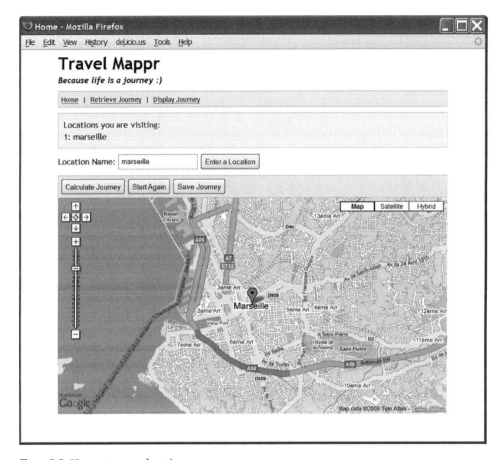

Figure 5-6. *User enters one location*

The Traveling Salesman Algorithm

When a user has entered a set number of locations and clicked the Calculate Journey button, we find the best journey with the "traveling salesman" algorithm. As the algorithm is quite large, we have split the code into three parts. We start the algorithm in Listing 5-13.

Listing 5-13. *The Traveling Salesman Algorithm Part 1*

```
1:    journey_combination : new Array(),
2:
3:    findBestJourney : function() {
4:
```

```
5:          // we won't calculate a journey if there is no journey to calculate
6:          if ( this.user_journey.length < 2 ) {
7:              alert( "Please enter at least 2 locations." );
8:              return;
9:          }
10:
11:         // we won't calculate the journey again if it has already been done.
12:         if ( this.best_journey.length == this.user_journey.length ) {
13:             return;
14:         }
15:
16:         // get all the journey combinations
17:         var num_locs = this.user_journey.length;
18:
19:         for ( var x = 0; x < num_locs; x++ ) {
20:
21:             from_here = this.user_journey[x];
22:
23:             for ( var y = x+1; y < num_locs; y++ ) {
24:
25:                 to_here = this.user_journey[y];
26:
27:                 current_journey = new Array();
28:
29:                 current_journey[ "from" ] = from_here;
30:                 current_journey[ "to" ] = to_here;
31:                 current_journey[ "journey_distance" ] = '';
32:
33:                 this.journey_combination.push( current_journey );
34:             }
35:         }
36:
37:         if ( this.getJourneyDistance() ) {
38:             this.calcTSP();
39:         }
40:
41:         return false;
42:     },
```

The variable at the top of Listing 5-13 holds all the journey combinations that the user has entered. The findBestJourney() function starts on line 3 with a couple of lines of error checking. Next, we work out all the combinations between the locations on line 17 to line 35. After that, we call getJourneyDistance() on line 37, which in turn makes the Google geocoding requests to fetch the distance for each pair of locations in journey_combination. Once that is done, we can start calculating the shortest distances between locations.

We continue from the previous listing with Listing 5-14.

Listing 5-14. *The Traveling Salesman Algorithm Part 2*

```
 1:    getJourneyDistance : function() {
 2:
 3:        // Start getting the journey distance. Once we have found a journey
 4:        // without any distance, let's just pick that one and fetch the
 5:        // journey distance from Google.
 6:        var do_journey = -1;
 7:
 8:        for ( var x = 0; x < this.journey_combination.length; x++ ) {
 9:
10:            if ( this.journey_combination[x][ 'journey_distance' ] == '' ) {
11:                // no journey distance here, so let's get it
12:                var do_journey = x;
13:                break;
14:            }
15:        }
16:
17:        if ( do_journey >= 0 ) {
18:
19:            // we found a journey to do
20:
21:            directions = new GDirections();
22:
23:            GEvent.addListener( directions, "load", function() {
24:
25:                // Get and fill journey distance. We always just
26:                // take the first journey
27:                this.journey_combination[do_journey]�Ш
[ 'journey_distance' ] = directions.getJourney(0).getDistance().meters;
28:
29:                // now let's find the next one
30:                this.getJourneyDistance();
31:            } );
32:
33:            direction_journey = 'from: ';
34:            direction_journey +=Ш
this.journey_combination[do_journey]['from']['coord'];
35:            direction_journey += 'to: ';
36:            direction_journey +=Ш
this.journey_combination[do_journey]['to']['coord'];
37:
38:            directions.load( direction_journey );
39:        }
40:
41:        return true;
42:    },
```

Notice that the getJourneyDistance() function in Listing 5-14 is recursive. The Ajax geo-coding call to the Google servers is asynchronous. We create a GDirections object on line 21, make the call to fetch the geocoding data, and then quickly carry on with the next location. The GEvent.addListener statement will automatically get the distance for us when the reply comes back.

OK, just to recap, we first work out all the combinations from one location to another and store this in the .journey_combination array. Next, we make geocoding requests to fetch the distance for all the location pairs in .journey_combination. Once all that is complete, we can start working out the shortest round-trip.

Working out the shortest round-trip starts with the calcTSP() function in Listing 5-15. Before we start, there are two important variables to mention: visited and best_journey. From their names, you can probably guess what they hold: locations already visited and the final path that we have worked out.

Listing 5-15. *The Traveling Salesman Algorithm Part 3*

```
 1:    // cities already visited
 2:    visited : new Array(),
 3:
 4:    // for holding the best journey
 5:    best_journey : new Array(),
 6:
 7:    calcTSP : function() {
 8:
 9:        var stopInfin = 0;
10:
11:        // while there is a next location to visit
12:        while ( this._visitNextCity() ) {
13:
14:            // temp var for holding the best (shortest)
15:            // nearest neighbor so far
16:            var nearest_neighbour = -1;
17:
18:            if ( stopInfin > 20 ) { return; }
19:            stopInfin++;
20:
21:            start_here = this._getNextNeighbour();
22:
23:            // get all neighbors that have not been visited from the
24:            // "start_here" location
25:            var neighbours = this._getNeighbours( start_here );
26:
27:            for ( var x = 0; x < neighbours.length; x++ ) {
28:
29:                if ( nearest_neighbour == -1 ) {
30:                    nearest_neighbour = neighbours[x];
31:                }
32:
```

```
33:                      // now find the shortest journey
34:                      if (    neighbours[x][ 'journey_distance' ] <
35:                              nearest_neighbour[ 'journey_distance' ] ) {
36:                          nearest_neighbour = neighbours[x];
37:                      }
38:                  }
39:
40:                  // we should now have the next nearest neighbor
41:                  this.best_journey.push( nearest_neighbour['to'] );
42:                  this._markVisited( nearest_neighbour['to'] );
43:              }
44:
45:          this._plotBestJourney();
46:      },
47:
48:      _visitNextCity : function() {
49:
50:          if ( this.visited.length == this.user_journey.length ) {
51:              return false;
52:          }
53:
54:          return true;
55:      },
56:
57:      _getNextNeighbour : function() {
58:
59:          var next_city = '';
60:
61:          if ( this.best_journey.length == 0 ) {
62:
63:              // init. We take the first journey as the starting point
64:              start_here = this.journey_combination[0]['from'];
65:              this.best_journey.push( start_here );
66:              this._markVisited( start_here );
67:
68:              next_city = start_here;
69:          }
70:          else {
71:
72:              // we pick the last city
73:              var last_loc = this.best_journey.length-1;
74:              next_city = this.best_journey[last_loc];
75:          }
76:
77:          return next_city;
78:      },
79:
```

```
80:     _markVisited : function( loc ) {
81:
82:          this.visited.push( loc['loc_name'] );
83:     },
84:
85:     _locVisited : function( loc_name ) {
86:
87:          for ( var x = 0; x < this.visited.length; x++ ) {
88:
89:               if ( loc_name == this.visited[x] ) {
90:                    return true;
91:               }
92:          }
93:
94:          return false;
95:     },
96:
97:     /*
98:      * Get all neighbors not visited
99:      */
100:    _getNeighbours: function( from_loc ) {
101:
102:         var result = new Array();
103:
104:         for ( var x = 0; x < this.journey_combination.length; x++ ) {
105:
106:              var next_loc = new Array();
107:              next_loc[ 'from' ] = from_loc;
108:              next_loc[ 'to' ] = (➥
this.journey_combination[x]['from']['loc_name'] ==➥
from_loc['loc_name'] ) ? this.journey_combination[x]['to'] :➥
this.journey_combination[x]['from'];
109:              next_loc[ 'journey_distance' ] =➥
this.journey_combination[x]['journey_distance'];
110:
111:              // check whether the location has been visited already
112:              if ( !this._locVisited( next_loc[ 'to' ][ 'loc_name' ] ) ) {
113:                   result.push( next_loc );
114:              }
115:         }
116:
117:         return result;
118:    },
```

Our calcTSP function starts with an outer loop on line 12. If there is a next location to visit, we carry on with the algorithm. Within the loop, we first pick a starting location using _getNextNeighbour on line 21. Next, we work out the nearest neighbor to that point using the _getNeighbours() function on line 25. This gets all the neighbors that haven't already been visited. From this, we use a simple bubble sort to work out the shortest distance to the next location. When we come around the loop the next time, we pick the last city we came from as the next starting point and start over again. Once we have visited all the locations, we plot the journey path on the map via the _plotBestJourney() function on line 45, which we will cover in the next section.

There are many functions that support calcTSP. These functions are described in Table 5-3.

Table 5-3. *Supporting Functions to calcTSP*

Function	Description
_visitNextCity	On line 48 in Listing 5-15. This function tells us whether there are any more locations to visit. Once there are no more locations to visit, we have found our shortest route.
_getNextNeighbour	On line 57 in Listing 5-15. This function provides us with the next location to visit, which is always the destination location of the last journey.
_markVisited	On line 80 in Listing 5-15. Once a location has been visited, this function marks that location, so that we do not visit the same location.
_locVisited	On line 85 in Listing 5-15. This tells us whether we have visited a location.
_getNeighbours	On line 100 in Listing 5-15. This gets all the neighbors that we have not visited. Using the result returned, we can then find the neighbor with the shortest route to the location.

Plotting the Journey

Using the Google Maps GDirections class, we can plot the path between the locations. Using the loadFromWaypoints method in the GDirections class, a blue path is marked on the map itself. The code is shown in Listing 5-16.

Listing 5-16. *Plotting the Journey*

```
1:    _plotBestJourney : function() {
2:
3:        var new_journey = new Array();
4:
5:        for ( var x = 0; x < this.best_journey.length; x++ ) {
6:
7:            direction_journey = this.best_journey[x]['coord'];
8:            new_journey[x] = direction_journey;
9:        }
10:
11:       // add the starting point back as starting position
12:       new_journey.push( this.best_journey[0]['coord'] );
13:
14:       directions = new GDirections( this.map );
15:
16:       var current_o = this;
17:
```

```
18:        // remove the default red markers
19:        GEvent.addListener( directions, "load", function() {
20:            current_o.map.clearOverlays();
21:        } );
22:
23:        // remove the last marker, so the first one would show up
24:        GEvent.addListener( directions, "addoverlay", function() {
25:            var num_markers = directions.getNumGeocodes();
26:            current_o.map.removeOverlay(➥
directions.getMarker(num_markers-1) );
27:        } );
28:
29:        directions.loadFromWaypoints( new_journey );
30:    },
```

Most of this code is devoted to organizing the locations in a format that will be suitable for use for the loadFromWaypoints() function. We first get the shortest route from the best_journey variable by looping through it on line 5. Then, on line 12, we trace a route from the end point back to the start so we have a loop. On line 14, we create a GDirections object for the plotting of the route. Next, starting from line 19, we need to carry out some housekeeping functions. Google automatically creates pushpin markers when we plot a location. We need to clear these, because the GDirections object creates additional markers that show the numeric order of the locations.

It is worth noting that for a lot of countries, the path and distance use the roads as the mode of travel, which is the route that we would prefer. However, in countries where Google doesn't have any road information, the straight path between the locations is used.

And that is just about it. We finish /app/webroot/js/site.js with the class-creation code shown here:

```
new TravelMapprManager( 'map_canvas' );
```

We're not quite finished yet on the client side, as there are two more buttons: Start Again and Save Journey. Start Again is pretty straightforward, as it just clears the variables and refreshes the map. Save Journey is a little more interesting. As shown in Listing 5-17, when saveJourney is called, we first check whether there is a journey to save. If there is, we basically create a JSON string format from the calculated route and insert it as a value in the hidden tag element with id locations, after which the form is submitted to the server. Using the journey we plotted earlier, Listing 5-18 shows the data format of the locations as a JSON string.

■**Note** What is a JSON string format? JSON stands for JavaScript Object Notation. It is a data format much like XML or even CSV. The popularity of its use came as a result of Ajax, since the format is native to JavaScript. It is also less verbose than XML.

Listing 5-17. *The saveJourney Function*

```
checkJourneyExists : function() {

    if ( this.best_journey.length == 0 ) {
        alert( 'No journey to save, create a journey first,\nor➥
maybe the journey has not been calculated yet.' );
        return false;
    }

    return true;
},

saveJourney : function(e) {

    if ( this.checkJourneyExists() ) {

        // create the json notation
        xml_loc = '{';

        for ( var x = 0; x < this.best_journey.length; x++ ) {
            xml_loc += '"' + x + '":';
            xml_loc += '{'

            xml_loc += '"id":';
            xml_loc += '""';

            xml_loc += ',';

            xml_loc += '"comments":';
            xml_loc += '""';

            xml_loc += ',';

            xml_loc += '"coord":';
            xml_loc += '"' + this.best_journey[x]['coord'] + '"';

            xml_loc += ',';

            xml_loc += '"loc_name":';
            xml_loc += '"' + this.best_journey[x]['loc_name'] + '"';

            xml_loc += '}'

            if ( x+1 < this.best_journey.length ) { xml_loc += ','; }
        }
```

```
        xml_loc += '}';

        $('locations').value = xml_loc;

        return true;
    }
    else {

        Event.stop(e);

        return false;
    }
}
```

Listing 5-18. *Our Journey Locations in a JSON String*

```
{

"0":{   "id":"",
        "comments":"",
        "coord":"43.298344,5.383221",
        "location_name":"Marseille" },

"1":{   "id":"",
        "comments":"",
        "coord":"48.856667,2.350987",
        "location_name":"Paris" },

"2":{   "id":"",
        "comments":"",
        "coord":"40.416741,-3.70325",
        "location_name":"Madrid"}

}
```

We can now plot a journey and see how it looks on screen. Let's assume our friends
are going to visit three locations: Marseille in France, Madrid in Spain, and Paris in France
again. After entering the three locations, our map application will look like the one shown in
Figure 5-7.

Now that we have completed the client side of the application, we'll jump across to the
server side and look at how a journey is saved into the database.

Figure 5-7. *A journey with three locations*

Journey Data

For our application, we need to save the journey details and also the tags associated with a journey. We also need to give users the ability to retrieve journeys for viewing and editing. Without further ado, we'll show you how these functions are done.

Saving a Journey

All our actions are contained in the one and only JourneysController in the application. Within that controller, we save a journey using the add_form() action, as shown in Listing 5-19. This is the target action for the Save Journey button on the client side. It parses the journey name, tags, and comments and also the journey details including the destination comments. The detail of the destinations arrives in the JSON format. We could have chosen XML or even some comma/semicolon type proprietary format. However, the JSON format seems to be the de facto format nowadays for web client/server data exchange. We set two variables to be used by the view: `locations` and `journey_id`.

Listing 5-19. *Saving Journeys*

```
function add_form() {

        // get the locations from the hidden form element
        $locations = json_decode( $this->data['locations'], true );
        $journey_id = null;
        $this->set(compact('locations','journey_id'));


}
```

Now let's look at the view that goes with the `add_form()` action. The `journey_id` is used to decide whether we are saving a new journey or editing an existing one. The same form is used to add or edit a journey. The view for `add_form()` action is shown in Listing 5-20. It is stored in `/app/views/journeys/add_form.ctp`. The output of the view is shown in Figure 5-8.

■**Note** We have noticed that as applications get more complex, they often branch out into separate add or edit action/view pairs. Be careful, as the code in the controller and view can get out of hand. Use components in the controller and view helpers or elements in the view where you can spot common code. In fact, we were pretty close to having two views, as we weren't sure whether to have the password field when editing a journey.

Listing 5-20. *The View for the add_form Action*

```
 1:    <?php
 2:        if ( !empty( $user_message ) )
 3:            echo $user_message;
 4:    ?>
 5:
 6:    <p>Fields marked with * are needed.</p>
 7:
 8:    <div>
 9:
10:    <?php
11:
12:        // Decide whether we're adding a journey or editing
13:        if ( $journey_id ) {
14:            echo $form->create( 'Journey',
15:                                 array(➥
'url' => '/journeys/edit/'.$journey_id ) );
16:        }
```

```
17:        else {
18:            echo $form->create( 'Journey',
19:                                array( 'url' => '/journeys/add' ) );
20:        }
21:
22:        echo '<div class="form_fields">';
23:        echo '<h5>Journey Name *:</h5>';
24:        echo $form->input( 'name', array(➥
'div' => false, 'label' => false ) );
25:        echo '</div>';
26:
27:        echo '<div class="form_fields">';
28:        echo '<h5>Password:</h5>';
29:        echo $form->password( 'password', array(➥
'div' => false, 'label' => false ) );
30:        echo '  <p>Used to retrieve your journey. If you do not enter your own
31:            password, one will be generated for you.</p></div>';
32:
33:        echo '<div class="form_fields">';
34:        echo '<h5>Tags:</h5>';
35:        echo $form->input( 'tags', array(➥
'div' => false, 'label' => false ) );
36:        echo '<p>Please separate tags with commas.</p></div>';
37:
38:        echo '<div class="form_fields">';
39:        echo '<h5>Notes:</h5>';
40:        echo $form->textarea(    'notes',
41:                                array(  'div' => false, 'label' => false,
42:                                        'rows' => '7', 'cols' => '60'
43:                                        ) );
44:        echo '</div>';
45:
46:        // locations
47:        echo $map->generateFields( $locations );
48:
49:        echo '<div class="form_fields">';
50:        echo $form->submit( 'Save Journey' );
51:        echo '</div>';
52:
53:        echo $form->end();
54:    ?>
55:
56:    </div>
```

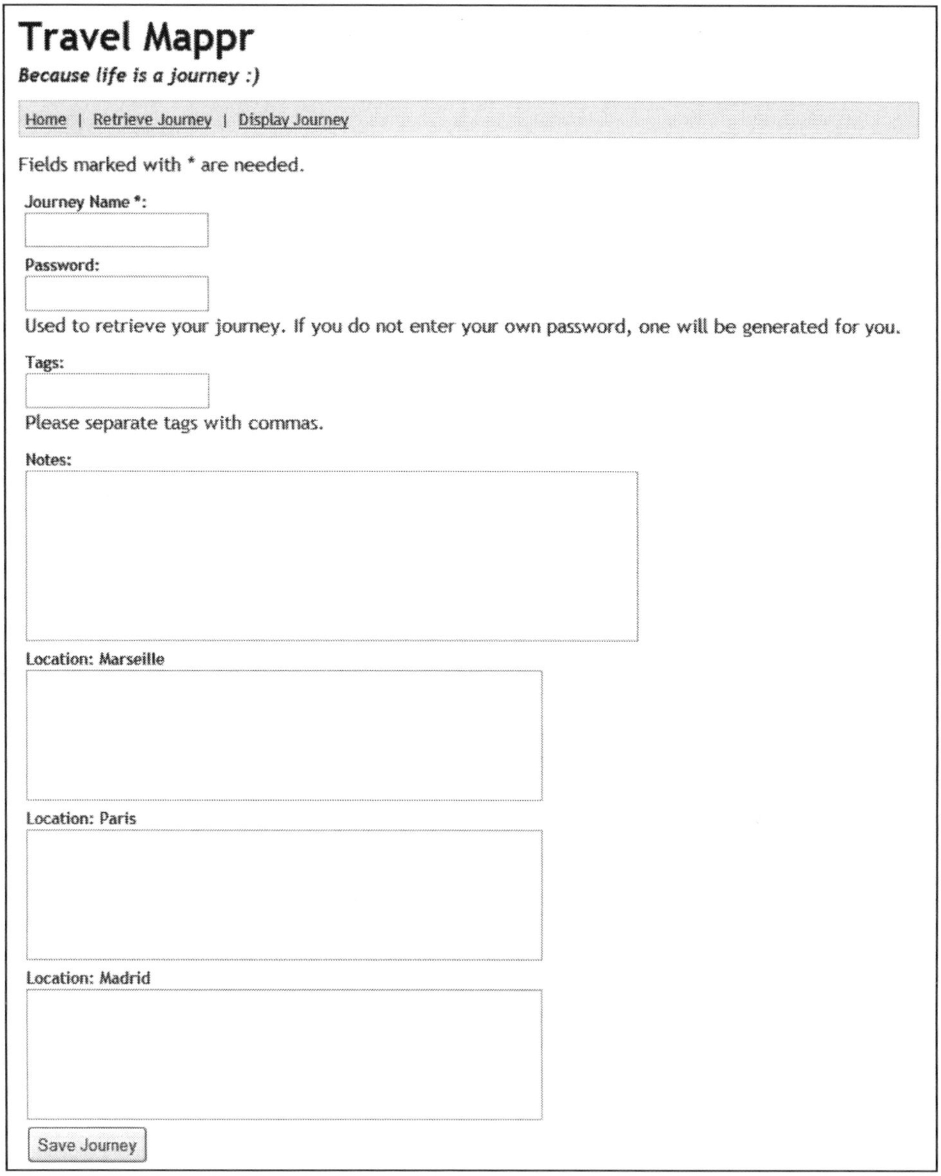

Travel Mappr

Because life is a journey :)

Home | Retrieve Journey | Display Journey

Fields marked with * are needed.

Journey Name *:

Password:

Used to retrieve your journey. If you do not enter your own password, one will be generated for you.

Tags:

Please separate tags with commas.

Notes:

Location: Marseille

Location: Paris

Location: Madrid

Save Journey

Figure 5-8. *The add_form view*

In the add_form() action, we decode the JSON locations details. These are then passed onto the view for display. In the view, we manage the layout of the elements ourselves by setting the div and label parameters to false. Each journey needs to have a password so a user can come back and edit a journey. In practice, you would probably create a user account and attach journeys to a particular user. However, to keep the application simple, we have attached a password to each journey instead.

We have created a view helper named MapHelper, which is stored in /app/views/helpers/map.php. In the MapHelper class, shown in Listing 5-21, we have a generateFields() method on line 5, which is used to help display the comment textarea tags that go with each location. Within the helper, we can use other helpers by including them in the $helpers array.

Listing 5-21. *The View Helper Class MapHelper (/app/views/helpers/map.php)*

```
1:    class MapHelper extends AppHelper {
2:
3:        var $helpers = array( 'Form' );
4:
5:        function generateFields( $locations ) {
6:
7:            $result = '';
8:
9:            for( $idx=0; $idx<sizeof( $locations ); $idx++ ) {
10:
11:                $id = $locations[$idx][ 'id' ];
12:                $coord = $locations[$idx]['coord'];
13:                $loc_name = $locations[$idx]['loc_name'];
14:                $comments = $locations[$idx]['comments'];
15:
16:                $json = json_encode( $locations[$idx] );
17:
18:                $result .= '<div class="form_fields">';
19:                $result .= '<h5>Location: '.$loc_name.'</h5>';
20:                $result .= $this->Form->textarea(   'notes',
21:                               array(  'value' => $comments,
22:                                       'name' =>➥
23:    "data[Journey][locations][".$idx."][comments]",
24:                                       'div' => false, 'label' => false,
25:                                       'rows' => '5', 'cols' => '50'
26:                                       ) );
27:
28:                $result .= '    <input type="hidden"
29:                               name="data[Journey][locations]['.$idx.'][data]"
30:                               value=\''.$json.'\' />';
31:                $result .= '</div>';
32:            }
33:
34:            return $this->output($result);
35:        }
36:    }
```

In Listing 5-20, the form is posted to the add() action on line 19. This is the action in the JourneysController that saves the journey when a user has entered the journey details. The add() action is shown in Listing 5-22.

Listing 5-22. *Saving the Journey Data*

```
1:    function add() {
2:
3:        // If no data is supplied, we just render the journey form
4:        if ( empty( $this->data ) ) {
5:            $this->redirect( '/', null, true );
6:        }
7:        else {
8:
9:            // Whether the save was successful
10:           $save_result = 1;
11:
12:           if ( $save_result ) {
13:
14:               // Check password
15:               $password = $this->data[ 'Journey' ][ 'password' ];
16:               if ( empty( $this->data[ 'Journey' ][ 'password' ] ) ) {
17:                   $password = rand( 1, 1000 );
18:               }
19:
20:               // Save journey
21:               $journey = array();
22:               $journey[ 'name' ] = $this->data[ 'Journey' ][ 'name' ];
23:               $journey[ 'notes' ] = $this->data[ 'Journey' ][ 'notes' ];
24:               $journey[ 'password' ] = md5( $password );
25:               $save_journey_result = $this->Journey->save( $journey );
26:
27:               // Journey didn't save properly
28:               if ( !$save_journey_result ) {
29:                   $save_result = 0;
30:               }
31:           }
32:
33:           if ( $save_result ) {
34:
35:               // Save locations
36:               $save_loc_result = $this->_save_locations(
37:                                   $this->data[ 'Journey' ][ 'locations' ],
38:                                   $this->Journey->id
39:                                     );
40:
41:               // Locations didn't save properly
42:               if ( !$save_loc_result ) {
43:                   $save_result = 0;
44:               }
45:           }
46:
```

```
47:            if ( $save_result ) {
48:
49:                // Save tags
50:                $save_tag_result = $this->_save_tags(
51:                                    $this->data[ 'Journey' ][ 'tags' ],
52:                                    $this->Journey->id
53:                                    );
54:
55:                // Tags didn't save properly
56:                if ( !$save_tag_result ) {
57:                    $save_result = 0;
58:                }
59:            }
60:
61:            if ( $save_result ) {
62:
63:                // Now render the success message view
64:                $this->set( 'journey_id', $this->Journey->id );
65:
66:                $this->set( 'password', $password );
67:
68:                $this->render( 'add_success' );
69:            }
70:            else {
71:
72:                $this->set( 'user_message',
73:                        'Please correct the form errors as shown below.' );
74:
75:                // We have to reform the location data
76:                $locations_for_form = $this->_reformat_locations(
77:                                    $this->data['Journey']['locations']
78:                                    );
79:                $this->set( 'locations', $locations_for_form );
80:
81:                $this->set( 'journey_id', '' );
82:
83:                $this->render( 'add_form' );
84:            }
85:        }
86:    }
```

On line 5, if no data is supplied, we simply redirect the user back to the home page, as we regard that as an error. If data is supplied, we save the three data sets into the tables journeys, locations, and tags. Note that in a production environment, these three units of code should be within a transaction block. If one fails, the previous save actions should be rolled back.

If everything has been saved OK, we display the add_success view on line 68. If not, we render the form again with error messages.

We have used two protected actions/functions to save the locations and tags: _save_ locations and _save_tags. The underscore prefix tells Cake that they are protected actions and should not be executed via any URL request.

Saving Tags

The tag data that goes with a journey is a set of comma-separated strings. These strings are split up and entered into the tags table separately. The tag-saving protected action is shown in Listing 5-23.

Note We could have placed the tags within a single database field in the journeys table and called it tags. However, this would not conform to the first normal form in database normalization, where each field must contain single, not multiple, values. We would run into trouble when we wanted to query the tags within a route.

Listing 5-23. *Saving the Journey Tags*

```
 1:    function _save_tags( $tags, $journey_id ) {
 2:
 3:        $tags_a = explode( ",", $tags );
 4:
 5:        for( $idx=0; $idx<sizeof( $tags_a ); $idx++ ) {
 6:
 7:            $db_tag = array();
 8:            $db_tag[ 'tag' ] = trim( $tags_a[$idx] );
 9:            $db_tag[ 'journey_id' ] = $journey_id;
10:
11:            // We need to create a new tag before saving another
12:            $this->Tag->create( $db_tag );
13:            $save_result = $this->Tag->save( $db_tag );
14:
15:            if ( !$save_result ) {
16:                return false;
17:            }
18:        }
19:
20:        return true;
21:    }
```

In Listing 5-23, we simply use the PHP explode() function to split the tags on line 3 and then loop through the strings and save the tags individually. When we are editing a journey, the saving or updating of the tags is done slightly differently, in that we first delete all the tags relating to the journey and then we save the updated tags as if they were new. We find this technique to be simpler to maintain and easier to read and reuse than the alternative method, where we update any tags that have been changed and delete any tags that have been removed.

Retrieving and Editing a Journey

The code to retrieve a journey is pretty simple. The action is shown in Listing 5-24. Yes, it's empty, because it's just a simple form with no other dependencies. The main view elements are shown in Listing 5-25. We have cut some of the HTML markup to simplify the view.

Listing 5-24. *The Controller Action to Retrieve a Journey*

```
function retrieve_form() {
}
```

Listing 5-25. *The View to Retrieve a Journey*

```
echo $form->create( 'Journey', array( 'url' => '/journeys/retrieve' ) );
echo $form->input( 'journey_id', array( 'div' => false, 'label' => false ) );
echo $form->input( 'password', array( 'div' => false, 'label' => false ) );
echo $form->submit( 'Retrieve Journey' );
```

The retrieve form simply renders a traditional HTML form with two input elements and a submit button.

The target of the form is the retrieve() action. The outline of the code is shown in Listing 5-26. It's very similar to the add action. If no data is supplied, we simply redirect the user back to the retrieve form. If data is supplied, we use Cake's find() model method to find the journey based on the journey ID and encrypted MD5 password. If a journey is found, we'll use the add_form action to display the results. If not, we will render the retrieve form with an error.

Listing 5-26. *Retrieving a Journey*

```
 1:    function retrieve() {
 2:        // If no data is supplied, we redirect user back to the retrieve form
 3:        if ( empty( $this->data ) ) {
 4:            $this->redirect( '/journeys/retrieve_form',null,true);
 5:
 6:        }
 7:        else
 8:        {
 9:            $journey_id = $this->data[ 'Journey' ][ 'journey_id' ];
10:            $password = $this->data[ 'Journey' ][ 'password' ];
11:            $journey = $this->Journey->find(
12:                                array( 'id' => $journey_id,
13:                                       'password' => md5( $password ) ) );
14:
15:            if ( $journey ) {
16:
17:                // Name of the journey
18:                $this->data['Journey']['name'] = $journey['Journey']['name'];
19:
```

```
20:                    // Tags relating to the journey
21:                    $this->data['Journey']['tags'] =➡
$this->_implode_tag( $journey['Tag'] );
22:
23:                    // Notes of the journey
24:                    $this->data['Journey']['notes'] =➡
$journey['Journey']['notes'];
25:
26:                    // Locations of the journey
27:                    $this->set( 'locations', $journey['Location'] );
28:
29:                    // Journey ID
30:                    $this->set( 'journey_id', $journey_id );
31:
32:                    $this->render( 'add_form' );
33:                }
34:            else
35:                {
36:                    $this->set( 'user_message',
37:                            '   Sorry, we couldn\'t
38:                                find your journey, or your password is
39:                                incorrect!' );
40:
41:                    $this->render( 'retrieve_form' );
42:                }
43:            }
44:    }
```

Viewing a Journey

Viewing a journey is similar to retrieving a journey, except we can only view the journey details
(and not edit them). The action is shown in Listing 5-27.

Listing 5-27. *The Action to Display a Journey*

```
1:    function display_journey( $get_journey_id = '' ) {
2:
3:        $journey_id = $get_journey_id;
4:
5:        if ( $this->data[ 'Journey' ][ 'journey_id' ] ) {
6:            $journey_id = $this->data[ 'Journey' ][ 'journey_id' ];
7:        }
8:
9:        // If no data is supplied, we redirect user back to the retrieve form
10:       if ( $journey_id ) {
11:
12:           $journey = $this->Journey->findById( $journey_id );
13:
```

```
14:            if ( $journey ) {
15:                $this->set( 'journey', $journey );
16:            }
17:            else {
18:                $this->set( 'user_message',
19:                        '  <div class="error-message">Sorry, we
20:                            couldn\'t find the journey!</div>' );
21:            }
22:        }
23:    }
```

The action handles both POST and GET scenarios. In the GET action, journeys can be displayed where the journey ID is within the URL request, as in /journeys/display_journey/1. In a POST action, the journey ID is stored within the $this->data variable.

In this action, we have used Cake's findBy<fieldName>(string $value) methods to retrieve the journey. The view is pretty straightforward and is shown in Listing 5-28. In this case, we have combined the display form with the view inserted below it. An example of the output is shown in Figure 5-9.

Listing 5-28. *The Journey View (/app/views/journeys/display_journey.ctp)*

```php
<?php

    if ( !empty( $user_message ) )
        echo $user_message;
?>

<p>Fields marked with * are needed.</p>

<div>

<?php

    echo $form->create( 'Journey',
                    array( 'url' => '/journeys/display_journey' ) );

    echo '<div class="form_fields">';
    echo '<h5>Journey ID: *<h5>';
    echo $form->input( 'journey_id', array( 'div' => false, 'label' => false ) );
    echo '</div>';

    echo '<div class="form_fields">';
    echo $form->submit( 'Display Journey' );
    echo '</div>';

    echo $form->end();
?>

</div>
```

```php
<!-- display journey here -->
<?php

    if ( isset( $journey ) ) {

        echo '<div class="display_journey_container">';
        echo '<h3>Your Journey Details</h3>';

        // journey name
        echo '<div class="form_fields">';
        echo '<h4>Journey Name:</h4>';
        echo $journey[ 'Journey' ][ 'name' ];
        echo '</div>';

        // journey notes
        echo '<div class="form_fields">';
        echo '<h4>Journey Notes:</h4>';
        echo str_replace( chr(10), '<br />', $journey[ 'Journey' ][ 'notes' ] );
        echo '</div>';

        // tag
        $tag = $journey[ 'Tag' ];
        $tag_str = '';
        for( $idx=0; $idx<sizeof( $tag ); $idx++ ) {

            $tag_str .= $tag[$idx][ 'tag' ];
            if ( $idx+1 < sizeof( $tag ) ) { $tag_str .= ','; }
        }

        echo '<div class="form_fields">';
        echo '<h4>Journey Tags:</h4>';
        echo $tag_str;
        echo '</div>';

        // locations
        $locations = $journey[ 'Location' ];

        for( $idx=0; $idx<sizeof( $locations ); $idx++ ) {

            echo '<div class="form_fields">';
            echo '<h3>Location: '.$locations[$idx][ 'loc_name' ].'</h3>';
            echo $locations[$idx][ 'comments' ];
            echo '</div>';
        }

        echo '</div>';
    }
?>
```

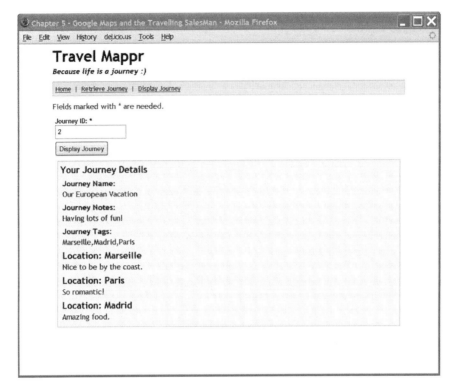

Figure 5-9. *Viewing a journey*

Summary

In this chapter, we have put together a simple travel log application. On the front end, we have used Google Maps to plot and work out a journey plan using purely JavaScript. On the server, we've created a journeys controller to handle saving and retrieving data. In the Cake models, we've used hasMany and belongsTo associations, as well as some simple validation. It's worth noting that some actions have more than one view.

Friends and family members can easily see what the travelers are up to by retrieving a journey, either via a URL or by using the display journey form. As a result of the feedback we got from our traveling friends, we have more tweaks and changes to implement, which we'll leave to you as an exercise. These are their comments:

- We would like to add a tag cloud so we can see what people are doing in general.

- We want to be able to just click the map instead of entering place names.

- We want to be able to enter comments for one destination only.

- We want to allow other people to enter comments. Also, each comment should be a separate, new entry.

- We want to see what other people are doing in similar destinations—something like a public gallery.

CHAPTER 6

■■■

Mashing Twitter with the Google Translator

For our fast-paced modern lifestyle, Twitter has filled a gap that fits between text messaging and blogging. You have a spare minute and want to let your pals know what you are doing or thinking, Twitter fits that need nicely. Twitter is a social networking and micro-blogging web application. You can post short messages to tell your friends and everyone else what you're up to right now. These short messages are referred to as *statuses, updates,* or *tweets.*

We can see Twitter being quite an addiction: Twitterdiction! In fact, we often view the Twitter public timeline, which is a listing of what people around the world are doing at that moment. However, quite a number of messages are in a foreign language. If a message has a cute picture, we cut and paste it into the Google Translate web site (`http://translate.google.com`) to see what it says. Wouldn't it be nice if we could do this translation automatically? Here's a stroke of luck: Google now has a language translation web service within the Google Ajax Language API. And in true Web 2.0 and Cake fashion, we can easily mash them together and bake some Cake!

In this chapter, we're going to cover quite a number of Cake topics. Twitter comes with an API that we can call from the server. The Google Ajax Language API can be called from the browser via Ajax or the server, but in this chapter, we'll be using only the server-side method.

So, let's get to creating our application, which we'll call Twitter Twister.

The Twitter API

The Twitter API comes with many methods. These methods are submitted via the principles of representational state transfer (REST). In most cases, this will be HTTP POST or GET—what most people have been using since their early days of web development. Twitter will also return the appropriate HTTP status code.

There are a few more items to be aware of when using the API:

- Twitter limits the number of requests to 70 requests per 60 minutes. Essentially, if you make one request per minute, you'll be OK.

- As users can post in many languages, the returned data from Twitter is encoded in UTF-8. As such, we must develop our application with this in mind.

- When Twitter returns an error, it will do so in the format you requested.

Within the Twitter API, we'll be using only one of the methods: the `public_timeline`. This returns the 20 most recent statuses from the server. This is the only method in the API that doesn't require authentication.

Calling the public timeline is easy. Using Cake's `HttpSocket`, you can fetch the most recent 20 statuses as follows:

```
App::import( 'HttpSocket' );

$http = new HttpSocket();

$request = array( 'uri' => ➡
'http://www.twitter.com/statuses/public_timeline.xml' );

$body = $http->request($request);
```

As you can see, requesting the public timeline is a simple case of supplying the `request` method with the URL. The $body variable will contain details of the 20 statuses in XML format, which we can easily handle in Cake or PHP. Listing 6-1 shows an example.

Listing 6-1. *Twitter XML Status Example*

```
 1:    <status>
 2:        <created_at>Thu Jul 10 21:31:17 +0000 2008</created_at>
 3:        <id>122039345</id>
 4:        <text>This is my first twitter!</text>
 5:        <source><a href="http://www.thisismyhomepage.com/">➡
my home page</a></source>
 6:        <truncated>false</truncated>
 7:        <in_reply_to_status_id>0123034190</in_reply_to_status_id>
 8:        <in_reply_to_user_id>123456</in_reply_to_user_id>
 9:        <favorited />
10:        <user>
11:            <id>9876543</id>
12:            <name>Me Myself</name>
13:            <screen_name>JustMe</screen_name>
14:            <location>London</location>
15:            <description>Take the Red Pill</description>
16:            <profile_image_url>http://s3.amazonaws.com/twitter_production/➡
17:    profile_images/9876543/mugshot.jpg</profile_image_url>
18:            <url>http://www.thisismyhomepage.com/</url>
19:            <protected>false</protected>
20:            <followers_count>111</followers_count>
21:        </user>
22:    </status>
```

On line 4, note the text tag, which is the tag that contains the Twitter status. Additionally, the tags `text`, `screen_name`, and `description` (on lines 4, 13, and 15, respectively) are the three XML tags that may contain foreign/multibyte characters. However, in our application, to keep things simple, we're just dealing with the `text` tag.

■**Tip** Some of the normal string manipulation functions do not always work on multibyte characters. For example, `strlen` may return different length sizes depending on whether the string is single or multibyte. Cake has a useful class called `Multibyte`, which contains some string-manipulation functions specifically written for multibyte characters, similar to PHP's `mbstring` module.

Now that we have covered the basics of the Twitter API, we can show you how the Google Ajax Language API works.

The Google Ajax Language API

The Google Ajax Language API is part of the Google Ajax API set of products. We'll call it the Google Translator for short, as that's its main feature.

The API allows you to translate or detect language text. The API commands can be called via Ajax, through other non-JavaScript environments like Flash, or on the server. For further details on using the Ajax calls, visit the Google Language API web site at (http://code.google.com/apis/ajaxlanguage/).

■**Caution** It must be said that the quality of the Google Ajax Language API translation can be quite poor. However, the service will serve our purposes, since we just want to get an idea of what's in the Twitter statuses.

To use the commands on the server side, again, we can employ Cake's `HttpSocket` class. For example, to translate "hello world," we use the code in Listing 6-2.

Listing 6-2. *Translating "Hello World"*

```
 1:    App::import( 'HttpSocket' );
 2:
 3:    $http = new HttpSocket();
 4:
 5:    $request = array(
 6:        'uri' => 'http://ajax.googleapis.com/ajax/services/language/translate?➥
v=1.0&q=hello%20world&langpair=en%7Cja',
 7:        'header' => array(
 8:        'Referer' => 'http://'.env('SERVER_NAME')
 9:        )
10:    );
11:
12:    $body = $http->request($request);
```

In Listing 6-2, we use the `translate` command and pass three parameters to it:

- v, for version `1.0` of the API

- q, for the `hello%20world` text we want to translate

- `langpair`, for the source language English (en) and target language Japanese (ja), separated by an entity-encoded vertical bar symbol: %7C

All the API commands respond in the JSON format, which we can easily decode using the PHP command `json_decode`.

Google's API documentation advises developers to make sure an HTTP referer header is always in place when making requests. This is shown in line 8 of Listing 6-2. Additionally, an API key should be sent. You can obtain a key from either of the following signup pages:

- Google Ajax Search (http://code.google.com/apis/ajaxsearch/signup.html)

- Google Maps (http://code.google.com/apis/maps/signup.html)

One useful feature is the language detection. If you do not know the original language that you want to translate, you can omit the source language in the `langpair` parameter. So, for example, we could simply write `langpair=%7Cja`. Now how cool is that!

■**Note** At the time of writing, the Google Ajax Language API is still quite new, and there don't appear to be any request limits. However, we can all be quite certain this will change at some point in the future.

Application Requirements

Even though we are essentially developing this application for fun, we still need to establish some requirements and consider usability.

The broad requirement is to give users the ability to view the current public timeline in any language by using the Google Translator to translate the status text. This simple statement gives us a starting point for scoping the application.

Scoping an application can be a lengthy task, involving many aspects, such as content, function, layout, wireframes, and site maps—just to mention a few. Since our application is quite small and should be fun, we will concentrate on the following simple functional requirements:

- Twitter has a usage limit. Considering the number of people who use Twitter, we definitely need to cache results. We will take advantage of Cake's cache helper to assist us.

- Even though there currently doesn't seem to be a usage limit on the Google Translator, we still need to cache results and save on bandwidth and the time it takes for the translation round-trip.

- Some people may want to view the translation on other devices. Since it is quite easy for Cake to provide data in different formats, we will add an RSS web feed service as well. We will use Cake's RSS helper.

- As we are translating the Twitter statuses, it makes sense to have the other parts of the site available in other languages as well. Using Cake's internationalization and localization classes, we can easily support this.

- Since we will be caching the results, we can also provide the ability to view past statuses.

Here are the details of these requirements:

- Each Twitter request we make will generate 20 statuses.

- A user comes to the site without specifying any language. The most recent 20 statuses in their original language are displayed on the first page. Since this happens to every user, we must always cache the results. We will be making requests to Twitter every 60 seconds. As such, we will cache the results every 60 seconds.

- We want the ability for any user to view past statuses as well as current statuses. Therefore, we will have a background process that will make Twitter requests and cache the results every 60 seconds, regardless of whether anyone is making a request to view statuses. In this way, we have separated the viewing of the statuses and the process that requests Twitter statuses.

- A user can select any language to view the current or past statuses. This language selection will also determine the language in which the rest of the site will be displayed.

In order to emphasize the raw nuts and bolts of the application, the interface layout will be kept as simple as possible. There will be two web pages:

- The first and main page will list 20 statuses in the selected language. We have sketched out a rough paper-and-pencil prototype in Figure 6-1. The top part consists of a header and tag line followed by a navigation area. We also allow the user to change the language at any point via a drop-down list on the right side of the page.

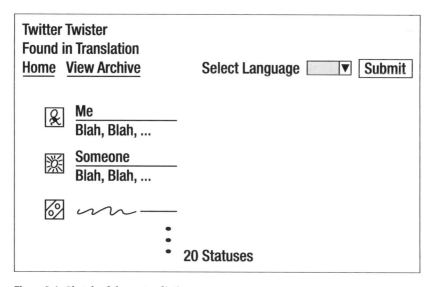

Figure 6-1. *Sketch of the status listing page*

- The second page will list the Twitter archives, which we have saved in the database. As shown in Figure 6-2, it will just list the date and time of each Twitter request. Each item in the list will be a link to the first view statuses page. This page will also have the drop-down list to allow the user to change the language.

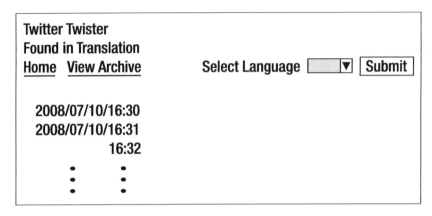

Figure 6-2. *Sketch of the archive listing page*

Application Structure

Each Twitter request we make will need to be stored in a database table. Remember that a single Twitter request to the public timeline returns 20 statuses. This naturally maps into a one-to-many relationship. Listing 6-3 shows the CREATE TABLE statements for both the twitter_requests and twitter_statuses tables.

Listing 6-3. *The twitter_requests and twitter_statuses Table Schemas*

```
CREATE TABLE `twitter_requests` (
  `id` int(11) NOT NULL auto_increment,
  `request_time` timestamp NOT NULL,
  PRIMARY KEY  (`id`)
);

CREATE TABLE `twitter_statuses` (
  `id` int(11) NOT NULL auto_increment,
  `twitter_request_id` int(11) NOT NULL,
  `t_created_at` timestamp NOT NULL,
  `t_id` varchar(50) collate latin1_general_ci NOT NULL,
  `t_text` varchar(255) character set utf8 collate utf8_unicode_ci NOT NULL,
  `t_source` varchar(255) collate latin1_general_ci NOT NULL,
  `t_truncated` varchar(255) collate latin1_general_ci NOT NULL,
  `t_in_reply_to_status_id` varchar(255) collate latin1_general_ci NOT NULL,
  `t_in_reply_to_user_id` varchar(255) collate latin1_general_ci NOT NULL,
```

```
  `t_favorited` varchar(255) collate latin1_general_ci NOT NULL,
  `t_user_id` varchar(50) collate latin1_general_ci NOT NULL,
  `t_user_name` varchar(255) collate latin1_general_ci NOT NULL,
  `t_user_screen_name` varchar(255) character set utf8 collate➡
utf8_unicode_ci NOT NULL,
  `t_user_location` varchar(255) collate latin1_general_ci NOT NULL,
  `t_user_description` varchar(255) character set utf8 collate➡
utf8_unicode_ci NOT NULL,
  `t_user_profile_image_url` varchar(255) collate latin1_general_ci NOT NULL,
  `t_user_url` varchar(255) collate latin1_general_ci NOT NULL,
  `t_user_protected` varchar(255) collate latin1_general_ci NOT NULL,
  `t_user_followers_count` varchar(50) collate latin1_general_ci NOT NULL,
  PRIMARY KEY (`id`)
);
```

In the `twitter_requests` table, the `request_time` field simply holds the time of the request. The `twitter_statuses` table will mainly hold all the data that has been returned by the Twitter request. Most fields are stored in the `latin1_general_ci` format collation. However, the `t_text`, `t_description`, and `t_user_screen_name` fields are stored in `utf8_unicode_ci`, since they will contain foreign characters. Notice that we're not using `utf8_unicode_bin`, as we may want to add search functionality to the fields later on; users expect searches to be case insensitive—`ci`.

The structure of how the translation will work is slightly trickier. When a Twitter request is made, the statuses returned will contain different languages. Do we also want to automatically translate them into all the other available languages? Pondering this point, we come up with a half yes and half no answer. Yes, we do want to translate them into other languages, but no, not immediately after fetching them from Twitter. This job should be spread over a period of time instead.

When a user does want to view the statuses in another language, whether they are current or past statuses, we will translate them on the fly and then cache the results. Thus, the first user who chooses to view a Twitter request in a specific language will need to endure the time delay that it takes to translate the 20 statuses. If we were running this application for real, we wouldn't want this to happen, as users would start to talk about how slow the site is to use.

When a status does get translated, the results are stored in the `twitter_translations` table, shown in Listing 6-4. This gives us a one-to-many relationship between `twitter_statuses` and `twitter_translations`, with one status having many different translations.

Listing 6-4. *The twitter_translations Table Schema*

```
CREATE TABLE `twitter_translations` (
  `id` int(11) NOT NULL auto_increment,
  `lang_from` varchar(10) collate latin1_general_ci NOT NULL,
  `lang_to` varchar(10) collate latin1_general_ci NOT NULL,
  `t_text_translation` varchar(255) character set utf8 collate➡
utf8_unicode_ci NOT NULL,
  `twitter_status_id` int(11) NOT NULL,
  PRIMARY KEY (`id`)
) ENGINE=MyISAM
```

The lang_from and lang_to fields will contain the language code to translate from and to, respectively. The lang_from field is, in a sense, redundant. When we are retrieving a translation of a status, we don't really need to know the language it was in, as we have a foreign key link to the twitter_statuses table, but we may need it in the future. The t_text_translation field will contain the actual translation, so it needs to be in utf8_unicode_ci.

Since localization will be involved somewhere, we see it as an advantage to have a language table that will help us bind different language areas together. Listing 6-5 shows the schema for this table, named languages.

Listing 6-5. *The languages Table Schema*

```
CREATE TABLE `languages` (
  `id` int(11) NOT NULL auto_increment,
  `lang_name` varchar(255) collate latin1_general_ci NOT NULL,
  `lang_code` varchar(10) collate latin1_general_ci NOT NULL,
  `google_lang_code` varchar(10) collate latin1_general_ci NOT NULL,
  PRIMARY KEY (`id`)
) ENGINE=MyISAM;
```

The languages table is essentially a lookup table for language codes. The lang_name field is for the name of the language, such as Japanese. The lang_code field is the three-letter ISO 639-3 language code used by Cake. The google_lang_code field is for the two-letter language code used by Google.

▓**Note** After much digging, we're still not sure why Google's language code has mostly two letters. We think it's a combination of codes, like the two-letter ISO 639-1 language code combined with locale names.

Figure 6-3 shows the relationships between the tables. The google_lang_code field in the languages table is linked to the lang_from and lang_to fields in the twitter_translations table. So we have a translation from one language to another language based on the google_lang_code entry. In the twitter_requests table, each request gives us many statuses, which are recorded in the twitter_statuses table, and each status has many different translations, which are recorded in the twitter_translations table.

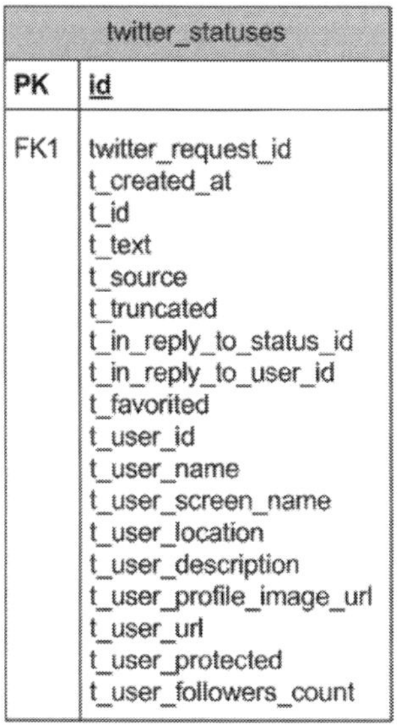

twitter_statuses	
PK	<u>id</u>
FK1	twitter_request_id t_created_at t_id t_text t_source t_truncated t_in_reply_to_status_id t_in_reply_to_user_id t_favorited t_user_id t_user_name t_user_screen_name t_user_location t_user_description t_user_profile_image_url t_user_url t_user_protected t_user_followers_count

Figure 6-3. *Database schema for all the Twitter Twister tables*

Cake Models

We now have enough information to build our model classes. As shown in the database schema (Figure 6-3), one Twitter request generates many Twitter statuses. This relationship is shown in the TwitterRequest model using the $hasMany variable, as shown in Listing 6-6.

Listing 6-6. *The TwitterRequest Model (/app/models/twitter_request.php)*

```php
<?php

class TwitterRequest extends AppModel {
    // Mainly for PHP4 users
    var $name = 'TwitterRequest';

    // Each journey has many locations and also many tags.
    var $hasMany = array(
        'TwitterStatus' => array(
        'className' => 'TwitterStatus',
        'order' => 'TwitterStatus.t_created_at'
        )
);
}

?>
```

The `twitter_statuses` table sits between the `twitter_translations` table and the `twitter_requests` table. One `twitter_statuses` record has many translations in the `twitter_translations` table. To complete the has-many relationship between the `TwitterRequest` and `TwitterStatus` models, we need to add the `belongsTo` relationship to the `TwitterStatus` Cake model, shown in Listing 6-7.

Listing 6-7. *The TwitterStatus Model (/app/models/twitter_status.php)*

```php
<?php

class TwitterStatus extends AppModel
{
    // Mainly for PHP4 users
    var $name = 'TwitterStatus';

    // Which db table to use
    var $useTable = 'twitter_statuses';

    var $hasMany = array(
        'TwitterTranslation' => array(
                            'className' => 'TwitterTranslation',
                            'foreignKey' => 'twitter_status_id' )
        );

    var $belongsTo = array(
        'TwitterRequest' => array(
                        'className' => 'TwitterRequest',
                        'foreignKey' => 'twitter_request_id' )
        );
}

?>
```

The `TwitterTranslation` model, shown in Listing 6-8, is quite simple, in that one single translation belongs to one Twitter status.

Listing 6-8. *The TwitterTranslation Model (/app/models/twitter_translation.php)*

```php
<?php

class TwitterTranslation extends AppModel
{
    // Mainly for PHP4 users
    var $name = 'TwitterTranslation';
```

```
    // Which db table to use
    var $useTable = 'twitter_translations';

    var $belongsTo = array(
        'TwitterStatus' => array(
                          'className' => 'TwitterStatus',
                          'foreignKey' => 'twitter_status_id' )
        );
}

?>
```

Note that we'll be adding some methods to the TwitterStatus and TwitterRequest models later in the chapter (see Listings 6-20 and 6-22).

Oddly, the Language model is the most complex out of the lot, as shown in Listing 6-9. Some of the code will make more sense when we explain caching later on.

Listing 6-9. *The Language Model (/app/models/language.php)*

```php
<?php

class Language extends AppModel
{
    // Mainly for PHP4 users
    var $name = 'Language';

    /*
    * Remove cache after database has been changed
    */
    function afterSave() {

        Cache::delete( 'getLang' );
    }

    /*
    * Get all the Twitter requests
    */
    function getLang() {

        $result = array();

        $allLang = $this->find( 'all' );

        foreach ( $allLang as $lang ) {

            $google_lang_code = $lang[ "Language" ][ "google_lang_code" ];
            $lang_name = $lang[ "Language" ][ "lang_name" ];
```

```
                    $result[ $google_lang_code ] = $lang_name;
        }

        return $result;
    }
}

?>
```

The `Language` model includes two methods: `getLang` and `afterSave`. `getLang` simply fetches all the Twitter requests using the `find` method. There is nothing surprising about the method, but bear in mind that the data it generates will be cached.

The `afterSave` method is a Cake model callback. The code within the method is executed whenever some data is saved into the database. In our case, we want to delete the cache that holds the data for the language drop-down list, so we can have an up-to-date list of languages.

▪**Caution** The `afterSave` method is called only if you execute the `save` model method. If you use the `query` method to execute raw SQL statements, `afterSave` won't get executed.

Internationalization and Localization

Internationalization (abbreviated as i18n) is the process of developing software so it is portable between different cultures without any change to its internal coding. *Localization* (abbreviated as l10n) is the process of adapting that software to any specific culture by using a predefined set of parameters called *locales*, normally stored in text files. In our case, a culture is defined by a number of parameters: its language, number format, date/time format, and currency.

Adding or changing the locale in Cake is quite easy. Note that in our application, i18n and l10n will be handling only the static text of the site—such as tag lines, error messages, and so on—so they are quite separate from the job of the Google Translator.

To get started, we first add the default language that we will use. In the `/app/config/core. php` file, we add the following line:

```
Configure::write( 'Config.language', "eng" )
```

▪**Tip** In a real application, you would probably want to override `Config.language` depending on where the user is connecting from. You can detect from a subdomain, the user agent header `HTTP_ACCEPT_LANGUAGE`, or any of the IP geolocation web services. You can add this in the `beforeFilter` so each action uses the correct language to display the view.

Next, we need to set up the locale files. For our application, we will have only two languages available: English and Japanese. We will create the two files as shown here:

```
/app/locale/eng/LC_MESSAGES/default.po
/app/locale/jpn/LC_MESSAGES/default.po
```

The cultural locale parameters are divided into categories. The LC_MESSAGES category basically handles text messages. Other categories exist, like LC_TIME to handle date and time formats, but we won't be using those in this chapter.

Cake's i18n and l10n modules will use the content within the .po files to map between languages.

The folder name of the language uses the three-letter ISO 639-3 language code. The same three-letter code is also used in the Config.language setting. If you want to expand the number of languages, either look in the Cake file /cake/libs/l10n.php or go to the official standards body web site http://www.sil.org/iso639-3/.

The .po portable object files are human-readable and editable. There were originally developed as part of the GNU gettext utilities for language translation.

Listings 6-10 and 6-11 show our two .po files.

Listing 6-10. *The English .po File*

```
msgid  "app_tag_line"
msgstr "Found in Translation!"
```

Listing 6-11. *The Japanese. po File*

```
msgid  "app_tag_line"
msgstr "混乱! 翻訳! 笑い!"
```

It's pretty obvious to see that app_tag_line will be used as the handle for the translations.

Now, to display the localized content, we use the global convenience function __(); for example, <?php __("app_tag_line") ?>. This will echo the msgstr text, which corresponds to the language that we have set in Config.language.

In the section "The Controllers" later in this chapter, we will go through how we have actually implemented i18n and l10n in our application.

■**Tip** In a production environment where there will be a lot of .po files, editing them should ideally be done with a .po file editor, such as Poedit. Also, as .po files may contain multibyte characters, remember to save them in UTF-8 format.

Web Services

In order to provide instant gratification for our application when people are away from their PCs, we will give users the option to view our application as an RSS feed. They will be able to easily see translated statuses when they are using a handheld device.

Adding different output formats for other devices to consume is a piece of cake! Or so we thought. . . .

We wrote a few different methods to achieve what we wanted. Starting with our first method, we saw that in the Cake documentation and some forums, the standard way to output RSS or any other format is to attach the format name you want at the end of the action as a file extension, like this:

```
/TwitterStatus/index.rss
```

In our case, we'll add the RSS feed to the index action. To get this to work, we need to tell the Router class about our new extension. We do this by adding the following line in /app/config/routes.php:

```
Router::parseExtensions( 'rss' );
```

Following this, we include the RSS helper in our app_controller.php file so we don't need to manually deal with any of the nitty-gritty RSS XML tags or headers.

Next, we need to have a specific layout for our RSS output. Under /app/views/layout/rss, we create a file called default.ctp. This is the layout that will surround the actual RSS data. As shown in Listing 6-12, we start off by adding the RSS header using the RSS helper. Next, we set up some basic channel data. And finally we echo the RSS document by passing $rss->document the $content_for_layout, which contains the list of statuses.

Listing 6-12. *The RSS Layout File (/app/views/layout/rss/default.ctp)*

```php
<?php
    echo $rss->header();

    if (!isset($channel)) {
        $channel = array();
    }

    if (!isset($channel['title'])) {
        $channel['title'] = $title_for_layout;
    }

    echo $rss->document($rss->channel(  array(),
                                        $channel,
                                        $content_for_layout );
?>
```

Before we proceed further, let's recap. We want to view the same data in different formats, while keeping the coding for the action unchanged. It will be the view that will change depending on the type of request. Now, having completed the layout part, we need to write the new RSS view. Under the controller view folder /app/views/twitter_status/, we need to create another folder called rss. In this folder, we create a file with the same name as the action, index.ctp. Listing 6-13 shows this file.

Listing 6-13. *The RSS View (/app/views/twitter_status/rss/index.ctp)*

```php
<?php

    function rssTransform( $current_status ) {

        return array('title' => $current_status['v_t_user_name'],
                     'link' => 'http://twitter.com/'.$current_status[➥
"v_t_user_screen_name" ],
                     'guid' => 'http://twitter.com/'.$current_status[➥
"v_t_user_screen_name" ],
                     'description' => $current_status['v_t_text'],
                     'pubDate' => $current_status['v_t_created_at'],
                     );

    }

    echo $rss->items( $statuses, 'rssTransform' );
?>
```

In Listing 6-13, the method $rss->items takes the $statuses array and loops through each status item through the function rssTransform, which sets up the RSS XML data tags—like title, link, and so on—in a form that the items method can use.

Finally, we need to add the built-in RequestHandler component, so it can pick out the correct view:

```
var $components = array( 'RequestHandler' );
```

And that is pretty much the standard way of adding an RSS feed to your data. When you specify the .rss extension, the class router parses the extension. If you don't tell Cake about the extension and you make an index.rss request, you will probably get an error like this:

```
The action index.rss is not defined in controller TwittertwisterController.
```

Once Cake knows about the extension through the Router class, the RequestHandler takes over and renders the view that corresponds to the extension.

We haven't quite finished with web services just yet. As we hinted early on, we ran into some trouble with our RSS feed. The problem starts when we add parameters to our URL action requests. For example, if want to view an archive Twitter request in another language, this is the URL we could use:

```
/TwitterStatus/index/lang:ja/id:1/
```

It's fine as it is, but if we want to view it in XML format, the URL would need to look like this (note the .rss extension):

```
/TwitterStatus/index/lang:ja/id:1/.rss
```

or even like this:

```
/TwitterStatus/index/lang:ja/id:1.rss
```

Basically, the `Router` class just parses out the extension at the end of the URL. We feel these are just too awkward looking. We want our URLs to look something like this instead:

```
/TwitterStatus/index/lang:ja/id:1/rss
```

Basically, we just add `/xml` instead of `.rss`.

To overcome this problem, we created two alternative methods. The first method is a bit hackish, while the second one works better.

The first method is quite easy. Using the `RequestHandler` component, we just add the following code snippet in the `beforeFilter` method in the `app_controller.php`:

```
// hackish!
if ( preg_match( '/\/rss$/', Router::url() ) ) {
    $this->RequestHandler->ext = 'rss';
}
```

`Router:url()`returns the requested URL, such as `/TwitterStatus/index/lang:ja/id:1/rss`. `preg_match` then matches for the ending `/rss`. If a match is found, we artificially set the extension variable `ext` to `rss`. We feel quite uneasy with this method, as we shouldn't really be setting class variables manually like this. But, hey, it works, and one alternative solution is better than none.

The second method we used to handle the `/rss` extension is easier and more obvious than the first. We just write a `mod_rewrite` rule in our root `.htaccess` file, as follows:

```
<IfModule mod_rewrite.c>
   RewriteEngine on
   RewriteRule    ^$ app/webroot/    [L]
   RewriteRule (.*)/rss$ app/webroot/$1/.rss [L]
   RewriteRule    (.*) app/webroot/$1 [L]
</IfModule>
```

The new rule is shown in bold. It matches anything ending with `/rss` and rewrites it in the `.rss` version. So if a user types

```
/TwitterStatus/index/lang:ja/id:1/rss
```

it gets translated to

```
/TwitterStatus/index/lang:ja/id:1/.rss
```

Using this `mod_rewrite` rule and the standard method to add web services, we feel this combination works well.

Caching

Our seemingly simple application has gotten a lot more complicated with the need to cache results. To start caching, we need to turn on Cake caching. This is done in the controller `/app/config/core.php`:

```
Configure::write('Cache.check', true);
```

We want to use the Cache helper. We'll just include it in app_controller.php, so all controllers in the future can have access to it. In our app_controller.php file, we simply add the following line:

```
var $helpers = array( 'Cache', 'Form', 'Html', 'Rss' );
```

Caching Views

Caching is a broad term. In our application, we're doing different types of caching, one of which is caching the views using Cake. This is where the output is saved, by default to /app/tmp/cache/views.

To cache a view, the setting is made in the action that corresponds to the view. In the controller, there are two different ways you can do this. One way is to set the cacheAction member variable, as in this example:

```
$cacheAction = array( 'TwitterRequest/view, 60 );
```

This caches the viewArchive action for 60 seconds.

We can also cache an action within the action function itself, like this:

```
$this->cacheAction = array( 'duration' => 60 );
```

This caches the current action for 60 seconds.

Caching Models

Cake goes through a lot of processing to build the object-relational mapping part of the MVC structure. To save on the execution time, you can cache the model data by setting the persistModel controller variable to true:

```
var $persistModel = true;
```

The cached model data is stored in the /app/tmp/cache/persistent folder.

■**Caution** If you change or add database fields, you must delete the cached data models. Be careful of cached data during your development. Sometimes you forget about your caching and then wonder why your changes are not showing up. Check your browser session cache and caching in Cake.

Caching Twitter and Google Translations

Once we get data back from Twitter and Google, that data is fairly permanent. The data we get is saved to the database in the three tables we have created. This is unlike some web caching, where data can be occasionally purged or destroyed.

In our application, the caching works in two levels. When a user requests the index page, Cake first checks to see whether the view is held in cache. If its not, the index action is called.

This then fetches the most recent statuses from the database. This data is essentially saved or cached in the database by the background cron process, which fetches the actual status messages from Twitter.

Caching and the Application Layout

Caching can bring up a lot of unforeseen problems within the application view. There are two main points to be aware of:

- We need to cache only some parts of a view. To achieve this, we use the Cake `<cake:nocache>This is not cached</cake:nocache>` tag to wrap content that we don't want to cache.

- Remember that no actions are called in the controller.

When we specify in the controller that we want to cache an action view, Cake will also cache the application layout. As such, we can't cache any dynamic content that changes within a session, whether in the action view or application layout.

As shown in the application layout in Listing 6-14, we don't cache our tag line, so we wrap it around the `<cake:nocache>` tag to say that it is not cached.

Listing 6-14. *Header HTML Code with the nocache Tag (in /app/views/layouts/base.ctp)*

```
<div class="header_wrapper">
    <h1>Twitter Twister</h1>
    <h2><i><cake:nocache><?__("app_tag_line")?></cake:nocache></i></h2>
</div>
```

Changing Languages

Since the HTML language selection drop-down list is displayed on every page within the application layout, we have pushed it out as a Cake element, as shown in Listing 6-15.

Listing 6-15. *Language Selection Form (/app/views/elements/lang_drop.ctp)*

```
<?php

    echo $form->create( 'Twittertwister',
                    array( 'url' => '/Twittertwister/changeLanguage',
                           'class' => 'lang_change_form'
                           ) );
?>

<cake:nocache>

<?php

    ClassRegistry::addObject( 'view', $this );
```

```
    echo $form->select( "Twittertwister.lang",
                        $session->read( "getLang" ),
                        $session->read( "userLang" ),
                        null,
                        true
                        );
?>

</cake:nocache>

<?php

    echo $form->submit( 'Change', array( 'label' => false,
                                         'div' => false
                                            ) );

    echo $form->end();
?>
```

The important part here is the <cake:nocache> tag. We don't want to cache the HTML drop-down list, because if a user changes the language, the newly selected item in the language should be selected and not a cached selection. However, we do want to cache the language data that was generated by the SQL find operation from the languages table list.

Some readers may notice this odd line of code:

```
ClassRegistry::addObject( 'view', $this );
```

When a view is rendered from the cache, the current view object isn't registered in Cake's global object register. As a result, some helpers that depend on the view object, such as the form helper, fail. Because of this, we need to manually register the current view object.

This highlights the complexity of caching. And in Cake, when an item is cached, no method in the controller is called. Therefore, we need to rely on session data as a conduit for any dynamic data that we need to pass to the view. As highlighted in the code, when we form the HTML select tag, we populate it with data that we saved into the Cake session. The getLang session variable holds the language data from the languages table, and userLang holds the current language that the user has selected.

Changing Locales

As no methods are called in the controller when data is cached, we need to set the new locale in the top part of the base layout file /app/views/layouts/base.ctp, as shown in Listing 6-16. When a user selects a new language, the cached page is presented while noncached content within the cached content is still being executed.

▓**Caution** Adding caching to our application was complex and time-consuming, mainly because we were also using other Cake features such as locales. If you are going to add caching, try to add it early on in your development. This will make your life easier when your application grows.

Listing 6-16. *Setting Locale in the Base View (/app/views/layouts/base.ctp)*

```
// ...
<cake:nocache>
<?php

    if ( $session->read( "userLocale" ) ) {
        Configure::write( 'Config.language', $session->read( "userLocale" ) );
    }

?>
</cake:nocache>
// ...
```

The Controllers

For our application, three controllers are used: TwittertwisterController, TwitterRequestController, and TwitterStatusController. Let's look at how each of these controllers works.

The Twittertwister Controller

The TwittertwisterController class file is shown in Listing 6-17. This is a base controller for the application. At present, it holds one action called changeLanguage, which changes the viewing language of the application.

Listing 6-17. *The TwittertwisterController Class (app/controllers/twittertwister_controller.php)*

```
 1:    <?php
 2:
 3:    class TwittertwisterController extends AppController {
 4:
 5:        var $name = 'Twittertwister';
 6:
 7:        var $uses = array();
 8:
 9:        /*
10:         * User specifically changed language
11:         */
12:        function changeLanguage() {
13:
14:            if ( $this->data[ "Twittertwister" ][ "language" ] ) {
15:                $this->Session->write(
16:                        "userLang",
17:                        $this->data[ "Twittertwister" ][ "language" ] );
18:            }
19:
```

```
20:              // We must also change the locale language
21:              $this->_changeSessionLocale(
22:                          $this->data[ "Twittertwister" ][ "language" ] );
23:
24:              $url = Router::parse( $this->referer() );
25:
26:              $url_str = '/'.$url[ 'controller' ].'/'.$url[ 'action' ].'/';
27:
28:              if ( isset( $url[ 'named' ][ 'id' ] ) ) {
29:                  $url_str .= 'id:'.$url[ 'named' ][ 'id' ].'/';
30:              }
31:
32:              // Set language parameter for action in calling page
33:              $url_str .= 'lang:'.$this->data['Twittertwister']['language'].'/';
34:
35:              // Redirect back to calling page
36:              $this->redirect( $url_str );
37:          }
38:
39:      /*
40:       * Change the locale
41:       */
42:      function _changeSessionLocale( $google_lang_code ) {
43:
44:              $lang = $this->Language->findByGoogleLangCode( $google_lang_code );
45:
46:              if ( $lang ) {
47:                  $this->Session->write( "userLocale",
48:                                  $lang[ 'Language' ][ 'lang_code' ] );
49:              }
50:          }
51:      }
52:
53:  ?>
```

This changeLanguage action is used by the language-selection form. Starting from line 12, this action takes the language code that the user has selected and changes the status viewing language on line 14 and the locale on line 21. From line 24 onwards, we redirect the users back to the page where they selected the language change, where they would view the same page they have selected in the new language.

The private method _changeSessionLocale on line 42 is used to change the web site locale. The language code used by Google was incompatible with the ISO 639-3 three-letter language code used by Cake's l10n. As a result, we needed to do some language code translation. We simply make a query to the languages table and get the three-letter code that corresponds with Google's two-letter code, and then save this into the session. We do this using Cake's model method findBy[field_name]([field_value]). Attach the field name in camel case as a suffix to the findBy keyword. In our case, the field name is google_lang_code, so the method name will be findByGoogleLangCode. We then supply the method with the value of the field as an argument.

The TwitterRequest Controller

The TwitterRequestController class is responsible for fetching Twitter statuses from the Twitter public timeline. The controller file app/controllers/twitter_request_controller.php is shown in Listing 6-18.

Listing 6-18. *The TwitterRequestController Class (app/controllers/twitter_request_controller.php)*

```
 1:    <?php
 2:
 3:    class TwitterRequestController extends AppController {
 4:
 5:        var $cacheAction = array( 'TwitterRequest/view' => '60' );
 6:
 7:        /*
 8:         * View entire archive
 9:         */
10:    function view() {
11:
12:            // Get all Twitter requests
13:            $allRequests = $this->TwitterRequest->find( 'all',
14:                                          array(  null,
15:                                                  null,
16:                                                  'recursive' => -1
17:                                                          ) );
18:
19:            $this->set( 'twitterRequests', $allRequests );
20:        }
21:
22:        /*
23:         * This should be called by cron every few seconds
24:         */
25:        function getTwitterRequests() {
26:
27:            $this->layout = 'blank';
28:
29:            $this->makeTwitterRequest();
30:        }
31:
32:        /*
33:         * This call the Twitter public timeline
34:         */
35:        function makeTwitterRequest() {
36:
```

```
37:              // Save the request header
38:              $this->TwitterRequest->saveRequest();
39:
40:              // Set up and execute the socket call
41:              $url = 'http://www.twitter.com/statuses/public_timeline.xml';
42:
43:              App::import( 'HttpSocket' );
44:              $http = new HttpSocket();
45:              $request = array( 'uri' => $url );
46:              $body = $http->request($request);
47:
48:              // Now save into db
49:              $this->TwitterStatus->saveStatuses( $body,
50:                                          $this->TwitterRequest->id );
51:          }
52:
53:      }
54:
55:    ?>
```

On line 5, we set $cacheAction to cache the viewArchive action to 60 seconds. We will explain this at the end of this section.

The controller contains two main actions: view and getTwitterRequests. The view action on line 10 lists all the Twitter requests in the database. As we are just listing the Twitter requests, we don't need the other tables that link to it, so we set recursive to -1. Remember that we have cached this action at the start of the controller to 60 seconds, so we are not regenerating the same query for different users. One obvious shortcoming with this action is the number of calls that will be returned. As we are making Twitter requests every 60 seconds, it would quickly generate a lot of requests. In fact, it probably won't take long before it would take more than 60 seconds to list all the status requests.

Line 25 starts with the getTwitterRequests action. This is essentially an action that we use during development to fetch statuses; however, it can still be used as the URL for a cron job entry. This action makes public timeline calls to Twitter requests every 60 seconds. The view in Listing 6-19 is even simpler. (If you use this in a cron entry, comment out the meta refresh, as that should be the job for cron.)

Listing 6-19. *The getTwitterRequests View (app/views/twitter_rquest/get_twitter_requests.ctp)*

```
<meta http-equiv="refresh" content="60">
```

The makeTwitterRequest action shown on line 35 of Listing 6-18 carries out the task of requesting the public timeline from Twitter. We start on line 38 by calling the saveRequest method in the TwitterRequest model, which is shown in Listing 6-20. On line 14 of this listing, the saveRequest method simply saves a record into the twitter_requests table by using the model's save method on line 20.

Listing 6-20. *The TwitterRequest Model with the saveRequest Method (app/models/twitter_request.ctp)*

```
1:    <?php
2:
3:    class TwitterRequest extends AppModel
4:    {
5:        // Mainly for PHP4 users
6:        var $name = 'TwitterRequest';
7:
8:        // Each journey has many locations and also many tags.
9:        var $hasMany = array(
10:                        'TwitterStatus' => array(
11:                            'className' => 'TwitterStatus',
12:                            'order'     => 'TwitterStatus.t_created_at' ) );
13:
14:        function saveRequest() {
15:
16:            // Each request must be saved in the twitter_requests table
17:            $reqData = array();
18:            $reqData[ 'request_time' ] = date( 'Y-m-d H:i:s', mktime() );
19:            $this->create( $reqData );
20:            $this->save();
21:        }
22:    }
23:
24:    ?>
```

Let's now go back to the `makeTwitterRequest` action in `TwitterRequestController` (Listing 6-18). Having now saved a request, we make a call to the Twitter public timeline using Cake's `HttpSocket` class. We fetch the statuses and save the results into the $body variable on line 46. The data returned will be in XML format. You can request the return format to be `json`, `rss`, or `atom` by appending those format strings as the extension instead of `xml`.

Finally, on line 49 of the controller, we save the status return message into the `twitter_statuses` table using the `TwitterStatus` model method `saveStatuses`. We will talk more about this method in the next section.

The TwitterStatus Controller

The `TwitterStatusController` class is the largest of the three controllers. It's responsible for displaying either statuses specified by the user or the most recent statuses that were fetched within the last minute. Listing 6-21 lists the controller with the actions omitted. As the controller is quite large, we will show each action in turn.

Listing 6-21. *The TwitterStatusController Class (app/controllers/twitter_status_controller.php)*

```
 1:    <?php
 2:
 3:    class TwitterStatusController extends AppController {
 4:
 5:        // View any particular Twitter request
 6:        var $currentTwitterReqId = '';
 7:
 8:        // actions ...
 9:
10:    }
11:
12:    ?>
```

On line 6, the $currentTwitterReqId variable holds the current Twitter request, if any. If a user has requested the home page, this would be empty, and the most recent statuses will be returned.

Before we talk about the controller's actions, let us first talk about the model. As shown in Listing 6-22, the model has only one method called saveStatuses. As we mentioned earlier, this method is used by the makeTwitterRequest action in the TwitterRequestController. It saves the statuses returned from a Twitter request.

Listing 6-22. *The TwitterStatus Model with the saveStatuses Method (app/models/twitter_status. ctp)*

```
 1:    <?php
 2:
 3:    class TwitterStatus extends AppModel
 4:    {
 5:        // Mainly for PHP4 users
 6:        var $name = 'TwitterStatus';
 7:
 8:        // Which db table to use
 9:        var $useTable = 'twitter_statuses';
10:
11:        var $hasMany = array( 'TwitterTranslation' => array(
12:                                    'className' => 'TwitterTranslation',
13:                                    'foreignKey' => 'twitter_status_id' ) );
14:
15:        var $belongsTo = array( 'TwitterRequest' => array(
16:                                    'className' => 'TwitterRequest',
17:                                    'foreignKey' => 'twitter_request_id' ) );
18:
19:        /*
20:        * Save statuses into database
21:        */
22:        function saveStatuses( $statuses, $twitterReqId ) {
23:
```

```
24:                 // Check we have a Twitter request id
25:                 if ( !is_numeric( $twitterReqId ) ) {
26:                     return;
27:                 }
28:
29:                 $xml = new SimpleXMLElement( $statuses );
30:
31:                 foreach ($xml->status as $status) {
32:
33:                     $statusData = array();
34:
35:                     $statusData[ "twitter_request_id" ] = $twitterReqId;
36:
37:                     $statusData[ "t_created_at" ] = $status->created_at;
38:                     $statusData[ "t_id" ] = $status->id;
39:                     $statusData[ "t_text" ] = $status->text;
40:                     $statusData[ "t_source" ] = $status->source;
41:                     $statusData[ "t_truncated" ] = $status->truncated;
42:                     $statusData[ "t_in_reply_to_status_id" ] =
43:                                             $status->in_reply_to_status_id;
44:                     $statusData[ "t_in_reply_to_user_id" ] =
45:                                             $status->in_reply_to_user_id;
46:                     $statusData[ "t_favorited" ] = $status->favorited;
47:
48:                     $statusData[ "t_user_id" ] = $status->user->id;
49:                     $statusData[ "t_user_name" ] = $status->user->name;
50:                     $statusData[ "t_user_screen_name" ] =
51:                                             $status->user->screen_name;
52:                     $statusData[ "t_user_location" ] = $status->user->location;
53:                     $statusData[ "t_user_description" ] =
54:                                             $status->user->description;
55:                     $statusData[ "t_user_profile_image_url" ] =
56:                                         $status->user->profile_image_url;
57:                     $statusData[ "t_user_url" ] = $status->user->url;
58:                     $statusData[ "t_user_protected" ] = $status->user->protected;
59:                     $statusData[ "t_user_followers_count" ] =
60:                                         $status->user->followers_count;
61:
62:                     $this->create( $statusData );
63:                     $this->save();
64:                 }
65:             }
66:
67:     }
68:
69:     ?>
```

The saveStatuses method starts on line 22. We take the statuses and parse the XML using PHP's SimpleXMLElement class. You can, of course, accomplish the same thing using Cake. Listings 6-23 and 6-24 show how to get the created_at field using Cake's XML classes.

Listing 6-23. *Using Cake's XML Class, Longer Version*

```
App::import( 'Xml' );
$xml_1 = new Xml( $statuses );

$node_1 = $xml_1->children( 'statuses' );
$node_2 = $node_1[0]->children( 'status' );
$node_3 = $node_2[0]->children( 'created_at' );
$created_at = $node_3[0]->children[0]->value;
```

Listing 6-24. *Using Cake's XML Class, Shorter Version*

```
App::import( 'Xml' );
$xml_1 = new Xml( $statuses );

$node_1 = $xml_1->child(0)->child(0)->children( 'created_at' );
$node_2 = $node_1[0]->child(0)->value;
```

Now we'll look at each of the actions in the TwitterStatusController:

The index() Action

The index action is shown in Listing 6-25.

Listing 6-25. *TwitterStatusController index Action*

```
 1:        function index( $twitterReqId = '', $transLang = '' ) {
 2:
 3:            // Override current Twitter request
 4:            if ( $twitterReqId ) {
 5:                $this->currentTwitterReqId = $twitterReqId;
 6:            }
 7:
 8:            if ( isset( $this->passedArgs['id'] ) ) {
 9:                $this->currentTwitterReqId = $this->passedArgs['id'];
10:            }
11:
12:            // If there is no id for the current request, then we assume
13:            // most recent statuses so we only cache for 60 secs
14:            if ( $this->currentTwitterReqId ) {
15:                // Cache it for a year
16:                $this->cacheAction = array( 'duration' => 31536000 );
17:            }
```

```
18:            else {
19:                $this->cacheAction = array( 'duration' => 60 );
20:            }
21:
22:            // Override current language view
23:            if ( $transLang ) {
24:                $this->currentLang = $transLang;
25:            }
26:
27:            if ( isset( $this->passedArgs['lang'] ) ) {
28:                $this->currentLang = $this->passedArgs['lang'];
29:            }
30:
31:            $this->__displayTwitters();
32:        }
```

On lines 4 and 8, we can override which Twitter request we want to view, via either the pretty URL method or the named parameter method. Both of the following examples would work:

twittertwister/index/1

or

twittertwister/index/id:1/

Following this on line 14, if the user has requested to view a particular Twitter request, we will cache it for a whole year. We wanted to cache it indefinitely, but we couldn't find an easy way except by hacking the Cake library files, which we definitely didn't want to do.

If a user hasn't requested a particular ID, then by default, the most recent statuses would be displayed. In this case, we cache it for 60 seconds, as new statuses are fetched from the Twitter servers every 60 seconds as well.

Next, we do the same check for the language selection. Once those two checks are complete, we display the Twitter statuses on line 31.

On line 27, even if a user has selected to view statuses in a language via the language drop-down list, he can still override the viewing language by passing a different language code via the URL, which overrides the $currentLang variable. For example, a Japanese user can still view a post in English by using a URL with a lang parameter in it set to en.

The __displayTwitters() Action

The private action __displayTwitters, shown in Listing 6-26, is the core of the application.

Listing 6-26. *TwitterStatusController __displayTwitters Action*

```
1:      function __displayTwitters() {
2:
3:              // We check whether a particular Twitter request was requested or
4:              // we just fetch the recent one
5:              $conditions = array();
6:
7:              if ( is_numeric( $this->currentTwitterReqId ) ) {
8:                      $conditions[ 'TwitterRequest.id' ] = ➥
$this->currentTwitterReqId;
9:              }
10:             else {
11:                     $conditions = array ();
12:                     $conditions[] = array(
13:                         "TwitterStatus.t_created_at <" => date(
14:                                             'Y-m-d H:i:00',
15:                                             strtotime( "-1 minute" )
16:                                             ) );
17:                     $conditions[] = array(
18:                         "TwitterStatus.t_created_at >" => date(
19:                                             'Y-m-d H:i:00',
20:                                             strtotime( "-2 minute" )
21:                                             ) );
22:             }
23:
24:             // Check to see if user has selected to view the statuses in
25:             // any particular language
26:             if ( $this->currentLang ) {
27:
28:                     $twitTransTable = array(
29:                         'TwitterTranslation' => array(
30:                                             'className' => 'TwitterTranslation',
31:                                             'foreignKey' => 'twitter_status_id',
32:                                             'conditions' => ➥
"TwitterTranslation.lang_to = '{$this->currentLang}'" ) );
33:
34:                     $this->TwitterStatus->bindModel(
35:                                             array( 'hasMany' => $twitTransTable ) );
36:             }
37:             else {
38:                 // No point getting translation, so lets unbind it
39:                 $this->TwitterStatus->unbindModel(
40:                     array( 'hasMany' => array( 'TwitterTranslation' ) ) );
41:             }
42:
```

```
43:                $min_statuses = $this->TwitterStatus->find( 'all',
44:                        array( 'conditions' => $conditions,
45:                                null,
46:                                'order' => 'TwitterStatus.t_created_at DESC'
47:                                ) );
48:
49:                // OK, now we got the status for the minute in question.
50:                // We check whether the language translation exists
51:                // in those statuses
52:                $statusesTrans = $this->__statusTranslate( $min_statuses );
53:
54:                // The view has no knowledge of what language
55:                // to display something
56:                $this->set( 'statuses', $statusesTrans );
57:        }
```

This method fetches Twitter statuses according to a number of query conditions, starting on line 5. We need to know what time period of statuses we want. Do we want archived statuses or the most recent statuses? When we are retrieving the most recent 20 statuses, we set it between 1 and 2 minutes behind the current time, so we will always get a full minute.

To make the query more efficient, if no language was selected, there is no need to try to fetch any associated translations, which is by default what would happen—see line 26 onwards. Therefore, we unbind any associations using the unbindModel method when no language was chosen. Once we have the statuses, on line 52, we make a call to _statusTranslate, which will translate any statuses if there are any. Finally, we set the view variable statuses so it's available to be displayed in any view.

The __statusTranslate() Action

The __statusTranslate private action, shown in Listing 6-27, is a supporting action to the __displayTwitters action. It helps us to translate statuses transparently, independent of the language in which the status is originally.

Listing 6-27. *TwitterStatusController __statusTranslate Action*

```
1:    function __statusTranslate( $statuses ) {
2:
3:        $result = array();
4:
5:        for( $idx=0; $idx<sizeof( $statuses ); $idx++ ) {
6:
7:            // Original language text
8:            $t_user_name = $statuses[$idx][ "TwitterStatus" ][ "t_user_name" ];
9:            $t_text = $statuses[$idx][ "TwitterStatus" ][ "t_text" ];
10:           $t_user_url = $statuses[$idx][ "TwitterStatus" ][ "t_user_url" ];
11:           $t_user_profile_image_url = ➥
$statuses[$idx][ "TwitterStatus" ][ "t_user_profile_image_url" ];
```

```
12:             $t_user_location =
13:                     $statuses[$idx][ "TwitterStatus" ][ "t_user_location" ];
14:             $t_user_screen_name =
15:                 $statuses[$idx][ "TwitterStatus" ][ "t_user_screen_name" ];
16:             $t_created_at = ➡
$statuses[$idx][ "TwitterStatus" ][ "t_created_at" ];
17:
18:             // We only check if there is a destination language specified
19:             // Check if there is a translation from the original to the
20:             // destination; if there is, we override, original text
21:             if ( $this->currentLang ) {
22:
23:                 if ( isset( $statuses[$idx][ "TwitterTranslation" ] ) ) {
24:
25:                     // Note we only translate status
26:
27:                     $trans_result = $this->_getStatusTranslation(
28:                                             $statuses[$idx] );
29:
30:                     if ( isset( $trans_result[ "t_text" ] ) ) {
31:                         $t_text = $trans_result[ "t_text" ];
32:                     }
33:                 }
34:             }
35:
36:             $current_result = array();
37:
38:             $current_result[ "v_t_user_name" ] = $t_user_name;
39:             $current_result[ "v_t_text" ] = $t_text;
40:             $current_result[ "v_t_user_url" ] = $t_user_url;
41:             $current_result[ "v_t_user_profile_image_url" ] =
42:                                         $t_user_profile_image_url;
43:             $current_result[ "v_t_user_location" ] = $t_user_location;
44:             $current_result[ "v_t_user_screen_name" ] = $t_user_screen_name;
45:             $current_result[ "v_t_created_at" ] = $t_created_at;
46:
47:             $result[] = $current_result;
48:         }
49:
50:         return $result;
51:     }
```

Basically, if there is a translation found for the status, we replace the original status with that translation. This happens on line 21. If a translation is not found, we will just display the status in its original language.

Additionally, we have formed a new result array to return on line 36. In that array, we prefix each key with v_ to make it clear that the array is to be used in the view.

Now that we have covered both __displayTwitters and __statusTranslate, the following view (/app/views/twitter_status/index.ctp), which displays the statuses, should make sense.

```php
<?php

    foreach ( $statuses as $current_status ) {

        echo '<div class="status_rec">';
            echo '<h3><a href="http://twitter.com/'.$current_status[➥
"v_t_user_screen_name" ].'" target="_blank">'.$current_status[➥
"v_t_user_name" ].'</a></h3>';
            echo '<hr align="left" noshade="" size=1 width="100%">';

            if ( $current_status[ "v_t_user_url" ] ) {
                echo '<a href="'.$current_status[ "v_t_user_url" ].'">➥
<img class="profile_img" src="'.$current_status[➥
"v_t_user_profile_image_url" ].'" align="left"></a>';
            }
            else {
                echo '<img class="profile_img" src="'.$current_status[➥
"v_t_user_profile_image_url" ].'" align="left">';
            }

            echo $current_status[ "v_t_text" ].'<br />';

            if ( $current_status[ "v_t_user_location" ] ) {
                echo '<b>From:</b> '.$current_status[ "v_t_user_location" ];
            }

        echo '</div>';
    }

?>
```

Here, we basically loop through the statuses and display the fields. Figure 6-4 shows an example of the translated statuses page.

Figure 6-4. *A translated statuses page*

The __getStatusTranslation() Action

The __getStatusTranslation action, shown in Listing 6-28, complements the previous two actions.

Listing 6-28. *TwitterStatusController __getStatusTranslation Action*

```
1:    function __getStatusTranslation( $statuses ) {
2:
3:        $result = array();
4:
5:        $transTo = $this->currentLang;
6:
7:        // 1. Check t_text translation. We always use the first one
8:        if ➡
( isset( $statuses[ "TwitterTranslation" ][0][ "t_text_translation" ] ) ) {
9:
10:           // Yes there is a translation. Let's use that
11:           $result[ "t_text" ] =
12:               $statuses[ "TwitterTranslation" ][0][ "t_text_translation" ];
13:        }
14:        else {
15:           $sourceLang = '';
16:
17:           // No there is no translation. Let's get one
18:
19:           // Start with t_text
20:           $t_text = $statuses[ "TwitterStatus" ][ "t_text" ];
21:           $google_trans_result =
22:                           $this->__translateText( $t_text, $transTo );
23:
24:           $result[ "t_text" ] = $google_trans_result[ "translation" ];
25:           $sourceLang = $google_trans_result[ "source_lang" ];
26:
27:           $this->__saveTrans( $sourceLang,
28:                               $transTo,
29:                               $result,
30:                               $statuses[ "TwitterStatus" ][ "id" ] );
31:        }
32:
33:        return $result;
34:    }
```

On line 8, if a translation already exists, we won't translate it. If there isn't a translation, we make the request to Google to translate the status, from line 14 onwards. If a translation is found, we always take the first translation, as we will explain shortly, in the description of the _saveTrans action.

The __translateText() Action

The private action in Listing 6-29 uses Cake's HttpSocket class methods to make translation requests to Google. Sometimes, the call may fail. In that situation, we still return the status minus the translation. We throttle the translation requests with a sleep period, as that helps the reliability of any immediate future requests.

Listing 6-29. *TwitterStatusController__translateText Action*

```
 1:    function __translateText( $transText, $destLang ) {
 2:
 3:        $result = array(    "translation" => "",
 4:                            "source_lang" => "",
 5:                            "response_status" => "" );
 6:
 7:        if ( empty( $transText ) ) { return ""; }
 8:
 9:        $params = array();
10:    $params[ "v" ] = "1.0";
11:    $params[ "q" ] = $transText;
12:    $params[ "langpair" ] = "|".$destLang;
13:    $params[ "key" ] = "!!!!!! Insert Your Google API Key Here !!!!!!";
14:
15:    $paramStr = $this->__constructURL( $params );
16:
17:        $url = ➥
"http://ajax.googleapis.com/ajax/services/language/translate?".$paramStr;
18:
19:        App::import( 'HttpSocket' );
20:        $http = new HttpSocket();
21:        $request = array(
22:            'uri' => $url,
23:            'header' => array(
24:            'Referer' => 'http://'.env('SERVER_NAME')
25:            )
26:        );
27:        $body = $http->request($request);
28:
29:        // Now, process the JSON string
30:        $json = json_decode( $body );
31:
32:        if ( isset( $json->responseStatus ) ) {
33:
34:            // Translation was good
35:            if ( $json->responseStatus == "200" ) {
36:                $result[ "translation" ] = $json->responseData->translatedText;
37:                $result[ "source_lang" ] = ➥
$json->responseData->detectedSourceLanguage;
38:                $result[ "response_status" ] = "200";
39:            }
40:            else {
41:                // We just fill with original
42:                $result[ "translation" ] = $transText;
43:                $result[ "source_lang" ] = "UNKNOWN";
44:                $result[ "response_status" ] = $json->responseStatus;
```

```
45:              }
46:          }
47:
48:          // We always wait for a bit before next action, 0.5 sec
49:          usleep( 500000 );
50:
51:          return $result;
52:      }
```

As this action is used by __getStatusTransation, which in turn saves it into the database,
we may occasionally see the value UNKNOWN in the twitter_translations table. In this chapter,
we won't be going into the reasons why some text doesn't get translated. Our goal is to translate some piece of text using Google. If the translation fails for some reason, we still return the
data in the same format, as if it were translated. This way, we have a log of the failure of the
translation, and the user still gets to see the original text, which we think is better than seeing
no status text or an empty translation display.

We start the action off on line 7. If no text is given, we just return an empty string. If
a string is given, we form the code to carry out the HttpSocket from line 9 to line 27. We then
decode the returned result on line 30 onwards. On line 13, remember to use your own Google
API key.

The __saveTrans() Action

There isn't much to the __saveTrans action, shown in Listing 6-30.

Listing 6-30. *TwitterStatusController__saveTrans Action*

```
1:     function __saveTrans( $sourceLang, $destLang, $transResult, ➥
$twitterStatusId ) {
2:
3:          // We first check whether the translation exists for the
4:          // "twitter_status_id" and "lang_to". Even if it does, we may
5:          // still have 2 or more of the same entries in the database.
6:
7:          $conditions = array (
8:                      "TwitterTranslation.twitter_status_id" => $twitterStatusId,
9:                      "TwitterTranslation.lang_to" => $destLang
10:                               );
11:
12:          $transExist = $this->TwitterTranslation->find(
13:                          'first', array( 'conditions' => $conditions ) );
14:
15:
16:          if ( empty( $transExist ) ) {
17:
18:              $statusTrans = array();
19:              $statusTrans[ 'lang_from' ] = $sourceLang;
20:              $statusTrans[ 'lang_to' ] = $destLang;
```

```
21:            $statusTrans[ 't_text_translation' ] = $transResult[ "t_text" ];
22:            $statusTrans[ 'twitter_status_id' ] = $twitterStatusId;
23:
24:            $this->TwitterTranslation->create( $statusTrans );
25:            $this->TwitterTranslation->save();
26:        }
27:    }
```

On line 12, we check if there are two or more of the same translation. If not, we enter the translation into the twitter_translations table on lines 24 and 25. Why would there be two or more of the same translation? Well, since we are not translating the statuses in a background process, any user who first brings up the statuses in a specific language would fire up the translation parts of the controller. As we are not using SQL transaction locks, there could easily be the situation where two or more users are requesting the same statuses at roughly the same time. Using transaction locks would hold up the rendering of the page. We don't feel they are necessary, as we can always write some housekeeping function to clear any duplicate entries. This is better than delaying the translation of the page.

The AppController

Along with our three controllers, the global AppController also plays a part in our application. Listing 6-31 shows the contents of the AppController file app/app_controller.php.

Listing 6-31. *The Application Base Controller (app/app_controller.php)*

```
1:     <?php
2:
3:     class AppController extends Controller {
4:
5:         // Default page title
6:         var $pageTitle = 'Chapter 6 - ➥
Mashing Twitter with the Google Translator';
7:
8:         // The view helpers that we'll use globally
9:         var $helpers = array( 'Cache', 'Form', 'Html', 'Rss' );
10:
11:        // Components that we'll often use
12:        var $components = array( 'Session', 'RequestHandler' );
13:
14:        // The default language to view the statuses
15:        var $currentLang = '';
16:
17:        var $uses = array( 'TwitterRequest', 'TwitterStatus',
18:                           'TwitterTranslation', 'Language' );
19:
20:        // We cache the models
21:        var $persistModel = true;
22:
```

```
23:        function beforeFilter() {
24:
25:            $cache_get_lang = Cache::read( 'getLang' );
26:
27:            if ( empty( $cache_get_lang ) ) {
28:
29:                // This is a site wide function
30:                Cache::write( 'getLang', $this->Language->getLang(), 0 );
31:            }
32:
33:            $session_get_lang = $this->Session->read( "getLang" );
34:
35:            if ( empty( $session_get_lang ) ) {
36:                $this->Session->write( "getLang", Cache::read( 'getLang' ) );
37:            }
38:
39:            // Hackish!
40:            /*
41:            if ( preg_match( '/\/rss$/', Router::url() ) ) {
42:                $this->RequestHandler->ext = 'rss';
43:            }*/
44:
45:            $this->__langChoice();
46:        }
47:
48:        function __langChoice() {
49:
50:            // If user has selected default viewing language
51:            if ( $this->Session->read( "userLang" ) ) {
52:                $this->currentLang = $this->Session->read( "userLang" );
53:            }
54:        }
55:
56:    }
57: ?>
```

Starting on line 9, we employ a number of view helpers. The cache helper helps us to cache the output view. The form helper is needed for the language selection drop-down list. The HTML helper is used for various HTML tags. And last, the RSS helper deals with the output needed for RSS requests.

We have also used a number of components. The Session component is used to store the language the user has selected and also the data generated from the language drop-down list. RequestHandler automatically handles user RSS web service requests by picking the correct layout and view. The RequestHandler will use the RSS layout under the layout folder. In the view, it will use the index.ctp in the /app/views/twittertwister/rss folder. Note, however, that beginning on line 40, we have used the alternative hack to get our /rss URL working. As we explained earlier, we want to have an RSS URL feed that ends with /rss. This method tricks the RequestHandler into thinking that the request has an rss extension.

Continuing our cache theme, on line 21, we are also caching the model using the persistModel variable. This will help to speed up the application. The code within the beforeFilter just caches the data from the language drop-down list. We have commented some code at the end of the method.

The beforeFilter finishes with a call to the __langChoice private method. If a user has previously selected a language via the top navigation drop-down list, this method makes sure that all the other controllers are aware of the chosen language. We assign the session userLang value to the global currentLang value.

Summary

In this chapter, we have successfully mashed two popular online applications. We have also covered a number of Cake topics, including caching. Its worth highlighting that *caching* is quite a loose term, with different meanings in different contexts, but the end result is always to save on some resource by not repeating the same action twice.

Additionally, we added i18n and l10n. Note that we will come back to this topic in Chapter 9, where we will add different languages to data that is stored in a database.

Since we have consumed two different web services, it seems only right that we also offer one as well. Adding the RSS web service feature was quite straightforward, except for our requirement that the URLs should end with /xml.

There are quite a number of features you could add to this application. The following are some suggestions:

- The view action could be split into years/months as one page, then days, then hours. Thus, you would only list up to 60 items in any one page. You could then have URLs like TwitterRequest/view/2008/08/03/14/00.

- You could further the cron background process and translate all archives into all languages gradually over a period of time. This would make the archive available via links instead of a drop-down list, so it would be search engine optimization–friendly.

- This is a big one: add the ability for users to write messages in their own language and post it to Twitter in the recipient's own language.

CHAPTER 7

■■■

Unit Testing and Web Testing

As you may have inferred, *unit testing* is the practice of testing individual units of code, to check that the application code works as expected. To help developers with their testing, CakePHP 1.2 includes integrated unit testing features. In this chapter, we'll show you how to use these features. We'll start by looking at a methodology that can provide some insight into the goals of unit testing.

Getting Programming Done

David Allen's productivity book, *Getting Things Done: The Art of Stress-Free Productivity* (Penguin, 2002), has attracted a lot of interest in the past few years. The methodology, abbreviated GTD, has become especially popular among the tech crowd. It's the primary subject of Merlin Mann's 43folders.com web site and many other blogs.

The GTD methodology might be summarized with these principles:

Define what done looks like: Visualize what your end goal is. Envision what it will take to get there. Allow your mind to brainstorm how to get yourself there.

Define what doing looks like: Decide what the next physical action is that will move you closer to your goal. What can you do to move closer to completion, based on your current priorities, resources, and context?

Unit testing helps you *define what done looks like* for your code. Unit testing gives you a specific goal to aim for as you code. It requires mental exertion up-front, as you decide specifically what your code should do, and then it "signals" to you in clear terms when you've reached your goal.

Over the life of your project, unit testing also provides one other GTD-like benefit: it helps you "get it all out of your head." The GTD methodology encourages you to write down all of your "open loops"—things, large and small, that you want to do or change—to free your mind. As you free your mind of trying to remember everything that's unfinished in your life, you'll have more mental energy for creativity.

Similarly, you may have noticed that when you refactor your code, especially in a dynamic, loosely typed language like PHP, you need to keep a lot in your head. You may wonder whether writing new code will break your existing code if you forget something. For example, have you ever had to rename a variable that was strewn throughout your code? Have you ever had to change all your <h2> elements to <h3> elements? If so, then you know the feeling. It's worrisome to refactor your code and wonder if it will still work afterwards. Unit testing provides an alert system and a security net to inform you when you've broken something and to catch you if you make a mistake. By freeing your mind from worrying whether you'll break something as you move forward, unit testing allows you to focus on the more creative aspects of your work.

Now that you have an idea about the benefits of unit testing, let's see how it works with a Cake application.

Our Case Study: An App Like In/Out

In April 2008, Jason Fried announced that his company, 37signals, uses a simple internal application called In/Out for communicating among team members (see http://www.37signals.com/svn/posts/976). In/Out shows what each team member is doing and what each has accomplished. Here, we'll build a similar application as our case study. We'll call it Accomplishments, and it will allow team members to create a log of tasks and projects they have accomplished. It won't have a real authentication system or security. For this example, we'll assume that it's being deployed on an intranet or otherwise secured.

Creating the Application

We'll start with a fresh installation of CakePHP 1.2, which includes integrated unit testing features, though we still need to install the unit testing framework. Figure 7-1 shows the green messages that indicate Cake is ready to use. We've set up caching, a MySQL database, and a custom security salt, so the development environment is ready to use.

For the application, we'll create an accomplishments table as shown in Listing 7-1.

Listing 7-1. *The accomplishments Table Schema*

```
1: CREATE TABLE `accomplishments` (
2:   `id` int(11) NOT NULL auto_increment,
3:   `team_member` varchar(30) NOT NULL,
4:   `description` varchar(140) NOT NULL,
5:   `created` datetime default NULL,
6:   `modified` datetime default NULL,
7:   PRIMARY KEY (`id`)
8: );
```

The table includes fields for a primary key, the team member's name (this table isn't normalized), a description of up to 140 characters (Twitter style), and created and modified dates.

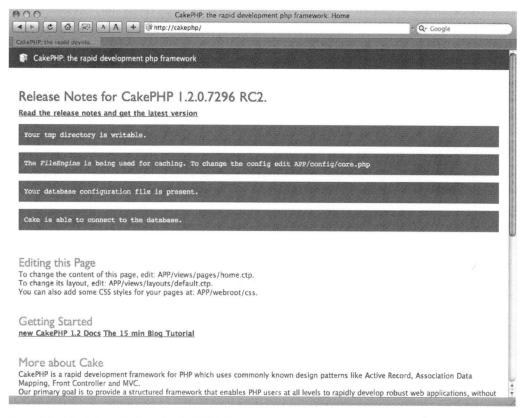

Figure 7-1. *A fresh installation of CakePHP 1.2*

A simple model will connect the application to our database. The Accomplishment model is shown in Listing 7-2.

Listing 7-2. *The Accomplishment Model (app/models/accomplishment.php)*

```
1: <?php
2:
3: class Accomplishment extends AppModel {
4:     var $name = 'Accomplishment';
5:
6: }
```

Next, we define an accomplishments controller, as shown in Listing 7-3.

Listing 7-3. *The AccomplishmentsController (app/controllers/accomplishment_controller.php)*

```
1: <?php
2:
3: App::import('Core', 'Sanitize');
4:
5: class AccomplishmentsController extends AppController {
6:     var $name = 'Accomplishments';
7:     var $helpers = array('Time');
8:
9:     function index() {
10:         if (empty($this->params['url']['team_member'])) {
11:             $this->redirect(array('action' => 'login'), 302);
12:         }
13:
14:         $this->set('my_accomplishments', $this->Accomplishment->find('all',
15:             array('conditions' => array("Accomplishment.team_member" => ➥
$this->Accomplishment->data['Accomplishment']['team_member']),
16:                 'order' => array('Accomplishment.created DESC'))));
17:
18:         $this->set('other_accomplishments', $this->Accomplishment->find('all',
19:             array('conditions' => array('not' => array( ➥
"Accomplishment.team_member" => $this-> ➥
Accomplishment->data['Accomplishment']['team_member'])),
20:                 'order' => array('Accomplishment.created DESC'))));
21:     }
22:
23:     function login() {
24:     }
25:
26:     function add() {
27:         if (!empty($this->data)) {
28:             $this->Accomplishment->save($this->data);
29:         }
30:         $this->redirect("/accomplishments/?team_member=" . ➥
$this->data['Accomplishment']['team_member'], 302);
31:     }
32: }
```

We load the Sanitize plugin in line 3 and the time helper in line 7, both of which will be used later. For simplicity, we'll store the user's name in the URL as a GET variable. In lines 10 through 12, we check that the GET variable team_member is not empty. If it is empty, the user is redirected to a login page.

With team_member in hand, the controller calls the model to get a list of accomplishments by the user (lines 14 through 16). The model is also called for a list of the other team members' accomplishments (lines 18 through 20).

Line 23 defines a login action. Line 26 defines an add action that will allow us to insert new accomplishments into our database.

The login view, shown in Listing 7-4, prompts for a username and submits it as a URL parameter (a GET variable). Both of our views use Cake's default layout and styling.

Listing 7-4. *The Login View (app/views/accomplishments/login.ctp)*

```
1: <?= $form->create('Accomplishment', array('type' => 'get', ➥
'action' => 'index')) ?>
2:
3:    <?= $form->input('team_member', array('label' => 'Please enter your name')) ?>
4:
5:    <?= $form->submit('Login') ?>
6:
7: </form>
```

In Listing 7-5, we define a view for our index page. This is what the user will see after logging in.

Listing 7-5. *The Main View (app/views/accomplishments/index.ctp)*

```
1: <h2>Team Accomplishments</h2>
2: <p>What have you done?</p>
3: <?= $form->create('Accomplishment') ?>
4: <?= $form->input('description') ?>
5: <?= $form->hidden('team_member', array('value' => ➥
$this->params['url']['team_member'])) ?>
6: <?= $form->submit('Post Accomplishment') ?>
7: </form>
8:
9: <h2>My Accomplishments</h2>
10:    <?php foreach($my_accomplishments as $accomplishment) : ?>
11:    <p><strong><?= Sanitize::html($accomplishment['Accomplishment'] ➥
['description']) ?></strong></p>
12:    <p><small><?= $time->niceShort($accomplishment['Accomplishment'] ➥
['created']) ?></small></p>
13:    <br/>
14:    <?php endforeach; ?>
15:
16: <h2>Others' Accomplishments</h2>
17:    <?php foreach($other_accomplishments as $accomplishment) : ?>
18:    <p><em><?= Sanitize::html($accomplishment['Accomplishment'] ➥
['team_member']) ?></em>: <strong><?= Sanitize::html( ➥
$accomplishment['Accomplishment'] ['description']) ➥
?></strong></p>
19:    <p><small><?= $time->niceShort($accomplishment['Accomplishment'] ➥
['created']) ?></small></p>
20:    <br/>
21:    <?php endforeach; ?>
```

In lines 3 through 7, we provide a form for entering new accomplishments. We then display a list of accomplishments by the user, in lines 9 through 14, and by the user's team members, in lines 16 through 21. You'll notice we're using the `Sanitize::html` method (lines 11 and 18) to prevent cross-site scripting (XSS) attacks. This is a good practice whenever you're echoing previously entered text back to the user.

We now have a working, admittedly simplistic, application. We can log in (see Figure 7-2) and begin using our application (see Figure 7-3).

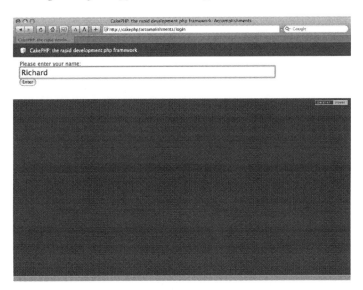

Figure 7-2. *Logging in to our new Accomplishments application*

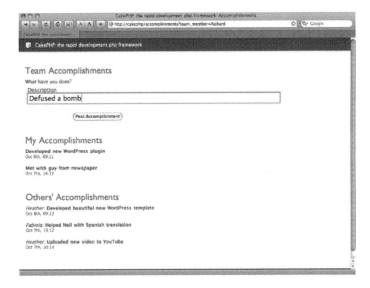

Figure 7-3. *Posting a completed accomplishment to our application*

EDITING YOUR HOSTS FILE

When working on a development machine, we find it convenient to create a hosts entry, or "mock domain," for each web site we're developing. This allows us to access the web site at a convenient address like http://cakephp/. You'll see this mock address used throughout this chapter.

You can create a similar mock domain by editing your hosts file, as follows:

- On Linux or a Mac, find and open the file /etc/hosts. On Windows XP, open the file C:\WINDOWS\system32\drivers\etc\hosts.

- At the bottom of the file, add a new entry, with the IP address 127.0.0.1 on the left, and the hostname cakephp (or whatever hostname you want) on the right, separated by space.

Assuming you already have your web server installed and running on your local machine, you should now be able to access your web site in your browser at the address http://cakephp/.

If you have multiple development web sites hosted on your local machine, you'll need to create a VirtualHost entry for each one in your Apache configuration file.

The rest of this chapter will assume you've created a host entry like our http://cakephp/ entry.

Adding Username Validation

With our simple application now running, let's suppose we want to add validation code to ensure that only alphabetic letters are acceptable for the username. We don't want to allow any numbers, symbols, or spaces in usernames. Listing 7-6 shows the validation code added to our Accomplishment model.

Listing 7-6. *Adding Username Validation to the Model (in app/models/accomplishment.php)*

```
 1: <?php
 2:
 3: class Accomplishment extends AppModel {
 4:     var $name = 'Accomplishment';
 5:
 6:     var $validate = array(
 7:         'team_member' => array(
 8:             'rule' => array('validUsername'),
 9:             'message' => "Invalid Username!"
10:         ),
11:     );
12:
13:     function validUsername($data) {
14:         return (preg_match('/^[A-Za-z]+$/', $data['team_member']));
15:     }
16: }
```

We could use Cake's built-in validation rules, but for the sake of discussion, we define our own custom method for validating the team_member field, in lines 6 through 11. This custom method, validUsername(), is defined in lines 13 through 15. It uses a regular expression to ensure that only uppercase and lowercase letters are allowed. In the real world, this method might connect to a centralized company directory web service to look up and validate the username.

Next, we'll modify our controller to do the validating, as shown in Listing 7-7 (additions shown in bold).

Listing 7-7. *The AccomplishmentsController Updated to Validate the team_member Name (app/controllers/accomplishment_controller.php)*

```
 1: <?php
 2:
 3: App::import('Core', 'Sanitize');
 4:
 5: class AccomplishmentsController extends AppController {
 6:     var $name = 'Accomplishments';
 7:     var $helpers = array('Time');
 8:
 9:     function index() {
10:         if (empty($this->params['url']['team_member'])) {
11:             $this->redirect(array('action' => 'login'), 302);
12:         }
13:
14:         $this->Accomplishment->set(array('Accomplishment' =>
array('team_member' => $this->params['url']['team_member'])));
15:
16:         if (!$this->Accomplishment->validates()) {
17:             $this->Session->setFlash('Invalid username: ' . Sanitize::html(
$this->Accomplishment->data['Accomplishment']['team_member']));
18:             $this->redirect(array('action' => 'login'), 302);
19:         }
20:
21:         $this->set('my_accomplishments', $this->Accomplishment->find('all',
22:             array('conditions' => array("Accomplishment.team_member" =>
$this->Accomplishment->data['Accomplishment']['team_member']),
23:                 'order' => array('Accomplishment.created DESC'))));
24:
25:         $this->set('other_accomplishments', $this->Accomplishment->find('all',
26:             array('conditions' => array('not' => array(
"Accomplishment.team_member" =>
$this->Accomplishment->data['Accomplishment']['team_member'])),
27:                 'order' => array('Accomplishment.created DESC'))));
28:     }
29:
30:     function login() {
31:     }
32:
33:     function add() {
34:         if (!empty($this->data)) {
35:             $this->Accomplishment->save($this->data);
36:         }
```

```
37:        $this->redirect("/accomplishments/?team_member=" . ↵
$this->data['Accomplishment']['team_member'], 302);
38:    }
39: }
```

In line 14, we load the `team_member` variable into the model. In line 16, we make sure the model validates. If the model does not validate, we know it must be an invalid username (because that's the only thing we've changed), so we set an error message and redirect to the login page (lines 17 and 18). We are performing the validation explicitly in the controller, as opposed to implicitly when the model attempts to save to the database, because we need a valid username before we can display accomplishments.

After adding username validation code, what if we discover that our code is too strict? What if we want to allow usernames with numeric digits? And, as a further complication, what if we don't want numeric digits at the beginning of the username? Suppose we want to accept a username like `jared11114`, but not `14031brittany`. This could quickly become complicated as we try to create an algorithm that will accept the usernames we want to accept and reject the usernames we want to reject. This is where unit testing comes in.

Using Cake's Unit Testing Framework

Begin by visiting `http://cakephp/test.php`, the location of Cake's testing interface. You should see the error message shown in Figure 7-4, indicating that SimpleTest is not yet installed.

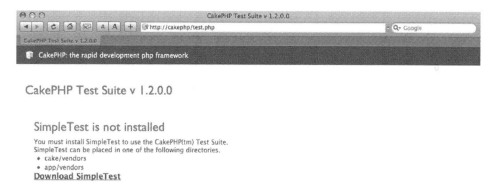

Figure 7-4. *You'll see this message if Cake's test interface, SimpleTest, is not yet installed.*

Installing SimpleTest

SimpleTest is the third-party unit testing library (created by Marcus Baker, a developer in London) that powers Cake's unit testing module. SimpleTest can be obtained from http://www.simpletest.org. As shown in Figure 7-5, the SimpleTest web site also offers a manual, a mailing list, and links to several articles and tutorials.

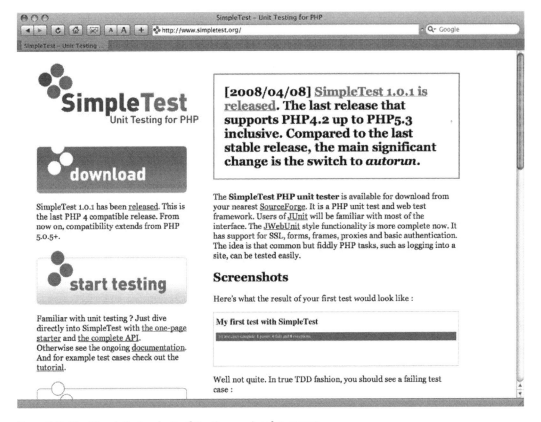

Figure 7-5. *The SimpleTest web site (http://www.simpletest.org)*

After downloading and uncompressing SimpleTest, installation is simple. Just copy the simpletest folder to either your vendors folder or your app/vendors folder, depending on whether you want the SimpleTest library to be available to all your applications or to only this application. In our development environment, this decision will make little difference. We'll flip a coin and copy simpletest to the vendors folder.

You'll also need to make sure the debug variable in app/config/core.php is greater than 0. Now when you revisit http://cakephp/test.php, you'll see a list of test groups and test cases, as shown in Figure 7-6. This means that SimpleTest has been successfully installed.

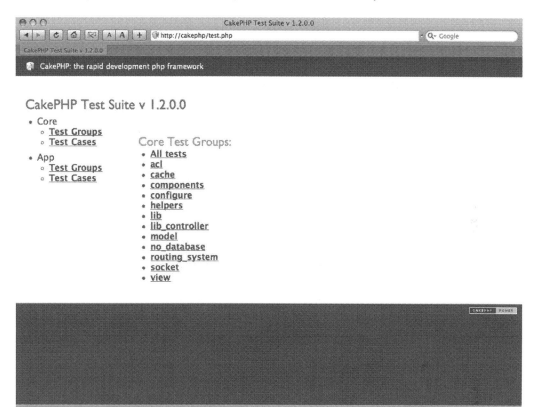

Figure 7-6. *SimpleTest is now successfully installed.*

You'll notice a list of several test groups and a longer list of test cases. These are the tests that come with every installation of Cake. They are designed to ensure the correct operation of the core Cake code. If you click the acl group, you may get a screen like the one shown in Figure 7-7, showing that 146 tests passed and 0 tests failed. In general terms, this means that Cake's ACL code is working correctly, according to the 146 criteria the Cake developers used to judge its correctness. This may not mean a lot to you now, but let's give the Cake developers a virtual pat on the back for creating code that passes their own tests, and we'll move along to create tests for our own code.

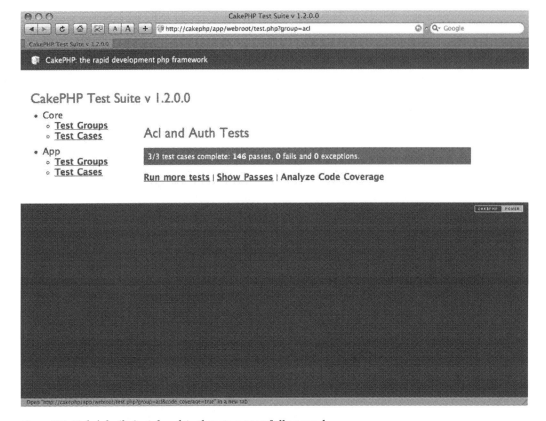

Figure 7-7. *Cake's built-in Acl and Auth tests successfully passed.*

Creating Your Own Unit Tests

The problem at hand is that we want to ensure that certain usernames are allowed in our application and certain usernames are not allowed. For example, adam, MATT, Sean, and BH44 are allowed; 97devin and Stukdog! are not. We want to ensure, in a systematic way, that our code accepts the good usernames and rejects the bad ones. To ensure this, we'll create unit tests.

Creating the Test File

We'll create a new test file at app/tests/cases/models/accomplishment.test.php. Every test file should end with the double extension .test.php, not just .php. The file name before the extension can be whatever you want. For convenience and as a matter of convention, we'll use the same name as our model. Listing 7-8 shows the accomplishment.test.php file.

Listing 7-8. *Our Test Module (app/tests/cases/models/accomplishment.test.php)*

```
 1: <?php
 2:
 3: App::import('Model', 'Accomplishment');
 4:
 5: class AccomplishmentTest extends Accomplishment {
 6:     var $name = 'AccomplishmentTest';
 7:     var $useDbConfig = 'test';
 8: }
 9:
10: class AccomplishmentTestCase extends CakeTestCase {
11:     var $fixtures = array( 'app.accomplishment_test' );
12:
13:     function testValidUsername() {
14:         $this->AccomplishmentTest =& new AccomplishmentTest();
15:
16:         $this->assertTrue($this->AccomplishmentTest->validUsername( ➥
array('team_member' => 'adam')));
17:         $this->assertTrue($this->AccomplishmentTest->validUsername( ➥
array('team_member' => 'MATT')));
18:         $this->assertTrue($this->AccomplishmentTest->validUsername( ➥
array('team_member' => 'Sean')));
19:         $this->assertTrue($this->AccomplishmentTest->validUsername( ➥
array('team_member' => 'BH44')));
20:         $this->assertFalse($this->AccomplishmentTest->validUsername( ➥
array('team_member' => '97devin')));
21:         $this->assertFalse($this->AccomplishmentTest->validUsername( ➥
array('team_member' => 'stukdog!')));
22:     }
23: }
```

In accomplishment.test.php, we define a new class called AccomplishmentTest, which extends the Accomplishment model class (lines 5 through 8). Similarly, your test classes should follow the same naming convention of <model class name>Test (although this is not required) and should extend your model's class.

Notice that we need to explicitly import our model (line 3). The Cake testing module doesn't make the automagic assumptions that Cake does elsewhere, to avoid muddying the testing environment. The test class also defines a new database configuration (line 7).

Next, we define a class called AccomplishmentTestCase, which extends CakeTestCase (line 10). Your test classes should follow the same naming pattern and extend CakeTestCase.

In the AccomplishmentTestCase class, we define a method called testValidUsername. Each method in a test case class should begin with test (as in line 13). The method testValidUsername begins by instantiating an object of the class AccomplishmentTest (line 14). Then six assertions are performed against the AccomplishmentTest object (lines 16 through 21). These assertions ensure that our validUsername method is behaving as expected. For example, if we pass in adam, MATT, Sean, or BH44, we expect validUsername to return true, so we use the assertTrue method to ensure it (lines 16 through 19). On the other hand, if we pass in 97devin or Stukdog!, we expect validUsername to return false, so we use the assertFalse method to ensure it (lines 20 and 21).

Creating a Test Fixture

To test a data model, as we are doing here, we need to create a test fixture. A fixture is a set of data used for testing purposes. It's called a *fixture* because it remains fixed across all tests, like the control group in a scientific experiment. Your fixture should use test data that approximates the breadth and variedness of your real data.

Test fixtures are created using PHP code that looks like SQL code. You define a multidimensional array to represent the database fields, and another array to represent the database records. The advantage of defining test data in PHP code, as opposed to in your database, is that it is less likely to be changed arbitrarily from the outside. It can also be versioned in a code-versioning system such as Subversion. Listing 7-9 shows a hypothetical test fixture, which would go in app/tests/fixtures/accomplishment_test_fixture.php, but we're not going to use this one in our example.

Listing 7-9. *A Hypothetical Test Fixture*

```
 1: <?php
 2:
 3: class AccomplishmentTestFixture extends CakeTestFixture {
 4:     var $name = 'AccomplishmentTest';
 5:
 6:     var $fields = array(
 7:         'id' => array('type' => 'integer', 'key' => 'primary'),
 8:         'team_member' => array('type' => 'string', 'length' => 30, 'null' ➥
=> 'false'),
 9:         'description' => array('type' => 'string', 'length' => 140, 'null' ➥
=> 'false'),
10:         'created' => 'datetime',
11:         'modified' => 'datetime'
12:         );
13:
14:     var $records = array(
15:         array('id' => 1, 'team_member' => 'Richard', 'description' => ➥
 'Wrote new unit tests for application.', 'created' => ➥
'2008-09-19 10:00:00', 'modified' => '2008-09-19 10:00:00'),
16:         array('id' => 2, 'team_member' => 'Steve', 'description' => ➥
'Prosecuted criminals.', 'created' => '2008-09-19 11:00:00', ➥
'modified' => '2008-09-19 11:00:00'),
17:         array('id' => 3, 'team_member' => 'David', 'description' => ➥
'Saved lives.', 'created' => '2008-09-19 12:00:00', 'modified' => ➥
'2008-09-19 12:00:00')
18:         );
19: }
```

Our particular unit tests don't need any data. We're simply testing the functionality of our validation method. So let's just punt and use a simpler test fixture, as shown in Listing 7-10.

Listing 7-10. *The Simpler Fixture Definition for This Example (app/tests/fixtures/accomplishment_test_fixture.php)*

```
1: <?php
2:
3: class AccomplishmentTestFixture extends CakeTestFixture {
4:     var $name = 'AccomplishmentTest';
5:     var $import = 'Accomplishment';
6:
7: }
```

Instead of defining data using PHP code, we'll simply indicate that we want the test fixture to import data from our production database table, Accomplishment (line 5), which we won't use anyway.

The test fixture uses the $test database connection defined in app/config/database.php if it is available. If not, it uses your production database connection, prepending the test tables with test_ to avoid overwriting your existing tables.

Running the Tests

Now that the tests are written and our fixture is set up, we can run our unit tests. Visit http://cakephp/test.php and then click Test Cases. You should see a test case entitled models / Accomplishment, as shown in Figure 7-8.

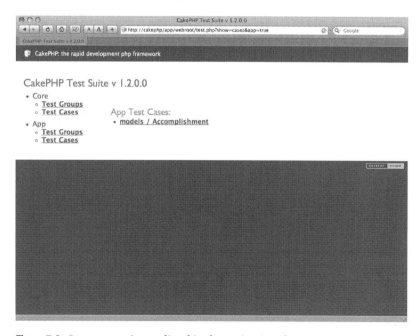

Figure 7-8. *Our test case is now listed in the testing interface.*

Now, the moment of truth! Click the models / Accomplishment link to see how our tests do. Figure 7-9 shows the result.

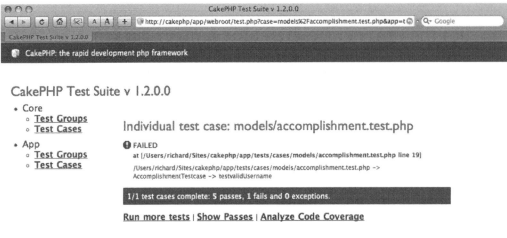

Figure 7-9. *Running our first test case*

You will see a lot of red! We failed our test, or more specifically, we failed one of the six tests, and it says the failure was in line 19 of `accomplishment.test.php`. Looking back at the code (Listing 7-8), we're not surprised that the test for the username BH44 failed, because we haven't yet coded `validUsername` to accept numeric digits.

Go to `app/models/accomplishment.php` and change the regular expression in line 14 from `/^[A-Za-z]+$/` to `/^[A-Za-z0-9]+$/` to allow digits in the username. Listing 7-11 shows this change.

Listing 7-11. *Modified Regular Expression to Accept Numbers in the Username (in app/models/ accomplishment.php)*

```
1: <?php
2:
3: class Accomplishment extends AppModel {
4:     var $name = 'Accomplishment';
5:
```

```
 6:    var $validate = array(
 7:       'team_member' => array(
 8:          'rule' => array('validUsername'),
 9:          'message' => "Invalid Username!"
10:       ),
11:    );
12:
13:    function validUsername($data) {
14:       return (preg_match('/^[A-Za-z0-9]+$/', $data['team_member']));
15:    }
16: }
```

With our new validUsername method, let's rerun our tests and see what we get. Refresh your browser.

As shown in Figure 7-10, once more, we see a lot of red, meaning our tests have failed again. But notice the failure is on a different line—line 20 instead of line 19. Our test for BH44 passed, but 97devin did not. You may have expected this, since our new regular expression wasn't sophisticated enough to reject usernames that begin with numeric digits, and our test case 97devin slipped through.

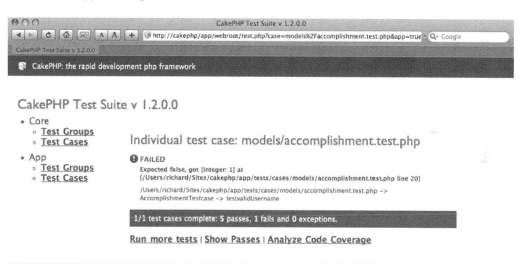

Figure 7-10. *Rerunning our test case to see if we've made progress*

Let's tweak our validUsername() method one more time and see if we can get it to behave as expected. We'll change the regular expression from /^[A-Za-z0-9]+$/ to /^[A-Za-z][A-Za-z0-9]+$/, as shown in Listing 7-12. This requires the first character of the username to be a letter, while any subsequent character can be a letter or a number. This also implies that our username must be at least two characters long, which is fine.

Listing 7-12. *Modified Regular Expression to Reject Usernames That Begin with a Number (in apps/models/accomplishment.php)*

```
 1: <?php
 2:
 3: class Accomplishment extends AppModel {
 4:     var $name = 'Accomplishment';
 5:
 6:     var $validate = array(
 7:         'team_member' => array(
 8:             'rule' => array('validUsername'),
 9:             'message' => "Invalid Username!"
10:         ),
11:     );
12:
13:     function validUsername($data) {
14:         return (preg_match('/^[A-Za-z][A-Za-z0-9]+$/', $data['team_member']));
15:     }
16: }
```

Refresh your browser again. Good news! Now all of the tests pass. We're rewarded with a green bar stating "6 passes, 0 fails and 0 exceptions," as shown in Figure 7-11.

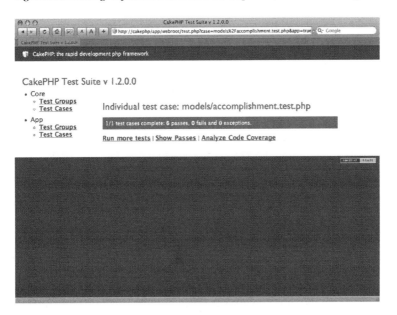

Figure 7-11. *Our tests now pass.*

Unit testing gives us confidence that our `validUsername` method now functions exactly as it should.

Using Assert Methods

Our unit tests used only two of about a dozen available `assert*` methods. Table 7-1 lists the `assert*` methods that you can use in your unit testing.

Table 7-1. *SimpleTest Assert Methods*

Method	Description
`assertClone( &$x, &$y [, $message = '%s'], $x, $y )`	Asserts that $x and $y should be clones of each other, meaning they are identical but not the same object
`assertEqual( $x, $y [, $message = '%s'] )`	Asserts that $x should be equal to $y
`assertFalse( $x [, $message = '%s'] )`	Asserts that $x should be false
`assertIdentical( $x, $y [, $message = '%s'] )`	Asserts that $x and $y should be identical, meaning they have the same value and are of the same type
`assertIsA( $object, $class [, $message = '%s'] )`	Asserts that $object should be of class $class
`assertNoPattern( $regex, $subject [, $message = '%s'] )`	Asserts that no portion of $subject should match the regular expression $regex
`assertNotA( $object, $class [, $message = '%s'] )`	Asserts that $object should not be of the class $class
`assertNotEqual( $x, $y [, $message = '%s'] )`	Asserts that $x should not be equal to $y
`assertNotIdentical( $x, $y [, $message = '%s'] )`	Asserts that $x should not be identical to $y, meaning it should either have a different value and/or be of a different type
`assertNotNull( $x [, $message = '%s'] )`	Asserts that $x should not be null
`assertNull( $x [, $message = '%s'] )`	Asserts that $x should be null
`assertOutsideMargin( $x, $y, $margin [, $message = '%s'] )`	Asserts that $x and $y should differ by more than $margin
`assertPattern($regex, $subject [, $message = '%s'] )`	Asserts that $subject should match the regular expression $regex
`assertReference( &$x, &$y [, $message = '%s'], $x, $y )`	Asserts that $x and $y should both refer to (be pointers to) the same object
`assertTrue( $x [, $message = false] )`	Asserts that $x should be true
`assertWithinMargin( $x, $y, $margin [, $message = '%s'] )`	Asserts that $x and $y should be within $margin of each other

Each assert method allows you to define an optional $message to be displayed when the assertion fails. You can optionally use the placeholder %s in your message to display the default error details.

Testing the Entire MVC System

The unit tests we wrote in the preceding example were for testing our model. But unit tests can also be written for testing controllers, views, plugins, and components.

The process for testing controllers, plugins, and components is similar to the process of testing models. Testing views, on the other hand, is a different beast, and we'll cover that in the next section.

Web Testing

The SimpleTest library that powers Cake's testing framework has a very cool web testing feature. It can simulate a user's navigation through a web site, allowing you to test your views and make sure your web site is working properly "from the outside." You might also call this a form of integration testing, since it can test the fitness and accuracy of the entire site, not just the individual units.

Creating Web Tests

Let's add a few web tests to our application, in app/tests/cases/models/accomplishment.test. php, as shown in Listing 7-13.

Listing 7-13. *The Class AccomplishmentWebTestCase (in app/tests/cases/models/accomplishment. test.php)*

```
24:
25: class AccomplishmentWebTestCase extends CakeWebTestCase {
26:     function testLoginGoodUsername() {
27:         $this->get('http://cakephp/accomplishments/');
28:         $this->setField('team_member', 'Richard');
29:         $this->click('Login');
30:         $this->assertText('Team Accomplishments');
31:         $this->assertText('My Accomplishments');
32:         $this->assertText("Others' Accomplishments");
33:     }
34:     function testLoginBadUsername() {
35:         $this->get('http://cakephp/accomplishments/');
36:         $this->setField('team_member', '97devin');
37:         $this->click('Login');
38:         $this->assertText('Invalid username');
39:     }
40: }
```

We define a class AccomplishmentWebTestCase, which extends CakeWebTestCase. The class contains two methods: testLoginGoodUsername will ensure that when we enter a valid username, we can log in, and testLoginBadUsername() will ensure that when we enter an invalid username, we are denied access.

You can probably guess what the code in Listing 7-13 does. In testLoginGoodUsername, we simulate a user going to the web site http://cakephp/accomplishments/, entering Richard into the team_member field, and clicking the Login button. We then assert that the resulting page contains three strings of text: Team Accomplishments, My Accomplishments, and Others' Accomplishments. The test could be more complex, but the presence of these three strings is likely to be a good indicator of whether the login was successful.

In testLoginBadUsername, we repeat the same simulation, this time entering the username 97devin, which we know to be unacceptable. We then test that the resulting page contains the text Invalid username, which we expect when the user is unable to log in.

Let's run our tests again, by visiting the test page http://cakephp/test.php, to see the results. As shown in Figure 7-12, we find that ten tests passed successfully, which include our six unit tests plus the four additional web tests we've just created.

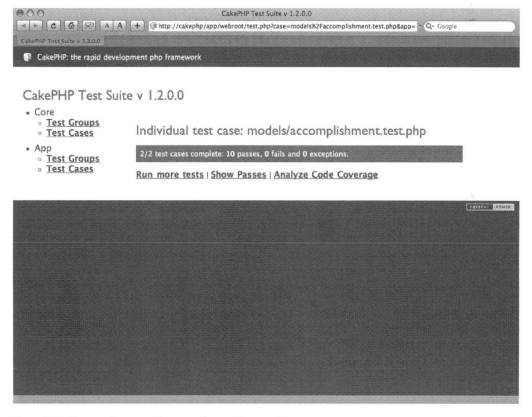

Figure 7-12. *Test results page after running our four web tests*

Web tests can be a powerful tool for ensuring that your web application is working correctly, in a holistic sense. With web tests, you can imitate the following user actions:

- Clicking links, clicking images, and submitting forms
- Clicking the back and forward buttons, and refreshing the page
- Sending and checking headers
- Sending, ignoring, and checking cookies
- Logging in using HTTP authentication
- Using a proxy

For a full list of available web testing methods, visit http://www.simpletest.org/api/ SimpleTest/WebTester/WebTestCase.html.

Web Testing Any Application

One very cool aspect of the web testing framework, which may already be apparent to you, is that you can test any feature of any web site, not just Cake web sites or web sites you own. For example, imagine setting up tests to ensure that your legacy corporate web site is up and running, that the password protection is working, and that private areas of your site are not publicly accessible. You could set up a cron job to run the tests regularly and e-mail you when there are abnormalities.

Listing 7-14 shows a hypothetical test for ensuring that the Wikipedia article on CakePHP mentions unit testing. As of this writing, unit testing is mentioned as a feature of CakePHP in the Wikipedia article. If this reference were ever removed, the following test would fail.

Listing 7-14. *A Hypothetical Test Case for Testing an External Web Site*

```
40:    function testWikipediaArticle() {
41:        $this->addHeader("User-Agent: CakePHP/SimpleTest");
42:        $this->get('http://en.wikipedia.org/wiki/Cakephp');
43:        $this->assertText('Unit testing');
44:    }
```

▓**Caution** If you use Cake's web testing features to test web sites that you don't own, you'll want to make sure you comply with their terms of usage.

Test-Driven Development

Test-driven development is a form of agile development that requires unit tests to be written before writing application code. Writing the unit tests before the actual code requires developers to think carefully about what the application should do. It also requires thinking about development with an eye to modularity; each unit should do something distinct and uncoupled from other units. In fact, someone else on your team could be the one to write the unit tests, while you write the code, or vice versa. The ensuing communication and coordination would be healthy.

Your lines of test code could easily outnumber your application code lines if you were to test every aspect of your application. This, of course, is not practical, nor is it smart business practice. You might consider writing tests only for the most important units of your code. What code might potentially cause the most damage if it were left to chance? Write unit tests for that code first. Also, as bugs are reported and fixed, write unit tests that ensure those bugs will not resurface in the future. This sort of testing is called *regression testing*, because it prevents your code from regressing to a prior, bug-laden state.

Imagine if your home appliances were wired directly into the electrical system without using plugs and sockets. Moving a lamp to a new room would be a huge pain. You would need to cut the wire and resplice it. It's much more convenient to use plugs and sockets. This also allows a separation of concerns; that is, if a lamp stops working, you can plug it into a different socket and see if it's the lamp or the socket that failed. Likewise, when your code is modular and decoupled, you can easily move it, use it elsewhere, and test it. Unit testing encourages this sort of modularity.

Summary

In this chapter, we have accomplished the following:

- Created a simple web application like the 37signals In/Out application

- Installed the SimpleTest unit testing framework

- Demonstrated how to run the built-in unit tests for Cake

- Created custom unit tests

- Modified the application code to pass unit tests

- Created web tests and run them against a web application

- Demonstrated how web tests can be used to test external web sites

- Explained when and why you should do unit testing

Unit testing can be a powerful practice for ensuring that your application code works as you expect. It can catch errors before you release new code, and save you time and energy by freeing your mind of concern. Cheers to your newfound freedom!

CHAPTER 8

■ ■ ■

A Cake Control Panel

Let us first say that there is no such feature as a Cake Control Panel in CakePHP, which is why we are creating one in this chapter.

Once you have developed several web sites, you will start to spot common functions that clients ask for time and again. Here are just some of the features clients typically request:

- Ability to update the content themselves

- Ability to have different categories of users, and allow only certain users to use particular features of the site; for example, allow only registered users to access special promotions

- Ability to change the web site configuration themselves

- Ability to view application statistics, such as number of users, last login, and so on

If your clients haven't asked for these functions yet, you can always turn them off temporarily, or maybe increase your income by selling them these extra cool features!

Developing a control panel for yourself makes a lot of sense. The same control panel can be used for different sites. You could say it's another form of the DRY principle.

Security is a basic functionality to have in any web site and also one of the most complex. If you're going to add a back-end administration area, or a control panel as we are calling it, this will be one of the functions that will be developed first.

In this chapter, we're just going to start the development of the control panel by writing a web-based front end that will allow a user to manage user security. Feel free to use the code in this chapter as a base for your own projects. We'll use several different Cake features, including the authentication (Auth) and access control list (Acl) components, and the Acl behavior, which also uses the Tree behavior.

Application Requirements

The security management function we are building in the control panel will have the following functions:

- Ability to add, edit, delete, and view user

- Ability to add, edit, delete, and view different user groups, such as administrators and ordinary users

- Ability to deny or allow a user or group access to controller actions

The Authentication and ACL Components

We'll start by talking a little about both the Auth and Acl components, and then we'll show you how we have combined them. We will warn you that although Cake's authentication component is easy to use, the access control list component is not that straightforward. However, using it is still much easier than writing the access-control code from scratch.

The Authentication Component

The reason for the Auth component is simple. It controls the login process and further controls access to controller actions. You can allow or deny access to certain actions using the component's allow and deny methods, but not on a per-user basis.

What the Auth component doesn't do is provide more granular access control between any one user and controller actions. This is where Cake's Acl component comes in.

To get started with the Auth component, you will first need a users table. The one for this chapter's application is shown in Listing 8-1.

Listing 8-1. *The users Table Schema*

```
CREATE TABLE `users` (
  `id` int(11) NOT NULL auto_increment,
  `username` varchar(255) NOT NULL,
  `password` varchar(255) NOT NULL,
  `group_id` int(11) NOT NULL,
  PRIMARY KEY (`id`)
)
```

The first three fields—id, username, and password—are mandatory for the Auth component. The password field is a hashed field. We have included the group_id field because we'll be adding user groups as well, so we can categorize users into groups.

The Access Control List Component

Cake's Acl component is a generic way to control the access rights between one entity and another entity. An entity can represent almost anything you want, but usually it will be users, user groups, and controller actions. For example, you can allow every developer access to a controller action, except for the new junior developer who just joined the team.

The security permissions between entities can be stored either in a text file in app/config/acl.ini.php or in a database. Here, we're just going to cover database storage, so we need to create the tables to store the permissions.

One way to create the database tables required by the Acl component is to use the cake command to do this automatically. To take this approach, in your command-line environment, go to your app folder and run the following command:

```
$   cake acl initdb
```

This will create three database tables:

- acos: This table holds the access control objects, which are the entities to be controlled, such as actions.

- aros: This table stores the access request objects, which are the entities that request access, such as users or groups.

- aros_acos: This is the link table between the acos and aros tables. An acos object (for example, a controller action) can be accessed by many aros objects (such as users). Conversely, an aros object (such as a user) can have access to many acos objects (such as controller actions).

If you want to create the tables manually, you can do that using the SQL statements in Listings 8-2, 8-3, and 8-4.

Listing 8-2. *The acos Acl Table Schema*

```
CREATE TABLE `acos` (
  `id` int(10) NOT NULL auto_increment,
  `parent_id` int(10) default NULL,
  `model` varchar(255) default NULL,
  `foreign_key` int(10) default NULL,
  `alias` varchar(255) default NULL,
  `lft` int(10) default NULL,
  `rght` int(10) default NULL,
  PRIMARY KEY (`id`)
)
```

Listing 8-3. *The aros Table Schema*

```
CREATE TABLE `aros` (
  `id` int(10) NOT NULL auto_increment,
  `parent_id` int(10) default NULL,
  `model` varchar(255) default NULL,
  `foreign_key` int(10) default NULL,
  `alias` varchar(255) default NULL,
  `lft` int(10) default NULL,
  `rght` int(10) default NULL,
  PRIMARY KEY (`id`)
)
```

Listing 8-4. *The aros_acos Table Schema*

```
CREATE TABLE `aros_acos` (
  `id` int(10) NOT NULL auto_increment,
  `aro_id` int(10) NOT NULL,
  `aco_id` int(10) NOT NULL,
  `_create` varchar(2) NOT NULL default '0',
  `_read` varchar(2) NOT NULL default '0',
  `_update` varchar(2) NOT NULL default '0',
  `_delete` varchar(2) NOT NULL default '0',
  PRIMARY KEY (`id`)
)
```

The acos and aros records are stored using Cake's own Tree behavior, which uses a binary tree data structure to store hierarchical data. One node (a record in our case) can have two children (records) below it, sometimes called the *left branch* and *right branch*. In turn, any one record can have a parent. Tables 8-1, 8-2, and 8-3 describe the important fields in each of these tables.

Table 8-1. *The acos Table Columns*

Column	Description
parent_id	ID of the parent acos record
model	Model name of the entity
foreign_key	Foreign key to the model record ID
alias	Unique name to identify the record
lft	ID of the left branch of the record
rght	ID of the right branch of the record

Table 8-2. *The aros Table Columns*

Column	Description
parent_id	ID of the parent aros record
model	Model name of the entity, which is normally User or Group
foreign_key	Foreign key to the model record ID, which is normally the ID of the user or group record
alias	Unique name to identify the record
lft	ID of the left branch of the record
rght	ID of the right branch of the record

Table 8-3. *The aros_acos Table Columns*

Column	Description
aro_id	Foreign key to the aros record ID
aco_id	Foreign key to the acos record ID
_create	Controls access to the add action—either 1 or 0
_read	Controls access to the index or view action—either 1 or 0
_update	Controls access to the edit action—either 1 or 0
_delete	Controls access to the remove action—either 1 or 0

Component Setup

To start using the Auth and Acl components, we need to declare their use. This is done in the global AppController file, app/app_controller.php, which is shown in Listing 8-5.

Listing 8-5. *Auth and Acl Components in the AppController Class (app/app_controller.php)*

```
1:    class AppController extends Controller {
2:
3:        var $pageTitle = 'Chapter 8 - The Cake Control Panel';
4:
5:        var $components = array( 'Auth', 'Acl' );
6:
7:        function beforeFilter() {
8:
9:            $this->Auth->authorize = 'actions';
10:
11:           $this->Auth->authError = '  You do not have permission to access
12:                                       the page you just selected.';
13:
14:           $this->Auth->loginRedirect = array( 'controller' => ➡
'ControlPanel',
15:                                               'action' => 'index' );
16:       }
17:
18:   }
```

We include the two components on line 5. There is also a beforeFilter, which is called before any other action. In it, we specify some Auth settings. The authorize parameter on line 9 is set to actions. This parameter controls how a user is authorized. Setting it to actions means we want the Acl component to authenticate the user for us automatically based on the entries in the users table. The authorize parameter can also be set to controller, crud, array, or object, as shown in Table 8-4.

Table 8-4. *Settings for the authorize Parameter in the Auth Component*

Values	Description
controller	Defines an isAuthorized action in your controller; the user is authenticated depending on whether the function returns true or false
actions	Uses the Acl's check method to authenticate users
crud	Also uses the Acl's check method to authenticate users
array('model'=> 'name')	Defines an isAuthorize (note no d at the end) action in another model
object	Uses the isAuthorized method in your own object to authenticate the user

The authError parameter on line 11 of Listing 8-5 is what gets displayed when a user does not have permission to view a controller action. The loginRedirect parameter on line 14 specifies the URL to redirect the user to once a user has logged in.

Control Panel Application Controllers

We will be using five different controllers in our application, as shown in Table 8-5.

Table 8-5. *The Controllers Used in Our Control Panel Application*

Controller	Description
ActionsController	Manages which of our controller actions will be security-managed
GroupsController	Manages user groups
UsersController	Manages users
ControlPanelController	Base controller for our application
WidgetsController	Sample controller to demonstrate the access control list security

The first three controllers are essential for the working of the application; the last two are mainly used to demonstrate our application. Now we'll look at each controller, starting with the base control panel controller.

The Control Panel Controller

The ControlPanelController, shown in Listing 8-6, is the base class for the application. It contains the first public page of the application.

Listing 8-6. *Control Panel Controller (app/controllers/control_panel_controller.php)*

```
1:     <?php
2:
3:     class ControlPanelController extends AppController {
4:
5:     var $name = 'ControlPanel';
6:     var $helpers = array('Html', 'Form');
7:
8:     var $uses = array( 'User' );
9:
10:        function beforeFilter() {
11:
12:            // Public access actions
13:            $this->Auth->allow( 'welcome' );
14:        }
15:
16:        // Public welcome page of control panel
17:        function welcome() {
18:
19:            // Check if the temporary user exists
20:            $tmpUser = $this->User->findByUsername( 'temp' );
21:
22:            if ( empty( $tmpUser ) ) {
23:
24:                $this->User->create();
25:                $this->User->save( array(    'username' => 'temp',
26:                                             'password' => ➥
Security::hash( 'temp', null, true ) ) );
27:            }
28:        }
29:
30:        // Page when logged in
31:    function index() {
32:
33:    }
34:
35:    }
36:    ?>
```

On line 13, we explicitly allow access to the welcome action. If you use an asterisk symbol, all actions will be accessible. Within the welcome action itself, we set up a temporary user, since we're starting off without any entries in the database tables. From line 20 onward, if we can't find a user called temp, we create a user called temp with the password temp. The welcome screen of the control panel is shown in Figure 8-1.

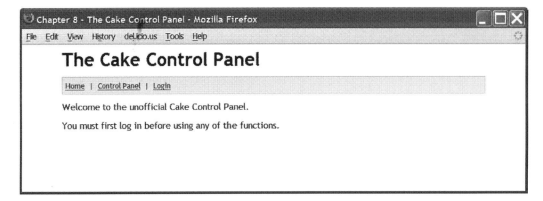

Figure 8-1. *The control panel welcome screen*

The Actions Controller

The actions controller is used to manage the access control objects—essentially, the controller actions that need security management. We can add or delete which functions within the whole application a user can or cannot access. This controller is shown in Listing 8-7.

Listing 8-7. *Actions Controller (app/controllers/actions_controller.php)*

```
 1:   <?php
 2:   class ActionsController extends AppController {
 3:
 4:       var $name = 'Actions';
 5:       var $helpers = array('Html', 'Form');
 6:
 7:       function beforeFilter() {
 8:
 9:           // We need to temporarily allow access during the setup
10:           $this->Auth->allow( 'index' );
11:       }
12:
13:       // Add and remove controller actions for Aco
14:       function index() {
15:
16:           if (!empty($this->data)) {
17:
18:               $this->_processActions();
19:           }
20:
21:           $this->_listActions();
22:       }
23:
```

```
24:         // Add or delete actions
25:         function __processActions() {
26:
27:             $securityAccess = $this->data['Actions']['SecurityAccess'];
28:
29:             $inflect = new Inflector();
30:
31:             foreach ( $securityAccess as $name_pair_key => $access_selection ) {
32:
33:                 $name_pair = explode( "__", $name_pair_key );
34:
35:                 $controller = $inflect->singularize( $name_pair[0] );
36:                 $action = $name_pair[1];
37:
38:                 if ( $access_selection == 'delete' ) {
39:
40:                     $aco = new Aco();
41:
42:                     $aco_record = $aco->find( array(
43:                                     "Aco.model" => $controller,
44:                                     "Aco.alias" => $action ) );
45:
46:                     if ( !empty( $aco_record ) ) {
47:
48:                         $delete_id = $aco_record['Aco']['id'];
49:                         $this->Action->Aco->Delete( $delete_id );
50:                     }
51:                 }
52:                 elseif ( $access_selection == 'include' ) {
53:
54:                     $parent_id = '0';
55:
56:                     // Find the parent. If no parent, we create one
57:                     $aco_parent = new Aco();
58:                     $aco_parent_record = $aco_parent->find(
59:                                     array( "Aco.model" => $controller,
60:                                            "Aco.alias" => $name_pair[0] ) );
61:
62:                     if ( empty( $aco_parent_record ) ) {
63:
64:                         $aco_parent = new Aco();
65:
66:                         $aco_parent->create();
67:                         $aco_parent->save( array(   'model' => $controller,
68:                                                     'foreign_key' => '',
69:                                                     'alias' => $name_pair[0],
70:                                                     'parent_id'     => ''
71:                                                     ) );
72:
```

```
73:                              $parent_id = $aco_parent->id;
74:                      }
75:                      else {
76:
77:                              $parent_id =  $aco_parent_record['Aco']['id'];
78:                      }
79:
80:                      // Now let's create the aco record itself
81:                      $aco = new Aco();
82:
83:                      $aco->create();
84:                      $aco->save( array(  'model' => $controller,
85:                                          'foreign_key' => '',
86:                                          'alias' => $action,
87:                                          'parent_id'        => $parent_id
88:                                          ) );
89:              }
90:          }
91:      }
92:
93:      function __listActions() {
94:
95:          // Get all the actions in the controllers
96:
97:          $actions = array();
98:
99:          App::import( 'File', 'Folder' );
100:
101:          $folder = new Folder( APP.'controllers/' );
102:          $folders = $folder->find();
103:
104:          foreach( $folders as $file  ) {
105:
106:              if ( is_file( APP.'controllers/'.$file ) ) {
107:
108:                  $file = new File( APP.'controllers/'.$file );
109:                  $file_contents = $file->read();
110:                  $file->close();
111:
112:                  // Get the controller name
113:                  $class_pattern = '/class [a-zA-Z0-9]*Controller ➥
extends AppController/';
114:                  preg_match($class_pattern, $file_contents, $matches);
115:                  $class_name_1 = str_replace( 'class ', '', $matches[0] );
116:                  $class_name = str_replace(
117:                          'Controller extends AppController',
118:                          '', $class_name_1 );
119:
```

```
120:                     // Get the action names
121:                     $pattern = '/function [a-zA-Z0-9]*\(/';
122:                     preg_match_all($pattern, $file_contents, $matches);
123:
124:                     // Now gather action details together
125:                     $action_group = array();
126:
127:                     $inflect = new Inflector();
128:                     $class_name_sing = $inflect->singularize( $class_name );
129:
130:                     $action_group[ 'name' ] = $class_name;
131:                     $action_group[ 'name_singular' ] = $class_name_sing;
132:                     $action_group[ 'actions' ] = $matches[0];
133:
134:                     $actions[] = $action_group;
135:                 }
136:             }
137:
138:         $this->set( 'actions', $actions );
139:
140:         // Get the full list of Aco records
141:         $aco = new Aco();
142:
143:         $aco_list = $aco->find('all');
144:
145:         $result = array();
146:
147:         $inflect = new Inflector();
148:
149:         foreach ( $aco_list as $current_aco ) {
150:
151:             $key_0 = $current_aco['Aco']['model'];
152:             $key_1 = $current_aco['Aco']['alias'];
153:
154:             $result[ $key_0.'__'.$key_1 ] = $current_aco;
155:         }
156:
157:         $this->set( 'aco_list', $result );
158:         }
159:     }
160:     ?>
```

The only action in this controller is the index action. Figure 8-2 shows the page produced by this listing.

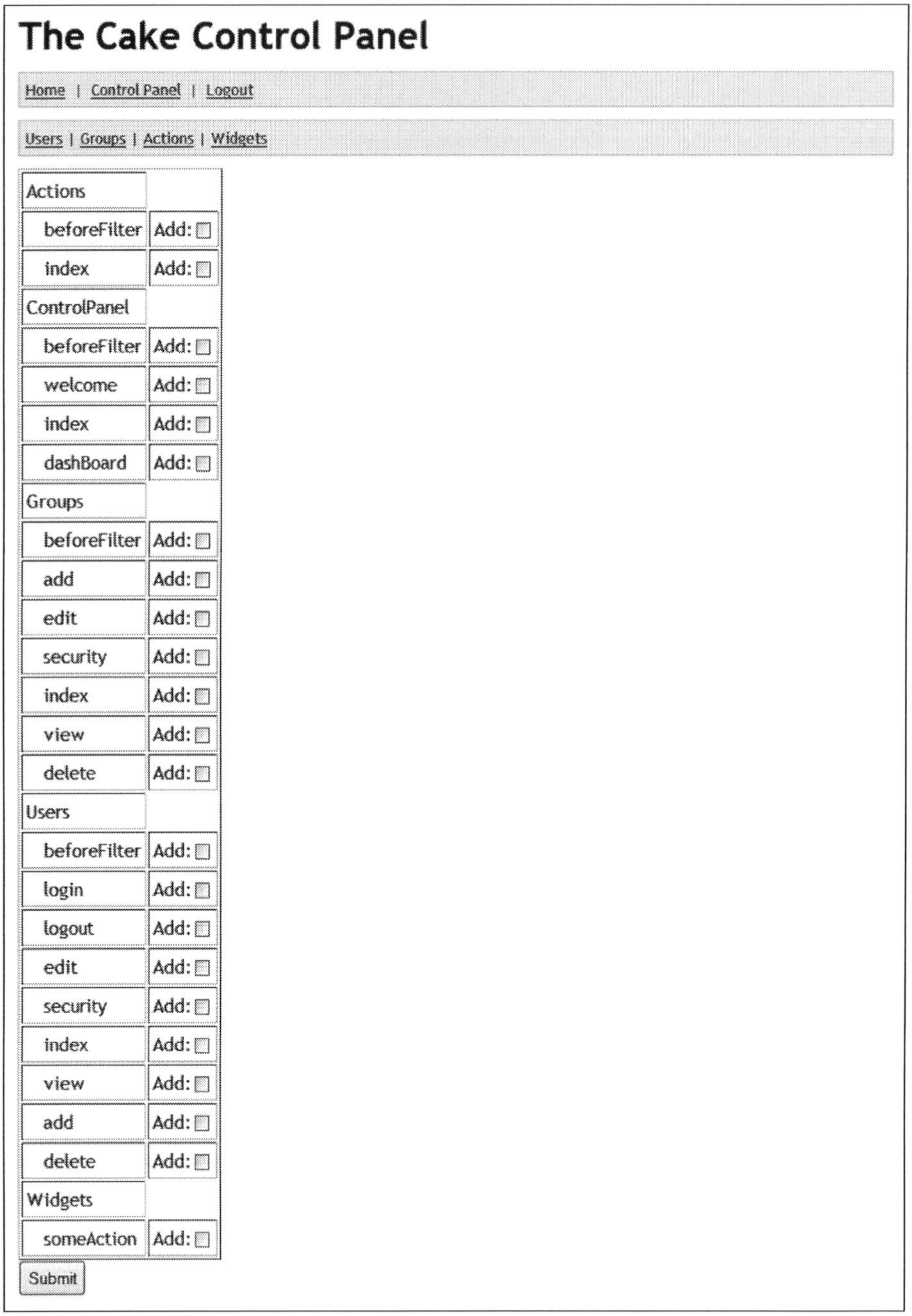

The Cake Control Panel

Home | Control Panel | Logout

Users | Groups | Actions | Widgets

Actions	
beforeFilter	Add: ☐
index	Add: ☐
ControlPanel	
beforeFilter	Add: ☐
welcome	Add: ☐
index	Add: ☐
dashBoard	Add: ☐
Groups	
beforeFilter	Add: ☐
add	Add: ☐
edit	Add: ☐
security	Add: ☐
index	Add: ☐
view	Add: ☐
delete	Add: ☐
Users	
beforeFilter	Add: ☐
login	Add: ☐
logout	Add: ☐
edit	Add: ☐
security	Add: ☐
index	Add: ☐
view	Add: ☐
add	Add: ☐
delete	Add: ☐
Widgets	
someAction	Add: ☐

Submit

Figure 8-2. *The index action in the actions controller*

In the Cake `Auth` component, if you set the `authorize` parameter to `crud`, Cake assumes you have all the CRUD (create, read, update, and delete) actions in your controller: `index`, `add`, `edit`, `delete`, and `view`. Cake will security-manage these actions for you using the fields `_create`, `_read`, `_update`, and `_delete` in the `aros_acos` table. However, when you set the parameter to `actions`, as we have for this application, you can security-manage any actions in your controller. Essentially, the `actions` value is more generic than the `crud` value in terms of the `Auth` security.

When the `authorize` parameter is set to `actions`, the `acos` table needs to be in a specific format, structured as follows:

```
Controller A
        Action 1
        Action 2
        Action 3
        . . .
Controller B
        Action 1
        Action 2
        Action 3
        . . .
```

There are only two levels. The top level is always occupied by the controllers, and the second levels form the controller actions that belong to the controller.

As an example, suppose we select only the last action in the control panel (Figure 8-2), by checking the someAction check box under Widgets and clicking the Submit button. This will generate the entries in the `acos` table shown in Figure 8-3.

← ↑ →	id	parent_id	model	foreign_key	alias	lft	rght
☐ ✎ ✕	1	0	Widget	0	Widgets	1	4
☐ ✎ ✕	2	1	Widget	0	someAction	2	3

Figure 8-3. *The acos table entries after choosing the someAction action*

Now that you've seen how the actions controller works, the code in Listing 8-7 will be easier to understand. On line 10, we temporarily allow access to the `index` action; otherwise, we wouldn't be able to use it.

The `index` action is fairly simple. It has two private methods: `__listActions` and `__processActions`. The `__listActions` action lists the actions available. The code for that starts on line 93. We use Cake's `File` and `Folder` convenience classes to get all the PHP files in the controller folder, and carry out a `preg_match` operation on the content of the files, matching controller names and action names. The following is a sample of the HTML code for the check boxes in Figure 8-2:

```
<input type="checkbox"
        name="data[Actions][SecurityAccess][Widgets__someAction]"
        label=""
        div=""
        value="include"
        id="ActionsSecurityAccessWidgetsSomeAction" />
```

The name attribute in this HTML code gives you an idea of the format of the data that will be returned to the action's __processActions method via the index action.

The __processActions method is responsible for adding and deleting entries in the acos table. Again, assuming we select the last entry in Figure 8-2 (someAction), the controller data will contain the following entry:

```
Array
(
    [Actions] => Array
        (
            [SecurityAccess] => Array
                (
                    [Actions__beforeFilter] => 0
                    [Actions__index] => 0
                    [ControlPanel__beforeFilter] => 0
                    [ControlPanel__welcome] => 0
                    [ControlPanel__index] => 0
                    [ControlPanel__dashBoard] => 0
                    [Groups__beforeFilter] => 0
                    [Groups__add] => 0
                    [Groups__edit] => 0
                    [Groups__security] => 0
                    [Groups__index] => 0
                    [Groups__view] => 0
                    [Groups__delete] => 0
                    [Users__beforeFilter] => 0
                    [Users__login] => 0
                    [Users__logout] => 0
                    [Users__edit] => 0
                    [Users__security] => 0
                    [Users__index] => 0
                    [Users__view] => 0
                    [Users__add] => 0
                    [Users__delete] => 0
                    [Widgets__someAction] => include
                )

        )
)
```

Once the form has been submitted, the function __processActions on line 25 kicks in. We start on line 31 by looping through the whole action list in the data variable. Each entry is composed of a name/value pair in the following format:

```
[controller]__[action] => [security_value]
```

In our example, the value is as follows:

```
[Widgets__someAction] => include
```

This tells us that the user wants to add the someAction action in the widgets controller into the acos table, so the user can allow or deny access to certain users or groups.

On line 38, if the user has selected to delete the acos entry, we simply find the acos entry and delete it using the model's delete method. If the user has decided to add the entry, we first check whether the controller parent record exists. If it doesn't, we create one. If it does exist, we need the ID for the action entry. Both entries are shown in Figure 8-3.

From line 141 onward, we fetch all the acos entries for the view so it can display an Add or Delete check box. If an entry doesn't exist, we display an Add check box. If an entry already exists, we display a Delete check box, as shown in Figure 8-4.

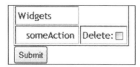

Figure 8-4. *The Delete check box option when the acos entry already exists*

To summarize, we now have one action called someAction in the widgets controller, which we can security-manage. If we didn't add that entry in the acos table, Cake's Auth component would always deny access to it, unless explicitly overridden by Auth's allow method.

The Groups Controller

The groups controller is an important element in our application. In Cake's Acl component, we can control groups of users simply by changing the security on the group itself, rather than changing the security on every individual in that group. This is due to the fact that we can layer groups in a hierarchical fashion. For example, we can have a root administrator, and below that role, a department administrator, followed by department users.

In the groups controller, we have the ability to list groups, add groups, edit groups, delete groups, and control the security access of groups.

We start the development of the controller by using the bake command to bake the code for the controller, model, and views. The code listing for the GroupsController class is shown in Listing 8-8.

Listing 8-8. *Groups Controller (app/controllers/groups_controller.php)*

```
1:    <?php
2:    class GroupsController extends AppController {
3:
4:        var $name = 'Groups';
5:        var $helpers = array('Html', 'Form');
6:
7:        function beforeFilter() {
8:
9:            // We need to temporarily allow access during the setup
10:           $this->Auth->allow( 'add', 'index' );
11:       }
12:
```

```
13:         function add() {
14:
15:             // For saving group
16:             if (!empty($this->data)) {
17:                 $this->Group->create();
18:                 if ($this->Group->save($this->data)) {
19:                     $this->Session->setFlash(➥
__('The Group has been saved', true));
20:                     $this->redirect(array('action'=>'index'));
21:                 } else {
22:                     $this->Session->setFlash(__('The Group could not be
23:                                     saved. Please, try again.', true));
24:                 }
25:             }
26:
27:             // For the group parent listing
28:             $groups = $this->Group->find('list');
29:             $this->set( 'parents', $groups );
30:         }
31:
32:         function edit($id = null) {
33:
34:             if (!$id && empty($this->data)) {
35:                 $this->Session->setFlash(__('Invalid Group', true));
36:                 $this->redirect(array('action'=>'index'));
37:             }
38:             if (!empty($this->data)) {
39:                 if ($this->Group->save($this->data)) {
40:                     $this->Session->setFlash(➥
__('The Group has been saved', true));
41:                     $this->redirect(array('action'=>'index'));
42:                 } else {
43:                     $this->Session->setFlash(__('The Group could not be saved.
44:                                     Please, try again.', true));
45:                 }
46:             }
47:             if (empty($this->data)) {
48:                 $this->data = $this->Group->read(null, $id);
49:             }
50:
51:             // For the parent group
52:             $groups = $this->Group->find('list');
53:             $this->set( 'parents', $groups );
54:         }
55:
56:         function security($id) {
57:
```

```
58:                if (!empty($this->data)) {
59:
60:                    // Let's get the Aro, i.e. the group
61:                    $aro_foreign_key = $this->data['Group']['id'];
62:
63:                    $aro = new Aro();
64:                    $aro_record = $aro->findByAlias( 'Group:'.$aro_foreign_key );
65:
66:                    $aro_alias = $aro_record['Aro']['alias'];
67:                    $aco_of_aro = $aro_record['Aco'];
68:
69:                    // Let's run through the security selection
70:                    $sec_access = $this->data['Group']['SecurityAccess'];
71:
72:                    $aco = new Aco();
73:                    $inflect = new Inflector();
74:
75:                    foreach ( $sec_access as $aco_id => $access_type ) {
76:
77:                        $aco_record = $aco->findById( $aco_id );
78:
79:                        $model_plural = ➥
$inflect->pluralize( $aco_record['Aco']['model'] );
80:
81:                            if ( $access_type == 'allow' ) {
82:                                $this->Acl->allow(  $aro_alias,
83:                          $model_plural.'/'.$aco_record[ 'Aco' ][ 'alias' ], '*');
84:                            }
85:                            elseif ( $access_type == 'deny' ) {
86:                                $this->Acl->deny(   $aro_alias,
87:                          $model_plural.'/'.$aco_record[ 'Aco' ][ 'alias' ], '*');
88:                            }
89:                    }
90:                }
91:
92:            // Let's gather the aco selections available
93:            $aco = new Aco();
94:
95:            // List the whole tree
96:            $aco_tree = $aco->generateTreeList();
97:
98:            // Now get the details of the Aco records
99:            $aco_records = $aco->find('all');
100:
101:            $this->set( compact( 'aco_tree', 'aco_records' ) );
102:
```

```
103:              $this->set( 'current_alias', ➥
$this->Group->name.':'.$this->Group->id );
104:
105:              if (empty($this->data)) {
106:                  $this->data = $this->Group->read(null, $id);
107:              }
108:          }
109:
110:          // The following was baked
111:
112:          function index() {
113:              $this->Group->recursive = 0;
114:              $this->set('groups', $this->paginate());
115:          }
116:
117:          function view($id = null) {
118:              if (!$id) {
119:                  $this->Session->setFlash(__('Invalid Group.', true));
120:                  $this->redirect(array('action'=>'index'));
121:              }
122:              $this->set('group', $this->Group->read(null, $id));
123:          }
124:
125:          function delete($id = null) {
126:              if (!$id) {
127:                  $this->Session->setFlash(__('Invalid id for Group', true));
128:                  $this->redirect(array('action'=>'index'));
129:              }
130:              if ($this->Group->del($id)) {
131:                  $this->Session->setFlash(__('Group deleted', true));
132:                  $this->redirect(array('action'=>'index'));
133:              }
134:          }
135:
136:      }
137:  ?>
```

When we first ran the application, we found ourselves in a catch-22 scenario: we couldn't log in because there were no users, but we had to log in to create a user. Of course, you can manually insert entries into the database using a tool like phpMyAdmin, but we wanted to automate processes as much as possible. So initially, we allow access to actions without the user needing to log in. This is done on line 10 in Listing 8-8.

The edit action beginning on line 32 is mostly based on baked code, with the exception of lines 52 and 53, which generate the parent drop-down list for the current group. This edit action follows the same pattern as the add action beginning on line 13, except on line 48, where we need to read the record into the data controller variable to be used in the edit form.

Adding a Group

We need to add some more lines of code into the model in order to get Cake's Acl component to work. Listing 8-9 shows the Group model.

Listing 8-9. *Group Model Class (app/models/group.php)*

```
1:    <?php
2:    class Group extends AppModel {
3:
4:        var $name = 'Group';
5:
6:        var $actsAs = array('Acl'=>'requester');
7:
8:        var $hasMany = array(
9:              'User' => array( 'className' => 'User',
10:                                 'foreignKey' => 'group_id',
11:                                 'dependent' => false,
12:                                 'conditions' => '',
13:                                 'fields' => '',
14:                                 'order' => '',
15:                                 'limit' => '',
16:                                 'offset' => '',
17:                                 'exclusive' => '',
18:                                 'finderQuery' => '',
19:                                 'counterQuery' => ''
20:                  )
21:        );
22:
23:        var $validate = array( 'title' => VALID_NOT_EMPTY );
24:
25:        function afterSave($created) {
26:
27:            if ( $created ) {
28:
29:                // It's a creation
30:
31:                $id = $this->getLastInsertID();
32:
33:                $aro = new Aro();
34:
35:                $aro->updateAll(    array('alias'=>'\'Group:'.$id.'\''),
36:                                array(  'Aro.model'=>'Group',
37:                                        'Aro.foreign_key'=>$id)
38:                                );
39:            }
40:            else {
41:
```

```
42:                // It's an edit; we have to update the tree
43:                $data = $this->read();
44:                $parent_id = $data['Group']['parent_id'];
45:
46:                $aro = new Aro();
47:
48:                $aro_record = $aro->findByForeignKey( $this->id );
49:                $parent_record = $aro->findByForeignKey( $parent_id );
50:
51:                if ( empty( $aro_record ) ) {
52:
53:                    // Orphaned child
54:                    $this->Aro->save( array(
55:                        'model' => $this->name,
56:                        'foreign_key' => $this->id,
57:                        'alias' => $this->name.':'.$this->id,
58:                        'parent_id'      => $parent_record['Aro']['id']
59:                    ) );
60:                }
61:                else {
62:
63:                    // Just moving nodes
64:                    $this->Aro->save( array(
65:                        'model' => $this->name,
66:                        'foreign_key' => $this->id,
67:                        'alias' => $this->name.':'.$this->id,
68:                        'parent_id'      => $parent_record['Aro']['id'],
69:                        'id'             => $aro_record['Aro']['id']
70:                    ) );
71:                }
72:            }
73:
74:        return true;
75:    }
76:
77:    function parentNode(){
78:
79:        // This should be the alias of the parent $model::$id
80:        $data = $this->read();
81:
82:        // This needs to be unique
83:        return 'Group:'.$data['Group']['parent_id'];
84:    }
85: }
86: ?>
```

On line 6 in Listing 8-9, we add the Acl behavior, providing it with the requester parameter value so it knows the Group model is an Aro entity. This behavior automatically deals with
the acos and aros entries. However, it doesn't quite do everything we need.

The Acl behavior automatically adds an entry into the aros table when we create a group by using the model's save method. Unfortunately, we need to update the entry with some additional details in order to get the Acl component to work properly, as follows:

- After a new aros record has been created via the save method, we need to update the alias field because the Acl component sometimes uses this field as a unique field when fetching nodes. The format of the alias field will be Group:[group_id], as shown in line 35 in Listing 8-9.

- When an existing record is being edited and saved, we need to manually update the parent_id field in the aros table as well.

We also need to include the parentNode method when using the Acl behavior. It needs to return the alias value of the parent aros record. Each group can have only another group entity as a parent, so the parent alias value will always be in the format Group:[group_id].

Line 25 in Listing 8-9 starts the afterSave operation. If it's a new record, we update the alias field with the unique string format Group:[user_id]. If it's an edit, we face a special scenario unique to the groups controller: if the parent was previously deleted, the children may have parent IDs pointing to nonexistent records; that is, they are orphaned. The Acl behavior does not automatically reassign orphaned children, so we must do that ourselves. The code between lines 40 and 71 in Listing 8-9 takes care of that scenario. Within that section of code, we also deal with the case of simply changing the parent; see line 64. It's worth noting that the Tree behavior will automatically adjust the other groups accordingly only when we are moving parents.

Group Security

The other important action in the groups controller is the security action. To explain this action, it's better to start from the group listing, as shown in the example in Figure 8-5.

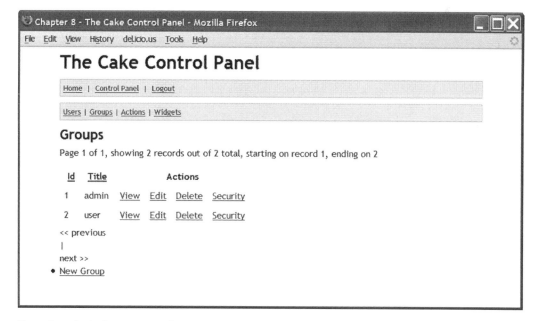

Figure 8-5. *The index action in the GroupController*

In Figure 8-5, you can see a Security link next to a group record. We simply added the new link into the baked view of the index action. When users click the Security link, they will be able to control the security settings relating to the group. Figure 8-6 shows the security page.

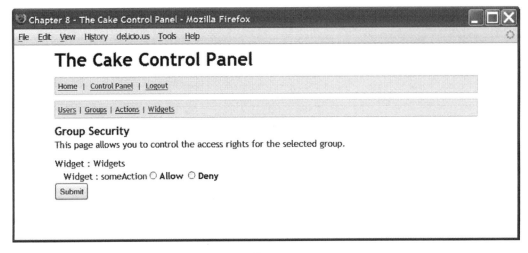

Figure 8-6. *The security action in the GroupController*

When you first bring up the security page, it will list all the access control objects that you can security-manage. In our case, it will list only the someAction action. This is handled from line 92 onward in Listing 8-8.

The Aco class has a method called generateTreeList, which generates the hierarchy of the tree. We also need the entire acos entry in order to know which actions have been granted and which ones have been denied.

Once a user has selected Allow or Deny, we process the entry from line 58 onward of Listing 8-8. It's similar to adding actions in the actions controller. We loop through the selection. If a user has selected Allow, we use this command:

```
$this->Acl->allow( [aro_alias], '[model_plaural]/[aco_alias]', '*');
```

If a user has selected Deny, we use this command:

```
$this->Acl->deny( [aro_alias], '[model_plaural]/[aco_alias]', '*');
```

In both the allow and deny methods, we are specifying a security relationship between the aros record and the acos record. The * is the standard value to use if the authorize parameter is set to actions. If it were set to crud, then you could specify which CRUD action to security-manage. But with the actions setting (sometimes called *actions mode*), the CRUD database columns must be all 1 values, all 0 values, or −1 values.

In Listing 8-8, the index, view, and delete actions are shown for the sake of completeness. Note that when we use the delete method to delete a group record, the Acl behavior also deletes the aros record and rearranges the tree accordingly.

The Users Controller

The users controller is essential for managing users. We will have the ability to list users, add users, edit users, delete users, and control the security access of users.

As with the groups controller, we get Cake to help us out by using the bake command to bake the code for the controller, model, and views. The code listing for the UsersController is shown in Listing 8-10.

Listing 8-10. *Users Controller (app/controllers/users_controller.php)*

```php
 1:    <?php
 2:    class UsersController extends AppController {
 3:
 4:        var $name = 'Users';
 5:        var $helpers = array('Html', 'Form');
 6:
 7:        function beforeFilter() {
 8:
 9:            // We need to temporarily allow access during the setup
10:            $this->Auth->allow( 'index', 'security',
11:                                'add', 'edit', 'delete');
12:        }
13:
14:        function login() {
15:
16:        }
17:
18:        function logout() {
19:
20:            return $this->redirect( $this->Auth->logout() );
21:        }
22:
23:        function edit($id = null) {
24:
25:            if (!$id && empty($this->data)) {
26:                $this->Session->setFlash(__('Invalid User', true));
27:                $this->redirect(array('action'=>'index'));
28:            }
29:            if (!empty($this->data)) {
30:
31:                // If no password is supplied, we don't change it
32:                if ( trim( $this->data['User']['password'] ) == ➥
Security::hash( '', null, true) ) {
33:                    unset( $this->data['User']['password'] );
34:                }
35:
```

```
36:                     if ($this->User->save($this->data)) {
37:                         $this->Session->setFlash( ➥
__('The User has been saved', true));
38:                         $this->redirect(array('action'=>'index'));
39:                     } else {
40:                         $this->Session->setFlash(__('The User could not be saved.
41:                                             Please, try again.', true));
42:                     }
43:                 }
44:             if (empty($this->data)) {
45:                 $this->data = $this->User->read(null, $id);
46:
47:                 // We set the password to nothing
48:                 // Passwords are only changed if you enter something
49:                 // since it's one way only!
50:                 $this->data['User']['password'] = '';
51:             }
52:
53:             // For the parent group
54:             $groups = $this->User->Group->find('list');
55:             $this->set( 'groups', $groups );
56:         }
57:
58:         function security($id) {
59:
60:             if (!empty($this->data)) {
61:
62:                 // Let's get the Aro, i.e., the group
63:                 $aro_foreign_key = $this->data['User']['id'];
64:
65:                 $aro = new Aro();
66:                 $aro_record = $aro->findByAlias( 'User:'.$aro_foreign_key );
67:
68:                 $aro_alias = $aro_record['Aro']['alias'];
69:                 $aco_of_aro = $aro_record['Aco'];
70:
71:                 // Let's run through the security selection
72:                 $sec_access = $this->data['User']['SecurityAccess'];
73:
74:                 $aco = new Aco();
75:                 $inflect = new Inflector();
76:
77:                 foreach ( $sec_access as $aco_id => $access_type ) {
78:
79:                     $aco_record = $aco->findById( $aco_id );
80:
```

```
81:                    $model_plural = ➡
$inflect->pluralize( $aco_record['Aco']['model'] );
 82:
 83:                    if ( $access_type == 'allow' ) {
 84:                        $this->Acl->allow( $aro_alias, ➡
$model_plural.'/'.$aco_record[ 'Aco' ][ 'alias' ], '*');
 85:                    }
 86:                    elseif ( $access_type == 'deny' ) {
 87:                        $this->Acl->deny( $aro_alias, ➡
$model_plural.'/'.$aco_record[ 'Aco' ][ 'alias' ], '*');
 88:                    }
 89:                }
 90:            }
 91:
 92:            // Let's gather the aco selections available
 93:            $aco = new Aco();
 94:
 95:            // List the whole tree
 96:            $aco_tree = $aco->generateTreeList();
 97:
 98:            // Now get the details of the Aco records
 99:            $aco_records = $aco->find('all');
100:
101:            $this->set( compact( 'aco_tree', 'aco_records' ) );
102:
103:            $this->set( 'current_alias', ➡
$this->User->name.':'.$this->User->id );
104:
105:            if (empty($this->data)) {
106:                $this->data = $this->User->read(null, $id);
107:            }
108:        }
109:
110:        // The following are baked
111:
112:        function index() {
113:            $this->User->recursive = 0;
114:            $this->set('users', $this->paginate());
115:        }
116:
117:        function view($id = null) {
118:            if (!$id) {
119:                $this->Session->setFlash(__('Invalid User.', true));
120:                $this->redirect(array('action'=>'index'));
121:            }
122:            $this->set('user', $this->User->read(null, $id));
123:        }
124:
```

```
125:        function add() {
126:            if (!empty($this->data)) {
127:                $this->User->create();
128:                if ($this->User->save($this->data)) {
129:                    $this->Session->setFlash(➥
__('The User has been saved', true));
130:                    $this->redirect(array('action'=>'index'));
131:                } else {
132:                    $this->Session->setFlash(➥
__('The User could not be saved. Please, try again.', true));
133:                }
134:            }
135:            $groups = $this->User->Group->find('list');
136:            $this->set(compact('groups'));
137:        }
138:
139:        function delete($id = null) {
140:            if (!$id) {
141:                $this->Session->setFlash(__('Invalid id for User', true));
142:                //$this->redirect(array('action'=>'index'));
143:            }
144:            if ($this->User->del($id)) {
145:                $this->Session->setFlash(__('User deleted', true));
146:                $this->redirect(array('action'=>'index'));
147:            }
148:        }
149:
150:    }
151:    ?>
```

Much of the code in Listing 8-10 follows the same pattern as the groups controller. On line 10, we temporarily allow access to some actions during the initial setup of the users.

The login and logout actions, on lines 14 and 18, respectively, are just stub functions that are needed in order for the Auth component to automatically log the user in and out.

The edit action on line 23 is mostly based on baked code. There are two sections worth noting. When a user edits user details, the password field is set to blank on line 50. If no password has been supplied in the form, we don't change the password; we simply check whether it is empty, on line 32. Passwords are hashed, so we never have the plain text of the original password. Therefore, we need to manually empty the password field; otherwise, Cake will fill it with the hashed password string. When we update the user details, and the user has provided a new password, the Auth component will automatically hash the password provided.

User Security

The security action is best explained by starting from the user listing (index action), shown in Figure 8-7, and the security form, shown in Figure 8-8.

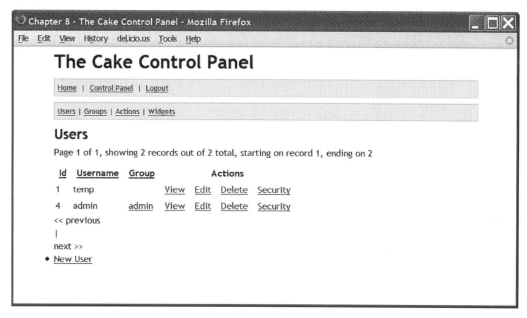

Figure 8-7. *The index action in the UserController*

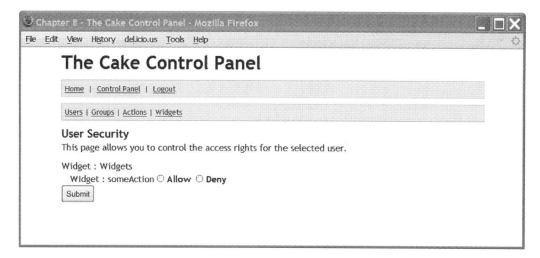

Figure 8-8. *The security action in the UserController*

The `security` action in the users controller, on line 58 of Listing 8-10, is similar to the security action in the groups controller. We display all the `acos` records, which we can security-manage. We allow the administrator to set whether the user should have access or not by selecting Allow or Deny. When we submit the form, the code beginning on line 60 in Listing 8-10 takes over. We loop over the selection, and depending on whether the user selected Allow or Deny, we use the `Acl` component's `allow` or deny method.

In Listing 8-10, the `index`, `view`, `add`, and `delete` methods are shown for the sake of completeness. As with the groups controller's `delete` action, when we delete a user record, the action also deletes the `aros` record and rearranges the tree accordingly.

Adding a User

The `User` model code for adding a user is similar in structure to that in the `Group` model. This code is shown in Listing 8-11.

Listing 8-11. *User Model (app/models/user.php)*

```
1:    <?php
2:    class User extends AppModel {
3:
4:        var $name = 'User';
5:
6:        var $actsAs = array('Acl'=>'requester');
7:
8:        var $belongsTo = array(
9:                'Group' => array('className' => 'Group',
10:                                 'foreignKey' => 'group_id',
11:                                 'conditions' => '',
12:                                 'fields' => '',
13:                                 'order' => ''
14:                )
15:        );
16:
17:        function afterSave($created) {
18:
19:            if($created) {
20:
21:                // It's a creation
22:
23:                $id = $this->getLastInsertID();
24:
25:                $aro = new Aro();
26:
27:                $aro->updateAll( array('alias'=>'\'User:'.$id.'\''),
28:                                 array(  'Aro.model'=>'User',
29:                                         'Aro.foreign_key'=>$id)
30:                                 );
31:            }
```

```
32:          else {
33:
34:              // It's an edit; we have to update the tree
35:              $data = $this->read();
36:              $parent_id = $data['User']['group_id'];
37:
38:              $aro = new Aro();
39:
40:              $aro_record = $aro->findByAlias( $this->name.':'.$this->id );
41:              $parent_record = $aro->findByAlias( 'Group:'.$parent_id );
42:
43:              if ( !empty( $aro_record ) ) {
44:
45:                  $parent_id = '0';
46:
47:                  if ( !empty( $parent_record ) ) {
48:                      $parent_id = $parent_record['Aro']['id'];
49:                  }
50:
51:                  // Just changing parents
52:                  $this->Aro->save( array(
53:                      'parent_id'         => $parent_id,
54:                      'id'                => $aro_record['Aro']['id']
55:                  ) );
56:              }
57:          }
58:
59:          return true;
60:      }
61:
62:      function parentNode(){
63:
64:          // This should be the alias of the parent $model::$id
65:          $data = $this->read();
66:
67:          // This needs to be unique
68:          return 'Group:'.$data['User']['group_id'];
69:      }
70:
71:  }
72:  ?>
```

After a save operation, whether it is creating a new aros record or editing an existing one, we still need to update some of the aros record ourselves.

Line 19 starts the afterSave operation. If it's a new record, we update the alias field with the unique string format User:[user_id].

Because of the hierarchical nature of aros records, we also need an action called parentNode. As in the Group model, this must return the unique alias value of the group, in the format Group:[group_id].

Testing the Control Panel

Now that we have all the code and tables in place, we can run a little test to check whether our access control list is working properly. Starting from a blank database, follow these steps:

1. Make sure all the database tables are blank. See the Records column in Figure 8-9.

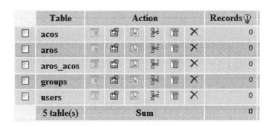

Figure 8-9. *Blank database tables*

2. Bring up the ControlPanel/welcome page (see Figure 8-1). This will automatically create the temp user entry in the users table and the aros table, as shown in Figures 8-10 and 8-11.

			id	username	password	group_id
☐	✎	✕	1	temp	055cd666a7840de8ae29d4477585480b08d1559c	0

Figure 8-10. *The temp user in the users table*

			id	parent_id	model	foreign_key	alias	lft	rght
☐	✎	✕	1	0	User	1	User:1	1	2

Figure 8-11. *The temp user in the aros table*

3. Log in with the temp user name and temp password.

Next, we start adding groups. Remember that we have temporarily allowed access to the add and index actions set in the beforeFilter method of the groups controller (see Listing 8-8, line 10). Remove this when you have all the groups and users in place.

4. Add a group called admin using the interface. Figure 8-12 shows the two entries in the aros table: one for temp and one for the admin group that you just added.

			id	parent_id	model	foreign_key	alias	lft	rght
☐	✎	✕	1	0	User	1	User:1	1	2
☐	✎	✕	2	0	Group	1	Group:1	3	4

Figure 8-12. *The admin group entry in the aros table*

5. Add another group called user. Figure 8-13 shows the aros table entries.

			id	parent_id	model	foreign_key	alias	lft	rght
☐	✎	✕	1	0	User	1	User:1	1	2
☐	✎	✕	2	0	Group	1	Group:1	3	4
☐	✎	✕	3	0	Group	2	Group:2	5	6

Figure 8-13. *The user group entry in the aros table*

Remember that we have temporarily allowed access to the add and index actions set in the beforeFilter method of the groups controller (see Listing 8-8, line 10). Remove this when you have all the groups and users in place.

6. Add the "real" admin user, using admin for the username, password, and group, as shown in Figure 8-14. Figure 8-15 shows the aros table entry.

Figure 8-14. *Adding an admin user*

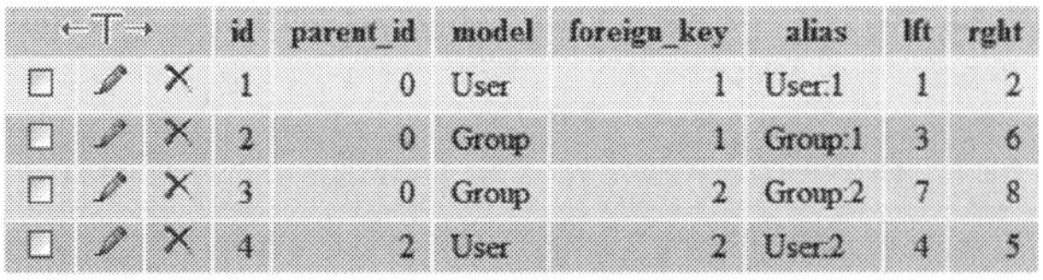

←T→			id	parent_id	model	foreign_key	alias	lft	rght
☐	✏	✕	1	0	User	1	User:1	1	2
☐	✏	✕	2	0	Group	1	Group:1	3	6
☐	✏	✕	3	0	Group	2	Group:2	7	8
☐	✏	✕	4	2	User	2	User:2	4	5

Figure 8-15. *The admin user entry in the aros table*

7. Log out, and then log back in using the `admin` username and password.

8. Delete the `temp` user using the Delete link.

9. Click the Actions link on the top menu, select the someAction action in the form, as shown in Figure 8-16, and then submit it.

Figure 8-16. *Selecting the someAction action*

10. Click the Groups link, and select the Security link for the admin group.

11. Check the Allow selection, as shown in Figure 8-17, and submit the form.

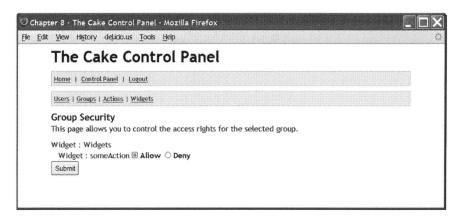

Figure 8-17. *Select the Allow check box.*

12. Click the Widgets link on the top menu. You should now have access to that page, as shown in Figure 8-18.

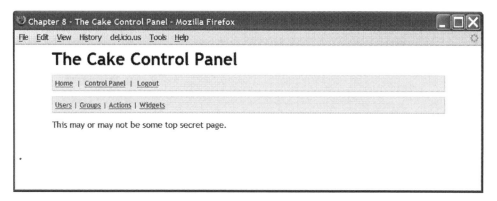

Figure 8-18. *Access allowed*

13. Return to the Security link for the `admin` group, and this time select Deny. Then submit the form.

14. Click the Widgets link again. Now you should be denied access, as shown in Figure 8-19.

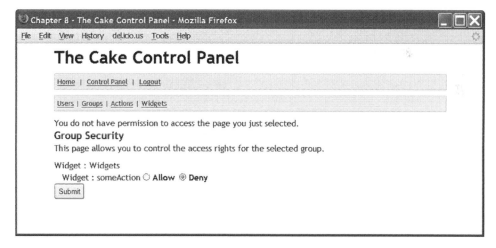

Figure 8-19. *Access denied*

By controlling the group, you indirectly control the users who belong to that group. However, you can also control individual security if necessary.

Summary

In this chapter, we used the idea of a control panel as a starting point for developing basic functions common to web applications. We began that process by using Cake's Acl component to develop a web front end to manage user and group security.

As we said, Cake's access control list is one of its most complex elements. Much of the complexity is due to its implicit link to other elements in Cake. Using the access control list functionality involves the Acl and Auth components. You also need the Acl behavior, which in turn uses the Tree behavior. On top of that, you still need to carry out some operations yourself. Furthermore, the Acl component behaves differently depending on the value of the authorize parameter. But despite this complexity, it's one of the most flexible security systems you can use. Once the basic system is up and running, it's much easier to change and adapt your access control list for other scenarios.

There are many other functions you can add to the access control list and to the control panel as a whole. Here are some ideas:

- Add a dashboard feature in the ControlPanelController class to list useful statistics about the application. For example, if the control panel is used for an e-commerce application, the dashboard could list the number of products sold, number of new users, and so on.

- Improve on the access control list. You may want a feature where you can drill down from the actions listings in the top menu and find out which aro entry has access or no access to that particular action.

- At the moment, if you delete an action from the acos list, security permissions on that list will no longer exist. It would be useful to have a feature that told the user which aros entities currently have permissions set on the action before deleting it.

- Once you have created the essential groups and users and also removed the temporary allow method in the controllers, these groups and users should remain permanent; no user should be able to delete them. You could modify the application so that the delete method would not affect these special groups and users.

CHAPTER 9

■■■

Translating Stories

In this chapter, we'll be writing a news story application in which the news stories will be available in other languages. There will also be an admin area, which will give translators the ability to translate stories from a base language (in our case, English) to another language. To protect the admin area, we will build a simple authentication system.

In Chapter 6, we covered Cake's internationalization features and demonstrated using .po files to display different languages. Using .po files is adequate for static text. However, if the data is stored in the database, you need to employ Cake's built-in Translate behavior. You'll see how that works in this chapter.

Application Structure

To start off, we need two database tables: stories and users. Naturally, stories will be used to store the stories, while users will be the admin users who will enter stories in different languages. There will also be two controllers to go with the two tables: StoriesController in /app/controllers/stories_controller.php and UsersController in /app/controllers/users_controller.php. The stories table schema is shown in Listing 9-1. We will discuss the users table later in the chapter, in the "Logging In" section.

Listing 9-1. *The stories Table Schema*

```
CREATE TABLE `stories` (
  `id` int(11) NOT NULL auto_increment,
  `title` varchar(255) NOT NULL,
  `body` mediumtext NOT NULL,
  PRIMARY KEY (`id`)
);
```

The two fields we need to be concerned with are title, which holds the story title, and body, which holds the actual story itself.

To use the Translate behavior, we need an extra table named i18n, which will be used to store the translation. The schema is shown in Listing 9-2.

Listing 9-2. *The i18n Table Schema*

```
CREATE TABLE `i18n` (
  `id` int(11) NOT NULL auto_increment,
  `locale` varchar(6) NOT NULL,
  `model` varchar(255) NOT NULL,
  `foreign_key` int(10) NOT NULL,
  `field` varchar(255) NOT NULL,
  `content` mediumtext,
  PRIMARY KEY (`id`)
);
```

This table has the following fields:

- locale: This is the language locale code. We need to decide which language the translation refers to. At present, unlike for language codes, there are no ISO locale standard codes; different software uses slightly different codes. In Cake, you can see the locale codes in the file /cake/libs/l10n.php. For further reading, http://www.openi18n.org is a good place to start.

- model: Since there could be many different tables using the Translate behavior, we need this field to identify the correct table via the model. In our case, our model will be Story.

- foreign_key: We need the id field to identify which record the translation relates to.

- field: This is the name of the field in the database table that needs translation. In our case, it will be either title or story.

- content: This contains the translation text itself.

Using this i18n table, we map one field in one record in our stories table to different translations. It's a one-to-many association.

The Translate Behavior

The Translate behavior provides the model class with a number of functions that assist with language translations in our own tables. It sits between the database and the controllers, transparently dealing with language translations between the two areas.

To use the Translate behavior, we start with a simple statement we insert into our story. php model file:

```
var $actsAs = array( 'Translate' => array( 'title', 'body' ) );
```

■**Note** You can add other behaviors to the model by appending the behavior name to the actsAs array variable. In our example, if we were going to add the Containable behavior, the actsAs variable would look like this: array('Translate' => array('title', 'body'), 'Containable');.

In this line, we bring in the Translate behavior, and tell it that we want the `title` and body fields in our `stories` table to be managed by the Translate behavior. When we say "managed," we mean that any model database function relating to the fields we specified should be transparently handled when there is a translation available. For example, when we use a `find( 'all' )` command, it will pick out the correct translation content relating to the language locale we specify.

Stories

Our application centers around the news stories to be translated. We need to add stories and translate them. Users will be able to view the stories either in their original language or a translated version. We will also add functionality to allow administrators to manage the stories.

▨**Note** To simplify our application, we have used Cake's `bake` command to generate most of the code relating to the controller and views. Additionally, we have created an admin section during the baking, so human translators can translate the stories from English into other languages.

Baking Cake

The bake command is a command-line tool that will generate the model, controller, and view files based on the database you created. For this chapter's application, we will use Cake's bake command to generate the Cake files relating to the administration of the stories. We're going to jump ahead a little by showing you the output of our bake session, in Listing 9-3.

Listing 9-3. *Output of the bake Session*

```
 1:    C:\chapter_9>cake\console\cake bake
 2:
 3:
 4:    Welcome to CakePHP v1.2.0.7296 RC2 Console
 5:    ---------------------------------------------------------------
 6:    App : app
 7:    Path: C:/chapter_9/app
 8:    ---------------------------------------------------------------
 9:    Interactive Bake Shell
10:    ---------------------------------------------------------------
11:    [D]atabase Configuration
12:    [M]odel
13:    [V]iew
14:    [C]ontroller
15:    [P]roject
16:    [Q]uit
17:    What would you like to Bake? (D/M/V/C/P/Q)
18:    > M
```

```
19:     -----------------------------------------------------------
20:     Bake Model
21:     Path: C:/chapter_9\app\models\
22:     -----------------------------------------------------------
23:     Possible Models based on your current database:
24:     1. I18n
25:     2. Story
26:     3. User
27:     Enter a number from the list above, type in the name of another model, ➡
or 'q' to exit
28:     [q] > 2
29:     Would you like to supply validation criteria for the ➡
fields in your model? (y/n)
30:     [y] > n
31:     Would you like to define model associations ➡
(hasMany, hasOne, belongsTo, etc.)? (y/n)
32:     [y] > n
33:
34:     -----------------------------------------------------------
35:     The following Model will be created:
36:     -----------------------------------------------------------
37:     Name:        Story
38:     Associations:
39:     -----------------------------------------------------------
40:     Look okay? (y/n)
41:     [y] > y
42:
43:     Baking model class for Story...
44:
45:     Creating file C:/chapter_9\app\models\story.php
46:     Wrote C:/chapter_9\app\models\story.php
47:     Cake test suite not installed.  Do you want to bake ➡
unit test files anyway? (y/n)
48:     [y] > n
49:     -----------------------------------------------------------
50:     Interactive Bake Shell
51:     -----------------------------------------------------------
52:     [D]atabase Configuration
53:     [M]odel
54:     [V]iew
55:     [C]ontroller
56:     [P]roject
57:     [Q]uit
58:     What would you like to Bake? (D/M/V/C/P/Q)
59:     > C
60:     -----------------------------------------------------------
61:     Bake Controller
62:     Path: C:/chapter_9\app\controllers\
```

```
63:     ------------------------------------------------------------------
64:     Possible Controllers based on your current database:
65:     1. I18ns
66:     2. Stories
67:     3. Users
68:     Enter a number from the list above, type in the name ➡
of another controller, or 'q' to exit
69:     [q] > 2
70:     ------------------------------------------------------------------
71:     Baking StoriesController
72:     ------------------------------------------------------------------
73:     Would you like to build your controller interactively? (y/n)
74:     [y] > y
75:     Would you like to use scaffolding? (y/n)
76:     [n] > n
77:     Would you like to include some basic class methods ➡
(index(), add(), view(), edit()))? (y/n)
78:     [n] > y
79:     Would you like to create the methods for admin routing? (y/n)
80:     [n] > y
81:     Would you like this controller to use other helpers ➡
besides HtmlHelper and FormHelper? (y/n)
82:     [n] > n
83:     Would you like this controller to use any components? (y/n)
84:     [n] > n
85:     Would you like to use Sessions? (y/n)
86:     [y] > n
87:
88:     ------------------------------------------------------------------
89:     The following controller will be created:
90:     ------------------------------------------------------------------
91:     Controller Name:  Stories
92:     ------------------------------------------------------------------
93:     Look okay? (y/n)
94:     [y] > y
95:
96:     Creating file C:/chapter_9\app\controllers\stories_controller.php
97:     Wrote C:/chapter_9\app\controllers\stories_controller.php
98:     Cake test suite not installed.  Do you want to bake ➡
unit test files anyway? (y/n)
99:     [y] > n
100:    ------------------------------------------------------------------
101:    Interactive Bake Shell
102:    ------------------------------------------------------------------
103:    [D]atabase Configuration
104:    [M]odel
105:    [V]iew
106:    [C]ontroller
```

```
107:    [P]roject
108:    [Q]uit
109:    What would you like to Bake? (D/M/V/C/P/Q)
110:    > V
111:    ---------------------------------------------------------------
112:    Bake View
113:    Path: C:/chapter_9\app\views\
114:    ---------------------------------------------------------------
115:    Possible Controllers based on your current database:
116:    1. I18ns
117:    2. Stories
118:    3. Users
119:    Enter a number from the list above, type in the name of ➥
another controller, or 'q' to exit
120:    [q] > 2
121:    Would you like to create some scaffolded views ➥
(index, add, view, edit) for this controller?
122:    NOTE: Before doing so, you'll need to create your ➥
controller and model classes (including associated models). (y/n)
123:    [n] > y
124:    Would you like to create the views for admin routing? (y/n)
125:    [y] > y
126:
127:    Creating file C:/chapter_9\app\views\stories\index.ctp
128:    Wrote C:/chapter_9\app\views\stories\index.ctp
129:
130:    Creating file C:/chapter_9\app\views\stories\view.ctp
131:    Wrote C:/chapter_9\app\views\stories\view.ctp
132:
133:    Creating file C:/chapter_9\app\views\stories\add.ctp
134:    Wrote C:/chapter_9\app\views\stories\add.ctp
135:
136:    Creating file C:/chapter_9\app\views\stories\edit.ctp
137:    Wrote C:/chapter_9\app\views\stories\edit.ctp
138:
139:    Creating file C:/chapter_9\app\views\stories\admin_index.ctp
140:    Wrote C:/chapter_9\app\views\stories\admin_index.ctp
141:
142:    Creating file C:/chapter_9\app\views\stories\admin_view.ctp
143:    Wrote C:/chapter_9\app\views\stories\admin_view.ctp
144:
145:    Creating file C:/chapter_9\app\views\stories\admin_add.ctp
146:    Wrote C:/chapter_9\app\views\stories\admin_add.ctp
147:
148:    Creating file C:/chapter_9\app\views\stories\admin_edit.ctp
149:    Wrote C:/chapter_9\app\views\stories\admin_edit.ctp
150:    ---------------------------------------------------------------
151:
```

```
152:    View Scaffolding Complete.
153:
154:    ---------------------------------------------------------------
155:    Interactive Bake Shell
156:    ---------------------------------------------------------------
157:    [D]atabase Configuration
158:    [M]odel
159:    [V]iew
160:    [C]ontroller
161:    [P]roject
162:    [Q]uit
163:    What would you like to Bake? (D/M/V/C/P/Q)
164:    >
```

As you can see, the bake command first asks what we would like to bake. We actually need to bake the story model first, before the controller or view. Line 46 confirms that the model has been created.

Next, we need to create the story controller, starting on line 69. The two most important questions are on lines 77 and 79: whether we want some basic class methods and admin routing. We say yes to both questions. The bake command will create the code for those actions for us.

We finish off by creating the views for the stories, beginning on line 109. On lines 121 and 124, we are asked about creating scaffolding views and the views for admin routing, and we say yes.

The code we have baked is shown at the end of this chapter.

Adding Stories

Our application will start with an empty i18n table and an empty stories table. So let's start at the beginning with adding a story. Listing 9-4 shows the admin_add action in /app/controllers/stories_controller.php, which adds a story.

Listing 9-4. *Adding a Story (in /app/controllers/stories_controller.php)*

```
1:    function admin_add() {
2:
3:        $this->_setI18nByLocale( 'en_us' );
4:
5:        if (!empty($this->data)) {
6:            $this->Story->create();
7:            if ($this->Story->save($this->data)) {
8:                $this->Session->setFlash(__( 'Story saved.', true ) );
9:                $this->redirect( array( 'controller' => 'Stories', ➡
'action' => 'index' ) );
10:           } else {
11:           }
12:        }
13:    }
```

In the `admin_add` action, the important method is the `setI10nByLocale` call on line 3. It's one of our own private methods, which is also housed within the `StoriesController`. Listing 9-5 shows this method.

Listing 9-5. *The setI10nByLocale Method (in /app/controllers/stories_controller.php)*

```
 1:    function _setI10nByLocale( $current_locale = null ) {
 2:
 3:        // Default locale is en_us
 4:        $locale = "en_us";
 5:
 6:        // Decide on session
 7:        if ( $session_locale = $this->Session->read( 'locale' ) ) {
 8:            $locale = $session_locale;
 9:        }
10:
11:        // User can override locale
12:        if ( $current_locale != '' ) {
13:            $locale = $current_locale;
14:        }
15:
16:        $this->Story->locale = $locale;
17:    }
```

The `_setI10nByLocale` method decides which locale, and thus which language, we'll be using in the Translate behavior. We start off with some default settings on line 4, and then we ask whether the locale has already been decided beforehand by checking the session on line 7. Line 16 sets the locale for the model.

In the `admin_add` action (Listing 9-4), we start off by setting the locale for the model so that the Translate behavior knows which locale we'll dealing with. The section of code after that is simply baked using Cake's bake command, which saves a record in the `Story` model. (See the "Baked Code" section at the end of this chapter for the actual baked version of the `admin_add` action.)

Now we enter three sample stories into our application. When the `save` command in the `Story` mode is called, we actually get a total of three different records for each story. We get the entry in the `stories` table, which we expect, but we also get two entries in the `i18n` table. The records for the three stories are shown in Figures 9-1 and 9-2.

←┬→			id	title	body
☐	✎	✕	1	Manned Mars Mission	After an epic 2 year voyage, our astronauts are a ...
☐	✎	✕	2	The Large Hydron Collider	Scientists working on the world's largest atom sma...
☐	✎	✕	3	Mind to Machine Programming	Neuro engineers have developed a new technique to ...

Figure 9-1. *The stories table records*

←T→			id	locale	model	foreign_key	field	content
☐	✐	✕	1	en_us	Story	1	title	Manned Mars Mission
☐	✐	✕	2	en_us	Story	1	body	After an epic 2 year voyage, our astronauts are a ...
☐	✐	✕	3	en_us	Story	2	title	The Large Hydron Collider
☐	✐	✕	4	en_us	Story	2	body	Scientists working on the world's largest atom sma....
☐	✐	✕	5	en_us	Story	3	title	Mind to Machine Programming
☐	✐	✕	6	en_us	Story	3	body	Neuro engineers have developed a new technique to ...

Figure 9-2. *The i18n table records for the title and body*

As it stands, the records in the i18n table just look like unnecessary duplication. However, the Translate behavior will show its usefulness when we start inserting other languages, as you'll see a little later in the "Translating Stories" section.

Administering Stories

Most CakePHP sites have a back-end administrative area. It would be convenient to have all actions come under one specific folder so administration can be more easily managed. There is a helpful feature in Cake that helps us with this. In the config/core.php file, we uncomment the following line of code:

```
Configure::write('Routing.admin', 'admin');
```

With this line uncommented, Cake will map all actions in the format admin_[*action_name*]() to the URL /admin/[*controller_name*]/[*action_name*]. For example, the admin_index action in the StoriesController would be accessed via /admin/Stories/index. However, Cake doesn't automatically password-protect those admin actions, so we will need to do that ourselves, as discussed in the "User Authentication" section.

Translating Stories

The first task for translating stories is to list them. We will list only the stories that need translating. This makes it slightly easier for the human translator to pick out which stories need translating. This is handled by using the admin_toTrans method, as shown in Listing 9-6.

Listing 9-6. *Listing Stories to Translate (in /app/controllers/stories_controller.php)*

```
1:   function admin_toTrans() {
2:
3:       $this->set('trans_lang', '');
4:       $language = '';
5:
6:       // Once user has picked the language, here we list the stories
7:       // that need translating
8:       if ( !empty( $this->params['url']['language'] ) ) {
9:           $language = $this->params['url']['language'];
10:      }
```

```
11:        elseif ( isset( $this->passedArgs[ 'language' ] ) ) {
12:            $language = $this->passedArgs[ 'language' ];
13:        }
14:
15:        if ( $language ) {
16:
17:            // The language we're using to translate the stories in
18:            $this->Story->transLanguage = $language;
19:            $this->set('trans_lang', $language);
20:
21:            // Get the language name, e.g., German
22:            $cat = $this->getLang( $language );
23:            $this->set('language', $cat[ 'language' ] );
24:
25:            // Which pagination method we're using
26:            $this->Story->usePaginate = 'paginateTranslation';
27:            $this->set('stories', $this->paginate());
28:        }
29:    }
```

In Listing 9-6, we start by initializing the variables on lines 3 and 4. Then we decide how the language code is picked out from the URL in the `if` statement on line 8. Once we know which language the user wants, we start retrieving the results using the controller `paginate` method on line 27.

Cake's `paginate` method turned out to be unsuitable for our needs. It lacks the functionality that returns only the stories that have not been translated in the language we chose—which is understandable, as that functionality is quite unique to our application. We had to override Cake's `paginate` method and write our own. We will go into the pagination a bit later, in the "Translation Pagination" section.

The story listing is shown in Figure 9-3. As you can see, each story has two links: View and Translate. Assuming we have a Japanese translator, she can view the story in English by clicking the View link. She can then click the Translate link to go to the story editing screen, as shown in Figure 9-4. A sample Translate URL link looks like this:

```
http://localhost/chapter_9/admin/stories/edit/2/trans_lang:jpn
```

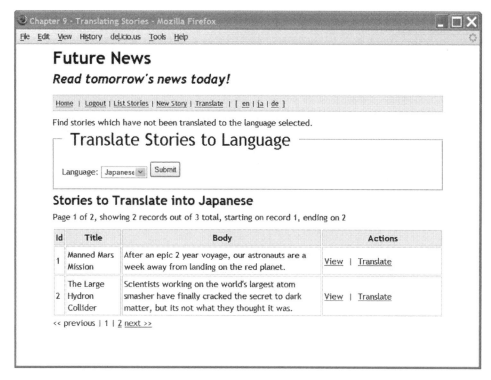

Figure 9-3. *Stories that need translating*

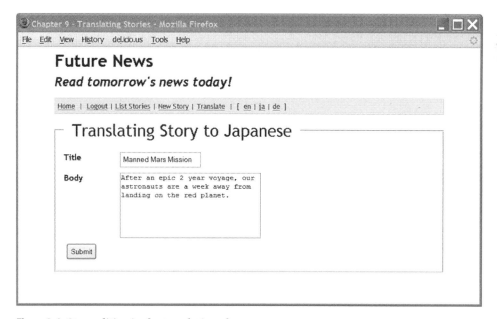

Figure 9-4. *Story editing in the translation phase*

For this form, we have simply used the baked `admin_edit.ctp` view. However, we have added a hidden tag named `trans_lang`, which holds the language code in which we want the story to be saved.

After the Japanese translator has translated the story and saved it, the Translate behavior creates two extra records: one for the title in Japanese and another for the body in Japanese. Figures 9-5 and 9-6 show how our i18n table looks now. You can see how our translation functions are taking place. We have a main story stored in `stories` and the language versions of those stories held in `i18n`. Notice that our story in the `stories` table is now in Japanese as well. This is a side effect of the Translate behavior; however, it will display the correct version when the specified locale is used.

←T→	id	title	body
☐ ✎ ✕	1	ãƒ²ãƒ‚ã‚¢ã‚¯ã‚	ã®ã²ã‚¢ æ‹ã£ãƒªãƒ¢ ã«ã«ã‚¯ã‚«‹ ãƒžãƒ«ãƒ¡ãƒ¼ãƒ«ã‚ ã‚ªãƒ¼ã…
☐ ✎ ✕	2	The Large Hydron Collider	Scientists working on the world's largest atom sma...
☐ ✎ ✕	3	Mind to Machine Programming	Neuro engineers have developed a new technique to ...

Figure 9-5. *The stories table after our first translation*

←T→	id	locale	model	foreign_key	field	content
☐ ✎ ✕	1	en_us	Story	1	title	Manned Mars Mission
☐ ✎ ✕	2	en_us	Story	1	body	After an epic 2 year voyage, our astronauts are a ...
☐ ✎ ✕	3	en_us	Story	2	title	The Large Hydron Collider
☐ ✎ ✕	4	en_us	Story	2	body	Scientists working on the world's largest atom sma...
☐ ✎ ✕	5	en_us	Story	3	title	Mind to Machine Programming
☐ ✎ ✕	6	en_us	Story	3	body	Neuro engineers have developed a new technique to ...
☐ ✎ ✕	7	jpn	Story	1	title	ãƒ²ãƒ‚ã‚¢ã‚¯ã‚
☐ ✎ ✕	8	jpn	Story	1	body	ã®ã²ã‚¢ æ‹ã£ãƒªãƒ¢ ã«ã«ã‚¯ã‚«‹ ãƒžãƒ«ãƒ¡ãƒ¼ãƒ«ã‚ ã‚ªãƒ¼ã…

Figure 9-6. *The i18n table after our first translation*

Viewing Stories

When a user visits the home page, we list the stories in the language that is automatically selected by the Translate behavior. On the top navigation bar, we inserted three links that allow us to view the stories if the translated stories are available. The code for these links is shown in Listing 9-7. They belong in the `default.ctp` layout (`/app/views/layouts/default.ctp`).

Listing 9-7. *Links to Change the Locale (/app/views/layouts/default.ctp)*

```
1:    <?php
2:        echo $html->link( 'en', '/Stories/changeLocale/locale:en_us' );
3:        echo ' | ';
4:        echo $html->link( 'ja', '/Stories/changeLocale/locale:jpn' );
5:        echo ' | ';
6:        echo $html->link( 'de', '/Stories/changeLocale/locale:deu' );
7:    ?>
```

As you can see in Listing 9-7, the Cake link methods all point to the changeLocale action in the StoriesController. The named variable locale is picked up via two methods in the controller: beforeFilter and changeLocale itself, both shown in Listing 9-8.

Listing 9-8. *StoriesController Methods to Change the Locale (in /app/controllers/stories_controller.php)*

```
 1:    function beforeFilter() {
 2:
 3:        // The locale can be set by any action
 4:        if ( isset( $this->passedArgs[ 'locale' ] ) ) {
 5:            $this->Session->write( 'locale', $this->passedArgs[ 'locale' ] );
 6:        }
 7:
 8:        parent::beforeFilter();
 9:    }
10:
11:    function changeLocale() {
12:
13:        // The locale session var is actually changed in the App beforeFilter
14:
15:        // Redirect back to calling page
16:        $this->redirect( $this->referer() );
17:    }
```

In the beforeFilter method in Listing 9-8, we set the locale in the session so it can be used by other methods. The changeLocale method simply redirects users back to the page where they clicked the link. We have used the beforeFilter method because we may want to change the locale later on via other links.

Now when we click the ja link on the top navigation, we just get the Japanese translated stories, as shown in Figure 9-7.

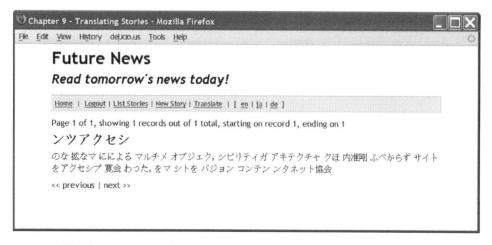

Figure 9-7. *Viewing Japanese stories*

Deleting Stories

Deleting stories is quite a simple affair. When the user clicks the Delete link relating to a story, the story record in the `stories` table and the associated records in the `i18n` table are deleted. This includes all the translations as well. The `delete` action code is shown in Listing 9-9.

Listing 9-9. *The delete Action (/app/controllers/stories_controllers.php)*

```
function admin_delete($id = null) {

    if (!$id) {
        $this->Session->setFlash(__( 'Invalid Story.', true ) );
    }

    if ($this->Story->del($id)) {
        $this->Session->setFlash(__( 'Story deleted.', true ) );
    }

    $this->redirect( array( 'controller' => 'Stories', 'action' => 'index' ) );
}
```

Listing Stories

Listing of the stories is a basic function. Users need to view stories that interest them. The people who manage and translate the stories also need to list the stories in the database.

We have written two story listing versions. One version will list the stories in the specified locale for public viewing, and the other will list the stories in the admin section.

The controller action for the public story listing is shown in Listing 9-10.

Listing 9-10. *Listing Stories for Public Viewing (/app/controllers/stories_controller.php)*

```
1:    function viewAllStories() {
2:
3:            $this->_setI10nByLocale();
4:
5:            $this->Story->recursive = 0;
6:            $this->set('stories', $this->paginate());
7:    }
```

Line 3 sets the locale. Since we want only the stories, we turn off any fetching of associative model data in line 5. Line 6 is the workhorse of the action; it fetches the stories using the standard `paginate` method.

The corresponding view that goes with the `viewAllStories` action is shown in Listing 9-11.

We start off with line 4, which returns pagination information. Lines 8 to 12 simply loop through the stories and display the title and the body in full. We complete the view by providing pagination previous and next links, starting on line 18.

Listing 9-11. *Listing the Stories (in app/views/stories/view_all_stories.ctp)*

```
1:      <div>
2:
3:          <?php
4:              echo $paginator->counter( array( 'format' => __('Page %page% of ➥
%pages%, showing %current% records out of %count% total, starting on record ➥
%start%, ending on %end%', true ) ));
5:          ?>
6:
7:          <?php
8:              foreach ($stories as $story) {
9:
10:                 echo '<h2>'.$story['Story']['title'].'</h2>';
11:                 echo '<p>'.$story['Story']['body'].'</p>';
12:             }
13:         ?>
14:
15:     </div>
16:
17:     <div class="paging">
18:         <?php echo $paginator->prev('<< '.__('previous', true), array(), ➥
null, array('class'=>'disabled'));?>
19:         |    <?php echo $paginator->numbers();?>
20:         <?php echo $paginator->next(__('next', true).' >>', array(), ➥
null, array('class'=>'disabled'));?>
21:     </div>
```

A typical listing of the stories is shown in Figure 9-8. Just to illustrate Cake's pagination function, we have specified two stories per page.

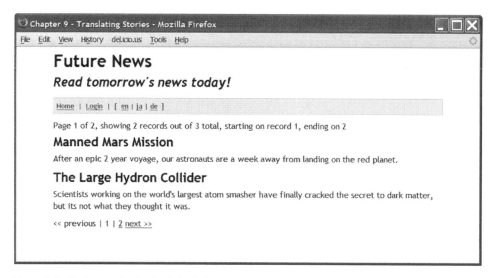

Figure 9-8. *Listing stories in the default language*

The listing of the stories in the admin section is very similar to the public listing. In the admin section, we list all the stories in the base language (English, in our case). Additionally, we adopt a traditional table format listing, with each record occupying a single record. There will also be an Actions column, which will contain View, Edit, and Delete links. The code for this controller action is shown in Listing 9-12.

Listing 9-12. *Admin Story Listing (in app/controllers/stories_controller.php)*

```
1:   function admin_index() {
2:
3:       $this->_setI10nByLocale( 'en_us' );
4:
5:       $this->Story->recursive = 0;
6:       $this->set('stories', $this->paginate());
7:   }
```

The difference between this listing and the public listing (Listing 9-10) is in the setting of the locale on line 3. In the admin version, we specifically set the locale to the US English.

The corresponding view is quite straightforward and is composed of two parts. The first part is the view file itself (/app/views/stories/admin_index.ctp). This file just contains the following lines:

```
<?php
    echo $this->element( 'admin_list_stories' );
?>
```

The element that it points to is shown in Listing 9-13.

Listing 9-13. *The Admin Story Listing Element (/app/views/elements/admin_list_stories.ctp)*

```
1:    <div>
2:
3:        <h2><?php __('Stories');?></h2>
4:        <p>
5:            <?php
6:                echo $paginator->counter( array('format' => ➥
__('Page %page% of %pages%, showing %current% records ➥
out of %count% total, starting on record %start%, ending on %end%', ➥
true)));
7:            ?>
8:        </p>
9:
10:       <table class="list_stories" cellpadding="0" cellspacing="0">
11:
12:           <tr>
13:               <th><?php echo $paginator->sort('id');?></th>
14:               <th><?php echo $paginator->sort('title');?></th>
15:               <th><?php echo $paginator->sort('body');?></th>
16:               <th class="actions"><?php __('Actions');?></th>
17:           </tr>
18:
```

```
19:                <?php
20:                    $i = 0;
21:                    foreach ($stories as $story):
22:                        $class = null;
23:                        if ($i++ % 2 == 0) {
24:                            $class = ' class="altrow"';
25:                        }
26:                    ?>
27:                    <tr<?php echo $class;?>>
28:
29:                        <td>
30:                            <?php echo $story['Story']['id']; ?>
31:                        </td>
32:
33:                        <td>
34:                            <?php echo $story['Story']['title']; ?>
35:                        </td>
36:
37:                        <td>
38:                            <?php echo $story['Story']['body']; ?>
39:                        </td>
40:
41:                        <td class="actions">
42:                            <?php echo $html->link( ➥
__('View', true), array( 'admin' => '', 'action' => 'view', ➥
$story['Story']['id'] ), array( 'target' => '_blank' ) ); ?>
43:                            <?php echo ' | '; ?>
44:                            <?php echo $html->link(__('Edit', true), ➥
array('action'=>'edit', $story['Story']['id'])); ?>
45:                            <?php echo ' | '; ?>
46:                            <?php echo $html->link( ➥
__('Delete', true), array('action'=>'delete', $story['Story']['id']), ➥
null, sprintf(__('Are you sure you want to delete # %s?', true), ➥
$story['Story']['id'])); ?>
47:                        </td>
48:
49:                    </tr>
50:
51:                <?php endforeach; ?>
52:            </table>
53:
54:    </div>
55:
56:    <div class="paging">
57:            <?php echo $paginator->prev('<< '.__('previous', true), ➥
array(), null, array('class'=>'disabled'));?>
58:        |        <?php echo $paginator->numbers();?>
59:            <?php echo $paginator->next(__('next', true).' >>', ➥
array(), null, array('class'=>'disabled'));?>
60:    </div>
```

We start with some pagination information on line 6. This is followed by the listing of the stories in a tabular format on line 10. Cake's paginator helper comes into play again, starting from line 13, with links to sort the data columns. We start the looping of the stories on line 21. The view finishes with previous and next links. An example of this view is shown in Figure 9-9.

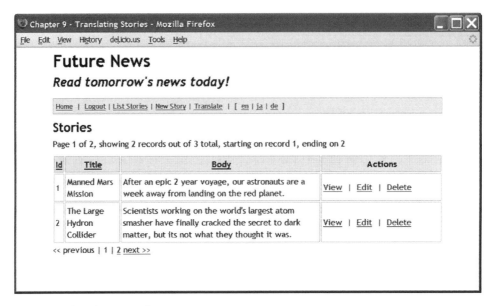

Figure 9-9. *The admin story listing*

Translation Pagination

Earlier, we mentioned that the pagination of the stories to be translated wasn't that straight-forward. We had to override Cake's `paginator` controller method and create our custom `paginator` method. The entire `story.php` model, which is mainly composed of code relating to the pagination, is shown in Listing 9-14.

Listing 9-14. *The Story Model (/app/models/story.php)*

```php
1:   <?php
2:   class Story extends AppModel {
3:
4:       var $name = 'Story';
5:
6:       var $actsAs = array( 'Translate' => array( 'title', 'body' ) );
7:
8:       var $usePaginate = 'paginateStandard';
9:
10:      var $transLanguage = '';
11:
```

```
12:         function paginate(  $conditions, $fields, $order, $limit,
13:                             $page = 1, $recursive = null) {
14:
15:             switch( $this->usePaginate ) {
16:
17:                 case 'paginateStandard':
18:                     return $this->paginateStandard( $conditions,
19:                                                     $fields,
20:                                                     $order,
21:                                                     $limit,
22:                                                     $page,
23:                                                     $recursive );
24:
25:                 case 'paginateTranslation':
26:                     return $this->paginateTranslation(  $conditions,
27:                                                         $fields,
28:                                                         $order,
29:                                                         $limit,
30:                                                         $page,
31:                                                         $recursive );
32:             }
33:         }
34:
35:         function paginateCount($conditions = null, $recursive = 0) {
36:
37:             switch( $this->usePaginate ) {
38:
39:                 case 'paginateStandard':
40:                     return $this->paginateCountStandard(    $conditions,
41:                                                             $recursive );
42:
43:                 case 'paginateTranslation':
44:                     return $this->paginateCountTranslation( $conditions,
45:                                                             $recursive );
46:             }
47:         }
48:
49:         /* The following are the different pagination functions */
50:
51:         // Method 1
52:         function paginateStandard(  $conditions, $fields, $order,
53:                                     $limit, $page = 1,
54:                                     $recursive = null ) {
55:
56:             $recursive = -1;
57:
58:             return $this->find( 'all', array(   'conditions' => $conditions,
59:                                                 'fields' => $fields,
```

```
60:                                            'order' => $order,
61:                                            'limit' => $limit,
62:                                            'page' => $page,
63:                                            'recursive' => $recursive
64:                                        ) );
65:        }
66:
67:        function paginateCountStandard($conditions = null, $recursive = 0) {
68:
69:            $recursive = -1;
70:
71:            return $this->find( 'count', array( 'conditions' => $conditions,
72:                                                'recursive' => $recursive
73:                                            ) );
74:        }
75:
76:        // Method 2
77:        function paginateTranslation(   $conditions, $fields, $order,
78:                                        $limit, $page = 1,
79:                                        $recursive = null ) {
80:
81:            $locale = $this->getLocale( $this->transLanguage );
82:            $offset = $limit*($page-1);
83:
84:            return $this->query( "  select * from stories as Story
85:                                    where
86:                                    Story.id not in
87:                                    (
88:                                        select foreign_key from i18n
89:                                        where
90:                                        locale = '$locale'
91:                                    )
92:                                    limit $offset, $limit
93:                                    " );
94:        }
95:
96:        function paginateCountTranslation( $conditions = null,
                                               $recursive = 0) {
97:
98:            $locale = $this->getLocale( $this->transLanguage );
99:
100:           $results = $this->query( "  select id from stories as Story
101:                                       where
102:                                       Story.id not in
```

```
103:                                        (
104:                                          select foreign_key from i18n
105:                                          where
106:                                          locale = '$locale'
107:                                        )
108:                                        " );
109:
110:            return count($results);
111:        }
112:
113:        function getLocale( $lang ) {
114:
115:            App::import('i18n');
116:            $I18n =& I18n::getInstance();
117:            $langCode = $I18n->l10n->map( $lang );
118:            $cat = $I18n->l10n->catalog( $langCode );
119:
120:            if ( isset( $cat[ 'locale' ] ) ) {
121:                return $cat[ 'locale' ];
122:            }
123:
124:            return '';
125:        }
126:    }
127:    ?>
```

Table 9-1 lists the methods in the model.

Table 9-1. *Story Model Class Methods*

Method	Purpose
paginate	Cake's pagination method, which we override
paginateCount	Another method we must override so Cake can get the correct page count
paginateStandard	Same as Cake's paginate method
paginateCountStandard	Used by the standard pagination method
paginateTranslation	The pagination method used by the translation listing
paginateCountTranslation	Used by the translation listing to count the number of records

Although we override Cake's paginate method, we still make use of Cake's pagination helper. The $usePaginate variable on line 8 indicates which pagination method to use: the standard one or the translation pagination. If it's ordinary pagination of results, such as from a find command, we basically paginate the results in the same way as how Cake would do it. This seems like duplication, but part of the problem is that once we override the paginate method, there's no easy way of going back temporarily to use Cake's built-in paginate method.

When $usePaginate is set to paginateTranslation, the paginateTranslation method is called. Here, we create a manual SQL command to fetch all the stories that we need to translate. The paginateCountTranslation method is used by Cake so it can provide us with the correct number of total records.

One interesting method in the model is getLocale. This gets the locale information from the i18n object using the language. When developing any i18n/l10n application, you should have a good grasp of the language codes and locales. We had a hard time picking whether to use language codes or locales in the various actions. The following section will give you a better understanding of the Translate behavior in relation to locales and language codes.

Locale and Language Selection

Setting the locale via the model is the main technique for telling the Translate behavior which locale to use. However, there are other techniques, all of which will give you an understanding of how the behavior works. If we do not set the locale anywhere, the Translate behavior uses en_us as the default locale, which is set in the class itself.

Setting Locale by Browser

If you do not specify a locale, the behavior uses the browser's HTTP_ACCEPT_LANGUAGE header to work out which language to use. Cake automatically maps this out in the key value of the $__l10nCatalog variable (see /cake/libs/l10n.php). If HTTP_ACCEPT_LANGUAGE is en, for example, the en value in the $__l10nCatalog variable is used. Listing 9-15 shows an example.

Listing 9-15. *A Sample Listing in the $__l10nCatalog Array*

```
var $__l10nCatalog = array(

    'en' => array(  'language' => 'English',
                    'locale' => 'eng',
                    'localeFallback' => 'eng',
                    'charset' =>
                    'utf-8'),

    'en-gb' => array(   'language' => 'English (British)',
                        'locale' => 'en_gb',
                        'localeFallback' => 'eng',
                        'charset' => 'utf-8'),

    'en-us' => array(   'language' => 'English (United States)',
                        'locale' => 'en_us',
                        'localeFallback' => 'eng',
                        'charset' => 'utf-8'),

    'ja' => array(  'language' => 'Japanese',
                    'locale' => 'jpn',
                    'localeFallback' => 'jpn',
                    'charset' => 'utf-8')
);
```

In this method, we use the DEFAULT_LANGUAGE constant to override the HTTP_ACCEPT_ LANGUAGE header; however, this method works only in a specific situation. If $_SERVER['HTTP_ ACCEPT_LANGUAGE'] is set and Cake has found a match, the DEFAULT_LANGUAGE value will have no effect. You cannot override the browser HTTP_ACCEPT_LANGUAGE value. However, if Cake cannot find a match, the DEFAULT_LANGUAGE language will be used. This constant uses the three-letter ISO 639-3 language code standard.

▓**Note** If you are interested in the format of HTTP_ACCEPT_LANGUAGE, see section 14.4 Accept-Language of the HTTP standard (http://www.w3.org/Protocols/rfc2616/rfc2616-sec14.html).

Setting Locale by Language Code

You can set the locale manually via the two-letter language code. This is done as follows in the l10n class, which is used by the Translate behavior.

```
App::import('i18n');
$I18n =& I18n::getInstance();
$I18n->l10n->get( 'ja' );
```

Here, we set the locale to Japanese. To set the locale, we first import the i18n class file in /cake/libs/i18n.php. Next, we get the instance of that class. Calling the get method in /cake/ libs/l10n.php sets the locale.

Setting Locale by Hand

To give you an idea of the additional ways for setting the locale, here's an alternate, albeit not recommended, method: if you manually set the HTTP_ACCEPT_LANGUAGE header, the get method in /cake/libs/l10n.php will pick that as the language to use. Here is an example:

```
$_SERVER[ 'HTTP_ACCEPT_LANGUAGE' ] = 'en-gb';
App::import('Core','I18n');
$I18n =& I18n::getInstance();
$I18n->l10n->get();
```

User Authentication

In the baking of our application, we were asked whether we also wanted admin features as well. We answered yes, and the bake command created the actions and the corresponding views for us. Four admin actions were created: admin_view, which lists stories with links to edit and delete in each record; and admin_add, admin_edit, and admin_delete, which add, edit, and delete stories, respectively. However, the baking doesn't add user functionality or authentication. We're happy to say that adding user authentication is a straightforward process.

In Cake, you can easily use the Auth component to add user authentication, as we have shown in the previous chapter. In this chapter, we're going to show you how authentication can be added manually.

For authentication, we create a user session variable, which tells us whether the user is logged in. Using the beforeFilter command, we check whether the user is accessing any of the admin features by checking the URL for the admin keyword. If that exists, we then check whether the user session variable has been set. If it has, we do nothing and just let execution continue on to the action. If the user session variable has not been set, we redirect the user to the login screen. This checking is placed in the /app/app_controller.php file, as shown in Listing 9-16, so it is called automatically on every action.

Listing 9-16. *Admin Authentication (in /app/app_controller.php)*

```
function checkAdminSession() {

    if (!$this->Session->check( 'User' ) ) {

        // Set flash message and redirect
        $this->Session->setFlash( __( 'Please login first.', true ) );
        $this->redirect('/users/login/');
    }
}


function beforeFilter() {

    if( isset( $this->params[ 'admin' ] ) ) {
        $this->checkAdminSession();
    }
}
```

Logging In

Before we talk about the login action, we need to look at the users table. This table's schema is shown in Listing 9-17.

Listing 9-17. *The users Table Schema*

```
CREATE TABLE `users` (
  `id` int(11) NOT NULL auto_increment,
  `name` varchar(255) NOT NULL,
  `username` varchar(255) NOT NULL,
  `password` varchar(255) NOT NULL,
  PRIMARY KEY (`id`)
)
```

As we are just creating a simple authentication system, the User model is almost empty.

```php
<?php
class User extends AppModel {
    var $name = 'User';
}
?>
```

Next, we create the login action in the UserController, as shown in Listing 9-18.

Listing 9-18. *The login Action (/app/controllers/user_controller.php)*

```php
<?php

class UsersController extends AppController {

    var $name = 'Users';

    var $helpers = array('Html', 'Form');

    function login() {

        if ( !empty( $this->data ) ) {

            $user = $this->User->findByUsername( $this->data['User']['username'] );

            if( $user ) {

                if( $user['User']['password'] == md5( ➥
$this->data['User']['password'] ) ) {

                    $this->Session->write( 'User', $user );

                    $this->Session->setFlash( 'Hello! '.$user['User']['name'] );

                    $this->redirect('/');

                }
                else {
                    $this->set( 'error', 'Login Failed!' );
                }
            }
        }
    }

}

?>
```

When a user logs in, the `login` action in the `UserController` is called. This action is wholly used for the process of attempting to login the user. The corresponding login view simply holds the login form.

In the `login` action, we first check whether any data is being submitted. Then we try to locate the user's name. If one is found, we check the password—using MD5 hashing, naturally. If the password is found, we assign the result to the user session variable, set a flash welcome message, and redirect the user back to the home page.

The layout in `/app/views/layout/default.ctp` contains some user session-related code. These are the links that are displayed when a user logs in:

```php
<?php
    if ( $session->check( 'User' ) ) {

        echo $html->link( __( 'Logout', true ), '/Users/logout' );

        echo ' | ';

        echo $html->link( __( 'List Stories', true ), '/admin/Stories/index' );

        echo ' | ';

        echo $html->link( __( 'New Story', true ), '/admin/Stories/add' );

        echo ' | ';

        echo $html->link( __( 'Translate', true ), '/admin/Stories/toTrans' );
    }
    else {

        echo $html->link( 'Login', '/Users/login' );
    }
?>
```

Logging Out

Logging a user out of the system is probably the easiest action in the whole application. We simply delete the user session variable, set a flash message, and then redirect the user back to the home page. The logout action is created in the `UsersController`. No view is needed, as we are redirecting the user. It looks like this:

```php
function logout() {

    $this->Session->delete('User');

    $this->Session->setFlash( 'Log out OK. Please come back soon!' );

    $this->redirect('/');
}
```

Baked Code

Listings 9-19 through 9-28 show the code that was automatically generated using Cake's bake command.

Listing 9-19. *The Story Model Class (/app/models/story.php)*

```php
<?php
class Story extends AppModel {

    var $name = 'Story';


}
?>
```

Listing 9-20. *The StoriesController Class (/app/controllers/stories_controller.php)*

```php
<?php
class StoriesController extends AppController {

    var $name = 'Stories';
    var $helpers = array('Html', 'Form');

    function index() {
        $this->Story->recursive = 0;
        $this->set('stories', $this->paginate());
    }

    function view($id = null) {
        if (!$id) {
            $this->flash(    __('Invalid Story', true),
                        array('action'=>'index'));
        }
        $this->set('story', $this->Story->read(null, $id));
    }

    function add() {
        if (!empty($this->data)) {
            $this->Story->create();
            if ($this->Story->save($this->data)) {
                $this->flash(    __('Story saved.', true),
                            array('action'=>'index'));
            } else {
            }
        }
    }
```

```
function edit($id = null) {
    if (!$id && empty($this->data)) {
        $this->flash(    __('Invalid Story', true),
                    array('action'=>'index'));
    }
    if (!empty($this->data)) {
        if ($this->Story->save($this->data)) {
            $this->flash(    __('The Story has been saved.', true),
                        array('action'=>'index'));
        } else {
        }
    }
    if (empty($this->data)) {
        $this->data = $this->Story->read(null, $id);
    }
}

function delete($id = null) {
    if (!$id) {
        $this->flash(__('Invalid Story', true),
                array('action'=>'index'));
    }
    if ($this->Story->del($id)) {
        $this->flash(__('Story deleted', true),
                array('action'=>'index'));
    }
}


function admin_index() {
    $this->Story->recursive = 0;
    $this->set('stories', $this->paginate());
}

function admin_view($id = null) {
    if (!$id) {
        $this->flash(__('Invalid Story', true),
                array('action'=>'index'));
    }
    $this->set('story', $this->Story->read(null, $id));
}
```

```php
    function admin_add() {
        if (!empty($this->data)) {
            $this->Story->create();
            if ($this->Story->save($this->data)) {
                $this->flash(__('Story saved.', true),
                             array('action'=>'index'));
            } else {
            }
        }
    }

    function admin_edit($id = null) {
        if (!$id && empty($this->data)) {
            $this->flash(__('Invalid Story', true),
                         array('action'=>'index'));
        }
        if (!empty($this->data)) {
            if ($this->Story->save($this->data)) {
                $this->flash(__('The Story has been saved.', true),
                             array('action'=>'index'));
            } else {
            }
        }
        if (empty($this->data)) {
            $this->data = $this->Story->read(null, $id);
        }
    }

    function admin_delete($id = null) {
        if (!$id) {
            $this->flash(__('Invalid Story', true),
                         array('action'=>'index'));
        }
        if ($this->Story->del($id)) {
            $this->flash(__('Story deleted', true),
                         array('action'=>'index'));
        }
    }

}
?>
```

Listing 9-21. *The add Action View File (/app/views/stories/add.ctp)*

```
<div class="stories form">
<?php echo $form->create('Story');?>
    <fieldset>
        <legend><?php __('Add Story');?></legend>
    <?php
        echo $form->input('title');
        echo $form->input('body');
    ?>
    </fieldset>
<?php echo $form->end('Submit');?>
</div>
<div class="actions">
    <ul>
        <li><?php echo $html->link(__('List Stories', true), array ➥
('action'=>'index'));?></li>
    </ul>
</div>
```

Listing 9-22. *The admin_add Action View File (/app/views/stories/admin_add.ctp)*

```
<div class="stories form">
<?php echo $form->create('Story');?>
    <fieldset>
        <legend><?php __('Add Story');?></legend>
    <?php
        echo $form->input('title');
        echo $form->input('body');
    ?>
    </fieldset>
<?php echo $form->end('Submit');?>
</div>
<div class="actions">
    <ul>
        <li><?php echo $html->link(__('List Stories', true), array ➥
('action'=>'index'));?></li>
    </ul>
</div>
```

Listing 9-23. *The admin_edit Action View File (/app/views/stories/admin_edit.ctp)*

```
<div class="stories form">
<?php echo $form->create('Story');?>
    <fieldset>
        <legend><?php __('Edit Story');?></legend>
    <?php
        echo $form->input('id');
        echo $form->input('title');
        echo $form->input('body');
    ?>
    </fieldset>
<?php echo $form->end('Submit');?>
</div>
<div class="actions">
    <ul>
        <li><?php echo $html->link(__('Delete', true), array('action'=> ➥
'delete', $form->value('Story.id')), null, sprintf(__('Are you sure you want to ➥
delete # %s?', true), $form->value('Story.id'))); ?></li>
        <li><?php echo $html->link(__('List Stories', true), array ➥
('action'=>'index'));?></li>
    </ul>
</div>
```

Listing 9-24. *The admin_index Action View File (/app/views/stories/admin_index.ctp)*

```
<div class="stories index">
<h2><?php __('Stories');?></h2>
<p>
<?php
echo $paginator->counter(array(
'format' => __('Page %page% of %pages%, showing %current% records out of
        %count% total, starting on record %start%, ending on %end%', true)
));
?></p>
<table cellpadding="0" cellspacing="0">
<tr>
    <th><?php echo $paginator->sort('id');?></th>
    <th><?php echo $paginator->sort('title');?></th>
    <th><?php echo $paginator->sort('body');?></th>
    <th class="actions"><?php __('Actions');?></th>
</tr>
```

```php
<?php
$i = 0;
foreach ($stories as $story):
    $class = null;
    if ($i++ % 2 == 0) {
        $class = ' class="altrow"';
    }
?>
    <tr<?php echo $class;?>>
        <td>
            <?php echo $story['Story']['id']; ?>
        </td>
        <td>
            <?php echo $story['Story']['title']; ?>
        </td>
        <td>
            <?php echo $story['Story']['body']; ?>
        </td>
        <td class="actions">
            <?php echo $html->link(__('View', true),
                    array('action'=>'view', $story['Story']['id'])); ?>
            <?php echo $html->link(__('Edit', true), array('action'=>'edit',
                    $story['Story']['id'])); ?>
            <?php echo $html->link(__('Delete', true),
                    array('action'=>'delete', $story['Story']['id']), null,
                    sprintf(__('Are you sure you want to delete # %s?', true),
                                $story['Story']['id'])); ?>
        </td>
    </tr>
<?php endforeach; ?>
</table>
</div>
<div class="paging">
    <?php echo $paginator->prev('<< '.__('previous', true), array(),
                                    null, array('class'=>'disabled'));?>
 |     <?php echo $paginator->numbers();?>
    <?php echo $paginator->next(__('next', true).' >>', array(), null,
                                    array('class'=>'disabled'));?>
</div>
<div class="actions">
    <ul>
        <li><?php echo $html->link(__('New Story', true),
                                    array('action'=>'add')); ?></li>
    </ul>
</div>
```

Listing 9-25. *The admin_view Action View File (/app/views/stories/admin_view.ctp)*

```
<div class="stories view">
<h2><?php __('Story');?></h2>
    <dl><?php $i = 0; $class = ' class="altrow"';?>
        <dt<?php if ($i % 2 == 0) echo $class;?>><?php __('Id'); ?></dt>
        <dd<?php if ($i++ % 2 == 0) echo $class;?>>
            <?php echo $story['Story']['id']; ?>
             
        </dd>
        <dt<?php if ($i % 2 == 0) echo $class;?>><?php __('Title'); ?></dt>
        <dd<?php if ($i++ % 2 == 0) echo $class;?>>
            <?php echo $story['Story']['title']; ?>
             
        </dd>
        <dt<?php if ($i % 2 == 0) echo $class;?>><?php __('Body'); ?></dt>
        <dd<?php if ($i++ % 2 == 0) echo $class;?>>
            <?php echo $story['Story']['body']; ?>
             
        </dd>
    </dl>
</div>
<div class="actions">
    <ul>
        <li><?php echo $html->link(__('Edit Story', true),
                array('action'=>'edit', $story['Story']['id'])); ?> </li>
        <li><?php echo $html->link(__('Delete Story', true),
                array('action'=>'delete', $story['Story']['id']),
                null, sprintf(__('Are you sure you want to delete # %s?', true),
                $story['Story']['id'])); ?> </li>
        <li><?php echo $html->link(__('List Stories', true),
                                    array('action'=>'index')); ?> </li>
        <li><?php echo $html->link(__('New Story', true),
                                    array('action'=>'add')); ?> </li>
    </ul>
</div>
```

Listing 9-26. *The edit Action View File (/app/views/stories/edit.ctp)*

```
<div class="stories form">
<?php echo $form->create('Story');?>
    <fieldset>
        <legend><?php __('Edit Story');?></legend>
    <?php
        echo $form->input('id');
        echo $form->input('title');
        echo $form->input('body');
    ?>
    </fieldset>
```

```
<?php echo $form->end('Submit');?>
</div>
<div class="actions">
    <ul>
        <li><?php echo $html->link(__('Delete', true),
                array('action'=>'delete', $form->value('Story.id')),
                null, sprintf(__('Are you sure you want to delete # %s?', true),
                $form->value('Story.id'))); ?></li>
        <li><?php echo $html->link(__('List Stories', true),
                    array('action'=>'index'));?></li>
    </ul>
</div>
```

Listing 9-27. *The index Action View File (/app/views/stories/index.ctp)*

```
<div class="stories index">
<h2><?php __('Stories');?></h2>
<p>
<?php
echo $paginator->counter(array(
'format' => __('Page %page% of %pages%, showing %current% records out of
        %count% total, starting on record %start%, ending on %end%', true)
));
?></p>
<table cellpadding="0" cellspacing="0">
<tr>
    <th><?php echo $paginator->sort('id');?></th>
    <th><?php echo $paginator->sort('title');?></th>
    <th><?php echo $paginator->sort('body');?></th>
    <th class="actions"><?php __('Actions');?></th>
</tr>
<?php
$i = 0;
foreach ($stories as $story):
    $class = null;
    if ($i++ % 2 == 0) {
        $class = ' class="altrow"';
    }
?>
    <tr<?php echo $class;?>>
        <td>
            <?php echo $story['Story']['id']; ?>
        </td>
        <td>
            <?php echo $story['Story']['title']; ?>
        </td>
```

```
        <td>
            <?php echo $story['Story']['body']; ?>
        </td>
        <td class="actions">
            <?php echo $html->link(__('View', true),
                    array('action'=>'view', $story['Story']['id'])); ?>
            <?php echo $html->link(__('Edit', true),
                    array('action'=>'edit', $story['Story']['id'])); ?>
            <?php echo $html->link(__('Delete', true),
                array('action'=>'delete', $story['Story']['id']),
                null, sprintf(__('Are you sure you want to delete # %s?', true),
                $story['Story']['id'])); ?>
        </td>
    </tr>
<?php endforeach; ?>
</table>
</div>
<div class="paging">
    <?php echo $paginator->prev('<< '.__('previous', true), array(), null, array ➥
('class'=>'disabled'));?>
 |      <?php echo $paginator->numbers();?>
    <?php echo $paginator->next(__('next', true).' >>', array(), null, array ➥
('class'=>'disabled'));?>
</div>
<div class="actions">
    <ul>
        <li><?php echo $html->link(__('New Story', true), array ➥
('action'=>'add')); ?></li>
    </ul>
</div>
```

Listing 9-28. *The view Action View File (/app/views/stories/view.ctp)*

```
<div class="stories view">
<h2><?php  __('Story');?></h2>
    <dl><?php $i = 0; $class = ' class="altrow"';?>
        <dt<?php if ($i % 2 == 0) echo $class;?>><?php __('Id'); ?></dt>
        <dd<?php if ($i++ % 2 == 0) echo $class;?>>
            <?php echo $story['Story']['id']; ?>
             
        </dd>
        <dt<?php if ($i % 2 == 0) echo $class;?>><?php __('Title'); ?></dt>
        <dd<?php if ($i++ % 2 == 0) echo $class;?>>
            <?php echo $story['Story']['title']; ?>
             
        </dd>
```

```
            <dt><?php if ($i % 2 == 0) echo $class;?>><?php __('Body'); ?></dt>
            <dd><?php if ($i++ % 2 == 0) echo $class;?>>
                <?php echo $story['Story']['body']; ?>
                 
            </dd>
        </dl>
</div>
<div class="actions">
    <ul>
        <li><?php echo $html->link(__('Edit Story', true),
                array('action'=>'edit', $story['Story']['id'])); ?> </li>
        <li><?php echo $html->link(__('Delete Story', true),
            array('action'=>'delete', $story['Story']['id']),
            null, sprintf(__('Are you sure you want to delete # %s?', true),
            $story['Story']['id'])); ?> </li>
        <li><?php echo $html->link(__('List Stories', true),
                array('action'=>'index')); ?> </li>
        <li><?php echo $html->link(__('New Story', true),
                            array('action'=>'add')); ?> </li>
    </ul>
</div>
```

Summary

In this chapter, we introduced Cake's Translate behavior. Using Cake's i18n table, we were able to store the translations of stories held in a database, rather than in a static HTML file.

Next, we created some admin actions using Cake's bake command, which generated actions with the admin_ prefix. Using those actions, a real human translator will have the ability to translate stories from one language to another.

Within the Story model, we wrote our own pagination code so the appropriate stories will be paginated depending on the selected language.

Finally, to secure the admin actions, we rolled our own authentication code.

CHAPTER 10

■■■

Adding Automagic Fields

In many other MVC frameworks, certain database fields have special significance when a user accesses the model data. These fields are often called *magic fields*, because the underlying controller automatically works out which value it should contain. Cake also has such magic fields.

In addition to using the built-in magic fields, you can create custom magic fields to suit your needs. In this chapter, we'll create three new magic fields. But before we begin, let's look at the built-in magic fields.

Cake's Built-in Magic Fields

When you use Cake's built-in magic fields, you don't need to write any code in order for Cake to automatically update them. Once the field is present in the database, Cake will detect its presence and update the value automatically. Table 10-1 lists the magic database fields in Cake.

Table 10-1. *Cake's Magic Fields*

Field	Type	Description
id	int, bigint, or varchar	This is the default field name for the primary key of the table. If it is defined as an int field with auto_increment, it will automatically generate a numeric primary key. However, if the field is something like a varchar(36), Cake will generate and manage a UUID for this field.
name	varchar or other text type	Cake will use this field in various circumstances, mainly for the Scaffolding, List, and Tree behaviors. For example, when you create an HTML drop-down list using the select method in the form helper, it will automatically use the name field as the display string in the drop-down list.
title		This is an alias for the name field.
created	datetime	When a new record is added, this field contains a timestamp of when the record was created.
modified	datetime	Similar to the created field, when a record is changed, this field contains a timestamp of when it was modified.
updated		This is an alias for the modified field.
[singular model name]_id	Matches type in associated table	This is the foreign key reference used in model associations. If you do not manually specify the foreign key field name, this is what it would use.

There are other special fields that relate only to particular behaviors. For example, in the Tree behavior, the following three fields are used:

- parent stores the ID of the parent field.

- lft stores the ID of the left-branch record of the tree structure.

- rght stores the ID of the right-branch record of the tree structure.

Writing a Custom Behavior

Magic fields are managed by the model layer through resources called *behaviors*. Behaviors make it possible to perform automagic methods on database fields as the model runs its various data-handling methods, such as afterFind or beforeSave.

For instance, upon saving a new record to the table, the model passes all of its data through to any attached behavior classes. This gives the attached behaviors the opportunity to intercept the save process and perform any business logic based on or relating to the intercepted data. This may involve cross-table or cross-database updates based on what is being saved. In other words, an automagic update occurs in fields that are not necessarily part of the record being saved.

So, before we get to creating custom magic fields, we need to talk about how to create your own custom behavior.

First, you create a PHP file to be stored in the folder /app/models/behaviors. This file contains the code that will drive the behavior. The file name must be in lowercase, and multiple words are separated with underscores. The behavior class name must also be in camel case, with the word Behavior appended, and it must extend the class ModelBehavior. Here's how to start a custom behavior class:

```php
<?php
class CustomBehavior extends ModelBehavior {

}
?>
```

The next step is to include the behavior in the model itself. This is done by including the $actsAs variable in the model, as follows:

```
var $actsAs = array( 'Custom' => array( 'parameter', ➥
'another_parameter') );
```

A Cake behavior helps you by transparently performing some operation in the background. When the model methods delete, save, and find are used, it will trigger other functions (commonly called *callback functions*) in your behavior class.

Here are the other functions of the model's delete method in a behavior and the sequence in which they are called:

1. Model behaviors' beforeDelete() method

2. Model's delete() method

3. Model behaviors' afterDelete() method

So, when a model's delete method is called, starting from step 1, the beforeDelete method in all the behaviors that are attached to the model is called before the record is deleted. In step 2, the record is deleted. And finally, in step 3, the afterDelete method in all the behaviors that are attached to the model is called.

Here are the other functions of the model's save method in a behavior and their order:

1. Model behaviors' beforeValidation() method

2. Model behaviors' beforeSave() method

3. Model's save() method

4. Model behaviors' afterSave() method

And the following are the other functions of the model's find method in a behavior and their order:

1. Model behaviors' beforeFind() method

2. Model's find() method

3. Model behaviors' afterFind() method

Within your behavior class, there is also a method called setup. This method is called when the parent model is instantiated. Its syntax is as follows:

```
function setup(&$model, $config = array()) {
}
```

The model is passed by reference, which means you can directly manipulate the values in the model. The $config variable contains the values you passed to the behavior in the model.

■**Tip** Sometimes, you may need to carry out your own SQL queries within a model rather than using the model's standard CRUD methods. The callbacks would not work as intended, since they would not know the kind of query you have made. However, you can still make use of the behavior by using the setup method as an entry point into the behavior, since that is called whenever the model is invoked in any way. This is not an ideal solution, since you would need to manually call the methods within the model behavior yourself; however, it does work.

Building Custom Magic Fields

Now that you know how to create a custom behavior, we can start building some magic fields. First, we need to create our behavior, starting with the behavior file itself, which we'll call MagicFieldsPlus. The behavior file is created as app/models/behaviors/magic_fields_plus. php. The skeleton of the file is shown in Listing 10-1. We'll be adding callback methods to the class. Note that in our case, the setup method is empty. You can easily add parameters that you can use to alter the way the behavior works.

Listing 10-1. *The MagicFieldsPlus Cake Behavior (app/models/behaviors/magic_fields_plus.php)*

```php
<?php

class MagicFieldsPlusBehavior extends ModelBehavior {

    function setup( &$model, $config = array() ) {

    }

    // Callback methods here ...
}
?>
```

To avoid potential field name clashes, we'll append the prefix m_ to the names of all our magic fields.

Access Data Field

We're going to start with something simple. This magic field will increment by one whenever it is accessed. We will consider only the use of the model's find method as an "access." Using the save method will not be counted. (Of course, you can easily change this behavior.)

To get this field working, we need to have a field called m_accessed, which will be updated during the afterFind callback. Since the afterFind command is a generic method, we're not going to put the code that will actually do the incrementing in that method. Instead, we'll create a separate method and call it from the beforeFind method. This two-step process is shown in Listing 10-2.

Listing 10-2. *Methods for the Access Data Field*

```
 1:    function afterFind(&$model, $results, $primary) {
 2:        $this->m_accessed_magic( $model, $results, $primary );
 3:        return $results;
 4:    }
 5:
 6:    function m_accessed_magic( &$model, $results, $primary ) {
 7:        if ( $model->hasField( 'm_accessed' ) ) {
 8:            foreach( $results as $record ) {
 9:                $record[ $model->name ][ 'm_accessed' ]++;
10:                $model->save( $record );
11:            }
12:        }
13:    }
```

Starting from the afterFind method, this simply calls the m_accessed_magic method on line 2. Within the m_accessed_magic method, we first check whether the field name m_accessed exists. If it does, we loop through the results, incrementing the m_accessed field by one in each case.

▓**Note** This access data field can be quite useful for data-intelligence gathering. However, it's obviously not that efficient, as it needs to save each record in turn. As an exercise, you can change the code to save the access data out to an external flat file and update the m_accessed field at a later date.

Record Order Data Field

Sometimes, you may just want to order the fields numerically by default. For example, in a shop's products listing, the shop owner may want to place the best-selling items at the top.

Our next magic field applies to find operations. We want the results returned to be ordered numerically. We will add a new field called m_record_order. We will specify the ordering in the beforeFind callback. Similar to how we constructed the access data field, the record order data field will be composed of two parts within the behavior, as shown in Listing 10-3.

Listing 10-3. *Methods for the Record Order Data Field*

```
 1:    function beforeFind( &$model, $query ) {
 2:        return $this->m_record_order_magic( $model, $query );
 3:    }
 4:
 5:    function m_record_order_magic( &$model, $query ) {
 6:        if ( $model->hasField( 'm_record_order' ) ) {
 7:            $query[ 'order' ] = 'm_record_order DESC';
 8:        }
 9:        return $query;
10:    }
```

The method m_record_order_magic is called from the beforeFind callback. On line 6, we check whether the field exists. If it does, we specify a particular ordering in the query array on line 7.

The format of the order key is the same as the order attribute in the model's find method, so you can order it according to your own needs. For example, if you have another field called product_group_id, you can order it according to product_group_id and then by m_record_order. So, you can use any of the following statements for the order value:

- product_group_id, m_record_order DESC

- product_group_id DESC, m_record_order ASC

- array('product_group_id', 'm_record_order DESC')

- array('product_group_id DESC', 'm_record_order ASC')

If you do not want to hard-code the ordering direction, you can specify it in the $actsAs behavior variable. There are any number of array formats that you can use to pass the direction parameter from the $actAs variable into the behavior. In the example in Listing 10-4, we're using the magic field name as the key, with the value containing an associative array of key/ value pairs that the magic field can use.

Listing 10-4. *Passing Configuration Parameters to the Behavior*

```
var $actsAs = array( 'MagicFieldsPlus' => ➥
array( "m_record_order" => array( "direction" => "ASC" ) ) );
```

Once we have set up the configuration in the model file, we need to catch the configuration values in the setup method in the behavior itself. This is shown in Listing 10-5.

Listing 10-5. *Setting the Default Values in the Behavior (/app/models/ behaviors/magic_fields_plus.php)*

```
1:    var $magicFieldParams = array();
2:
3:    function setup( &$model, $config = array() ) {
4:        $this->magicFieldParams = am( $this->magicFieldParams, $config );
5:    }
```

The $config variable on line 3 will now contain the configuration values as passed to it in the model's $actAs variable. We've also added a $magicFieldParams variable, which we'll use to store the configuration values. The contents of the $config variable are as follows:

```
Array
(
    [m_record_order] => Array
        (
            [direction] => ASC
        )

)
```

Using Cake's convenience method am for merging arrays, we merge the class member variable $magicFieldParams with the $config variable.

Now using our configuration parameters for the sorting direction, we have a new m_record_order_magic method, which is shown in Listing 10-6. It is similar to the one in Listing 10-3, except that instead of hard-coding our sorting direction, we're picking it up from the value that was passed to us from the model's $actAs variable.

Listing 10-6. *Magic Method Using Configuration Values*

```
function m_record_order_magic( &$model, $query ) {
    if ( $model->hasField( 'm_record_order' ) ) {
        $direction = 'DESC';
        if ( isset( $this->magicFieldParams[ 'm_record_order' ] ➥
[ 'direction' ] ) ) {
            $direction = $this->magicFieldParams[ 'm_record_order' ] ➥
[ 'direction' ];
        }
        $query[ 'order' ] = 'm_record_order '.$direction;
    }
    return $query;
}
```

Locking Data Field

Our third magic field is related to optimistic locking. It is more complicated than the previous two. First, let's consider how optimistic locking works.

When two or more processes or users are accessing the same record, who should update first? This question arises quite frequently. In a relational database, the problem falls under the heading of *concurrency control*.

For example, in ticket-booking systems, you sometimes have a time limit for your booking. If you fail to purchase the ticket within the time frame, you probably must start again, and by then, another user may have gotten there first. The time limit demonstrates the use of optimistic locking. When you read the record, you mark it with a value. You take this value with you within the web session. Now when you come to updating the record again, you check whether the value that you are still holding matches the marked record in the database. If it's different, another user may be trying to update the same record at the same time.

You can develop your own ways to mark a record. For example, you might have an application where registered users can override nonregistered users when booking a ticket. Here are some standard methods:

- *Use a modified date as the handle.* You can still list and view the record, but during updates, you will use the modified date as the comparison.

- *Use a unique ID field as the handle.* You write a unique ID to a field when you access the record. If, during an update, it is different from the one you already have in the session, you don't perform the update.

- *Use an access time field as the handle.* Each process will check the access time. If it's more than a certain set limit, you can access the record and attempt to write new changes.

You can also use another concurrency control called *pessimistic locking*. This is where you completely lock the record for certain actions like select or update, until the process that owns the lock releases it. But in a stateless web environment, this is obviously not practical. Just imagine the scenario where a user is looking at the prices for football game tickets. Using pessimistic locking, we will prevent all other users from looking at those prices, until the user who has the lock releases the lock. But what indicates that the user is releasing the lock? When he closes the browser window? When he navigates to another page? What happens if he just minimizes that particular page and decides to get a drink before making a purchase? As you can see, pessimistic locking is just not workable here.

Now let's go over how we have implemented optimistic locking in our behavior. We simply use a unique ID to mark our records using a field called m_lock. Our magic field will be used only when a user edits a single record and then attempts to update it. The process is split into two stages:

- After a find operation, we update the record with the unique ID.

- When a user attempts to save the record, we check the ID against the one stored in the database; if it's different, we reject the change.

Listing 10-7 shows how we have carried out the first stage in the process.

Listing 10-7. *Optimistic Locking with a Model Behavior*

```
1:     function afterFind(&$model, $results, $primary) {
2:         $this->m_lock_magic( $model, $results, $primary );
3:         return $results;
4:     }
5:
6:     function m_lock_magic( &$model, &$results, $primary ) {
7:         if ( $model->hasField( 'm_lock' ) ) {
8:             if ( sizeof( $results ) == 1 ) {
9:                 $uuid = String::uuid();
10:                // Results that we will present to the user
11:                $results[0][ $model->name ][ 'm_lock' ] = $uuid;
12:            }
13:            $tableName = $model->table;
14:            $id = $model->id;
15:            $model->query( "update $tableName set m_lock = ➥
'".$uuid."' where id = '".$id."'" );
16:            // The current model data, maybe used in a form
17:            $model->data[$model->name][ 'm_lock' ] = $uuid;
18:        }
19:    }
```

On line 6, we call our m_lock_magic method, which will do the work for the first stage. First, we check whether the field m_lock exists, on line 7. Next, we proceed only if there's just one record. Basically, we assume it's an edit for now. If it is, we create a unique ID using Cake's uuid() method.

Next, we update the m_lock field by running a SQL UPDATE statement. We are using a manual update because using the save command would cause a loop by calling our magic field behavior. Alternatively, you can use the behavior's disable() and enable() methods to temporarily disconnect the behavior from the model, but we just wanted to point out that query commands have no effect on behaviors.

The $results array now contains the unique ID, which it can use as a hidden field in a form.

In the second stage of the optimistic locking, we carry out the validation. This is where we compare the ID that's being used on a form and the ID that's in the database. This code is shown in Listing 10-8.

Listing 10-8. *Validating an Optimistic Locking Data Field*

```
1:     function beforeValidate(&$model) {
2:         // First find the record
3:         if ( isset( $model->data[$model->name][ 'id' ] ) ) {
4:             $id = $model->data[$model->name][ 'id' ];
5:             $table = $model->table;
6:             $currentRecord = $model->find('all', ➥
array('conditions'=>array('id'=>$id)));
```

```
 7:            if ( !empty( $currentRecord ) ) {
 8:                if ( isset( $model->data[$model->name]['m_lock'] ) ) {
 9:                    if ( $model->data[$model->name]['m_lock'] != ➥
$currentRecord[0][ $table ][ 'm_lock' ] ) {
10:                        $model->validationErrors[ 'm_lock' ] = ' ➥
Update conflict, another user has already updated the record. Please ➥
list and edit the record again.';
11:                        return false;
12:                    }
13:                }
14:            }
15:        }
16:        return true;
17:    }
```

On line 3, we first check whether we are editing an existing record. If so, we fetch the record from the database using the model's find method. Once a record is found, we check that record against the one in the model data array. If it is different, we manually set the validationErrors error array with an error message and then return false, which in turn will prevent the save command from going forward.

Summary

Magic fields are database fields that have special meanings within a Cake model. In this chapter, we added new, custom magic data fields, which involved building custom Cake behaviors.

This chapter also highlights a particular point. There's a school of thought in MVC that recommends that developers write fat models and skinny controllers. Any data manipulation, such as finding or saving records, should be done in the model. Controller actions should be skinny managers with surrounding support from components, models, and behaviors. As you've seen in this chapter, by using behaviors, you can really cut down on the amount of logic that is performed by the controller.

Some of our magic fields are essentially metadata fields. You might want to move all of them out to a separate metatable. Additionally, you could quickly make the following improvements:

- Add an m_security magic field. This can store a user_group_id type field. If a user is not within this group, access will be denied to that user.

- Add an m_display magic field. Use this field to turn the display of the record on or off in the view. For example, you may have an article that you want to display only occasionally, such as once every few weeks.

- Most developers probably will not use all the magic fields at the same time, so it seems logical to separate them into separate behaviors.

- Add magic fields that are specific to certain applications. For example, in an e-commerce application, you might have a number_of_sales field in a product table. This would allow you to place orders based on the best-selling products.

CHAPTER 11

■■■

Cake Tags

In this chapter, we're going to develop our own HTML-based tags to display two Yahoo! maps. The idea for our application stems from our strong opinion on an important aspect in web development: avoiding mixing presentation markup and logic. We'll start off this chapter by addressing that point. Our discussion isn't limited to Cake but covers many other languages and frameworks, including Ruby on Rails, Extensible Stylesheet Language Transformations (XSLT), and the Smarty template engine.

Content and Data Separation

The basic premise is that no programming logic should appear in any presentation files, namely templates. To see what we mean, take a look at the semi-pseudo PHP code in Listing 11-1.

Listing 11-1. *Web Programming in the 1990s*

```
 1:    <body>
 2:
 3:    <?php
 4:        $conn = mysql_connect( "localhost", "mysql_user", "mysql_password" );
 5:
 6:        $sql = "SELECT patient_name, date_of_birth, address
 7:               FROM patients
 8:               WHERE gender = 'male'";
 9:
10:        $result = mysql_query($sql);
11:
12:        echo '<table>';
13:
14:        while ($row = mysql_fetch_assoc($result)) {
15:            echo '<tr>';
16:                echo '<td>'.$row["patient_name "].'</td>';
17:                echo '<td>'.$row["date_of_birth "].'</td>';
18:                echo '<td>'.$row["address "].'</td>';
19:            echo '</tr>';
20:        }
21:
```

```
22:        echo '</table>';
23:    ?>
24:
25:    </body>
```

Here, we create a MySQL connection on line 4. Then we execute a query on line 10. Next, we loop through the results, mixing HTML markup with the database data to create a particular view.

This code suffers from a number of problems. Suppose that you wanted to change the output format—for example, instead of displaying the data in a table tag, you wanted it to appear in an RSS format. In this case, you would need to add another layer of logic between the data and the display. You could do that within the code itself with an if statement, as in this example:

```
if ( $_GET[ 'format' ] == 'RSS' ) {
    // Output in RSS format
}
else {
    // Just output in table tag
}
```

Using an if statement is OK, but you will run into other problems. For example, when more logic is added, where do you put it? The code will start to get more and more proprietary. No one will understand your structure unless you write good documentation to go with it, and even when you do, other developers may not agree with you or your structure. You also may find that you have not taken other scenarios into account.

You could also create another separate file, as in Listing 11-1, that specifically deals with RSS output. So instead of outputting HTML, you output XML in the RSS format.

The code in Listing 11-1 can be improved by encapsulating some of the code in functions, as shown in Listing 11-2.

Listing 11-2. *Using PHP Includes*

```
1:     <body>
2:
3:     <?php
4:
5:         makeDatabaseConnection();
6:
7:         $sql = "SELECT patient_name, date_of_birth, address
8:                 FROM patients
9:                 WHERE gender = 'male'";
10:
11:        $result = mysql_query($sql);
12:
13:        if ( $_GET[ "format" ] == "XML" ) {
14:            displayXML( $result );
15:        }
```

```
16:        else {
17:            displayHTML( $result );
18:        }
19:    ?>
20:
21:    </body>
```

This is better, and using an MVC pattern helps, but developers can still develop proprietary designs within the controller. And with such proprietary designs, documentation should be written, but sadly, often it is not.

■**Note** As a brief diversion, there's an entertaining take on the separation of data and content on `http://www.youtube.com/watch?v=6gmP4nkOEOE`.

We jump ahead now to the use of MVC in the web development process. In basic terms, the controller delegates incoming requests and funnels them to the appropriate end point, which is normally an action in a class. The model handles the data, and the view is responsible for the return format to the recipient. However, the solution still has a problem: in too many cases, we see developers putting more and more logic into the view. Plus, it's often difficult to distinguish whether a piece of code relates to the application or to the view—for example, when there is some specific data or code that's just used for a particular format. And with time pressures, it's often easier to place it in the view.

Our Cake tags approach is one small step toward addressing the problem. Following from the previous examples, Listing 11-3 shows how Cake tags would do it.

Listing 11-3. *Using Cake Tags*

```
<body>
    <ct plugin="DatabaseAccess" controller="DbRecords" ➥
action="listRecords" table="patients" gender="male"/>
</body>
```

Our idea in using tags isn't new, of course. ColdFusion has used it since the 1990s, and Java has JSP tags. For example, in ColdFusion, you can send an e-mail message using the following tag:

```
<cfmail to="another@example.com" from=another2@example.com ➥
subject = "Hello Friend!">How are things?</cfmail>
```

View Template

The best place to start explaining how we wrote our Cake tags is from the view. In this application, our Cake tags will be available to use in any view. We're going to create a sample page in `/app/views/pages/home.ctp`, Cake's default home page.

A Cake tag is essentially an XML wrapper for Cake plugins, where the output from the plugin replaces the Cake tag. We could have used any number of ways of interfacing the tag with Cake, but plugins seem generic enough. Additionally, we envisage some point in the future where the Cake tags can be used as a clean interface between third-party code (Cake plugins) and Cake itself. We can even go one step further and imagine a framework where we can add Cake plugins in a visual development environment and specify the attribute values using a form-based user interface.

Now back to our application. In it, we will have a Yahoo! Maps plugin. This plugin will display a geographical map location, which we specify, much the same as with Google Maps. How the Yahoo! Maps plugin is written will be explained a little later, in the "Cake Plugins" section. From our view in Listing 11-4, using our tag method, we will make two requests to display the Yahoo! maps via our Cake tags on lines 3 and 7.

Listing 11-4. *The Home Page (/app/views/pages/home.ctp)*

```
1:    <h3>My Vacation Destinations</h3>
2:
3:    <ct plugin="Yahoomaps" controller="Maps" action="display" ➥
latitude="48.856925" longitude="2.341210" />
4:
5:    <br />
6:
7:    <ct plugin="Yahoomaps" controller="Maps" action="display" ➥
location="San Francisco" />
8:
9:    <br />
```

From this listing, you can see that our Cake tags are named ct (for Cake tag, of course). We'll be using standard XML syntax format for the tags.

A Cake tag is formed with a single XML tag, with no tag end. The attributes are used to pass key value parameters to the Cake plugin. Table 11-1 describes these attributes.

Table 11-1. *Cake Tag Attributes*

Attribute	Description
plugin	The name of the plugin that we are calling
controller	The controller within the plugin that we are calling
action	The action within the controller that we are calling
Others	Passed into the plugin as named parameters, which can be accessed via Cake's passedArgs controller variable

If you ran the code in Listing 11-4 as it is, without overriding Cake's view, it will just display "My Vacation Destinations" in the h3 tag format, which is not very useful.

Our goal is to display two Yahoo! maps, one after the other. In order for that to happen, we must override Cake's view class so we can parse our Cake tags, as described next.

Cake View Class Extension

Using your own view is quite simple, as shown in Listing 11-5.

Listing 11-5. *Overriding Cake's View*

```
 1:    <?php
 2:
 3:    App::import( 'View', 'CakeTags', array( 'file' => 'cake_tags.php' ) );
 4:
 5:    class AppController extends Controller {
 6:
 7:        var $pageTitle = 'Chapter 11 - Cake tags';
 8:
 9:        var $view = 'CakeTags';
10:    }
11:    ?>
```

First, in the global controller /app/app_controller.php, we import the view using Cake's
App::import command (line 3 in Listing 11-5). Next, we set the name of our view class in the
controller to our own on line 9.

■**Note** If you set the Controller's autoRender variable to false, no view is rendered, regardless of
whether the view was overridden or not.

Next, we create our new view class, as shown in Listing 11-6.

Listing 11-6. *Our New View Class (/app/views/cake_tags.php)*

```
 1:    <?php
 2:
 3:    class CakeTagsView extends View {
 4:
 5:        function render($action, $layout, $file) {
 6:
 7:            $result = parent::render($action, $layout, $file);
 8:
 9:            $result = $this->_renderCt( $result );
10:
11:            return $result;
12:        }
13:
14:        function _renderCt( $output ) {
15:
```

```
16:            $result = $output;
17:            $match = 1;
18:            $offset = 0;
19:
20:        while ( $match ) {
21:
22:            preg_match("/<ct ([\w]+)[^>]*\/>/", $result, ➥
$match, PREG_OFFSET_CAPTURE, $offset );
23:
24:            if ( $match ) {
25:
26:                $plugin = $controller = $action = $params = '';
27:
28:                $tag = $match[0][0];
29:                $offset = $match[0][1];
30:
31:                $xml = new SimpleXMLElement( $tag );
32:
33:                foreach( $xml->attributes() as $attr => $value ) {
34:
35:                    switch ($attr) {
36:
37:                        case 'plugin':
38:                            $plugin = $value;
39:                            break;
40:
41:                        case 'controller':
42:                            $controller = $value;
43:                            break;
44:
45:                        case 'action':
46:                            $action = $value;
47:                            break;
48:
49:                        default:
50:                            $params .= $attr.':'.$value.'/';
51:                            break;
52:                    }
53:                }
54:
55:                if ( $controller && $action ) {
56:
57:                    $tagResult = $this->requestAction( ➥
'/'.$plugin.'/'.$controller.'/'.$action.'/'.$params, array( 'return' ) );
58:
59:                    $result = str_replace( $tag, $tagResult, $result );
60:                }
61:            }
```

```
62:                  else {
63:                       break;
64:                  }
65:             }
66:
67:             return $result;
68:        }
69:   }
70:
71:   ?>
```

Our view class name must be in the format [*YourViewName*]View and it must extend Cake's
View class. The next step is to override the render method. In line 7, we first render the real
view using Cake's render command. On line 9, we intercept the output and parse the ct tags.
This is done using our _renderCt method, starting from line 14. (If you were to comment out
line 9, it would be as if you had not changed any of Cake's original view output.)

In the _renderCt method, we take the output of the view after Cake has rendered it, parse
any ct tags we find, and call the relevant plugin as specified in the ct tag attributes. We continuously loop through the output and parse and replace the ct tags until there are no more
ct tags to process. The ct tags are simply matched with the regular expression in the following
line of code:

`/<ct ([\w]+)[^>]*\/>/`

Once a match is found, we attempt to fill the four main variables: $plugin, $controller,
$action, and $params. PHP's SimpleXMLElement class is used to extract all the attributes.
Once the $controller and $action values are in place, we call the actions by using the
$this->requestAction call. In line 59, we simply replace the whole ct tag with the output of
the $this->requestAction call.

In line 57 of Listing 11-6, we make a request to a particular action in a Cake plugin. If you
were to build your own Cake tag, it would need to be a Cake plugin, so line 57 could access that
action in the URL format /plugin/controller/action/params.

Cake Plugins

Next, to create our Yahoo! Maps plugin, we first create a folder called yahoomaps in the app/
plugins folder. Within that folder, we create several files and folders, which will resemble
a Cake application folder structure, as follows:

```
Yahoomaps
    yahoomaps_app_controller.php
    yahoomaps_app_model.php
    controllers
        maps_controller.php
    models
    views
        maps
            display.ctp
```

The two main files we are concerned with are maps_controller.php and display.ctp. The maps_controller.php file is shown in Listing 11-7.

Listing 11-7. *Map Controller (maps_controller.php)*

```php
<?php

class MapsController extends GoogleMapsAppController {

    var $uses = null;

    function display() {

        // do longitude
        $longitude = '-0.127144';

        if ( isset( $this->passedArgs['longitude'] ) ) {
            $longitude = $this->passedArgs['longitude'];
        }

        $this->set( 'longitude', $longitude );

        // do latitude
        $latitude = '51.506325';

        if ( isset( $this->passedArgs['latitude'] ) ) {
            $latitude = $this->passedArgs['latitude'];
        }

        $this->set( 'latitude', $latitude );

        // Location can also be specified
        // which overrides the long and lat values
        $this->set( 'location', '' );

        if ( isset( $this->passedArgs['location'] ) ) {
            $this->set( 'location', $this->passedArgs['location'] );
        }
    }
}

?>
```

To be honest, this example isn't terribly exciting. The display method simply acts as a proxy for passing values from the ct tag to the view. If no longitude or latitude values are passed, we use some default values, which at present are set to London. However, don't underestimate what you can actually do. Since you can essentially invoke any plugin, controller, or action, you can wrap any functionality behind a Cake tag.

The other two files, yahoomaps_app_controller.php and yahoomaps_app_model.php, are shown in Listings 11-8 and 11-9, respectively. These are the global controller and model files, similar to the app_controller.php and app_model.php files. In Listing 11-8, we need the JavaScript helper to display the Yahoo! Maps API JavaScript files.

Listing 11-8. *Yahoo! Maps Controller (yahoomaps_app_controller.php)*

```php
<?php
    class YahooMapsAppController extends AppController {
        var $helpers = array( 'Javascript' );
    }
?>
```

Listing 11-9. *Yahoo! Maps Model (yahoomaps_app_model.php)*

```php
<?php
    class YahooMapsAppModel extends AppModel {

    }
?>
```

You can achieve more complex operations in other scenarios. Here are some examples:

- Display the current shopping basket, with the total number of products and a total cost, as follows:

  ```
  <cf plugin="Ecommerce" controller="Basket" action="display" skin="minimalist" />
  ```

- Display the products available as a tree menu:

  ```
  <cf plugin="Ecommerce" controller="Products" action="listProductsTree" />
  ```

- Display the Twitter public timeline messages in 3D using a Flash 3D display engine called Papervision3D:

  ```
  <cf plugin="Twitter" controller="StatusMethods" action="public_timeline" ➥
  format="paperVision3D" />
  ```

Yahoo! Maps

Adding Yahoo! Maps is similar to adding Google Maps. We start by including Yahoo!'s JavaScript Map API. Listing 11-10 shows the view.

Listing 11-10. *Yahoo! Maps View (/app/plugins/yahoomaps/views/maps/display.ctp)*

```
 1:    <?= $javascript->link( 'http://api.maps.yahoo.com/ajaxymap➥
?v=3.8&appid=[you own api key]' ) ?>
 2:
 3:    <style type="text/css">
 4:    #map{
 5:      height: 75%;
 6:      width: 100%;
 7:    }
 8:    </style>
 9:
10:    <?php
11:        $uuid = String::uuid();
12:        echo '<div id="'.$uuid.'"></div>';
13:    ?>
14:
15:    <script type="text/javascript">
16:
17:        // Create a map object
18:        var map = new YMap(document.getElementById('<?php echo $uuid; ?>'));
19:
20:        // Zoom Control
21:        map.addZoomLong();
22:
23:        // Add map type control
24:        map.addTypeControl();
25:
26:        // Set map type to either of: YAHOO_MAP_SAT, ➥
YAHOO_MAP_HYB, YAHOO_MAP_REG
27:        map.setMapType(YAHOO_MAP_REG);
28:
29:        // Display the map centered on a geocoded location
30:        <?php
31:            if ( $location ) {
32:                echo "map.drawZoomAndCenter( '".$location."', 3 );";
33:            }
34:            else {
35:                echo "map.drawZoomAndCenter( ➥
new YGeoPoint( ".$latitude.", ".$longitude." ), 3 );";
36:                //echo "map.drawZoomAndCenter( ➥
new YGeoPoint( 16.773480, -97.747175 ), 3 );";
37:            }
38:        ?>
39:
40:    </script>
```

When including the API, you need to provide your application ID, which you can get from `http://www.developer.yahoo.com/maps/`.

Next, we create the `div` container, which will hold the map, on lines 10 through 13. Since this plugin may be included in the same view more than once, we create a unique ID for the `<div>` element using Cake's `uuid()` string method.

Just to recap, the output from Listing 11-10 will replace the `ct` tag that called for it. A sample output of the two Yahoo! maps is shown in Figure 11-1.

Figure 11-1. *Using Cake tags to display Yahoo! maps*

Our Yahoo! Maps example is quite simple. We can easily specify other parameters to pass to Yahoo! Maps. For example, to add a zoom level, our Cake tag would look like this:

```
<ct plugin="Yahoomaps" controller="Maps" action="display" ➥
location="San Francisco" zoom="2" />
```

On line 32 in Listing 11-10, the `drawZoomAndCenter` command would now look like this:

```
echo "map.drawZoomAndCenter( '".$location."', '".$zoom."' );";
```

And in the `display` action in Listing 11-10, we would need to capture the zoom value and pass it to the view with the following lines of code:

```
// Do zoom
$zoom = '3';

if ( isset( $this->passedArgs['zoom'] ) ) {
    $zoom = $this->passedArgs['zoom'];
}
$this->set( 'zoom', $zoom );
```

Summary

In this chapter, we have shown how you can override Cake's output. Additionally, we created a Cake plugin that displays Yahoo! maps.

We mentioned early on that the whole Cake tags idea is a small step toward solving the problem of content and data separation. In our view, this is a big problem, because so many modern applications need to talk to other applications. Good separation of these two layers is vital in web development. However, at some stage, you will inevitably need to mix them. The questions will be how much and where. One thing is certain: you should never put any presentational markup in the controller. With Cake, use Cake elements and helpers to reduce the size of your views.

CHAPTER 12

■■■

Dynamic Data Fields

In this chapter, we'll present a snippet of an e-commerce feature. We will supply enough code and explanation to allow you to use this feature in a real-life project. Our feature centers on product searching. We take a nontraditional approach to this feature, basing it on dynamic data fields. We'll start off by reviewing how product searches are usually conducted.

Traditional Product Searching

While shopping online, many e-commerce sites allow you to narrow down the product range by selecting specific attributes of interest. For example, you can narrow down the search to just a particular brand or a particular price range. Figures 12-1 and 12-2 show typical product filtering on Amazon and Kelkoo, respectively.

Figure 12-1. *Amazon product filtering*

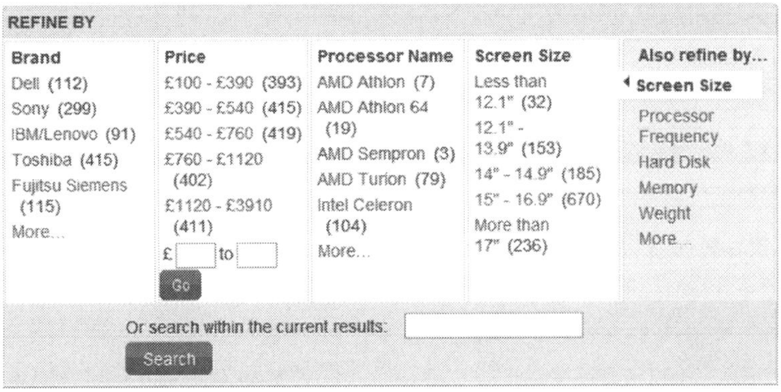

Figure 12-2. *Kelkoo product filtering*

Traditionally, to provide such a feature, you would put the products and their attributes in a single table, as shown in Listing 12-1.

Listing 12-1. *A Typical Products Table*

```
CREATE TABLE `products` (
  `id` int(11) NOT NULL auto_increment,
  `title` varchar(255) NOT NULL,
  `price` float NOT NULL,
  `stock_qty` int(11) NOT NULL,
  `color` varchar(255) NOT NULL,
  `size` varchar(255) NOT NULL,
  PRIMARY KEY (`id`)
);
```

You would then create a form that contained hard-coded fields that users could select. These fields would be passed to a standard SQL SELECT statement via a POST action, and the filtered results would be returned.

The traditional method works well if the products are mostly the same or you have only a few hundred products. However, if you want to build a more flexible system and be able to handle a much larger product base with attributes that vary widely, you need a different approach.

The Dynamic Data Approach

Our method turns the traditional products table on its side. For example, in the traditional table, the price field occupies one column on its own, with the prices running down the table, as shown in Figure 12-3.

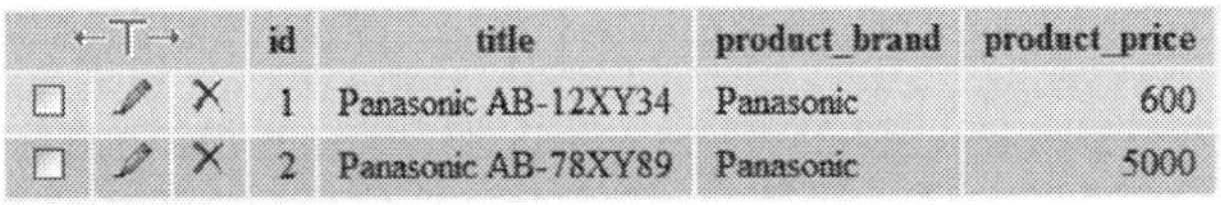

			id	title	product_brand	product_price
☐	✎	✕	1	Panasonic AB-12XY34	Panasonic	600
☐	✎	✕	2	Panasonic AB-78XY89	Panasonic	5000

Figure 12-3. *A table with a traditional price field*

In our approach, we have the price field as a data type in itself, and create a separate record for each price based on that price field data type, as shown in Figure 12-4. Our price field now is essentially dynamic data. We can add and delete it as if it were ordinary data. Taking this concept further, we can dynamically create table data fields.

←T→	id	title	field_type_group_id	product_field_group_id
☐ ✎ ✕	1	Product Brand	4	1
☐ ✎ ✕	2	Product Price	1	1

Figure 12-4. *The price field as a database record*

From an e-commerce standpoint, we can now create thousands or millions of products with varying properties. Each property or attribute would be a record in itself.

Considerations for Using the Dynamic Data Approach

Since we're moving away from the standard way of creating relational tables, we need to consider the implications of taking this approach. There are both advantages and disadvantages.

Our approach has the following disadvantages:

- Filtering data using the standard WHERE clause conditions will not work in some circumstances. For example, the simple SQL statement select * from products where price > 10 and color = 'red' will not return the desired results, because there are no price and color fields. We could still achieve the same results using other means, but it would involve more code and more SQL statements.

- Programming other e-commerce features becomes much more complicated. For example, a simple SQL statement like select * from products would not return the results we want. To get this data, we would need to make further SQL queries.

- Code maintenance becomes more difficult. Developers are familiar with the traditional way in which SQL statements interact with code.

The advantages of the dynamic data approach are as follows:

- You can create dynamic tables and data fields based on the attributes of products. Indeed, you can also create dynamic forms (although that isn't our goal in this chapter's example).

- You can create automatic validation since you are controlling the data type of the field. (We won't cover that feature in this chapter, but you can easily add it.)

- What wasn't practically possible previously using standard SQL methods is now possible—namely, mixed data sets.

Our dynamic data field technique is recommended only if the ability to have dynamic fields is a core feature of your application. If you have several hundred brands or products, it's still much better to create separate tables as and when needed, such as products_shoes, products_televisions, products_hats, and so on (although, honestly, that solution isn't that attractive either when the number of tables increases).

The Product Database Design

Most of our tables will be metatables—tables that hold data that describes other data. For example, the integer value 42 may numerically represent anything, but if we attach an attribute called `price` to it, then 42 numerically represents price. The attribute is the metadata. As we've said, creating dynamic data fields is a complicated business. To achieve our aim, we have created nine tables, as shown in Figure 12-5.

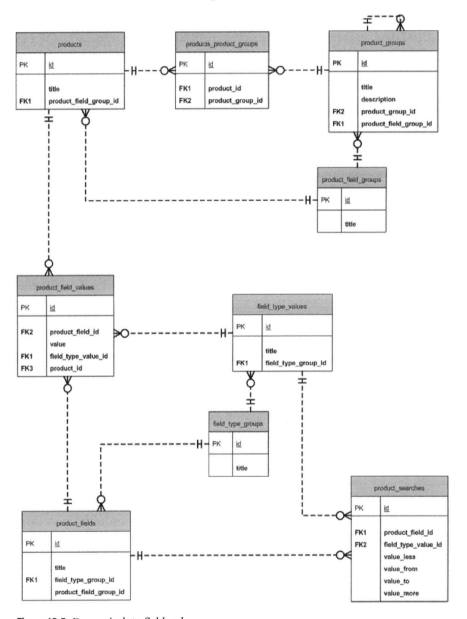

Figure 12-5. *Dynamic data fields schema*

We will now describe the type of data each table will contain and show some examples. This will give you enough information to allow you to adapt the code to suit your own needs.

The field_type_groups Table

The field_type_groups table is used to group the different data types, as shown in the example in Figure 12-6. For example, a price field is a decimal field; a free-form text field, such as the description of a product, is a varchar type; and a drop-down field of brand names is an enumerated type. Table 12-1 describes the two fields in this table.

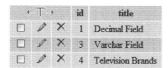

Figure 12-6. *Sample data in the field_type_groups table*

Table 12-1. *The field_type_groups Table Fields*

Field	Description
id	Unique primary key field
title	Name of the field type

The field_type_values Table

The field_type_values table holds the actual data types, as shown in the example in Figure 12-7. It's used with the field_type_groups table. It exists mainly for the benefit of enumerated types. Each field in this table is described in Table 12-2.

←T→			id	title	field_type_group_id
□	✎	✕	3	Panasonic	4
□	✎	✕	4	Samsung	4
□	✎	✕	5	[DECIMAL]	1
□	✎	✕	6	[VARCHAR]	3

Figure 12-7. *Sample data in the field_type_values table*

Table 12-2. *The field_type_values Table Fields*

Field	Description
id	Unique primary key field
title	Name of the data type
field_type_group_id	Foreign key to field_type_groups

The products Table

Each product will have one entry in the products table, as shown in the example in Figure 12-8. All the other tables are ultimately used to support this single table. Table 12-3 shows the fields in the products table.

←T→	id	title	product_field_group_id
☐ ✐ ✗	1	Panasonic AB-12XY34	1
☐ ✐ ✗	2	Panasonic AB-78XY89	1

Figure 12-8. *Sample data in the products table*

Table 12-3. *The products Table Fields*

Field	Description
id	Unique primary key field
title	Name of the product
product_field_group_id	Foreign key to product_field_groups

The products_product_groups Table

The products_product_groups table links the products table and the product_groups table. The products and product_groups table have a many-to-many relationship: one product can belong to many product groups, and a product group can contain many products. In Cake, this association is called has and belongs to many (HABTM). For example, SD memory cards can be used in many devices, such as cameras and computers, and devices like cameras and computers can take different types of SD memory cards. An example of the products_product_groups table is shown in Figure 12-9. Each field is described in Table 12-4.

←T→	id	product_id	product_group_id
☐ ✐ ✗	1	1	1
☐ ✐ ✗	2	1	9
☐ ✐ ✗	3	2	1
☐ ✐ ✗	4	2	9

Figure 12-9. *Sample data in the products_product_groups table*

Table 12-4. *The products_product_groups Table Fields*

Field	Description
id	Unique primary key field
product_id	Foreign key to products
product_group_id	Foreign key to product_groups

The product_fields Table

The product_fields table holds the name of the data fields, as shown in the example in Figure 12-10. Table 12-5 describes the four fields in this table.

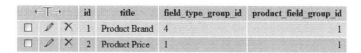

← T →		id	title	field_type_group_id	product_field_group_id
☐	✎ ✕	1	Product Brand	4	
☐	✎ ✕	2	Product Price	1	1

Figure 12-10. *Sample data in the product_fields table*

Table 12-5. *The product_fields Table Fields*

Field	Description
id	Unique primary key field
title	Name of the data field
field_type_group_id	Foreign key to field_type_groups
product_field_group_id	Foreign key to product_field_groups

The product_field_groups Table

The product_field_groups table is essentially used to hold together the different data fields in the product_fields table, as shown in the example in Figure 12-11. Table 12-6 describes the fields in this table.

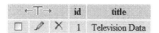

← T →		id	title
☐	✎ ✕	1	Television Data

Figure 12-11. *Sample data in the product_field_groups table*

Table 12-6. *The product_field_groups Table Fields*

Field	Description
id	Unique primary key field
title	Name of the grouping of the field (like a table name)

The product_field_values Table

After the products table, product_field_values is the second most important table, as it holds the attribute data for each product. Figure 12-12 shows an example of the table. Each of its fields is described in Table 12-7.

←T→	id	product_field_id	value	field_type_value_id	product_id
☐ ✎ ✗	1	1	Panasonic	3	1
☐ ✎ ✗	2	2	600	5	1
☐ ✎ ✗	3	1	Panasonic	3	2
☐ ✎ ✗	4	2	5000	5	2

Figure 12-12. *Sample data in the product_field_values table*

Table 12-7. *The product_field_values Table Fields*

Field	Description
id	Unique primary key field
product_field_id	Foreign key to product_fields
value	Value of the data itself—probably the most important field
field_type_value_id	Foreign key to field_type_values
product_id	Foreign key to products

The product_groups Table

The product_groups table is one found in many other applications. It simply groups the products and puts the groups in a hierarchical structure. The product_group_id field points back to itself and is used to record the hierarchy structure. Figure 12-13 shows an example of this table. Each field in the product_groups table is described in Table 12-8.

←T→	id	title	description	product_group_id	product_field_group_id
☐ ✎ ✗	1	LCD Displays		9	1
☐ ✎ ✗	6	Home	All Products	0	0
☐ ✎ ✗	9	Televisions		8	0
☐ ✎ ✗	8	Electronics		6	0
☐ ✎ ✗	13	Computer Monitors		8	0

Figure 12-13. *Sample data in the product_groups table*

Table 12-8. *The product_groups Table Fields*

Field	Description
id	Unique primary key field
title	Name of the group of products
description	Description of the group
product_group_id	Foreign key to product_groups
product_field_group_id	Foreign key to product_field_groups

The product_searches Table

The product_searches table holds the search criteria for each product group, as shown in the example in Figure 12-14. Table 12-9 describes the fields in this table. The fields that begin with value_ are used in price range search filtering. For example, if value_from is 100 and value_to is 500, then one of the search fields would allow you to search for products with the price range between $100 and $500. You'll see the code that uses these fields later in this chapter, in Listing 12-4 starting on line 39.

			id	product_field_id	field_type_value_id	value_less	value_from	value_to	value_more
☐	✎	✕	1	1	3				
☐	✎	✕	2	1	4				
☐	✎	✕	3	2	5		500	1000	
☐	✎	✕	6	2	5		1001	10000	

Figure 12-14. *Sample data in the product_searches table*

Table 12-9. *The product_searches Table Fields*

Field	Description
id	Unique primary key field
product_field_id	Foreign key to product_fields
field_type_value_id	Foreign key to field_type_values
value_less	Used for price range filtering; filter for values less than this limit
value_from	Used for price range filtering; filter for values from this limit
value_to	Used for price range filtering; filter for values to this limit
value_more	Used for price range filtering; filter for values more than this limit

Baking for This Application

Using Cake's bake command, we generated all the models for this application automatically. Even more important is that we also created the associations in the models automatically. To generate the associations, we named the foreign key using the naming convention [foreign_table_singular]_id.

Regarding the controllers, we have baked only the products controller. In it, we will create two actions: the search action for searching and the addData action for adding a product. Because of the architecture of our tables, we cannot simply use the automatically generated add action to add products. However, that add action will still help us to some extent, as you'll see when we discuss adding products later in this chapter.

We have also baked some views, but again, only for the products.

Building the Product Search Feature

One of the main objectives of our dynamic data field approach is to allow flexible product searches. Users can refine their search to a narrow set of desired attributes. For our search feature, we need to create the search form and code the search process.

Creating the Product Search Form

Listing 12-2 shows the products controller for our application.

Listing 12-2. *The Products Controller (/app/controllers/products_controller.php)*

```
 1:    <?php
 2:    class ProductsController extends AppController {
 3:
 4:        var $name = 'Products';
 5:        var $helpers = array( 'Html', 'Form');
 6:
 7:        var $uses = array( 'Product', 'ProductSearch', 'ProductGroup',
 8:                           'ProductFieldValue', 'ProductField',
 9:                           'FieldTypeValues' );
10:
11:        function search() {
12:
13:            if ( isset( $this->params['form']['product_group_id'] ) ) {
14:
15:                $searchResult = $this->Product->doSearch( ➥
$this->params['form'] );
16:
17:                $this->set( 'search_results', $searchResult );
18:            }
19:
20:            $this->_listProductSearch();
21:        }
22:
23:        function _listProductSearch() {
24:
25:            // At the moment, this is hard coded to a default value of 1
26:            // but you may want to change this to your product group id
27:            $productGroupId = '1';
28:
29:            if ( isset( $this->passedArgs[ 'productGroupId' ] ) ) {
30:                $productGroupId = $this->passedArgs[ 'productGroupId' ];
31:            }
32:
33:            // Get the end node group
34:            $productGroup = $this->ProductGroup->findById( $productGroupId );
35:
```

```
36:                 $this->set( 'product_group', $productGroup );
37:
38:                 $this->set( 'product_fields',
39:                         $this->ProductField->searchFilters( $productGroup ) );
40:         }
41:
42:         function addData() {
43:
44:             if (!empty($this->data)) {
45:
46:                 $fieldData = $this->data[ 'Product' ]['data_fields'];
47:
48:                 foreach( $fieldData as $fieldVal ) {
49:
50:                     if ( is_array( $fieldVal ) ) {
51:                         list( $key, $value ) = each( $fieldVal );
52:
53:                         $fieldData2Split = explode( ",", $key );
54:                         $product_field_id = $fieldData2Split[0];
55:                         $field_type_value_id = $fieldData2Split[1];
56:                     }
57:                     else {
58:                         $fieldData2Split = explode( ",", $fieldVal );
59:                         $product_field_id = $fieldData2Split[0];
60:                         $field_type_value_id = $fieldData2Split[1];
61:                         $value = ➥
$this->getFieldTypeValue( $field_type_value_id );
62:                     }
63:
64:                     $data = array();
65:                     $data[ 'ProductFieldValue' ][ 'product_field_id' ] = ➥
$product_field_id;
66:                     $data[ 'ProductFieldValue' ][ 'value' ] = $value;
67:                     $data[ 'ProductFieldValue' ][ 'field_type_value_id' ] = ➥
$field_type_value_id;
68:                     $data[ 'ProductFieldValue' ][ 'product_id' ] = ➥
$this->data[ 'Product' ]['product_id'];
69:
70:                     $this->ProductFieldValue->create( $data );
71:                     $this->ProductFieldValue->save();
72:                 }
73:             }
74:
75:             if ( isset( $this->passedArgs[ 'productFieldGroupId' ] ) ) {
76:
77:                 $productFieldGroupId = $this-> ➥
passedArgs[ 'productFieldGroupId' ];
78:
```

```
79:                    // Let's find all the data fields
80:                    $productFields = $this->ProductField-> ➥
findAllByProductFieldGroupId( $productFieldGroupId );
81:
82:                    // Next we need the values relating to the data fields
83:                    foreach( $productFields as &$field ) {
84:
85:                        $fieldTypeGroupId = $field[ 'FieldTypeGroup' ][ 'id' ];
86:
87:                        $fieldTypeValues = $this-> ➥
FieldTypeValues->findAllByFieldTypeGroupId( $fieldTypeGroupId );
88:
89:                        $field[ 'FieldTypeValues' ] = $fieldTypeValues;
90:                    }
91:
92:                    $this->set( 'field_type_values', $productFields );
93:                }
94:
95:            $productId = '';
96:            if ( isset( $this->passedArgs[ 'productId' ] ) ) {
97:                $productId = $this->passedArgs[ 'productId' ];
98:            }
99:
100:            $this->set( 'product_id', $productId );
101:
102:        }
103:
104:        function getFieldTypeValue( $field_type_value_id ) {
105:
106:            $result = '';
107:
108:            $fieldTypeValues = $this->FieldTypeValues-> ➥
findById( $field_type_value_id );
109:
110:            if ( !empty( $fieldTypeValues ) ) {
111:
112:                if ( isset( $fieldTypeValues ➥
[ "FieldTypeValues" ][ "title" ] ) ) {
113:                    $result = $fieldTypeValues[ "FieldTypeValues" ][ "title" ];
114:                }
115:            }
116:
117:            return $result;
118:        }
119:    }
120:    ?>
```

We have created a search action in the products controller to handle searches, on line 11. Line 20 carries out the task of listing the product search fields in the _listProductSearch method. On line 23, we find all the data fields for a particular product group. On line 27, we assume the default product group ID is 1. If no productGroupId value has been specified, then the products with a productGroupId of 1 will be shown. In practice, this value would be passed to the function via the URL, maybe as a named parameter. For example, you may have a page with different product group types, and one URL might look like this:

```
http://localhost/chapter_12/Products/search/productGroupId:42/
```

This URL would then list all the products with a productGroupId value of 42.

Once we retrieve the productGroupId, on line 30, we simply get details about the group for display in the view. Line 38 does the main work and fetches the product fields.

Finding the search fields is carried out by the ProductField model, shown in Listing 12-3. Remember that the search fields are not hard-coded; they are generated dynamically.

Listing 12-3. *ProductField Model (/app/models/product_field.php)*

```php
1:   <?php
2:   class ProductField extends AppModel {
3:
4:       var $name = 'ProductField';
5:
6:       var $belongsTo = array(
7:           'FieldTypeGroup' => array('className' => 'FieldTypeGroup',
8:                                  'foreignKey' => 'field_type_group_id',
9:                                  'conditions' => '',
10:                                 'fields' => '',
11:                                 'order' => ''
12:          ),
13:          'ProductFieldGroup' => array('className' => 'ProductFieldGroup',
14:                                 'foreignKey' => 'product_field_group_id',
15:                                 'conditions' => '',
16:                                 'fields' => '',
17:                                 'order' => ''
18:          )
19:      );
20:
21:      var $hasMany = array(
22:          'ProductFieldValue' => array('className' => 'ProductFieldValue',
23:                                 'foreignKey' => 'product_field_id',
24:                                 'dependent' => false,
25:                                 'conditions' => '',
26:                                 'fields' => '',
27:                                 'order' => '',
28:                                 'limit' => '',
29:                                 'offset' => '',
```

```
30:                              'exclusive' => '',
31:                              'finderQuery' => '',
32:                              'counterQuery' => ''
33:              ),
34:          'ProductSearch' => array('className' => 'ProductSearch',
35:                              'foreignKey' => 'product_field_id',
36:                              'dependent' => false,
37:                              'conditions' => '',
38:                              'fields' => '',
39:                              'order' => '',
40:                              'limit' => '',
41:                              'offset' => '',
42:                              'exclusive' => '',
43:                              'finderQuery' => '',
44:                              'counterQuery' => ''
45:          )
46:      );
47:
48:      function searchFilters( $searchField ) {
49:
50:          // We get the fields relating to this product group
51:          $productFields = array();
52:
53:          if ( $searchField['ProductGroup'][ 'product_field_group_id' ] ) {
54:
55:              $productFieldGroupId = ➥
$searchField['ProductGroup'][ 'product_field_group_id' ];
56:
57:              $fields = ➥
$this->findAllByProductFieldGroupId( $productFieldGroupId );
58:
59:              foreach( $fields as $product_field ) {
60:
61:                  $productFields[] = ➥
$product_field[ 'ProductField' ][ 'id' ];
62:              }
63:          }
64:
65:          // Next, for each field, we get the search criteria, e.g., list of
66:          // brand names, price range, etc.
67:          $fieldRefine = array();
68:
69:          foreach( $fields as $productField ) {
70:
71:              $productFieldId = $productField[ 'ProductField' ][ 'id' ];
72:
```

```
73:                $fieldSelection = ➥
$this->ProductSearch->findAllByProductFieldId( $productFieldId );
74:
75:                $fieldValues = array();
76:
77:                foreach( $fieldSelection as $selection ) {
78:                    $fieldValues[] = $selection;
79:                }
80:
81:                $productField[ 'field_selections' ] = $fieldValues;
82:
83:                $fieldRefine[] = $productField;
84:            }
85:
86:            return $fieldRefine;
87:        }
88:
89:    }
90:    ?>
```

At the beginning of the file, we have created some associations that correspond to the diagram shown earlier in Figure 12-5. The important code begins on line 48 with the searchFilters method. First, we get the fields relating to the product group, starting on line 53. Next, starting on line 69, we get the search criteria for each field. For example, if the field is about brand names, we need a list of all the brands. If it is a price field, we need to get the search range of the price field. Figure 12-15 shows an example of the form displaying these criteria.

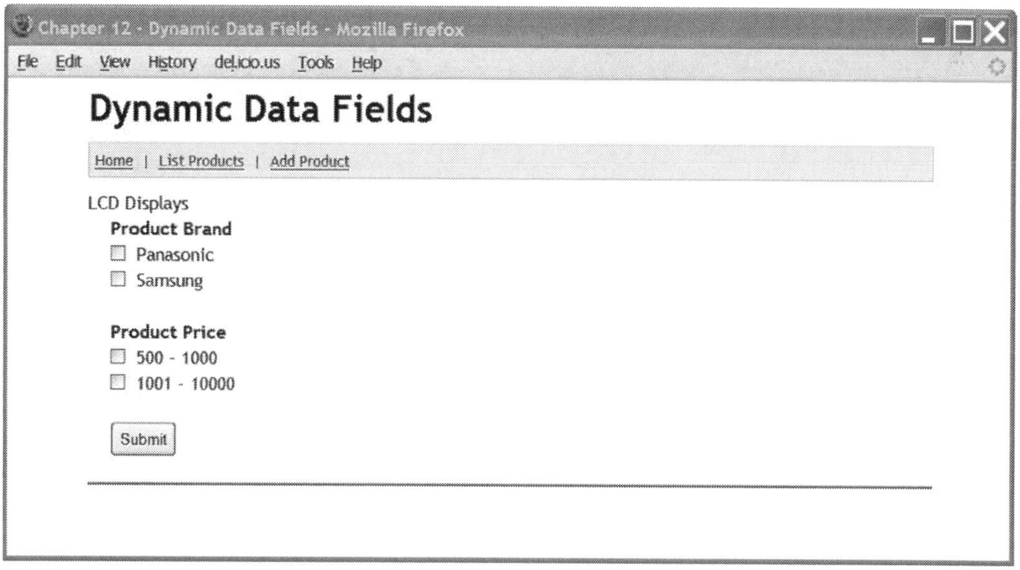

Figure 12-15. *The dynamic search form*

Let's now look at the view that corresponds to the search form, which is shown in Listing 12-4. The file is split into two sections: lines 1 through 105 list the search fields relating to the product group, and lines 107 through 140 list the products found.

Listing 12-4. *Search Action View (/app/views/products/index.ctp)*

```
 1:    <?php
 2:
 3:        echo $form->create( 'Product',
 4:                            array( 'url' => '/Products/search/' ) );
 5:
 6:    ?>
 7:
 8:    <?php echo $form->create('Product');?>
 9:
10:    <?php
11:
12:        if ( isset( $product_group ) ) {
13:
14:            $product_group_id = $product_group['ProductGroup'][ 'id' ];
15:
16:            echo $form->hidden( 'product_group_id',
17:                                array(  'name' => 'product_group_id',
18:                                        'value' => $product_group_id ) );
19:        }
20:    ?>
21:
22:    <?php
23:
24:        if ( isset( $product_group ) ) {
25:
26:            // List the product group
27:            echo $product_group['ProductGroup'][ 'title' ];
28:        }
29:
30:        echo '<br />';
31:
32:        echo '<div id="product_search">';
33:
34:            if ( isset( $product_group ) ) {
35:
36:                foreach( $product_fields as $product_field ) {
37:
38:                    echo ➥
'<b>'.$product_field[ 'ProductField' ][ 'title' ].'</b><br />';
39:
40:                    $field_selections = $product_field[ 'field_selections' ];
41:
```

```
42:                             foreach( $field_selections as $field_value ) {
43:
44:                                 $title = $field_value[ 'FieldTypeValue' ][ 'title' ];
45:                                 $id = $field_value[ 'ProductSearch' ][ 'id' ];
46:                                 $product_field_id = ➥
$field_value[ 'ProductSearch' ][ 'product_field_id' ];
47:
48:                                 if ( $title == '[DECIMAL]' ) {
49:
50:                                     // We take it from the range
51:                                     $value_less = ➥
$field_value[ 'ProductSearch' ][ 'value_less' ];
52:
53:                                     if ( $value_less ) {
54:
55:                                         echo $form->checkbox( '', ➥
array( 'name' => 'field_selection['.$product_field_id.'][]', 'value' => $id ) );
56:
57:                                         echo '<'.$value_less.'<br />';
58:                                     }
59:
60:                                     $value_from = ➥
$field_value[ 'ProductSearch' ][ 'value_from' ];
61:
62:                                     if ( $value_from ) {
63:
64:                                         echo $form->checkbox( '', array( ➥
'name' => 'field_selection['.$product_field_id.'][]', 'value' => $id ) );
65:
66:                                         echo $value_from;
67:
68:                                         $value_to = ➥
$field_value[ 'ProductSearch' ][ 'value_to' ];
69:
70:                                         if ( $value_to ) {
71:
72:                                             echo ' - '.$value_to.'<br />';
73:                                         }
74:                                     }
75:
76:                                     $value_more = ➥
$field_value[ 'ProductSearch' ][ 'value_more' ];
77:
78:                                     if ( $value_more ) {
79:                                         echo $form->checkbox( '', array( ➥
'name' => 'field_selection['.$product_field_id.'][]', 'value' => $id ) );
80:
```

```
81:                                echo '>'.$value_more.'<br />';
82:                            }
83:                        }
84:                        else {
85:
86:                            // For ordinary lists, e.g. brand names
87:                            $id = $field_value[ 'ProductSearch' ][ 'id' ];
88:
89:                            echo $form->checkbox( '', array( ➥
'name' => 'field_selection['.$product_field_id.'][]', 'value' => $id ) );
90:
91:                            echo ➥
$field_value[ 'FieldTypeValue' ][ 'title' ].'<br />';
92:                        }
93:                    }
94:
95:                    echo '<br />';
96:                }
97:
98:                echo $form->end('Submit');
99:            }
100:
101:        echo '</div>';
102:
103:
104:
105:    ?>
106:
107:    <br />
108:    <hr width="100%" color="#555555">
109:    <br />
110:
111:    <?php
112:
113:        if ( isset( $search_results ) ) {
114:
115:            foreach( $search_results as $a_result ) {
116:
117:                $product_fields = $a_result[ 'product_fields' ];
118:
119:                if ( isset( $product_fields[0][ 'Product' ][ 'title' ] ) ) {
120:                    $product_title = $product_fields[0][ 'Product' ][ 'title' ];
121:                    echo '<p>'.$product_title.'</p>';
122:                }
123:
124:                foreach( $product_fields as $product_field ) {
125:
```

```
126:                    $field_title = $product_field[ 'ProductField' ][ 'title' ];
127:
128:                    switch ( $field_title ) {
129:
130:                        case 'Product Brand':
131:                            echo '<p><b>Brand:</b> '.$product_field ➥
[ 'ProductFieldValue' ][ 'value' ].'</p>';
132:                            break;
133:
134:                        case 'Product Price':
135:                            echo '<p><b>Price:</b> '.$product_field ➥
[ 'ProductFieldValue' ][ 'value' ].'</p>';
136:                            break;
137:                    }
138:                }
139:            }
140:        }
141:
142:    ?>
```

Lines 12 to 19 simply store the product group ID in a hidden field, so that when we perform the search, we know on which product group we're searching. The `if` statement on line 24 echoes the name of the product group—for example, Plasma TVs. On line 36, the big outer `foreach` loop goes through each field and displays the relevant filter input box and the label that goes with it.

Inside the big `foreach` loop on line 42, we have an `if` statement on line 48 that decides on the data type of the data field. If it's a decimal, we assume it's a price range filter. We then go through the `value_` variables to find what kind of range we should display. If it's not a decimal, we assume it's an enumerated list, like brand names or shoe sizes. We then go into the `else` block on line 84, where we echo a check box and the title of the field type.

Processing the Search

In the previous section, we showed you how the search form was created. We'll now explain how the search actually works. Referring to the products controller in Listing 12-2, on line 15, you can see that all the work to search for the products is done within the `Product` model. The code for the `Product` model is shown in Listing 12-5.

Listing 12-5. *Product Model (/app/models/product.php)*

```
1:    <?php
2:    class Product extends AppModel {
3:
4:        var $name = 'Product';
5:
6:        var $belongsTo = array(
7:                'ProductFieldGroup' => array('className' => 'ProductFieldGroup',
```

```
 8:                           'foreignKey' => 'product_field_group_id',
 9:                           'conditions' => '',
10:                           'fields' => '',
11:                           'order' => ''
12:              )
13:         );
14:
15:         var $hasMany = array(
16:             'ProductFieldValue' => array('className' => 'ProductFieldValue',
17:                          'foreignKey' => 'product_id',
18:                          'dependent' => false,
19:                          'conditions' => '',
20:                          'fields' => '',
21:                          'order' => '',
22:                          'limit' => '',
23:                          'offset' => '',
24:                          'exclusive' => '',
25:                          'finderQuery' => '',
26:                          'counterQuery' => ''
27:              )
28:         );
29:
30:         var $hasAndBelongsToMany = array(
31:             'ProductGroup' => array('className' => 'ProductGroup',
32:                          'joinTable' => 'products_product_groups',
33:                          'foreignKey' => 'product_id',
34:                          'associationForeignKey' => 'product_group_id',
35:                          'unique' => true,
36:                          'conditions' => '',
37:                          'fields' => '',
38:                          'order' => '',
39:                          'limit' => '',
40:                          'offset' => '',
41:                          'finderQuery' => '',
42:                          'deleteQuery' => '',
43:                          'insertQuery' => ''
44:              )
45:         );
46:
47:         function doSearch( $formValues ) {
48:
49:             $result = array();
50:
51:             $productGroupId = $formValues[ 'product_group_id' ];
52:
53:             if ( isset( $formValues[ 'field_selection' ] ) ) {
54:
```

```
 55:                  $result = $this->getFieldSelection(
 56:                              $productGroupId,
 57:                              $formValues[ 'field_selection' ] );
 58:
 59:              // We need to add the field information to each product
 60:              $result = $this->addFieldInformation( $result );
 61:          }
 62:
 63:          return $result;
 64:      }
 65:
 66:      function addFieldInformation( $products ) {
 67:
 68:          foreach( $products as &$current_product ) {
 69:
 70:              $productId = $current_product['id'];
 71:
 72:              $productFields = $this->ProductFieldValue-> ➥
findAllByProductId( $productId  );
 73:
 74:              $current_product[ 'product_fields' ] = $productFields;
 75:          }
 76:
 77:          return $products;
 78:      }
 79:
 80:      function getSearchCriteria( $fieldSelection ) {
 81:
 82:          $selectionFlat = array();
 83:
 84:          $idx = 0;
 85:
 86:          foreach( $fieldSelection as &$currentSelection ) {
 87:
 88:              for( $idx2=0; $idx2<sizeof( $currentSelection ); $idx2++ ) {
 89:
 90:                  $selectionValue = $currentSelection[$idx2];
 91:
 92:                  $sql = "    select * from product_searches
 93:                              where
 94:                              id = '$selectionValue'
 95:                              ";
 96:
 97:                  $searchs = $this->query($sql);
 98:
 99:                  $selectionFlat[$idx][$idx2] = $searchs[0];
100:              }
101:
```

```
102:                    $idx++;
103:            }
104:
105:            return $selectionFlat;
106:        }
107:
108:        function getFieldSelection( $productGroupId, $fieldSelection ) {
109:
110:            $result = array();
111:
112:            // Get all products within the group
113:            $products = $this->ProductGroup->findById( $productGroupId );
114:
115:            $searchCriterias = $this->getSearchCriteria( $fieldSelection );
116:
117:            // Now walk through each product to filter out
118:            // according to user selection
119:
120:            foreach( $products[ 'Product' ] as $currentProduct ) {
121:
122:                $productId = $currentProduct[ 'id' ];
123:                $productFieldGroupId = $currentProduct ➥
[ 'product_field_group_id' ];
124:
125:                $sql = "    select * from product_fields
126:                            inner join product_field_values ➥
on product_field_values.product_field_id = product_fields.id
127:                            inner join field_type_values on ➥
field_type_values.id = product_field_values.field_type_value_id
128:                            where
129:                            product_fields.product_field_group_id = ➥
'".$productFieldGroupId."' and
130:                            product_field_values.product_id = '".$productId."'
131:                            ";
132:
133:                $productFields = $this->query($sql);
134:
135:                $topLevelMatches = 0;
136:
137:                // Walk through each field
138:                foreach( $productFields as $field ) {
139:
140:                    // Now match against the selection
141:                    // Top level groups must match with an "AND"
142:                    // e.g., brand, price, etc.
143:                    // While second level groups match with an "OR"
144:                    // e.g., Panasonic, Sony, etc.
145:
```

```
146:                        // Start with top level
147:                        for( $idx=0; $idx<sizeof( $searchCriterias ); $idx++ ) {
148:
149:                               $subLevels = $searchCriterias[$idx];
150:                               $subLevelMatching = 0;
151:
152:                               // Sub level
153:                               for( $idx2=0; $idx2<sizeof( $subLevels ); $idx2++ ) {
154:
155:                                   if (   (   $subLevels[$idx2] ➥
['product_searches'][ 'product_field_id' ] ==
156:                                          (   $field ➥
[ 'product_field_values' ][ 'product_field_id' ] ) ) )
157:                                   {
158:                                       // User selected this field to filter
159:                                       // Check if selection matches this field
160:
161:                                       if ( ➥
$field[ 'field_type_values' ][ 'title' ] == '[DECIMAL]' ) {
162:
163:                                           $valueLess = ➥
$subLevels[$idx2]['product_searches'][ 'value_less' ];
164:
165:                                           if ( $valueLess ) {
166:                                               if ( $field ➥
[ 'product_field_values' ][ 'value' ] < $valueLess ) {
167:                                                   $subLevelMatching = 1;
168:                                               }
169:                                           }
170:
171:                                           $valueFrom = $subLevels ➥
[$idx2]['product_searches'][ 'value_from' ];
172:                                           $valueTo = $subLevels ➥
[$idx2]['product_searches'][ 'value_to' ];
173:
174:                                           if ( ( $valueFrom ) && ( $valueTo ) ) {
175:                                               if (   ( $field ➥
[ 'product_field_values' ][ 'value' ] > $valueFrom ) &&
176:                                                      ( $field ➥
[ 'product_field_values' ][ 'value' ] < $valueTo ) )
177:                                               {
178:                                                   $subLevelMatching = 1;
179:                                               }
180:                                           }
181:
182:                                           $valueMore = $subLevels ➥
[$idx2]['product_searches'][ 'value_more' ];
183:
```

```
184:                                    if ( $valueMore ) {
185:                                         if ( $field ➡
[ 'product_field_values' ][ 'value' ] > $valueMore ) {
186:                                              $subLevelMatching = 1;
187:                                         }
188:                                    }
189:                               }
190:                          else {
191:
192:                               // If plain id selection, e.g., brand names,
etc.
193:                               if (    $field ➡
[ 'product_field_values' ][ 'field_type_value_id' ] ==
194:                                    $subLevels ➡
[$idx2]['product_searches'][ 'field_type_value_id' ] ) {
195:
196:                                         $subLevelMatching = 1;
197:                                    }
198:                               }
199:                          }
200:                     }
201:
202:                // Count how many
203:                if ( $subLevelMatching ) {
204:                     $topLevelMatches++;
205:                }
206:           }
207:      }
208:
209:      if ( $topLevelMatches == sizeof( $searchCriterias ) ) {
210:           $result[] = $currentProduct;
211:      }
212:      }
213:
214:      return $result;
215:      }
216:
217:  }
218:  ?>
```

The search starts with doSearch on line 47. Starting on line 55, the getFieldSelection method gets the fields that were selected. As you may notice, we have used some raw SQL queries, which is sometimes necessary with such a complex system.

The getFieldSelection method also does the work of finding the products. On line 113, we first get all the products within the product group. Next, on line 115, we get the search criteria that the user selected. Then, beginning on line 120, we walk through each product and check it against the search criteria.

On line 125, we get all the data fields for the product. Then, on line 138, we take each field and try to match it against the search criteria values.

Let's consider the example shown earlier in Figure 12-15. If a user selects Panasonic and the price range 500–1000, that means she wants to find Panasonic Plasma TVs in the price range of $500 to $1,000. However, if the user also selects Samsung, that means she wants to find Panasonic or Samsung Plasma TVs in the price range of $500 to $1,000. Since we cannot use an ordinary SELECT statement with AND and OR operators in the WHERE clause, we need to write the code to perform the equivalent functionality of these two operators. This is done from line 147 to line 212.

Adding a Product

The process of adding a product is carried out in two stages: we add entries in the products and products_product_groups tables and then add the product data. (This could be combined into one step, but we'll leave that as an exercise for those who are interested.)

Creating Table Entries

First, we need to create an entry in the products table. This is quite simple, as we will use the action /Products/add that we baked, as mentioned earlier in the chapter. (We have not altered any of the baked code.) Figure 12-16 shows an example of the form, where we are adding a Panasonic AB-WOW product.

The important point regarding the products table is the relationship it has with the product_groups table. During the baking process, Cake generated the relevant associations for us. Because it knows about the associations, Cake will automatically carry out many operations for us, including the following:

- In the view of an add action, a multiselect field is automatically generated so users can select more than one entry in the product group, as shown in Figure 12-16.

- During the save process, entries for the other tables are automatically created. In Figure 12-16, we have selected two product groups. The model's save method will actually create three records: one for the products table and two for the products_ product_groups link table.

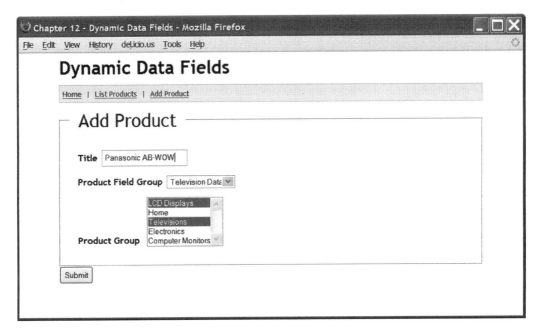

Figure 12-16. *The add product form*

Entering Product Data

Now we have created an entry in the products table for the new product, and we have also created two entries in the products_product_groups table. So, we know to which product group the product belongs. However, we still need to enter the actual data for the product, such as its price and specific attributes. For this task, we need to write specific code.

Figure 12-17 shows the form that lists the products. Most of what you see in Figure 12-17 is baked. The exception is the Add Data link in the middle of the Actions column. For each product, we need to add the data for the product attributes. For example, clicking the Add Data link for the Panasonic AB-WOW entry will take you to the form shown in Figure 12-18.

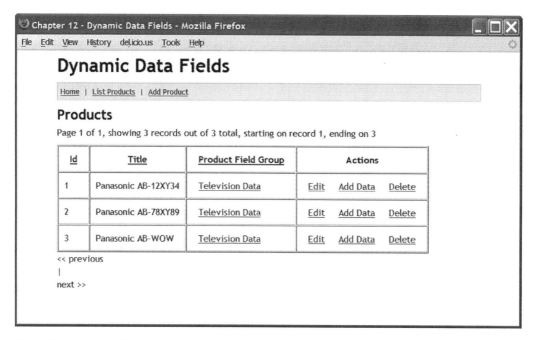

Figure 12-17. *Listing of the products*

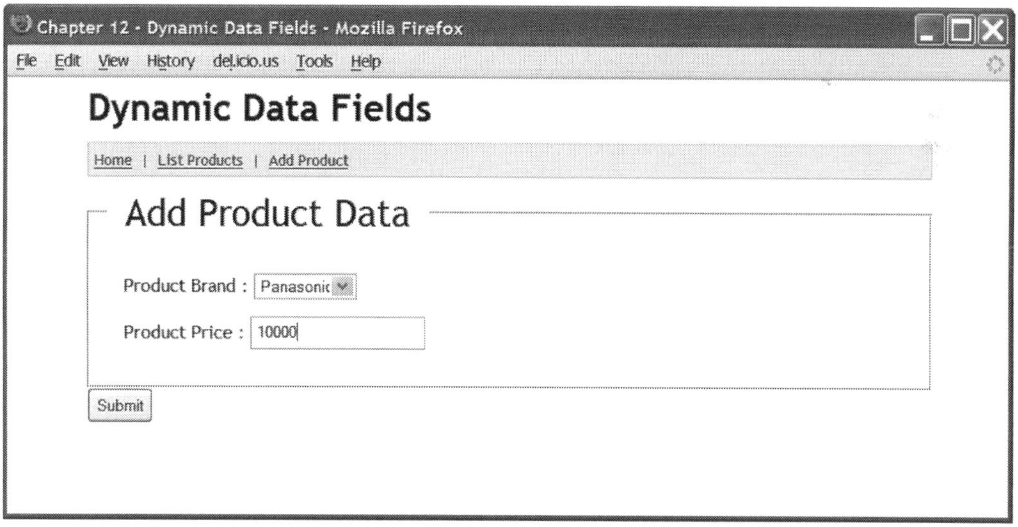

Figure 12-18. *Adding data for a product*

The Add Data link is in the following format:

```
/Products/addData/productId:6/productFieldGroupId:2
```

As you can see from the link, there is an addData action in the products controller (shown earlier in Listing 12-2). We pass into the action two named parameters: productId and productFieldGroupId. The code for the addData action is shown on line 42 in Listing 12-2.

When the product data is returned, it goes into the if statement on line 44 in Listing 12-2. To give you a better understanding of the code, the following is an example of the $this->data variable as used on line 44:

```
1:    Array
2:    (
3:        [Product] => Array
4:            (
5:                [data_fields] => Array
6:                    (
7:                        [0] => 3,4
8:                        [1] => Array
9:                            (
10:                               [4,5] => 50
11:                            )
12:
13:                        [2] => Array
14:                            (
15:                               [5,5] => 8
16:                            )
17:
18:                    )
19:
20:                [product_id] => 6
21:            )
22:
23:    )
```

In this listing, the Product key has two elements: data_fields and product_id. We need the product_id so we know to which product the data is attached. The data_fields element contains the product data itself. The numeric order in the data_fields element is not important; the important part is the value. If the value is an array (see line 50 in Listing 12-2), then the key is composed of two values in the format [product_field_id, field_type_value_id]. Thus, we have all the information we need about the data: the data itself, the data type, and the field it is. If the value is not an array, then it's coming from a select list (in our example, the brand names). In this case, we will just have the [product_field_id, field_type_value_id] pair. It won't have a value, since we already know the value, as it is in the enumerated list. Remember that the data fields are not hard-coded, so they don't actually exist in the database as real data columns. As far as the database is concerned, these fields are just data.

The view that generated Figure 12-18 is shown in Listing 12-6. The form simply sends the data back to itself in the addData action. In the products controller in Listing 12-2, the data starts getting processed on line 44 onward.

Listing 12-6. *AddData View (/app/views/products/add_data.ctp)*

```
1:    <div class="products form">
2:    <?php echo $form->create('Product',array( ➥
'url' => '/Products/addData' ));?>
3:        <fieldset>
4:            <legend><?php __('Add Product Data');?></legend>
5:        <?php
6:
7:            if ( isset( $field_type_values ) ) {
8:
9:                foreach( $field_type_values as $field ) {
10:
11:                    $fieldTypeValues = $field[ 'FieldTypeValues' ];
12:
13:                    $productFieldId = $field[ 'ProductField' ][ 'id' ];
14:                    $productFieldTitle = $field[ 'ProductField' ][ 'title' ];
15:                    $productFieldTitle_2 = low( $productFieldTitle );
16:                    $productFieldTitle_2 = r( " ",
17:                                                            "_",
18:                                                            $productFieldTitle_2 );
19:
20:                echo '<div class="form_field">';
21:
22:                    echo $productFieldTitle.' : ';
23:
24:                    // Check type of data
25:                    if ( sizeof( $fieldTypeValues ) == 1 ) {
26:
27:                        // Get field type value id
28:                        $FieldTypeValueId = ➥
$field[ 'FieldTypeValues' ][0][ 'FieldTypeValues' ][ 'id' ];
29:
30:                        // It's a basic data type like int or a string
31:                        // and not a list of data items
32:
33:                        echo $form->input( '', array(   'label' => false,
34:                                                        'div' => false,
35:                                                        'name' => ➥
'data[Product][data_fields][][ '.$productFieldId.','.$FieldTypeValueId.']' ) );
36:                        echo '<br />';
37:                    }
38:                    else {
39:                        // We'll assume it's a list of data items
40:                        // Let's gather the data together
41:                        $listItems = array();
42:                        foreach( $fieldTypeValues as $fieldValue ) {
43:
```

```
44:                                    $id = $fieldValue[ 'FieldTypeValues' ][ 'id' ];
45:                                    $title = ➥
$fieldValue[ 'FieldTypeValues' ][ 'title' ];
46:
47:                                    $listItems[ $productFieldId.','.$id ] = $title;
48:                                }
49:
50:                                echo $form->select( '',
51:                                                    $listItems,
52:                                                    null,
53:                                                    array( ➥
'name' => 'data[Product][data_fields][]' ) );
54:                                echo '<br />';
55:                            }
56:
57:                        echo '</div>';
58:                    }
59:                }
60:
61:        ?>
62:        </fieldset>
63:    <?php echo $form->hidden(   'product_id',
64:                               array( 'value' => $product_id ) ); ?>
65:
66:    <?php echo $form->end('Submit');?>
67:    </div>
```

Summary

Now that we're at the end of the chapter, we hope you are still with us. As we said at the beginning of the chapter, our design is quite complex because we are essentially trying to do some of the job that the SQL engine usually does for us. Essentially, we have carried out some research and development work. And along the way, we've used Cake's has-and-belongs-to-many association, as well as raw queries using the query function. By stepping out of the norm, we can see how Cake responds to new ideas.

This chapter contains the skeleton of an application. You can take the code in numerous directions. For example, in the product_groups table, instead of using a single product_group_id field to represent a hierarchical tree structure, you could use the preorder tree traversal algorithm (see http://www.sitepoint.com/article/hierarchical-data-database). This ordering method allows you to fetch all products with certain attributes under a complete branch. For example, you can list all televisions between the price range of $500 and $1,000. You can achieve the same result using a single product_group_id field, but it would involve more code and more SQL statements.

Additionally, you might add a back-end administration area, where administrators can easily manage products, product groups, and search criteria.

CHAPTER 13

∎∎∎

Captcha

Nowadays, most developers would not leave any web forms open to unlimited submission. Some safety measure must be put in place to prevent web forms from being used for spamming.

While some people focus on building creative web sites and extending the capability of the Internet, others spend considerable amount of time trying to crack and compromise the information on web sites. Spamming is a huge problem. A recent statistic from Sophos research revealed that during the first quarter of 2008, 96.5 percent of all e-mail was spam (`http://www.sophos.com/pressoffice/news/articles/2008/07/dirtydozjul08.html`)!

Spambots are everywhere. They simply engage in the process of filling out web forms as if they were customers. For example, a spambot could send thousands of spontaneous e-mail messages by filling out your contact form or your blog comment form, if that form is not protected.

You've probably encountered web sites where you're required to interpret some obfuscated characters and input them for validation when a web form is submitted. You will most often see this type of protection on high-profile sites like Google's Gmail and Yahoo! Mail. This fuzzy character output is called a *Captcha*.

In this chapter, we will briefly look at the various types of Captchas used as a means of protecting web forms. We'll then focus on the ASCII Art Captcha technique and implement an ASCII Art Captcha component.

Captcha Implementations

The term *Captcha* was coined in 2000 by Luis von Ahn, Manuel Blum, Nicholas J. Hopper, and John Langford. It is a shortened acronym for Completely Automated Public Turing Test to Tell Computers and Humans Apart. The purpose of a Captcha is to prevent automatic form submission by spambots or similar intrusion programs.

In 1950, the brain behind the advent of Captcha, Professor Alan Turing, wrote an article called "Imitation Game" to describe how machines can demonstrate intelligence similar to humans. In 1997, Alta Vista created an early spam-blocking measure. Now Captchas are common. There is even a company (reCAPTCHA, at `http://recaptcha.net/`) that offers Captcha security as a web service. Figure 13-1 shows an example of a reCAPTCHA Captcha box.

Figure 13-1. *A reCAPTCHA box*

Captcha Types

There are different types of Captchas and consequently many ways of implementing them. This presents us with many options when it comes to blocking spammers from using robots for submitting web forms. The following list describes some of the common implementations of Captcha designed to completely block automatic programs from web form submission.

Alphanumeric images: The most common Captcha implementation is the appearance of a random selection of distorted images made up of alphanumeric values. As humans, we can easily recognize distorted image characters, but spambots cannot. It's more challenging for spambots to crack the Captcha when the image characters are overlapping or distorted with lines across the characters.

Picture images: Another Captcha implementation uses a set of various images, such as animal images (a bird, a fish, an elephant, and so on) or furniture (table and chairs, for instance). You're expected to recognize the objects by their names and enter their names into an input box.

Audio: This technique involves embedding an audio (sound) to pronounce some words or random letters and digits. You're expected to type the words into an input box. Unfortunately, this requires some audio player, which not everyone has. Also, it makes things difficult for people with hearing problems.

Question/answer: A question-and-answer technique involves asking a user a question. If it's a difficult question, some potential users may be blocked from form submission.

Math problems: Using this technique, you are given a mathematical question (such as 56 minus 30), and you are expected to input the resulting value before you can submit the web form.

ASCII Art: This technique displays a set of fonts that are created from a combination of characters artistically designed to form gigantic versions of some keyboard characters (A–Z, 0–9, @, and so on). This set of fonts is called the ASCII Art characters.

The Captcha implementation presented in this chapter uses ASCII Art, so we'll take a closer look at that approach.

ASCII Art Captcha

Although most of the standard Captchas on the Internet display graphic characters, users sometimes find it difficult to decipher all the characters correctly, perhaps due to their screen resolution, sight, or both. Many people find it is easier to recognize ASCII Art characters compared to their graphic counterparts.

■**Note** ASCII Art is the creation of images by using the strokes of the characters defined by the ASCII Standard as lines and shading. It is a mini-industry in itself. For more information, just search for "ASCII Art" on the Internet. You can start by going to http://chris.com/ascii/ for some enlightening information.

As new ways of protecting web information are evolving, so are techniques for cracking that protection. Spammers are finding ways of decoding them, typically using optical character recognition (OCR) programs. Not many web forms use ASCII Art, so many deciphering spambot programs find it difficult to decode.

Another advantage ASCII Art Captchas have over graphics-based Captchas has to do with external libraries. Some of the graphics-based Captchas rely on PHP extensions (for example, the PHP GD library). The ASCII Art Captchas do not rely on any external library for their operation. They simply rely on your design of the characters.

One of the major characteristics of a Captcha is its look and feel. It includes the overlapping of characters and lines that touch the characters. To some extent, this characteristic is dependent on the spacing between characters and the fonts of the individual characters. One of the advantages of using ASCII characters is that you have total control over the look and feel of the characters.

ASCII Art Captchas offer a very strong way of thwarting spambots. First, the spambot would need to decipher which keyboard characters are used to compose a single individual character. A single font character could combine some hash (#) characters, some pipe (|) characters, a few ampersands (&), and so on. Additionally, spambots face the problems of determining the start and end of characters, actual borders or coordinates of each character, and the position of the random text, as well as distinguishing the background noise from the character.

In our ASCII Art Captcha implementation outlined in this chapter, our array of fonts will define all characters of the alphabet from A–Z and the numbers 0–9. With this array of fonts, you can modify the characters to suit your own preferences. Here is an example of a constructed font character:

```
#!#!#!#!#!#
    #!#
    #!#
    #!#
    #!#
    #!#
    #!#
```

This is clearly a letter *T*. It's constructed using a combination of the hash (#) and exclamation point (!) characters.

A Captcha Component

Now we will take you through implementing an ASCII Art Captcha. This technique will involve the creation of an array of fancy fonts (ASCII Art) using our own custom keyboard character combinations. Our Captcha characters will be randomly drawn from the array of the ASCII Art fonts, distorted, and finally displayed on a simple web form.

The Captcha program will be rolled into a component, so that it can be reused when required in other Cake applications. Table 13-1 describes the properties of the ASCII Art Captcha component.

Table 13-1. *The Properties of the Captcha Component*

Property	Description
fonts	Consists of ASCII Art characters. Each character is built by putting together some keyboard characters to form a whole character. You can create your own pattern of characters to replace these fonts. As the name implies, the individual characters of the fonts are determined from the standard alphanumeric values A–Z and 0–9.
noiseChars	Defines a set of characters that includes a dash (-) character stored as an array that is used as the background of ASCII Art characters.
numberChar	A numeric value that must be greater than zero. It's used to determine the total number of characters in the CAPTCHA string text.

Of course, you can add to the list of the properties—for example, include background coloring—to intensify security.

The ASCII Art Component Class

Our component class is named AsciiArtsComponent. Listing 13-1 shows the properties in this class.

Listing 13-1. *The Beginning of the AsciiArtsComponent Class (app/controllers/components/ascii_captcha.php)*

```php
<?php
class AsciiArtsComponent extends Object {
    var $noiseChars = array( ' ', "=", "-", ":" );
    var $asciiFonts = array();
    var $numberChar = 6;
?>
```

The AsciiArtsComponent class contains three properties:

- $noiseChars is assigned an array of four ASCII characters: (' ', "=", "-", ":"). These characters are randomly used to distort the Captcha characters.

- $asciiFonts is initially assigned an empty array. This property will later contain a list of all the defined ASCII Art characters for A–Z and 0–9.

- $numberChar is assigned an integer 6, which specifies the total number of characters that will constitute the Captcha.

Now that we've dealt with the component properties, let's look at the functionality that we'll implement to build the ASCII Art Captcha. This functionality includes generating random text from the ASCII character fonts, distorting the randomly generated text, and writing the text to the screen.

Next up in our component class is Cake's startup function, as shown in Listing 13-2.

Listing 13-2. *AsciiArtsComponent's Startup Method*

```
function startup(&$controller) {
    $this->data = $controller->data;
}
```

You should be familiar with the startup method by now. In this case, it gives the AsciiArtsComponent access to the properties of its parent controller, which is the CaptchaController object. For example, it enables you to access a form object data ($this->data) submitted to a controller within a component.

Next, the initialize method performs a similar task to the beforeFilter method of the controller. This method contains logic that must be run before any component functionality is run. We initialize the $fonts property with a set of ASCII Art characters. This font property contains an array of the ASCII Art characters that we created from different sets of characters. For example, Listing 13-3 shows the first two elements of the $fonts array.

Listing 13-3. *AsciiArtsComponent's Initialize Method*

```
function initialize() {
$fonts['A'] =
"   @@@
   @@-@@
  @@---@@
@@- ---@@
@@@@@@@@@
@@- - -@@
@@-----@@ ";

$fonts['B'] =
"@@@@@@@@
@@------@@
@@---- -@@
@@@@@@@@@
@@------@@
@@- ----@@
@@@@@@@@@";

// Other alphabet characters follow...

}
```

Listing 13-3 shows the created ASCII Art characters for the first two elements (A and B) of the $fonts array variable ($fonts['A'],…..$fonts['Z'], $fonts['0'],…..$fonts['9']). In total, the $fonts array contains 36 elements. We are going to randomly draw a number of characters from this array, based on the $numberChar property of the component.

Next in this class is the getCaptcha method, which returns a Captcha string, as shown in Listing 13-4.

Listing 13-4. *AsciiArtsComponent's getCaptcha() Method*

```
function getCaptcha() {
        $result = array();
        $captchaChars = array_rand( $this->asciiFonts, $this->numberChar );

        for ($idx = 0; $idx < sizeof( $captchaChars ); $idx++) {
           $capChar = $captchaChars[$idx];
           $result[ $capChar ] = $this->asciiFonts[ $capChar ];
        }

        $result = $this->addNoise( $result );

        return $result;
}
```

The first statement in this method initializes the $result variable with an empty array. This variable will eventually contain the final result of this function. Next, we use the PHP function array_rand to randomly select a list of characters from this function's first argument, $this->asciiFonts. The total number of characters selected is determined by the second argument, $this->numberChar, which has a default value of 6. In this case, a set of six randomly selected characters is stored in the $captchaChars array variable.

Next, we use a for loop to store each character in $capChar variable. That variable is used as a key to pull the corresponding ASCII Art characters from the $asciiFonts array, and then stored in the $result array variable. The for loop's maximum iteration is based on the number of elements in the $captchaChars array variable.

Finally, we use the addNoise method to distort the ASCII Art characters and return the final Captcha result to be used in the CaptchaController object.

The next method in our component class is addNoise, which takes an array of the randomly selected ASCII Art characters and returns a distorted version of the character, as shown in Listing 13-5.

Listing 13-5. *AsciiArtsComponent's addNoise() Method*

```
function addNoise( $captchaStrings ) {

        $result = array();

        foreach( $captchaStrings as $capChar => $ascii ) {

            for ($idx = 0; $idx < strlen( $ascii ); $idx++) {
```

```php
            if ( $ascii[$idx] == ' ' ) {

                $noiseChar = array_rand( $this->noiseChars, 1 );
                $ascii[$idx] = $this->noiseChars[$noiseChar];
            }
        }

        $ascii = str_replace( chr(13), ' ', $ascii );

        $result[ $capChar ] = $ascii;
    }

    return $result;
  }
}
?>
```

In Listing 13-5, we first set the $result variable to an empty array. Next, we use the foreach loop to iterate the list of the ASCII Art characters stored in $captchaStrings, and then use an inner for loop to iterate each ASCII Art character and check whether a character is empty or a whitespace character. If a character is a whitespace character, the program randomly selects a replacement character from the $noiseChars array variable. The final $ascii character is stored and returned as the $result array variable.

Now that we are finished with the AsciiArtsComponent properties and methods, let's move to the controller that employs the services of this component to provide security against a spambot's submission of our sample form.

The Captcha Controller

Next, we will create the CaptchaController class that displays a form to test our Captcha. It starts as shown in Listing 13-6.

Listing 13-6. *The Beginning of the CaptchaController Class (app/controllers/captcha_controller.php)*

```php
<?php
class CaptchaController extends AppController {
    var $name = 'Captcha';
    var $uses = array('Captcha');
    var $helpers = array( 'Form', 'Html', 'Session');
    var $components = array( 'Session', 'RequestHandler', 'AsciiArts');
```

In Listing 13-6, we declare the helpers and components to aid some of the functions implemented in the controller. Notice that we've included our AsciiArts component.

Next in the controller is the beforeFilter function, which is invoked before any of the controller functionality is called to set the heading information for our screen, as shown in Listing 13-7.

Listing 13-7. *CaptchaController's beforeFilter Method*

```
function beforeFilter() {
    $actionHeading = 'ASCII Arts CAPTCHA!';
    $actionSlogan = 'Please fill in ASCII Arts text';
    $this->set(compact('actionHeading','actionSlogan'));
}
```

Next, we will create the index function, which renders a simple HTML form to do a Captcha test, as shown in Listing 13-8.

Listing 13-8. *CaptchaController's index Function*

```
function index() {
    $captcha = $this->AsciiArts->getCaptcha();
    $string = implode("",array_keys($captcha));
    $this->Session->write('string', $string);
    $this->set(compact('captcha','string'));
}
```

The index method starts by setting the $captcha array variable with the list of ASCII Art characters retrieved by using the getCaptcha method of the AsciiArtsComponents object. Next, using the PHP implode function, we obtain all the keys of the elements of the $captcha array variable with an empty string; this is the ASCII value of the Captcha characters. We then store the keys in the $string variable written to a string Session variable. We will use the characters stored in a Session object to validate the input a user has entered on a web form. We then make the $captcha and $string variables available to the app/views/captcha/index.ctp view code, which is shown in Listing 13-9.

Listing 13-9. *The Captcha Test View (app/views/captcha/index.ctp)*

```
<fieldset>
    <legend> <?php __("$actionHeading");?> </legend>
    <?=$actionSlogan;?>
    <br />
    <?php

    e("<pre><table><tr>");
    foreach($captcha as $key => $val) {
        e('<td style="font-size: 10px;">'.$val.'</td>');
    }
    e("</tr></table><pre>");
        echo $form->create('Captcha', array('url'=>'/captcha/check'));
        echo $form->error( 'Captcha.text' );
        echo $form->input( 'Captcha.text', array( ➥
'id' => 'text', 'label' => 'Text:', 'size' => '50', ➥
'maxlength' => '255', 'error' => false ) );
        echo $form->end( array( 'label' => ' Submit ' ) );
    ?>
</fieldset>
```

In Listing 13-9, the page heading and slogan were rendered using the variables set in the beforeFilter method of the controller. Next, we use the foreach loop to display the ASCII Art characters stored in the $captcha array variable. Finally, we create a Captcha form containing an input text field to accept user input. The user is expected to correctly enter the ASCII Art character displayed above the input element. The view is shown in Figure 13-2.

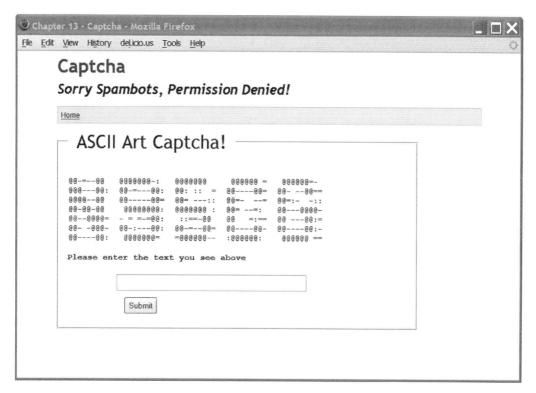

Figure 13-2. *The Captcha test form*

When a user clicks the Submit button, the form submission is handled by the check function declared in the component, as shown in Listing 13-10.

Listing 13-10. *The check() Function in the CaptchaController Class (app/controllers/captcha_controller.php)*

```
function check() {
    if (!empty($this->data['Captcha']['text'])) {
        if ($this->data['Captcha']['text'] == $this->Session->read('string')) {
            $this->Session->setFlash(
                __('<h1>You have entered the right characters</h1>', true));
            $this->redirect(array('action'=>'index'));
```

```
        } else {
            $this->Session->setFlash(
                __('You have entered the wrong characters. Please try again.', true));
            $this->redirect(array('action'=>'index'));
        }
    } else {
        $this->Session->setFlash(
                __('You need to enter the correct characters. ➡
Please try again.', true));
        $this->redirect(array('action'=>'index'));
    }
}
```

In the check function, we first check if the submitted data ($this->data['Captcha']
['text']) is not empty. If it's empty, the appropriate error message is stored in the Session
object, and the Captcha form is displayed with the preset error message. If it's not empty, we
first check if the input value entered by the user is equal to the ASCII Art characters stored in
the Session object. If they are not equal, the error message is set, using the setFlash method
of the Session object. Otherwise, the success message is set for display in the Captcha view, as
shown in Figure 13-3.

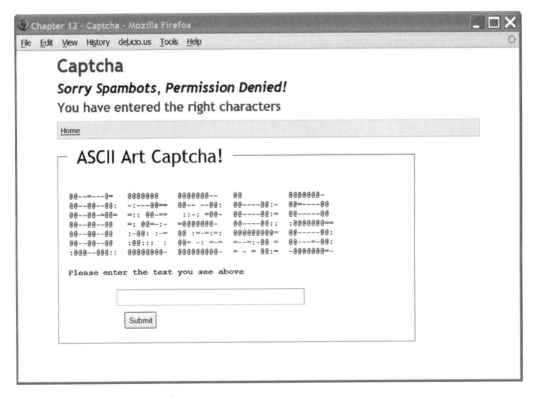

Figure 13-3. *The screen showing the success message*

Summary

In this chapter, we addressed the need to thwart spammers when collecting information using web forms. We concentrated on safeguarding form data against machine-code intruders such as spambots, who can act like humans and fill in web forms. We took a brief look at the various types of Captchas that can be implemented.

We chose to implement an ASCII Art Captcha. We created an ASCII Art component. This component contains properties and functionality that enable our Captcha controller to create a simple human test via a web form that randomly displays a set of ASCII Art characters on the screen. Finally, appropriate messages are displayed after a user has entered text.

There are many possible ways you can improve on our Captcha component. Here are some suggestions:

- Increase the security by replacing a random number of the @ characters that are used as the character for the fonts with other ASCII characters. Replace only a few; replacing too many characters will render the ASCII Art representation unrecognizable.

- Increase the security even more by using JavaScript to output the font characters.

- Instead of using the fonts we have created, create your own fonts.

And do keep in mind that for every security measure, there will always be some counter-measure. Never underestimate the resolve of the enemy!

Index

You Need the Companion eBook

Your purchase of this book entitles you to buy the companion PDF-version eBook for only $10. Take the weightless companion with you anywhere.

We believe this Apress title will prove so indispensable that you'll want to carry it with you everywhere, which is why we are offering the companion eBook (in PDF format) for $10 to customers who purchase this book now. Convenient and fully searchable, the PDF version of any content-rich, page-heavy Apress book makes a valuable addition to your programming library. You can easily find and copy code—or perform examples by quickly toggling between instructions and the application. Even simultaneously tackling a donut, diet soda, and complex code becomes simplified with hands-free eBooks!

Once you purchase your book, getting the $10 companion eBook is simple:

❶ Visit **www.apress.com/promo/tendollars/**.

❷ Complete a basic registration form to receive a randomly generated question about this title.

❸ Answer the question correctly in 60 seconds, and you will receive a promotional code to redeem for the $10.00 eBook.

THE EXPERT'S VOICE™

2855 TELEGRAPH AVENUE | SUITE 600 | BERKELEY, CA 94705

Offer valid through 06/09.

13944866R10229

Made in the USA
Lexington, KY
29 February 2012

The Psychotherapy
Documentation Primer

Third Edition

The Psychotherapy Documentation Primer

Third Edition

Donald E. Wiger

WILEY

John Wiley & Sons, Inc.

Library of Congress Cataloging-in-Publication Data

Wiger, Donald E., 1953-

The psychotherapy documentation primer / Donald E. Wiger. — 3rd ed.

   p. cm.

Includes index.

ISBN 978-0-470-90396-4 (pbk)

ISBN 978-1-118-16787-8 (ebk)

ISBN 978-1-118-16785-4 (ebk)

ISBN 978-1-118-16786-1 (ebk)

1. Psychiatric records. 2. Mental health services—Medical records. 3. Mental health services—Management. I. Title.

RC455.2.M38W543 2011

616.890068—dc23   2011025718

10 9 8 7 6 5 4 3 2

Contents

Preface

THANK YOU FOR your interest in mental health documentation. Perhaps you are a student preparing for a challenging and rewarding career; or you might be in the field and enhancing your skills. No matter what level of preparation you have in mental health treatment, this text is designed to bring you up to date in current documentation practices.

Those who oppose the tasks of documentation might make statements such as "I entered this field to help people, not to fill out paperwork." Of course, none of us looks forward to paperwork and documentation, but it is a part of today's requirements from third-party payers, reviewers, and professional boards. Documentation is an important aspect of, not an option in, the practice of mental health. On a positive note, having documentation requirements in mind while conducting therapy helps therapists keep on target to meet the specific goals and objectives of treatment.

If this is your first training in documentation, there is much to learn, but I have done my best to present the material in an interesting manner that makes practical sense. Several real-life examples and explanations are provided to help integrate the material.

The first edition of this book covered documentation in the basic areas of clinical service. It was well received primarily because there is not much published on this topic. The second edition was published shortly after several Health Insurance Portability and Accountability Act (HIPAA) procedures were necessary to document; plus, additional clinical examples of documentation were provided. This current third edition of *The Psychotherapy Documentation Primer* provides the same basic paradigms of documentation as the previous editions, with two additional chapters—"The Art and Science of Psychological Assessment and Treatment" and "Ethical Considerations in Documentation"—and a significantly expanded documented client chart in Appendix A, which integrates the material taught throughout the book. Several examples from previous editions were left unchanged because there was no need for revision.

Donald E. Wiger

How This Book Came Into Being
A Lesson in Making a Really Bad Negative Into a Really Good Positive

IN THE EARLY 1990s I started a solo mental health practice. The start-up operation was with no clients, no money, no office furniture, but lots of enthusiasm and dedication. I worked out a deal with a sympathetic landlord so that I wouldn't have to pay rent for the first few months. The furniture for the office came from my home. Fortunately, growth took place quickly, and within the first year there were two additional full-time employees. The rate of growth skyrocketed because we incorporated sound business principles and emphasized customer service. Now we could afford nice furniture at home and at the office.

Due to our specialization at that time, most of our billing was to Medicaid. Our rather sudden volume of business led to fairly high payments from Medicaid, raising a red flag to them for an audit. When I received notice of an audit, I wasn't worried because we had records for every client and most likely underbilled, rather than overbilled. So, a few weeks later, when the auditors showed up for their scheduled review, we were naively proud to show them that there were indeed proper intake notes, treatment plans, and progress notes.

The auditors never mentioned the rapid growth of the clinic or the fact that complete records existed for every client. During the audit we weren't sure what they were attempting to find. The auditors copied several files and informed us that we would meet with them again in about a month. Since they gave us no feedback, we weren't sure if we would receive accommodations or reprimands.

For the next month we did business as usual and practically forgot about the audit. But when the auditors showed up for the feedback session, our lives changed. The auditors informed us that there were no financial improprieties, and there were no records missing. We had not billed for any dates of service for which there were no records and we had not overbilled for any procedures. So far, so good. But then they opened their briefcases with seemingly hundreds of progress notes in which they said were "not in compliance." My initial thoughts were "Not in compliance with what?" I was not taught how to write progress notes in my graduate training, my internship, or my previous employment. I simply wrote down what the client and I did in the session. My problem was that I didn't know what I didn't know, which is commonly called "ignorance." The old saying "Ignorance of the law is no excuse" was staring me in the face. The other old adage, "Ignorance is bliss," is not true.

The auditors kindly and respectfully explained that my progress notes stunk. Their point was that just because services took place doesn't mean that there is documented evidence that psychotherapy was *necessary*. They unsympathetically admonished me that my records must document *medical necessity*. I had never heard of this term. It sounded like something someone would say in a medical office, not a counseling clinic. I thought to myself, "Medical necessity: We don't provide medical services." The auditors went on to say that even though the assessments adequately explained the clients' diagnoses, the progress notes did not recurrently confirm the diagnosis and need for continued treatment. My progress notes merely documented that treatment took place.

They explained to me that the documented content of each session must match the goals and objectives written in the treatment plan. I had never heard of treatment plan *goals and objectives* the way in which they meant. Their main point was that my progress notes for every session did not clearly describe current symptoms and impairments listed in the treatment plan. That is, every progress note should validate the current need for services, and the services performed must be appropriate for the client's problem areas. Even if a client is severely impaired mentally, if it is not empirically documented in every progress note, there is no evidence for the need for psychotherapy. If it isn't written down, it doesn't exist. I wasn't taught this in graduate school.

There would be a payback to Medicaid for every progress note that did not meet this criterion. Although our treatment was appropriate and our clients' outcomes were positive, our progress notes did not specifically address medical necessity. We covered the contents of the sessions only. Bottom line: We documented the wrong material. Perhaps we should have spent more time reading Medicare's bulky manual. I was convinced that our clients needed mental health services, but the documentation didn't provide the evidence the auditors wanted. We had done nothing clinically, morally, or ethically wrong, but documentation is not about such skills; it is about empirical evidence. Being a good therapist is not enough.

This lack of appropriate documentation cost me thousands of dollars in paybacks to Medicaid. Fortunately, I was put on a payment plan; otherwise I would have gone out of business. At the time, the effects of this audit seemed like the worst thing that could have happened to me. I had no one to blame but myself. I couldn't tell the auditors that it wasn't my fault because no one had taught me how to document psychotherapy appropriately; as a mental health professional, it was my responsibility to be accountable for my work.

The lessons learned from the audit inspired me to study everything I could about documentation. There wasn't much information available except in written materials from accreditation agencies, provider manuals from insurance companies, and some literature. With this information I revised our clinical forms to make sure that the information obtained accurately covered what was needed. After sharing this information with colleagues, I was asked to present local seminars. This eventually led to national seminars in documentation. Before I knew it, my forms were published. The forms book is now in its fourth edition (Wiger, 2010). However, documentation is more than filling out forms. This led to another book—this book, which is its third edition. Now I'm glad that I was audited. The payback was worth the lesson. A negative can become a positive if you don't become negative!

CHAPTER 1

Introduction

W<small>E ARE LIVING</small> in the age of professional accountability. In addition to mental health workers, professionals such as politicians, executives, clergy, educators, and people from most walks of life have increasing demands placed on them to demonstrate that they have practiced their profession effectively and ethically. In the past few years an increasing number of well-known public figures have filled the headlines and court dockets due to compromising their professional standards. Colleges and professional schools have increased their required ethics courses. Many mental health licensing boards require ongoing ethics training as part of their mandatory continuing education.

Standards of accountability in the mental health profession come from a number of sources. State boards, such as those for psychology, social work, professional counselors, and marriage and family therapy, have specific guidelines for licensees. Accrediting agencies, such as the Commission of Accreditation for Rehabilitation Facilities and The Joint Commission, and third-party payers, such as insurance companies and managed care organizations, maintain specific documentation requirements to assure accountability.

Such regulations help curtail the rising costs of mental health services, which have skyrocketed due to factors such as inflation and increased mental health insurance benefits available to consumers. Current standards of third-party payers hold that services must be medically necessary in order to be covered for payment. Both third-party payers and regulatory agencies impose strict requirements in which each step of the clinical process must be clearly documented. Therefore, appropriate documentation and communicating evidence of clients' needs for services are crucial for a clinic's financial and professional survival.

Learning appropriate documentation procedures goes far beyond meeting professional regulations or requirements for payment of services.

Accurate recording procedures provide clear evidence of what takes place in mental health sessions. Without accurate documentation, there is not a clear record of what takes place in therapy; thus, it is difficult to evaluate therapeutic effectiveness. Sloppy clinical procedures are not only unfair to the client but may border on malpractice. During third-party audits or clinical reviews, among others, proper documentation validates that appropriate treatment took place. When sound documentation procedures are followed, a written record of treatment will be available for review of (1) therapeutic effectiveness, (2) appropriateness of services, (3) continuity of services, and (4) evaluation of therapeutic outcomes, setting a high standard for mental health treatment.

When documentation is poor, there is no clear written evidence of the course of therapy. With or without documentation requirements, responsible clinicians will continue to provide clients with valuable services.

Documentation procedures can affect the financial condition of a clinic. It is not uncommon for an insurance provider to audit records. When records do not adequately demonstrate that services were necessary, on target, or concordant with the presenting problem or diagnosis, it is possible that the clinic will have to pay back money received from the insurance company. Such audits have put some clinics out of business.

In the past, third-party payers simply paid therapists when an insurance claim was made. Due to escalating costs, managed care was necessary and subsequently flourished. Today, third-party payers no longer blindly accept billing for any psychotherapy services. They require specific types of evidence demonstrating the client's need for services and the therapeutic effectiveness in order to pay for the treatment. Without knowing proper documentation procedures and how to present a case on paper, the therapist is vulnerable to appearing to be "out of compliance" or providing "unnecessary services," even if the treatment is exceptional. If it isn't written down, it doesn't exist.

Although most mental health professionals are properly schooled in conducting psychotherapy, few receive any training in documenting the evidence of their treatment. It is not uncommon for therapists new to the field to become discouraged when exposed to the "other responsibility" of treatment: documentation. However, when properly trained, therapists soon realize the benefits of documentation. Not only do they become more confident in meeting third-party requirements, but they also become more aware of their clients' progress. Learning documentation procedures is a win-win situation.

Documentation is atheoretical. It is not psychotherapy. That is, it does not follow a certain theoretical school of thought. It is presented as *behavioral evidence,* in measurable terms; however, it has nothing to do with behavioral therapy. The clinician may conduct psychotherapy from any effective type of treatment (e.g., cognitive, behavioral, dynamic, rational-emotive, solutions focused, etc.). Managed care companies, along with other third-party payers and accrediting organizations, are open to this variation, provided that the improvements in client functioning are documented in behavioral terms. The evidence is presented in terms of objective client behaviors, not opinions or speculation. Evidence of alleviation of specific client impairments is required. Third-party payers ask: "What changes in behavior are taking place as the result of therapy?"

Regulatory agencies require that the same measuring stick is used to assess the effects of therapy regardless of the treatment modality employed. The current measurement standards in mental health require that clinical documentation be observable and measurable and provide behavioral evidence of therapeutic progress.

Documentation begins at the first interview. The several documentation procedures conducted throughout therapy are interrelated. The information collected in the initial interview is necessary for writing the treatment plan. The treatment plan provides a guideline for the course of therapy, which is documented in the progress notes. Progress notes are necessary for writing a revised treatment plan. All of the information collected is needed in writing the discharge summary and assessing outcomes as outlined in Figure 1.1.

The documentation procedure examples provided in this text represent a course of treatment for a client with depression. In addition, Appendix A provides documentation examples for a client with panic disorder with agoraphobia.

This text begins by teaching the rationale and examples of documentation for each step of the therapeutic process. It also provides training as to what documentation is required for third-party payers and accreditation agencies.

Initial	Diagnostic Interview
	Treatment Plan
	Progress Notes
Cycles of	Treatment Plan Revisions/Updates
	Progress Notes
End	Discharge Summary

Figure 1.1 Course of Documentation

Source: Reprinted with permission of John Wiley & Sons, Inc.

HIGHLIGHTS OF CHAPTER 1

- Accurate and specific documentation procedures are necessary for ethical, professional, and financial reasons.
- Third-party payers and accrediting agencies are becoming more stringent in documentation procedures.
- The intake, treatment plan, progress notes, revised treatment plan, and discharge summary are interrelated. Although they are independent documents, they represent a continuous process in therapy and documentation.
- Each step in the counseling procedures has specific documentation procedures. Not following them could be detrimental to the client, the therapist, and the clinic. Likewise, all can benefit when appropriate procedures are followed.

QUESTIONS

1. In the medical model of documentation, the means by which a therapist documents therapy
   a. depends on the theoretical school of thought.
   b. is atheoretical.
   c. is not important.
   d. incorporates documenting impairments rather than strengths.
2. A current requirement by most third-party payers to cover mental health services is documenting
   a. that personal growth will take place in therapy.
   b. that a preexisting condition was not present.
   c. proof of insurability.
   d. medical necessity.
3. When audited by a third-party payer, client files that are found not to be compliant with documentation standards
   a. typically result in loss of licensure.
   b. are a minor concern to most clinicians.
   c. may be subject to repaying funds to the third-party payer.
   d. are clear violations of confidentiality.
4. Typically, the evidence a third-party case manager uses to determine that the treatment plan has been followed is found
   a. in the progress notes.
   b. by interviewing the client.
   c. through determining the number of sessions that have been conducted, to date.
   d. in the initial summary report.
   Answers: 1b, 2d, 3c, 4a

CHAPTER 2

The Art and Science of Psychological Assessment and Treatment

There is no pretense that reason and reason alone, or that science and science alone, can prevail by themselves in any kind of human relationship, personal or therapeutic.

—James Mann, *Time-Limited Psychotherapy*

MENTAL HEALTH CLIENTS desire a treating professional who is caring, empathic, and able to help them work through issues. However, they do not want treatment from someone who fully plays it by ear or says whatever comes to mind. A certain degree of professionalism and knowledge is expected. Yet clients do not desire someone who is so scientific or technical that the human element is lost. A combination of art and science is necessary in the delivery of mental health services (Walborn, 1996).

Mental health professionals vary tremendously in their views of how to accurately collect diagnostic information and conduct therapy. Everyone falls somewhere on the continuum between viewing and practicing the field as an art versus a science. On one extreme we have those who believe and practice psychology based on their gut feelings, intuition, and inner gift of helping others. The other extreme consists of those who adhere closely to a scientific medical model. If one was to observe professionals from each of the two extremes, it would seem as if they were in different professions. Most of us are somewhere in between, relying on both the lessons of scientific research and our clinical acumen and insight.

The clinical practices in the field of psychology follow the same pendulum as other historical trends. Sometimes the pendulum swings toward hard science, but eventually, when it becomes too regimented, we miss the good old days and gradually return to the softer sciences and less empirical methods.

When the pendulum swings too far to that side, we realize that we need more empirical research for our practices, and the pendulum reverses.

PRACTICE OF MENTAL HEALTH AS AN ART

Many experienced and successful therapists view their clients as unique individuals and believe that placing them into a diagnostic category is counterproductive and impersonal. Such therapists tend to reject any requirements of placing a diagnosis on clients because it provides no more than a label that serves little or no therapeutic purpose. They realize that clients' concerns are likely multifaceted. Thus, assigning a label is pointless.

Their documentation generally consists of present feelings and listings of insights gleaned by clients. Both the assessment and treatment are feelings and insight oriented. This modality has been around for years and has a long history of success. During a typical assessment in such a model, the therapist would not focus on empirically validating a diagnosis to fit outside criteria but rather would attempt to soothe the client and provide hope and direction for the future. A number of therapeutic interventions often are used during the initial assessment session to develop rapport. Focusing on clients' immediate and long-term needs are crucial. The requirements of validating a diagnosis based on the text revision of the fourth edition of the *Diagnostic and Statistical Manual of Mental Disorders* (*DSM-IV-TR*; American Psychiatric Association, 2000) are viewed as secondary to providing hope.

The greatest strengths therapists have are the ability to focus on the here-and-now, empathy, insight, instilling hope, and providing guidance and emotional support. They tend to be patient with clients and allow them to progress at their own rates. They tend to reject any third-party restrictions on the modality and number of sessions allowed for treatment.

For example, if a child is referred for problems with temper tantrums, the therapist could focus on the child's feelings and attempt to discover why the child tantrums. It would be important to develop a trusting relationship in order for the child to be able to gradually trust the therapist and his or her interventions. One of the primary goals of the therapist would be to discover the root cause of the tantrums and help the child work through these issues. An effective therapist would be skillful in human relationship skills to help the child become more positively effective.

PRACTICE OF MENTAL HEALTH AS A SCIENCE

Psychology is also practiced from an empirical point of reference. Therefore, scientific principles are the primary modality of assessment and treatment. Human behavior is viewed as being subject to scientific laws in which people are viewed as fairly predictable if we knew enough about them. The causes and treatment of maladaptive behaviors can be understood if the appropriate information is collected. Every behavior and emotion has a cause and an effect on the individual. Changing behavior requires making modifications in clients' external and/or internal environment.

A common paradigm for treatment is the A-B-C model (antecedents-behavior-consequences). The antecedents are the events that take place that trigger the behavior. The consequences are the rewards or punishments received after the behavior takes place. The consequences might come from others or the physical environment, or be viewed subjectively by clients. A behavior can be changed if either the antecedents and/or the consequences are altered. A behavior remains the same or escalates if the antecedents and consequences remain the same. For example, if a child receives attention only when misbehaving, the child will continue to misbehave as long as attention is received.

Let us return to the child being evaluated for temper tantrums. The examiner, from a scientific perspective, would inquire about what takes place before the tantrums to determine what can be altered to avoid such situations; plus, information would be gathered to determine the consequences for tantrumming in order to determine what rewards or punishments (intrinsic or extrinsic) could be increased to help prevent tantrums.

INTEGRATING THE ART AND SCIENCE OF MENTAL HEALTH

Few people practice at the extreme end of the art/science continuum (see Figure 2.1). The schools of thought vary significantly in their viewpoints. For example, radical behaviorism holds to a strict scientific viewpoint of practicing psychology while humanistic and existential viewpoints fall on the art side of clinical practice. The cognitive-behavioral school of thought incorporates and integrates each stance. Most modern practitioners claim to be eclectic, picking and choosing what works best for them and their clients. Within each school of thought, there is variation among practitioners.

Therapy and documentation are two very different skills to learn. A therapist has a choice of literally hundreds of theoretical frameworks or any combination. Therapy can range from an intuitive to a regimented approach. In Walborn's (1996) excellent text, *Process Variables*, the effectiveness of the major therapies are compared and contrasted. It turns out that the mode of therapy is not what leads to client change. Rather, Walborn lists four process variables that, if they occur, no matter what type of therapy (art versus science), client change will take place. These variables include: (1) the theoretical relationship, (2) cognitive insight and change, (3) emotions in therapy, and (4) client expectations. Walborn describes how even though

| As an Art | 1 | 2 | 3 | 4 | 5 | 6 | 7 | 8 | 9 | 10 | As a Science |

| | Humanistic/
Existential | | Cognitive/
Behavioral | | Behaviorial | |
| | 1-4 | | 3-8 | | 7-10 | |

The differences and overlap in the practice of psychology as an art versus science from three theoretical points of view. The numbers used are for example only, and are not based on specific published material.

Figure 2.1   Range of Practice in Mental Health Treatment

the therapies appear to be quite different, they each treat the various components of the process variables. Thus, it is not the therapies in themselves that lead to client change but the common therapeutic processes they have in common. This is not to say that all therapies are the same. Although the various therapies hold different views of what is necessary for client change, the process variables that lead to client change are common between the therapies.

DOCUMENTATION IN THE LIGHT OF ART VERSUS SCIENCE

It is clear that therapists differ immensely regarding what should take place in a counseling session. This difference allows clients to receive treatment in a manner that best suits their needs. It allows therapists to practice therapy according to their particular style. However, documentation is not about theory and does not follow a school of thought. Documentation is no more than the written evidence of objective observations and data. With good documentation, client progress and course of therapy can be fairly well understood by both the therapist and a third party. It can be especially helpful when a new therapist takes over the case. Without good documentation, the client's new therapist, for the most part, has to start over.

Documentation is used for several purposes, including (1) objectively monitoring progresses and setbacks in treatment; (2) monitoring the effectiveness of current interventions; (3) working collaboratively with other professionals; and (4) audits from third parties such as payers, accreditation reviews, and professional review boards and for legal matters. Very few therapists enjoy documentation; however, many therapists who have not done a good job of documenting have realized its importance when their charts were audited.

The type of therapy you provide does not affect what third parties require for documentation. Documentation is atheoretical. It takes that same amount of time to document if you conduct therapy as an art or science. However, when you learn what is expected in documentation, it can be surprising how little time it takes. Usually you can complete all or most of your documentation before the session is over. Most types of documentation require little or no time after the session.

HIGHLIGHTS OF CHAPTER 2

- There is no set or standardized means of conducting psychological services.
- Those who consider psychotherapy an art believe in gut feelings, intuition, and insight that lead to client change.
- Those who view conducting psychological services as a science value the scientific method, in which objective data are incorporated into treatment.
- Other schools of thought combine treatment as both an art and science.
- Although the various theoretical perspectives may seem different, their common process variables contribute to client change.
- No matter what therapeutic orientation a therapist follows, documentation is atheoretical, and current standards require an empirical format.

QUESTIONS

1. Which of the following best represents a statement from someone who views psychotherapy as an art? "Today we worked on . . .
   a. . . . identifying how he she feels rewarded by excessively washing her hands."
   b. . . . expressing latent emotions."
   c. . . . identifying what factors lead to outbursts at work."
   d. . . . identifying rational behaviors."
2. Which of the next treatment strategies would most likely be incorporated by someone from a scientific perspective of psychological treatment?
   a. Dream interpretation.
   b. Psychiatric hospitalization.
   c. A-B-C model.
   d. Expressing empathy
3. According to this text, the most current documentation
   a. is atheoretical.
   b. should correspond the theoretical model used in treatment.
   c. is important, thus it requires much of the therapist's time.
   d. Each of these answers.

4. Process variable research
   a. maximizes the differences between psychological therapies.
   b. suggests that there are very different processes that take place in the various therapies.
   c. suggests that documentation can be either written as an art or science.
   d. integrates the similarities between psychological therapies.

   Answers: 1b, 2c, 3a, 4d

CHAPTER 3

Overview of Current Documentation Procedures and Third-Party Requirements

D OCUMENTATION PROCEDURES HAVE changed dramatically since the 1970s and 1980s. Previously, requirements consisted of no more than verifying that an interview took place, making a diagnosis, perhaps making a treatment plan, and writing rudimentary progress notes. Since there were few specific standards, documentation was a matter of subjective opinion. Although clinical judgment always will be an extremely important part of understanding client behaviors, there must be a balance of incorporating universal procedures (e.g., criteria based on the text revision of the fourth edition of the *Diagnostic and Statistical Manual of Mental Disorders* [*DSM-IV-TR*], professional regulations, accreditation requirements) when documenting services. Insurance companies that paid for mental health services listed few or no documentation requirements to validate a diagnosis or the client's need for services. Clients receiving mental health services seldom knew their diagnosis or even if there was a formalized, written treatment plan. Now the client's input is an important part in formulating, following, and revising the treatment plan.

Today, in the age of professional accountability, clinical proficiency is necessary but not sufficient in providing all aspects of mental health services. Third-party payers demand evidence that demonstrates both the need and the effectiveness of mental health treatment. Insurance companies or accreditation agencies do not interview a client to determine the effectiveness of services. (However, at times, outcomes surveys are sent to clients.) Rather, they rely on written documentation from the therapist. Therefore, if services are not documented properly, the most skillful therapist could appear on paper to be ineffective with clients. This can lead to significant multifaceted

11

losses (termination of services, loss of insurance contract, reimbursement to the insurance company) to the therapist. In some cases, very poor documentation has been reported to professional boards, leading to reprimands, required supervision, and continuing education. Like it or not, documentation is a necessary part of the training of mental health professionals.

Some therapists become upset when they see a client for a few sessions and then are required to request an authorization for additional services. If therapists are not proficient in documentation procedures, it is possible that further services could be denied even if the client highly needs treatment. Case managers reviewing the case for the third-party payer have nothing else to review other than a therapist's written evidence. The case managers do not provide a separate diagnostic interview with the client to verify the information. When third-party reviewers decline additional services, the rejection is more likely due to inadequate documentation rather than a refusal to allow treatment for a needy client. The adage "If it isn't written down, it doesn't exist" holds especially true for clinical documentation. A client with severe mental health problems who receives therapy from a therapist without adequate documentation skills could be denied services due to the therapist's lack of documentation skills. Thus, poor documents ultimately can lead to termination of insurance payments for mental health services.

When a file is audited or reviewed, no assumptions are made regarding the need for services, what took place in a session, or what progress has occurred. This information must be documented. Auditors or reviewers do not attend therapy sessions to assess therapeutic effectiveness. The only effective means of communication therapists have with auditors is *written documentation*. This book provides examples and explanations of how to document the entire course of therapy.

WHAT WE OUGHT TO DO VERSUS WHAT WE WERE TAUGHT TO DO

Current documentation procedures required by third parties and accrediting agencies follow a medical model in which evidence of therapeutic effectiveness is based on observable and measurable client behaviors rather than being based solely upon subjective measures, such as intuition and insight. Undoubtedly clinical intuition and insight are necessary clinical skills, but they are not sufficient for empirical documentation. Therapists are trained from a wide range of theoretical perspectives, dealing with mild to severe degrees of client impairment and dysfunction. Therapists trained from a perspective emphasizing personal growth, increased insight, and clinical intuition are likely to be less comfortable learning documentation procedures from a medical model than those trained from a scientific practitioner model. Their type of treatment is not the issue, for it may very well be as effective or even more effective than other means of treatment. However, the issue is documentation of the effects of therapy, not the mode of therapy.

The criteria for the medical, or scientific practitioner, model is based on diagnostic criteria found in the *DSM-IV-TR* (American Psychiatric Association, 2000). This text provides instruction in documentation that will be especially helpful to those whose training did not include a scientific practitioner model.

Typically third-party payers do not reimburse for services unless such services are demonstrated as being medically necessary. Those who are trained to provide counseling that may be therapeutically helpful (e.g., personal growth counseling, relationship therapy) but is not medically necessary are likely to find the material found in this text as challenging to their basic assumptions. Adequate documentation skills are necessary for a clinic's financial survival if they receive third-party payment. Documentation training will help ease the conflict of determining which services are covered by insurance.

MENTAL HEALTH GRADUATE TRAINING

Graduate school mental health training emphasizes the theory and practice of psychotherapy. Training includes obtaining knowledge and understanding in a wide spectrum of clinical perspectives, assessment, interviewing, testing, diagnosis, ethics, statistics, research, and other areas. Developing the numerous skills is quite time consuming, providing little time for therapists to learn the mechanics of clinical practice, including documentation skills. Training in "treatment planning" certainly involves planning a client's treatment, but usually it does not involve how to write an observable and measurable treatment plan or document client behaviors during treatment. Students are taught how to treat clients but not necessarily how to communicate in writing what will be conducted in therapy, what was conducted in therapy, and how to integrate the two.

It is clearly the intention of graduate school educators that students will learn documentation skills, but the training does not neatly fit into one particular graduate school course . . . and when considering the numerous required courses, there is usually no room for additional courses in most training programs. Even if documentation procedures are not taught specifically, it is usually assumed that students will be taught these procedures during their practicum and/or internship experiences. Oftentimes, though, documentation training does not take place here either, because typically, in an internship, the graduate student sees clients pro bono or for a reduced fee rather than through third-party payment; therefore, their documentation is not subject to third-party payer regulations. In addition, their clinical supervision focuses on the quality of therapy and case conceptualization skills, which, in themselves, are arduous tasks to master. For these reasons, students' documentation skills typically are not scrutinized with the same rigor by their clinical supervisors as they would be by a third-party payer. Nevertheless, documentation training in graduate school is on the rise due to the realities in the field.

THIRD-PARTY PAYERS AND MANAGED CARE

Third-party payment to mental health providers is a phenomenon that has been increasing in significance since the 1980s. Lobbying on the part of mental health professionals and employers has led to the inclusion of mental health care in many healthcare insurance packages. However, more recently, mental health coverage has been increasingly restricted. There was a time in which, if a client's insurance policy covered mental health services, he or she could receive seemingly unlimited services from a provider of choice. Mental health providers simply filled out insurance forms and soon received payment. Not surprisingly, some people with minor diagnoses spent several years in counseling, with no review of therapeutic effectiveness. As a result, the cost of mental health benefits skyrocketed, and third-party payers had no choice but to find means to lower mental health costs to remain competitive and stay in business. Managed care, with its focus on cost containment, was the end result.

More than any other change agent, managed care has transformed the scope and nature of mental health services. Before managed care existed, it was possible to receive insurance benefits for nonmedically necessary counseling services. Costs increased dramatically. Thus, psychological services such as for personal growth, relationship therapy, and psychoeducational services now are not generally covered by insurance. This author is not negating the positive and life-changing effects of these types of counseling but is simply noting current third-party criteria.

Managed care has reduced the types of services available to those viewed only as medically necessary, and it requires that therapists must, on an ongoing basis, demonstrate that services are medically necessary. When there is not sufficient evidence that a client's impairments are reduced as a result of mental health treatment, services are to be discontinued. Without appropriate documentation, there is no means to gauge the effects of treatment.

Although practitioners from different treatment modalities disagree about which therapeutic methods lead to effective change, documentation is theoretically neutral. Good documentation skills enable therapists from any school of thought to demonstrate the need for services and demonstrate therapeutic effectiveness. Therapists from all schools of thought can learn to document therapeutic progress and not worry about their insurance claims being rejected due to insufficient documentation.

The intent of managed care is to provide affordable services to clients and reduce unnecessary services. The quality of documentation is the sole means of determining whether services are medically necessary. Therapists who learn appropriate documentation procedures typically have no problem receiving payment for services and receiving authorization for continued services.

MEDICAL NECESSITY

The concept of "medical necessity" has dramatically influenced current third-party reimbursement procedures for mental health services. Mental health services are considered medically necessary when the client is significantly impaired in areas such as social, occupational, educational, or other types of functioning and when, without mental health services, the client is not likely to improve or return to premorbid functioning. Prior to adopting the medical necessity model, third-party payers paid for services when qualified clinicians diagnosed clients with a mental health disorder. This is still part of the process, but receiving a diagnosis alone is not sufficient to guarantee payment for services. A person who endorses a number of symptoms of, for example, major depressive disorder might be functioning adequately socially and occupationally and in other areas. Simply experiencing some mental health symptoms may not fit the third party's criteria for coverage of mental health services. That is, services might be helpful but may not be necessary. One could say that there are two types of counseling services: those that are medically necessary (which would qualify for insurance payment) and those that are not necessary (not qualify for insurance payment), both of which are helpful to the client.

Criteria for diagnosing a mental health diagnosis also have been in transition. Several years ago, the typical procedure for making a diagnosis was simple endorsement of mental health symptoms that defined a diagnosis. For example, if a client endorses having a number of symptoms of depression, such as weight loss, low appetite, sadness, decreased concentration, and decreased sleep, in the past it was likely that a diagnosis would be given solely based on symptoms. However, today simply endorsing symptoms is not enough because it does not imply the degree (i.e., mild to severe) of the symptoms or their effect on the client's functioning. Current diagnosis procedures must validate both the existence and the degree of symptoms, plus demonstrate that there are resultant impairments as a result of the mental health disorder.

The degree to which symptoms affect the client's behavior and functioning is much more significant than acknowledging that symptoms exist. To qualify for treatment reimbursement, symptoms must be documented so that a third-party review can understand their impact on the client. Thus, clinicians also must learn to document the onset, frequency, antecedents, intensity, and duration of symptoms plus the resulting functional impairments.

MENTAL HEALTH CRITERIA

Some third-party payers provide vague criteria for reimbursement for mental health services, supplying few if any examples of what is expected in documentation. There are no clear statutory requirements other than from state-funded Medicaid. Medicaid provider manuals range in specificity from state to state. Some states that licensed mental health facilities periodically audit charts to monitor the quality of services. State licensure boards typically publish some guidelines for documentation, but not at the specificity of managed care or accrediting agencies.

Few widely accepted standards of documentation exist. Even the standards from accreditation agencies (e.g., Commission of Accreditation for Rehabilitation Facilities [CARF] and The Joint Commission), which publish extensive manuals of standards, there is room for subjective interpretation. This writer recalls a previous accreditation visit in which the auditors sent from the accreditation agency appeared to have difficulty agreeing on rating various charts.

Third-party payers have different specific requirements for reimbursement of services from state to state and company to company, but many of the guidelines are fairly consistent, such as:

1. Services must be medically or therapeutically necessary.
2. Services must be directed toward a diagnosable mental illness or disorder.

Comparison to Documentation in Other Fields

When someone has an auto accident and has insurance coverage to pay for the car being repaired, the insurance company will not accept a bill from the repair shop until evidence of what repairs took place is provided. Methods of documentation may include photographs of the damage and a detailed list of services that are concordant with acceptable standards. Likewise, when a dentist performs certain services, X rays first must be sent to the insurance company as evidence of the need for services. In the delivery of mental health services, it is not possible to take photographs or X rays of the problems; therefore, we provide written documentation that follows the same general principles.

3. Services must be consistent with the diagnosis and degree of impairment.
4. There must be documentation of reasonable progress consistent with the treatment of the disorder.
5. The treatment plan must include specific discharge criteria written in behavioral terms.
6. Services must be directed specifically toward the diagnosis.
7. To receive continued services, there must be documented evidence of continued impairment.
8. The progress notes must clearly reflect the treatment plan goals and objectives.

Without such criteria, there is no clear means of documenting that the services being rendered are needed. Although specific regulations of third-party payers regarding forms, frequency of reports, and so forth may differ in some areas, the overall information requested is remarkably similar.

CRITERIA FOR CLINICAL SIGNIFICANCE

The *DSM-IV-TR* states:

> The definition of mental disorder in the introduction to *DSM-IV-TR* requires that there be clinically significant impairment or distress. To highlight the importance of considering this issue, the criteria sets for most disorders include a clinical significance criterion (usually worded ". . . causes clinically significant distress or impairment in social, occupational, or other important areas of functioning"). This criterion helps establish the threshold for the diagnosis of a disorder in those situations in which the symptomatic presentation by itself (particularly in its milder forms) is not inherently pathological and may be encountered in individuals for whom a diagnosis of "mental disorder" would be inappropriate. (p. 8)

O-F-A-I-D PROCEDURE

The acronym O-F-A-I-D (of aid) is a helpful procedure that may be used throughout the course of therapy to help provide measurable evidence of client progress. The collected information also helps confirm a diagnosis and demonstrate outcomes of treatment. The O-F-A-I-D acronym stands for

Onset
Frequency
Antecedents
Intensity
Duration

Term	Description
Onset	Date or time period when symptoms and impairments began
Frequency	How often symptoms occur
Antecedents	Events or stressors leading to onset/exacerbation of symptoms
Intensity	Severity of symptoms (e.g., mild, moderate, severe, or 1–100)
Duration	How long symptoms last

EXAMPLE OF DOCUMENTATION WITH O-F-A-I-D PROCEDURE

Client with Depression   Nora W. states that she has been depressed for the past year since her child was removed from the home by social services (onset). She states that she feels depressed over 90% of the time (frequency). She becomes increasingly more depressed when she sees little children, who remind her of her child who is currently placed in foster care (antecedents). When asked about the level of her depression, she states that, on a 1 to 100 scale, it is usually around 85–90 (intensity). She further adds that bouts of depression, in which she isolates herself in her room up to 10 hours per day (duration).

Client with Panic Attacks   Halle P. began having panic attacks when he lost his job six months ago (onset). Currently he has an average of 3 panic attacks per day (frequency). Panic attacks typically take place when he leaves the house, when the phone rings, or when he someone comes to his door (antecedents). He describes the effects as severe, rating them as a 95 on a scale of 1 to 100 (intensity). He states that his panic attacks last an average of 20 minutes (duration).

Use of the O-F-A-I-D Procedure in Validating a Diagnosis   Although validating a diagnosis is discussed in more detail in Chapter 7, a brief explanation of this procedure is given at this time of validating a diagnosis with the O-F-A-I-D procedure. The *DSM-IV-TR* lists specific requirements that must be met in order to make a diagnosis. The specific types of requirements vary by diagnosis; however, the O-F-A-I-D procedure is helpful in validating or providing supportive evidence that the diagnosis given to a client matches specific *DSM-IV-TR* criteria. (See Table 3.1)

The *DSM-IV-TR* suggests that it is possible for a person to experience symptoms of a disorder but not be diagnosed as such because symptoms are not severe enough. Inadequate documentation, however, can make clients appear to be less afflicted than they actually are. If medical necessity is not

Table 3.1

Example of Use of O-F-A-I-D Procedure in Validating a Diagnosis of
Major Depressive Disorder

DSM-IV-TR criteria for diagnosis	Example of validation
Depressive symptoms or lack of pleasure for at least 2 weeks	"Client has been depressed for the past 8 months." (*onset*)
Depressed most of the time	"Client states that she is depressed 5 or more days per week." (*frequency* and *duration*)
	No *DSM-IV-TR* requirement for antecedents for this diagnosis
Qualifiers of *Mild, Moderate, Severe,* and other descriptors	"Level of depression is Severe, due to significant impairments socially and occupationally." (*intensity*)

Note: Not every facet of O-F-A-I-D is required in this case.

Source: Reprinted with permission of John Wiley & Sons, Inc.

found to be evident due to insufficient or inadequate documentation, reimbursement will be denied. The next examples highlight incidents where medical necessity is not adequately documented.

Depression

- *Poorly documented symptoms.* "The client is depressed, withdrawn, suffers from lack of sleep and fatigue, feels anxious, and has feelings of confusion."
- *Specific problems with the documentation.* This statement does not provide adequate documentation for a diagnosis because it lists only symptoms. Impairments are not validated. It is possible that the client is functioning adequately because the severity of symptoms is minimal. According to this documentation, the client *might* need services, but it is uncertain. The evidence presented is not quantifiable.

  A normal life stressor could lead to these symptoms. At times, people experience some degree of these symptoms and are not considered psychopathological. For example, if a person fails an important college exam, it is possible that the person, for a few days, could feel down, avoid others, lose some sleep, and feel tired. These symptoms, on paper, might look like a depressive disorder, but when considering other factors, such as duration and intensity of symptoms, they appear to be a normal reaction to a normal life stressor. In this case, the listed symptoms are expected, given the situation.
- *Properly documented example.* "The client meets criteria for major depression as evidenced by feeling depressed most of the time for the past 2 months, withdrawing from almost all people, daily suicidal ideations,

sleeping less than 3 hours per night, physical and mental fatigue, and increased worrying. There is resulting educational and social impairment in that he has not attended college classes in over 1 month and usually stays in his room by himself, avoiding friends and family."

Panic Attacks

- *Poorly documented example.* "The client has panic attacks."
- *Specific problems with the documentation.* This statement also does not provide enough information to warrant a diagnosis of a mental disorder. The label "panic attacks" could be explained using the O-F-A-I-D procedure to provide a clearer picture of the history and level of symptomology. Most people have had at least one panic attack in their lives, but it does not constitute a panic disorder. Others have frequent, debilitating panic attacks causing significant dysfunction that interferes with a wide array of daily activities. The main problem with this statement is that it could apply to someone with panic attacks of any degree, whether very mild or severe. The description is missing evidence of the *DSM-IV-TR* criteria for a panic disorder and the resulting impairments.
- *Properly documented example.* "The client has experienced panic disorder without agoraphobia. Symptoms last at least 30 minutes, and have occurred at least twice per day for the past year. Symptoms are evidenced by palpitations, hot flashes, sweating, chest pains, dizziness, trembling, and fleeing the situation. During the past 3 months, panic attacks have increased in duration and intensity, resulting in avoiding any new or stressful situations and leaving work early approximately 3 to 4 times per week. He has gone to the emergency room 3 times in the past month, believing that he was going to die."

Adjustment

- *Poorly documented example.* "The client is having trouble coping with a recent divorce and death of a loved one."
- *Specific problems with the documentation.* This statement does not justify the need for treatment. These are normal life stressors or events that many people experience. There is no evidence of abnormal impairments or a need for mental health services. It is expected that a person would have difficulty coping with a recent divorce and the death of a loved one, but there is no documented evidence of a mental health disorder. Although mental health counseling might be needed, there is no supporting evidence.
- *Properly documented example.* "The client is experiencing an adjustment disorder with depressed mood as evidenced by increased depression,

withdrawal, and difficulties coping. Symptoms have occurred since the onset of two major stressors in the past 3 months including the death of his mother and his divorce. Affective impairment is noted as evidenced by feeling dysphoric most of the time and having difficulties feeling motivated to work, shop, or resume usual activities. Concerns include crying several times per day, missing work at least twice per week, and avoiding all social supports."

- *Poorly documented example.* "The client goes to work only 1 or 2 days per week, has no friends, and has not phoned any family members for more than 2 months."

- *Specific problems with the documentation.* In this case, functional impairments might exist, but no mental disorder is documented. The impairment must be the result of a mental disorder to demonstrate medical necessity for receiving mental health treatment. Otherwise, services other than mental health may be needed. The documentation also does not indicate whether these behaviors represent a significant change in functioning or if the client simply chooses to work temporary jobs sporadically and prefers to be alone. One cannot assume psychopathology based on a lifestyle that is not mainstream.

- *Properly documented example.* "The client has felt depressed for the past 3 weeks as evidenced by suicidal ideations, feeling hopeless and worthless, and excessive eating. There is resulting affective, cognitive, educational, and physical impairment as evidenced by constant fatigue, missing school 50% of the time from lack of sleep (average 3 hrs./night), decreased concentration (unable to comprehend after reading more than 3–4 minutes at a time), weight gain of 12 pounds in past 3 weeks, and increased negative self-statements noted by others."

Figure 3.1 provides a helpful format to use when documenting a client's symptoms and resulting impairments or dysfunctions. Documentation procedures that state only whether symptoms exist can be compared to stating that an automobile tire is low on air. Most automobile tires are low on air at some time. This may be because the automobile has hit a bump, due to cold weather, or even due to normal wear. Just because a tire is low on air does not always mean the driver cannot drive the car. The severity of the problem depends, in part, on how low tire is on air. A tire that is designed to have 32 pounds per square inch (psi) of air pressure will likely work fine if the pressure is anywhere from 25 to 40 psi. But if the air pressure is, for example, 2 psi, the car is not drivable and is in need of services before the car can be driven again. Other descriptors, such as how long there has been trouble with the tire losing air, how often it must be filled up, and the condition of the tire, will help you make a more informed decision about whether to continue

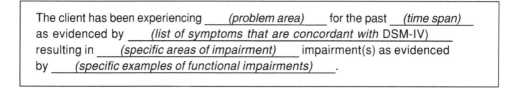

> The client has been experiencing ____*(problem area)*____ for the past ___*(time span)*___ as evidenced by ____*(list of symptoms that are concordant with* DSM-IV)____ resulting in ____*(specific areas of impairment)*____ impairment(s) as evidenced by ____*(specific examples of functional impairments)*____ .

Figure 3.1 Suggested Format for Documenting Client Symptoms and Functional Impairments

Source: Reprinted with permission of John Wiley & Sons, Inc.

driving the car or to take it in for service. Likewise, listing vague mental health symptoms alone does not provide enough specific information to make a diagnosis or plan treatment.

Figure 3.2 illustrates the difference between simply listing a client's symptoms and documenting the impacts of those symptoms by adding

	Profile 1 Listing Symptoms Only	
Client A		**Client B**
Depressed mood		Depressed mood
Social withdrawal		Social withdrawal
Suicidal ideations		Suicidal ideations
Lack of pleasure		Lack of pleasure
Poor concentration		Poor concentration
Weight gain		Weight gain

Profile 2 Listing Additional Descriptors for Clients A and B Documents Difference in Diagnosis and Medical Necessity

Client A		**Client B**
Onset:	4 years ago	12 years ago
Frequency:	2 episodes since onset	2–3 episodes/year (cycling)
Duration:	Episodes last ≤ 2 weeks	Episodes last 30–45 days
Severity:	Mild	Severe, occasional psychotic features
Extent of impaired function:	Sometimes late for work	Recently fired from job, 8 job losses, no
	No job losses	friends, 4 suicide attempts, 6
	Sometimes avoid friends	hospitalizations for depression, currently
	No hospitalizations	in bankruptcy, emerging panic
	Gained 10 lbs. in past	symptoms, gained 35 lbs. in past 6 months
	6 months	

Figure 3.2 Two Profiles of Clients Presenting With Major Depression

Source: Reprinted with permission of John Wiley & Sons, Inc.

qualifiers to demarcate additional dimensions of impairment. Profile 1 represents two clients appearing to suffer from the same problem. Notice the difference, however, when further descriptors are added in Profile 2.

Adding the descriptors of the O-F-A-I-D procedure provides evidence that Client B is more severely impaired than Client A. Documentation procedures that address only symptomology miss this important distinction. For this reason, it is difficult to make a clear diagnosis when only symptoms are described. Likewise, it is difficult to convince third-party payers that a diagnosis (or treatment) is warranted when only symptoms are documented.

In addition, when documentation of specific functional or behavioral impairment is lacking, there is meager evidence to use in determining the type and number of services most appropriate for the client. The *DSM-IV-TR* states: "Making a *DSM-IV* diagnosis is only the first step in a comprehensive evaluation. To formulate an adequate treatment plan, the clinician will invariably require considerable additional information about the person being evaluated beyond that required to make a *DSM-IV* diagnosis" (p. xxxv).

Appropriate documentation for diagnosis, treatment planning, and reimbursement requires specifying the degree to which symptoms are impairing various areas of the client's functioning. Current standards in documentation incorporate the level of functional impairment as the measurement standard of the effects of mental illness symptoms. Incorporating impairments and dysfunctions presents a clearer picture of a client's mental status. Also, decisions regarding the medical necessity of treatment are more clearly communicated, and treatment planning may be written and understood more clearly.

FUNCTIONAL IMPAIRMENTS

Functional impairments are significant dysfunctions in daily living impacting affective, cognitive, occupational, social, and/or other functioning for which the client needs mental health services (i.e., medical necessity is demonstrated) to adequately return to normal or previous levels of functioning. In other words, without such services, the client is likely to remain dysfunctional. For example, a currently depressed person might have a history of going to work and working productively five days per week. Since the onset of depression, however, the client has been attending work only two to three days per week, resulting in significantly decreased production, and is in jeopardy of termination. This same client also may be experiencing increased social withdrawal and avoiding previous friends, thereby cutting off potential social supports. Areas of impairment for this client are described as *occupational* and *social*. Other areas of impairment due

Occupational	"Work production for the client has decreased by more than 75% since the death of his spouse, resulting in potential termination if quota is not met by July 10th."
Academic	"Recent school reports indicate that client is angry at classmates, teachers, and family members almost all of the time making it difficult to concentrate on academics. Grades have dropped two letter grades in the past two terms."
Social	"Client has not left her house nor contacted any family members in the past five months, since panic attacks began. Previously client was highly involved socially and with her family."
	"Client is ostracized by classmates due to hyperactivity and immature behaviors on the playground. Frustration, aggressive outbursts, and temper tantrums have increased."
Affective	"Client reports significant sadness, boredom, and grief, resulting in increased suicidal threats."
Physical	"Client reports inability to perform usual activities of daily living, extreme fatigue, increased headaches, loss of 40 lbs. due to low appetite, and dizziness since losing his job."
Combinations	"Client's mother indicates that he is failing in school, has lost all of his friends, has been fired from his job, and has been arrested for marijuana possession for the third time. Before he was injured in the auto accident he received As and Bs in school, seldom missed work, and had no history of drug or alcohol use."

Figure 3.3 Examples of Functional Impairments
Source: Reprinted with permission of John Wiley & Sons, Inc.

to depression could exist also, including physical, affective, cognitive impairments, and any other aspect in which a person's activities of daily living are restricted due to a mental disorder. Figure 3.3 provides various examples of functional impairments.

Because current documentation guidelines (medical model) require providing observable and measurable evidence of changes in functional impairments resulting from treatment, the diagnostic interview should include obtaining baseline measures of the client's degree of functional impairment.

ASSESSMENT PROCEDURES

The initial diagnostic session is the backbone of clinical assessment; the foundation of treatment. Assessment procedures provide a clinical history and current snapshot of the purpose for which services are needed. Several aspects of the client's life are reviewed and subsequently integrated in a diagnostic summary that considers a full range of function status. Without the assessment, there would be no identification of client strengths, weaknesses, preferences; thus, no information would be available to provide an accurate treatment plan. Figure 3.4 lists CARF requirements for the initial assessment.

---

1. The organization continuously conducts assessments or obtains information for each person served:
   a. In a manner that is respectful and considerate of that person's specific needs.
   b. That identifies the expectations of the person served.
   c. That provides for the use of assistive technology or resources, as needed, in the assessment process.
   d. That is responsive to the changing needs of the person served.
   e. That includes provisions for communicating the results of the assessment to:
      1. Personnel.
      2. The person served.
      3. Appropriate others.
   f. That provides the basis for legally required notification, when applicable.
2. Assessments are conducted by qualified personnel:
   a. Knowledgeable to assess the specific needs of the persons served.
   b. Trained in the use of applicable tools.
3. The assessments include information obtained from:
   a. The person served.
   b. Family members, when applicable or permitted.
   c. Friends or peers, when appropriate and permitted.
   d. Other appropriate and permitted collateral sources.
4. The primary assessment gathers sufficient information to develop an individualized, person-centered plan for each person served, including information about the person's:
   a. Personal strengths.
   b. Individual needs.
   c. Abilities and interests.
   d. Preferences.
   e. Presenting problems.
   f. Urgent needs, including suicide risk.
   g. Previous behavioral health services, including:
      1. Diagnostic information.
      2. Treatment information.
      3. Efficacy of current or previously used medications.
   h. Physical health history and current status.
   i. Diagnosis(es).
   j. Mental status.
   k. Current level of functioning.
   l. Pertinent current and historical life situation information, including his or her:
      1. Age.
      2. Gender.

Figure 3.4   Overview of CARF (2004) Standards for Assessment

Source: Used by permission of the *Behavioral Health Standards Manual*, Commission on Accreditation of Rehabilitation Facilities. Copyright 2011.

3. Employment history.
4. Legal involvement.
5. Family history.
6. History of abuse.
7. Relationships, including natural supports.
m. Issues important to the person served.
n. Use of alcohol, tobacco, and/or other drugs.
o. Need for, and availability of, social supports.
p. Risk-taking behaviors.
q. Level of educational functioning.
r. Advance directives, when applicable.
s. Medication use profile.
t. Medication allergies or adverse reactions to medications.
u. Adjustments to disabilities/disorders.
5. The primary assessment:
a. Is conducted within specific time frames.
b. Results in the preparation of an interpretive summary that is:
1. Based on the assessment data.
2. Used in the development of the treatment plan.
3. Identifies any co-occurring disabilities/disorders that should be addressed in the development of the individual plan.

Figure 3.4 Continued

INTEGRATING CONFLICTING OBSERVATIONS, CLIENT STATEMENTS, MENTAL STATUS EXAM, PREVIOUS RECORDS, AND TESTING

All client files contain some conflicting information. Always expect there to be differences in areas such as current versus previous diagnoses, observations versus test results, verbal versus nonverbal behaviors, or any other possible areas. Conflicting information comes for a variety of reasons, including variable client behavior, different viewpoints from different therapists, marginal validity of tests conducted, faking good, faking bad, test/interview anxiety, effects of medications, actual client change, substance abuse, and more.

Therapists must prioritize the various types of information they receive about a client. Prioritizing the relevancy of information requires experience and judgment. However, a few rules of thumb are suggested.

CURRENT INFORMATION

In most situations, the most recent information best reflects the client's current behaviors. This statement is most accurate when the client is self-referred for treatment and the purpose is to receive treatment and get better.

Current testing and observations, in such cases, provide the best indication of the client here-and-now. Older information could be detrimental if significant client change has taken place. Too many clients make a number of positive improvements, but old records with diagnoses that are no longer applicable become monkeys on their backs. For example, it has become a common (although not suggested) practice to retain previous diagnoses in current records. Some therapists denote them as "history of (name of diagnosis)" while others simply keep the diagnosis without validating whether it is current. The practice of retaining older unverified diagnoses can lead to several problems in the client's records and implications of multiple diagnoses when it might not be accurate. Often, when clients have a record of multiple diagnoses, it is due to being given different diagnoses by different therapists over the years. It is important to clearly validate current symptoms and impairments of every diagnosis you list. If you do not agree with a previous diagnosis, make a clear notation of it in the records to prevent the diagnosis from remaining in the client's records perpetually.

Recently a young man requested a psychological evaluation because he was having trouble getting into the military due to his current records listing multiple diagnoses. His diagnoses were clearly secondary to stressors and reactions from a disruptive childhood, not due to current behaviors. His emotional, behavioral, educational, vocational, and social functioning was now within normal limits. His previous diagnoses were no longer applicable. His new diagnosis was "no diagnosis."

However, when there is the possibility of secondary gain, such as avoiding prosecution, receiving financial benefits, being exempt from a difficult task, or any other circumstances in which the results could affect an outside decision, caution must be taken to avoid overdiagnosing or underdiagnosing. In such cases it is suggested that the use of collateral informants and previous history be given equal or more weight than the present data.

Psychological Testing

Usually psychological tests confirm what has been discovered in the verbal assessment. Tests can be very helpful in providing additional insight into client concerns. It is the therapist's responsibility to opine how valid a test is for a particular person. Simply because a test is deemed "valid" for certain groups and circumstances does not mean that it is valid for everyone in all situations. Each edition of a psychological test seeks to improve its validity and reliability. There is no blanket validity for any test for every individual.

Several factors can affect the validity of a test for a particular individual. Some of these factors include the person's emotional state at the time of taking the test, reading level, motivation, time constraints, knowledge of the

English language, cultural factors, personality variables, history of test exposure, the purpose for taking the test, and more. When any of these variables is significant, it can greatly affect the tests results. Thus, a person taking a test at one time could score differently on another test administration due to factors that related not to the test but to the client. It is suggested that a statement of the therapist's opinion of validity of the testing situation should accompany every report.

Some tests, such as the Minnesota Multiphasic Personality Inventory, 2nd edition, the Beck Anxiety Inventory, and the Beck Depression Inventory, 2nd edition, are designed to provide the client's level of functioning at the time of taking the test or near proximity; thus, variation is expected depending on the client's mental state at that time. However, other tests, such as academic tests or tests of intellectual functioning, are based on stable traits. That is, results should be similar over time, unless factors that lead to cognitive declines have taken place, such as a traumatic brain injury, onset of dementia, or severe depression or anxiety. Thus, if a client has had no significant events that would lead to cognitive declines, cognitive or academic test results should be fairly consistent. When significant changes take place in testing results, the validity of the testing should be questioned if there are no alternative explanations.

Collateral Information

Collateral information is provided by others who know the client's history and present behaviors. These "others" typically include family, friends, or associates. Due to the extent of their relationships with the client, much information can be gained regarding any changes in functioning and current areas of impairment. One must be cautious because collaterals are not professionals and have personal relationships with the clients in which the information might be overly subjective.

Historical Records

Information in historical records includes previous information from professionals who have treated the client. Common sources of records include medical doctors, mental health professionals, teachers, and case workers. Typically, newer information is the most valid. However, even newer information sometimes conflicts, especially when a client presents differently to different providers. This could be evidence of a personality disorder, bipolar disorder, medication noncompliance, malingering, or situational stress. Most of the time historical records are fairly consistent and help determine the chronicity of a disorder. A therapist should never ignore or dismiss conflicting records.

TREATMENT PLANNING

Although the collection of clinical information is ongoing, the information gathered in the initial diagnostic assessment is most crucial because it directly affects the treatment plan, progress notes, and subsequent reports. The treatment plan is based on the diagnostic assessment. All information written in the treatment plan must correspond to the assessment and information gathered in therapy sessions. That is, targeted issues for treatment should be examined carefully in the intake and subsequent sessions rather than simply appearing in the treatment plan without written justification that a need for treatment exists.

The treatment plan is a dynamic document that is subject to revisions as treatment progresses and as more information is learned about the client. A static treatment plan, in which no revisions are made over time, is no more than an exercise in wasted time and effort. A well-formed treatment plan is crucial to ensuring reimbursement for services because it provides a blueprint of therapy. Like a teacher's lesson plan, it outlines the recipient's needs and functioning level and describes in a step-by-step to meet the intended goals via specific objectives. Likewise, properly written progress notes are important because they are the sole source of documentation that treatment plan goals and objectives are being met.

POTENTIAL FINANCIAL IMPACT OF POOR DOCUMENTATION

In the not-so-distant past, third-party reimbursement for mental health services was virtually guaranteed. Today, however, the quality of documentation directly affects the financial status of the clinic and the therapist. The effect of an audit can result, and often has, resulted in therapists being required to return thousands of dollars in funds to third parties when client charts are not in compliance with accepted standards. Too many clinics have gone bankrupt because they were unable to return funds to an insurance company after an audit. Keep in mind that paybacks do not always indicate that treatment was unwarranted or that a therapist was unscrupulous. It is possible for therapists to provide appropriate treatment but be penalized financially due to insufficient documentation of the effects of treatment.

One common auditing procedure used by third-party payers is to audit a set number of charts and use that as the basis for determining what percentage of files at the clinic are not in compliance with documentation procedures. For example, if 100 charts are audited and 20 are determined not to demonstrate medical necessity for services, the insurance company may determine that 20% of all monies it paid to the clinic during the audit period (often one to three years) must be paid back. In this case, if a clinic employs five therapists who each see an average of ten patients from the auditor's insurance company per week, the total number of visits would look like this:

5 therapists
× 10 Clients per week (from the insurance provider conducting the audit)
× 52 Weeks per year
× 3 Years (audit period)
7, 800 Client visits reimbursed by the insurance provider

This results in a total of 7,800 client visits in the three-year period. If the insurance company reimbursed the clinic $60 per visit, the total payment to the clinic in the three-year period would be $468,000. An audit resulting in 20% noncompliance would suggest a 20% payback totaling $93,600 plus interest. One therapist (of the five), at this rate, would owe the insurance company $18,200 for seeing only ten clients per week from one paying source. Many therapists would have tremendous difficulty paying back such an audit. If the clinic is footing the bill, there are two usual payback procedures: The insurance company deducts payment from its future reimbursements to the clinic, or the clinic pays back a set amount monthly. Either procedure makes it difficult to meet payroll until the amount is paid off (which often is the time for another audit).

There should be clear contractual or employment contract provisions between a clinic and its therapists to determine who is responsible for audit paybacks. When therapists are paid based on a commission of fees received, contracts generally state that the clinician will pay back the income received from the specific files under audit. For example, if the clinician is paid 55% of money received for services, his or her payback amount would be 55% of the total payback for his or her portion of the audit. The procedure is more difficult for clinics that pay therapists salaries; in most such cases, the clinics bear the brunt of the entire payback. Fortunately, clear and thorough documentation drastically reduces the possibility of making paybacks to third parties. Thus, this situation can be avoided if clinics provide training in documentation and monitor therapists' documentation by providing feedback.

Accurate documentation procedures not only help a clinic remain in business but also provide for clinical and ethical responsibility. They aid in accurate diagnosis, treatment planning, continued demonstration of need for services, and validating the effects of therapy. Documentation skills do not add to the level of paperwork in the therapeutic process. On the contrary, when good documentation procedures are adopted, the time needed to chart a case accurately decreases.

Audits are not the only potential concern for financial impact. Other areas of possible concern include potential loss of accreditation, loss of referrals from other professionals who require empirical evidence, and professional boards, such as in ethical inquiries or complaints.

LEGAL ISSUES IN DOCUMENTATION

A major focus in the study of litigation in mental health malpractice has been examining psychological records (Fulero & Wilbert, 1998). Over- and under-documentation poses different sets of problems. Documenting everything that takes place in treatment may violate client confidentiality in areas that are not necessary to document whereas underdocumenting may fail to document that specific services are taking place. In a 1998 study, Fulero and Wilbert found that more than 50% of therapists surveyed withheld nothing in their patients' records. Other therapists endorsed withholding information in patients' records regarding, among others:

1. Speculations or opinions
2. Others' names
3. Keep no or minimal records anyway
4. Anything damaging
5. Highly personal information
6. Infidelity
7. Sexual preference or behavior
8. Process notes
9. Diagnostic labels
10. Criminal behaviors

Soisson, VandeCreek, and Knapp (1987) reviewed cases in which records influenced the outcomes of malpractice suits. They noted that in a malpractice claim, the plaintiff must demonstrate that:

1. The practitioner (defendant) owed a duty to the client (plaintiff) based on an established therapeutic relationship.
2. The quality of care provided by the practitioner fell below the standard of care expected of the average practitioner.
3. The patient suffered or caused harm or injury.
4. The practitioner's dereliction of duty was the direct cause of harm or injury (Cohen, 1979).

The most common grounds for malpractice are identified as:

1. Unauthorized release of information
2. Negligent treatment of suicidal or aggressive patients
3. Sexual relations between patient and therapist

4. Failure to diagnose adequately
5. Improper hospitalization of a patient.

In each of these examples, thorough clinical documentation is crucial in the psychotherapist's defense. Specific information in the patient's record may demonstrate that effective therapeutic principles were followed but the client did not comply or was not honest in the clinical presentation.

In cases of suicide, the practitioner or agency has not been held legally responsible when records indicate that adequate assessment and treatment procedures were conducted (*Dalton v. State*, 1970; *Johnson v. United States*, 1976). Without adequate documentation, therapists have been held accountable in litigation. Likewise, adequate records, but with poor follow-up of the clinical observations, may put the therapist in jeopardy.

Gutheil and Appelbaum (1987) state that clinical records should be written from the perspective of future readers. Soisson et al. (1987) suggest that in the case of a suicidal client, documentation should include an assessment of the risk, options considered for the prevention of suicide, and possible treatments (including advantages and disadvantages).

The treatment process is a series of systematic procedures in which most aspects of the client's life are examined in order to rule out specific areas of impairment that might otherwise be overlooked. The biopsychosocial assessment is designed to integrate past and present behaviors. It is the first clinical procedure in the assessment and treatment process.

HIGHLIGHTS OF CHAPTER 3

- Clinical skills, in themselves, are not sufficient to obtain extended services for clients when third-party payers are involved. Documentation skills are needed to demonstrate accountability.
- Graduate school training in mental health services often has assumed that documentation skills are being learned at internship sites, but this may not be the case.
- Although any level of counseling may be helpful to clients, third-party reimbursement generally requires that mental health services be medically necessary.
- In mental health, medical necessity is demonstrated by the existence of a mental health disorder resulting in significant functional impairments and when, without treatment, the client is not likely to improve or return to premorbid functioning in a timely manner.
- Collecting information from several sources inevitably will lead to obtaining conflicting information. Integrating this information is an important part of professional competence.

- Without documentation of functional impairments, it is difficult to assess the need for mental health services.
- Indicators such as onset, frequency, duration, intensity, and duration (O-F-A-I-D procedure) significantly increase the specificity of documentation of the diagnosis, symptoms, and impairments.
- Documentation skills can improve with adequate training and simplified procedures.
- Mental health services from any school of thought can be documented in measurable and behavioral terms.
- Poor documentation significantly increases a clinician's chances of being held liable in litigation.
- Therapists are encouraged to conduct therapy from their choice of schools of thought, but documentation procedures are written according to a medical model in behavioral terms (scientific practitioner).

QUESTIONS

1. When third-party payment is involved, clinical skills are necessary for _____ while documentation skills are necessary for _____
   a. therapeutic progress, termination of services.
   b. rapport, therapeutic progress.
   c. therapeutic progress, continuation of services.
   d. continuation of services, termination of services.
2. Stringent documentation requirements are considered important at this time because they help
   a. control mental health costs.
   b. demonstrate the need for services.
   c. provide specific diagnostic information.
   d. all of these.
3. Which of the next statements best describes the concept of *medical necessity*?
   a. Without mental health services, the client will remain dysfunctional.
   b. Without mental health services, the client could develop medical problems.
   c. Services are necessary because of the client's current medical condition.
   d. Services are necessary to enhance the client's self-concept.
4. What is the primary purpose of the O-F-A-I-D procedure?
   a. To aid the client in therapy.
   b. To obtain objective information about client behaviors.
   c. To prove that a client needs services.
   d. To provide information beyond the requirements of the *DSM-IV-TR*.

5. Which of the following best represents a functional impairment?
    a. The client's symptoms include low appetite, poor sleep, worrying, frustration, and low self-esteem.
    b. The client doesn't feel as happy as in the past and therefore desires counseling.
    c. The client is in danger of losing another job due to excessive absences due to depression.
    d. The client quit his job due to boredom. He is now looking for a job but is unemployed.
6. The potential consequences of lack of documentation in cases such as suicide or homicide could lead to
    a. loss of licensure.
    b. significant ethical and legal issues.
    c. financial consequences.
    d. all of these.

Answers: 1c, 2d, 3a, 4b, 5c, 6d

CHAPTER 4

Ethical Considerations in Documentation

THICAL GUIDELINES VARY somewhat from state to state among mental health organizations. However, the ethical practices from the major mental health associations and boards, such as the American Psychological Association (APA), National Association of Social Work (NASW), National Association of Marriage and Family Therapists (NAMFT), National Association for Alcohol and Drug Abuse Counselors (NAADAC), American Mental Health Counselors Association (AMHCA), and National Board for Certified Counselors (NBCC), provide similar rules and guidelines for accepted ethical practices. Since this text focuses on documentation, only ethical principles regarding documentation are emphasized. Other aspects of ethics are not covered in this text. Several texts dedicated to ethics are available (Allan & Love, 2010; Fisher, 2009; Koocher & Keith-Spiegel, 2008).

DOCUMENTATION ETHICAL PRINCIPLE 1: "DO NO HARM. HELP YOUR CLIENT BY PROVIDING APPROPRIATE DOCUMENTATION"

The practice of mental health assessment and documentation ultimately is to benefit clients. Documentation must be accurate and objective. It must be free from any bias, beliefs, or stereotypes held by the mental health professional. Although therapy has a fair amount of room for choosing the various modalities of treatment, documentation must be neutral or value free. It can be compared to the evidence a lawyer presents in court. The attorney does not say "Based on my opinion, understanding of the law, and professional qualifications, I believe that my client is innocent." The attorney must provide specific evidence by established rules of the profession. Attempting to persuade a judge based solely on an opinion, not facts, is risky. Likewise, it is in the mental health client's best interest that therapists provide documentation that is empirical, not solely opinionated or nonempirical.

Good documentation is not a narrative or list of the client's general concerns or the therapist's opinion based on a gut feeling. Obviously the therapist's opinions are important, but they must be supported with evidence. Documentation must contain empirical confirmation of the client's issues that both fit the text revision of the fourth edition of the *Diagnostic and Statistical Manual of Mental Disorders* (*DSM-IV-TR*) (American Psychiatric Association, 2000) criteria for the disorder and describe the client's resulting impairments due to the mental health disorder (or lack thereof).

Principle 1 is crucial to a client's well-being because it is possible that services could be discontinued due to inadequate documentation. A client with several and persistent mental illness could be denied much-needed services if poor documentation is presented.

Putting it Into Practice 4.1

Which of the next examples of documentation would best aid the client applying for disability benefits?

Scenario 1. "Della Smith is diagnosed with major depressive disorder. She has had a number of stressors in her life, which has led to feeling down. She states that she is depressed and doesn't believe that she is able to work. She believes that life has been unfair to her. She has many regrets for past behaviors. She endorses several symptoms of depression. She states that doesn't feel good emotionally. It is possible that if she didn't have so many stressors at home that she might be able to maintain competitive employment effectively. She has difficulty dealing with her children, who have oppositional defiant disorder and attention-deficit/hyperactivity disorder, which is a full-time job in itself. In addition, she is stressed due to marital conflict. She notes that she did not like her past few jobs because they were boring and did not match her level of education. She goes to counseling to work on self-esteem and motivation. She is clearly disabled from working because there are only 24 hours in a day, and she is too involved in stressful activities at home. After a thorough review of her life, I believe that she should receive disability benefits."

Scenario 2. "Della Smith is diagnosed with major depressive disorder due to the following symptoms and impairments. She notes being depressed at least 80% of the time for the past 9 months. Other symptoms include a lack of pleasure; weight loss of 12% in the past 4 months; daily crying spells; sleeping an average of 3 hours per night compared to 8 hours previously; decreased concentration which led to being fired at work after 3 reprimands for making too many errors; decreased self-esteem; psychomotor retardation; and loss of appetite, in which she notes now forcing herself to eat 1 meal per day but had previously eaten 3 full meals daily. She further states that she is withdrawing from her friends, whom she had previously enjoyed socializing with at least twice per week. She has been hospitalized twice in the past month for suicidal intent and cutting. Her level of depression has increased significantly. Weekly counseling and med management has not been effective. Several modes of counseling have been attempted, but there has been little or no progress. Therefore, it is my opinion that she is not capable of gainful employment at this time."

Each of these scenarios describes the same person in about the same number of words, but with different proficiencies in documentation. In Scenario 1, the mental health professional seems to be unclear regarding impairments in the client's life other than being too busy with family issues. There is no evidence of a disabling condition other than an opinion of a mental health disorder. The reader has not been given adequate information to form an opinion if the client is mentally disabled or if there are other factors that would make it difficult to work at this time. Thus, even if the client is suffering from debilitating depression, it is likely that she will not receive disability benefits due to the therapist's lack of documentation skills. Can poor documentation do harm to the client?

Scenario 2 provides an endorsement of *DSM-IV-TR* symptoms that match the diagnosis, plus a description of how the client is impaired due to the mental health disorder. The therapist provides a basis for the opinion rather than a statement with no substance.

DOCUMENTATION ETHICAL PRINCIPLE 2: "REPORT DATA ACCURATELY, NOT CONVENIENTLY"

It can be tempting to cover up or delete conflicting information in an assessment or when conducting therapy. For example, it is not unusual to obtain conflicting results when a battery of psychological tests has been administered. Likewise, in therapy, clients can present conflicting information week to week or within the same session. The ethical issue emerges when the mental health professional must decide what to do with this information. The inexperienced psychologist conducting an assessment could be tempted to emphasize only those test results that coincide with his or her diagnosis or opinion. However, such a practice can lead to incorrect conclusions. Many times it is the so-called conflicting data that is the key to the client's concerns. Do not ignore conflicting or treat it as outlying or erroneous data.

Conflicting information can be indicative of a number of clinical concerns. Clients with personality disorders, especially borderline, antisocial, and histrionic, typically struggle with issues in coping and living fairly conflicted lives. Extreme variances in behavior are not conflicts of information but rather evidence of the disorder due to behavioral and emotional instability. Most clients behave differently in times of high versus low stress. Many clients have ups and downs in their lives in which they can seem like different people from one session to the next.

Another cause of conflicting information could be that it is not conflicting at all. Like anyone else, therapists are not all-knowing individuals with perfect mental health. No one is errorless in their procedures. Therapist variables are likely the least likely to be recognized (especially by the therapist him- or herself). However, errors can be made in test administration, scoring, and understanding or comprehending what the client is divulging. Other therapist variables, such as unfinished business, current stressors, prejudices, having similar mental health concerns, or other personal and cognitive factors, can distort the therapist's assessment and treatment of the client.

A thorough assessment nearly always contains conflicting information from either source (client and/or therapist). The more experienced you are in assessment and assessment tools, and the higher degree of personal insight you possess, the more capable you are to handle conflicting information. Whenever you are uncertain in these areas, collaborate with others who are more experienced and can provide objective supervision and consultation. Not even the most experienced professionals are exempt from being helped by others. Some people refer to experienced therapists who guide other therapists as "therapist's therapists."

Putting it Into Practice 4.2

Psychological evaluation referrals often come from caseworkers or caregivers for people with mental retardation (MR). In many localities, if a client is tested on a standardized test and obtains an IQ of 70 or less, he or she qualifies for a number of services for people with developmental disabilities. The IQ score is often the sole criterion required by referral sources. This presents a dilemma for the assessor, because the *DSM-IV-TR* criteria refer not only to a client's level of intellectual functioning or IQ; the client's level of adaptive functioning is equally important in a diagnosis of MR.

There are a number of ethical concerns in this type of evaluation; thus, clear documentation is crucial to provide the most accurate information. Consider the next example, which took place recently.

I received a referral from a county caseworker for a periodic evaluation for a client diagnosed with MR. The state required that people receiving services for MR are reevaluated every 5 years. Previous records noted IQ scores in the upper-60s range quite consistently over a period of more than 20 years. The client has received services such as living at group homes, vocational enclave services, disability payment, medical insurance, and social work services. Things were going well, and now the evaluation was due. The previous evaluations were conducted by different psychologists. The only test given was the Wechsler Adult Intelligence Scale (WAIS); because the IQ scores were less than 70, the diagnosis of mild MR remained. No one rocked the boat.

Because the *DSM-IV-TR* requires a more than just an IQ test, I administered a WAIS-IV and the Vineland Adaptive Behavior Scales (VABS-expanded edition). The VABS is a test of the client's adaptive behaviors in areas such as communication, socialization, daily living skills, and a composite score. The information is provided by interviewing caregivers. I was able to administer the VABS to the social worker and a staff member at the group home who had known the client for 6 years.

The IQ score, as in the past, was in the upper 60s, but the VABS standard scores were in the upper 70s to low 80s, which are in the borderline range. Thus, there was conflicting information between the IQ scores and adaptive functioning. The practical question to ask is: What best represents a client's functioning, an IQ test or the client's level of functioning in several areas of daily life? This is conflicting test information, because now the client does not have adaptive functioning test scores in the MR range, but the IQ scores are below that level.

I looked further into the client's history and discovered that when he was in school, his main concern was academics. He learned to give up easily and developed an aversion to tests. He was always in special education due to a learning disability. He was never considered mentally retarded until he was an adult, when he was referred for vocational testing. The diagnosis was based solely on an IQ in the 60s range.

I later administered a test of academic functioning, which yielded scores in most areas of academics in the standard score ranges of 45 to 50. He was not mentally retarded; he had a severe learning disability. His WAIS-IV full-scale IQ was an underrepresentation of his functioning due to a learning disability and an aversion to testing. A close look at his previous scores provided more evidence that it was his verbal, academic deficiencies that led to a full-scale IQ in the 60s range. His nonverbal scores were much higher. But due to incomplete testing, he had spent most of his life in a group home.

However, this man had been in different group homes for 20 years and was receiving services designed for people with developmental disabilities; no one wanted to listen to my reasons why I believed that his appropriate diagnosis was not MR. He remains in the group home based on his IQ score. I am not sure what ever happened to my report. Since that time I have not received referrals from that source.

DOCUMENTATION ETHICAL PRINCIPLE 3: "DUAL RELATIONSHIPS: DOUBLE TROUBLE"

If you have any relationship to the client, do not perform psychological services unless it is absolutely necessary. The relationship you have with the client will interfere with your objectivity. Whether the service you provide is a consultation, therapy, or a psychological evaluation, the established dynamics of your relationship will prevent it from becoming a proper objective therapeutic relationship. Even if you have never met the client, but he or she is an associate or relation of someone in your sphere of friends or relatives, it is best to refer the client elsewhere.

There are exceptions to this rule, but they are rarities. For example, in a crisis situation when a person needs immediate psychological comfort, the person's emotional needs will outweigh the fact that she is your neighbor. But it is best to refer the person elsewhere for future services.

Putting it Into Practice 4.3

A few years ago a relative of a friend of mine, who knew that I perform psychological evaluations, phoned me to set up a psychological evaluation for one of his relatives. The relative needed a psychological report at the request of his disability attorney.

Part of me wanted to help him because he was related to my close friend, but that is the problem! My human nature could get in the way and prevent me from assessing his condition objectively. It would be tempting to view him as more disabled than he really was in order to be a good friend by helping him obtain disability benefits. It could be stressful in our relationship if my report did not suggest a disability, especially if my friend wanted to do his relative a favor by him receiving benefits due to my evaluation. So, at the expense of placing potential stress on the friendship, I explained the ethics of the situation and gave my friend's relative a list of three other psychologists who conduct similar evaluations. I still have the friend. The relative was evaluated elsewhere.

DOCUMENTATION ETHICAL PRINCIPLE 4: "ALL PEOPLE ARE CREATED EQUAL. TREAT PEOPLE HOW YOU WANT TO BE TREATED"

One of the worst potential enemies of a mental health worker is his or her own prejudices. However, typically we are not aware of them because, as humans, we view the world through our subjective reality. That is, the way we view the world is normal. Our prejudices and biases affect how we view and treat other people and ourselves. People's race, religion, national origin, body size, hygiene, sexual identity, income, and a host of other differences can adversely affect the way they are treated by others. We are influenced on these factors by a multitude of sources, such as our parents, siblings, teachers, the media, our own experiences, and much more. Any unfair prejudices that have been learned must be reconciled or unlearned. If we are to help clients change, we must be willing to change ourselves; otherwise, our distorted views will interfere with our ability to help others. It is clearly unethical to provide mental health services to someone toward whom you have unresolved negative prejudices. Although it might not be possible to rid ourselves completely of all biases, we must begin with awareness. Whenever any level of prejudice may get in the way of fair mental health treatment, refer the client elsewhere.

Putting it Into Practice 4.4

In my clinical practice, we train several practicum students every year. On their first day, they are given a lecture about treating people with dignity and respect. They will see people from all walks of life. Some of the people they see will have recently been released from prison for terrible crimes; others are dirty, smelly, and typically are rejected by others. Some are quite wealthy and uppity. People from a variety of religious, political, and ethnic backgrounds will come for services. The students are told that they do not have to personally like every client, but they must make all effort to treat every client positively and equally.

This positive and respectful treatment of clients who differ from the student's historical beliefs eventually can lead to personal and professional growth. Perhaps clients from other backgrounds might have been treated poorly by most other people, but not in our clinic. Over the years, some of these students have told me that they learned much about themselves and learned to be more tolerant of others by treating them well. It brought out the good side in their clients. They learned to be more understanding after objectively listening to the clients' stories rather than prejudging them.

Any of us, given the right set of unfortunate circumstances, could become homeless and needy. The adage "Do unto others as you would have them do unto you" clearly applies in psychological practice.

DOCUMENTATION ETHICAL PRINCIPLE 5: "COMPETENCY: LEARN BEFORE YOU EARN"

Becoming licensed does not suggest competency in all areas of mental health treatment. One must have appropriate experience, training, supervision, or consultation to perform any task involving any assessment or therapy independently. Be aware of your limitations, and correct any statements made about you by others that do not represent your qualifications. For example, if clients call you "Doctor" and you do not have a doctoral degree, inform them that you do not have a doctoral degree and tell them how to address you.

One must keep up to date with advances in areas of competence. Typically this is done by taking continuing education courses. Simply taking a course in cognitive testing does not qualify one for interpreting neuropsychological tests. Taking a few therapy courses does not qualify one to conduct a psychoanalysis. As in many professions, mental health professionals are required to receive supervised training and regularly receive continuing education to enhance their skills and develop new practices.

No one wants to be accused of malpractice. It can ruin both a reputation and a career. Malpractice insurance can cover financial consequences, but it does not cover a damaged reputation for practicing in an area of incompetency. Before you practice in any area of mental health treatment, be able to provide evidence that would satisfy both yourself and any reviewer of your competencies. It is suggested that for every type of treatment you provide and for every test you administer, keep a log of how and when you received competency (i.e., supervision, number of procedures, training). In addition, retain the evidence that you received the training. Keep all certificates and evidence of the training. Ask other professionals what training and experience they received before they practiced independently.

Putting it Into Practice 4.5

Example of a Log of Competencies

COMPETENCY 1: ADMINISTERING AND INTERPRETING TESTS OF INTELLECTUAL FUNCTIONING

Training	Date	Experience/training	Supervisor
University of California	2005	Cognitive Assessment 6002	Dr. Smithberg
Diagnostic practicum	2007/8	Administered, scored and interpreted 48 cognitive tests 22 WAIS-IV 13 WISC-IV 4 WPPSI-III 9 Stanford-Binet_IV	Dr. Laliani
Doctoral internship	2010/11	Administered, scored, interpreted 64 cognitive tests 30 WAIS-IV 12 W WISC-IV 8 WPPSI-III 24 Stanford-Binet IV	Dr. Stevens

continued

continued

Continuing education Seminar	10/7/10	6-hour seminar "Advanced Training in Cognitive Assessment	Dr. Richfield
Continuing education Seminar	6/4–5/11	2-day seminar "Neuropsychometric Aspects of WAIS-IV Interpretation"	Dr. Brainerd

COMPETENCY 2: CONDUCTING INDIVIDUAL PSYCHOTHERAPY
(COGNITIVE-BEHAVIORAL MODEL)

Training	Date	Experience/Training	Supervisor
University of California	2006	Cognitive-Behavioral Therapy 7111	Dr. Excelsior
Therapy practicum	2008	Conducted cognitive/behavioral therapy for 41 clients	Dr. Winona
Doctoral internship	2010/11	Conducted cognitive-behavioral therapy for 90 clients	Dr. Edina
Continuing education Seminar	8/18/10	6-hour seminar "Current Trends in Cognitive/ Behavioral Therapy"	Dr. Dilworth

DOCUMENTATION ETHICAL PRINCIPLE 6:
"CONFIDENTIALITY: NOT EVERYTHING IS CONFIDENTIAL"

Many clients believe that everything they tell a therapist is confidential. This is not always the case, such as when there is a court order for the records, suicidality, intent to harm to others, billing to third parties, and certain medical emergencies. National and state mental health boards and texts about the topic cover this aspect of mental health treatment quite thoroughly.

Each client must be provided, in verbal and/or written form, the details regarding the limits of confidentiality and disclosures of information. It is suggested that clients sign in their charts that they understand these limits and have received the appropriate information.

At times clients will tell you information that they have never told anyone else, and they do not want anyone ever to know about it. You, as a therapist, must make a choice either to not record this information in the progress notes or to inform the client that whatever is discussed will be written down. Each course of action has its ramifications, merits, and drawbacks. If you choose to not record the information, your files are incomplete, and you are following the client's wishes. But if you record it, others could have later access to the material that the client does not want disseminated. Such material can be placed in psychotherapy notes, as discussed in Chapter 9.

When third parties request client records, they may no longer make a blanket request for the entire record as in the past. The appropriate procedure is to request only what is necessary for the use intended. For example, if the third party needs only the results of a particular test or a current diagnosis, no other information should be sent. Progress notes are never to be sent unless the client gives specific written permission.

Whenever any confidential topics are discussed or when there is a request for records, clearly document it in the files. Make a list of each source requesting the records, and keep the request in the client's file. Never send records to a source in which the client has not specifically named you or your agency to send such information. In addition, be sure that the signed release form has been filled out for the time period allowed (typically one year). If the request has expired, notify the sender to have it updated with a new client signature.

Putting it Into Practice 4.6

Limits of Confidentiality: A "Blanket Release" Covers Nothing

I received a request for a release of information from a mental health agency. The form was addressed to "All providers for (John Doe)." The client signed the form, and it was sent to various providers who have treated him. Neither my name nor the name of my clinic was listed on the signed form. I phoned the person requesting the information, stating that this blanket release of information was not acceptable. He stated that the client said that he could contact and receive information from "all providers." He then went on to say that since we have previously provided services, we were required to send him the information. I politely refused to send him information without a release form directly naming my agency. About a week later I received another letter from the same provider. It contained the same form, but the name of my clinic was written under the previous request to all providers. I phoned him again and said that I must have the client's signature, not simply my name added by him to the old form without the client signing specifically for my agency to receive the information. A few days later the client phoned me and asked why I had refused to turn over his records. I explained the circumstances, and he understood. Then I sent the client a release of information form, which he properly signed and returned to me, and then I released the records.

DOCUMENTATION ETHICAL PRINCIPLE 7:
"CULTURAL CONCERNS: BE ETHNICALLY ETHICAL"

"Culture" is a multifaceted word. It can refer to the ethnicity, way of life, values, attitudes, traditions, beliefs, customs, and/or identity for a group of people. Accepted behaviors in one culture could be construed as pathological in another. Certain nuances, such as eye contact and personal space boundaries, can lead people from different cultures to feel uneasy with one another. Religious beliefs can lead to wars. Skin color can lead to ostracism.

No one would disagree that cultural differences can lead to gross misunderstandings. For example, in some cultures eye contact is considered disrespectful, but in others it implies confidence. Mental health professionals are not exempt from miscues in interpreting cultural cues. No one can learn the nuances of every culture, but we all can learn how to identify cultural differences and recognize them for what they are, not as abnormal behavior.

The primary focus of this text is not about cultural differences, but readers must be aware of the possible effects they may have on mental health diagnosis and treatment. See Sue and Sue (2008) for training about several cultures, their behaviors, and beliefs.

Learning about cultural diversity can straddle both the cognitive and affective domains of a therapist. Emotionally, it can challenge our presuppositions and prior beliefs about the culture. Cognitively, there is much to learn, and the learning process can be confusing, because often there are cultures within cultures. Therefore, blanket statements such as "This culture believes that women are secondary to men" might be a learned stereotype of a culture but may be true only for a small percentage of that culture. Such stereotypes are concomitant with statements such as "All Americans are rich," an untrue belief held by some in other parts of the world.

Experience, observations, and asking several questions are perhaps the best way to learn about various cultures. Always reserve judgment until you are able to verify if "unusual" statements made by a client are culturally accepted or not. At the same time, do not assume that unusual behaviors a client discusses can be attributed to cultural differences.

Therapists often need foreign-language interpreters to communicate with non–English-speaking clients. They can be an excellent resource to learn about client cultures and to ask questions regarding some of the statements made.

Putting it Into Practice 4.7

A client had moved to America several years ago as a refugee due to persecution in her country. She was referred for an evaluation due to psychotic symptoms in which she stated that she was hearing voices. She recently had been diagnosed with schizophrenia by another mental health worker because of her statements about voices. The worker referred her for a full evaluation.

While living in a refugee camp prior to moving to the United States, she had been beaten a number of times and had witnessed severe war atrocities. During the interview, she endorsed most symptoms of posttraumatic stress disorder over the years. She had been in counseling, in which several improvements were noted, leading to terminating services about two years previously.

When asked about the voices, she stated that she had recently moved to a different house. She noted that since moving to the house, she "hears voices." She denied hearing voices prior to moving into the house. It seemed unusual (from my cultural perspective) to hear voices due to changing residences, especially because there was no previous evidence of a thought disorder.

My experiences and training suggested that her set of beliefs, not a psychotic disorder, were the cause of her "schizophrenia." To validate this, I asked the interpreter about the client's statements. The translator noted that it is not unusual in her culture to move into a new place and hear voices. The translator described them as a cultural belief of spirits of people who had lived there in the past. No efforts had been taken to remove the spirits. The interpreter stated that the client's belief was that when the spirits were removed, the voices would go away. That is, according to her cultural/religious belief, there was nothing unusual happening.

HIGHLIGHTS OF CHAPTER 4

- A therapist can provide excellent services, be well respected in the field, and treat clients with excellent outcomes. But without adequate documentation of the treatment, services could be discontinued, funds could have to be repaid, and ethical charges could be filed.
- There will always be conflicting information when treating clients. Seeming contradictions should not be ignored but rather integrated into the client's treatment. Sources of conflict may be due to client or therapist variables.
- Unless there is an emergency and no alternatives, do not provide mental health services to clients for whom there is any possible dual relationship.
- Treat all people equally with dignity and respect. If you cannot perform this function with certain clients, refer them to others for treatment.
- Do not practice independently in areas outside of your level of competency. Keep a record of how you attain, develop, and maintain your competencies. The most common means of developing competencies are by training and supervised experiences.
- Inform each client of the limits of confidentiality. There are very strict rules regarding the confidentiality of information. Be careful to comply with professional, Health Insurance Portability and Accountability Act, state, and professional guidelines.
- Cultural differences must be understood and respected in the diagnosis and treatment of mental health. Cultural sensitivity is a key component the ethical treatment of clients.

QUESTIONS

1. Which of the next statements best represents a possible ethical problem due to not providing the best documentation? "She should remain on a medical leave because she is . . .
   a. severely depressed."
   b. suicidal."

    c. not ready to go back to work."

    d. very disoriented."

2. What is the most ethical thing to do in this situation? John is an experienced therapist. When he was in high school, he was assaulted by a person from Beronia. Today he conducted a counseling intake from someone from Beronia and took an immediate dislike to the client. He should

    a. tell the client of his bias and be careful not to let it interfere with the therapy.

    b. call his supervisor to sit in for a few sessions.

    c. refer the client to another therapist.

    d. work on his own issues with while treating the client.

3. Which of these dual relationships is the most acceptable ethically?

    a. You provide counseling for a relative whom you had previously never met.

    b. You spouse's boss asks you to provide counseling for a major client of your spouse.

    c. Your neighbor is suicidal and is sent to the hospital where you work. You are the only therapist on duty at the time. You counsel the person one time and make a referral.

    d. You are physically attracted to a client and plan on requesting a date sometime after the counseling is terminated.

4. Jerry's competency in providing hypnotherapy was questioned by client who filed a complaint to the board of psychology. What should Jerry present to the board in his defense?

    a. Provide a list of satisfied clients who have benefited from hypnotherapy.

    b. Hire an attorney who has experience in defending therapists who practice hypnotherapy.

    c. Produce a list of professional character references.

    d. Provide a detailed account of his training, supervision, and experience.

Answers: 1c, 2b, 3c, 4d

CHAPTER 5

The Biopsychosocial Assessment

THE BIOPSYCHOSOCIAL ASSESSMENT provides background information regarding several areas of the client's functioning. The bulk of the information is obtained through questioning in the initial interview and through forms the client fills out. Additions and revisions are made throughout treatment. Information covered includes biological (or physical), psychological, and social. Biological information includes information about the client's family, development, education, employment, legal, and other medical history. Psychological information focuses on previous and current psychological status and treatment. Social information includes the client's social supports and stressors.

Information regarding both the client's strengths and weaknesses should be collected for each aspect of the biopsychosocial assessment. Data about the client's strengths is helpful in treatment by incorporating positive aspects in the client's environment. For example, if the client has a supportive social network, treatment might include incorporating these people. Documenting and incorporating weakness is important in selecting what type(s) of treatment would be most suitable for the client.

General demographic information, such as number of years of schooling, may be obtained in pre-interview questionnaires. The clinician reviews this information for clinical significance and incorporates it into the assessment when helpful. If the information suggests therapeutic significance, it may be incorporated in the treatment plan.

It is important to avoid redundancy when gathering information. If clients fill out information forms prior to the initial interview, do not ask them for the same information in the interview unless it is being expanded. If the same questions are asked in presession questionnaires, phone screenings, and the diagnostic assessment interview, nothing new is learned and time is wasted. Moreover, the client is likely to become frustrated.

Rather, each method of information gathering should integrate, expand, and add to on data already collected. For example, instead of asking about a client's marital status at each stage of information gathering, the initial phone screening might determine the marital status; a presession questionnaire might identify relationship issues; and the clinician might probe stressors, strengths, and dynamics of the relationship (if applicable) in the diagnostic interview.

The diagnostic assessment is not intended to be a counseling session. Focusing on counseling during the initial interview may be counterproductive because the time is needed to collect discrete types of information. However, a clinician who skillfully conducts the diagnostic interview in both an empathic and a professional manner can assure clients that they are understood and allow them to leave the interview ready for treatment. Thus, the diagnostic session ultimately may have the effect of a productive counseling session even though no therapy was offered. After a successful interview, a client feels understood.

Each individual piece of information collected in the biopsychosocial assessment, in itself, may not seem significant but, when taken together, helps present a clear clinical picture of the client. At this point, the therapist is no longer dealing with unrelated data but with the whole person in the realm of his or her past and present environment.

CONDUCTING THE BIOPSYCHOSOCIAL ASSESSMENT

Prior to conducting the initial interview, it is necessary to obtain the client's informed consent. The therapist should begin by tellling the client of the purpose of the interview and how results will be disseminated. Written statements in the initial interview, such as, "The client acknowledges and understands the benefits and risks of providing the information requested in this evaluation and has agreed to allow results to be shared with . . ." document informed consent. Some clinicians have clients sign that they have had the information explained to them. A summary of the Health Insurance Portability and Accountability Act of 1996 (HIPAA) guideline for dissemination of information is found in Appendix C.

All of the information should be reviewed to produce a diagnosis and subsequent treatment plan. Some clinicians prefer to mail all pre-interview questionnaires to clients and have them filled out prior to the first meeting. Others ask clients to come early to the initial interview to fill out the questionnaires.

Using preformatted questionnaires can save time for the clinician. For example, Figures 5.1 and 5.2 follow similar formats that allow the clinician to

Adult Personal History Form

Case No. _05398JD_

Client's Name _John Doe_   Date _5-3-05_

Gender __F _✓_M   Date of Birth _2-15-1967_   Age _45_

Form completed by (if someone other than client)_____

Address _34567 Main Street_____

City _Longview_____   State _CA_   Zip _99999_

Phone (Home) _(555)-555-1213_   (Work) _(555) 555-1211_   ext. _9876_

IF YOU NEED ANY MORE SPACE FOR ANY OF THE FOLLOWING QUESTIONS PLEASE USE THE BACK OF THE SHEET

Primary reason(s) for seeking services: __Addictive behavors   __Alcohol/drugs
__Anger management   __Anxiety   __Coping   _✓_Depression
__Eating disorder   __Fear/phobias   __Mental confusion   __Sexual concerns
__Sleeping problems   __Other mental health concerns (specify)_____

FAMILY INFORMATION

Relationship	Name	Age	Living Yes	Living No	Living with you Yes	Living with you No
Mother	Debra Doe	X		✓		✓
Father	Robert Doe	X		✓		✓
Spouse	None (1-Deceased 2-Divorced)		①✓	②✓		✓
Children	Cynthia Doe	16	✓			✓
	Victoria Doe	13	✓			✓

Significant Others (Brothers, Sisters, Grandparents, Step-relatives, Half-relatives. Please specify relationship.)

Relationship	Name	Age	Living Yes	Living No	Living with you Yes	Living with you No
Brother	Raymond Doe	48	✓			✓

Page 1

Figure 5.1 Personal History Form

Source: Reprinted with permission of John Wiley & Sons, Inc.

Marital Status   (more than one answer may apply)

__Single

__Divorce in process
Length of time_____

__Unmarried, living together
Length of time_____

__Legally married
Length of time_____

__Separated
Length of time_____

✔Divorced
Length of time **4 yrs.**

✔Widowed
Length of time **10 mos.**

__Annulment
Length of time_____

Total number of marriages ____

Assessment of Current Relationship (if applicable)   __Good   __Fair   ✔Poor **with ex-wife**

Parental Information
✔Parents legally married **(now deceased)**
__Parents have even been separated
__Parents ever divorced

__Mother remarried: Number of times_____
__Father remarried: Number of times_____

Special circumstances (e.g. raised by person other than parents, information about spouse/children not living with you, etc.)
_____
_____

DEVELOPMENT

Are there special, unusual, or traumatic circumstances that affected your development: ✔No   __Yes
If Yes, which type(s) of child abuse? __Sexual ✔Physical __Verbal.   Abuse was as __Victim   __Perpetrator
Other childhood issues: __Neglect __Inadequate nutrition   __Other (specify)_____
Comments re: Childhood development **My father often beat me up when I was a teenager**
_____
_____

SOCIAL RELATIONSHIPS

Check how you generally get along with other people: (check all which apply)
✔Affectionate   __Aggressive   __Avoidant   __Fight/argue often   __Follower
✔Friendly   __Leader   __Outgoing   ✔Shy/withdrawn   __Submissive
__Other (specify)_____
_____

Sexual Orientation: **heterosexual**   Comments:_____

Sexual Dysfunctions? ✔No   __Yes (describe)_____

Any current or history of being as sexual perpetrator? ✔No   __Yes (describe)_____
_____

CULTURAL / ETHNIC

From which cultural or ethinic group, if any, do you belong? **WASP**_____
Are you experiencing any problems due to cultural or ethnic issues? ✔No   __Yes (describe)_____
_____

Other cultural / ethnic information:_____
_____

Page 2

Figure 5.1   Continued

SPIRITUAL / RELIGIOUS

How important to you are spiritual matters? __Not __Little __Moderate ✓Much
Are you affiliated with a spiritual or religious group? ✓No __Yes (describe)_____
Were you raised within a spiritual or religious group? __No ✓Yes (describe) **very strict**
Would you like your spiritual/religious beliefs incorporated into the counseling? __No ✓Yes (describe) **I would like honest, ethical practices.**

LEGAL

Current Status
Are you involved in any active cases (traffic, civil, criminal)? __No ✓Yes
If Yes, please describe and indicate the court and hearing/trial dates and charges_____
Child support hearing in two weeks

Are you presently on probation or parole? ✓No __Yes
If Yes, please describe_____

Past History

Traffic violations	__No ✓Yes	DWI, DUI, etc.	✓No __Yes
Criminal involvement	✓No __Yes	Civil involvement	✓No __Yes

If you responded Yes to any of the above, please fill in the following information.

Charges	Date	Where (city)	Results
Speeding 45 in a 30	1985	Cambridge	Paid Fine

EDUCATIONAL

Fill in all that apply   Years of education __12__   Currently enrolled in school ✓No __Yes
✓High School grad/GED   __Vocational: Number of years____   Graduated __No __Yes   Major____
                 __College: Number of years____   Graduated __No __Yes   Major____
                 __Graduate: Number of years____   Graduated __No __Yes   Major____
Other training_____
Special circumstances (e.g. learning disabilities, gifted, etc.) **Average grades when in school**

EMPLOYMENT

Begin with most recent job, list job history:

Employer	Dates	Title	Reason left the job	How often miss work?
4M	1987-Present	Miller		lately 2days/wk
Stanford's	1984-1987	Laborer	new Job	seldom
Mengers	1979-1984	Laborer	new Job	seldom
Pollies	1975-1979	Sales	new Job	seldom

Currently: ✓FT __PT __Temp __Laid-off __Disabled __Retired __Social Security __Student
__Other (describe)_____

Page 3

Figure 5.1 Continued

MILITARY

Military experience? __No ✓Yes   Combat experience? ✓No __Yes   Where?_____

Branch __Army_____   Discharge date __1990__

Date drafted_____   Type of discharge __honorable__

Date enlisted __1985_____   Rank at discharge __Sergeant__

LEISURE / RECREATIONAL

Describe special areas of interest or hobbies (e.g., art, books, crafts, physical fitness, sports, outdoor activities, church activities, walking, exercising, diet/health, hunting, fishing, bowling, traveling, etc.)

Activity	How often now?	How often in the past?
Sports events	none	weekly
outdoor activities	seldom	weekly

MEDICAL / PHYSICAL HEALTH

Check all that apply and describe below:

__AIDS	__Constipation	__Hepatitis	__Sore throat
__Alcoholism	__Chicken Pox	__High blood pressure	__Scarlet Fever
__Abdominal pain	__Dental problems	__Kidney problems	__Sinusitis
__Abortion	__Diabetes	__Measles	__Small Pox
__Allergies	__Diarrhea	__Mononucleosis	__Stroke
__Anemia	__Dizziness	__Mumps	__Sexual problems
__Appendicitis	__Drug abuse	__Menstrual pain	__Tonsillitis
__Arthritis	__Epilepsy	__Miscarriages	__Tuberculosis
__Asthma	__Ear infections	__Neurological disorders	__Toothache
__Bronchitis	__Eating problems	__Nausea	__Thyroid problems
__Bed wetting	__Fainting	__Nose bleeds	__Vision problems
__Cancer	✓Fatigue	__Pneumonia	__Vomiting
__Chest pain	__Frequent urination	__Rheumatic Fever	__Whooping cough
__Chronic pain	__Headaches	__SexuallyTransmitted Diseases	__Other (describe)
__Colds/Coughs	__Hearing problems	__Sleeping disorders	

List any current health concerns __low energy_____

List any recent health or physical changes_____

Nutrition

Meal	How often (times per week)	Typical Foods Eaten	Typical amount eaten	Comments
Breakfast	7 / week	cold cereal	__No __Low ✓Med __High	
Lunch	6 / week	Soup- sandwich	__No __Low __Med ✓High	
Dinner	7 / week	meat-potatoes-veg	__No __Low __Med ✓High	
Snacks	20 / week	Junk food	__No __Low __Med ✓High	high appetite

Current Prescribed Medications	Dose	Dates	Purpose	Side Effects
None				

Current Over-the-counter Meds	Dose	Dates	Purpose	Side Effects
None				

Figure 5.1   Continued

Are you allergic to any medications or drugs? ✓ No __ Yes (describe)_____

	Date	Reason	Results
Last physical exam	2011	regular check-up	good health
Last doctor's visit	2007	strep throat	given antibiotic - OK
Last dental exam	2012	regular check-up	no problems
Most recent surgery	none		
Other surgery	none		
Upcoming surgery	none		

Family history of medical problems __Mother had thyroid condition._____

_____

_____

Please check if there have been any recent changes in the following
__ Sleep patterns   ✓ Eating patterns   __ Behavior   ✓ Energy level
__ Physical activity level   __ General disposition   ✓ Weight   __ Nervousness / tension

Describe changes in areas in which you checked above __Gaining weight from overeating and__
__underactivity. Low energy: Don't feel like doing things._____

CHEMICAL USE HISTORY

	Method of use and amount	Frequency of use	Age of first use	Age of last use	Used in last 48 hours		Used in last 30 days	
					Yes	No	Yes	No
Alcohol	lite social drinking	Rare	21	55		✓		✓
Barbiturates								
Valium/Librium								
Cocaine/Crack								
Heroin/Opiates								
Marijuana								
PCP/LSD/Mescaline								
Inhalants								
Caffeine								
Nicotine								
Over the counter								
Prescription drugs								
Other drugs								

Substance of preference

1. __None_____   3. _____

2. _____   4. _____

Page 5

Figure 5.1   Continued

Substance Abuse Questions

Describe when and where you typically use substances Rare social drinking

Describe any changes in your use patterns None

Describe how your use has affected your family or friends (include their perceptions of your use)

Reason(s) for use:

    __Addicted   __Build confidence   __Escape   __Self-medication

    ✓Socialization   __Taste   __Other (specify)

How do you believe your substance use affects your life? not

Who or what has helped you in stopping or limiting your use?

Does (Has) someone in your family (present/past) have (had) a problem with drugs or alcohol? ✓No __Yes (describe)

Have you had withdrawal symptoms when trying to stop using drugs or alcohol? ✓No __Yes (describe)

Have you had adverse reactions or overdose to drugs or alcohol? (describe) NO

Does your body temperature change when you drink? ✓No __Yes (describe)

Have drugs or alcohol created a problem for your job? ✓No __Yes (describe)

COUNSELING / PRIOR TREATMENT HISTORY

Information about client (past and present):

	No	Yes	When	Purpose ~~Where~~	Your reaction or overall experience
Counseling/Psychiatric treatment		✓	2000	Depression	It was helpful.
		✓	age 13	Problems with father	Things got better. Don't remember
Suicidal thoughts/attempts	✓				
Drug/Alcohol treatment	✓				
Hospitalizations	✓				
Involvement with self-help groups (e.g. AA, Al-Anon, NA, Overeaters Anonymous)	✓				

Figure 5.1   Continued

Information about **family / significant others** (past and present):

	No	Yes	When	Where	Your reaction or overall experience
Counseling/Psychiatric treatment	✓				
Suicidal thoughts/attempts	✓				
Drug/alcohol treatment	✓				
Hospitalizations	✓				
Involvement with self-help groups (e.g. AA, Al-Anon, NA, Overeaters Anonymous)					

Please check behaviors and symptoms that occur to you more often than you would like them to take place:

__Aggression	__Dizziness	__Irritability	__Sleeping problems
__Alcohol dependence	__Drug dependence	__Judgment errors	__Speech problems
__Anger	__Eating disorder	__Loneliness	✓Suicidal thoughts
__Antisocial behavior	__Elevated mood	__Memory impairment	__Thoughts disorganized
__Anxiety	✓Fatigue	__Mood shifts	__Trembling
✓Avoiding people	__Gambling	__Panic attacks	✓Withdrawing
__Chest pain	__Hallucinations	__Phobias/fears	__Worrying
__Cyber addiction	__Heart palpitations	__Recurring thoughts	__Other (specify)
✓Depression	__High blood pressure	__Sexual addiction	
__Disorientation	__Hopelessness	__Sexual difficulties	_____
__Distractibility	__Impulsivity	__Sick often	_____

Briefly discuss how the above symptoms impair your ability to function effectively. I don't feel like seeing anybody or going to work. Too many bad things have happened to me. I want to get better.

Any additional information that would assist us in understanding your concerns or problems I feel abandoned by life.

What are your goals for therapy? Feel good about myself

Do you feel suicidal at this time? ✓No   __Yes (explain)_____

FOR STAFF USE

Sigmund Z. Adler, PhD

Therapist's Signature/Credentials   Date 5-3-12

Physician's Comments Have reviewed intake material and agree with treatment considerations and diagnoses. Recommend med referral.

Physical Exam: ✓Required   __Not Required

Carl J. Erikson, MD

Physician's Signature and Credentials   Date 5-10-12

Certifies case assignment. level of care and need for exam

Figure 5.1   Continued

Adult Initial Assessment

Client's Name __John Doe__   Date __5-17-05__

Starting Time __10:00__   Ending Time __11:30__   Duration __90 minutes__

Session Type __✓__ 90801   __Other_____

A. BIOPSYCHOSOCIAL ASSESSMENT

1) Presenting Problem __Depressed mood, fatigue, social withdrawal,__
__lack of motivation__

2) Signs and Symptoms (DSM based) . . . . **Resulting in Impairment(s)**

(Include current examples; for treatment planning)   (e.g. social, occupational, affective, cognitive, physical)

The client describes feeling depressed for the past 10 months, since the
death of his wife, as evidenced by usual dysphoric mood, low motivation,
social withdrawal, decreased concentration, fatigue, and anhedonia. It
has resulted in affective, occupational, and social impairment, as
evidenced by missing 10 days of work in the past month, significantly
decreased production at work, avoiding friends and activities
previously enjoyed on a regular basis, and sitting home most of the time.

3) History of presenting problem

Events, precipitating factors or incidents leading to need for services __Spouse passed away__
__10 months ago. Since then symptoms of depression have__
__increased.__

Frequency/Duration/Severity/Cycling of symptoms __Depressed most of the time. Current__
__episode is not cyclical. Previously treated for depression in 1993__
__after divorce.__

Was there a clear time when Sx worsened? __Death of spouse__

Family mental health history __None Known__

Page 1

Figure 5.2   Initial Intake Including Biophysical Assessment

Source: Reprinted with permission of John Wiley & Sons, Inc.

4) CURRENT FAMILY AND SIGNIFICANT RELATIONSHIPS   See Personal History Form

No close family relation

Strengths/support _____

Stressors/problems Ex-Spouse & children avoid him leading to shame

Recent changes 2nd spouse died. Was in a functional relationship

Changes desired Desires to restore relationship with children and spend more time.

Comment on family circumstances Feels abandoned by all family, no support

5) CHILDHOOD / ADOLESCENT HISTORY   See Personal History Form

(Developmental milestones, past behavioral concerns, environment, abuse, school, social, mental health)

Normal developmental milestones. States that he was physically abused as a child. Brief counseling at age 13 dealing with issues with father. Average school grades. Describes his family as "dysfunctional." Parents divorced when he was teenager, stayed with mother.

6) SOCIAL RELATIONSHIPS   See Personal History Form

Currently avoids most people.

Strengths/support One close friend

Stressors/problems Refusing invitations from friends. Doesn't feel like socializing.

Recent changes Until depressed was much more active socially

Changes desired Increase time with friends

7) CULTURAL / ETHNIC   See Personal History Form

No significant cultural/ethnic practices

Strengths/support N/A

Stressors/problems N/A

Beliefs /practices to incorporate into therapy No

8) SPIRITUAL / RELIGIOUS   See Personal History Form

strong fundament Christian beliefs

Strengths/support Belief in God as source of strength

Stressors/problems Not involved in any activities

Beliefs /practices to incorporate into therapy Undecided

Recent changes No longer attending church activities

Changes desired Undecided

9) LEGAL   See Personal History Form

No criminal history. Minor traffic violation. Upcoming Child Support hearing.

Status/impact/stressors Much stress over court meeting in 2 weeks.

Page 2

Figure 5.2   Continued

10) EDUCATION   See Personal History Form

High school graduate - Average intelligence.

Strengths Would like to take public speaking course someday

Weaknesses None

11) EMPLOYMENT / VOCATIONAL   See Personal History Form

Has worked as laborer most of life   Jobs last 4-10 years

Strengths/ support History of stable employment all of life.

Stressors/problems Missing approx. 10 days of work per month. Low production.

12) MILITARY   See Personal History Form

Army 4 years Honorable discharge.

Current impact None Known.

13) LEISURE / RECREATIONAL   See Personal History Form

None at present

Strengths/ support History of regular involvement recreationally.

Recent changes Dropped almost all activities since spouse died.

Changes desired Wants to return to previous activities.

14) PHYSICAL HEALTH   See Personal History Form

No Known health problems. Has set up appt for physical and
med eval. No medications.

Physical factors affecting mental condition None Known

15) CHEMICAL USE HISTORY   See Personal History Form and Substance Abuse Addendum

Occasional social drinking. No increase since death of spouse.
No history of CD.

Patient's perception of problem None

16) COUNSELING / PRIOR TREATMENT HISTORY See Personal History Form: Client and Family

Previous diagnosis of "dysthymia" five years ago when receiving marital
counseling. Brief counseling as teenager. 6 months counseling for
depression in 2000. Counseling helpful.

Benefits of previous treatment Returned to premorbid functioning in 6 months.

Setbacks of previous treatment None Known

Page 3

Figure 5.2   Continued

B. DIAGNOSTIC INTERVIEW

MOOD   (RULE IN AND RULE OUT SIGNS AND SYMPTOMS: VALIDATE WITH DSM)

Predominant mood during interview___**Depression**_____

Current Concerns   (give examples of impairments (i), severity (s), frequency (f), duration (d)

Adjustment Disorder (w/in 3 months of identified stressor, Sx persist < 6 months after stressor, marked distressed)
__Depressed   __Anxiety   __Mixed Anxiety & Depression   __Conduct   __Emotions & Conduct   __Unspecified
Specify disturbance: __Acute (<6 months) ✓ Chronic (>6 months)
_____**Criteria not met**_____

Impairment(s) _social _occupational/educational _affective _cognitive _other _____

Examples of impairment(s)_____

Major Depression (2 or more wks): ✓Usually depressed or ✓anhedonia. (4+ of following): ✓wght +/- 5%/month, ✓appetite⊖-,
__sleep +/-, __psychomotor +/-, ✓fatique, ✓worthlessness/guilt, ✓concentration, ✓death/suidal ideation.
Other; _crying spells,✓withdrawal, _add'l. sx _____

Impairment(s)✓social ✓occupational/educational ✓affective _cognitive _other _____
Examples of impairment(s) **Avoiding friends, missing work 10 days of past month**
Low production (previously "high producer")

Dysthymia (2 or more years): ✓ depressed most of time. (2+ of following): ✓Low/high appetite or eating, __ In/hypersomnia, ✓ low
energy/fatigue, ✓low self-esteem, ✓low concentration/decisions, ✓hopelessness. Other **Previous diagnosis of**
dysthymia. Endorses symptoms as occurring since teenager.
Impairment(s) _social _occupational/educational ✓affective _cognitive _other _____
Examples of impairment(s) **Feels sad most of the time**

Mania (3+): __Grandiosity, __low sleep, __talkative, __flight of ideas, __distractibility, __goals/agitation, __ excessive pleasure.
_____**Denies**_____

Impairment(s) _social _occupational/educational _affective _cognitive _other _____
Examples of impairment(s)_____

Panic Attacks (4+, Abrupt development of): __palpitations, __sweating, __trembling, __shortness of breath, __feeling of choking,
__chest pain, __nausea, __dizziness, __light-headed, __derealization, __fear of losing control, __fear of dying, __numbness, __chills /hot flashes
_____**Denies**_____

Impairment(s) _social _occupational/educational _affective _cognitive _other _____
Examples of impairment(s)_____

Anxiety (GAD: 3+, most of time, 6 months): __restlessness, __easily fatigued, __concentration, __irritability, __muscle tension, __sleep disturbance
_____**Denies**_____

Impairment(s) _social _occupational/educational _affective _cognitive _other _____
Examples of impairment(s)_____

Other Diagnostic Concerns or Behavioral Issues
(E.g., __Dissociation, __Eating, __Sleep, __Impulse control, __Thought disorders, __Anger, __Relationships, __Cognitive, __Phobias,
__Substance Abuse, __Medical conditions, __Somatization, __Phobias, __Sexual, __PTSD.etc.)
_____**Denies each**_____

Impairment(s) _social _occupational/educational _affective _cognitive _other _____
Examples of impairment(s)_____

USE ADDITIONAL PAPER AS NECESSARY

Page 4

Figure 5.2   Continued

more easily access information when writing reports, treatment plans, and reviewing cases. Figure 5.1 provides an example of a client personal history form. Figure 5.2, an example of an initial intake, which also includes biopsychosocial information, is a report the therapist fills out after collecting sufficient information from the client. Some clinicians do not formally conduct a biopsychosocial assessment but prefer a structured or unstructured initial interview. There are no universally accepted formats for documenting a biopsychosocial assessment, but several exist commercially and in various texts. *The Clinical Documentation Sourcebook*, 4th edition (Wiger, 2010) provides mental health forms, examples of how to fill them out effectively, and a computer disk to aid in the documentation process.

There are three commonly accepted steps for conducting a biopsychosocial assessment:

1. Determining the presenting problem
2. Recording the history
3. Determining client strengths and limitations

STEP 1: DETERMINING THE PRESENTING PROBLEM (SIGNS AND SYMPTOMS)

The presenting problem is the client's description of the problem rather than the clinician's opinion or diagnostic statements. It is recorded in the section of the psychological report commonly labeled "Signs and Symptoms." Although the terms "signs" and "symptoms" generally are combined or used synonymously, the text revision of the fourth edition of the *Diagnostic and Statistical Manual of Mental Disorders* (*DSM-IV-TR*; American Psychiatric Association, 2000) defines "signs" as "an objective manifestation of pathological condition. Signs are observed by the examiner rather than reported by the affected individual" (p. 827) whereas "symptoms" are defined as "a subjective manifestation of a pathological condition. Symptoms are reported by the affected individual rather than observed by the examiner" (p. 828).

The clinician elicits symptoms from the client, including descriptors such as onset, frequency, antecedents, intensity, and duration (O-F-A-I-D procedure), plus notes the resulting impairments in an effort both to determine the appropriate diagnosis and to demonstrate medical necessity for services. The presenting problem should be reflected in the treatment plan; however, this may not be possible when the client is in denial or noncompliant. Clinical noncompliance is especially difficult in cases of third-party reimbursement because this client is likely to deny that impairments exist; thus there may be no clear evidence of medical necessity. Chapter 9 discusses documentation for the noncompliant client.

Throughout this book we will follow John Doe, a client with depression, through the course of therapy to illustrate the proper documentation process at each stage. Additional case examples will further illustrate correct and incorrect documentation techniques.

Presenting Problem and Signs   The first step in the diagnostic intake session is to determine the client's presenting problem and record signs and symptoms.

THERAPIST (T): What brings you here today?
JOHN DOE (JD): I've been feeling down lately.

Clarification   If the presenting problem is unclear, the therapist should seek clarification.

T: Tell me what you mean by "feeling down."
JD: I feel like no one cares about me, I'm sad, and I don't want to go to work anymore.

Onset   Next the therapist determines the onset of the problem.

T: How long have you been feeling this way?
JD: I've been just fine all of my life, but for the past ten months I have had no motivation.

Antecedents   The therapist should also investigate whether a specific event (antecedent) occurred that brought on the presenting problem.

T: Did something happen last year?
JD: Yes, my wife died, and now I just can't do anything.

Specific Examples of Impairments   Once the presenting problem is determined, the therapist should find out how the problem is impairing the client's normal functioning.

T: How has this affected your performance at work?
JD: Over the past several months I keep missing more and more work. I'm now on probation at work and could lose my job if I don't improve. My production is the lowest in my department.
T: How many days of work have you missed this month?
JD: At least ten.

T: What were your reasons for missing work?

JD: I just didn't feel like getting up, I have no motivation . . . I have no energy, so I called in sick or made something up.

T: Is there anything you enjoy doing at this time?

JD: No, nothing is pleasurable.

Frequency   It is necessary at this point for the therapist to determine how frequently the problem occurs or impacts the client's functioning.

T: How often do you feel depressed?

JD: I'm depressed almost all of the time. Seldom a day goes by in which I'm not sad all day long. I just can't think straight or keep my mind on things.

Comparison to Premorbid Functioning   Finally, the therapist compares the client's current state to premorbid functioning to determine a baseline for treatment.

T: How were things at work for you before your wife passed away?

JD: It was hard, but I did as well as anyone else, I seldom missed any work, and I was up for a promotion because of seniority.

T: Describe your social life before your wife passed away.

JD: I was outgoing. I went out with friends at least twice a week and loved to play on sports teams at least one time every week.

T: What is currently happening in your life socially?

JD: I sit home alone every evening and weekend. I avoid people at work and cringe at the thought of having to be with people.

T: Are there any other areas in which your life has changed in the past 10 months?

JD: No, that's about it.

The next example illustrates poor documentation of John Doe's signs and symptoms discussed in the diagnostic assessment interview:

> Client is feeling down. Missing work. Few activities. Wife died. Problems at work.

This statement summarizes the topics and current stressors discussed during the intake session but does not demonstrate medical necessity for treatment. Mental health concerns are implied but not documented. In this instance, the vagueness of the documentation rather than the therapist's ability ultimately will jeopardize the client's chances of receiving mental health services when the therapist petitions for preauthorization for treatment. Even if the client receives services, the therapist ultimately might wind up repaying the insurance company the cost of service if audited.

A case manager or an auditor does not have access to a session transcript to review the many concerns brought up in the interview. In this case, in a short time period, the therapist has solicited adequate information to validate medical necessity for services; however, due to the therapist's poor documentation skills, there is no evidence of significant impairment in the client's functioning.

Do not blame the auditor or case manager for denying services for a needy client if the documentation does not clearly portray the medical necessity for services. Clients in need of mental health treatment are best served by therapists who can both deliver quality mental health services and document the scope of services.

The next example provides a somewhat better documentation for John Doe's problem but still does not clearly describe the medical necessity for treatment:

> Client claims to feel depressed since death of his spouse last year. He is not performing adequately at work and has no current friendships.

Although this example somewhat documents areas of impairment (affect, occupational, and social), it does not provide diagnostic information concordant with the interview narrative. For example, it is expected that a person would feel depressed after the death of a spouse as part of the normal grieving process; however, John Doe's level of depression is more severe than this documentation suggests. Stating that a person has no current friendships might hint at social concerns but in itself does not provide evidence for medically necessary treatment.

The next example illustrates the proper documentation of John Doe's signs and symptoms. It identifies stressors, time periods, symptoms, and impairments noted in the interview. It also provides baseline data for later assessments of the effects of treatment. Taken together, these signs and symptoms suggest that treatment is medically necessary to restore John Doe to normal functioning.

> The client describes feeling depressed most of the time (*frequency*) for the past 10 months (*onset*), since the death of his wife (*antecedents*), as evidenced by usual dysphoric mood, low motivation, social withdrawal, decreased concentration, fatigue and lack of pleasure (*DSM-IV-TR validation of symptoms*). It has resulted in affective, occupational, and social impairment (*impairments*) as evidenced by missing 10 days of work in the past month, significantly decreasing production

at work, avoiding friends and activities previously enjoyed on a regular basis, and sitting home most of the time.

This portion of the diagnostic interview does not go so far into depth as to rule out specific disorders but instead focuses on signs and symptoms of the presenting problem. The presenting problem supplies baseline information that provides initial direction for the diagnostic interview. Further evidence of specific issues, personality disorders, and other concerns will be elicited later in the interview. Additional diagnostic information also will continue to be formulated throughout therapy.

STEP 2: RECORDING THE HISTORY OF PRESENT ILLNESS

The client's personal history provides valuable information regarding the his or her past and present behaviors. It may be helpful in predicting future performance. Information such as strengths and stressors that tend to alleviate or increase problem areas are necessary in completing a treatment plan that is designed specifically for the client's needs. Previous mental health and physical health diagnoses help the therapist recognize behavior patterns that may be dysfunctional. Information may come from a variety of sources and draw from several domains in the client's life. Regulatory agencies, such as The Joint Commission (TJC), require that the assessment process address a number of areas (see Figure 5.3).

In addition to recording the information shown in Figure 5.3, the therapist documents how these areas are impacting the client's current functioning. The information is integrated directly into the treatment plan and incorporated into therapy. Figure 5.4 describes the type of information that should be elicited and demonstrates its clinical significance.

The next dialogue between John Doe and his therapist demonstrates how to elicit specific client information related to the domain areas shown in

Family and Significant Relationships	Military
Childhood and Adolescent History	Leisure/Recreational
Social Relationships	Physical Health
Cultural/Ethnic	Chemical Use
Spiritual/Religious	Counseling/Prior Treatment
Legal	History
Employment/Educational	

Figure 5.3   Domain Areas that Must Be Investigated in Biopsychosocial Assessment
Source: Reprinted with permission of John Wiley & Sons, Inc.

Solicited Information	Clinical Significance
Strengths/supports	Incorporate into treatment plan to most effectively integrate client's existing strengths and supports available from a wide range of areas.
Stressors/problems	Identify current problem areas that may be contributing to the client's mental health issues; also important diagnostically to justify an adjustment disorder.
Recent changes	Change in itself, whether viewed as positive or negative, often results in a stressful reaction. Note the client's reaction to changes and the permanence of the changes.
Changes desired	Document in the objectives section of the treatment plan and implement using various intervention techniques.
Specific beliefs or practices	Cultural, ethnic, and religious beliefs and practices should be identified prior to beginning treatment. Lack of knowledge in these areas is usually counterproductive, especially when counseling practices might contradict deep-rooted systems or beliefs.
Development —Past behavioral concerns —Past abuse —School issues —Social information —Mental health —Family dynamics	The clinical use of previous history is important because it may provide clues as to the etiology of current behaviors, responses, coping mechanisms, strengths, and disabilities. It helps the therapist to understand difficult developmental issues affecting current behaviors. Much of this information can be obtained from documents filled out by the client prior to the intake session.

Figure 5.4 Type of Information Solicited for Biopsychosocial Domains and Its Clinical Significance

Source: Reprinted with permission of John Wiley & Sons, Inc.

Figure 5.3 to use in treatment planning. It defines measurable behaviors that both John Doe and the therapist view to be helpful in restoring and maintaining appropriate mental health. The therapist does not provide therapy at this point but rather identifies target information for future sessions and current diagnostic significance.

Family and Significant Relationships

T: Tell me about your family.

JD: Since my wife died . . . my second wife . . . I haven't been in contact with her family. I have two children from my first marriage, but they live with their mother.

T: How about your immediate family?

JD: They moved across the country a few years ago. They can't afford to visit me. The last time I saw them was at my wife's funeral. We've never been that close, though.

T: Do you have any friends here?

JD: I see one of my high school friends about once every month or two.

T: When you need to talk to someone about personal issues, who is available or with whom do you feel comfortable?

JD: Certainly not my first wife. She has always poisoned our two children against me so much that they don't even want to visit me on weekends. My ex-wife digs it in that I'm depressed and not a good example for the children.

T: Do you have any relatives you can talk to?

JD: Sometimes I phone my brother in Detroit to complain about things, but he seems to side with my ex-wife. They used to date. I think they're still in touch.

T: What about your friend?

JD: Our relationship is mainly competitive . . . you know . . . like playing pool and shooting hoops. Lately, though, I've canceled our engagements. When we're together, we want to have fun. If we talked about problems, it would take away from the escape.

T: So are you saying that being with your friend helps on another level?

JD: What do you mean?

T: It sounds like being with him is a helpful escape from your problems.

JD: I never thought of it that way . . . yes.

T: Tell me more about how your children impact or affect your mood.

JD: I just feel lower and lower. I sit home and mope and feel so bad that I'm embarrassed to see the children. I used to take them at least two places every week. It's not happening. Nothing good is happening with my family. I have a dead wife, an ex-wife, and an ex-family.

T: It sounds like things used to be much better. What changes would you like to see in your relationships?

JD: If I could change anything it would be to have fun with my children.

T: How much time do you now spend with your children?

JD: About two hours a week when they want to see me.

T: How much time would you like to spend with them?

JD: At least ten hours a week, doing things we used to do. I have liberal visitation rights . . . at least on paper.

T: What about your relationships with other people in your life?

JD: I would like to spend more time with my best friend. Things always feel better when we go out and spend time together. It takes my mind off of things.

T: How often do you see him now?

JD: Not in the last three months.

T: How often would you like to see your friend?

JD: At least once or twice a month.

Childhood and Adolescent History

T: Tell me about your childhood.

JD: For the most part it was fairly uneventful. My parents got along about half the time. I had friends and did well in school. I never got in trouble with the law or in school.

T: Did you ever see a counselor or have any emotional or behavioral problems when you were a child or adolescent?

JD: Well, once when I was about 13 I threatened suicide when my father punished me for something I didn't do.

T: Go on.

JD: My father always accused me of not being obedient and then beat me. He did this several times when I was younger. My mother eventually kicked him out of the house. After that our home life was tolerable.

T: You mentioned threatening suicide.

JD: I was so stressed out that I didn't feel I could go on any longer. School was getting to be too difficult, I hated my father, and my friends made fun of me because they often heard my parents fighting. I just wanted to give up. I really wouldn't have killed myself, but I didn't want to be around, either. My mother took me to a counselor and after about two or three months I felt better.

T: How has handling change been for you at other times?

JD: Actually, I've never been good at changes. I usually get depressed and isolate myself. I don't like any challenges. I like feeling comfortable and secure.

T: How was your school and social life as a child?

JD: I always had friends after my father left. People treated me okay. Things were then calmer at our house. I had average grades in school. It was okay.

Social Relationships

T: Tell me about your social life.

JD: What social life? I have none.

T: Are you presently involved in any activities or see any other people than those you mentioned?

JD: No, not really. I don't feel like it.

T: How long has it been since you did any socializing?

JD: Not since my wife died. Most of our friends were married; now we have nothing in common.

T: Is there anything you miss about being with people or going out?

JD: I used to like just talking to people, I was a real people person. I could talk to anybody. But it's like I forgot how or have no motivation to do it.

T: How would you like things to be?

JD: I guess if things were better, I'd like to be involved in some sort of recreational activity but not yet.

Cultural/Ethnic Beliefs

T: Do you have any cultural or ethnic beliefs or practices which would be helpful for me to know or which would be helpful to the counseling processes?

JD: No, not really . . . I'm a White, middle-class, Anglo-Saxon Protestant.

Spiritual/Religious Beliefs

T: Are there any spiritual or religious beliefs that would be helpful for me to know?

JD: Yes, I am a born-again Christian. I always pray before I make a major decision. I was raised with very strict rules of conduct and do not want any advice in counseling that would violate biblical principles.

T: Could you give me an example of what you mean?

JD: Sure. I don't believe in premarital sex; therefore, I hope you don't say I should seek sexual fulfillment in that manner. But at the same time, I believe that there is strength available from God if I put him first in my life and read positive passages from the Bible.

T: Tell me more about how the spiritual aspects of life can be positive for you.

JD: Although I haven't been to church since my wife died, I believe that Christians can help and support each other. I used to be very involved in church but stopped going when she died.

T: Do you think that this could be another avenue to help you at this time?

JD: I don't know if I'm ready yet.

T: What changes, if any, would you like to see in this area?

JD: Well, I used to feel more inner peace when I went to church. I don't want to talk about this now.

Legal Concerns

T: Are there any current legal concerns affecting you in any way?

JD: No, I've never been arrested for anything other than minor traffic violations.

T: Is there any court involvement at all at this time?

JD: Well, yes, I'm going through some child-support battles. We will go to court again in about two weeks.

T: How is this affecting you?

JD: Every day it annoys me. I can't afford the amount of support she is asking for. I feel like when I go to work, my check is totally to pay for a house I no longer live in. So why should I even go to work? It's not fair at all. I'm still paying for funeral expenses. How can I have a life if all I do is pay money to my ex-wife to support children who don't even want to visit me?

T: It sounds like you are really frustrated about this.

JD: Yes . . . there is no room for me anymore. I can't do anything . . . it's like they own me, and the law is on their side.

Employment/Educational History

T: You said before that you have been missing a lot of work. Tell me more about it.

JD: I just have no motivation to go to work. Nothing is satisfying anymore. I used to be a top producer, but now it just doesn't matter because I have no reason to get ahead. The more I make, the more my ex-wife gets and the more frustrated I become. Most of the time I'm just too down to feel like I'd be any good at work. What good could I do at work if I can't produce? I guess I'm just a loser, what else can I say?

T: What do you want it to be like at work?

JD: I wish that things were like the way they were before. I made good money . . . I was needed . . . I had goals . . . I never missed work. I really want to be that way again. That's why I'm here. I need a boost.

T: Are there any changes you would like to see educationally?

JD: I have always wanted to take a course in public speaking, but believe me, I'm in no mood right now to do that . . . maybe someday.

T: Someday?

JD: Yes, when I feel better about life.

Military History

T: I see on your personal information form that you were in the military. How was it for you?

JD: It was a learning experience. I did my time and survived. I didn't see any action. It was a job. It paid for my schooling. No problems.

Leisure/Recreational Activities

T: What sort of things do you do for fun?
JD: Well, right now just about nothing, anymore.
T: Anymore?
JD: I used to be involved in plenty of activities.
T: Tell me about them.
JD: Okay. My second wife, the one who died, and I used to go to at least one sports event every two weeks, and we went to one cultural event every two weeks. The sports were for me and the culture was for her. Actually, after a while we began to enjoy things together.
T: It sounds like you used to be pretty active in a number of areas.
JD: That's right . . . I used to be.
T: Tell me some more of the activities you used to like.
JD: Golfing, bowling, football games, basketball, antique stores, concerts, and going for walks.
T: That's quite a list. Do you miss some of them now?
JD: I do, but I always did them with her. About the only fun I have is with my best friend now and then.

Physical Health

T: How is your physical health?
JD: Oh, it's always been pretty good . . . lately I've felt fatigued, but I'm pretty healthy.
T: When was your last physical or visit to the doctor?
JD: About two years ago I had a physical for work. Everything was fine.
T: Do you have a history of any physical problems?
JD: No, I've always been in good health.
T: How about your family, such as your parents, siblings, or grandparents?
JD: Well, my father and grandmother had some thyroid problems, but I don't know too much about it. Overall, we're a pretty healthy family.

Chemical Use

T: Do you use alcohol or any other drugs?
JD: Yes, I drink socially on occasion, but it is not a problem.
T: How often is that?
JD: Oh, I might drink a few beers once every few months.
T: How does it affect you, or why do you drink?
JD: Just to fit in socially. I don't even enjoy the taste especially.

T: When did you have your last drink?

JD: About six months ago. I had one glass of wine at an office party.

T: Have you ever had any problems with alcohol or any other drugs?

JD: No, I've never even been drunk. I've never tried any other street drugs.

T: Is there any chemical abuse history in your family?

JD: Not that I know of.

Counseling/Prior Treatment History

T: I noticed on your information form that you were in counseling about five years ago. Tell me about it.

JD: Well, I saw Dr. Wilson for individual therapy about five years ago for depression after my first wife and I were talking about a separation. It was similar to now. I just had no motivation to do anything, and I started missing work. Also, I already told you about some counseling as a teenager.

T: How did the therapy with Dr. Wilson turn out for you?

JD: We met every week for about six months. About half the time my wife attended the sessions. She suggested that I visit the psychiatrist for medications, but I was afraid to so I didn't. Toward the end of counseling things seemed to get back to normal in our marriage, and I stopped missing work.

T: Was there anything in the counseling that was especially helpful?

JD: I don't remember the specifics, but Dr. Wilson often suggested things we could work on together to help the relationship. It seemed to work . . . at least for a while.

T: Do you remember if a diagnosis was given?

JD: I believe she said "dysthymia" or something like that.

T: Later we'll go over this and see how it relates to you today. It would be helpful if we could write to Dr. Wilson for your previous counseling records. Would that be all right?

JD: Sure.

T: Tell me about the other time you were in counseling.

JD: Like I mentioned before, I went to counseling at age 13 because I had to please my father. You know, it made me appear as the sick person, instead of him.

T: Do you think it was helpful being there?

JD: No, not then, but counseling was okay back then.

Interview information can be the most important data available to the clinician. Therefore the quality of the information and how it is used is crucial to the assessment and treatment plan process.

Strengths	Weaknesses
Recreational activities with best friend take his mind off problems	Little family contact
Motivated to increase time with others	His children avoid him
History of having friendships	Childhood relationship problems with father
Strengths in religious/spiritual beliefs	History of difficulty coping with change
Law abiding	Little/no social life at this time
History of stable work record	Stressed due to upcoming court visit (child support)
History of good physical health	Missing much work lately
No history of chemical dependency	Current low energy
Successful counseling in past	Low motivation
Good insight	

Figure 5.5 Documenting John Doe's Strengths and Weaknesses
Source: Reprinted with permission of John Wiley & Sons, Inc.

STEP 3: DETERMINING CLIENT STRENGTHS AND LIMITATIONS

Throughout the entire interview, client strengths and weaknesses are assessed in all areas examined. TJC requires that this information be incorporated into the treatment plan. The previous interview questions can help a therapist document client strengths and weaknesses so that they can be incorporated into counseling (see Figure 5.5).

Although every client strength and weakness is not written directly in the treatment plan, the plan reflects these capabilities in order to provide more efficacious treatment. For example, if a client has good insight, the therapist might consider using insight-oriented therapy in treatment. If a client has severe cognitive deficits but responds well to specific, concrete behavioral intervention, behavior therapy could be more fitting. Clients with supportive social contacts would most likely respond well to incorporating this support into the treatment, whereas someone with a social phobia might panic if others were included immediately.

Information about client strengths and limitations may be solicited from a variety of sources, including observations, questioning during the interview, prediagnostic questionnaires, collateral information (such as reports from other providers or family members), or psychological testing. As with most clinical information, knowledge of the client's strengths and weaknesses increases with time and rapport and may be incorporated into treatment throughout the course of therapy. Figure 5.6 lists categories similar to *DSM-IV-TR*'s examples of impairments and represents common strengths and limitations to consider during treatment planning.

Social

Accepts feedback	Helpful
Accepts responsibility for own behavior	Impulse control
Appropriately accesses support system	Listens to others
Articulate	Maintains appropriate boundaries
Assertive	Makes own decisions
Aware of impact on others	Organization membership(s)
Congruent	Outgoing
Dependable	Respectful
Empathic	Sense of humor
Establishes appropriate boundaries	Sensitive
Friendly	Sharing
Fun-loving	Supports others
Genuine	Tolerant of others
Good hygiene	Willing to please
Has long-term relationships	

Occupational/Educational

Abstract thinker	Good follower
Adapts to changes	Good leader
Articulate	Hard worker
Assertive	Independent
Attention span good	Learns fast
Aware of impact on others	Logical
Bright	Organized
Common sense good	Reads well
Concentration	Reliable
Concrete thinking	Stable employment
Cooperative	Team player
Creative	Uses lists
Dedicated	Willing to please
Dependable	Works hard
Goal focused	Writes well

Affective

Accepts feelings in self	Empathic
Accepts feelings in others	Expresses emotions
Aware of feelings	Integrates thinking and feeling
Aware of impact of feelings on behavior	Range of feelings available
Emotions appropriate	Tolerates emotional discomfort

Cognitive

Abstract thinker	Insight into own behavior
Attention/concentration	Insight into others' behaviors
Aware of how thoughts affect feelings	Intelligent

Figure 5.6 Examples of Areas of Client Strengths or Limitations that May Be Incorporated into the Treatment Plan

Note: Provided by Danielle Jordan, PhD.

Aware of how thoughts affect behaviors	Logical
Clear imagery	Memory
Creative	Positive self-dialogue
Delays decision making	Reality testing intact
Flexibility in thinking	Reflects on own behavior
Physical	
Eats well	Healthy
Endurance	Maintains normal weight
Exercises regularly	Solid sleep

Figure 5.6 Continued

SNAPS

In addition to collecting specific diagnostic information, a thorough assessment includes obtaining sufficient details about the client's strengths, needs, abilities, and preferences (SNAPs; Wiger & Huntley, 2002). The SNAPs information may be collected from multiple sources (e.g., client statements during the interview, forms filled out by the client before or after the interview, collaterals, observations, previous records) and is incorporated into treatment to best suit client needs. Such information aids in viewing and understanding clients more in terms of people rather than diagnoses.

STRENGTHS

Strengths were discussed in Step 3 on pages 72–73.

NEEDS

Client needs are specific areas that are current deficits in the client's life. Although therapists cannot treat every client need, all needs can be addressed through actions such as referrals, handouts, additional services, homework assignments, and specific treatment plan objectives. Client needs could range from basic necessities, such as food, shelter, and clothing, to education, to finding a physician, to leaving an abusive relationship.

ABILITIES

Client abilities can be a significant component in successful mental health treatment. The question "What is the client able to do?" is addressed in the treatment plan. If a therapist inappropriately suggests a behavior that the client is not able to do, no positive results will take place. For example, if attending a specific group seems likely to help the client, but the client is not able to get on a bus or get a ride there, nothing would become of the strategy. Some therapists suggest that clients read certain books as bibliotherapy, but if they are not able to afford the books, nothing will be accomplished.

PREFERENCES

Historically, some therapists have overlooked client preferences. Treatment may involve a number of preferences in which the client is given a choice in areas such as type of therapy, frequency and time of visits, use of collaterals, and treatment plan objectives. Too many clients have terminated therapy prematurely because the entire therapeutic process was dictated by the therapist and no choices were available.

PSYCHOLOGICAL REPORT

Report writing is one of the most important skills a mental health professional can learn. The psychological report typically is the only mechanism of communicating a client's psychological, cognitive, personality, adaptive, and other types of functioning. A mediocre report reflects directly on the perceived clinical ability of the writer. A concise, insightful, information-filled report speaks highly about the clinician and typically will generate future referrals. Ultimately the psychological report must be beneficial to the client.

The psychological report (see example in Appendix A) is also known as an integrated summary, a psychological evaluation, a consultative examination, or a clinical assessment. It provides a technically accurate yet concise overview of the client's psychological functioning. The psychological report integrates all aspects of the information collected during pre-interview screening and the initial intake. Several different psychological report formats exist, but the specific order in which the information is presented is not as important as the overall content and integration of material. Reports must be understood easily by both mental health professionals and nonclinicians. Unclear reports result in uncertainty or vagueness about the client's condition, loss of future referrals, and, often, much postreport time spent answering questions that could have been covered in the report.

Different readers focus on different aspects of the report, depending on their level of understanding and reason for reading it. Some readers focus on raw data and observations whereas others prefer reading the diagnosis and recommendations. Overall, the report should be written so that the client can understand it; however, the report should also provide enough details to portray an accurate clinical picture. Using excessive technical jargon is unnecessary, especially because the report is meant to be summative. There are at least six sources for integrating information into the psychological report, including:

1. Clinical information collected by the clinician during the interview
2. Biographical information collected from pre-interview screening, such as information gathered in forms or telephone prescreening
3. Information from other professionals who have treated the client
4. Behavioral observations made during the initial interview
5. Test results (e.g., personality, cognitive, behavioral, adaptive functioning)
6. Information from collaterals, such as significant others, teachers, bosses, friends, or family members

Effective writing skills are necessary to clearly integrate the several sources of information. In addition, reporting raw data from tests or observations is meaningless without integration and interpretation. Consider the difference among the next three statements:

1. "The client's MMPI-2 score indicated elevated scores in the 2, 4, and 7 scales."
2. "The client's MMPI-2 score suggested concerns with depression, anger, and anxiety. People with similar profiles tend to exhibit behavior cycles of acting out, guilt, and subsequent depression."
3. "The client's MMPI-2 score indicated elevated scores in the 2, 4, and 7 scales, suggesting concerns with depression, anger, and anxiety. People with similar profiles tend to exhibit behavior cycles of acting out, guilt, and subsequent depression."

The first statement might be significant to someone trained in using the Minnesota Multiphasic Personality Inventory. The second statement is understandable to people not trained in clinical interpretation. Both types of information are found in statement 3, which is intended to be understood by any reader; however, statements in this format tend to be longer than the others. Reports can be tailored to the audience. If a report has only one intended type of readership, such as mental health professionals only, simple language included solely for the sake of explanation of clinical terms can be omitted; in this case, statement 1 would be the appropriate description.

Factors influencing the report's format include its purpose (the referral question), the writer's theoretical orientation, the intended audience, and writing style. The same writer often writes reports that look different depending on the purpose for which the reports will be used. For example, if a report is intended primarily for the client's parent to read, it will most likely be summative rather than providing extensive test results or uninterpreted data. A report that is written for professionals may contain extensive clinical terminology and test scores. This text is not concerned about the particular format used to write the report; rather, it focuses on how to properly document information included in the report.

Psychological reports also vary in length. If a clinician includes all of the information gathered about a client, the report could easily reach 25 or more pages. Clinicians who provide little technical information and instead focus on integrating results could produce reports of only a few pages. This writer suggests providing adequate details pertaining to the referral question and summarizing other areas. For example, some clinicians administer a standard test battery to every client as a screening process. If the referral question is "Does this person qualify for an anger management group?" it may not be important to extensively interpret intellectual tests. But in the case of a brain injury, the interpretation of these tests may be extremely important. When I receive a referral for a psychological evaluation, I discuss with the referral source what types of information are desired in the report.

In the not-so-distant past, clinicians routinely administered a standard battery of tests to clients. However, due to payment authorization issues, the practice of administering a seemingly unlimited number of tests has declined. Often clinicians decide which specific tests and procedures to administer after sufficient rule-in/rule-out questions (described in Chapter 7) have been answered and a clearer clinical picture is presented. In actual clinical practice, it is becoming more common to have each intended test preapproved to secure preauthorization of payment.

Diagnostic and biopsychosocial information continues to be collected and revised throughout the course of therapy, and adjustments to the treatment plan are made as needed. Some clinicians prefer to wait a few weeks before filling out a biopsychosocial report until they have received adequate collateral information and have attained sufficient information in the sessions. Once the initial biopsychosocial assessment is complete, the next step in the initial intake is to conduct a mental status exam. Chapter 6 introduces several components that can be used to determine a client's current mental state.

HIGHLIGHTS OF CHAPTER 5

- The biopsychosocial assessment provides historical information from several areas of a client's life. Both strengths and weaknesses are incorporated into treatment planning.

- Biopsychosocial information may be gathered from several sources including questionnaires, clinical questioning, and collateral information.
- Although the purpose of the diagnostic interview is to gather information, it can be both informative and therapeutic by increasing client insight due to the nature of the questions and answers.
- The documentation of both signs and symptoms provides current information regarding mental health symptoms from the client's and the therapist's perspective.
- The only clinical information available to a third-party auditor or case manager is that which is furnished by the therapist; therefore, inadequate documentation will result in denial of services.
- The best predictor of future behavior is past behavior.
- Three steps of conducting a biopsychosocial assessment include collecting information for (1) the presenting problem, (2) history, and (3) strengths and weakness.
- Assessing client strengths and weakness helps determine which types of interventions may be the most appropriate.
- The psychological report should be written in a level of technical language concordant with the intended reader(s).

QUESTIONS

1. The biopsychosocial assessment focuses on
   a. background information.
   b. current mental status.
   c. clinical diagnosis.
   d. future behaviors.
2. Signs are_____; symptoms are_____.
   a. endorsed by the client; . . . observed by the clinician.
   b. observed by the clinician; . . . endorsed by the client.
   c. physical; . . . psychological.
   d. observable; . . . implied.
3. Which of the next statements best incorporates portions of the O-F-A-I-D procedure?
   a. The client has been depressed since his divorce.
   b. The client is depressed almost all of the time.
   c. The client is severely depressed.
   d. All of these.
4. How are client strengths and weaknesses typically incorporated into a treatment plan?
   a. They are specifically listed in the treatment plan.

b. They are incorporated into the treatment strategies.

c. Only weaknesses are incorporated because of the medical model.

d. Only strengths are incorporated due to a positive focus.

5. Which of the following is NOT part of the biopsychosocial assessment?

a. Spiritual matters.

b. Drug and alcohol use.

c. Clinical observations.

d. Friendships.

6. Written psychological reports should

a. be written in a concise, scientific, and technical manner.

b. primarily focus on the diagnosis.

c. be read only by professionals.

d. be written at a level concordant with the readers' level of under-standing.

Answers: 1a, 2b, 3d, 4b, 5c, 6d

CHAPTER 6

The Mental Status Exam

THE MENTAL STATUS exam (MSE), an essential part of the diagnostic interview, is administered through both questioning and observations. Whereas the biopsychosocial assessment focuses primarily on history, the MSE's focal point is the client's current mental state. It includes making several observations about the client designed to clarify, validate, and compare clinical information that has been received. MSE observations sometimes seem to contradict previous records because they represent the client's mental status here and now rather than in the past. That is, a typically normal-functioning client could, during a time of stress, exhibit significant mental health or behavioral concerns during the MSE and return to normal functioning rather quickly when the stressor has alleviated. Likewise, a typically dysfunctional client can present in a functionally appropriate manner at the time of the interview. Therefore, a psychological report that integrates historical and MSE information provides a wealth of clinical information.

The MSE was adapted from the physical examination, which reviews major organ systems, while the MSE reviews major psychiatric functions. MSE formats, such as the Mini Mental Exam (Folstein, Folstein, & McHugh, 1975), are widely used. However, most MSEs are conducted informally. In general, the greater degree of mental impairment, the more focus the MSE receives. That is, if a client's concerns are minor affective issues or behavioral problems, the MSE may not reveal any specific mental status issues other than the current affective state. But clients presenting with severe psychotic, cognitive, behavioral, or affective concerns may readily display mental status concerns.

It is not common to administer a MSE to children under age 12–13; however, observations and parental statements tend to focus on the similar information. Many clinicians never formally conduct a MSE, but their clinical observations and notations serve the same purpose. This writer suggests incorporating a separate topic of mental status exam in psychological reports because it assures the reader that the information in that section is a current mental status snapshot rather than historical information.

Whether conducted formally or informally, the MSE evaluates items such as the client's appearance, posture, speech, and judgment. It is not conducted at a specific time during the diagnostic interview but is administered throughout the intake session as observations are noted. Nevertheless, mental status observations generally are documented in a separate section of the psychological report.

If an MSE is not conducted, there is an increased risk of misdiagnosis, especially for clients with poor insight or thought disorders or who are in denial. For example, a client might deny being upset or agitated, but the clinician may observe several such behaviors during assessment. Simply considering client responses to questions posed will not help therapists reach a diagnosis in such cases. The observations and clinical interpretive skills employed in the MSE will aid in differential diagnosis and will provide the therapist with cues regarding how to proceed with the intake.

As noted, MSEs are available in a variety of formats, but they seek similar information. Frequently, the information gathered in the MSE is presented as a checklist of items the clinician observes and documents in the assessment. The areas most commonly reported in an MSE include:

- Appearance
- Activity level
- Speech/Language
- Attitude toward the examiner
- Affect/Mood
- Stream of consciousness
- Sensorium/Cognition

APPEARANCE

Descriptors of appearance should be objective and include physical aspects, such as the client's neatness and cleanliness of dress, grooming, hygiene, body odor, and apparent health. An unusual appearance could signify a number of concerns. For example, loud, expensive, or bright clothing is not unusual during a manic episode or may suggest a Cluster B personality disorder, or nothing at all.

Inappropriate clothing might represent cognitive concerns or confusion of thought. Impeccable dressing, or a client who constantly straightens an article of clothing, might indicate obsessive/compulsive concerns. Depression, substance abuse, a thought disorder, or dementia might be depicted in clothing that is noticeably soiled, wrinkled, or foul in odor. However, a client's appearance alone should not be the basis of a diagnosis. The client's subculture, background, socioeconomic status, and current life situation must be taken into account before passing judgment. Never base a diagnosis solely on one type of observation. The liberty of individual and cultural differences always must be factored in before assigning a label to someone who happens to be different from the typical population you serve. Those who conduct psychological interviews cannot allow their personal worldview to influence their observations of clients. Open-mindedness and specific training in diversity are crucial for mental health professionals. Consider a therapist's observations about the appearance of a client:

> Helen L. appeared at the interview wearing worn jeans and several layers of soiled clothing. She was 5 feet tall, weighed 120 lbs., and seemed to be poorly nourished. She appeared to be at least 15 to 20 years older than her chronological age of 48, as evidenced by a slumped posture, yellowed teeth, a rosy complexion, and disheveled hair. She appeared to be in below-average health. There was a strong smell of alcohol on her clothing.

This information is written in a fairly objective manner and makes no judgments; however, it could easily lead to premature conclusions. More information is needed regarding the client's current situation. Consider how your evaluation (professionally and personally) of the client in the narrative might change if the description was preceded by the any of these statements:

1. The client is applying for a job as a salesperson.
2. The client, a civil engineer, sustained a head injury from an assault when he was robbed of his possessions and clothing. Apparently, he was found and taken care of in an abandoned building by unknown persons.
3. The client was diagnosed with cancer six months ago.
4. This is the client's tenth time in conduct disorder treatment.
5. Three months ago, on the way to a "Helping Humanity" volunteer weekend, the client was backing up his car and accidentally hit a child.

The client's posture may also indicate a variety of nonverbal attitudes, pain disorders, or levels of affect (e.g., slumped signifying depression; leaning forward signifying interest; erect signifying anxiety or other concerns). Changes in the client's body position during the interview may signal pain, anxiety, or feelings of discomfort. It is not helpful to make premature judgments; rather, it is best to make ongoing hypotheses that can be ruled in and ruled out as more information is received.

Other information that can be gleaned from observing a client's appearance includes a description of whether the appearance matches the person's chronological age, facial expressions, level of eye contact, or any other unusual physical characteristics that could indicate psychological or physical dysfunction. It is not necessary to list every possible observation; rather, the clinician should report only those that may be clinically significant or affect the validity of the interview.

When the client's appearance appears to be normal, do not assume that the reader of the report will know this; rather make statements such as "The client appeared at the interview looking his chronological age. His posture, health, grooming, and hygiene appeared to be within normal limits."

ACTIVITY LEVEL

Activity level, body movements, and motor behaviors may reflect a wide range of psychological concerns. The clinician should report any unusual movements; otherwise, the report should indicate that the client did not exhibit abnormal body movement behaviors. Numerous clinical terms are available to describe various body movement behaviors; however, it is best to describe them in layman's terms. This makes reports more readily understandable yet preserves clinical integrity.

Some clinicians choose to incorporate technical terms in the report or describe behaviors in simpler terms, depending on the intended reader. Table 6.1 demonstrates the difference between clinical terminology and everyday language. Although the same message is being presented, the level of understanding is more widespread using everyday language.

Normal activity level might be described with statements such as:

No concerns were noted in the client's activity level. There were no unusual gestures or mannerisms. His activity level was within normal limits. He was not limp, rigid, lethargic, combative, or hyperactive. He did not appear to be preoccupied or easily distracted. He sat still the entire time. He appeared to be relaxed and alert. Accessory movements were within normal limits.

It is not likely that every behavior listed in the next observations would be listed in every report, but those that are clinically significant warrant mention.

SPEECH/LANGUAGE

A client's speech provides important mental status and diagnostic information. The term "speech aphasia" describes problems with grammar, word usage, and sentence structure. Unusual speech patterns may indicate affective, neurological, psychotic, physical, or cognitive dysfunction. Clinicians

Table 6.1

Possible Observations of a Client's Appearance

Topic	Examples of observations	Narrative examples: "The client('s) . . .
Age	Younger/Older	. . . appears to be at least 10 years older than her chronological age."
Posture	Erect/Slumped/Shifting	. . . exhibited a slumped posture during the entire interview."
Grooming	Poor/Neat	. . . was groomed very poorly, as evidenced by . . . (give examples of the grooming)."
Hair	Clean/Dirty/Disheveled	. . . hair was uncombed, oily, and disheveled."
Nails	Clean/Dirty/Bitten/Long/Neatly trimmed	. . . nails were very short, dirty, and appeared to be bitten."
Odor	Strong body odor/Smell of alcohol	. . . body odor was very strong, suggesting poor hygiene." (Note: consider cultural factors before making such statements.)
Health	Good/Poor	. . . appeared to be in good health." (Note: Do not make a medical-like diagnosis of good health. Simply make an observation of the appearance.)
Weight	Under/Over	. . . was morbidly obese, weighing 380 lbs."

Source: Reprinted with permission of John Wiley & Sons, Inc.

must be careful not to pass judgment based on speech patterns alone but rather use such information as a piece of the puzzle to be integrated and concordant with other observations.

It can be difficult to differentiate between speech problems resulting from organic versus psychiatric etiology. Although symptoms tend to overlap, organic speech problems tend to be progressive, unless they follow a traumatic event, such as a stroke. Psychiatric speech problems, however, tend to coincide with psychiatric episodes.

Although no clear standards are defined, the MSE should report any departures from what is considered functional. Because such information is based on opinion, observed examples should be provided. If no abnormal speech behaviors are evident, the therapist should note this as well. For example, the therapist might record: "The patient expressed a normal range of vocabulary, volume, reaction time, details, pace, pitch, articulation, and spontaneity," or "No speech concerns were noted."

When abnormal speech patterns exist, further observations should be reported, such as whether speech is pressured, hesitant, monotonous, slurred, stuttered, cluttered, or mumbled, and whether repetitions, neologisms, difficulties with word finding, or echolalia are present. In such cases, the therapist should document specific examples and incorporate them into the diagnostic summary.

Language observations go beyond specific areas of speech. Therapists should evaluate and record the client's level of comprehension throughout the interview and document the client's ability to understand simple to complex requests or points of conversation.

ATTITUDE TOWARD EXAMINER

The client's attitude toward the examiner is important in assessing areas such as relationship to authority, social behaviors in new situations, prognosis of treatment, and accuracy of information. In addition, personality disorder variables often are reflected in the client's attitude. Assessment is possible across several dimensions that should be considered on a continuum and include aspects such as level of interest, cooperation, frankness, defiance, evasiveness, defensiveness, guardedness, manipulation, hostility, hesitance, ability as historian, and sense of humor.

In the case of a cooperative client, a statement such as "The client was cooperative, friendly, provided adequate historical information, and did not appear to be guarded or defensive" portrays a reasonable picture. When the client is not cooperative, the clinician should document abnormal behavior. For example, a clinician might write:

> Esther G. entered the office yelling at the receptionist, "All psychologists should be locked up." During the interview, she refused to answer over half of the questions, stating that they are no one's business. She made little eye contact and sat facing away. At one point she stated that she had not consumed alcohol in over six months; however, there was a strong odor of alcohol on her breath and clothing, noticed by three staff members and this therapist.

Therapists should integrate the purpose of the interview when making attitudinal observations. For behavioral disorders, clinicians should note observations relating to symptoms of the presenting problem. Some children (and adults) will behave differently in the waiting room than in the presence of the interviewer, so it is important to include observations of the client's behavior during the interview as well as before and after the session, when possible. For example, children with conduct disorder may behave well during the interview but punch their parents or steal a magazine on the way out of the office. Likewise, children with attention-deficit/hyperactivity disorder (ADHD) may show no signs or symptoms of inattention or hyper-activity during the interview, but school records may indicate strong concerns. The text revision of the fourth edition of the *Diagnostic and Statistical*

Manual of Mental Disorders (*DSM-IV-TR;* American Psychiatric Association, 2000) states that even though few or no symptoms may be observed in the clinician's office, a disorder still may be present.

In cases in which clinicians do not directly observe signs of a disorder, it is important to gather more information than usual from collaterals, such as family members or teachers. Generally a provisional diagnosis and accompanying statements, such as "as per history" or "as per parent, but not observed during the interview," are used; a therapist may write, for example: "314.01 ADHD, Provisional, as per history (parents' comments, school records, psychiatrist's report), not observed during the interview."

An example of describing all areas of the client's attitude toward examiner is:

> He was cooperative and attentive and seemed interested in the interview. He appeared to be an adequate historian. He did not appear to be defiant, guarded, defensive, evasive, hostile, or manipulative.

AFFECT AND MOOD

Although the terms often are used interchangeably, affect and mood reflect the emotional state of the client from different perspectives. "Affect" refers to the clinician's observations of the client's emotional state, whereas "mood" represents the client's endorsement of symptoms. Affect and mood are usually congruent but, in cases of denial, defensiveness, or confusion, the clinician's observations may differ from the client's statements.

Affective observations include behavioral notations of the client's temperament during the examination. The next descriptors often are used in describing various aspects of affect.

RANGE OF AFFECT

The affective range is on a continuum and is depicted from flat to normal. Flat affect is the total lack of affective responses. Blunted affect is characterized as a severely reduced level of affect. Restricted affect is a level noticeably below normal. Normal affect indicates that a typical and expected amount of affect was observed.

APPROPRIATENESS OF AFFECT

The appropriateness of affect is the correspondence or correlation between the client's thoughts and speech and the observed level of affect. For example, it would be unusual for a client to describe the recent traumatic loss of a loved one while giggling. Although appropriateness often is inconsistent in cases such as guardedness or denial, it also may indicate psychopathology.

INTENSITY OF AFFECT

Affective intensity is characterized as the strength of emotional responses. For example, a person who sobs intensely with extreme emotional expression is described as having strong intensity whereas someone who expresses little affect would be described as displaying mild intensity.

MOBILITY OF AFFECT

Mobility of affect refers to the time span between changes in emotional expression. For example, decreased mobility (also referred to as constricted mobility) could refer to someone who does not show normal and expected changes in affect as topics of conversation change. Increased mobility or lability is exhibited by abrupt changes in emotional states, such as going from laughing to crying to anger in an unusually short time period.

Other descriptors of affect include psychomotor behaviors, level of anxiety, irritability, and anger expression. For example, if a client appears to be anxious but denies such concerns, the report might state:

> Jack B. often fidgeted with his fingers and bit his fingernails. On four occasions, he appeared perplexed and stuttered slightly. He often checked his watch, stating that he must get home before the rush hour or something bad might happen. But, when asked if he describes himself as nervous, anxious, or worried, he adamantly denied any such concerns.

MOOD

Mood is assessed by asking the client about his or her typical and current emotional state. This information is crucial diagnostically and is essential for the rule-in/rule-out process discussed in Chapter 5. Scores of human moods exist; however, most clinicians thoroughly assess emotional symptoms related to the *DSM-IV-TR* diagnoses. That is, although moods such as joy, surprise, and elation may be prevalent, they typically are not symptomatic of psychopathology, unless they are in excess or debilitating.

STREAM OF CONSCIOUSNESS

Stream of consciousness, also called flow of thought, is determined by observing speech patterns, which are presumed to indicate thought processes. Table 6.2 highlights relevant observations that can be made about a client's speech.

Table 6.2

Clinical Observations and Everyday Language Definitions of Observable Body Movements

Clinical Terminology	Everyday Language
Akathisia	The client reports feeling restlessness in legs since the onset of neuroleptics.
Akinesia	Few movements were noticed in areas such as arm movement when walking and eye blinking.
Athetoid movements	Slow, involuntary, snakelike movements were observed in the client's arms.
Choreiform movements	Quick, jerky, involuntary movements were noticed in the client's limbs.
Dystonia	The client's head remained twisted for several minutes, during which time the client's tongue remained stuck out.
Hypokinesia	Very few body movements were noticed such as the client's arms rarely moved when the client walked.
Masked facies	There was no facial expression.
Psychomotor agitation	The client had difficulties sitting still and appeared restless and tense.
Psychomotor retardation	Body movements and speech patterns were slow.
Waxy flexibility	Client's body position, in which arms were extended upward, remained unchanged despite all attempts to change it by staff.

Source: Reprinted with permission of John Wiley & Sons, Inc.

FLIGHT OF IDEAS

An excessive number of ideas and rapid change in idea content denote a flight of ideas. In a flight of ideas, the content of one idea may have a relationship with the next idea, or an idea may last for less than one sentence. Consider this example:

> We went to the store in the van. Traveling is just great. I love visiting the mountains, especially in the summertime. Oh, yes, the weather is great.

ASSOCIATIONS

The term "loose associations" refers to unrelated ideas that occur in the same sentence or within a few sentences. The words are coherent, but the content is not related and does not follow a logical sequence. Other types of associations (e.g., clang, derailment, tangentiality, etc.) also exist. Therapists should record specific examples in the psychological report. Other observations include excessive rambling, coherency of speech, logical speech, neologisms, cause and effect, and relevance of speech. These behaviors are rare and can indicate severe psychopathology. Consider the next example.

> Why is whatever might be kind to others. You might think and do why not cobetize the plemil.

THOUGHT CONTENT

Observations of thought content in psychology refer to intrusive thoughts, unusual thoughts, destructive thoughts, or false beliefs that may preoccupy the client. Common preoccupations include obsessions; compulsions; phobias; or homicidal, suicidal, or antisocial thoughts. Thought disturbances, such as delusions of grandeur, persecution, or somatic concerns, also may be observed and recorded. Clinicians also should document ideas of reference, such as thought broadcasting, bizarre ideations, and unusual content. Consider this example:

> Connie B. states that she is constantly being watched by "agents of evil from another dimension." She further states that she has seen them in the television and they are trying to recruit and possess her. She believes that if she "gives in" she will lose her soul.

HALLUCINATIONS

Hallucinations may be distortions of any of the five senses (optic, auditory, olfactory, tactile, or gustatory). Before noting such observations, the clinician should be sure to consider cultural and spiritual issues and should make certain that the client understands the context behind such questioning. For example, if a highly religious person is asked "Do you ever hear voices that no one else hears?" an affirmative answer does not necessarily imply a thought disorder. Instead, it could reflect a religious experience, organicity, or a transient symptom of a severe affective disorder.

No matter what kinds of hallucinations are reported, it is important to document the degree of the disturbance clearly. Simply stating that hallucinations exist does not present a clear clinical picture. As with other signs and symptoms, it is important to document the onset, frequency, antecedents, intensity, duration, and resulting impairments of the hallucinations. Other notations of clinical significance related to hallucinations include depersonalization, derealization, déjà vu, overvalued ideas, and illusions, all of which suggest issues of perception.

SENSORIUM/COGNITION

This section of the MSE elicits information regarding the client's orientation, concentration, attention span, memory, and ability to hold a normal conversation.

ORIENTATION × 3

The term "orientation × 3" refers to the client's knowledge of the current time, place, and person. The therapist typically asks the client to state the time of day, date, year, and season; the name of the clinic and the city where the interview is taking place; and the client's name and the names of other important people in the client's life. Disorientation indicates cognitive dysfunction that could stem from a number of etiologies.

ATTENTION AND CONCENTRATION

Attention is the ability to focus on a given task whereas *concentration* is the ability to sustain attention over a period of time. The MSE measures attention and concentration by recording the client's ability to perform various mental tasks. Examples of common attention/concentration tasks in the MSE include:

- Serial threes beginning with 1
- Serial sevens backward from 100
- Mathematical calculations
- Verbal tasks backward
- Repeating digits

Serial Threes Clients are asked to count to 40 by threes beginning with 1 (e.g., 1, 4, 7, 10). The common margin of error is 0 to 2 mistakes, with an average of 2 to 3 seconds between digits. It is important to record in the report the number of errors as well as the time that elapses between digits; the client's level of persistence, anxiety, and frustration; and any strategies the client uses to perform the calculations.

Serial Sevens from 100 Backward Serial sevens from 100 backward is more difficult than serial threes. The normal margin of error is 0 to 2 mistakes, with an average of 3 to 6 seconds between digits. For this test, the client is asked to count backward from 100 by sevens. The clinician should make similar observations as the ones suggested for serial threes.

Mathematical Calculations   Depending on the client's level of education, the clinician can present mathematical calculations that are typically beyond rote memory. For example, adult clients might be asked to solve problems such as 65/5 and 12 × 6. Much simpler problems, such as asking a first grader to add 3 + 4, are given to children.

Verbal Tasks Backward   Most adults are able to spell words, such as WORLD or EARTH, forward, but during times of difficulty with concentration, errors are common when spelling words backward. Be sure to evaluate or estimate the client's intellectual level and any learning disabilities prior to making conclusions regarding such tasks. It is best to ask clients first to spell the words forward before attempting to spell them backward. If clients are not able to spell the word forward, choose a simpler word or select a new task. Other tasks include operations such as saying the months of the year backward or tasks that are not a challenge when recalled forward but are not typically performed backward.

Repeating Digits   The average adult is able to repeat five to seven digits forward and four to six digits backward. The Wechsler intelligence test manuals provide child and adult norms for digit span. To administer the test, the therapist repeats an increasing number of digits, spaced one second apart and beginning with two digits forward, to the client. The tone of the examiner's voice typically drops on the last digit to signify the end of the list. The client then repeats the digits back to the therapist in the same order. After a limit has been reached, the client is asked to repeat another set of digits backward.

JUDGMENT

Judgment is assessed by asking the client direct questions about hypothetical situations in which choices of judgment must be made. Questions from the Wechsler comprehension subtests commonly are used. Clinicians should bear in mind that although many clients are aware of what should be done in a particular situation, in real life they seldom take the best course of action. Thus, obtaining an accurate history of client behaviors will better support the clinician's determination of the client's judgment.

It is common to ask hypothetical questions, such as "What would you do if you were the first one in a theater to see smoke and fire coming from under one of the exit doors?" Observations include the quality of the answer and whether the answer is unusual. For example, if the client answers, "I'd yell fire," it is not an unusual response, but it may indicate lack of planning or impulsivity. An answer of "I'd just leave" can lead to the question "What about the other people?" Some clients will respond, "I would warn them as I left," whereas others would respond, "That's their problem." The query, in this case, provides valuable clinical information.

INSIGHT

A client's level of insight is important in assessing treatment prognosis. Lower levels of insight generally indicate that the client will be less aware of psychological problems. Many therapists use more behavioral counseling methods for clients with poor insight and more cognitive methods for those with higher levels of insight. Levels of insight may vary from session to session or depending on the problem being addressed and include:

1. Complete denial
2. Slight awareness
3. Awareness, but blames others
4. Intellectual insight, but few changes likely
5. Emotional insight and understanding that changes can occur

Figure 5.2 in Chapter 5 includes a mental status checklist on which the therapist documents various mental status dimensions. Some of the information is asked directly of the client whereas other information is observed.

The clinician can review and integrate the biopsychosocial assessment, MSE, and other data collected from phone screens, presession questionnaires, and so on in order to validate the diagnosis and demonstrate medical necessity for treatment. Chapter 7 explains the validation process.

HIGHLIGHTS OF CHAPTER 6

- The MSE provides an index of the client's current mental condition. It is like a snapshot of the moment rather than being historical in nature.
- The MSE is based on behavioral, physical, and affective observations of the client and specific client statements.
- MSE observations may vary from one session to the next, based on current mental status.
- Several specific MSE procedures are employed to provide consistency in the information collected.
- Observed speech, attitude, cognition, and affective observations are major components of the MSE.
- Thought content generally is assessed by the client's speech and language.
- The client's attitude and level of insight may be indicators of prognosis in therapy.

QUESTIONS

1. Which of the next statements best represents *medical necessity* in mental health services?
   a. Both therapy and medications are suggested.
   b. Without therapy, the client is likely to remain functionally impaired.
   c. A medical opinion is needed.
   d. Medical, not psychological, services are needed.
2. The *mental status exam* is intended to provide a(n)
   a. summary of the client's past mental health history.
   b. description of the reasons the client has come to therapy.
   c. current picture of the client's current mental state.
   d. overview of the client's past and present mental state.
3. Which of the next statements best represents a description of a client's affect?
   a. Client states that she is depressed, anxious, and irritable.
   b. Client states that she has previous diagnoses of depression and anxiety.
   c. Client appears to be depressed, anxious, and irritable.
   d. Each of the above demonstrates a client's affect.
4. In a mental status exam, the client's *stream of consciousness* is evaluated by his or her
   a. speech.
   b. history.
   c. affect.
   d. IQ.
5. The client's mental status is evaluated
   a. only during the mental status exam in the initial interview.
   b. throughout treatment.
   c. only when revising a treatment plan.
   d. historically, every fourth session.
6. A client presents with slurred speech. This provides evidence of
   a. alcoholism.
   b. brain damage.
   c. a communication disorder.
   d. need more information.

   Answers: 1b, 2c, 3a, 4a, 5b, 6d

CHAPTER 7

Validating a Diagnosis

A MONG THE SEVERAL purposes of the diagnostic interview is the need to document the medical necessity for services and solicit information to produce an accurate and effective treatment plan. Although the diagnostic interview is not structured to be a counseling session, the manner in which information is solicited can be quite therapeutic for the client. If the therapist has a clear understanding of the text revision of the fourth edition of the *Diagnostic and Statistical Manual of Mental Disorders* (*DSM-IV-TR*; American Psychiatric Association, 2000) and psychopathology and shows empathy for the client's situation, the result often will increase client cooperation and insight.

The *DSM-IV-TR* states:

> In the *DSM-IV-TR*, each of the mental disorders is conceptualized as a clinically significant behavioral or psychological syndrome or pattern that occurs in an individual and that is associated with present distress (e.g., a painful symptom) or disability (i.e., impairment in one or more important areas of functioning) or with significantly increased risk of suffering death, pain, disability, or an important loss of freedom. (p. xxxi)

The volume further explains that the syndrome must not be based on an expected culturally sanctioned behavior or a response to an event that would lead to an expected emotional reaction. The documentation process continuously monitors impairments and progress to justify the medical necessity of services.

Each *DSM-IV-TR* disorder is characterized by various diagnostic criteria, such as symptoms, time frames, and impairments. Many disorders list a specific number of symptoms that must be present to justify the diagnosis. Symptom endorsement is necessary but not sufficient to make a diagnosis.

Mental health diagnoses are not to be given in a cookbook-like fashion. That is, the process of formulating a diagnosis is not simply a matter of word processing in which a client endorses enough symptoms until the best-fitting diagnosis is given. Questionnaires that base a diagnosis solely on endorsed symptoms clearly do not match the *DSM-IV-TR* criteria, because there are several factors other than simply endorsing symptoms to consider when formulating a diagnosis.

The *DSM-IV-TR* cautions that the diagnostic criteria are guidelines meant to enhance communication among clinicians. The accuracy of *DSM* diagnoses is an ongoing work. Each revision since the first *DSM* has added specificity and has attempted to be a result of collaboration between mental health professionals. It is intended that subsequent editions will be more accurate than the current edition. Because mental health diagnoses are constructs rather than absolutes, there will always be disagreements and inaccuracy. If a specific diagnosis was given for every possible mental health problem, there would be thousands of diagnoses, if not more, because each would be somewhat different. Even in the most recent *DSM*, the *DSM-IV-TR*, several diagnoses are similar and often confused by professionals (e.g., dysthymic disorder versus adjustment disorder, chronic with depressed mood; or major depressive disorder, with psychotic features versus schizoaffective disorder).

It would be unwise and confusing to define a new diagnosis each and every time someone's symptoms vary from someone else's. Thus, when making a diagnosis, the clinician selects a diagnosis that is the best *DSM-IV-TR* fit to the client. The closer the fit, the more valid the diagnosis for a client. Many diagnoses are symptomatically composed of endorsing at least a minimal number of symptoms out of a select list listed for each diagnosis in the *DSM-IV-TR*. Thus, clients assigned the same diagnoses may have a number of symptoms in common and some not in common. Without this diagnostic system, there would have to be a separate diagnosis for every combination of symptoms. That is, two people with the same diagnosis could function at different levels and have somewhat different symptoms. However, there are more similarities than differences between diagnoses.

Consider the color designated as blue. It is a description of a wide array of hues and brightnesses, not a specific wavelength of light. There are numerous shades and brightnesses of blue that are different on the color spectrum, but they still are commonly referred to as blue for the sake of communication. Similarly, a *DSM-IV-TR* diagnosis suggests a general category that aids in communication between professionals rather than an exact description of symptoms for each diagnosis. For example, we use general terms for such mental health concerns as depression and anxiety, or we use diagnostic terms, such as major depressive disorder, but the terms in themselves provide direction only, not specificity. Thus, a diagnosis is important for communication and to provide general information, but a thorough diagnostic assessment is necessary to clearly define the client's concerns.

Some clients exhibit significant symptoms of a diagnosis, but they may be short of the specified number of necessary symptoms noted in the *DSM-IV-TR*. The *DSM-IV-TR* allows for clinical judgment in making a diagnosis when the individual does not clearly meet the diagnostic criteria but the clinician believes that the diagnosis is warranted.

The *DSM-IV-TR* follows a common format for classifying disorders. Although some *DSM-IV-TR* disorders contain additional headings, the basic outline for each is:

Common *DSM-IV-TR* Disorder Classification Headings
Code number
Name of diagnosis
Diagnostic features
Associated features and disorders
Associated descriptive features and mental disorders
Associated laboratory findings
Specific age and gender features
Prevalence
Course
Familial pattern
Differential diagnosis
Diagnostic criteria

ESSENTIAL SYMPTOMS

Essential symptoms of a diagnosis are symptoms that must be present to make a diagnosis. These symptoms are listed in the Diagnostic Features section for each *DSM-IV-TR* diagnosis. For example, the *DSM-IV-TR* lists the essential features of dysthymic disorder as "a chronically depressed mood that occurs for most of the day more days than not for at least 2 years (children, 1 year) (Criterion A)" (p. 376). If an adult has felt depressed most of the time for only one year, the diagnosis is not dysthymic disorder. Also, the diagnosis cannot be made if the adult has been depressed two or more years but only sporadically. Other essential symptoms are listed, but not all are required to be present to validate the diagnosis.

Primary and Secondary Essential Symptoms

The terms "primary essential symptoms" and "secondary essential symptoms" are not found in the literature but are used in this text to more clearly differentiate between two discrete types of essential symptoms. Some *DSM-IV-TR* classifications break down essential symptoms into two types but do not define them. The first type includes symptoms (herein referred to as primary essential symptoms) that must be present to validate a diagnosis. The *DSM-IV-TR* lists these symptoms first under the heading "Diagnostic Features." The second type includes symptoms (herein referred to as secondary essential symptoms) of which only a certain number must be present to validate the diagnosis. The *DSM-IV-TR* combines both types, referring to them interchangeably as essential symptoms. Every *DSM-IV-TR* diagnosis features primary essential symptoms, but not all list secondary essential symptoms.

For example, to diagnose a client with conduct disorder, the client must exhibit the essential symptom of "a repetitive and persistent pattern of behavior in which the basic rights of others or major age-appropriate societal norms or rules are violated" (*DSM-IV-TR*, APA, 2000, p. 93). Other *DSM-IV-TR* disorders include both primary and secondary essential symptoms. In this case, the client must exhibit the primary symptom(s) but exhibit only a certain number (dictated by the *DSM-IV-TR*) of the other essential symptoms listed (secondary essential symptoms). For example, the *DSM-IV-TR* criteria for Oppositional Defiant Disorder (313.81) include primary essential symptoms of a recurrent pattern of negativistic, defiant, disobedient, and hostile behavior toward authority figures that persists for at least six months. In addition, during this period, four or more of these secondary essential symptoms must be validated:

> (1) often loses temper, (2) often argues with adults, (3) often actively defies or refuses to comply with adults' requests or rules, (4) often deliberately annoys people, (5) often blames others for his or her mistakes or misbehavior, (6) is often touchy or easily annoyed by others, (7) is often angry or resentful, (8) is often spiteful or vindictive. (p. 102)

Each of the validated symptoms must result in disturbance in behavior that causes clinically significant impairment in social, academic, or occupational functioning.

In the previous example, eight secondary essential symptoms of oppositional defiant disorder are listed, but only four or more must be present, along with the primary essential symptom, to validate the symptoms of a diagnosis. It is, therefore, possible that two people with the same diagnosis could have no overlap in secondary essential symptoms. Even people with the same symptoms could experience different functional impairments. Thus, it is important to ensure that a diagnosis is documented carefully so that the treatment plan can be tailored to the individual client. A treatment plan that addresses a generic oppositional defiant disorder diagnosis is not individually targeted and may not successfully return the client to normal functioning.

ASSOCIATED SYMPTOMS

Associated symptoms are symptoms present in, or attributable to, a diagnosis but not essential to formulating the diagnosis. They are often vegetative symptoms (e.g., weight loss, insomnia, and diminished libido; Maxmen & Ward, 1995). The *DSM-IV-TR* lists various associated symptoms for most diagnoses. These symptoms are not used to validate a diagnosis but provide useful information for planning treatment and understanding the nature of the client's issues. Associated symptoms within a given diagnosis can vary among individuals. Symptoms not specifically listed in the *DSM-IV-TR* but that contribute to the client's functional impairments of a valid diagnosis may be added to the treatment plan.

Figure 7.1 describes the various symptoms associated with dysthymic disorder. According to the *DSM-IV-TR*, the first essential symptom (primary essential symptom #1) must be present, along with two or more other essential symptoms (secondary essential symptoms #2–#7) to validate a diagnosis.

Associated symptoms provide more information specifically about the client's situation. In this case, if the symptom in criterion A were present

---

A. *Primary Essential Symptoms*
   (Necessary to validate a diagnosis)
   1. Depressed most of day, for more days than not, as indicated either by subjective account or observation by others, for at least 2 years; and
B. *Secondary Essential Symptoms*
   Presence, while depressed, of two or more of the following in order to validate a diagnosis
   2. Poor appetite or overeating
   3. Insomnia or hypersomnia
   4. Low energy or fatigue
   5. Low self-esteem
   6. Poor concentration or difficulty making decisions
   7. Feelings of hopelessness
C. *Associated Symptoms*
   (Not sufficient to validate a diagnosis, but typically associated with the diagnosis)
   1. Feelings of inadequacy
   2. Generalized loss of interest or pleasure
   3. Social withdrawal
   4. Feelings of guilt or brooding about the past
   5. Subjective feelings of irritability or excessive anger
   6. Decreased activity, effectiveness, or productivity

Figure 7.1 *DSM-IV-TR* Symptoms of Dysthymic Disorder

Source: Reprinted with permission from the *Diagnostic and Statistical Manual of Mental Disorders, Fourth Edition, Text Revision* (Copyright © 2000). American Psychiatric Association.

along with all of the symptoms in criterion C, yet no symptoms from criterion B were evident, the *DSM-IV-TR* does not allow the diagnosis. (However, the *DSM-IV-TR* does allow for clinical judgment in making a diagnosis when an insufficient number of symptoms are endorsed.)

To validate the diagnosis in Figure 7.1, the clinician should first document criterion A (primary essential symptoms) and then document at least two of the symptoms listed in criterion B (secondary essential symptoms). The clinician may also document any symptoms from criterion C (associated symptoms), although these do not need to be present to diagnose the disorder. In addition to documenting these symptoms, the clinician must elicit information regarding how these effects of dysthymic disorder are impairing and causing distress in the client's life socially, occupationally, or in other areas.

This book follows the *DSM-IV-TR*'s definition of essential and associated symptoms; however, this book differentiates between the two types of essential symptoms listed in the *DSM-IV-TR* by calling them primary essential symptoms and secondary essential symptoms. In the example of dysthymic disorder symptoms (Figure 7.1), the *DSM-IV-TR* combines the primary and secondary essential symptoms, referring to them as essential symptoms. The diagnostic portion of the initial interview is designed to rule in and rule out clinical syndromes. Crucial information is provided for clinical dialogue, treatment planning, and third-party review. The information gathered in the initial interview drives the treatment plan; therefore, it must be clinically specific.

During the diagnostic interview, the clinician should ask specific questions to validate the symptoms and criteria of a diagnosis. This process of ruling in and ruling out often accounts for as much as 30% to 40% of the interview time. As noted previously, it is crucial to ask questions regarding the onset, frequency, antecedents, intensity, and duration (O-F-A-I-D procedure) of each symptom.

IMPAIRMENTS

Typically, when clients request mental health services, they suffer from dysfunction or impairments in their lives. They may have been exhibiting symptoms for a significant period of time without seeking services; however, when clients experience increasing dysfunction or impairments in their lives, the need for services becomes more pressing. That is, it is more common to hear a client's presenting problem in the initial interview as "My life is falling apart . . . I might lose my job and family"(impairments) than to hear "I am losing weight, not sleeping well, and I have low self-esteem" (symptoms). For example, the symptom of sleeping only a few hours per night is an impairment only if it negatively impacts the client's adaptive functioning. Some people can get by with very little sleep, while others require many hours in order to function adequately. As symptoms increase in intensity, impairments become more apparent. One major difference between symptoms and impairments is that symptoms tend to be at a micro level, affecting specific client behaviors, while impairments are more global, affecting major areas of the client's life. Endorsement of symptoms without resulting impairments typically suggests that the level of symptoms is not at a level of severity in which services are medically necessary.

The *DSM-IV-TR* requires that clinically significant distress or impairment resulting in social, occupational, or other important areas of functioning exist before a diagnosis may be made. That is, endorsement of symptoms, alone, is not sufficient to make a clinic diagnosis. A mental health diagnosis is made by a combination of related symptoms and their resulting impairments. Examples of these impairments should be documented to validate the medical necessity for treatment. The level of impairment or dysfunction is a good indicator of the severity of symptoms.

EXAMPLES OF INTEGRATING DIAGNOSIS, SYMPTOMS, AND IMPAIRMENTS

EXAMPLE 1

Vickii, age 24, has been diagnosed with Dysthymic Disorder (300.4; diagnosis). She describes the onset of her depression as 3 years ago when she moved out on her own. She feels depressed at least 75% of the time. There has never been more than a 2- to 3-week period in this time frame in which she has not felt depressed (primary essential symptoms). Ongoing symptoms include poor appetite, fatigue, and feelings of hopelessness (secondary essential symptoms). She further adds that she often isolates herself from others, and does not want to do much but sit around the house (associated symptoms). She has never received another diagnosis of depression or mania, nor is her depression the result of a medical condition or substance abuse (additional validation of diagnosis). Prior to impairment, she rarely missed work and surpassed her job quotas most of the time. Over the past 2 years, she has missed increasingly more work due to fatigue and low motivation. Last week she was given a warning at work due to absenteeism and significantly decreased productivity (occupational impairment). Previously, she was involved in sports teams and usually spent about 2 evenings per week with friends. Now she socializes about 1 evening per month, other than eating lunch daily with coworkers (current functioning compared to previous functioning). She describes herself as "lonely" and "not very interested in other people" (social impairment). She states that she "just feels numb" and does not care much about what happens in her future (affective impairment). Although she knows she must eat, she states that she is seldom hungry and has steadily lost about 5 to 10 pounds per year (possible physical impairment).

EXAMPLE 2

Chandler C., age 7, is diagnosed with Attention-Deficit/Hyperactivity Disorder, Predominantly Inattentive Type (314.00; diagnosis). He is described and observed by his parents, teacher, and school counselor as having persistent patterns of attention significantly below what is expected for his level of development (primary essential symptoms). Observations by this examiner and review of records from his school and parents' collateral information indicate examples of symptoms of difficulties paying attention to details at home and school, poor attention span, lack of follow-through with homework or household chores, inability to keep track of possessions, and distractibility and forgetfulness during daily activities (secondary essential symptoms). He is reported to be prone to temper tantrums, stubbornness, and bossiness (associated symptoms). His parents first noticed most of these symptoms about the age of 4 or 5. Teachers began informing his parents of these issues in the first grade (additional validation of diagnosis). Although educational testing indicates a normal range of intellectual functioning, he is performing academically significantly below grade level. He is not learning age-appropriate material and has been referred to the EBD program at school (educational impairment). In school activities, he is often ridiculed by his classmates for not paying attention. Subsequently, he has no friends and often is teased by his classmates, resulting in social withdrawal and low self-esteem (social and affective impairment).

RULE-IN/RULE-OUT PROCESS

The next illustration provides insight into the logic of the rule-in/rule-out process. If a person in Europe wanted directions to 525 Main Street in North St. Paul, MN, USA, she would format the information in her computer search in a logical progression. That is, she should not only enter "525" or even "525 Main St." because there are likely thousands of 525 Main Streets in the world. Instead, the progression of information would be (1) USA, (2) Minnesota, (2) North St. Paul, (4) Main St., and (5) 525. Thus, she is able to avoid this address in several cities, states, or countries asking where a 525 Main Street is located. A logical progression of questions avoids redundancy.

This illustration employs deductive rather than inductive methods of reasoning; that is, moving from general to specific questioning to reach a conclusion. This type of reasoning holds true for the diagnostic interview as well. If a clinician asks for information based on secondary essential and associated symptoms alone, it will be difficult to make a diagnosis because many *DSM-IV-TR* disorders have similar or related secondary and associated symptoms. For example, symptoms such as social withdrawal, low self-esteem, irritability, restlessness, fatigue, guilt, negativism, sleeping problems, weight changes, and poor concentration are clinically significant but are associated with several disorders, including various types of depression, anxiety, pain disorders, and thought disorders. Soliciting information about only these symptoms would be like asking how to find 525 Main St. The person may never get home or may end up in the wrong place because the question was not specific. Diagnostically, misdirection may or may not become an issue of litigation, but it certainly raises ethical and treatment issues.

A more efficient means of ruling in or ruling out a specific diagnosis is to first survey the primary essential symptoms of various *DSM-IV-TR* disorders. Interviewing clients regarding these symptoms differentiates the diagnostic categories, is time efficient, eliminates redundancy, and covers the spectrum of disorders. Figure 7.2 demonstrates a poor example of ruling in or ruling out specific disorders.

Although the dialogue in Figure 7.2 may suggest therapist empathy for the client's problem, it provides little diagnostic information. If the therapist assumes that the client's responses to the questions suggest dysthymic disorder, it may be accurate, but several other diagnoses have not been ruled out. For example, the symptoms endorsed in the figure could suggest other DSM-IV-TR diagnoses as well, including any depressive disorder, an adjustment disorder, various personality disorders, or fatigue.

T: Do you feel tired at times?
C: Yes.
T: Are there times when you just want to be left alone?
C: Yes.
T: Does your self-esteem seem to drop when you feel down?
C: You hit the nail on the head.
T: Do you feel uptight when you are under stress?
C: That's exactly it!
T: Is it harder to cope when you are under stress?
C: Yes. You seem to know exactly how I feel.

Figure 7.2 Poor Example of Rule-in/Rule-out Process
Source: Reprinted with permission of John Wiley & Sons, Inc.

T: Do you feel sad often?
C: Yes.
T: Are you often anxious?
C: Yes.
T: Do you ever have panic attacks?
C: No.
T: Have you been avoiding people lately?
C: I think so.

Figure 7.3   Better but Still Insufficient Example of Diagnosing a Disorder
Source: Reprinted with permission of John Wiley & Sons, Inc.

Even a person with no clear mental health diagnosis who is undergoing normal life stressors might complain of these symptoms. In this case, the Barnum effect (Klopfer, 1960), in which overdiagnosis is possible due to vague specification of symptoms, is clearly evident. The therapist is asking questions that a majority of people, with or without psychopathology, would endorse. The client believes that the therapist is right on target, but diagnostically there is no clear target. That is because the therapist is using an inductive rather than a deductive model of questioning.

Figure 7.3 illustrates a better approach to diagnostic questioning but still does not produce a definitive diagnosis. The clinical questions in the figure have more direction than those in Figure 7.2, but they are posed randomly. In this case, the client acknowledged feelings of depression and anxiety, but the clinician did not determine their effects, significance, or relationship with the presenting problem. Eventually these questions will have to be repeated and more specific information requested.

A better way to solicit client information and approach a diagnosis is to use the rule-in/rule-out process. As shown in Figure 7.4, the *DSM-IV-TR* is divided into 17 diagnostic categories. Each of the diagnostic categories contains diagnostic features unique from other categories. The rule-in/rule-out process allows the clinician to target information gathering and determine what information should be pursued and what is not as important, based on the client's reported symptoms and observable signs.

The clinician rarely needs to systematically go through all 17 diagnostic categories for each client. The nature of the client's presenting problem nearly always directs the focus of the interview. For example, a client who initially presents with complaints of depressed mood most likely is suffering from a mood disorder. As the interview progresses, it becomes clear whether concerns in other areas not initially presented by the client also exist.

1. Disorders Usually First Diagnosed in Infancy, Childhood, or Adolescence
2. Delirium, Dementia, and Amnestic and Other Cognitive Disorders
3. Mental Disorders Due to a General Medical Condition
4. Substance-Related Disorders
5. Schizophrenia and Other Psychotic Disorders
6. Mood Disorders
7. Anxiety Disorders
8. Somatoform Disorders
9. Factitious Disorders
10. Dissociative Disorders
11. Sexual and Gender Identity Disorders
12. Eating Disorders
13. Sleep Disorders
14. Impulse-Control Disorders Not Elsewhere Classified
15. Adjustment Disorders
16. Personality Disorders
17. Other Conditions That May Be a Focus of Clinical Attention

Figure 7.4 *DSM-IV-TR* Diagnostic Categories

Source: Reprinted with permission of John Wiley & Sons, Inc.

STEPS OF RULE-IN/RULE-OUT PROCESS

STEP 1: RULE IN/RULE OUT PRIMARY ESSENTIAL SYMPTOMS

Let us return to John Doe's intake session. The therapist asks a series of questions designed to rule in or rule out different categories of *DSM-IV-TR* disorders. Keep in mind that the therapist already ruled out a substance abuse problem earlier in the interview.

Review of Presenting Problem   First, the therapist reviews the client's presenting problem.

THERAPIST (T): You stated before that you are here because of depression.
JOHN DOE (JD): Yes, I've felt that way too many times in my life.
T: Have you ever been treated for any other mental health concerns?
JD: Just for the depression with Dr. Wilson five years ago that I told you about.
T: Are there any other concerns besides depression?
JD: I don't think so. The depression is bad enough.

Rule Out Anxiety Disorders   The next questions rule out the possibility that the client is suffering from an anxiety disorder.

T: How about anxiety?
JD: What do you mean?

T: Do you often worry excessively, feel nervous, restless, or panicky?

JD: No, not often. Every once in a while I worry, but no more than anyone else with financial problems.

T: Do you have any history of panic attacks?

JD: What do you mean?

T: Do you ever experience symptoms such as dizziness, chest pain, difficulties breathing, or feeling out of control?

JD: Oh, maybe once or twice in my life, but not to that extent. I guess I'm not a worrier.

Rule Out Cognitive Disorders   Next the therapist rules out cognitive disorders, such as delirium, dementia, amnesia, and so on. (Information from the mental status exam is also used to rule out these disorders.)

T: Do you have problems with memory or concentration, or have people made comments about this to you?

JD: No, not really, actually, my memory and concentration are pretty good.

Rule Out Physical Conditions   The therapist also wants to rule out physical conditions that might produce a mental disorder.

T: You stated before that you are in pretty good health. Have you noticed any changes in your health or physical condition lately?

JD: I get tired or fatigued more easily, but it's not that bad.

T: How long have you felt more fatigued?

JD: Probably since I realized how depressing things are for me. I think it's because I used to be so active, and now I just don't feel like it. I'll get over it.

Rule Out Somatoform Disorders   Next the therapist rules out somatoform disorders.

T: For most of your teen or adult life, have you had a history of concerns such as frequent headaches, stomachaches, nausea, diarrhea, or memory lapses?

JD: No, not more than anyone else. I've always been healthy.

Rule Out Psychotic Disorders   The therapist also rules out schizophrenia and other psychotic disorders.

T: Have you ever, or do you ever hear voices, and no one is there?

JD: Oh no!

T: Do you ever see things that no one else sees?

JD: What do you mean?

T: Like shadows walking on the wall or images that no one else sees but you.

JD: No, nothing at all like that.

T: Do you ever experience any unusual body sensations, smells, tastes, or feelings?

JD: Not at all.

Rule Out Mania   Now the therapist rules out mania.

T: Are there times in which you feel full of energy, maybe have little or no need for sleep, and feel like you are on top of the world?

JD: I wish I felt that way. No, not at all.

Rule Out Dissociation   The therapist then rules out dissociation.

T: Do you ever feel like you have left your body or do you feel like you are someone else?

JD: Not at all, what you see is what you get!

T: Have you ever had times when it felt like you just were not there, but your body was going through the motions?

JD: No, never.

Rule Out Eating Disorders   Next the therapist rules out eating disorders.

T: Do you have any concerns in any of the following areas: eating, such as throwing up, or eating too much or too little?

JD: My appetite is high and I've gained weight, but I'm not throwing up or binge eating.

T: Have you had any eating problems in the past?

JD: When I get depressed I gain weight.

Rule Out Sleeping Disorders   And the therapist rules out a sleeping disorder.

T: Do you have problems falling asleep, sleeping too much or too little?

JD: Well, since my wife died, I've been waking up about an hour earlier than I'd like, but I'm getting used to it.

T: Once you fall asleep, do you have any problems with terrors, nightmares, or sleepwalking?

JD: No, I don't.

Rule Out Sexual or Gender-Identity Disorders   Next the therapist rules out sexual or gender-identity disorders.

T: Do you have any sexual concerns or problems with sexual behavior?
JD: I've had no sex life since my wife died, but there are no sexual problems.

Rule Out Impulse Control Disorders   The therapist also rules out impulse control disorders.

T: Are any of your behaviors difficult to control or do they get out of hand?
JD: No, this is not a problem.
T: Are there any areas of your life in which others have told you that you spend too much time or effort?
JD: What do you mean?
T: Like gambling, drugs, alcohol, sexual behaviors, or even time on the computer . . . anything like that?
JD: No, not at all.

Rule Out Adjustment Disorders   Finally, the therapist rules out adjustment disorders.

T: Have there been any other major stressors or changes in your life in the past six months that are difficult to cope with now?
JD: None that I can think of.

These diagnostic questions were designed to rule in or rule out primary essential symptoms of most *DSM-IV-TR* disorders. Before making a diagnosis, the therapist wanted to rule out other *DSM-IV-TR* disorders, such as anxiety, panic attacks, cognitive issues, physical concerns, somatization, thought disorders, mania, dissociation, eating disorders, sleeping problems, sexual issues, and adjustment problems.

Notice that the clinician did not ask detailed questions about John Doe's depression, other than requesting a history of the problem and eliciting his concerns about it. At this point, the clinician strongly suspects a mood disorder and has ruled out most other categories of *DSM-IV-TR* disorders.

Step 2: Rule In/Rule Out Secondary Essential Symptoms

The clinician believes that John Doe is suffering from a mood disorder and has ruled out nonmood disorders. But more specific information is needed to make a differential diagnosis. The next step is to rule in or rule out specific mood disorders, specifically a depressive disorder. The clinician ruled out a bipolar disorder during step 1. The information collected earlier in the interview, as well as knowledge of specific *DSM-IV-TR* criteria of the various mood disorders, also will be helpful in making a diagnosis. Questions in step 2 focus on symptomology, onset, frequency, duration, and severity of John Doe's impairments. Next the therapist incorporates the appropriate aspects of the O-F-A-I-D technique to provide much more specific diagnostic information.

T: I would like to ask you some more questions about your sadness or depression.
JD: Go ahead.

Onset   First, the therapist finds out how long John Doe has felt depressed.

T: How long have you felt this way?
JD: All of my life. I've never really been happy. I've never really felt good about myself. I'm a failure . . . but I function. . . . That's all I do. It's just that now things are building up, and I need help. My rut is deeper than usual.

Differential Diagnosis   The next questions seek to verify the diagnosis of a specific disorder.

T: Have there ever been any extended periods of time when you were not depressed, say for more than two months?
JD: No, none that I can remember. Sometimes when major life events are taking place, like my graduation or getting married, I've felt better for a few weeks or so, but this is unusual.
T: Tell me more about how the depression now is different than your usual mood.
JD: Like I said before, I'm usually able to function, but now I don't want to. I'm down and don't feel like getting up. There's too much pressure. I'm alone, no one cares. I feel like I'm bottoming out. It's like . . . what's the use?
T: It sounds like you are usually down on yourself and look at life as hopeless, but now things are much worse than usual.
JD: That's exactly what I'm saying.

Frequency   Next, the therapist determines how often John Doe feels depressed.

T: How often do you feel down or depressed?
JD: I feel down about every day.
T: How often do you not feel depressed?
JD: Maybe once a week.
T: What is it like then?
JD: I feel almost normal . . . like I might get ahead someday. I go shopping and take care of the things I should have done the rest of the week.

Most Recent Onset or Cycling of Symptoms   Now the therapist needs to determine how long this most recent bout of severe depression has lasted.

T: Since you have felt depressed, has there been a time in which symptoms became noticeably worse?

JD: Yes, at first after her death I was handling it, but it has been getting much worse lately.

T: How long has it been worse like this?

JD: Probably about two months.

T: And nothing happened out of the ordinary two months ago?

JD: No, things just kept building up, and I began giving up.

T: Is the feeling similar to when you received counseling from Dr. Anderson five years ago?

JD: Yes, but even worse . . . at least I was married then.

Clarification of Symptoms   Next the therapist clarifies John Doe's specific symptoms.

T: Do you ever have thoughts of suicide or dying?

JD: Sometimes I think it would be better for everyone if I wasn't around. I've even thought of ways to die.

T: Do you have a plan for suicide?

JD: Oh no. I would never commit suicide. I believe in God. I couldn't . . . wouldn't . . . do it.

T: Are you sure?

JD: Yes, for certain, but thanks for asking.

T: How is your appetite?

JD: I eat and eat and eat. It's never been so bad. Just six months ago I weighed 160 pounds, now I weigh almost 190.

T: Is there anything enjoyable in your life at this time?

JD: Yes, I do enjoy reading and watching movies—they seem to be an escape.

Clarification of Impairments   Now the therapist clarifies how depression is affecting John Doe.

T: Has your depression affected any other areas of your life?

JD: What do you mean?

T: For example, you mentioned that you are on probation at work due to excessive absences. When I ask, "Are there any other areas in your life which have been affected by your depression?" I mean areas such as your social life, your physical health, or your thinking.

JD: I sometimes don't pay attention to things, and people think I'm forgetful. It's probably because I just don't care.

T: Do you have these times of confusion or poor concentration only when you are depressed or at other times, also?

JD: It's only when I'm the most depressed . . . maybe once or twice a month since I've been down. It's part of the reason I'm missing so much work. I'm afraid.

T: For most of your life have you done well or had difficulty making decisions?

JD: It's always been a real chore. I change my mind because I believe my decisions are wrong. I never really make up my mind.

T: Tell me more about your social life.

JD: What social life? In the past few months I haven't returned any phone calls. Like I said before, I don't even spend time with my best friend. I've become a recluse. I haven't felt like getting out. I wouldn't even know what to say to someone if I were introduced to someone new. What would I talk about? My life is about as boring as it gets.

With these questions, the therapist has successfully ruled in both major depressive disorder and dysthymic disorder. Some of the symptoms and impairments were validated in the initial screening, whereas others were validated when the therapist explored symptoms of specific mood disorders. As you can see from the *DSM-IV-TR* description of essential symptoms (Figure 7.5), the diagnosis is valid for both disorders.

STEP 3: DETERMINE ASSOCIATED SYMPTOMS

The two diagnoses of dysthymic disorder and major depression were ruled in during the interview via steps 1 and 2. Now sufficient information is available for the treatment plan. Other questions posed in the interview could include eliciting additional associated symptoms to aid in providing a clearer understanding of the client's issues. Clinicians also may focus on items of interest helpful within their school of thought. For example, those from a systems approach will focus on the role of the family and significant others whereas those from a dynamic approach will show more interest in how the client's early environment has impacted his or her current state.

LIMITATIONS OF THE DIAGNOSTIC INTERVIEW

The diagnostic interview is subject to limitations of validity and reliability. It is as valid as the *DSM-IV-TR* is valid in its diagnostic categories; however, some *DSM-IV-TR* diagnoses are more valid than others. For example, some

Diagnosis #1	Major Depressive Disorder

Must exhibit symptom in Criteria #1 and at least four symptoms from Criteria #2.

Criteria Met (X)	DSM-IV-TR Essential Symptoms Criteria
	Criteria #1 (Primary Essential Symptom)
X	Usual depressed mood or lack of pleasure, continuously for two or more weeks, resulting in social, occupational, and affective impairment or distress.
	Criteria #2 (Secondary Essential Symptoms)
X	Weight gain of over 5% per month
X	Increased appetite
	Insomnia or hypersomnia
	Psychomotor agitation or retardation
X	Fatigue
X	Worthlessness or guilt
X	Poor concentration
X	Thoughts of death/suicide

Diagnosis #2	Dysthymic Disorder

Must exhibit symptom in Criteria #1 and at least two symptoms from Criteria #2.

Criteria Met (X)	DSM-IV-TR Essential Symptoms Criteria
	Criteria #1 (Primary Essential Symptom)
X	Depressed more days than not for at least two years
	Criteria #2 (Secondary Essential Symptoms)
X	Poor appetite or overeating
	Insomnia or hypersomnia
X	Low energy or fatigue
X	Low self-esteem
	Poor concentration or difficulty making decisions
X	Feelings of hopelessness
	Other DSM-IV-TR Criteria
X	Not symptom-free for more than two months in past two years
X	Disorder not better accounted for by other DSM-IV-TR conditions

Figure 7.5   Diagnosing John Doe with Major Depressive Disorder and Dysthymic Disorder

Source: Reprinted with permission of John Wiley & Sons, Inc.

disorders, such as major depressive disorder, list clear symptoms that must be evident to make a valid diagnosis. To justify the diagnosis, the clinician compares the client's symptoms to the symptoms listed under the specific disorder in *DSM-IV-TR*. Thus, this diagnosis is not likely to arouse much disagreement among professionals because its symptoms are clear cut.

Other *DSM-IV-TR* disorders do not have such straightforward symptoms, and many disorders have symptoms that overlap with those of other disorders. In these cases, clinicians may disagree on a diagnosis based on seemingly minor points. Some examples of disorders that have overlapping symptoms, thereby limiting the validity of their diagnosis, include:

- Bipolar disorder and borderline personality disorder
- Schizo-affective disorder and major depression with psychotic features
- Major depression: mild, recurrent type, and dysthymic disorder

The reliability of a diagnostic interview depends on the clinician's knowledge of psychopathology and consistency of the examination. The clinician should always ask clients the same general set of questions when ruling in or ruling out various disorders. When different sets of questions are posed to different clients, important diagnostic questions may be forgotten to be asked; thus, misdiagnosis could occur. Thorough knowledge of psychopathology and the *DSM-IV-TR* enables clinicians to stay on target. Memorizing specific symptoms of the major mental disorders is a crucial time-saving skill that enables experienced clinicians to perform the rule-in/rule-out process quickly.

This chapter has provided information to help formulate an accurate diagnosis. The next step in helping the client return to normal functioning is to formulate an individualized and detailed treatment plan.

HIGHLIGHTS OF CHAPTER 7

- In order for a diagnosis to be validated, there must be a sufficient number of symptoms and resulting impairment to meet diagnostic criteria in the *DSM-IV-TR*. Both symptoms and impairments should be clearly documented throughout the course of therapy until the diagnosis is no longer relevant.
- *DSM-IV-TR* diagnoses are broken down into essential and associated symptoms.
- Essential symptoms are those that must be prevalent in order to give a diagnosis.
- Associated symptoms do not validate a diagnosis but often are present when a diagnosis occurs.
- Interviewing time can be more efficient when essential symptoms are determined before associated symptoms because most associated symptoms are common to several diagnoses.
- The rule-in/rule-out process in diagnostic interviewing saves much time in the interview process by systematically validating the existence (or

lack of) of *DSM-IV-TR* essential and associated symptoms and the subsequent diagnosis.

- The mere existence of symptoms does not validate mental health problems unless the symptoms are significantly impairing to the individual.
- The diagnostic interview is limited by both its validity and its reliability.

QUESTIONS

1. Which of these interview questions best represents potential problems due to the *Barnum effect*?
   a. Do you experience auditory hallucinations when you are severely depressed?
   b. Does your level of depression cause you to miss a significant amount of work?
   c. How long do your panic attacks generally last?
   d. Do you get upset when you don't get your way?
2. The diagnostic interview incorporates a procedure in which the client is asked whether he or she is experiencing various symptoms. Deciding on the subsequent questions is determined by the answers to the earlier questions. This process is called
   a. rule-in/rule-out.
   b. symptom evaluations.
   c. backtracking.
   d. goal development.
3. Which of these descriptors of behaviors is suggested in the text as helpful in determining both a specific diagnosis and a level of functional impairment?
   a. Essential and associated symptoms.
   b. Diagnosis and treatment.
   c. Treatment plan, progress notes, discharge summary.
   d. Onset, frequency, antecedents, intensity, and duration.
4. What is clearly wrong with the next statement? *"Pat endorses symptoms of social withdrawal, low motivation, low self-esteem, sleeping problems, and irritability; therefore she meets criteria for dysthymic disorder."*
   a. The symptoms do not match that of a person with the diagnosis.
   b. The essential symptoms criteria are not met.
   c. No associated symptoms are mentioned.
   d. All of the above.
5. Which of the following best represents an associated symptom?
   a. Depressed most of the time.
   b. Prominent hallucinations.

    c. Low motivation.

    d. Daily panic attacks.

6. What is meant by this statement? "The diagnosis has been ruled out."

    a. The diagnosis will be given.

    b. There is clearly a different diagnosis that should be given.

    c. There is not enough evidence to give the diagnosis.

    d. The diagnosis next must be ruled in.

Answers: 1d, 2a, 3d, 4b, 5c, 6c

CHAPTER 8

Formulating a Treatment Plan

W HY IS TREATMENT planning necessary? It ensures accountability, clarity, communication, compensation, competency, compliance, consistency, dialogue, direction, documentation, ethics, evaluation, focus, goals, integration, justification, measurement, monitoring, needs, objectives, planning, preferences, record keeping, standardization, strategies, strengths, symptoms, and validation.

Formal treatment plan writing in the mental health field is a relatively recent development. Prior to the 1970s, formalized treatment plans were not part of the mental health delivery system. Early treatment plans provided little information other than vague acknowledgments that psychotherapy would occur. As managed care has increased the requirements for clinical efficacy, the quality of treatment plans has improved. The advent of managed care and regulatory agencies, such as the Commission of Accreditation for Rehabilitation Facilities (CARF), The Joint Commission (TJC), Tricare, and Medicare, have led to increasingly more stringent accountability procedures; therefore, detailed treatment planning is now an important part of the therapeutic process. Currently, regulatory agencies and third-party payers have similar requirements in treatment plan writing.

A survey conducted in seminars between 1994–1998 by this author of more than 2,000 mental health professionals revealed that less than 3% of currently practicing mental health professionals (e.g., psychologists, social workers, licensed marriage and family therapists, and counselors) were formally trained or supervised in accountability procedures such as treatment plan and progress note writing. A myriad of texts have been written about mental health treatment and how to conduct therapy, but few teach how to write and follow treatment plans or document the course of therapy.

COMPUTERIZED TREATMENT PLANNING

Siegel and Fischer (1980) noted that the treatment plan is the most frequently consulted portion of a client's chart. One of the biggest complaints about writing detailed treatment plans is the time it takes to develop them (Galasso, 1987; Ormiston, Barrett, Binder, & Molyneux, 1989; Walters, 1987). Fortunately, research in computerized treatment planning has flourished, and computer-generated treatment plans have become an effective and time-saving resource to clinicians.

Some early computer programs developed canned treatment plans that were designed to fit *Diagnostic and Statistical Manual* criteria for various diagnoses; however, they did not provide for the client's individual needs or alleviating functional impairments. Some facilities use these treatment plans with potentially disastrous results. For example, a therapist might diagnose a client with dysthymic disorder and then pull out a "dysthymia treatment plan" from a packet of several diagnostic choices. To begin treatment, the therapist would fill in the client's name and sign the prewritten plan. Although treatment plans of this variety are better than no treatment plan, they are designed to address global symptoms of a diagnosis and do not consider the client's special needs and desires. These types of plans do not allow therapists to develop a collaborative and individualized plan for treating specific clients who may have unique symptoms and impairments.

Widespread accepted standards and language in treatment plan writing is occurring, however, and computer software development over the past 10 to 15 years has provided some promising solutions. Today's computerized treatment plans have added more options for the therapist to individualize treatment. The Therascribe® treatment planner (Jongsma, 2008) has received positive reviews because it allows the clinician to customize the course of treatment based on the client needs and it follows current guidelines. It is user-friendly and saves considerable time in the treatment plan writing process.

Except for guidelines for each agency, little has been published that demonstrates how to write treatment plans with measurable and observable objectives that meet current managed care criteria. This chapter shows how to integrate current agency and managed care requirements into properly documented, individualized treatment plans.

GETTING STARTED

Treatment plan objectives should be formulated as an incremental plan to alleviate a client's functional impairments associated with documented symptoms of a disorder listed in the text revision of the fourth edition of the

Diagnostic and Statistical Manual of Mental Disorders (*DSM-IV-TR*; American Psychiatric Association, 2000). It is important that treatment plans be designed to address client needs rather than simply the diagnosis.

Writing treatment plans is easiest for clinicians who are thoroughly familiar with the *DSM-IV-TR* and competent in diagnostic interviewing techniques. Excellent texts that integrate both areas include Morrison's *DSM-IV Made Easy* (1995), Othmer and Othmer's *Clinical Interview Using DSM-IV-TR* (2002), and Groth-Marnat's *Handbook of Psychological Assessment*, 5th ed. (2009).

TREATMENT PLAN DEVELOPMENT

Both a poor and an excellent treatment plan take relatively the same amount of time to write. Actually, a writer with little or improper training in treatment plan writing may take significantly more time to write the plan than a trained writer because of not knowing what to write down. Sufficient training and understanding of treatment plan writing enables one to write an effective treatment plan in a brief time period, in the session with the client, providing results that are therapeutic to the client and in compliance with third-party requirements.

Typically, the initial treatment plan is written in the second session or after the initial assessment is complete. The client's cooperation and corroboration are essential. The therapist goes over the diagnostic information collected in the initial session and collaborates with the client concerning what impairments will be addressed in treatment.

An individualized treatment plan is based on detailed and accurate clinical information that corresponds with the client's strengths, needs, abilities, preferences (SNAPs) plus symptoms and respective functional impairments. Treatment plans formulate strategies to alleviate these impairments by incorporating client variables that would result in the most effective treatment. The chance of misdiagnosis and unresponsive treatment increases if essential symptoms, resulting impairments, and other client variables are not validated or incorporated into the treatment plan.

Historically, third-party payers have focused on the Axis I diagnoses as the primary determinant for reimbursement and the number of authorized sessions. Today, nearly all third-party payers still require an Axis I mental health diagnosis before authorizing for mental health services; moreover, there is a trend to exclude reimbursement for a growing number of specific Axis I diagnoses (e.g., conduct disorder, not-otherwise-specified diagnoses, and adjustment disorders). It is important for therapists to familiarize themselves with the specific authorization procedures and any exceptions for receiving services of each third-party payer. At times it is possible to receive authorization for services when a diagnosis is not covered but the documentation demonstrates medical necessity of services.

Reimbursement for services is most affected by the degree of functional impairment resulting from the mental disorder. Treatment handbooks, such as Roth and Fonagy's *What Works for Whom?* (2005) and Barlow's *Clinical Handbook of Psychological Disorders* (2007), provide information regarding the average number of visits and types of therapy indicated for various disorders; however, the diagnosis itself does not determine the level of mental health services needed. For example, it is possible for two people to be diagnosed with the same disorder but exhibit different levels of impairment. Other factors could impact these individuals' functioning, including history, personality, social supports, genes, and life stressors, among others. For two people with the same diagnosis, one might receive therapy to return to normal functioning whereas the other could decompensate. One of the several purposes of the diagnostic interview is to document this information and provide appropriate treatment recommendations.

A well-thought-out treatment plan addresses the individual's strengths and limitations. It goes beyond diagnosis, symptoms, and impairments. Addressing only *DSM-IV-TR* symptoms may be technically correct but may not meet a client's therapeutic needs. Earlier this book described how to solicit and clearly document detailed examples of a client's level of functioning and contributing factors to mental health concerns in the initial interview. Although symptoms and functional impairments are similar concepts, fundamental differences exist. Symptoms are described in distinct terms by which a mental or physical disorder is defined whereas impairments are problem areas or functional limitations in life that are adversely affected by the symptoms.

The client's SNAPs should be accounted for in the treatment plan. TJC requires that the client actively participate in designing the treatment plan. Similar to building a house from a blueprint, both the buyer (client) and architect (therapist) work together to develop a mutually satisfying product. When people build a home, most have a fairly good idea of what they want it to look like. Likewise, many, but not all, people entering therapy have an idea of what they want to accomplish. Therefore, the architect (therapist) does not simply hand them a plan and say, "Here is your plan." Rather, therapists provide helpful guidance, based on their training and experience, in which they consider the strengths and limitations of the client's ideas. Together they will develop a realistic and workable plan within reach of the client and within the expertise of the therapist.

Third-party requirements also can affect treatment plan development. For example, third parties often limit the number of sessions per year they will reimburse. Thus, if the insurance company limits reimbursement to 12 sessions per year, and the client is unable to pay for additional sessions, the treatment plan should be written to realistically utilize the 12 allotted sessions and provide for closure for the treatment at the end of session 12. If the client needs additional sessions, the therapist should help him or her obtain them either through a request for additional services or by other available means.

Situational variables that can affect the length of treatment also should be considered when planning treatment. For example, if a client will commit only to two months of therapy because of an impending move, the treatment plan should be realistic, given this limitation. Lofty goals will lead to an unfulfilled course of therapy.

GOALS AND OBJECTIVES

Treatment plan *goals* are the desired outcomes of therapy for various aspects of functional impairment. *Objectives* are incremental steps used to accomplish treatment plan goals. Without specific goals and objectives to provide direction, treatment may be vague and lack direction. Measurable and observable objectives allow the therapist and the client to evaluate the effectiveness of interventions, client progress, level of treatment, and the appropriate time of termination. In addition, regular evaluation of the client's progress toward goals can serve as a motivator for the client to stay on target with treatment issues. Effective treatment plans answer these questions: Why am I in therapy? What will we talk about and do? How do I know how well therapy is working? How will we know when therapy should terminate? Progress notes, which are discussed in Chapter 9, document that the treatment plan is being followed.

A number of publications and agencies recommend guidelines for developing treatment plans. For example, the *Consolidated Standards Manual* (TJC, 2011) presents standards for mental health services, including assessment, treatment planning, time frames, and discharge status. CARF treatment plan standards are listed in Figure 8.1. Medicare also has guidelines for clinicians to follow when preparing treatment plans and requires plans to include both long-range and short-range goals (Medicare, 1984).

The therapist and the client work together to establish treatment goals. Therapeutic interventions, treatments, or strategies are not goals; rather, they are the therapeutic means by which the goals and objectives will be achieved. Part of the intake process should include discussing what changes the client would like to make and how they might be accomplished. Some treatment strategies designed to accomplish the client's goals are implemented in the session throughout treatment and others are implemented outside the session (e.g., homework or referrals).

1. The individual plan is developed with the active participation of the persons served, and:
    a. Is prepared using the information from the primary assessment and interpretive summary.
    b. Is based on the needs and desires of the persons served and focuses on his or her integration and inclusion into:
        1. The local community.
        2. The family, when appropriate.
        3. Natural support systems.
        4. Other services needed.
    c. Involves the family of the person served, when applicable or permitted.
    d. Identifies any needs beyond the scope of the program.
    e. Specifies the services to be provided by the program.
    f. Specifies referrals for additional services.
    g. Is communicated to the person served in a manner that is understandable.
    h. When possible, is provided to the person served.
    i. Is reviewed periodically with the person served for continuing relevance and is modified as needed.
2. The individual plan contains the following components:
    a. Goals that are:
        1. Expressed in the words of the person served.
        2. Reflective of the informed choice of the person served or parent/guardian.
        3. Appropriate to the person's culture.
        4. Appropriate to the person's age.
        5. Based on the person's:
            a. Strengths.
            b. Needs.
            c. Abilities.
            d. Preferences.
    b. Specific service or treatment objectives that are:
        1. Reflective of the expectations of:
            a. The person served.
            b. The treatment team.
        2. Reflective of the client's expectations.
        3. Reflective of the person's development.
        4. Reflective of the person's culture and ethnicity.
        5. Reflective of the person's disabilities/disorders or concerns.
        6. Understandable to the person served.
        7. Measurable.
        8. Achievable.
        9. Time specific.
        10. Appropriate to the treatment setting.

Figure 8.1 Overview of CARF (2004) Standards for Treatment Planning (Individual Plan)

Source: Used by permission of the Behavioral Health Standards Manual, Commission on Accreditation of Rehabilitation Facilities. Copyright © 2011.

c. Frequency of specific treatment interventions.
d. Information on, or conditions for, transition to other services.
e. When applicable, identification of:
    1. Legal requirements.
    2. Legally imposed fees.
4. Signed and dated progress notes document:
    a. Completion of the individual plan.
    b. Significant events or changes in the life of the person served.
    c. The delivery of services that support the individual plan.
5. A designated individual(s) in coordinating services for each person served by:
    a. Assuming responsibility for ensuring the implementation of the individual plan.
    b. Ensuring that the person served is oriented to his or her services.
    c. Promoting the participation of the person served on an ongoing basis in discussions of his or her plans, goals, and status.
    d. Identifying and addressing gaps in the service provision.
    e. Sharing information on how to access community resources relevant to his or her needs.
    f. Advocating for the person served, when applicable.
    g. Communicating information regarding progress of the person served to the appropriate persons.
    h. Facilitating the transition process, including arrangements for follow-up services.
    i. Involving the family or legal guardian, when applicable or permitted.
    j. Coordinating services provided outside of the organization.
    k. Identifying the process for after-hours contact.

Figure 8.1 Continued

In most cases, goals should reflect the alleviation of unwanted symptoms by attaining positive functional behaviors. TJC requires that treatment plan goals be linked to living, learning, and work activities. In addition, objectives should be written in observable, measurable terms so that outcomes can be evaluated impartially. For example, the goal "increase positive social interactions" might be achieved through specific objectives (attained by the client) such as "attend one social function per week" or "attend weekly social skills group meeting." Treatment strategies might include therapist interventions such as "positive reinforcement of target behaviors" or "role playing means of meeting new people."

Treatment plans are revised as the client progresses in meeting objectives. TJC standards indicate that treatment goals should be evaluated and revised periodically. TJC does not impose a specific time frame for periodic evaluation; however, managed care companies often require treatment plan revisions after a set number of sessions or a given time period, such as every three months, every six to ten sessions, or whenever best suits the client's needs.

A key factor to ensuring the client's successful accomplishment of objectives is how they are written. When objectives are either too simple or too difficult, clients will not be appropriately motivated to accomplish them. For example, extremely low expectations or easy objectives provide clients with little motivation to change behavior. Overly high expectations, however, can produce anxiety, resulting in client avoidance of the objective targets. Thus, the client's input is necessary in creating the objectives.

Likewise, vague and unclear objectives may lead to lengthy treatment but provide little or no direction regarding how they will help the client reach treatment goals, thereby reducing the probability of behavioral change. The obvious problem of establishing vague objectives, such as "increase social interactions," is the difficulty in demonstrating significant change. For example, because the word "increase" is not quantified, even change of .001% implies attainment of the objective. Change of this magnitude will most likely not significantly alter the client's level of impairment. Specific objectives clarify progress in treatment. Thus, clearly written treatment plan objectives that require a moderate amount of effort to achieve provide the greatest probability of success.

As noted, treatment plans are not static. As objectives are accomplished, they are revised to more closely reach the stated goal. If each objective is a step toward the goal, then the last objective best reflects the goal (Goodman, Brown, & Dietz, 1992). This does not mean that every change in a treatment plan requires that a new form be filled out. Incremental revisions may be noted in progress notes or in a designated section of the treatment plan. Treatment plan itself is revised only as necessary (e.g., as required by third parties or institutional policies or when writing a prior authorization request). Treatment plans extend for a specified period or number of sessions, after which they are to be revised per the third party's specific requirements to reflect therapeutic progress.

The timing of treatment and the number of steps needed to accomplish treatment goals are highly related to the client's degree of impairment. Figure 8.2 depicts the relationship between goals and objectives by illustrating how incrementally more challenging objectives will help a client reach a target number of initiated social interactions. Figure 8.3 features objectives that demonstrate incremental steps toward a goal of systematic desensitization to airline travel. Although a treatment plan would not be rewritten every time an objective is reached, the progress notes could document revisions to it.

Figures 8.2 and 8.3 illustrate how incremental objectives are used to help clients reach a goal. If, for example, the client in Figure 8.2 initially was given the objective of flying in a plane, it might be overwhelming. Incremental objectives allow the client to gradually make therapeutic progress.

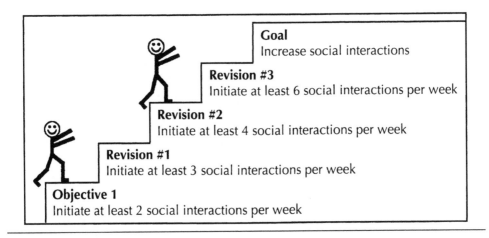

Figure 8.2 Revising Objectives to Reach Targeted Goals: Increase Social Interactions

Source: Reprinted with permission of John Wiley & Sons, Inc.

Other variables, such as the client's motivation, insight, and cooperation and rapport with the therapist, as well as the therapist's clinical skills, must be considered in the timing of treatment plan objectives. In many managed care settings in which the number of sessions is limited, time becomes a precious commodity.

Cognitive dissonance (tension caused by a conflict between one's established beliefs/attitudes/behaviors and opposing beliefs/attitudes/behaviors) often

Figure 8.3 Revising Objectives to Reach Targeted Goal: Systematic Desensitization to Airplane Travel

Source: Reprinted with permission of John Wiley & Sons, Inc.

occurs when the therapist's training does not match current third-party documentation requirements. The dissonance often results in stress, discomfort, complaining, and worrying in the therapist. It can be reduced when specific training and experience in current documentation and time-limited therapeutic procedures are provided. The dissonance often stems from stress induced from lack of training; therefore, additional training will help change the therapist's attitude and behaviors.

TREATMENT PLAN REQUIREMENTS OF THIRD-PARTY PAYERS

Third-party payers, such as insurance companies and managed care providers, have their own rules and regulations regarding development and maintenance of treatment plans. Figure 8.4 depicts common requirements.

BEHAVIORAL OBJECTIVES: MEASURABLE AND OBSERVABLE

Terms such as "measurable" and "observable," as required by managed care companies and regulatory agencies, follow the scientific practitioner model, in which empirical or observable evidence is crucial to outcomes. Vague treatment plans, for example, might include vague objectives, such as "increase communication skills." In this case, the concept of communication skills is not clear. The term "communicate" might be interpreted as anything from a client's poor speech patterns to his or her ability to express emotions. Specificity is needed. In addition, because the objective is stated in relative

---

Competence: The service provider must have appropriate credentials to perform the indicated type of service and must be competent in the area of expertise for the particular mental disorder.

Medical Necessity: There must be documentation of dysfunction or functional impairment resulting from a mental disorder (defined in *DSM* or ICD) that significantly interferes with the client's activities of daily living.

Goals/Objectives: The treatment plan must include specific, attainable, observable, and measurable goals and objectives.

Treatment: Level and amount of treatment must be concordant with intensity of impairment. Type of treatment must be consistent with acceptable procedures that reliably predict outcomes. Treatment is directed toward the active signs of a disorder.

Ongoing Documentation: Progress notes must follow specific treatment plan objectives designed to alleviate functional impairments that have been clearly documented in the assessment and in the treatment plan.

Figure 8.4 Third-Party Payer Requirements for Treatment Plan Development and Maintenance

Source: Reprinted with permission of John Wiley & Sons, Inc.

terms, measurement is illusive. As noted earlier, objectives incorporating words such as "increase," "decrease," "add," "change," and so on, with no further clarification, are vague because they do not quantify or give helpful direction to the degree of change.

It is suggested that the clinician first determine the symptoms of the disorder to formulate a *DSM-IV-TR* diagnosis and then question the client about functional impairments (e.g., social, occupational, physical) due to the effects of the mental health disorder. The clinician then should determine baseline measures for the functional impairments and set goals and incremental objectives for treatment.

It is difficult to measure and observe symptoms, but the resulting impairments are easily documented in a measurable manner. For example, documenting that a client is 75% depressed is a poor way to provide measurable evidence of impairment because the construct of depression is too vague to quantify. But the behavioral effects of depression can be quantified by stating, for example, "The client misses school 75% of the time due to depression."

SUBJECTIVE UNITS OF DISTRESS

The impact of symptoms can be estimated using subjective units of distress (SUDs), which are measured on a scale of 1 to 100. Clients periodically are asked to rate their level of distress for variables such as anxiety, fear, depression, and so on. Clinicians who utilize this technique will ask clients to rate their SUD levels at the onset of therapy and then ask them to reassess those levels as therapy progresses to evaluate the effects of treatment. The treatment plan can incorporate goals and objectives based on a client's SUD levels. For example, the treatment plan might state:

> Anxiety level when leaving the house. Current SUD: 90. Goal: 30. Four-week objective: 70.

Figure 8.5 illustrates a client's SUD using a graph.

VARYING BELIEFS AND PROCEDURES

Some therapeutic schools of thought claim that incorporating measurable outcomes contradicts their basic tenet of therapy. This statement might be true if measurable outcomes focused on symptoms rather than impairments. For example, many insight-oriented clinicians do not view therapeutic progress in terms of reducing symptoms. They believe that "symptom substitution" will occur; that is, new symptoms emerge as others decline. They do not focus on symptoms because they believe that the underlying

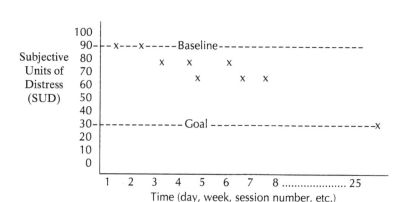

Figure 8.5 Graphic Representation of Subjective Units of Distress
Source: Reprinted with permission of John Wiley & Sons, Inc.

causes of the symptoms should be the focus of therapy. Therefore, a systematic measurement of symptoms becomes moot. Thus, advocates from a number of treatment modalities ask, "If we must validate a diagnosis with symptoms but do not believe that outcomes should be measured based on symptom changes, what else is there to measure?" To answer this question, it is necessary to point out that at least three processes take place in mental health treatment, regardless of the clinician's therapeutic orientation: (1) assessment, (2) treatment, and (3) discharge. Each part of treatment avails itself to different types of documentation.

ASSESSMENT

The assessment phase involves determining whether the client needs mental health services. That is, the clinician ascertains by various means the degree to which problem areas exist. A major point of the assessment is to validate the diagnosis of a disorder via symptoms and resulting impairments. No matter what theoretical orientation the therapist supports, certain criteria within the theoretical model are used to determine whether a client would benefit from mental health services. The same measures used to determine whether services are needed also can be used to determine when services are no longer necessary.

TREATMENT

The specific procedures in the treatment phase vary depending on which mode of therapy is used. The clinician documents changes in impairments throughout the course of therapy. Whether the clinician's type of treatment intends to modify behaviors, clarify cognitions, increase insight, or focus on the future is not important in documenting behavioral change. What matters is documenting that the treatment employed is alleviating the impairments that made treatment necessary.

Analogously, there are several means of traveling across the country, including, but not limited to airplane, bus, automobile, motorcycle, bicycle, and walking. Although each mode of transportation is quite different, requiring different preparations, experiences, and time allotments, each eventually will get the person across the county. The various providers of transportation may disagree as to what mode is the best, but what matters is whether the person makes it across the country. Each transportation provider describes how the trip is made through its mode of transportation. Likewise, even though the mental health schools of thought might vary significantly in the preparations, experiences, and time allotments, they each intend to obtain the client's original intention: reach the goal.

DISCHARGE

If treatment goes a full course, it lasts until the client is able to function adequately in those areas that were previously impaired. Documentation is provided by regularly evaluating progress toward the goals of the treatment plan.

VALIDATING CHANGE

Validating changes in impairments is a simple documentation task compared to quantifying symptoms. Different therapeutic schools of thought approach the process of charting a client's impairments in the same way; it is simply part of documenting a client's presenting problem and goals. During therapy, changes in these impairments can be achieved and measured by the objectives listed in the treatment plan. For example, the vague objective to "increase social interactions" could be revised to "initiate an average of 2 new social interactions per week by August 10." When the client accomplishes this objective, it could be revised again to "initiate 3 social interactions per week by October 15." Thus, the objective remains concrete and targeted, and the effectiveness of treatment is easily measured. How these objectives are achieved is not important from a documentation standpoint. For example, some therapists might use session time to teach clients to be more socially outgoing whereas others might focus on client thought patterns, such as negative thoughts in social situations. Still others may explore how a client's early life experiences influence his or her ability to interact with others. The treatment plan simply provides examples of behaviors for which changes will be documented to validate therapeutic progress.

A major point of documentation is to provide evidence of the effectiveness of treatment. Clinicians should be careful to select objectives that are consistent with their treatment methods. The probability of success is increased when the client is instrumental in formulating objectives.

Precautions must be taken against overmeasuring goals and objectives. Not all behaviors are measurable in clearly quantifiable terms; however, it is advisable to do so whenever possible. For example, it is difficult to quantify behaviors such as level of insight, respect for authority, level of self-esteem, mental confusion, and ability to concentrate.

INSIGHT-ORIENTED THERAPY AND TREATMENT PLANNING

Perhaps the most resistance to incorporating observable and measurable outcomes in treatment plans comes from therapists who conduct insight-oriented therapy. The issue arises not due to problems with the treatment but rather due to theoretical conflicts. Documenting the level of insight is not subject to clear quantification, and the concept of symptom reduction might not fit into the theoretical frame of reference. These clinicians find the medical model of reference incompatible with treating intrapsychic conflicts. Nevertheless, Gabbard (2005) notes that treatment plans are an integral part of the mental health service system, just as psychodynamic theory is a major part of psychiatry; therefore, the two must be integrated.

Allen, Buskirk, and Sebastian (1992) discuss and provide examples of treatment plans developed at the Menninger Clinic, in which therapists provide traditional psychodynamic treatment but document client progress in behavioral terms. Figure 8.6 depicts typical psychodynamic target areas that can be documented in the listed behavioral terms. Eight problem domains of focus are shown in Figure 8.7.

Self-concept and identity
    Low self-esteem/self-confidence
    Unclear/unstable identity/sense of self
    Uncertain masculine/feminine identity
    Self-concept and identity disrupted by dissociation

Interpersonal relationships
    Excessive interpersonal isolation
    Unstable relationships

Figure 8.6 Psychodynamic Target Areas in Treatment Plan Writing
Source: J. G. Allen, J. R. Buskirk, and L. M. Sebastian (1992).

Hypersensitivity to rejection and perceived abandonment
Inability to function autonomously
Excessive dependency
Continual perception of victimization/abuse/exploitation
Extreme distrust of others
Extreme hostility in interactions with others
Oppositionalism/indirect opposition to demands
Dishonest behavior
Extreme self-centeredness/arrogance
Hypersensitivity to criticism
Deficient social skills

Thinking and cognition
Impaired contact with reality
Disorganized thinking
Failure of accommodation to cognitive deficits
Flashbacks with confusion of past and present

Emotional functioning
Depressed mood
Suicidal intentions/preoccupation
Mood-related withdrawal from people/activities
Hyperactivity/euphoria
Tension/fearfulness/panic
Excessive and unrealistic guilt feelings
Mood swings

Impulse regulation/addiction
Impulsivity
Substance abuse (specify)
Self-injurious behavior
Violence
Flight/elopement
Inhibition/overcontrol

Adaptive skills
Impairment in activities of daily living
Impairment in academic/vocational skills
Poor medication compliance

Family
Lack of age-appropriate autonomy
Alienation from family
Marital difficulties
Parenting problems
Poor family alliance with treatment team

Other (including medical)

Figure 8.6   Continued

Example #1

Problem focus

Severe dissociation and discontinuity in identity associated with profoundly impaired interpersonal and vocational functioning. Manifested by amnesia, loss of job, propensity to be exploited by others, and inability to take care of basic needs.

Long-range goal

Patient will establish and maintain continuous self-awareness and develop a coherent sense of self.

Short-term goals (objectives)

1. Patient will report discontinuities in experience (amnesia) to self.
2. Patient will make a list of alter personalities and describe each.
3. Patient will initiate communication among alter selves.
4. Patient will identify alter personalities for staff.
5. Patient will keep a journal to record experience of alter personalities.
6. Patient will verbalize awareness of situations/feelings that trigger emergence of alter personalities.
7. Patient will take responsibility for actions.
8. Patient will verbalize understanding of the origins of his/her alter personalities/fugue states.

Example #2

Problem focus

Impaired contact with reality and extreme social isolation. Manifested by paranoid delusions, auditory hallucinations, inability to leave the house and to function at work, and deterioration of personal hygiene.

Long-range goal (a)

Patient's perception will be accurate.

Short-term goals (objectives)

1. Patient will take medication as prescribed and report effects.
2. Patient will plan and carry through a schedule of activities.
3. Patient will check out perceptions and assigned nursing/activity therapy staff.

Long-range goal (b)

Short-term goals (objectives)

1. Patient will compare beliefs with those of other patients.
2. Patient will discuss unrealistic beliefs and the psychological basis.

Figure 8.7   Example of Psychodynamic Treatment Plan

Source: J. G. Allen, J. R. Buskirk, and L. M. Sebastian (1992).

TYPES OF MEASUREMENT

Four traditional types of data can be measured: nominal, ordinal, interval, and ratio. A seldom-noted type of data, ordinal-metric (Wiger & Solberg, 2001), also may be helpful in documentation. Behavioral objectives can incorporate nominal, ordinal, ordinal-metric, or interval data. Ratio data are not used as they require an absolute zero, which is not a behavioral concept; interval is the highest measure available in behavioral data. Nominal data in treatment objectives demonstrate whether a behavior takes place. Ordinal data suggest increases or decreases in behaviors but do not quantify the amount of behavioral change. Ordinal-metric data are a cross between ordinal and interval data. Interval data allow observers to determine the amount of behavioral change; thus, these data are more precise than ordinal data. Table 8.1 illustrates the various means by which objectives may be measured.

Table 8.1
Methods for Measuring Behavioral Objectives

Type of measurement	Definition of objective	Sample statement of objective	Use
Time frames (Nominal data)	Objectives are identified by time periods in which behaviors will be evidenced/decreased.	Client will remain sober for at least 30 days. Target date: July 9.	Easy to document by collaterals. Time is quantified, not the behavior.
Specific completion of assignments or tasks (Nominal data)	Documenting for med. evaluation, therapeutic contracts, homework, etc.	Client will visit psychiatrist by Dec. 12 for med. evaluation	Documents assignments given and additional services needed.
Specific outcomes (Nominal data)	Denoting whether or not behaviors have occurred.	Client will make no suicide attempts in next 60 days. Target date: February 12.	Generally objectives are rated by others. Used in day care or in residential settings.
Increase in frequency (Ordinal data)	Increases in positive behaviors	By May 8 the client will discuss in each group on average three incidents when he has not acted impulsively after getting his way.	Use when the goal is to increase frequency of behaviors.

Note: Material adapted in collaboration with Steve Friedman, MA.

continued

Table 8.1
Continued

Type of measurement	Definition of objective	Sample statement of objective	Use
Decrease in frequency (Ordinal data)	Decreases in negative target behaviors	The client will decrease suicidal threats to no more than 1/week by Dec. 12.	Use when the goal is to eliminate or decrease frequency of behaviors.
Baseline comparisons (Interval data)	Comparing levels of behaviors to a baseline measure	Client will increase positive statements to family. Current (baseline): 1/week Objective: 4/week by June 3.	Denoted in casenotes or graphs. Client easily visualizes progress as objectives are incrementally increased.

Treatment strategies incorporated in the treatment plan should reflect interventions that have been proven efficacious in the field. Clinicians should avoid including vague treatment strategies, such as no other indicators than "individual therapy," because they do not adequately describe what interventions are taking place. Information in the treatment plan about specific interventions should include:

1. Type of therapy (e.g., individual, group, or family)
2. School of thought (e.g., psychoanalytic, rational-emotive, or cognitive-behavioral)
3. Therapeutic techniques (e.g., role playing, dream interpretation, or positive regard)
4. Homework assignments
5. Any other interventions taking place inside or outside of the session

TREATMENT PLAN FORMATS

Treatment plan formats vary, but, at minimum, headings for symptoms, goals/objectives, and treatment strategies (or similar nomenclature) are suggested. Some therapists include a separate column to list a time frame for attaining each objective. Others incorporate the same time period (e.g., eight weeks, a particular date, or number of sessions) for the entire treatment plan rather than setting separate time frames for reducing impairments. Some treatment plans include a column that lists specific services and providers to comply with TJC standards. Master treatment plans, such as those used in multidisciplinary settings, note which provider in the facility (and his or her area of specialty) will provide specific services and how often the services will be performed. When only one therapist provides services, as in private practice, no such notation is needed.

This text adopts the treatment plan format outlined in *The Complete Adult Psychotherapy Treatment Planner* (Jongsma & Peterson, 2006). This format complies with most third-party standards in which problem areas, goal, objectives, interventions, and diagnosis are listed.

COMMON PROBLEMS IN TREATMENT PLAN WRITING

If a therapist regards a treatment plan as an unnecessary document that is filled out simply because it is required by a third party, it will be of little or no benefit to the client because of the therapist's attitude toward having to fill out a perceived useless document. Without proper training regarding the benefits of treatment plans, therapists are likely to resist investing much energy into their formulation. No matter whether writers have excellent or poor writing skills; they must be cognizant of the treatment plan's importance to do justice to its creation.

Treatment plan writing is subject to several potential problems. Documenting in a manner that complies with one or more regulatory agencies and third-party payer requirements and incorporating the requirements into a brief document requires creativity, writing skills, and knowledge of psychopathology and client-change agents.

Therapists who lack training in how to integrate diagnosis and treatment strategies produce poorly documented treatment plans. Problems begin when the clinical assessment is unclear. Vague assessment procedures contribute to vague treatment plans, which lead to unfocused treatment. Other factors, such as nonmeasurable objectives and undefined treatment strategies, also lead to treatment with uncertain outcomes.

Problems also arise when the treatment plan does not correspond with the *DSM-IV-TR* diagnosis. Although treatment plans are not written for a diagnosis (they are written for client's specific strengths, needs, abilities, and preferences), they should reflect the diagnosis and resulting impairments. That is, the treatment plan for a depressed client's should address alleviating symptoms and impairment indicative of depression, not simply addressing vague or global problem areas that do not necessarily represent mental health symptoms or impairments.

Not only should therapeutic interventions listed in the treatment plan be concordant with acceptable procedures in the mental health profession; they also should be of proven effectiveness for the specific problems being treated. Generic treatment for all clients and problem areas is insufficient.

The number of goals and objectives should be consistent with the level of care and number of sessions allowed. Setting too many goals may overwhelm the client, and there may not be enough time to address each goal adequately in the allotted number of sessions. In addition, focusing too much on outcome measures may lead to treating symptoms rather than treating the client. However, underfocusing on outcomes promotes lack of therapeutic direction.

A well-written treatment plan is assessable. A reviewer should be able to read a treatment plan, then look at subsequent progress notes and treatment updates, and have a good idea of its effectiveness. Some common problems with treatment plans include:

- Vagueness
- Not indicative of the assessment
- Not incorporating both strengths and weakness
- Not addressing functional impairments
- Not reflecting the diagnosis
- Unrealistic (over-/underambitious)
- Not assessable

TREATMENT PLAN WRITING

The content of the initial treatment plan is based on information obtained in the diagnostic interview, psychological testing, collateral reports, observations, and previous treatment records. The treatment plan summarizes and prioritizes this information. Jongsma and Peterson (2006) suggest that therapists follow seven steps in developing the treatment plan.

STEP 1: PROBLEM SELECTION

Problem selection involves deciding which problem areas will be the focus of therapy. Although several problems may exist, they should be prioritized so that services will help the client most effectively. Problem areas should be expressed in behavioral terms. Remember that the treatment plan should list only problems that most effectively validate the diagnosis and document specific examples of functional impairments secondary to the mental health disorder.

STEP 2: PROBLEM DEFINITION

The problems in step 1 should be defined according to the client's particular issues. Rather than resorting to generic definitions, problems should align with symptoms of a specific *DSM-IV-TR* or International Statistical Classification of Diseases and Related Health Problems, 10th Revision (ISCD-10) disorder and thereby correspond with a specific diagnosis. This specificity ensures that guidelines, such as TJC, are followed and that treatment is concordant with the diagnosis. Remember that problem areas should reflect areas of impairment in the client's life for which services are being sought. To ensure appropriate communication among mental health professionals, problems should be defined according to *DSM-IV-TR* terminology.

STEP 3: GOAL DEVELOPMENT

Goals are broad descriptions of the desired outcome for each problem area. They specify behavior changes that the client must attain to demonstrate that treatment is working. Therapeutic techniques or strategies are used to reach goals but do not represent attainment of those goals. For example, the statement "Read 2 books about codependence" is not a goal because it does not suggest a behavior change; rather, it is a treatment *strategy*.

STEP 4: OBJECTIVE CONSTRUCTION

Objectives are incremental steps to reaching goals. They must be observable and measurable to meet the requirements of third-party reviewers and fit a scientific-practitioner model. They directly correspond to the impairments (e.g., social, occupational, affective, physical) by which the diagnosis was validated. Generally, each goal should have at least two written objectives. Each objective should include a target date for attainment, at which time progress is evaluated and objectives are revised to meet the underlying goals more appropriately.

STEP 5: INTERVENTION CREATION

Interventions represent the treatment strategies conducted or guided by the therapist. Interventions should be empirically valid and not contraindicated or experimental. Each objective should have at least one intervention. Documentation of therapeutic interventions should include the type of therapy (e.g., individual, group, collateral, family), treatment modality (e.g., psychodynamic, cognitive-behavioral, humanistic), and specific interventions common to the school of thought (e.g., role playing, dream interpretation, or bibliotherapy).

STEP 6: DIAGNOSIS DETERMINATION

The symptoms included in the treatment plan must be concordant with a *DSM-IV-TR* diagnosis. Few, if any, insurance companies will reimburse treatment without an Axis I diagnosis. Note: This author suggests that the diagnosis be determined *prior* to writing the treatment plan; however, step 6 is included to ensure that the treatment plan targets the client's diagnosis.

Step 7: Saving Time in Writing Treatment Plans

Both CARF and TJC (accrediting agencies) recommend that the client take an active part in establishing treatment plan goals and objectives. Some clinicians take time between sessions to write their treatment plans without consulting clients. A potential problem with this method is that it may leave out the client's SNAPs and could ignore important client needs.

Typically the first session with the client is reserved for the diagnostic interview or assessment. The second session is dedicated to writing the treatment plan, in which the clinician and the client review the assessment material from the first session and cooperatively write the treatment plan together. This method increases client involvement in the treatment process and saves time. The session is usually quite therapeutic, providing clear client understanding of the direction for therapy and a better understanding for the therapist of the client's goals for treatment. The amount of time spent with the client in writing the treatment plan is affected by the client's level of motivation, insight, and cognitive functioning. It is advisable to spend less time and effort writing treatment plans in sessions with clients with severe cognitive deficits, active psychotic concerns, or low motivation to be in treatment. In such cases, clients typically need more direction from the therapist.

An example of a dialogue between the therapist and a client in collaborating in treatment plan writing is presented next.

Therapist (T): In our initial meeting last week, you mentioned a number of areas of change you would like to see in your life. Today we are going to work on writing your treatment plan so we can plan what we will work on in therapy.

Client (C): In the past I never had to help write the treatment plan. I just signed it and never saw it again. Can you just write one for me and start counseling?

T: That would be easy, but a treatment plan is designed to reflect what you want to accomplish in therapy. If we discuss your goals for therapy together, we are more likely to stay on target by treating specific problem areas that brought you to therapy. If not, it is very easy to go off in tangents in which therapy might take much longer than what is needed.

C: I see. It makes sense. So where do we start?

T: Well, we can first work on issues that are either most important, most stressful, or even lesser severe items if you want to ease yourself into the process of therapy.

C: What do you think I should do?

T: I can certainly help you with that decision, but I think it would mean more to you if we first looked at your ideas.

C: Okay. How about my panic attacks when I go outside. I'd like to learn to control them . . . and even have them eventually go away. Can we start there?

T: Sounds good. In the treatment plan we have areas called goals and objectives. Goals are the overall outcomes or results of therapy that you desire. Objectives are step-by-step means of reaching these goals. (Therapist takes out a treatment plan form.) Here we have three columns, "Problem," "Goals/Objectives," and "Treatment Strategies." You mentioned that one of your problems is having panic attacks. Let's start there by writing "Panic Attacks" in Column 1: Problems.

C: You're right, panic attacks are a problem. (Therapist writes "Panic Attacks" in the first column.) So what do we put in the column marked "Goals/Objectives"?

T: Actually you already answered part of the question. You said that you want to alleviate the panic attacks. Let's make that Goal 1. (Therapist writes "Goal 1: Alleviate Panic Attacks in Column 2.)

C: So what about the objectives?

T: Good question. Let's look at our notes from last week. You said that panic attacks typically last about 30 minutes. Is that correct?

C: Yes, more or less, but 30 minutes is about average.

T: Objectives are specific behavioral improvements that you are trying to accomplish in a given time period. The goals are accomplished by gradually meeting various objectives that are increased each time they are reached. The final objective is to reach the goal. How would you like to set some objectives to be accomplished in the next four weeks? That doesn't mean that we'll be finished in four weeks, but it gives us more direction and it brings us closer to the goal.

C: That sounds good. So what can we do in the next four weeks with my panic attacks?

T: Currently your panic attacks last for about 30 minutes. How about trying to cut down the time to less than 15 minutes by our session on September 30? Does this seem reasonable to you?

C: Yes, it does. But what happens if I don't reach the objective or if I do much better?

T: Objectives are just estimates of what we believe can reasonably be accomplished. They can be revised periodically based on your progress.

C: It's good that there is room for not following the plan exactly.

T: How does this sound to you for Goal 1, Objective 1a: "Decrease duration of panic attacks from an average of 30 minutes to no more than 15 minutes, by September 30." (Therapist writes this as the first objective under Goal 1.)

C: Yes, I would like that. It seems reachable, not too simple, not too difficult . . . I hope!"

T: Usually there are about three objectives for every goal. We do this to try to work on the problem by more than one means. You mentioned that panic attacks take place about three times per day. Perhaps we could have an objective to decrease the number of panic attacks per day.

C: Okay. How about going from three panic attacks per day to no more than one per day?

T: All right. Under the first goal we'll write Objective 1b as "Decrease frequency of panic attacks from an average of 3/day to no more than 1/day by September 30." (Therapist writes the objective under the second objective.)

C: What about a third objective?

T: It would be good to learn different means of relaxation when you feel panic symptoms emerging. How does that sound to you?

C: Could we make that Objective 1c?

T: Yes, that would be fine. There are five relaxation techniques that I teach in therapy. It would be too much to teach them in one or two sessions. It is better to learn, practice, and master them one at a time to be most effective. I believe that it would be reasonable to learn two of them by September 30. How does that sound to you?

C: I'm willing to learn and practice them if it helps.

T: We'll write Objective 1c as "Learn and implement 2 relaxation techniques to help prevent panic symptoms by September 30. (Therapist writes the objective under Objective 1c.)

C: What will we do to reach these goals and objectives?

T: The third column of the treatment plan is labeled "Treatment Strategies." It describes what we will be doing in therapy to attain the goals and objectives. This represents what we will do in and out of the counseling sessions.

C: What else is in the treatment plan?

T: We will now set up goals and objectives.

At this point, the treatment plan, paraphrased from the preceding dialogue, looks like this:

Problem	Goals/Objectives	Treatment Strategies
1. Panic attacks occurring on an average of 3x/week for 30 minutes	Goal 1. Alleviate panic attacks Obj 1a. Decrease duration to < 15 minutes by Sep 30 Obj 1b. Decrease frequency to 0–1 per day by Sep 30 Obj 1c. Learn 2 relaxation methods by Sep 30	Cognitive therapy Teach relaxation Med referral Homework Bibliotherapy

REVISED TREATMENT PLANS

Treatment plans are not static documents. As treatment progresses, the objectives, treatment strategies, and circumstances change; thus, the treatment plan must reflect these modifications. There are three ways to revise a treatment plan: treatment plan revisions, revised treatment plans, and treatment plan updates. A revised treatment plan can be as simple as written notations in the progress notes, to writing a new treatment plan separately.

Treatment plan revisions are used to describe any changes that have taken place since the original treatment plan or previous update was written. The updates typically are written in the progress notes and might be listed in a treatment plan update form, if one is used. For example, using the previous treatment plan example, an update could be as simple as "Revise Objective 1a to decrease duration of panic attacks to < 8 minutes." If the goal for a problem area has been met, it could be written as "Goal 1, "Alleviate panic attacks met." Or, if additional problem areas and goals are set, they would be added to the treatment plan.

Revised treatment plans reflect current progress. They generally include a brief narrative of progress to date. Objectives that have been met are revised to more closely reflect goals. Those that have not been met are reviewed to determine whether other interventions could be more helpful. New objectives also may be introduced into the treatment plan at this point. A revised treatment plan, then, is similar to the original treatment plan, but it reflects the client's current state of functioning. Most of the information in a revised treatment plan is taken from the periodic treatment plan revisions. It is common to revise treatment plans every 60 to 90 days. As with initial treatment plans, revised treatment plans are formulated collaboratively by the client and the therapist.

Treatment plan updates are similar or identical to a preauthorization for additional services report. Overall, an update is a summary of how treatment plan objectives have been met to date, providing evidence of the effectiveness of the therapeutic interventions.

A properly documented treatment plan provides a solid foundation for documenting the course of therapy. Once the treatment plan has been developed, the next step is to put the plan into action. To keep therapy time efficient and on track and to qualify for reimbursement, clinicians must document that the plan is being followed and that progress is being made. Progress notes serve this purpose. Progress notes are the only documentation that shows third-party reviewers the degree to which treatment is effective. Chapter 9 demonstrates how to write effective progress notes that are concordant with the treatment plan.

HIGHLIGHTS OF CHAPTER 8

- Although a relatively new procedure, the treatment plan is the most frequently consulted treatment document.
- There is a major difference between planning treatment and writing a treatment plan.
- Because a diagnosis is based on the *DSM-IV-TR*, the treatment plan also validates *DSM-IV-TR* principles.
- Treatment plans are designed to provide observable and measurable treatment outcome measures that demonstrate alleviation of functional impairments.
- Both the client and the therapist take an active part in treatment plan formulation.
- Treatment plans are highly individualized and incorporate several client and therapist variables, situational concerns, and third-party regulations.
- The client ultimately sets goals and objectives.
- Goals reflect overall outcomes in therapy whereas objectives are incremental, objective, and measurable steps by which goals are attained.
- Objectives are revised periodically as treatment progresses toward goals.
- There are several ways to measure objectives, which allows for variations in techniques and schools of thought.

QUESTIONS

1. Which of the following best represents a treatment plan *objective*?
   a. Eliminate depression.
   b. Return to work at least 30 hours per week.
   c. Initiate cognitive therapy.
   d. Prozac, 40 mg.
2. Which of the following best represents a treatment plan *goal*?
   a. Return to work full time.
   b. Begin psychoanalysis.
   c. Visit physician for evaluation.
   d. Enter group therapy for 12 weeks.
3. Which of the following provides the best example of a measurable behavioral *objective*?
   a. Continue therapy.
   b. Increase sense of well-being.
   c. Discuss previous treatment.
   d. Spend at least three hours per week outdoors.

4. What is wrong with this treatment plan objective? Objective: Increase euthymic mood.
   a. It is too vague.
   b. It is difficult to measure.
   c. Both of these.
   d. Nothing; it is a good objective.
5. The treatment plan is designed primarily to be based on
   a. specific client needs.
   b. the diagnosis.
   c. the therapist's specialty.
   d. the therapist's theoretical school of thought.
6. Treatment plan revisions typically are written in
   a. the form of a new treatment plan.
   b. homework assignments by the client.
   c. the initial diagnostic interview and accomplished gradually throughout treatment.
   d. the progress notes, then incorporated into the revised treatment plan.

   Answers: 1b, 2a, 3d, 4c, 5a, 6d

CHAPTER 9

Writing Progress Notes

PROGRESS NOTES VERSUS PSYCHOTHERAPY NOTES

Before discussing progress notes, we must make a distinction between progress notes and psychotherapy notes. This distinction has come about due to guidelines from the Health Insurance Portability and Accountability Act of 1996 (HIPAA) in which psychotherapy notes are not considered information to be released to the client or to others.

Psychotherapy notes are kept separate from the client's record and are not intended for release to anyone. They are used for the benefit of the therapist to keep track of important information not included in the progress notes.

HIPAA 45 CFR 164.501

The term "psychotherapy notes" refers to notes recorded (in any medium) by a healthcare professional documenting or analyzing the contents of conversation during a private counseling session or a group, joint, or family counseling session that are separated from the rest of the individual's medical record. Psychotherapy notes do not include medication prescription and monitoring, counseling session start and stop times, the modalities and frequencies of treatment furnished, results of clinical tests, and any summary of these items: diagnosis, functional status, the treatment plan, symptoms, prognosis, and progress to date.

This chapter focuses on standard formats for progress notes, not psychotherapy notes. Psychotherapy notes, by definition, are not designed to be documentary evidence. Progress notes provide evidence not only that a session took place but also of the effects of treatment. They are the record for documenting the session's length, type, content, interventions, and therapeutic progress. Because progress notes are the primary source for documenting what happens in therapy and the level of progress being made, they are a primary document reviewed by auditors. Clinicians must be certain, therefore, that progress notes do not simply imply session content but rather fully document it.

From the progress notes, a reader should be able to ascertain the client's diagnosis, current issues, and effects of therapy. Progress notes correspond with the client's presenting problems and the diagnosis. These notes also document a client's functional impairments that have led to the medical necessity for services, plus the course of treatment toward alleviating those impairments. For example, if a client is diagnosed with depression, the progress notes should primarily reflect treatment for depression and not other areas (unless they, too, have been included in the treatment plan). That is, areas treated must be in the treatment plan.

Progress notes have gained increasing importance over the years. Older methods merely documented that a session was held and informed the reader to some degree of what happened in the session. Today, progress notes are an essential documentation tool. Third-party criteria for progress notes have become progressively more stringent in terms of accountability because traditionally there has been little documented evidence of the effects of therapy. Requirements for demonstrating outcomes in mental health treatment are increasing (Wiger & Solberg, 2001).

Third-party requirements, whether they are from regulatory agencies or third-party payers, demand behavioral evidence to demonstrate accountability for services. For financial reasons, third-party payers cannot provide unlimited mental health benefits. Regulatory agencies set high standards to raise the level of accountability and professionalism in the mental health field. Therapists must clearly document that the treatment plan is being followed and that services are being directed toward the active symptoms of the diagnosis, what progress is being made, and how goals and objectives are being addressed.

WHY WRITE PROGRESS NOTES?

In addition to third-party requirements regarding the use of progress notes, there are other benefits to writing progress notes as well. Progress notes establish the therapist's accountability to the client. Keeping therapy on track and steadily noting progress by following the treatment plan assures cost effectiveness in treatment. Progress notes are designed to provide evidence that the services being conducted are efficacious.

Should there be payment for sessions that are off target and do not address the client's mental health impairments? Insurance auditors would say no.

Their reasoning is likened to this question: Should mechanics be paid for charging you for an hour's labor when they did not work on what you have agreed to fix or just sat around socializing during the hour? Socializing with a client is not psychotherapy. Building rapport is much more than "socializing." It is not simply getting the client to talk with you and is not to be the focus of several sessions. Rapport is built up as therapy takes place. Psychotherapy is professionally focused treatment on the client's mental health impairments. From an auditor's viewpoint, any progress notes that do not provide evidence of such treatment are questionable.

It is unlikely that, over any length of time, therapists can remember the specific points and interventions in every session. When reviewing a client's chart (i.e., intake notes, previous records, treatment plan, psychotherapy notes, progress notes, and updates) prior to a session, therapists can refresh their memories as to the client's ongoing concerns, treatments employed, homework assignments, and progress toward treatment plan goals. A therapist who does not remember the content of previous sessions is likely to be viewed in a different light by a client from a therapist who is up to date with the treatment provided thus far.

Well-kept progress notes may help protect the therapist from litigious or ethical problems that might arise without adequate documentation. For example, in the beginning of this writer's career as a psychologist, a client attempted suicide the day after an intake session. The client's family contacted me immediately, asking how I did not discover this potential problem during the intake interview. My notes indicated that I posed a number of questions regarding suicide, but the client denied that there were such concerns. The suicidal attempt was a reaction to a crisis that had taken place the day after the evaluation. Although suicide is extremely difficult to predict (Hillard, 1985; Maltsberger, 1988; Wiger & Harowski, 2003), therapists must document observations and client statements regarding such issues carefully.

Progress notes are also helpful when a client is transferred to another therapist. Clear progress notes alert the new therapist to specific issues that have been addressed and the types of interventions that work best for the client. Without sufficient records of treatment, the client basically would have to start over when changing therapists, leading to unnecessary, wasted time at the client's expense. Transitioning from one therapist to another is enough of an ordeal for a client; it should not be exacerbated by poor communication between the therapists involved.

Progress notes also establish baseline behaviors to help evaluate progress and setbacks. A review of the data documented in the progress notes is perhaps one of the best means of evaluating treatment outcomes. Notations such as compliance, attendance, insight, alleviation of impairments, cyclical behaviors, and much more provide helpful information to best serve the client.

HIPAA regulations have changed the availability of progress notes to someone requesting a client's health records. Historically, when a client's medical information was requested, it was common to copy the entire file. HIPAA requires that the *minimum* necessary information be sent to someone requesting medical records. In addition, progress notes are to be kept separate from the client's main file. Progress notes may be sent when asked for specifically, with the client's (or designated representative's) permission.

WHAT CONSTITUTES A GOOD PROGRESS NOTE?

Although not every progress note, from every session, covers each of these topics, overall they should address these ten questions:

1. What content or topics were discussed in the session?
2. How did the session address treatment plan objectives?
3. What therapeutic interventions and techniques were employed, and how effective were they?
4. What clinical observations (behavioral, affective, etc.) were made?
5. What progress or setbacks occurred?
6. What signs and symptoms of the diagnosis are present, increasing, decreasing, or no longer present?
7. How are treatment plan goals and objectives being met at this time?
8. What is the current medical necessity for services?
9. What is being done outside the session to increase effectiveness of therapy?
10. What are the client's current limitations and strengths?

Answering these questions documents that appropriate treatment is being provided. A pattern of documentation should be established so that each question is addressed adequately over the course of therapy. Let us consider each question individually.

What Content or Topics Were Discussed in the Session?

Historically, progress notes have provided a summary of what took place in the session. Although this information is important, it does not always document medical necessity. Statements should be objective and factual, including information regarding current, ongoing, or historical events in the client's life. In addition, validation of the diagnosis and evidence that the treatment plan is being followed are important aspects of progress notes. Documenting session content is necessary but not sufficient if nothing else is written in the progress notes.

Content-wise, progress notes should include the main topics discussed in the session. If more than one topic is discussed, each topic should be listed in the order in which it was addressed. Topic areas should coincide with the areas of strength and weakness addressed in the treatment plan. If topic areas do not seem to relate to the primary purpose of treatment, the purpose and medical necessity for covering the topic should be documented. If these areas are continued to additional sessions, they should be added to treatment plan revisions.

Examples of content-oriented progress note statements include:

- Discussed ways in which family of origin influences current behaviors.
- Session focused on the 4 times client has been in the hospital for suicidal gestures.
- Client asked for help exploring problems coping with rejection.

How Did the Session Address Treatment Plan Objectives?

As noted, one of the main functions of progress notes is to document that treatment plan goals and objectives are being addressed. Progress notes should specify which treatment plan objectives are being treated and how they are progressing.

If, for example, a treatment plan addresses the client's depressed mood in each problem area, goal, and objective, but progress notes document that communication skills in the client's marriage are the focus of treatment, treatment plan goals and objectives are not being addressed or met. To avoid this situation, it is helpful to assign a number or letter to each treatment goal and objective and to list in the progress notes which ones are being treated each session. It is common to denote the goal as a number and the related objectives as alphabetical characters after the number. For example:

Goal 1: Increase self-esteem.
Objective 1a: Initiate at least 2 positive behaviors per week.
Objective 1b: Employ at least 3 assertive behaviors per week.

In this case, the progress note statement could read: "Worked on Objective 1b by role playing various assertive behaviors." Additional statements could indicate specific issues and interventions being employed to address treatment objectives.

WHAT THERAPEUTIC INTERVENTIONS AND TECHNIQUES WERE EMPLOYED, AND HOW EFFECTIVE WERE THEY?

Progress notes include descriptions of the specific therapeutic interventions taking place during the session. Some treatment strategies are more effective than others, depending on the diagnosis and client variables. In addition, some treatment strategies are experimental, and others have been demonstrated to be nonefficacious in certain therapeutic situations. It is not unusual for a third-party insurance or managed care contract to state specifically that the policy does not cover experimental therapeutic procedures.

The treatment plan lists which therapeutic school of thought and procedures will be employed in the treatment. Progress notes verify that the procedures are being used and demonstrate the outcomes of implementing the procedures. Such documentation helps the clinician evaluate the effectiveness of treatment and decide whether changes to the treatment plan should be made.

Documenting specific treatment interventions also helps the therapist keep the session on track and therapeutic. Without such documentation, sessions could deteriorate to chitchat or discussions irrelevant to treatment. Examples include:

> Utilized empty chair technique to help client with closure from divorce. Client wept though the entire procedure, later stating that he felt better because he had been holding in too many feelings.

> Client states that she does not want to practice relaxation techniques in the sessions anymore because they make her more upset.

WHAT CLINICAL OBSERVATONS (BEHAVIORAL, AFFECTIVE, ETC.) WERE MADE?

The therapist's clinical observations are crucial in evaluating the course of therapy and in assessing the client's current condition. Notations should include clinically significant observations of verbal and nonverbal behaviors. Observations should be integrated with the client's presenting problem and diagnostic concerns. For example, if a client is diagnosed with depression, progress notes should regularly assess the client's level of depression. It is expected that the client would appear less depressed as therapy progresses. Unless progress notes document these observations, there is no way to assess the efficacy of treatment.

Examples of clinical observations include:

> The client appeared depressed as evidenced by slumped posture, crying often, and a blunted affect.

The client appeared anxious as evidenced by speaking more rapidly than usual, hyperventilating, sweating, and getting out of the chair four times.

The child continues to demonstrate defiant behaviors as evidenced by yelling at her mother three times during the session, telling this therapist to "stuff it," and refusing to answer questions over 50% of the time.

Each of these progress note statements documents observations that validate the diagnosis and treatment plan. Without statements of this nature, a third-party auditor or insurance case manager may not find sufficient evidence to warrant payment for additional services. In some legal and ethics cases, treatment has been rendered to a client but the progress notes did not clearly document that a disorder existed or was properly treated. Results have led to licensure issues, malpractice, or other disciplinary measures. Concise documentation helps solve all of these issues.

What Progress or Setbacks Occurred?

Because behavioral health insurers routinely rely on a scientific model to substantiate treatment and because a significant number of clients utilize such insurance to pay for treatment, therapists must use the scientific model to document a client's impairments and the medical necessity for treatment. In this model, treatment that does not alleviate or reduce impairments is not considered helpful and should be discontinued or modified.

Consider a person with a broken leg who visited the doctor at regular intervals for treatment. It would be expected that the patient's medical charts would document the specific medical procedures and service, plus the timely improvements in the patient's condition. If the broken bone began to deteriorate, we would expect it to be clearly documented to help determine necessary changes in the treatment. When the patient returns to normal functioning and the leg is healed, the appointments would end. The physician would not continue treating the leg after recovery took place. What is there to treat besides the physician's income? Mental health services documentation follows a similar logic.

Except for possible booster or checkup sessions, when clients are no longer impaired mentally, therapy is discontinued. Third-party payers generally will stop reimbursing treatment that does not document alleviation of impairments after a number of sessions or after various interventions have been attempted without positive results. There are a number of reasons why clients might not improve or might even decompensate in therapy. In such cases, the therapist should document each attempt to revise the client's treatment (e.g., new strategies, increased number of sessions, additional services, change in environment, medications, change therapists, other referrals). When no progress takes place despite the increased efforts, decisions must be made regarding future treatment. At some point, though, the possibility of discontinued payment could become a concern.

Conversely, it is also possible for a client to progress in leaps and bounds due to excellent treatment and high client motivation to change but have difficulties in an audit because of poorly written progress notes. In such cases, the therapist is advised to seek supervision in documentation procedures because both the client and the therapist suffer. Too many promising therapists have become discouraged or left the field due to factors other than their counseling ability. These "other factors" can be learned.

Clinical setbacks do not necessarily indicate that treatment is of poor quality. Setbacks might occur because additional stressors develop during the course of therapy, treatment strategies are not the best fit for the client, the client-therapist match is not optimum, the client is noncompliant, or a number of other reasons. Documenting setbacks is important because setbacks raise red flags indicating that changes are likely needed. Good documentation explains how clinical setbacks were handled and how subsequent changes affected the client's condition.

Clear documentation of progress and setbacks makes it easier for the clinician to consult with other professionals about the case. Examples of progress note statements of progress and setbacks include:

> Progress is evidenced by client's initiating discussions in session, displaying a normal affect, and no longer crying during session when discussing losing his job.

> The client states that she has been more depressed and frustrated in the past 3 weeks because her family is protesting her attempts to be more assertive.

> The child's mother states that target behaviors in school (hitting teacher, stealing, and destroying property) have escalated to the point of being suspended from school.

What Signs and Symptoms of the Diagnosis Are Present, Increasing, Decreasing, or No Longer Present?

The medical model requires documenting the presence or absence of symptoms and impairments reflective of the need for services. Just as a diagnosis is validated by the presence of symptoms and impairments, progress is assessed by alleviation of symptoms and impairments. In effect, the initial diagnostic interview identifies symptoms and impairments, and treatment attempts to resolve or alleviate them. Most psychotherapies do not actively or specifically focus on symptoms alone as part of the therapeutic process. Symptoms and impairment reduction is a documentation procedure, not necessarily a therapeutic technique.

There is a notable difference between a medical model of therapy and a medical model of documentation. A medical model of documentation can be used for any type of therapy, whether the treatment focuses on symptoms, insight, the relationship, cognitions, behavior, or anything else. No matter what theoretical model is practiced, the client will have some sort of measure of the level of therapeutic progress. For example, if a client who previously experienced an average of three panic attacks per day prior to therapy now reports having one or none per day, symptoms have been reduced. The client's primary concern is not the type of treatment used; what is important is the decrease in panic attacks. Thus, although the medical model is used to document the effects of therapy, it is not needed to determine the process or method used in treatment.

Clients have a reason for coming to therapy. Generally, something in their lives is not going well. Issues might be related to emotional, social, occupational, or other aspects of their lives. The reason a client comes to therapy is called the *presenting problem*. If clients are able to detect that they need services due to subjective levels of symptoms and impairments, they also will know when they are getting better. Effective progress notes document these changes in client symptoms and impairments. For example:

> The client claims to be symptom-free of binging and purging for the past 2 months.

> Since the onset of therapy, the client claims to feel increasingly more irritable most of the time.

> The client states that she is no longer depressed most of the time. Previously she endorsed feeling depressed at least 6 days per week. Currently she states that she feels depressed no more than 1–2 days per week.

How Are Treatment Plan Goals and Objectives Being Met at This Time?

Progress notes regularly evaluate the effectiveness of therapy. Measurable and observable treatment plan objectives provide the best evidence of therapeutic effectiveness. Progress note statements may be evaluative or summative, or they may provide current information about the client's progress. Statements of this nature are helpful in making treatment plan revisions. For example:

> Four out of 5 treatment goals have been met to date. Client states he is feeling much better and is considering discharge in the next 2 weeks.

Objective 2b, "attend work at least 3 days per week," is met and being revised to "attend work at least 4 days per week."

Little progress has been made in the past 2 months of treatment, due to noncompliance.

Considerable setbacks are noted in Objective 3b in which the homework assignments appear to be too stressful for client. Client appears to be more anxious socially since given the assignment of greeting 3 neighbors per day. The treatment strategies for this objective will be changed to bibliotherapy and role playing at this time.

WHAT IS THE CURRENT MEDICAL NECESSITY FOR SERVICES?

Most insurers require evidence of medical necessity in order to reimburse mental health services. Thus, progress notes should document the medical necessity of services needed by recording the client's functional impairments caused by the mental illness.

According to a medical model, when a client is no longer functionally impaired, services are no longer necessary. Documentation of functional behaviors thus helps the therapist and the client to decide when treatment can be terminated. When treatment plan goals, objectives, and discharge criteria are written clearly and understood by both the client and the therapist, vagueness about termination decreases.

Some therapy, however, is not considered medically necessary by third-party payers, including counseling solely for personal growth, psychoeducational treatment, treatment for non-Axis I disorders, relationship therapy, and other types of therapy in which the client is not significantly impaired by a mental disorder. Although clinicians need not necessarily steer clear from those types of therapy, they may have to tell patients that they may have to pay the bill themselves. Unfortunately, some third-party payers forbid their contracted therapists from charging for mental health services that are not medically necessary. Some examples of documenting continued medical necessity include:

The client has experienced an average of 5 panic attacks daily, lasting 20–30 minutes, leading to going home from work early most days or missing work most days.

Since the onset of medication and insight-oriented therapy, the client has been able to get out of bed at least 3 days per week but remains unable to go to classes.

Discussed termination of services due to significant progress in meeting therapeutic goals, which has led to a return to normal functioning socially and occupationally.

WHAT IS BEING DONE OUTSIDE THE SESSION TO INCREASE EFFECTIVENESS OF THERAPY?

Although most psychotherapy occurs at the clinician's office, progress is not measured solely in the context of isolated in-office sessions. The clinician can observe progress in session, but most indices of progress are statements reported by the client or collaterals about behaviors that occur outside the session. Thus, it is important to document these statements as well. Such documentation may include compliance and progress of homework assignments, behaviors generalized from the sessions, and interventions utilizing collaterals. For example:

> Client reports initiating 3 conversations at school party, as rehearsed in the previous session. He describes decreased anxiety resulting from rehearsal.

> Client's spouse reports enhanced marital satisfaction due to increased positive remarks made since onset of marital therapy.

> Compliance in homework assignments remains at over 80%.

WHAT ARE THE CLIENT'S CURRENT LIMITATIONS AND STRENGTHS?

Throughout the course of therapy, a client's limitations and strengths will change. Strengths will increase due to compliance with effective therapy. But as the effects of therapy impact the client's family and other environmental systems, certain stressors also will increase. Behavioral changes in one family member are most likely to disrupt the family system in one way or another.

Even the most dysfunctional client possesses strengths that can be incorporated into the treatment process. Client strengths should be assessed throughout the therapeutic process and incorporated into treatment even though weaknesses and impairments often seem to be the focus of therapy in a medical model. Documenting client strengths and stressors could include statements such as:

> The client continues utilizing social supports, such as family and friends, when feeling an urge to consume alcohol.

> The client is improving in reducing levels of anxiety by utilizing relaxation techniques employed in therapy.

> Although the client is learning new coping mechanisms, his family is refusing to trust him to be alone by himself. Much frustration is reported.

> The client describes feeling much better and more comfortable around others since volunteering at the youth center using his carpentry skills.

OTHER ITEMS PROGRESS NOTES SHOULD ADDRESS

In addition to the items already discussed, progress notes should include other important information, such as:

1. *Type of sessions being conducted (e.g., individual, family, group).* Progress notes should list specific types of therapy and therapeutic techniques and describe their effectiveness. Some auditors validate the type of therapy via progress notes. For example, if a therapist bills an insurance company for individual psychotherapy but progress notes document that the client is receiving marital counseling, reimbursement may be denied. (Few insurance companies pay for marital counseling.) Billing an insurance company for marital or couple's counseling as individual or family counseling is considered insurance fraud.

2. *Goals and objectives addressed in the session.* Third-party payers provide guidelines such as "Progress notes must reflect the objectives of the treatment plan." Some progress note forms allow space to list the treatment plan objectives being addressed in the session. Even if the form does not have space for this, clinicians should consider listing session objectives to keep sessions on target and provide evidence that the treatment plan objectives were followed.

3. *Time frame of the session: date, starting time, ending time, duration.* Each progress note should list the time frame of the session. This author recalls an audit in which the evaluator complained that noting the length of a session as "1 hour" was not sufficient, stating "How do I know the session lasted one hour unless you write down both the starting and ending times?"

4. *Signature and credentials of the therapist (initials only are insufficient).* After the session, the therapist should sign the progress note with his or her full signature, including professional credentials (degree and licensure), which denotes professional responsibility for the session. Just as a check cannot be cashed without a valid signature, initials are not sufficient for such an endorsement.

POORLY WRITTEN PROGRESS NOTES VERSUS WELL-WRITTEN PROGRESS NOTES

Figure 9.1 illustrates the difference between a poorly documented progress note and a properly documented one. The next dialogue between a client and his therapist provides background for the documentation:

CLIENT (C): I'm so upset about everything that has been happening to me.
THERAPIST (T): Tell me what you mean.

Poorly Written Progress Note

We talked about issues at home and on the job. Increased fears and marriage problems. Spouse is cheating on him. Not communicating well. Complaining about spouse, job, and police.

The progress note does not depict the medical necessity of services. Although the content might be accurate, it is unclear diagnostically, symptomatically, and therapeutically, and it does not depict current impairments. Even though significant impairments may exist, the evidence provided is so poor an auditor would most likely state that there is lack of justification to continue services. Statements such as "spouse is cheating on him" may or may not be accurate, so therefore should be written as a belief, quote, or not at all. None of the questions listed on page 148 were addressed.

Properly Documented Progress Note

Client appeared nervous, tense, and guarded, noting several current stressors. Was easily upset and agitated when discussing ongoing issues. Recently fired from job. Much blaming of others (ex-employer, spouse, police) of following him, spying on him, being unfaithful to him or trying to harm him. Often got up and looked out of the window for police. Confirms having a longstanding history of not trusting others.

Although progress note remarks are brief, they more clearly indicate current impairments, validate diagnostic criteria, and demonstrate the need for further services. The progress note briefly discussed a possible antecedent (recently fired from his job), resulting exacerbation of nontrusting behaviors (increased paranoia with ex-employer, spouse, and police), and impairments (distrust, checking behaviors, affective concerns).

Figure 9.1   Progress Note Statements

Source: Reprinted with permission of John Wiley & Sons, Inc.

C: Ever since I was fired from my job, everyone is out to get me.

T: Everyone?

C: Yes. My ex-boss at work won't pay for unemployment compensation. My wife thinks I'm a bum. The police are following me. My food tastes funny, if you know what I mean. My children don't want to play with me. Yes, everyone is out to get me.

T: How long have you believed that people are out to get you?

C: Well, I've never trusted anyone completely (speaking more rapidly), but I knew for sure a few months ago when my boss warned me that people at work were complaining about my so-called attitude, as she puts it. I told her what I thought about the situation, and they fired me. (In a much louder voice) I knew it would happen.

T: What about the police following you?

C: Oh, yes. Yesterday I noticed police driving by the house at least four times (carefully looks out the window). They were acting like they weren't looking for me, but I know their tactics. I'm sure they're bugging my phone. Have they talked to you about me?

T: And the food tasting funny?

C: My wife does all of the cooking. There's something different in the taste the past few months. I'm sure she's in on it too. Who knows who she's sleeping with now?

T: Now?

C: Yes, we've been married only one year. It's my second marriage. . . . I've always wondered why she doesn't answer the phone when I call her in the afternoon. Come on, let's get real (sarcastically). We all can add two plus two. I won't get near her or any of my so-called friends. Just leave me alone.

SCIENTIFIC METHOD

According to the scientific method, measurements are based on a baseline behavior, and subsequent measures determine a client's degree of change. Without a baseline measure, the level of change is difficult to assess. Baselines may be established in the diagnostic interview and throughout therapy, and progress note documentation can incorporate changes to the baselines. Two documentation methods utilizing the scientific model are commonly used: the comparative method and behavioral charts.

COMPARATIVE METHOD

In the comparative method, the clinician documents various baseline measures that depict current impairments. These measures may be documented in the intake notes, psychological report, treatment plan, or progress notes. A progress note might report: "Since the onset of Ritalin (15 mg × 2), the client's teacher reports the client being on task 80% of the time compared to 50% prior to treatment."

BEHAVIORAL CHARTS

With behavioral charts, the therapist, client, or collaterals chart progress throughout therapy. When therapists are writing progress notes, they refer back in writing to the chart. An excellent use of charting to document therapeutic progress incorporates treatment plan goals and objectives throughout therapy. Figure 9.2 illustrates how one picture is worth 1,000 words.

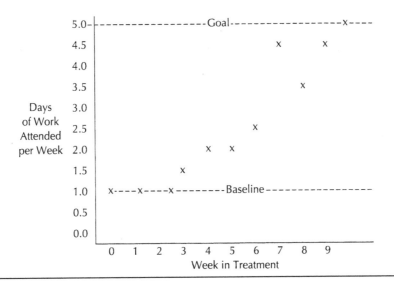

Figure 9.2 Charting Client Progress over Course of Therapy
Source: Reprinted with permission of John Wiley & Sons, Inc.

PROGRESS NOTE FORMATS

Clinicians use several formats or means of organizing progress notes. The specific format is not important as long as accurate documentation takes place. There is no universally approved progress note format. Typically, therapists within a particular clinic tend to use the same format for consistency.

The most popular formats are SOAP and DAP. SOAP (subjective, objective, assessment, plan) progress notes contain four sections while DAP (data, assessment, plan) progress notes include three categories.

SOAP	**DAP**
Subjective	Data
Objective	Assessment
Assessment	Plan
Plan	

The assessment and plan portions of both DAP and SOAP notes are identical. The only difference between SOAP and DAP progress notes is how session content is organized in the notes. A DAP progress note lists all session content as data; SOAP progress notes break down session content data into two types: subjective and objective.

SESSION DATA

SOAP Progress Notes   The subjective data of SOAP notes are not quantifiable or measurable; rather, they include subjective statements reflecting the client's condition. Information includes statements presented to the therapist, such as the presenting problems; statements from others, such as family or other collaterals; and historical data (e.g., family background, medical history, and social structure). Examples of subjective data include:

- The client reports feeling sad most of the time.
- He states that he is from a dysfunctional family.
- Several physical concerns were reported, such as . . .

The objective section of SOAP notes represents observable, verifiable, and quantifiable data. Objective data provide specific information that can be compared to previous data or used as a baseline for future objective observations. Examples of objective data include:

- Current score on the Beck Depression Inventory was 13, which is significantly lower than 28, recorded 2 months ago.
- She appeared dysphoric the entire session.
- On 3 occasions he cried, stating that he wants to give up trying.

DAP Progress Notes   The DAP format is becoming more popular and is considered by many to be more user friendly than the SOAP format. For this reason, this book utilizes the DAP format. For DAP progress notes, the therapist does not have to separate two types of data (subjective and objective) into different parts of the note. This is beneficial, as some statements, such as "The patient appeared confused, as evidenced by rambling 50% of the session," contain both subjective and objective information that is difficult to separate.

ASSESSMENT

The assessment section of the progress note (the same for SOAP and DAP formats) is a written evaluation of the current session and how it relates to the cumulative scope of therapy. It presents the therapist's evaluation of the effects of therapy, based on the documented information from previous and current sessions. Nine types of information are documented in this section:

1. Effects or results of the current session
2. Therapeutic progression
3. Client's level of cooperation/insight/motivation

4. Client progress and setbacks
5. Areas requiring more clinical work
6. Effectiveness of treatment strategies
7. Completion of treatment plan objectives
8. Changes needed to keep therapy on target
9. Need for diagnostic revisions

Although it is not necessary to address each area in every progress note, each should be covered sufficiently over the course of therapy. The statements in the assessment section are summaries of the information in the data section. Consider each item individually:

1. *Effects of the current session.* Comments assessing the effectiveness of the session are limited to data collected during the specific session. These comments are not meant to assess the cumulative effects of the course of treatment. For example:
   - The session seemed helpful in eliciting the client's feelings about how he resents his family intruding on his marriage.
   - The session was not helpful in building rapport.
2. *Therapeutic progress.* Statements assessing the course of therapy document the overall effects of therapeutic interventions (rather than the effects of the current session, as in area 1). Third-party reviewers regularly request this information. When progress notes consistently document the course of therapy, the clinician does not have to search for this information because it will be located in the assessment portion of each progress note. For example:
   - The client continues to show steady progress in therapy.
   - Group therapy has not been beneficial to this point.
3. *Client's level of cooperation/insight/motivation.* Client variables require the clinician's careful attention. An excellent therapist will be ineffective without mutual cooperation. The client's level of motivation and insight should be assessed to help evaluate whether the current regimen of treatment is sufficient. For example:
   - The client appears to have adequate insight into the nature of his therapeutic issues.
   - Level of cooperation has increased in the past month, leading to increased compliance in homework assignments and behavioral changes.
4. *Client progress and setbacks.* It is crucial to document both progress and setbacks. Such documentation provides regular assessments of what positive and negative outcomes have occurred since the onset of treatment. If only progress is documented, it appears that there is no need for

continued services. If only setbacks are documented, it appears that therapy is not helping. For example:

○ The client has increased suicidal threats, posing an increased risk to herself.

○ Significant client progress is noted in reducing anxiety and worrying.

5. *Areas requiring more clinical work.* Throughout therapy, clients will experience ongoing changes and stressors in their lives. New issues will surface, and others will be alleviated. As clients progress through therapy, new stressors will develop due to behavioral and environmental changes resulting from the effects of therapy. For example, if a client is taught to be more assertive, it may impact the dynamics of the client's family, thereby raising new therapeutic issues. Certain issues that may have been considered minor in the original assessment may develop into significant problem areas. Impairments apparent at the time of the initial assessment might have only a marginal impact on the client's current functioning level. Current documentation of medical necessity is based on client impairments; therefore, impairments should be assessed periodically to help determine the current need for services. The original treatment plan may suffice for a certain period of time, but eventually the clinical direction will need to be revised. The assessment section allows clinicians to note changes in the client's life that may require revising the treatment plan. For example:

○ Slight progress has taken place in alleviating temper tantrums, but school reports indicate continued need to focus on his bullying behavior.

○ The client's excessive drinking of alcohol and not looking for a job continue to cause severe financial and family problems that attribute to client's anxiety and depression.

○ The client no longer reports having panic attacks prior to meeting new people.

6. *Effectiveness of treatment strategies.* Treatment strategies also should be assessed periodically. Strategies that are particularly effective or ineffective should be noted and, if necessary, revised. Documenting whether treatment strategies work benefits future treatment providers who work with the client. For example:

○ Most progress has occurred when the client is given a homework assignment that corresponds to the session topic.

○ Client seems to lack insight, but behavioral strategies are effective in meeting treatment plan goals.

○ Hypnotherapy has not proven to be effective to date.

7. *Completion of treatment plan objectives.* Third-party reviewers require periodic updates to the treatment plan. The underlying question focuses on whether the goals and objectives are being met. If they are not being

met, or if progress is slower than expected, services may not be considered cost effective. Thus, other services may be more efficacious for the client and should be considered. For example:

- ○ Treatment plan objectives 2a, 3b, and 4a have been accomplished.
- ○ Client has not been able to return to college by the target date, due to excessive social anxiety.

8. *Changes needed to keep therapy on target.* Therapy is a dynamic process. Problem areas and objectives change on a regular basis. Every setback and achievement sets new directions, no matter how slight. Assessment of needed changes provides a periodic look at the direction therapy is heading and what overall changes will most benefit the client. For example:

- ○ The client is under significant stress at this time, and monthly psychotherapy is not sufficient to meet her therapeutic needs.
- ○ The client seems to be uncomfortable disclosing personal information to a male therapist. This therapist suggests referral to a female therapist.

9. *Need for diagnostic revisions.* As more information is gathered about the client and as life stressors change, the clinician may revise a diagnosis based on recent information. Some disorders go into remission whereas others no longer fit time frames specified by the text revision of the fourth edition of the *Diagnostic and Statistical Manual of Mental Disorders.* The specific reasons for changing a diagnosis should be listed in the data (DAP format) section, but the overall assessment of the client should be listed in the assessment section. Some clinicians periodically assess the current diagnosis by validating current symptoms and restating the diagnosis in the assessment section. For example:

- ○ Based on additional information, the diagnosis of oppositional defiant disorder will be revised to conduct disorder.
- ○ The client continues meeting criteria for bipolar II disorder.

PLAN

The plan section of progress notes is also identical for SOAP and DAP formats. Just as the assessment is based on the data (subjective and objective types for SOAP notes), the plan is based on the assessment. The plan section of the progress notes documents the focus of future treatment based on the client's current functioning level. Noting future plans for therapy also helps the therapist keep track of treatment options and follow up on assignments. It includes plans for use inside and outside of the session, such as:

- Homework assignments
- Upcoming interventions

- Content of future sessions
- Treatment plan revisions
- Referrals

Homework Assignments   Homework assignments include any assigned tasks to be completed outside of the counseling session. They range from behavioral assignments, to charting progress, to reading, to meditating. Homework should relate to the treatment plan and be designed to increase functioning. When therapists assign homework, they should write it down in the plan section, so they can review it prior to the next session and be prepared to discuss it during the session. For example:

- The client will write a letter to his parents describing his thoughts and feelings about how they treat his sister better than him.
- Continue logging feelings of anger.
- Lent client a copy of *I'm OK, You're OK* to discuss next week.

Upcoming Interventions   There are times when a therapist decides to try a new treatment strategy in a future session. When planning future session topics or interventions, it is helpful to discuss them in advance with the client. For example:

- Next session: incorporate role playing of assertiveness with best friend.
- Practice systematic desensitization during the next several sessions.

Content of Future Sessions   Treatment plans generally list at least two or three problem areas that will be addressed during the course of therapy. It is possible to dwell on one problem area for the duration of treatment and never address other areas of the treatment plan. To avoid this, it is helpful to plan in advance when some or all of the client's problems will be discussed and then periodically review the treatment plan with the client to ensure that problem areas are being addressed adequately. For example:

- Next session: Treatment plan problem area 2, binge eating.
- Continue treatment of self-esteem issues.

Note, however, that treatment should not be so regimented and pre-planned that the treatment plan becomes more important than the client's current needs. Especially when new issues or stressors arise between sessions, the content of what was planned for the session may seem irrelevant compared to the client's current needs. Therefore, stay on target with the treatment plan, but be flexible.

Treatment Plan Revisions   Treatment plans are designed to be revised when the client's level of impairments change. This does not mean that the treatment plan must be rewritten each time any progress or setbacks occur. As objectives are met (or not met), they should be revised in an effort to meet treatment goals. New treatment strategies may be added as more information about the client is learned. For example:

- Current objective: Maximum of 5 panic attacks daily. Revised objective: Maximum of 2 panic attacks daily.
- New objective: Apply for a minimum of 3 employment positions per week.

Referrals   Any referrals or additional services suggested that affect current treatment also should be documented in the plan section. For example:

- Referred to Dr. Smith for med evaluation.
- Referred client to Alcoholics Anonymous.

Third-party payers often ask if a medical or psychiatric referral was given, so it is important to note referrals in the client's chart. The data section of future progress notes will document the effects of client compliance with the referral. Figure 9.3 provides a DAP progress note for John Doe.

John Doe's progress note follows specific treatment plan objectives and interventions. It validates continued medical necessity by providing examples of current symptoms and impairments concordant with the diagnosis. The treatment is directed toward active symptoms of the diagnosis and demonstrates therapeutic benefits and setbacks.

CONFIDENTIALITY ISSUES AND PROGRESS NOTES

HIPAA regulations have clearly changed the nature of accessibility of progress notes. In client files, psychotherapy notes are now kept separately from the rest of the file. A separate authorization for records specifically requesting and allowing progress notes is required. Thus, if an "entire file" is copied, progress notes typically are not to be included, due to their confidential nature.

This does not mean that progress notes are not subject to audit, nor does it suggest that they are not important. In fact, progress notes are some of the most crucial documents in a client's file. However, access to progress notes is more limited than to the rest of the file due to the personal information that might be disclosed in them. They must be requested separately.

Some clinicians argue that progress notes should be vague and unrevealing to protect the confidential nature of the session. This argument would be valid

PROGRESS NOTES

Client: John Doe   Date: 3-6-05

Diagnosis: Major Depression, Dysthymia

Treatment Plan Objectives: (1) Identify sources of depression, (2) Describe/ understand conflicts with children

DATA: Current Beck Depression Inventory Score: 29. Previous week 27. Did not complete homework assignment due to "low motivation and too many stressors this week." Client reports a very difficult week in which he missed work 50% of the time. Is complying with Prozac (20 mg. $\times$ 2), which he began taking two weeks ago. No noticeable benefits or side effects yet. Very dysphoric over feelings of rejection from family. Often cried when relating feelings of worthlessness. Discussed suicidal contract and steps to follow if feeling suicidal. Gave him another copy of emergency contact phone numbers. Interventions included discussing specific antecedents leading to depressive thoughts and cyclical patterns recurring much of his life. Identified three areas that typically lead to depressed mood: (1) perceived rejection, (2) gives up easily leading to guilt, and (3) thoughts of childhood abuse. Role played having a discussion with his children about his depression and his desire to return to previous functioning. Appeared less depressed during the intervention. Client states that on a scale of 100, usual level of depression is at 85 (baseline was 90, last week was 68, objective is 50). Attended a full session of individual psychotherapy.

ASSESSMENT: A very difficult week in which he seems to be regressing into some negative thought patterns that have usually led to depression. Increased occupational and social impairment. Session seemed helpful in increasing insight and increasing hope.

PLAN: Client will attempt to discuss his depression with his children to increase their understanding that he is not upset with them. Continue keeping journal, which we will review next session. Set up med review with Dr. Anderson.

Time Started: 10:00 A.M.	Time Ended: 10:52 A.M.	Duration: 52 minutes
Type: 90844	Next Session: 3-13-05	Time: 10:00 A.M.
		Date: 3-6-05

_____
Therapist's Signature and Credentials

Figure 9.3   Example of Progress Note for John Doe

Source: Reprinted with permission of John Wiley & Sons, Inc.

if progress notes were meant to disclose confidential material. Well-written progress notes do not need to include potentially damaging confidential information about clients. Some clinicians were trained to produce progress notes that could serve as transcripts of their sessions with clients. These types of progress notes could violate a client's confidentiality if released and are unnecessary. Other types of progress notes focus on psychological processes rather than the resolution of client problems. These progress notes do provide evidence of personal growth and various processes taking place in the session but do not demonstrate the alleviation of impairments.

Progress notes can be detailed and thorough without sacrificing the client's integrity or confidentiality. A careful look at progress notes requirements reveals that rarely, if ever, do third parties require clinicians to provide a detailed history of client behaviors (outside the session) in progress notes. Historical information is crucial in the course of therapy, but it is not clearly diagnostic or necessary in documentation. Therefore, there is no merit in recording specific aberrant or private behaviors, thoughts, or concerns that could lead to embarrassment or potential legal jeopardy. VandeCreek and Knapp, cited in Soisson, VandeCreek, and Knapp (1987), suggest that records should leave out emotional statements, certain personal problems, information about illegal behavior, sexual practices, or other information that may harm the client or others. None of the procedures outlined in this book is designed to raise confidentiality concerns; rather, all are intended to document the efficacy of therapy through evidence of client change.

Other issues arising in progress notes include the client's right to access the information. Although patient records are the property of the provider, the patient controls its dissemination and access to individual records (Soisson et al., 1987). In almost all states, patients have direct access to their records except in cases in which the records could be harmful to the patient.

When patients inspect records and disagree with their content, they have the right to dispute that content and request needed corrections. See Wiger (2010) for clinical forms available designed to fit HIPAA criteria for clients' right to disagree or amend records. See Appendix C for a summary of HIPAA procedures. Such practices increase the clinician's awareness of, and responsibility for, keeping accurate records, adding to accountability in the profession.

COMMON PROBLEMS WITH PROGRESS NOTES

VAGUENESS

The most common problem with progress notes is vagueness. Progress note statements such as "discussed emotions," "went over problems," and "practiced communicating" are common but reveal little clinical information and do not document medical necessity of services or treatment progress.

PROGRESS NOTES UNRELATED TO TREATMENT PLAN GOALS

Another red flag for auditors is raised when progress notes do not address the client's diagnosed problem, describe the medical necessity for treatment, or reflect the treatment plan. Figure 9.4 illustrates two examples of progress notes that provide interesting anecdotal information but lack evidence of medical necessity. In addition, the notes raise concerns about potential confidentiality violations and provide little information regarding treatment implications.

Example A

Poor example of progress note statement

"Client's deceased uncle, Jay Doe, sexually molested him twenty years ago."

Problems with this statement

1. Does not document how this event affects the client at this time (lacks medical necessity).
2. Implicates the uncle (by name) because it is written as a definitive statement. It is possible that the incident did not take place. In such cases, it is better to quote patient directly. Otherwise, if the client, another relative, or the court were to gain access to the client's file, this potentially unmerited and libelous accusation could be used against the client.

Clinically relevant progress note statement

"Client reports a traumatic incident twenty years ago at age 15, in which he states a deceased relative 'sexually molested' him, currently resulting in recurring nightmares, social withdrawal, and fear of older men."

Why this statement is relevant

The historical incident is alluded to; however, the current symptoms and impairments resulting from the alleged incident are the focus of the progress note. For some, experiencing a severe stressor will not cause a mental health problem; in this case, the effects of stress did cause mental health issues.

Example B

Poorly written progress note statement

"We discussed various problems."

Problems with this statement

1. The statement is vague; thus, there is no way of knowing how this fits the goals and objectives written in the treatment plan.
2. There is no reference to therapeutic techniques or interventions employed in treating the client's problems.

Figure 9.4   Poorly Documented Progress Note Statements

Source: Reprinted with permission of John Wiley & Sons, Inc.

Clinically relevant progress note statement
"Due to increasing social withdrawal and avoidance at work and other areas, we role-played two ways to socially interact with coworkers. Client appeared tense and said, 'What do I have to offer?' Client appeared more confident after role-playing work situations. He stated that he will attempt these strategies by next session and report level of progress."

Why this statement is relevant
This example provides detail without potentially breaking confidentiality if an outside source had access to the record. It documents that social and occupational impairments are currently taking place and validates dysphoric observations. The effects of treatment strategies were noted, evaluated, and incorporated into the client's life.

Note: When the law requires reporting an incident such as child abuse, intended suicide, intent to harm someone, or taking illegal drugs during pregnancy, it is suggested that the clinician quote what the client stated in the session. The client must be warned of limits to confidentiality prior to receiving services.

Figure 9.4 Continued

Noncooperative Clients

It is difficult to document impairments, progress, and compliance adequately when the client is unwilling to disclose information. This dilemma makes it more difficult to demonstrate the medical necessity for services. For example, a client with paranoia is unlikely to disclose debilitating thoughts and behaviors to a therapist (due to the paranoia). In addition, court-referred clients who deny problems with domestic violence, chemical dependency, perpetrator issues, or other criminal areas for which they are in treatment tend to admit little or nothing about the behavior in question. Some non-cooperative clients claim to have a rapid cure in an effort to terminate therapy.

Although insurance companies initially will reimburse treatment based on a diagnosis, they will continue paying based only on the effectiveness of treatment. Thus, for noncooperative clients for whom it is difficult to document the course of treatment properly, therapists might:

- Inform the client that third-party reimbursement depends on accurate diagnosis, client cooperation, therapeutic progress, and documented decreases in impairment. Thus, cooperating in this process is crucial when there is third-party payment. Further inform the client that even if he or she decides to pay cash, the referral source (i.e., a judge or probation officer) may require evidence of progress as part of the rehabilitation process. If the client still refuses to cooperate, other forms of rehabilitation (incarceration, day treatment, and so forth) may be required.

- Increase the use of collaterals in therapy when the client may be attempting to cooperate but has poor insight. Collaterals may be useful in documenting behavioral changes outside of the counseling sessions. The use of charts and behavioral change graphs provide evidence of progress. For example:
  - ○ Client's spouse states that he previously consumed at least 2 quarts of vodka per day. Since the onset of treatment and med. management, he has remained dry.
  - ○ There have been 2 incidents of temper outbursts (verbal) in the past month. She states that prior to treatment, temper outbursts (physical and verbal) occurred almost daily.

Therapists should be careful about accepting third-party payment for clients who do not want to be in therapy. Poor rates of compliance impede adequate documentation of progress, and it is challenging to elicit information about the client's ongoing impairments and progresses. If such cases are audited, there is a possibility that payback will be required, resulting in financial losses for not adhering to HIPAA procedures. Worse yet, some third parties contractually prohibit clinics from billing clients for penalties issued due to an audit. Even when back-billing clients is allowed, the chances of collection are low, considering the fact that the therapy may have been conducted a few years prior to the audit. Finally, it is always more difficult to collect payment from clients who did not want to be in therapy in the first place.

SAVING TIME IN WRITING PROGRESS NOTES

Approximately 75% of more than 2,500 therapists surveyed by this author say they write their progress notes after the session. These therapists note that they prefer waiting until after the session ends because:

- I can't attend to my client if I'm writing notes.
- Clients will hold back information or become self-conscious if they believe that I am writing down everything that they say.
- They will ask me what I am writing down, become interrupted, and won't concentrate on the session.
- I wait until I'm finished with the session so I can integrate the whole picture of what was said.

Others write brief notations during the session and integrate them afterward. Few therapists surveyed claimed to write the bulk of their progress notes during the session. Although there is nothing improper with any of these methods, writing progress notes during the session is a time-saver. Imagine clinicians who see six to eight clients a day and save writing progress notes for all clients until the end of the day. The clinicians may get a week or two behind and realize there are 30 or more progress notes to write. Now they need a full day to catch up. Additionally, remembering specifically what took place in each session becomes a mammoth task, typically leading to confabulation.

To avoid having to remember specific details about a session several hours to weeks later and to avoid falling behind, writing progress notes during the session can be a life-saver. Although the concerns mentioned earlier about writing progress notes during the session are valid, with practice, in-session note taking can be used positively and can enhance empathy. When the clinician nonverbally suggests that what the client says is important (by showing interest when writing things down), clients often encourage this practice. Writing a progress note takes only a small fraction of the session time because only the data section is completed during the session. The assessment and plan sections are completed when the client leaves. For example, in Figure 9.3, the data section consists of less than 15 sentences. Thus, fewer than one sentence would need to be recorded about every three minutes.

Data are specific pieces of information that do not require continuity or interrelationships; thus, the data section does not have to read like an ongoing narrative. The data are integrated and used to formulate the assessment section of the progress note after the session. The assessment and plan sections can be written as the client leaves the room. The average time to write these sections is generally less than 5 minutes. If a session lasts 45 minutes, and it takes 5 minutes to write the assessment and plan sections, the clinician still has 10 minutes for a breather before seeing the next client. No additional time is needed later in the day, and no catch-up time at the clinic is needed.

Another advantage of writing progress notes during the session is that the therapist can more easily quote clients directly and document observations. Much of this information becomes lost if writing is deferred for several minutes, hours, or days.

After reading this far, you are well on your way to ensuring that you will never be held responsible for third-party paybacks. Unfortunately, sometimes even the best-planned treatment does not fully alleviate a client's symptoms or impairments in the allotted time frame. In such cases, clinicians must request additional treatment for the client. Convincing third parties that additional therapy is medically necessary is challenging but can be accomplished if the right procedures are followed.

HIGHLIGHTS OF CHAPTER 9

- Accurate progress notes are crucial because they are the only evidence of progress, therapeutic procedures, and current mental condition.
- Although progress notes are detailed, they do not need to reveal information that might potentially harm the client or others.
- HIPAA regulations require that a separate request is made for progress notes. Psychotherapy notes are kept in a separate file.
- Vague or incomplete progress notes could lead to legal, ethical, or reimbursement issues.
- Well-written progress notes enable a new therapist to resume therapeutic services quickly during times of therapist transition.
- Progress notes reflect the client's progress in specific treatment plan objectives.
- Standard progress note formats, such as SOAP and DAP, follow the scientific method in which the effects of treatment are assessed and a plan is made for future interventions.
- Time can be saved by writing progress notes during the session.
- Progress notes are not written from a particular theoretical school of thought but rather simply are behavioral evidence of the progress from any therapeutic viewpoint.
- Research indicates that therapists can learn new ways to write progress notes when appropriate feedback is available and procedures are simplified.

QUESTIONS

1. Which of these statements best represents the data from a DAP progress note?
   a. Client states, "I feel much better this week."
   b. Therapist states, "Observations suggest improvement in affect."
   c. Therapist states, "Based on new information, diagnosis is changed to . . ."
   d. Therapist states, "Test scores indicate improvements in subjective well-being."
2. Which of these statements best represents the assessment from a DAP progress note?
   a. Beck Depression Inventory (BDI) score = 21.
   b. Client cried uncontrollably when role playing saying good-bye to loved one.
   c. Significant improvements in ability to resolve stressors at home.
   d. Revise treatment plan objective 3c to . . .

3. Which of these statements best represents the plan from a DAP progress note?
   a. The homework assignment for next week is to . . .
   b. The homework assignment for this current session was to . . .
   c. The homework assignment was detrimental because . . .
   d. The homework assignment indicated a significant increase in positive behaviors in the classroom.
4. What is wrong with the next progress note statement that is placed in the data section? *"The client has improved significantly in assertiveness skills."*
   a. It is a good data statement.
   b. It adds no significant client information.
   c. It is too judgmental.
   d. It is not data.
5. How might well-written progress notes help protect a therapist from ethical/legal/financial problems?
   a. They document that appropriate therapeutic and procedural steps were taken prior to a client attempting suicide.
   b. They demonstrate that the treatment was medically necessary.
   c. They provide evidence that the treatment provided was concordant with acceptable procedures in the field.
   d. Each of these.
6. A mental health therapist receives a request for medical information for "the entire record." According to HIPAA regulations, what information CANNOT be sent in this situation?
   a. Testing.
   b. Progress notes.
   c. Treatment plans.
   d. Diagnostic summary.

   Answers: 1a, 2c, 3a, 4d, 5d, 6b

CHAPTER 10

Documenting the Need for
Additional Services

INSURANCE AND MANAGED care companies typically request a written request for additional services once a previously allowed number of services have been utilized. It is not uncommon for a third-party payer to authorize about four to eight sessions initially and then require documentation that additional services are medically necessary. The content and quality of this written request directly affects the third-party payer's decision to pay for additional services. It is the most crucial piece of documentation material needed to continue services. The therapist's writing style and documentation are an important part of this aspect of the treatment process. A sample preauthorization request can be found in Appendix A.

Since the third-party case manager does not have direct contact with the client, the only information available is the written mental health records. A patient may be in dire need of services, but if the therapist does not adequately document this need, services likely will be denied. The third party should not be blamed or held responsible for denying services when documentation does not clearly demonstrate medical necessity. Thus, learning adequate documentation techniques is an obligation to clients, not an unnecessary task or merely an additional skill to learn.

Although it might be difficult for some therapists to accept the current documentation requirements, they are a reality, necessary to function within today's standards. On a positive note, those who learn to document well rarely have difficulties obtaining services for clients who need additional treatment. Effective clinical skills are necessary, but not sufficient, in securing ongoing mental health care for clients. Therefore, therapists must be trained and supervised in documentation procedures.

Information commonly requested by third-party payers is not difficult to provide if adequate records have been kept. Therapists should not have to rely on their memory about what took place in previous sessions to demonstrate that services are necessary; rather, existing documentation that has been kept throughout treatment should be the reference. For example, progress notes and treatment plan updates regularly document medical necessity and the need for continued services.

Several types of information typically are requested in a preauthorization for additional services request.

- *Mental health diagnosis.* The preauthorization request should include the most current diagnosis. Any diagnosis changes should be incorporated into the treatment plan and clearly explained. In addition, some third-party payers no longer provide payment for certain diagnoses, such as not-otherwise-specified diagnoses, behavioral behaviors, adjustment disorders, or other diagnoses with a Global Assessment of Functioning (GAF) over 60.

- *Service dates and current number of sessions used.* This type of information should correspond with the dates on the progress notes. Third-party payers pay special attention to this information as the number of sessions increases by comparing the number of sessions used to national averages of sessions for various diagnoses. For example, the expected number of sessions for treatment of a mild adjustment disorder would be much less than for someone suffering from post-traumatic stress disorder. If the number of sessions is significantly more than average, it is important to clearly document any special circumstances that demonstrate a need for additional services. There have been cases in which some managed care companies have not renewed providers' contracts because the clinicians consistently used more sessions than the norm.

- *Current mental status and diagnosis documentation.* This information is crucial for obtaining additional services. The key term is *current*. Clinicians must provide an up-to-date validation of the patient's condition. It should reflect progress and setbacks that have occurred since the onset of treatment. If there is no current documented evidence of a mental health diagnosis, services may be terminated.

- *Current functional impairments.* Since part of the definition of medical necessity includes functional impairments, services should be able to continue when the patient continues being impaired but shows progress since the onset of treatment. Thus, the clinician should document and validate the current impairments rather than listing those at the onset of treatment.

- *Therapeutic/behavioral progress and regressions.* Some therapists view reporting progress and setbacks as a Catch-22 situation. That is, if clinicians emphasize current impairments and regressions as evidence that additional services are needed, it will appear that no progress has occurred and make services appear unhelpful on paper. If clinicians emphasize great leaps and progresses, it may appear that no further services are needed.

Both progress and setbacks need to be balanced in the request for additional services report. When progress has occurred but setbacks and impairments still exist, which is often the case, clinicians should provide evidence of both. Ideally, the clinician would document client progress as the result of achieving some treatment plan goals and objectives and document setbacks and continued impairments as areas that have not yet been treated in therapy or as new stressors that have emerged. In this scenario, there is evidence that treatment is working, but more services are necessary to deal with issues not yet treated.

The clinician must exercise ethics in this documentation to prevent painting a picture of the client on paper different from what is actually the case. There may a temptation to overdocument in order to obtain more services. A good check and balance is to share reports of progress and setbacks with the client.

- *Patient's willingness to accomplish treatment goals and objectives.* Client cooperation is necessary in the counseling process. The preauthorization request should include specific examples of client cooperation in areas such as attending sessions, homework cooperation, therapeutic compliance, and behavioral changes outside the session.
- *Revised or updated treatment plan.* Treatment plans are made to be revised. Plans without revisions imply that no progress has taken place. Objectives should be revised periodically as clients more closely reach the goals set in the treatment plan.
- *Objective discharge criteria.* Discharge criteria are difficult to determine. Vague statements suggesting discharge criteria, such as "attain 80% of goals," mean very little clinically. The best descriptions are in behavioral terms, suggesting alleviation of functional impairments that led to the medical necessity for services.

HIGHLIGHTS OF CHAPTER 10

- Most third-party payers request written evidence (a preauthorization request) regarding the effectiveness of treatment in order to reimburse services after a few visits.

- The therapist's documentation and writing skills can directly impact the chances of the client receiving additional services.
- The preauthorization request provides an overview of the client's current mental condition compared to his or her condition at the onset of services, thus measuring clinical effectiveness.
- Both setbacks and progress in therapy are documented to demonstrate the need for additional services and the benefits of services rendered to date.
- The preauthorization request should demonstrate that treatment has focused on the diagnosis by means of the treatment plan.

QUESTIONS

1. How can a client who severely needs additional mental health services be turned down by a case manager from a third-party payer?
   a. Lack of specific documentation
   b. Lack of demonstration medical necessity of services
   c. Lack of evidence of functional impairments
   d. All of these
2. When applying for approval for additional client services, why should both progress and setbacks be documented?
   a. They show both what has been accomplished and what needs to be accomplished in treatment.
   b. Never document setbacks or lack of progress because it implies that treatment is not effective.
   c. Never document progress because it implies that the client is now functioning adequately.
   d. It does not matter which one you document as long as there is evidence that you desire additional services.
3. Why might a client with a diagnosis of major depressive disorder and a GAF of 88 be denied additional services?
   a. Major depression is not a serious disorder, as schizophrenia is.
   b. A client with a GAF of 88 would receive additional services.
   c. A client with a GAF of 88 is not likely to have significant impairments.
   d. A client with a diagnosis of major depressive disorder would not have a GAF of 88.
4. Which of the next statements represents the best discharge goal?
   a. Complete eight sessions of psychotherapy.
   b. Return to work full time.
   c. Finish discussing disruptive childhood.
   d. They are all good discharge goals.

5. What is suggested by this statement: "Effective clinical skills are necessary but not sufficient when working with-third party payers"?
   a. Good therapy skills are not enough if you do not get along with case managers.
   b. The third-party payer must know that you work well with people or you will not receive referrals.
   c. Third-party payers desire that your treatment is effective, not just sufficient.
   d. Although a therapist might possess excellent clinical skills, clients may not receive an adequate number of services if the therapist has not learned appropriate documentation skills.

   Answers: 1d, 2a, 3c, 4b, 5d

APPENDIX A

Putting it All Together
Documented Chart for Mental Health Services

DIAGNOSTIC ASSESSMENT REPORT

Name: <u>Judy Doe</u>   Chart # <u>JD0533</u>   DOB: <u>2-8-88</u>   DOE <u>3-5-11</u>
   Presenting Problem: Panic Attacks, Alcoholism, Decreased Cognitive functioning

SIGNS AND SYMPTOMS

Judy Doe, a Caucasian female, age 23, never married, was referred by her primary physician, Dr. Reynolds, due to anxiety, substance abuse, and to rule out any cognitive deficits that could be secondary to substance abuse or anxiety.

She states that she feels anxious and usually panics whenever she is in public places where she may not be able to flee the situation immediately. She further notes a history and current excessive usage of alcohol. She states, "I want to be calm and not have to rely on booze to get there." She adds that she is worried that her abuse use of alcohol and subsequent blackouts might have led to cognitive declines.

During the interview she appeared to be highly anxious. She often fidgeted, breathed rapidly, and stuttered a few times. She reported having a panic attack in the waiting room prior to the interview. There was a faint smell of alcohol on her breath. She took about 3 breath mints during the interview.

She began experiencing panic attacks 3 months ago, approximately 1 month after losing her job as a videographer, which she held for about 1½ years. She currently experiences up to 3–4 panic attacks per day, each lasting 20–30 minutes. When she has panic attacks, she reports shortness of breath, choking sensations, palpitations, dizziness, chills, and a feeling of doom. Since her first panic attack in public 2 months ago, she refuses to go to public places, such as malls or grocery stores, unless she first has a few drinks. She notes that otherwise it would be too anxiety provoking. At home she experiences fewer panic attacks except when the doorbell or phone rings. She will not go out with her friends or relatives and states that she is afraid to apply for another job, noting that she is a "mess-up" and "no one wants to hire a has-been." She was fired from her last job due to excessive absences and coming into work intoxicated "one too many times."

Her use of alcohol began when she moved away from a small town to Los Angeles to attend college. She states that she isn't sure whether she began drinking to help alleviate anxiety, or whether it was due to feeling accepted by others at her college. However, since her first year of college, she states that she has become more dependent on alcohol to function vocationally and socially. By the middle of her second year in college she dropped out, stating that she couldn't handle it anymore. She moved back to the safety of her supportive family.

She believes that since she frequently drinks alcohol until she blacks out, there could be "brain atrophy." She adds that she is having increased difficulty in short-term memory, concentration, and remembering basic academic material that she knew well in the past.

REVIEW OF RECORDS

Records available to this psychologist included an evaluation report by Dr. Monteroni, from Century School District, dated 3-3-05 when she was being evaluated for intellectual, academic, and vocational functioning to help her decide on what might be the best fit in college. WAIS-IV results noted the following standard scores: VCI-103, PRI-109, WMI-100, PSI-102, FSIQ-105. All scores were within normal limits, with relative strengths in nonverbal areas. Woodcock Johnson scores of academic functioning were all within normal limits. There was no evidence of a learning disability.

Clinical notes written on 2-15-11 from her primary physician, Dr. Reynolds, noted issues with anxiety and substance abuse. At that time she was not formally diagnosed or treated for with mental illness or chemical dependency. She had stated the she would think about med trials but wanted to receive this present evaluation first. No other records were available.

HISTORY OF PRESENT ILLNESS

Judy Doe reports no known family history of mental health treatment or problem areas. She has never attended a counseling session, nor has she been previously diagnosed with a mental health disorder or chemical dependency.

Most of her life she has been somewhat withdrawn and anxious in public, viewing herself as shy until she drinks alcohol. She reports that she began feeling increasingly more anxious at work when a college graduate was hired in a position similar to hers. The college graduate eventually was promoted in the company due to exceptional work quality. Judy Doe became fairly upset and admits that her work quality suffered from her increased amount of worrying about her job and the effects of using alcohol so frequently. She began making a greater number of errors and missing work due to headaches, upset stomach, and making up stories why she couldn't come too work when she had been hung over. She received 2 reprimands at work for smelling of alcohol. After another college graduate was hired, she states her work quality became "poor." She eventually was fired when she went into work intoxicated.

Since leaving her job, her anxiety level has increased. She feels incapacitated in her ability to work competitively with people who are more highly trained than she is. She worries excessively that if she were able to go back to work, she would just get fired again. She describes having increased problems concentrating and short-term memory loss, stating, "I feel like I have dementia or something like that."

One month ago she filled out 3 job applications and received a phone call for an interview. On the day of the job interview she arrived at the building of the meeting, panicked, and drove home. When she arrived home she drank a pint of vodka to relieve her anxiety. On her next job interview she tried to alleviate her anxiety by having a few drinks before the meeting, but the interviewer commented that she seemed to "have a buzz," and she was not offered the position. She has now given up trying to get a job, stating, "I'm either to anxious or too drunk."

BIOPSYCHOSOCIAL ASSESSMENT

Judy Doe is the youngest of 5 children and describes her family as close knit. Her parents have been married for 40 years. She reports that she is from a functional family who treated her "too well" as a child. She describes herself as "daddy's girl" and "the baby of the family." Until she began working full time, her parents took care of all expenses. She lived at home, expense-free, until 2 years ago when she went off to college.

She currently lives alone in an apartment. Her parents and most of her siblings live within 5 miles of her. She talks with them on the phone regularly but since experiencing panic attacks has not visited them. Although she describes her family as supportive, she is beginning to feel alienated from them because recently they held an intervention with her about her drinking. She states that she was embarrassed and didn't know that they were aware of her problem. They offered to pay for counseling. Now she doesn't feel like she is part of the family because of how they singled her out by having an intervention.

As a child she had few friends and was not involved in any school activities or outside events. She was often teased due to her small size and occasional stuttering. Her older siblings often protected her from teasing and ridicule from children in school, but she often worried about what would happen if they were not present. She dated a few times as a teenager and early adult but was involved in no serious relationships. She states that she is too reserved and afraid to phone any of her acquaintances or former work associates to enhance her social life, but she wishes she would be able to learn how to make friends.

She has a best friend, whom she has known for over 10 years, who recently moved to New York due to a job transfer. She has not made any new friends since dropping out of college. She sometimes talks with one of her neighbors, a family friend. Historically she has attended religious services with her family, but not in the past several months. She states that being around people in church is "both anxiety producing and comforting." Her spiritual beliefs and practices are very important to her, and she views them as a definite strength. She describes the people at her place of worship as friendly. She has been asked to join a singles group there but hasn't yet made up her mind. She has considered attending an AA group at the church but fears being judged.

Prior to going to college she was more active in outside activities. She visited the zoo by herself. At times she would take her two nieces with her. She played on a neighborhood softball team, but her friend who urged her to join the team with her moved away. She did not continue with the team. Since returning from college she has attended family social functions, such as birthday parties, but is not willing to go to events not involving her family. About a year ago she went camping with her sisters and their families. However, she notes that she would sneak off and drink.

Her last physical evaluation was conducted 6 months ago by Dr. Reynolds, of Main Health Clinic. She states that exam indicated no health concerns, but she informed the doctor about her anxiety and substance abuse. A further evaluation was suggested. No medications were prescribed. She is allergic to penicillin. Her weight is within normal limits for her height. She was hospitalized once in her life for a tonsillectomy at age 9. She visits the dentist once per year for routine checkups. She reports no significant history of any physical injuries.

Currently, she drinks at least a 6-pack of beer daily. She drinks a pint of vodka plus the beer on weekends or when she feels stressed. She experiences blackouts, but because she lives alone, no one knows the extent of her drinking. Over the past 6 months she is requiring more alcohol to get the desired effect. Without alcohol she feels jittery, withdraws from people, and usually thinks about getting her next drink. She reports withdrawal symptoms when not drinking.

Although she has never been in counseling, she believes it will be helpful because her friend successfully went through counseling following her divorce. She further states that she knows that there is a connection between her anxiety, alcohol use, and concentration problems. She states that she wants to get her life back. She is willing to receive MICD (Mental Illness—Chemical Dependency) treatment. She is looking for a female therapist "who understands what it is like being the youngest in a family of high achievers."

MENTAL STATUS EXAM

CLINICAL OBSERVATIONS

She appeared at the interview neatly dressed and groomed. Her posture and health seemed to be within normal limits. Her nails were very short, as if bitten. She looked her chronological age. There were no unusual mannerisms or gestures. She was alert. Her gait was normal. She sat somewhat rigidly and did not appear relaxed. Initially she rarely looked at this psychologist, but her eye contact increased as the interview progressed.

Her speech was clear and easily understood, but soft in volume. She expressed a normal range of vocabulary, pronunciations, and details. A few times during the interview her speech was hesitant and stuttered. Her speech was not mumbled or slurred.

She was cooperative, answering every question. She seemed somewhat inhibited socially, as evidenced by not initiating interactions but rather responding only when spoken to. She did not appear to be defensive, defiant, manipulative, or hostile. She seemed to be interested in the interview process.

STREAM OF CONSCIOUSNESS

There was no evidence of a thought disorder. She was logical, coherent, and remained on target. No concerns were noticed regarding issues with thought processes, content of thought, thought disturbances, hallucinations, illusions, delusions, or depersonalization. She denies any history of suicidal thoughts, preoccupations, or detachment.

Affect/Mood

Affective observations included a restricted range of affect. Her mobility and intensity of affect were within normal limits. No psychomotor concerns were observed. She appeared to be anxious, as evidenced by often fidgeting with her fingers, and hesitancy in her speech. She asked to go to the rest room 2 times during the interview. She did not appear to be irritable or angry.

She states that she is able to show a normal range of affect around her family but not "outsiders." She denies having any anger management issues. When she is upset she usually holds it in rather than expressing it to others. She denies currently feeling depressed but claims to be frustrated with herself due to being fired from her job and dropping out of college. She does not endorse symptoms suggesting a depressive disorder, mania, or PTSD.

She currently endorses symptoms and impairments concordant with panic disorder with agoraphobia. Symptoms include abrupt development of heart palpitations, sweating, shortness of breath, chest pain, a feeling of choking, dizziness, and chills. She reports that she has an average of 3 panic attacks per day, each taking place when she has been in public or worries about social situations. Her panic attacks last from 10–30 minutes. She describes the severity of panic attacks at 80 out of 100, which she labels as "severe." She has not been able to feel comfortable in social settings, noting major impairments in which she feels isolated and is not able to apply for work. This leads to increased anxiety over finances.

She denies any history or current usage of any illegal drugs or prescribed medications. She states, "My problem is booze." She endorses the several symptoms of alcohol dependence, including: (1) increased tolerance, with an increased need for higher amounts to become intoxicated; (2) withdrawal symptoms when not using, leading to increased use of alcohol to relieve withdrawal symptoms; (3) typically drinking significantly larger amounts than she intends to drink; (4) a history of unsuccessful attempts to stop or reduce her drinking; and (5) loss of her job and quitting school due to the effects of alcohol.

She further states that for most of her life she only gets involved in activities if she is sure that she will be accepted and liked. In social situations she is often preoccupied with thoughts that people will criticize or reject her. On 2 occasions she stated that she is "not as good as other people" academically, socially, and on the job. She has taking relatively few risks in her life. She meets criteria for avoidant personality disorder.

Sensorium/Cognition

She was in touch with reality, able to hold a normal conversation, and was oriented × 3. Attention and concentration were within normal limits as evidenced by adequately counting to 40 by threes beginning with one and counting backward by sevens from 100 in a normal time period. She repeated 6 digits forward and 4 digits backward, which is within the normal range. She correctly spelled the words STOP and WORLD forward and backward. She recalled 3 out of 3 words after 5 minutes and 2 out of 3 words after 30 minutes. She remembered the names of previous teachers, historical events in her life, recent meals, and her activities of the past weekend. Short-term, long-term, and immediate memory were intact.

She appeared to have average intelligence. Her level of judgment and abstract thinking were within normal limits. She seems to have appropriate insight into the nature of her concerns, stating that she wants learn how to cope with stress, manage her anxiety, stop drinking, and develop healthy friendships.

TESTING

MINNESOTA MULTIPHASIC PERSONALITY INVENTORY-2 (MMPI-2)

MMPI-2 results appear to be valid. She finished the testing in a normal time span, responding to every question. The validity scales suggest that she sees herself as experiencing a significant number of emotional concerns at this time, which is concordant with the presenting problem.

The basic clinical scales indicate a 7–0 profile with a slightly elevated 2 scale. People with similar profiles tend to have issues with insecurity, social withdrawal, lack of drive, shyness, and a lack of assertiveness and confidence. The most notable elevation in the profile suggests concerns with anxiety, which is often indicated by long-standing patterns of worrying and poor coping mechanisms. Similar profiles also may indicate concerns with passive aggression. Supplementary and content scales provided similar mental health concerns. It is further noted that she endorsed significant elevations in the substance abuse related scales. MMPI-2 results were concordant with her presenting problem.

WECHSLER ADULT INTELLIGENCE SCALE-IV (WAIS-IV)

WAIS-IV results noted the following index scores: VCI—102, PRI—82, WMI—97, PSI—81, FSIQ—85. Perceptual Reasoning and Processing Speed are significantly lower than other scores, suggesting relative concerns in nonverbal areas. Verbal scores are within normal limits. Concerns are noted when comparing current testing to her WAIS-IV scores from 2005, as there has been a significant drop in nonverbal areas and in her processing speed. Such scores are concordant with effects of alcoholism.

TrailMaking A & B

TMA = 32 seconds, 0 errors; TMB = 94 seconds, 4 errors

TMA results note no concerns in single tasking. However, when required to multitask in TMB, her ability to quickly process information and perform a nonverbal task declined significantly.

SUMMARY AND DIAGNOSIS

Judy Doe was referred by her primary physician for psychological consultation due to presenting with panic attacks, alcoholism, and decreased cognitive functioning. Symptoms began when she moved to college after she graduated high school. She dropped out of college and returned home and found a job as a videographer. Symptoms increased significantly after losing her job 4 months ago due to substance abuse issues. She is no longer looking for work due to anxiety, substance abuse, and difficulties concentrating. She has no counseling history, nor are there any known mental health concerns in her family.

She describes her childhood history in positive terms. Being the youngest, her family often took care of most of her needs. Her family is currently supportive. As well, she has one lifelong friend who recently moved out of state.

The MSE indicated a normal appearance, speech, and attitude toward this examiner. There was no evidence of a thought disorder. She appeared anxious and was fidgety during the interview. MSE observations suggested concerns with anxiety, social introversion, and alcohol dependence. MMPI-2 testing was concordant with her presenting problems. Cognitive testing noted declines in nonverbal cognitive functioning compared to records of previous testing. She endorsed symptoms and impairments indicating Alcohol Dependence, Panic Disorder with Agoraphobia, Avoidant Personality Disorder, and a rule out of a cognitive disorder, secondary to alcoholism or anxiety.

She is in need of mental health and chemical dependency treatment. It is suggested that she receives (1) at least 12 sessions of individual psychotherapy focusing on means of coping with stressful situations and panic attacks; (2) at least 6 sessions of family therapy with her parents and siblings to work on family dynamics and expectations; (3) a full chemical dependency (CD) assessment from a local CD treatment center to evaluate her need for, and level of, CD treatment; (4) a psychiatric referral for an evaluation of medications for anxiety and panic attacks; and (5) a neurological referral due to rule out any organicity secondary to excessive use of alcohol.

It is the opinion of this psychologist that her cognitive declines could be due to factors other than substance abuse. Her level of anxiety clearly may affect her current level of concentration and cognitive functioning. As improvements in mental health functioning take place, her cognitive status will be monitored. Thus, her current diagnosis of a cognitive disorder is tentative.

Axis I:	Diagnosis	Code
	Panic Disorder with Agoraphobia	300.21
	Alcohol Dependence	303.90
	R/O Cognitive Disorder NOS, secondary to alcoholism	294.9
Axis II:	Avoidant Personality Disorder	302.81
Axis III:	Defer to Physician	
Axis IV:	Unemployment, few friends	
Axis V:	GAF = 50 (current) 65 (highest in past year)	

Ronald Obama Lincoln, PhD, LP   3-5-11
Signature and Credentials of Therapist   Date

INDIVIDUAL TREATMENT PLAN

Client: Judy Doe   Chart #: JD0533   Date: 3-12-11

Axis I:	Diagnosis	Code
	Alcohol Dependence	303.90
	Panic Disorder with Agoraphobia	300.21
	R/O Cognitive Disorder NOS, secondary to alcoholism	294.9
Axis II:	Avoidant Personality Disorder	302.81
Axis III:	Defer to Physician	
Axis IV:	Unemployment, few friends	
Axis V:	GAF = 50 (current) 65 (highest in past year)	

Therapist Ronald Obama Lincoln

Estimated # of Sessions Individual <u>12–16</u> Group___ Family <u>4–6</u> Other _____

Impairments <u>X</u> Social <u>X</u> Occupational___ Academic___ Physical <u>X</u> Affective___ Other_____

Strengths/Abilities <u>Close family ties, strong religious beliefs, willing to work hard</u>

Needs <u>Social outlets, employment, assertiveness training, sobriety</u>

Preferences <u>Prefers individual therapy, midafternoon appointments, family involvement</u>

Initial GAF <u>50</u> Target GAF <u>70+</u> Other Outcome Measures <u>See treatment plan objectives.</u>

TP Problem #1 <u>Panic attacks in social situations</u>
Frequency: <u>3/day</u> Duration: <u>30 minutes</u> Severity: <u>SUD = 80</u> Target date

Goal 1:	<u>Alleviate panic attacks</u>	<u>7-15-11</u>
Objective 1a	<u>Decrease number of panic attacks to 2 or less per day.</u>	<u>5-13-11</u>
Objective 1b	<u>Decrease length of panic attacks to 15 minutes or less.</u>	<u>5-13-11</u>
Objective 1c	<u>Decrease severity of panic attacks to SUD level of 60 or less.</u>	<u>5-13-11</u>

Treatment Strategies/Interventions: <u>Med referral, relaxation training, guided imagery, bibliotherapy</u>

Dates of Completed Goals/Objectives
Objectives: 1a <u>5-13-11</u> 1b <u>5-6-11</u> 1c <u>5-6-11</u> Goal 1 <u>Met at discharge</u>
Comments <u>1a revised to 1 or less per day; 1a revised to 5 minutes or less; 1c revised to SUD of 50 or less</u>

TP Problem #2 <u>Decreased social contacts due to anxiety and panic, social impairment</u>
Frequency: <u>1/month</u>   Duration: <u>5 minutes</u> Severity: <u>NA</u>   Target date

Goal 2:	<u>Increase positive social contacts.</u>	<u>7-15-11</u>
Objective 2a	<u>Increase social contacts to at least 1/wk.</u>	<u>5-6-11</u>
Objective 2b	<u>Increase time spent with others socially to at least 20 minutes.</u>	<u>5-6-11</u>
Objective 2c	<u>Invite at least 1 person to social activity every other week.</u>	<u>5-6-11</u>

Treatment Strategies/Interventions   <u>Role playing, empty chair, relaxation techniques</u>

Dates of Completed Goals/Objectives
Objectives: 2a <u>5-6-11</u> 2b <u>5-6-11</u> 2c <u>5-27-11</u> Goal 2 <u>Partially met at discharge</u>
Comments <u>2a revised to 2 contacts; 2b revised to 40 minutes; 2c revised to weekly</u>

TP Problem #3 <u>Excessive dependency on family of origin</u>

Frequency: <u>Asks for advice daily</u>   Duration: <u>NA</u> Severity: <u>NA</u>   Target date

Goal 3:	<u>Increase independent behaviors.</u>	7-15-11
Objective 3a	<u>Engage in at least 1 new behavior that is safe but somewhat risky emotionally.</u>	5-20-11
Objective 3b	<u>Decide which jobs to apply for without consulting or depending on others.</u>	5-6-11
Objective 3c	<u>Keep a daily journal of functional and dysfunctional thoughts.</u> <u>Increase positive thoughts. Discuss in therapy</u>	Ongoing

Treatment Strategies/Interventions <u>Role playing, homework assignments, journaling</u>

Dates of Completed Goals/Objectives
Objectives: 3a <u>5-20-11</u>   3b <u>5-6-11</u>   3c ____ Goal 3 Met at discharge
Comments_____

TP Problem #4 <u>Excessive use of alcohol</u>   Target Date
<u>Refer to substance abuse counselor for CD treatment.</u>   3-12-11
<u>Maintain treatment coordination with substance abuse counselor.</u>
<u>CD treatment plan by others.</u>

Comments: <u>She received a CD evaluation, attended 1-1 counseling, and is attending AA and MICD group. She has remained abstinent.</u>

TP Problem #5 <u>Refer neurological evaluation with MD.</u>   3-12-11
<u>Treatment plan by others.</u>

Comments: <u>She received a neurological evaluation. No concerns noted by neurologist.</u>

Discharge Criteria <u>Return to work or college. No more than 1 panic attack per week, which is of brief duration. Notable increasing in self-esteem in which client is able to assert herself in occupational and family situations. Initiate social interactions at a comfortable level. Coordination of services with CD treatment to monitor their treatment objectives as it relates to mental health counseling.</u>

Discharge Plan (Planning with client begins in initial session: Fill in those that apply.)

Social   Client will feel comfortable in social situations by learning various social skills, with no notable impairments.

Vocational   Client will return to work full time.

Treatment   Treatment plan goals and objectives will be met at a level suitable to the client.

Recreational   Client will seek out and continue in recreational activities to increase social andleisure activities.

Physical   Client will learn relaxation techniques to increase physical well-being.

Environmental   Client will learn to avoid environments in which have led to previous bouts of alcohol abuse.

I have discussed the above information, various treatment strategies, goals, and objectives, possible outcomes, and discharge planning. I have received and/or read my copy of my rights as a client and procedures for reporting grievances. I concur with the diagnosis, treatment plan, and discharge plan.

Additional Client Comments and Input_____

Client's Signature   *Judy Doe*   Date 3-12-11

Guardian's Signature _____   Date_____

Therapist's Signature   *Ronald Obama Lincoln, PhD, LP*   Date 3-12-11

Supervisor's Signature   *Hillary Washington Carver, MD*   Date 3-13-11

PROGRESS NOTES

Client: <u>Judy M. Doe</u>   Chart # <u>JD0533</u>   Session # <u>1</u>   Date: <u>3-19-11</u>

Diagnosis: Panic Disorder with Agoraphobia, Avoidant Personality Disorder, Alcohol Dependence, R/O Cognitive Disorder NOS, secondary to alcoholism

Objectives for Session: (1) relaxation techniques, (2) med referral, (3) anxiety sources

DATA: First therapy session since intake. On time. Signed release of information with Dr. Erikson. Reviewed limits of confidentiality. Reviewed MMPI-2 results, which suggested anxiety, shyness, lack of assertiveness, and substance abuse. She concurred with results. Client reports a daily average of 5 panic attacks each lasting 20–25 minutes in past week, each time when anticipating going to public places. She states, "I just can't stop them from happening . . . the harder I try, the worse they get. . . . I'll never get a job." Insists on keeping therapy sessions in the midafternoon when there is little traffic. Practiced muscle relaxation in 3 major muscle areas and deep breathing exercises. Initially became more tense when trying to relax. Eventually stated that she felt "more relaxed." Has mixed feelings regarding daily telephone calls from her family, stating that she needs but resents their help. Discussed feelings of dependency and need for approval. She replied, "That's what families are for." Attended a full session of individual psychotherapy. Topics included test results, relaxation, and family dynamics. She has made appointments with neurologist and substance abuse counselor.

ASSESSMENT: Slight increase in number of panic attacks. Somewhat pessimistic about employment at this time. Seemed tense in learning relaxation techniques; eventually soothed. Supportive family but concerns with dependency. Her attempts to curtail panic attacks increase anxiety.

PLAN: Will practice 2 relaxation techniques daily. Will write diary of feelings after talking with family on telephone. Next session: Continue relaxation training and family dynamics, review diary.

Time Started: 1:30 P.M	Time Ended: 2:15 P.M.	Duration: 45 minutes
Type: 90840	Next Session: 3-26-11	Time: 1:30 P.M.

Ronald Obama Lincoln, PhD, LP   Date: 3-19-11
Therapist's Signature and Credentials

PROGRESS NOTES

Client: <u>Judy M. Doe</u>   Chart # <u>JD0533</u>   Session # <u>2</u>   Date: <u>3-26-11</u>

Diagnosis: Panic Disorder with Agoraphobia, Avoidant Personality Disorder, Alcohol Dependence, R/O Cognitive Disorder NOS, secondary to alcoholism

Objectives for Session: (1) relaxation techniques, (2) family dynamics

DATA: Session 2. Med evaluation will be this week with Dr. Erikson. Compliant with homework assignment. Has not looked into any job possibilities. Reports 4 panic attacks this week, in which she tried repeating relaxation techniques. Although these techniques did not stop them, they may have decreased duration of attacks from 20–30 minutes to about 15 minutes on average. Stated that she feels helpless during an attack and "always" phones her family when in distress. Journaling notations indicate relief of stress when in contact with family. Brought up increasing resentments toward family due to "taking care of me . . . I want to make my own mistakes." Family will be incorporated as future collaterals in treatment. Reviewed and refined 2 relaxation techniques. Used guided imagery techniques in imagining going to grocery store. Some resistance but followed through. Gave her a handout of assertiveness training group at Main Hospital. Attended full session. She had gone to 1 individual session with LADC. She will join a CD treatment group with MICD concerns that meets 3 times per week. Upcoming appointment with neurologist on 4-15-11.

ASSESSMENT: Cooperative and motivated to change but has difficulties acknowledging dependence on family for stress alleviation. Guided imagery techniques were helpful. Deep breathing seems more effective than muscle relaxation at this time. Somewhat reluctant to join group therapy at this time.

PLAN: Assigned reading of *Take Control of Your Anxiety*. Client will discuss collateral sessions with family parents and 2 sisters. No changes in objectives.

Time Started: 1:30 P.M.	Time Ended: 2:15 P.M.	Duration: 45 minutes
Type: 90840	Next Session: 4-2-11	Time: 1:30 P.M.

Ronald Obama Lincoln, PhD, LP   Date: 3-26-11
Therapist's Signature and Credentials

REQUEST FOR ADDITIONAL SERVICES

Client: Judy M. Doe   Chart # JD0533   Date: 3-26-11

Axis I:	Diagnosis	Code
	Alcohol Dependence	303.90
	Panic Disorder with Agoraphobia	300.21
	R/O Cognitive Disorder NOS, secondary to alcoholism	294.9
Axis II:	Avoidant Personality Disorder	302.81
Axis III:	Defer to Physician	
Axis IV:	Unemployment, few friends	
Axis V:	GAF = 50 (current) 65 (highest in past year)	
	Hours used to date: 4: 2 individual, 2 family	
	Hours requested: 10: 6 individual, 4 family	

History: No prior mental health treatment, self or family. Describes self as typically shy and nervous prior to onset of panic symptoms. Fired from job 4 months ago due to coming to work intoxicated and excessive absences. Since losing job experiences panic attacks when leaving the house. Too anxious/fearful to apply for jobs. Increased concerns with concentration and short-term memory lost.

Diagnostic Features: Panic symptoms include shortness of breath, choking feeling, palpitations, feelings of doom, dizziness, and chills. Onset: 1-11. Frequency: 3/day. Duration: 20–30 minutes. Severity: moderate. History of social avoidance, with increasing severity.

Current Stressors/Impairments: Currently unemployed and under financial stress. Increasing level of panic attacks, anxiety, and worrying causing inability to go on job interviews. No social supports outside of her family, on whom she is dependent. Avoiding most people.

Progresses/Setbacks in Therapy: Client reports decreased duration of panic attacks due to relaxation techniques. Gaining insight into family dynamics leading to dependency. Considering assertiveness group. Cooperative, motivated to change. Somewhat reluctant to try new techniques.

Treatment Plan Revisions: No revisions at this point. Presently working on current objectives.

Referrals/Medications: Referred to Dr. Erikson for physical exam and med. evaluation. Appointment on 4–22. No Hx of meds. Signed release of information with Dr. Erikson.

Referred to Debra Burrows, LADC for CD treatment, currently in MICD treatment group. Referred to Dr. Lockery for neurological exam.

Discharge Plans: 80% of treatment plan goals met. Reduce number and duration of panic attacks to <2 per week lasting less than 10 minutes. Learn relaxation and coping techniques to control anxiety. Regularly search for employment and attend job interviews. Decrease dependency on family. Increase social interactions and assertiveness such as initiating at least one social interaction daily.

Ronald Obama Lincoln, PhD, LP   Date: 3-26-11
Therapist's Signature and Credentials

PROGRESS NOTES

Client: Judy M. Doe   Chart # JD0533   Session # 9   Date: 7-26-11

Diagnosis: Panic Disorder with Agoraphobia, Avoidant Personality Disorder, Alcohol Dependence, R/O Cognitive Disorder NOS, secondary to alcoholism

Objectives for Session: (1) review of all treatment plan objectives, (2) increase social contacts.

DATA: Session 12. Reviewed treatment plan objectives to date. (1) Has become proficient in muscle relaxation. (2) Has reduced number and duration of panic attacks—currently averaging no more than 2 panic attack weekly, duration 2–3 minutes. (3) Receiving medications from MD. (4) Significant improvements implementing new coping mechanisms. (5) Has initiated approximately 1 social contact daily, with minimal anxiety. Discussed discharge, with booster sessions as needed. Appeared much calmer than in initial sessions. Has attended assertiveness group 5 weeks in a row in which she is beginning to enjoy the exercises. Experiencing some stress when attempting to assert own opinions toward family. Continued exploring family dynamics and social avoidance issues. She has been on her job now for 2 weeks in which she notes mild anxiety, but not at a level that she would miss work or relapse. Her CD counselor notes significant progress in treatment. She notes that she has stayed abstinent and does not crave or need alcohol to be around other people. She further notes that she no longer has difficulty concentrating, and her memory has improved as she becomes less anxious. She was administered 2 executive functioning tests in which results were within normal limits, noting significant improvements.

ASSESSMENT: The major treatment plan objectives on target for date. Medications effective; no side effects. Continued difficulties with assertiveness and social avoidance, but not at a debilitating level. There is no evidence of a cognitive disorder. The previous cognitive concerns do not appear to be organic but due to her stress and anxiety. Treatment is no longer medically necessary. Ready for discharge.

PLAN: Discharge, with booster sessions as needed. Plan follow-up visit in 60 days.

Time Started: 1:30 P.M.   Time Ended: 2:15 P.M.
Duration: 45 minutes   Type: 90844
Next Session: Follow up in 60 days

Ronald Obama Lincoln, PhD, LP   Date: 7-26-11
Therapist's Signature and Credentials

DISCHARGE SUMMARY

Client's Name Judy Doe   DOB 2-8-82 Chart # JD0533   Date: 7-26-11

		Diagnosis	Code
Initial Diagnosis	Axis I:	Alcohol Dependence	303.90
		Panic Disorder with Agoraphobia	300.21
		R/O Cognitive Disorder NOS, secondary to alcoholism	294.9
	Axis II:	Avoidant Personality Disorder	302.81
	Axis III:	Defer to Physician	
	Axis IV:	Unemployment, few friends	
	Axis V:	GAF = 50 (current) 65 (highest in past year)	

		Diagnosis	Code
Discharge	Axis I:	Alcohol Dependence, early full remission	303.90
Diagnosis		Panic Disorder with Agoraphobia, mild	300.21
	Axis II:	Avoidant Personality Disorder	302.81
	Axis III:	Defer to Physician	
	Axis IV:	Few friends	
	Axis V:	GAF = 70 (current) 70 (highest in past year)	

SERVICES AND TERMINATION STATUS

Opening Date: <u>3-5-11</u> Termination Date: <u>7-26-11</u>
  Total Number of Sessions: <u>12 Individual 6 Family</u>

Which of the following services were used during the client's stay?

<u>X</u> Individual
__Group
<u>X</u> Family
<u>X</u> Psychiatric
<u>X</u> Psych. Testing
<u>X</u> Other (specify) Referral to neurologist for evaluation of cognitive declines

Overall status at termination

<u>X</u> Improved
__No Change
__Regressed
__Unknown

Reason(s) for termination

<u>X</u> Treatment plan objectives completed
__Client referred for other services (specify) _____
__Client terminated against recommendation
__Client withdrew (specify reason) _____
__Other (specify) _____

Presenting Problem and Assessment (Subjective Evaluation: Summarize specific symptomology, onset, duration, intensity and frequency of symptoms. Include client's assessment of presenting problem and reason(s) for seeking services.)

Client was referred by her primary physician for mental health counseling due to panic attacks, substance abuse, and cognitive declines. She consumed excessive amounts of alcohol since moving away to college 6 years ago. She has a history of social avoidance and panic attacks with agoraphobia. She dropped out of college and returned home due to such issues. She lost her last job due to missing too much work and coming into work intoxicated. Panic attacks at the time of initiating services took place about 3x/day, lasting about 30 minutes. She was drinking 12 beers per day plus a pint of vodka on weekends. She further noted increased problems concentrating and in short-term memory.

Clinical Course (Impact of services upon each problem identified in treatment plan. What clinical interventions were utilized to improve the client's condition in regard to specific problem areas?)

She received 12 sessions of individual counseling and 6 sessions of family counseling, plus she was referred for CD counseling and a neurological evaluation. She has learned to identify stressors that lead to panic attacks and consuming alcohol. She continues attending AA meetings 1–2 times per month. Cognitive/behavioral and family therapy was helpful in increasing her insight into the nature of her anxiety and substance abuse. As she become less anxious and abstained from alcohol, her level of concentration and memory returned to premorbid levels. The neurological evaluation noted no concerns.

Medical/Psychiatric Status (Was the client seen by the psychiatrist for either a psychiatric evaluation or medications? Please describe discharge medications, dosages, instructions, and any psychiatric referral planning.)

She continues to receive psychiatric services for med management once every 3 months. Currently she is taking Xanax, .5mg PRN. On average, she has been taking it about 3×/wk.

Strengths (e.g., family support, motivated, insightful)

Her family continues to be a significant source of strength. She phones them when she is tempted to use alcohol. She is very insightful as to triggers that lead to anxiety and drinking alcohol.

Needs (e.g., housing, meds, transportation)

Her greatest need is to develop sober friendships and remain employed. Although her family continues to help her financially, she does not want to be dependent on them.

Abilities (various skills)

She has advanced clerical skills. She enjoys studying and reading. She has the ability to return to college and do well.

Preferences (e.g., follow-up treatment, changes)

She prefers to continue receiving psychiatric services, attend AA, and have counseling booster session as needed. She desires to be med-free within a year.

Posttermination Plan (Include referrals, appointments, disposition, client's reaction)

No additional referrals have been made. An appointment has been made with this clinic for a follow-up visit in 60 days. See Preferences, above.

Client's Statement Regarding Satisfaction of Treatment Rendered

Counseling has been very helpful for me. I no longer have to rely on alcohol to relieve my anxiety. I have learned how to cope when I feel anxious and panicky. If problems come up, I will make another appointment. Judy Doe

Endorsements

Therapist

Ronald Obama Lincoln, PhD, LP   Date: 7-26-11
Therapist's Signature and Credentials

Supervisor
I concur with the Final Diagnosis and Posttermination Plan, as delineated.
Comments: Everything appears to be in order.

Hillary Washington Carver, MD   Date: 7-29-11

Supervisor's (Signature and Credentials)

APPENDIX B

Overview of Outcome Measures

The material in this appendix provides an overview of outcomes, but it is not intended to present a complete description of how to conduct an outcome study. See Wiger and Solberg (2001) for training in several aspects of outcomes.

Prior to the late 1970s to early 1980s, mental health services represented only 3% to 4% of the healthcare dollars spent by employers. But mental health costs have skyrocketed by as much as 30% to 40% per year, and mental health services grew to nearly 35% of the money spent on healthcare by the early 1990s (Lyons, Howard, O'Mahoney, & Lish, 1997). To reduce costs, services were limited and subject to increasing guidelines for approval. Outcome measures have developed to help determine the most efficient means of providing quality services. The basic questions being asked in outcomes measures are, "What evidence is there that psychotherapy is working?" and "What types of mental health services work most effectively for whom?" As outcomes measures research has developed, issues have arisen regarding what needs to be measured and how it will be helpful. Table B.1 provides eight principles of outcomes measurement.

According to Browning and Browning (1996), developers of the Browning Outcomes Survey Scale (BOSS), the best judge of therapeutic outcomes is the person who received services; therefore, much of outcomes measurement is based on self-report. The BOSS comes in three versions: intake, discharge, and six-month follow-up. Both Likert ratings for quantification and comment sections for quality are included for each of several dimensions. The authors suggest sharing the findings regularly with case managers in either a summary format or by providing a copy of the instrument. Copies of the BOSS are available from Duncliff's International at 1-800-410-7766.

Lyons et al. (1997) suggest three dimensions of satisfaction based on the Medical Outcomes Study developed by the Rand Corporation (Ware & Hays, 1988). These dimensions include technical quality, competence, interpersonal

Table B.1

Principles of Outcome Measurement

What to Measure

Principle 1.   Define the goals and objectives of the service and measure their clinical aspects. Do not measure what is irrelevant to these goals and objectives.

Principle 2.   Determine what is important to consumers, providers, and customers of the services, and attempt to include these in the measurement.

Principle 3.   Determine what is possible and practical to measure. Try not to overreach in any single effort. Multiple short-term studies are often more feasible and of greater value than comprehensive but overly complicated long-term efforts.

How to Measure

Principle 4.   Know the existing measurement choices. Do not create a new measure needlessly. Choose measures with relevant databases that provide norms and benchmarks against which to assess consumers.

Principle 5.   Decide who should provide assessments of clinical status based on the nature of the treatment and the characteristics of the consumers served.

Principle 6.   Choose measures that are reliable, valid, brief, and easy to use.

When to Measure

Principle 7.   Always measure at the earliest possible time. Assessment at the initiation of treatment is essential for estimating change.

Principle 8.   Measure again on a fixed schedule, particularly when the end of treatment is not predictable. This method allows statistical options for estimating end-of-treatment clinical status.

Source: Reprinted with permission of John Wiley & Sons, Inc.

quality, access, and availability and choice of services. Examples of areas to assess are found in Figure B.1.

The material in Figure B.1 is not intended to be a formal outcomes questionnaire; rather, it provides helpful guidelines regarding the type of information that can aid in an outcomes assessment. The formatting of the questions can range from yes/no questions, to a Likert scale, to a narrative.

TYPES OF DATA USED IN DOCUMENTING OUTCOMES

YES/NO QUESTIONS

Yes/no questions in outcomes measurement are calculated by the percentage of its survey items either endorsed as "yes" or "no" (or similar contrasting terms, such as agree/disagree, positive/negative, improved/declined, etc.).

Examples of Technical Quality Dimensions

Were the educational materials helpful?

Were the medications explained to you?

Did you understand the possible side effects of your prescription when you finished your visit?

Was the equipment in good working condition?

Were the program's policies explained to you?

Was the billing procedure accurate?

Examples of Competence Dimensions

Did you feel your therapist was qualified to provide the care you needed?

Did you find the hospital staff sufficiently well trained?

Did your therapist discuss your treatment plan with you in a manner that you could understand?

Was the intake worker able to provide sufficient information about the available services?

To what degree were you confident that the program staff were skilled in their professions?

Examples of Interpersonal Competence Dimensions

Did you feel that your case manager was concerned with your well-being?

Did you experience your therapist as warm and supportive?

Did you feel comfortable talking to program staff?

Did program staff listen to you when you had a question or concern?

Did you feel that your problems were being taken seriously?

Examples of Access to Care Dimensions

Was the geographical location of your therapist convenient?

How long did you have to wait to see the crisis worker? How did you feel about the wait?

How many days passed between the time you called to request services and when you were able to see your therapist? How did you feel about this amount of time?

How did you feel about the costs of your treatment?

How did you feel about the copayment?

How did you experience the process of obtaining treatment?

Did you have any concerns about the confidentiality of the service? Were these concerns communicated and addressed?

Figure B.1   Suggested Dimensions of Client Satisfaction in Outcomes Studies

Source: Reprinted with permission of John Wiley & Sons, Inc.

For example, a question like, "Did your therapist seem to listen to your concerns?" requests either a positive or negative response, with no in-between choices.

The main problem with yes/no questions is that they assume a person totally agrees or totally disagrees with the statement. A "no" answer implies that the therapist did not listen at all to the client's concerns whereas a "yes"

---

1. Pretreatment, midtreatment, discharge, and posttreatment scores
2. Treatment variables (type of, number of sessions)
3. Clinician variables (style, empathy, background, education, experience)
4. Diagnosis (chronic, acute, onset, duration, intensity of symptoms, impairments)
5. Demographic variables (age, race, socioeconomic status, previous treatment)
6. Treatment/medication compliance (attendance, compliance in homework, meds, interventions)

Figure B.2   Use of Likert Ratings in Outcomes Measurement
Source: Reprinted with permission of John Wiley & Sons, Inc.

answer implies no problems in this area. When a client fills out a questionnaire with this format (called *ipsative*), there is no place for partial agreement. That is, the client who believes that the therapist listened some of the time faces a dilemma as to how to answer the question. Results allow the researcher to have a general idea of outcome measures, but the degree is unknown.

Likert Scale Ratings

Likert ratings provide answers on a continuum in which a degree of agreement or disagreement with a statement is possible. For example, the wording of the outcomes measures question, "Did your therapist seem to listen to your concerns?" would have to be changed to a statement, because a level of agreement is needed. For example, a Likert rating scale could be incorporated for the statement, "The therapist seemed to listen to my concerns." Likert ratings are numerical ratings in which the client's level of agreement is analyzed. When the highest point on the scale is an odd number, there is a midpoint in which the client is neutral in the response. A Likert scale of 1 to 7 is commonly used. Some Likert scales use an even number of items, in which there is no mid- or neutral point. Data from Likert ratings, such as those found in Figure B.2, can be used for several possible outcome measures.

Figure B.3 provides an example of Likert rating items.

Use of Outcome Data

Ultimately outcome measures most benefit the client by providing evidence of the most cost-effective treatment by the most qualified professionals. The process of collecting and utilizing outcomes data helps make this possible.

Please circle the response which most closely indicates your level of agreement or disagreement with the following statements.

Highly Disagree 1	*Moderately Disagree 2*	*Slightly Disagree 3*	*Neutral 4*	*Slightly Agree 5*	*Moderately Agree 6*	*Highly Agree 7*

"I was given choices about my treatment."

| 1 | 2 | 3 | 4 | 5 | 6 | 7 |

"The therapist explained the benefits and risks of therapy to me."

| 1 | 2 | 3 | 4 | 5 | 6 | 7 |

"I was treated with respect and dignity by the therapist."

| 1 | 2 | 3 | 4 | 5 | 6 | 7 |

"The therapist listened to my concerns."

| 1 | 2 | 3 | 4 | 5 | 6 | 7 |

"The treatment plan was clearly explained to me."

| 1 | 2 | 3 | 4 | 5 | 6 | 7 |

"Services were performed in a time-efficient manner."

| 1 | 2 | 3 | 4 | 5 | 6 | 7 |

"The clinic's policies were clearly explained to me."

| 1 | 2 | 3 | 4 | 5 | 6 | 7 |

"The counseling was directed toward helping my problem areas."

| 1 | 2 | 3 | 4 | 5 | 6 | 7 |

"I was satisfied with the counseling I received."

| 1 | 2 | 3 | 4 | 5 | 6 | 7 |

"The services I received were helpful."

| 1 | 2 | 3 | 4 | 5 | 6 | 7 |

"I would return to the therapist for services in the future if needed."

| 1 | 2 | 3 | 4 | 5 | 6 | 7 |

Figure B.3 Example of Likert Scale Items in Outcome Measures

Source: Reprinted with permission of John Wiley & Sons, Inc.

On an individual level, outcomes data can be useful to the client/consumer, as a motivator that therapy is working and that it is cost effective. Properly conducted outcome studies are intended to result in the therapist changing interventions that are not helpful and maintaining interventions that result in progress. Third-party payers benefit in that they are assured that their funds are being used to benefit clients who have paid for such services. When outcome measures indicate lack of progress, it provides a flag that current interventions are not alleviating the client's impairments. In general, third-party payers request individual outcome measures on a client-by-client basis. Outcomes training found in Wiger and Solberg (2001) teaches how to collect outcomes data in all aspects of treatment, such as the interview, treatment plan, and progress notes, and through standardized outcome measures.

APPENDIX C

Overview of HIPAA Guidelines in Mental Health Settings

The information in this appendix is not intended to constitute comprehensive training in the Health Insurance Portability and Accountability Act of 1996 (HIPAA); rather, it briefly summarizes the rationale for the guidelines. HIPAA guidelines specifically state that there are no approved training courses, and consumers are cautioned to be aware of programs that present themselves as such.

The U.S. Department of Health and Human Services (HHS) implemented HIPAA in 1996. HIPAA is designed both to protect people's health information and to provide standardized means of regulating the flow of information. Its major purposes are to: (1) protect individuals from losing their health insurance when they change jobs, (2) allow medical savings accounts, (3) help prevent abuse and fraud, and (4) simplify health insurance administrative procedures. Prior to HIPAA regulations, there were about 400 different formats of electronic claims submission in the United States. Since the enactment of HIPAA, providers must adhere to standard codes and are not allowed to modify or use additional code sets; thus uniformity and cost savings are assured. Complete rules may be found on the Office of Civil Rights (OCR) Web site at http://www.hhs.gov/ocr/hipaa.

HIPAA's "Privacy Rule" refers to the standards of disclosure of "protected health information" by "covered entities" (those subject to the regulations). Covered entities include healthcare clearinghouses, health plans, and healthcare providers who transmit health information electronically or use billing services that transmit electronically.

The covered entity must have a written contract with each business associate to safeguard the protected health information. All individually identifiable health information held or transmitted by a covered entity or its business associate (nonmember of covered entity's workforce who has access to protected health information; e.g., billing service, utilization review) requires this contract. The OCR Web site provides a sample at www.hhs.gov/ocr /privacy/hipaa/understanding/coveredentities/contractprov.html. Health-care providers who are covered entities must disclose protected health information in two broad situations. These include providing the information to (1) the individual (or personal representative) who requests their records and (2) to HHS in a compliance action. The covered entity may disclose protected health information without the individual's consent in certain situations.

1. The individual who is the subject of the protected health information (i.e., client, patient) is not required to authorize information sent to self.
2. Treatment, payment, and healthcare operations. Protected healthcare information that is used in the normal operation of providing services, consultation, and referral does not need a specific authorization.
3. Payment operations, such as premiums, determination of benefits, and billing services are not subject to an authorization.
4. Healthcare operations, such as quality improvement, case management, competency assurance activities (e.g., credentialing, accreditation), audits, reviews, insurance functions, business development, and administrative activities, may use a "limited data set" in which records are "de-identified" (patient information does not include identifying information, such as name, Social Security number, or other specific identifiers).
5. The public interest can override confidentiality in situations such as when the health, welfare, or safety of others may be in jeopardy. Certain civil operations, such as court orders, crimes, and essential government services necessary for the public's best interest, do not require an individual's authorization for disclosing protected health information.

The covered entity is required to treat the individual's "personal representative" with the same rights as the individual in matters of disclosure. The personal representative is legally allowed to make healthcare decisions for the individual, except in cases of suspected abuse. In general, parents are the personal representatives of their minor children and have access to protected health information, except in cases where the law would allow discretion on behalf of the licensed healthcare professional.

DISCLOSURE OF INFORMATION

A written authorization from the individual (or authorized representative) to the covered entity must precede a release of protected healthcare information. The content of the authorization must be in specific terms, written in plain language. The authorization must designate which information is being requested (rather than asking for an entire file), include an expiration date, and describe the individual's right to revoke the authorization.

In most cases, an individual must consent to disclose psychotherapy progress notes. Exceptions include ongoing psychotherapy with the originator of the progress notes, training, legal matters brought by the individual, legal reasons, and for the public interest.

The practice of routinely requesting an individual's entire record is discouraged. The Privacy Rule requires limiting the amount of information disclosed to the "minimum necessary." The covered entity is required to develop and implement policies to set guidelines for determining the minimum amount of information necessary for the intended purpose of the disclosure. Policies and procedures must be established regarding which persons or categories of persons in the covered entity's workforce will have access to which level of protected health information in order to perform their duties adequately. When covered entities receive requests for specific information, it can be assumed that the level of information requested is reasonable.

Covered entities are required to provide a notice of privacy practices that describes people's rights to privacy, the duties of the covered entity, and the complaint process. This notice must be distributed to individuals at their first encounter (e.g., office, electronic, mailing). It must be posted in a prominent space where individuals can read it. The covered entity must make reasonable efforts to obtain an individual's signature that the notice was received.

The covered entity has the right to review their own medical records (designated health set). However, the covered entity may choose to not disclose (1) psychotherapy progress notes, (2) information from legal proceedings, and (3) laboratory results, when doing so is deemed as not being in the individual's best interest.

Individuals have a right to amend information in their protected health information when they consider the information to be inaccurate or incomplete. If the information is amended, reasonable efforts must be made to provide the revised information to those identified by the individual as in need of the information and to others who rely on this information for treatment. When the request for an amendment is denied, the individual has the right to make a statement of the disagreement that will be included in the record.

Glossary

A

ABSTRACTIVE CAPACITY: A person's ability to think abstractly. Children often think concretely, whereas an average adult is able to think conceptually rather than perceptually.

Documentation Examples:
In the MSE, the clinician often asks the client to interpret various proverbs that could be interpreted either concretely or abstractly. An abstract interpretation of "The early bird catches the worm," could be, "Those who get up early have the best opportunities," whereas a concrete interpretation is generally more literal. A child or an adult with limited intelligence or brain damage might interpret this proverb as, "Birds catch worms in the morning." Tests of abstract thinking may also indicate signs of a thought disorder. Responses such as, "Birds who fly never die if they eat a worm every day to keep the doctor away," generally indicate concerns beyond the normal range of concrete vs. abstract thought patterns.

ACCREDITATION: An external review process in which a provider of services has been approved by an outside source that sets acceptable standards of performance in which consumers can make decisions about the provider.

ACTIVITY LEVEL: A series of observations in the mental status exam including notations regarding a client's mannerisms, gestures, degree of relaxation versus tenseness, eye contact, vigilance, gait, degree of boredom, attentiveness, and body movements.

Documentation Examples:
Increased activity level: "Increased activity level was observed as evidenced by several body movements, tenseness, often getting out of the chair, and hypervigilance."

Decreased activity level: "The client's activity level appeared decreased as evidenced by low attention span, masked facies, psychomotor retardation, and slow speech."

AFFECTIVE OBSERVATIONS: The client's degree of affect (emotions) as observed by the clinician. See *appropriateness of affect, intensity of affect, mobility of affect, predominant mood,* and *range of affect.*

Documentation Examples:
Depressed mood: "The client appeared dysphoric as evidenced by blunted affect, low mobility of affect, restricted range of affect, few facial expressions, and crying at times."

Anxious mood: "The client appeared anxious. Observations included low eye contact, sweating, irritability, and overworrying."

APPEARANCE: Objective observations made by the clinician describing the client's grooming, manner of dress, hygiene, posture, health, demeanor, and apparent age.

Documentation Examples:
Appearance suggesting depressed mood: "Client appeared at the interview appearing dysphoric as evidenced by disheveled hair, slumped posture, beard stubble, and lack of facial expression."

Appearance suggesting mania: "The client wore extremely bright clothing not suggestive of his usual appearance. Activity level was increased."

Appearance suggesting thought disorder, dementia, or possible substance abuse: "The client appeared at the interview with a soiled winter coat (in the summertime), mismatched socks, and no shoelaces. There was a strong body odor. He appeared to be in poor health, looking approximately 15 years older than his chronological age."

APPROPRIATENESS OF AFFECT: Affective observations indicating the concordance among the client's stated mood, speech, and ideas.

Documentation Examples:
Example 1: "Although the client stated that she was severely depressed and suicidal, she often spoke in an animated manner, joked, and seemed to be somewhat flirtatious."

Example 2: "The client sat in the interview calmly, appearing relaxed, but stated that he was extremely worried and having panic symptoms."

ASSESSMENT: The continuous process in integrating clinical data to form an objective clinical opinion. Assessment data in mental health comes from sources such as observations, information gathered from others, and standardized testing. Simply reporting data is not an assessment. Generally, the more effectively the data are integrated, the better the assessment. Assessment information is used to determine the most appropriate treatment for the client.

ASSOCIATED SYMPTOMS: Symptoms that are often linked to a mental health disorder but not used in validating a diagnosis because they are prevalent in several disorders.

Documentation Examples:

Examples of associated symptoms: Social withdrawal, difficulties coping, low self-esteem, fatigue, irritability, difficulty concentrating.

ATTENTION OR ATTENTION SPAN: The ability to cognitively focus on a stimulus when in an aroused state. Common mental status exam tasks to assess attention include incrementally repeating numbers (digit span) forward and backward. Other indices include the examiner's observations of the client's level of attention in holding a conversation.

Documentation Examples:

Low attention span: "Client's attention span appeared to be significantly below average, as evidenced by asking to have several questions repeated, repeating 3 digits forward and 2 digits backward, and often staring into space."

ATTITUDE TOWARD EXAMINER: The client's general attitude observed during the interview. Descriptions include aspects such as cooperation, level of interest, guardedness, defiance, humor, defensiveness, evasiveness, suspiciousness, manipulative, and level of historical information provided. The validity of the interview is affected by this variable.

Documentation Examples:

Negative attitudinal concerns: "Attitudinal concerns were noted during the interview in which the client made several defiant comments, refused to supply background information, made several derogatory comments, and stated that he does not trust anyone with a tie."

Positive attitude: "The client was cooperative, answered every question, provided detailed historical information, and seemed interested throughout the interview."

AXIS I: MENTAL DISORDERS: A *DSM* diagnosis describing a mental health diagnosis. All mental health diagnoses in the *DSM-IV-TR* are considered Axis I, except personality disorders and mental retardation.

AXIS II: PERSONALITY DISORDERS AND MENTAL RETARDATION: *DSM* diagnoses of personality disorders and mental retardation.

AXIS III: PHYSICAL CONDITIONS AND DISORDERS: *DSM* diagnoses of a physical nature. These may or may not have a bearing on mental disorders. Mental health professionals generally defer this diagnosis to a physician or refer to information received from a physician.

Axis IV: Psychosocial and Environmental Problems: A *DSM* axis that includes a listing of current stressors in the client's life that may be contributing to mental health issues.

Axis V: Global Assessment of Functioning: An overall *DSM* assessment of the client's current level of functioning on a 100-point scale. It also allows for noting changes in functioning over a period of time.

B

Biopsychosocial Assessment: An ongoing assessment of the client's biological, psychological, and social functioning.

C

CARF: The Commission of Accreditation of Rehabilitation Facilities is a private accrediting agency for healthcare organizations designed to improve the quality of care from member organizations to the public.

Clinical Observations: Any observations made by the therapist regarding client behaviors. Typical observations include aspects such as affect, appearance, activity level, speech, and attitude toward examiner.

Clang Association: A type of loose association in which statements are interrelated by their sounds rather than their meanings.

Example:
"I went to Brent at Trent and spent the rent in a dent by a tent."

Cognition: Mental processing of information involving memory and thinking. Mental status observations include indices such as the client's apparent contact with reality, orientation × 3, attention, and concentration.

Collateral Information: Background and clinical information about the client provided by other people, such as other professionals, family members, and significant others.

Compulsions: Repeated physical or mental acts viewed as not useful to the client. Examples include behaviors such as repeatedly washing hands, locking doors, checking that appliances are turned off, or other excessive behaviors of clinical significance.

Concentration: The ability to focus attention over a period of time. Mental status exam measures of concentration typically include tasks such as counting by serial threes beginning with 1 or counting backward by sevens from 100.

Documentation Examples:
Poor concentration: "Client's concentration seemed to be significantly below average, as evidenced by not being able to count by serial threes beginning with one and sometimes forgetting the topic of a question asked after providing only part of the answer."

Adequate concentration: "The client's level of concentration appeared to be within normal limits as evidenced by rapidly counting backward from 100 by sevens in a normal time period, making zero errors."

CONFIDENTIALITY AGREEMENT: An agreement between the therapist and the client that the information disclosed to the therapist will not be shared with other people without the client's consent. State laws impose certain limits of confidentiality that should be disclosed to the client prior to receiving services.

D

DAP NOTES: A progress note format in which three distinct sections are outlined including data, assessment, and plan.

DATA: Specific information, such as observations, test scores, client statements, and collateral information, that is used to form an assessment.

DELUSIONS: Untrue or incorrect beliefs that are not religiously or culturally approved. Contrary evidence does not change these beliefs. Common types of delusions include paranoid, grandeur, nihilistic, and somatic.

DEPERSONALIZATION: A subjective experience of feeling detached or outside of one's body or in a dream.

DERAILMENT: A loosening of associations depicted by unrelated thoughts. Clients jump from one thought to another without a logical transition, which is likened to a train jumping off the rail.

Example:
A client might say, "I balloon never before Sally pepper chair over there."

DISCHARGE: The time in which the clinician or treatment center no longer holds responsibility for the care of the patient. Generally a discharge summary report accompanies discharge.

E

ECHOLALIA: Recurring repetitions of another person's speech.

EFFECTIVENESS: The level in which clinical interventions and care are provided in accordance to the current level of knowledge and practice in the field. Greater effectiveness produces greater outcomes and less level of risk.

EFFICACY: The level of positive outcomes for the client resulting from treatment.

EFFICIENCY: The correspondence between the resources used in providing treatment and the outcomes of treatment. Sometimes called the cost-effectiveness ratio or cost/benefits ratio in which the results of treatment are compared to the cost of treatment.

Essential Symptoms: *DSM-IV-TR* symptoms that must be prevalent for a diagnosis to be made. Also called core symptoms.

Euphoria: An elevated normal mood state but not a manic state. Euphoria often is described as a state of happiness.

Euthymic: A normal range of mood states.

F

Flight of ideas: A rapid succession of interconnected ideas in which the client's conversation changes quickly. The topic of conversation may change from sentence to sentence, but logic is retained.

G

Goals: The client's overall desired outcomes from therapy, or the endpoints of various objectives in therapy.

H

Hallucinations: Perceptual disturbances without corresponding outside stimulation. Hallucinations are associated with all five of the senses. They are often associated with psychosis.

HIPAA: The Health Insurance Portability and Accountability Act created in 1996 by the U.S. Department of Health and Human Services. HIPAA is designed both to protect people's health information and to provide standardized means of regulating the flow of information.

Health Maintenance Organization (HMO):   A source that arranges or provides coverage of health services to members.

I

Illusion: A misperception or distortion of an outside stimulus.

Example:
Trees blowing in the wind may be perceived as demons or giants.

Immediate Memory: Memories recently stored.

Example:
In the mental status exam, the clinician may ask the client to remember three unrelated words after 5- and 30-minute intervals.

Impairments: Areas in a person's life that are not functional; therefore, treatment is "medically necessary." Also called functional impairments.

Commonly documented areas of impairment include social, occupational, affective, physical, and academic.

Example:
"Due to increased irritability and aggression over the past year, the client currently has no friends or social supports. He has not been involved in any social activities for several months and is becoming increasingly more withdrawn, resulting in social impairment."

INTENSITY OF AFFECT: The strength of affective expression. Often it is measured on a continuum from mild to strong.

L

LOOSE ASSOCIATIONS: The absence or loss of logical connectedness in speech. Speech transitions seem to have little association.

Example:
"I like bananas because they taste good and children walk to school."

M

MALINGERING: The intentional presentation of signs and symptoms of a mental disorder. It generally is intended to achieve some sort of gain or to avoid unpleasant circumstances.

MEDICAL MODEL: A model in which mental health service delivery is viewed as treating pathology and documentation consists of symptoms reduction.

MEDICAID: A federally funded, state-administered program that provides healthcare benefits to people with low incomes.

MEDICAL NECESSITY: Mental health services are considered medically necessary when significant dysfunction or impairments exist that result from a diagnosable mental disorder. Services are needed either to restore functioning or prevent deterioration.

MEDICAL RECORD: The client's record of documented clinical information related to services provided.

MOBILITY OF AFFECT: The rate in which a person moves from one type of affect to another. For example, if a client moves rapidly from dysphoria to euphoria, it would be described as lability or increased mobility. Little or no mobility is described as constricted or fixed.

MOOD: The client's description of his or her current or usual affective state.

MOOD DISORDER: Classified as diagnoses in mania, depression, or both. Also called affective disorder.

MSE: Mental status exam.

N

NEOLOGISMS: New or nonsense words used by the client but not recognized as words by others.

Example:

"The cirplexanity of the situation leads to additional recountations."

O

OBJECTIVES: Sequential steps by which treatment plan goals are met. Each objective, when attained, is revised to more closely reach the goal.

OBSESSIONS: Intrusive and persistent unwanted thoughts that will not go away despite attempts to suppress them and despite knowledge that the thought is not reality based or is out of proportion to reality.

ORIENTATION: A person's ability to understand his or her connection in relation to aspects such as time, place, and person. In the mental status exam, the clinician generally states that the person is "oriented × 3" when referring to orientation in all three areas.

OUTCOMES: The empirical results of a course of treatment in which outcomes criteria set by the reviewer are evaluated.

P

POVERTY OF SPEECH: The client's speech has little depth or meaningful information. Sometimes little is spoken, whereas others may speak full sentences.

PREOCCUPATION: A recurrent theme, thought, or idea often prevalent in the client's conversations or thoughts.

Example:

"They're evil. This world is wicked. I dream about the awful things happening. My friends, family, and everyone . . . they're all evil. I always know when the bad people are coming."

PRESENTING PROBLEM: The client's statement of the problem area or reason for seeking services. It is not a diagnosis, but problem areas will be assessed to help determine the need for services.

PROGNOSIS: The clinician's opinion as to the probability of the client leaving services with a positive outcome. Typical descriptions include poor, marginal, guarded, moderate, good, and excellent. It is common for the clinician also to include qualifiers, such as compliance, to the prognosis for areas such as medications, treatment, or changes in areas such as behaviors or education.

PROVISIONAL DIAGNOSIS: A diagnosis qualifier that is given when there is yet insufficient information to warrant a full diagnosis.

PSYCHOMOTOR AGITATION: A behavioral observation in the mental status exam in which the client appears to have difficulties sitting still or attending to tasks and/or appears tense.

PSYCHOMOTOR RETARDATION: A behavioral observation in the mental status exam in which the client's movements and other behaviors are slow.

R

RANGE OF AFFECT: The client's ability to express a variety of affective responses in various situations. Affect often is described as normal, restricted, blunted, or flat.

RECENT MEMORY: Memories of recent events in the client's life. Mental status exam questions regarding the client's memory of recent meals and events of the past weekend typically are asked.

REMOTE MEMORY: Memories of historical events in the client's life. Mental status exam questions for remote memory include the name of the street clients grew up on, previous teachers' names, or asking someone born prior to the mid-1950s what they were doing when they heard that President Kennedy was shot.

S

SIGNS: Characteristics of a mental disorder that are observed objectively by the clinician.

SNAPs: An acronym for the client's strengths, needs, abilities, and preferences, in which these characteristics are incorporated into the client's treatment.

SOAP NOTES: A progress note format in which four distinct sections are outlined: subjective, objective, assessment, and plan.

SOMATOFORM DISORDER: A variety of physical disorders with emotional origins.

SYMPTOMS: Characteristics of a mental disorder reported by the affected individual.

T

THIRD-PARTY PAYER: A source such as an individual, organization, or government entity that has agreed or is obligated to pay for part of all of a recipient's healthcare services.

THOUGHT CONTENT: Generally refers to types of thoughts the client experiences. The mental status exam often includes questions regarding obsessions, compulsions, phobias, suicidality, homicidality, and antisocial thoughts.

THOUGHT DISORDER: Encompasses disorders of thought or perception, such as schizophrenia or psychotic disorders.

THOUGHT DISTURBANCES: Thoughts that are intrusive, such as delusions (persecutory, grandeur, and somatic) or ideas of reference (thought broadcasting, thought control, or bizarre thoughts).

THOUGHT PROCESSES: The manner in which thoughts are interconnected. It is measured in the mental status exam by aspects of the client's speech, such as number of ideas, flight of ideas, relevance, coherence, derailment, neologisms, and associations.

TJC: The Joint Commission is a private accrediting agency for healthcare organizations designed to improve the quality of care from member organizations to the public.

TREATMENT PLAN: A systematic plan, formulated by the client and therapist, in which the client's diagnosis, problem areas, goals and objectives, treatment strategies, and anticipated closure dates are delineated. It becomes an agreement, similar to a contract, for the course of therapy.

U

UTILIZATION REVIEW: An examination of the use and costs of medical service considering its appropriateness, efficiency, and level of treatment. It typically is referred to as an audit.

References and Suggested Readings

Allan, A., & Love, A. (2010). *Ethical practice in psychology: Reflections from the creators of the APS code of ethics*. Hoboken, NJ: Wiley.

Allen, J. G., Buskirk, J. R., & Sebastian, L. M. (1992). A psychodynamic approach to the master treatment plan. *Bulletin of the Menninger Clinic, 56*, 487–510.

American Psychiatric Association. (2000). *Diagnostic and statistical manual of mental disorders* (4th ed., text revision). Washington, DC: American Psychiatric Association.

Barlow, D. H. (Ed.). (2007). *Clinical handbook of psychological disorder: A step-by-step treatment manual* (4th ed.). New York, NY: Guilford Press.

Brown, S. L. (1991). *The quality management professional's study guide*. Pasedena, CA: Managed Care Consultants.

Browning, C. H., & Browning, B. J. (1996). *How to partner with managed care*. New York, NY: Wiley.

Cohen, R. J. (1979). *Malpractice: A guide for mental health professionals*. New York, NY: Free Press.

Commission on Accreditation of Rehabilitation Facilities. (2010). *Behavioral health standards manual*. Washington, DC: Author.

Dalton v. State, 308 N.Y.S 2d 411 (1970).

Fisher, C. B. (2009). *Decoding the ethics code: A practical guide for psychologists* (2nd ed.). Thousand Oaks, CA: Sage.

Folstein, M. F., Folstein, S. E., & McHugh, P. R. (1975). Mini-mental state: A practical method for grading the cognitive state of patients for the clinician. *Journal of Psychiatric Research, 12*, 189–198.

Frederiksen, L. W., Richter, W. T., Jr., Johnson, R. P., & Solomon, L. J. (1982). Specificity of performance feedback in a professional service delivery setting. *Journal of Organizational Behavior Management, 3*, 41–53.

Fulero, S. M., & Wilbert, J. R. (1998). Record keeping of clinical and counseling psychologists: A survey of practitioners. *Professional Psychology Research and Practice, 19*, 658–660.

Gabbard, G. O. (2005). *Psychodynamic psychiatry in clinical practice* (4th ed). Washington, DC: American Psychiatric Press.

Galasso, D. (1987). Guidelines for developing multi-disciplinary treatment plans. *Hospitals and Community Psychiatry, 38*, 394–397.

Goldstein, G., & Hersen, M. (2000). *Handbook of psychological assessment* (3rd ed.). New York, NY: Pergamon Press.

Goodman, M., Brown, J., & Dietz, P. (1992). *Managing managed care: A mental health practitioner's survival guide*. Washington, DC: American Psychiatric Press.

Grant, R. L. (1981). The capacity of the psychiatric record to meet changing needs. In C. Siegel & S. K. Fischer (Eds.), *Psychiatric records in mental health care*. New York, NY: Brunner/Mazel.

Groth-Marnat, G. (2009). *Handbook of psychological assessment* (5th ed.). Hoboken, NJ: Wiley.

Gutheil, T. B., & Applebaum, P. S. (1987). *The clinical handbook of psychotherapy and the law* (2nd ed.). New York, NY: McGraw-Hill.

Hillard, J. R. (1995). "Predicting suicide." *Psychiatric Services, 46*(3), 223–225.

Johnson v. United States, 409 F. Supp. 1283 (M.D. FA. 1976).

Joint Commission on Accreditation of Healthcare Organizations. (2011). *Standards for behavioral health care*. Oakbrook Terrace, IL: Author.

Jongsma, A. E. (2008). *Therascribe 5.0. The computerized assistant to the psychotherapy treatment planner*. Hoboken, NJ: Wiley.

Jongsma, A. E., & Peterson, L. M. (2006). *The complete adult psychotherapy treatment planner* (4th ed.). Hoboken, NJ: Wiley.

Jongsma, A. E., Peterson, L. M., & McInnis, W. P. (2006a). *The adolescent psychotherapy treatment planner* (4th ed.). Hoboken, NJ: Wiley.

Jongsma, A. E., Peterson, L. M., & McInnis, W. P. (2006b). *The child psychotherapy treatment planner* (4th ed.). Hoboken, NJ: Wiley.

Kennedy, J. A. (2003). *Fundamentals of psychiatric treatment planning* (2nd ed.). Washington, DC: American Psychiatric Press.

Klopfer, W. G. (1960). *The psychological report*. New York: Grune & Stratton.

Koocher, G. P., & Keith-Spiegel, P. (2008). *Ethics in Psychology: Professional Standards and Cases*. New York, NY: Oxford University Press.

Lezak, M. D., Howieson, D. B., & Loring, D. W. (2004). *Neurological assessment* (4th ed.). New York, NY: Oxford University Press.

Lovett, S. B., Bosmajian, C. P., Frederiksen, L. W., & Elder, J. P. (1983). Monitoring professional service delivery: An organizational level intervention. *Behavior Therapy, 14*, 170–177.

Maltsberger, J. T. (1988). Suicide danger: Clinical estimation and decision. *Suicide and Life-Threatening Behavior, 18*(1), 47–54.

Mann, J. (1973). *Time-limited psychotherapy*. Cambridge, MA: Harvard University Press.

Maxmen, J. S., & Ward, N. G. (1995). *Essential psychopathology and its treatment* (2nd ed.). New York, NY: Norton.

Medicare program: Prospective payment for Medicare final rule. (1984). *Federal Register, 49*, 234–240.

Morrison, J. R. (1993). *The first interview*. New York, NY: Guilford Press.

Morrison, J. R. (1995). *DSM-IV made easy*. New York, NY: Guilford Press.

Ormiston, S., Barrett, N., Binder, R., & Molyneux, V. (1989). A partially computerized treatment plan. *Hospital and Community Psychology, 40*, 531–533.

Othmer, E., & Othmer, S. C. (2002). *The clinical interview using DSM-IV-TR*. Washington, DC: American Psychiatric Press.

Patterson, R., Cooke, C., & Liberman, R. (1972). Reinforcing the reinforcers: A method of supplying feedback to nursing personnel. *Behavior Therapy, 3,* 444–446.

Phares, E. J. (1988). *Clinical psychology: Concepts, methods, and profession* (3rd ed.). Pacific Grove, CA: Brooks/Cole.

Roth, A. D., & Fonagy, P. (2005). *What works for whom? A critical review of psychotherapy research* (2nd ed.). New York, NY: Guilford Press.

Siegel, C., & Fischer, S. K. (1980). *Psychiatric records in mental health care.* New York, NY: Brunner/Mazel.

Slovenko, R. (1979). On the need for record keeping in the practice of psychiatry. *Journal of Psychiatry and Law, 7,* 339–340.

Soisson, E. L., VandeCreek, L., & Knapp, S. (1987). Thorough record keeping: A good defense in a litigious era. *Professional Psychology: Research and Practice, 14,* 498–502.

Soreff, S. M., & McDuffee, M. A. (1993). *Documentation survival handbook: A clinician's guide to charting for better care, certification, reimbursement, and risk management.* Seattle, WA: Hogrefe & Huber.

Stout, C. E. (1997). *Psychological assessment in managed care.* New York, NY: Wiley.

Sturm, I. E. (1987). The psychologist in the problem-oriented record (POR). *Professional Psychology Research and Practice, 18,* 155–158.

Sue, D., & Sue, D. (2008). *Counseling the culturally diverse* (5th ed.). New York, NY: Wiley.

Trzepacz, P. T., & Baker, R. W. (1993). *The psychiatric MSE.* New York, NY: Oxford University Press.

Walborn, F. (1996). *Process variables: Four common elements of counseling and psychotherapy.* Pacific Grove, CA: Brooks/Cole.

Walters, S. (1987). Computerized care plans help nurses achieve quality patient care. *Journal of Nursing Administration, 16,* 33–39.

Ware, J. E., Jr., & Hays, R. P. (1988). Methods for measuring patient satisfaction with specific medical encounters. *Medical Care, 26,* 393–402.

Wiger, D. E. (2010). *The clinical documentation sourcebook* (4th ed.). Hoboken, NJ: Wiley.

Wiger, D. E., & Harowski, K. J. (2003). *Essentials of crisis counseling and intervention.* Hoboken, NJ: Wiley.

Wiger, D. E., & Huntley, D. K (2002). *Essentials of interviewing.* Hoboken, NJ: Wiley.

Wiger, D. E., & Solberg, K. B (2001). *Tracking mental health outcomes.* Hoboken, NJ: Wiley.

Zuckerman, E. L. (2006). *Clinician's thesaurus: The guidebook for writing psychological reports* (6th ed.). New York, NY: Guilford Press.

Zuckerman, E. L. (2008). *The paper office: Forms, guidelines, and resources* (4th ed.) New York: Guilford Press.

Index